Theory of
MENTAL TESTS

WILEY PUBLICATIONS
IN PSYCHOLOGY

Herbert S. Langfeld
Advisory Editor

Theory of
MENTAL
TESTS

HAROLD GULLIKSEN

PROFESSOR OF PSYCHOLOGY, PRINCETON UNIVERSITY
RESEARCH ADVISER, EDUCATIONAL TESTING SERVICE
PRINCETON, NEW JERSEY

New York · JOHN WILEY & SONS, Inc.
London · Sydney

BOOKS BY H. GULLIKSEN AND S. MESSICK
Psychological Scaling

BY H. GULLIKSEN
The Theory of Mental Tests

COPYRIGHT, 1950
BY
JOHN WILEY & SONS, INC.

SIXTH PRINTING, JANUARY, 1967

PRINTED IN THE UNITED STATES OF AMERICA

Preface

The material in this book is based on my several years' experience in construction and evaluation of examinations, first as a member of the Board of Examinations of the University of Chicago, later as director of a war research project developing aptitude and achievement tests for the Bureau of Naval Personnel, and at present as research adviser for the Educational Testing Service. Collection and presentation of the material have been furthered for me by teaching courses in statistics and test theory at The University of Chicago and now at Princeton University.

During this time I have become aware of the necessity for a firm grounding in test theory for work in test development. When this book was begun the material on test theory was available in numerous articles scattered through the literature and in books written some time ago, and therefore not presenting recent developments. It seemed desirable to me to bring the technical developments in test theory of the last fifty years together in one readily available source.

Although this book is written primarily for those working in test development, it is interesting to note that the techniques presented here are applicable in many fields other than test construction. Many of the difficulties that have been encountered and solved in the testing field also confront workers in other areas, such as measurement of attitudes or opinions, appraisal of personality, and clinical diagnosis. For example, in each of these fields the error of measurement is large compared to the differences that the scientist is seeking; hence the methods of dealing with and reducing error of measurement developed in connection with testing are pertinent. Methods of adjusting results to take account of differences in group variability have been developed in testing, and they are helpful in arriving at appropriate conclusions whenever the apparent results of an experiment are affected by group variability. If measurements in any field are to merit confidence, the scientist must demonstrate that they are repeatable. Thus the theoretical and experimental work on reliability as developed for tests may be utilized in numerous other areas, as, for example, clinical diagnosis or personality appraisal. In any situation where a single decision or a diagnosis is made on the basis of several different types of evidence, the material on weighting methods is applicable.

As the writing of the book progressed, there were several developments that seemed especially interesting to me from a technical point of view. The basic formulas of test theory are derived from two different sets of assumptions. In Chapter 2 the derivation is based on a definition of random error, with true score being simply a difference between observed and error score. In Chapter 3 the same formulas are derived from a definition of true score, error being the difference between observed and true scores. The treatment of the effects of test length and of group heterogeneity in terms of invariants may enable workers in the field of statistical theory to furnish test technicians with appropriate statistical criteria for this invariance. The distinction between explicit and incidental selection and the development of the theory of incidental selection for the multivariate case may facilitate the proper use of corrections for restriction of range. It was especially interesting to me to work on the beginning of a rationale for power tests that are partly speeded, as given in Chapter 17. This theory should help in determining test time limits and their effect on estimates of reliability. The initiation of a systematic mathematical theory for item analysis, as indicated in Chapter 21, should help in constructing tests that are suited for different specific purposes. I hope that the discussion of weighting methods presented in Chapter 20 will assist in clarifying problems in this field.

Illustrative computing diagrams are given for those formulas simple enough to be changed into a linear form. In general, if we work with curved lines on a computing diagram, the labor of computing a large number of points for each line is prohibitive for the individual worker. If the diagram can be made up of straight lines, it is necessary to compute only one or two points for each line, and a graph of the proper size and scaled with values appropriate for any particular operation can be set up in a few hours. To be used for actual computing, such diagrams must be much larger than the illustrative ones given here. A minimum size of 8 by 10 inches and a large size of 20 by 30 inches will usually be found suitable. I hope that the diagrams given here will illustrate the principles of construction so well that any worker who has occasion to use any one of these formulas a great number of times can construct a larger and more detailed diagram with a scale appropriate to his own problem.

The major part of this book is designed for readers with the following preparation:

1. A knowledge of elementary algebra, including such topics as the binomial expansion, the solution of simultaneous linear equations, and the use of tables of logarithms.

2. Some familiarity with analytical geometry, emphasizing primarily the equation of the straight line, although some use is made of the equations for the circle, ellipse, hyperbola, and parabola.

3. A knowledge of elementary statistics, including such topics as the computation and interpretation of means, standard deviations, correlations, errors of estimate, and the constants of the equation of the regression line. It is assumed that the students know how to make and to interpret frequency diagrams of various sorts, including the histogram, frequency polygon, normal curve, cumulative frequency curve, and the correlation scatter diagram. Familiarity with tables of the normal curve and with significance tests is also assumed.

A brief résumé of the major formulas from algebra, analytical geometry, and statistics that are assumed in this book is given in Appendix A.

In order to include a more complete coverage of some major topics in test theory, certain exceptions were made to the foregoing requirements.

1. Chapter 5, sections 3 and 4, assumes an elementary knowledge of analysis of variance, including a first-order interaction.

2. Chapter 10, section 4, assumes a knowledge of the least squares procedure for fitting a second-degree curve.

3. Chapter 13 assumes an understanding of the elements of matrix theory.

4. Chapter 14 assumes the ability to use determinants for those cases involving more than three variables. For the case of three tests, the formulas of Chapter 14 are written without the use of determinantal notation.

5. Chapter 20, sections 2 and 4, assumes a knowledge of maxima and minima in calculus and of the solution of simultaneous linear equations by determinants.

6. Chapter 20, sections 12 and 13, assumes an understanding of the use of the Lagrange multiplier in solving a matrix equation.

The rest of the material in the book has been written so that the parts requiring advanced preparation may be omitted without disturbing the continuity of the material.

My suggestion is that students with the minimum preparation in elementary algebra and statistics should omit the following material:

Chapter 5 (sections 3 and 4), Chapter 10 (section 4), Chapter 13, and Chapter 20 (sections 1 to 4, 12, and 13). If lack of time makes it necessary to curtail assignments still further, Chapters 3, 7, 14, and 17 may be omitted also without disturbing the continuity of the treatment. Advanced students whose preparation includes calculus, matrix theory, and analysis of variance may not need to study Chapters 2, 6, and 11.

HAROLD GULLIKSEN

Princeton, New Jersey
August, 1950

Acknowledgments

Professor L. L. Thurstone encouraged me in the writing of this book. The material presented here, particularly in the earlier chapters, has drawn very heavily upon his teaching, and in particular upon his now unavailable book *Reliability and Validity of Tests*. I profited greatly from long association with Professor Thurstone, first as his student and assistant and later as his colleague. This association gave me the opportunity to observe at first hand his methods in the development of new quantitative techniques for the solution of psychological problems. His developments are among the major contributions that give us confidence that psychology is beginning to take its place among the older sciences.

I am also especially pleased to be able to present the work of Dr. S. S. Wilks, which furnishes a statistical criterion for parallel tests, and the extension of this work by Dr. D. F. Votaw, Jr., to the more general criteria for compound symmetry, which gives a statistical criterion for equal validities of parallel tests. The work of Dr. W. G. Mollenkopf, given in Chapter 10, is a contribution to the theory of the variation in the error of measurement. The methods Dr. L. R. Tucker has developed for equating tests seem to me to be better than previous methods. It is my feeling that these contributions mark a distinct advance in the development of test theory.

My thanks are due Dr. S. S. Wilks for reading and criticizing several sections of the manuscript dealing with developments made by him; Dr. D. F. Votaw, Jr., for criticizing the material on compound symmetry; Dr. W. G. Mollenkopf for a careful review of and valuable comments on several of the chapters; and Dr. Irving Lorge for reviewing the manuscript. Many errors and ambiguities have been eliminated from the text by this help.

I am indebted to Dr. L. R. Tucker for permission to utilize his material on equating of tests, prior to its publication by him, and for assistance on the derivations concerned with the problem of weighting to maximize reliability of a composite.

I wish to acknowledge assistance from the Princeton University Research Fund of Princeton University toward the preparation of this manuscript; to express my appreciation to Professor Herbert S. Langfeld for suggesting that I write this book; and to thank Mr. Henry Chauncey for his interest in the development and practical application of these formulas in test theory.

I wish also to thank the Princeton University Press, the editors of the *Annals of Mathematical Statistics*, the editors of *Psychometrika*, and the National Defense Research Committee for permission to adapt material from their publications for use here.

H. G.

Symbols

Although certain chapters required a special set of symbols, generally the following notation is used in this book.

$X, Y, Z,$ or W denotes the gross score or raw score on a test.

i and j are subscripts designating persons.

g and h are subscripts designating tests.

$x, y, z,$ or w denotes deviation scores, the gross score minus the mean.

N denotes total number of persons in a group.

n denotes the number of persons in a subgroup.

K denotes the number of items in a test, or the number of tests in a battery.

k denotes the number of items in a subtest.

T equals the gross true score.

t equals the deviation true score, the gross true score minus the mean of these scores.

E equals the gross error score (random error).

e equals the deviation error score (since the average error is zero, $E = e$).

$M, m, \overline{X}, \overline{Y}$ equal the sample mean.

$S, s, \breve{X}, \breve{Y}$ equal the sample standard deviation.

r and R equal a sample correlation coefficient.

μ equals the population mean.

σ equals the standard deviation for the population.

ρ equals the correlation for the population.

ς equals the covariance for the population.

Contents

Contents

CHAPTER

1

Introduction

It is interesting to note that during the 1890's several attempts were made in this country to utilize the new methods of measurement of individual differences in order to predict college grades. J. McKeen Cattell and his student Clark Wissler tried a large number of psychological tests and correlated them with grades in various subjects at Columbia University; see Cattell (1890), Cattell and Farrand (1896), and Wissler (1901). The correlations between the psychological tests and the grades were around zero, the highest correlation being .19. A similar attempt by Gilbert (1894), at Yale, produced similarly disappointing results.

Scientific confidence in the possibilities of measuring individual differences revived in this country with the introduction of the Binet scale and the quantitative techniques developed by Karl Pearson and Charles Spearman at the beginning of the twentieth century. Nearly all the basic formulas that are particularly useful in test theory are found in Spearman's early papers; see Spearman (1904a), (1904b), (1907), (1910), and (1913). Since then development of both the theory and the practical aspects of aptitude and achievement testing has progressed rapidly. Aptitude and achievement tests are widely used in education and in industry.

Since 1900 great progress has been made toward a unified quantitative theory that describes the behavior of test items and test scores under various conditions. This mathematical rationale applicable to mental tests should not be confused with statistics. A good foundation in elementary statistics and elementary mathematics is a prerequisite for work in the theory of mental tests. In addition, as the theory of mental tests is developed, the necessity arises for various statistical criteria to determine whether or not a given set of test data agrees with the theory, within reasonable sampling limits. The theory, however, must first be developed without consideration of sampling errors, and then the statistical problems in conjunction with sampling can be considered.

This book deals with the mathematical theory and statistical methods used in interpreting test results. There are numerous non-quantitative problems involved in constructing aptitude or achievement tests that are not considered here. Non-quantitative problems such as choice of item types or matching the examination to the objectives of a curriculum are discussed in the University of Chicago *Manual of Examination Methods* (1937); Engelhart (1942 and 1947); Hawkes, Lindquist, and Mann (1936); Hull (1928); Orleans (1937); Ruch (1929); and others. Therefore, no attempt is made here to familiarize the student with the various psychological and educational tests now available or with the scope of the many testing programs. Such material is surveyed in yearbooks by Buros (1936), (1937), (1938), (1941), and (1949); Hildreth (1939); Lee and Symonds (1934); the National Society for the Study of Education, the 17th Yearbook (1918); Ruger (1918); Whipple (1914), (1915); Freeman (1939); Mursell (1947); Ross (1947); Goodenough (1949); Cronbach (1949); and other general textbooks listed in the bibliography.

In constructing tests, analyzing and interpreting the results, there are five major types of problems:

1. Writing and selecting the test items.
2. Assigning a score to each person.
3. Determining the accuracy (reliability or error of measurement) of the test scores.
4. Determining the predictive value of the test scores (validity or error of estimate).
5. Comparing the results with those obtained using other tests or other groups of subjects. In making these comparisons, it is necessary to consider the effect of test length and group heterogeneity on the various measures of the accuracy and the predictive value of the test scores.

In dealing with any given test these problems would arise chronologically in the order in which they are given above. However, the theory of the selection of test items depends upon comparing them with some test score or scores; therefore it is convenient to consider first the theory dealing with the accuracy of these test scores. Similarly the evaluation of experimental methods of determining reliability and the discussion of practical methods of setting up parallel tests depend upon a theoretical concept of reliability and of parallel tests. Therefore, instead of beginning with practical problems of item selection, experimental methods of determining reliability, or of setting up parallel tests, we shall begin with the theoretical constructs.

An ideal model will be set up giving the measures of accuracy of test scores and the theoretical effects of changes in test length and in group heterogeneity. The theory of these changes will be derived from assumptions regarding parallel tests and selection procedures, without inquiring very closely into the experimental methods that are appropriate for realizing these assumptions. Beginning with Chapter 14, various practical problems relating to the construction of parallel tests, criteria for parallel tests, experimental methods of determining reliability, etc., will be considered. It is felt that postponing such practical considerations until the latter part of the book has the advantage of giving the student a firm foundation in theory first. Then on the basis of this familiarity with the ideal situation, various practical procedures can be evaluated in terms of the closeness with which they approximate the theoretically perfect method. To consider practical experimental procedures without such a grounding in the theoretical foundation leaves these procedures as approximations to something that is not yet clearly stated or understood.

The basic theoretical material on accuracy of test scores is presented in Chapters 2 through 5, which deal with the topics of test reliability and the error of measurement. The effect of test length upon reliability and validity is considered in Chapters 6 through 9, and the effect of group heterogeneity on measures of accuracy in Chapters 10 through 13. In these chapters we give only a theoretical definition of parallel tests, and we define reliability as the correlation between two parallel forms. This simplified presentation of the concept of parallel tests and of reliability makes it possible to concentrate on the theory of test reliability and test validity before taking up the short-cuts and approximations that are frequently used in actual practice. Practical problems of criteria for parallel tests are given in Chapter 14, and experimental methods of determining reliability when a parallel form is not used are considered in Chapters 15 and 16. Methods of scoring, scaling, and equating tests are considered in Chapters 18 and 19. Problems dealing with batteries of tests are considered in Chapter 20, and problems of item selection in Chapter 21.

2

Basic Equations Derived
from a Definition of Random Error

1. Introduction

We shall begin by assuming the conventional objective testing procedure in which the person is presented with a number of items to be answered. Each answer is scored as correct or incorrect, and a simple or a weighted sum of the correct answers is taken as the test score. The various procedures for determining which items to use and the best weighting methods will be considered later. For the present we assume that the numerical score is based on a count, one or more points for each correct answer and zero for each incorrect answer, and we turn our attention to the determination of the accuracy of this score.

When psychological measurement is compared with the type of measurement found in physics, many points of similarity and difference are found. One of the very important differences is that the error of measurement in most psychological work is very much greater than it is in physics. For example, Jackson and Ferguson (1941) resorted to specially constructed "rubber rulers" in order to reduce the reliability of length measurements to values appreciably below .99. The estimation of the error in a set of test scores and the differentiation between "error" and "true" score on a test are central problems in mental measurement.

2. The basic assumption of test theory

It is necessary to make some assumption regarding the relationship between true scores and error scores. Let us define three basic symbols.

X_i = the score of the ith person on the test under consideration.
T_i = the true score of the ith person on this test.
E_i = the error component for the same person.

In defining these symbols it is assumed that the gross score has two components. One of these components (T) represents the actual ability of the person, a quantity that will be relatively stable from test to test

4

as long as the tests are measuring the same thing. The other component (E) is an error. It is due to the various factors that may cause a person sometimes to answer correctly an item that he does not know, and sometimes to answer incorrectly an item that he does know. So far, it will be observed, there is no proposition subject to any experimental check. We have simply said that there is some number T that would be the person's correct score, and that the obtained score (X) does not necessarily equal T.

It is possible to make many different assumptions regarding the relationship between the three terms X, T, and E. The one made in test theory is the simplest possible assumption, namely, that

$$(1) \qquad X_i = T_i + E_i \quad \text{or} \quad E_i = X_i - T_i.$$

This equation may be regarded as an *assumption* that states the relationship between true and error score; or it may be regarded as an equation *defining* what we are going to mean by error. In other words, once we accept the concept of a true score existing that differs from the observed score, we may then say that the difference between these two scores is going to be called error.

3. The problem of determining characteristics of true and error score

It may be noted that so far we have but one equation with two unknowns $(T$ and $E)$. It cannot be solved to determine the values of T and of E for the person. If we test additional people, the situation does not become any more determinate. Each new score brings one new equation, like equation (1), and also two new unknowns. However, we may note that with measures on many persons we would have three frequency distributions—the distribution of X's, of T's, and of E's. Let us investigate to see if we can learn something about the characteristics or parameters of these frequency distributions. Can we determine or make reasonable assumptions about the means, the standard deviations, or the intercorrelations of these three distributions?

There are two equivalent approaches to the problem of determining the characteristics of the distributions of T and E.

1. A definition of error score is given, and the true score is regarded simply as the difference between the observed score and the error score. Intuitively this approach is somewhat unsatisfying, since the main attention is concentrated upon the error part, which is to be ignored, and the important component (true score) is just what happens to be left over. However, the basic equations can be derived quite simply from this assumption.

2. The other approach is to define the true score and then to let the difference between observed and true score be called error. This approach is probably intuitively more satisfying, since attention is first concentrated upon getting a reasonable true score, and the error is a remainder. However this approach results in much more difficult equations. Since the first approach is the simpler to follow, let us consider it next.

4. Definition of random errors

In this approach to the problem of determining the means, the standard deviations, and the intercorrelations of true, observed, and error scores, we define more carefully just what is meant by error. In dealing with errors of measurement, it is necessary to recognize that there are two basic types of error. They are termed random or chance errors, on the one hand, and constant or systematic errors, on the other.

If measurements are consistently larger than they should be or are consistently smaller than they should be we have what is termed "constant error." For example, if a tape measure has stretched with use and age, measurements made with it would be smaller than those made with an accurate tape, and there would be a systematic negative error. The error would be negative because it is customary to measure error as "the obtained measure minus the correct measure." The terms random, chance, or unsystematic errors on the other hand refer to discrepancies that are sometimes large and sometimes small, sometimes positive and sometimes negative.

The basic assumptions of test theory deal with the definition and the estimation of chance errors. These "random errors" are the only errors that will be explicitly considered in test theory. For many purposes, constant errors can be ignored, since the process of establishing test norms takes care of constant errors that may appear in the gross score on the test.

Since we are dealing with random errors, it is not unreasonable to assume that over a sufficiently large number of cases the average error of this type will be zero. We may write this assumption,

(2) $$M_E = 0,$$

and note that the larger the number of cases in the distribution, the closer will this assumption be approximated. This equation may also be regarded, not as an assumption, but as a part of the definition of random errors. By random errors we mean errors that average to zero over a large number of cases. Stating more exactly, we can say that the mean error will differ from zero by an amount that will be smaller than any assigned quantity however small, if the number of cases is sufficiently large. In actual practice, however, it is customary to assume that equation 2 holds exactly for any particular sample that is being considered.

Turning to a consideration of the relationship between error score and true score, we can see that there is no reason to expect positive errors to occur oftener with high than with low true scores, and that the same holds for negative errors. Likewise there is no reason to expect large errors to occur oftener with low than with high true scores. It is reasonable to assume that as the number of cases increases the correlation between true and error scores approaches zero. We may write the equation

(3) $$r_{TE} = 0$$

and note that it comes closer and closer to being correct as the number of cases increases. Like equation 2, equation 3 is not so much an assumption as a definition. If the errors correlate with true score, they are not random errors. In such a case there is a systematic tendency for persons with high scores (or low scores) to have the larger errors. In practice it is assumed in testing work that equation 3 holds for any given set of test data.

The only other equation needed to define random error relates to the correlation between error on one test and error on another parallel test. As before, we can point out that there is no reason to expect a relationship, and that if a relationship existed between error scores on one test and error scores on a second test, we should have some systematic and predictable source of error and not a random error. In other words, by definition the correlation between two sets of random errors is zero or approaches zero as the number of cases increases. We may use the subscripts 1 and 2 to represent any two parallel tests and write

(4) $$r_{E_1 E_2} = 0.$$

Again, as before, we note that strictly speaking this assumption is true only as the number of cases approaches infinity. In practice, however, it is assumed to hold for any given set of test data.

We may summarize the foregoing material in the following three definitions of random error:

> *The mean error is zero (equation 2). The correlation between error score and true score is zero (equation 3). The correlation between errors on one test and those on another parallel test is zero (equation 4).*

We should finally note again that actually these definitions do not hold unless the number of cases is very large, but that in practice it is customary to assume that they hold for any given set of test data.

5. Determination of mean true score

In order to determine the mean true score we note from the definition of equation 1 that

(5)
$$T_i = X_i - E_i.$$

Summing both sides gives

(6)
$$\sum_{i=1}^{N} T_i = \sum_{i=1}^{N} (X_i - E_i).$$

Removing the parentheses and omitting the subscripts and limits (since they are all identical), we have

(7)
$$\Sigma T = \Sigma X - \Sigma E.$$

Dividing by N (the number of cases) to obtain the mean gives

(8)
$$M_T = M_X - M_E.$$

Using equation 2, we can see that

(9)
$$M_T = M_X.$$

The mean true score equals the mean observed score. Equation 9 is based only on the definition of equation 1 and the assumption of equation 2.

6. Relationship between true and error variance

Next let us determine the relationship between the standard deviations of the true, the error, and the observed scores. From the definition of equation 1 and from equation 9 we may write

(10)
$$X - M_X = T + E - M_T.$$

Let us use lower-case letters to represent deviation scores. That is,

(11)
$$x = X - M_X.$$

(12)
$$t = T - M_T,$$

and since M_E equals zero from the definition of equation 2, we have

(13)
$$e = E.$$

Substituting equations 11, 12, and 13 in equation 10 gives

(14)
$$x = t + e.$$

Squaring and summing gives

(15) $$\Sigma x^2 = \Sigma(t + e)^2.$$

Removing the parentheses gives

$$\Sigma x^2 = \Sigma t^2 + \Sigma e^2 + 2\Sigma et.$$

Dividing both sides by N, we have

(16) $$s_x^{\;2} = s_t^{\;2} + s_e^{\;2} + 2r_{te}s_ts_e.$$

Substituting the definition of equation 3 in equation 16 gives

(17) $$s_x^{\;2} = s_t^{\;2} + s_e^{\;2}.$$

The variance of the observed scores is equal to the sum of the true variance and error variance. It should be noted that equation 17 may be derived solely from the definition of equation 1 and the assumption of equation 3.

The relationship between these three variances is shown in Figure 1. Such a diagram can readily be constructed to cover any particular set

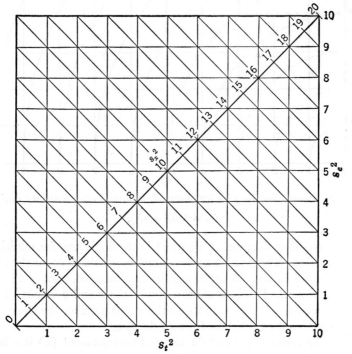

FIGURE 1. Computing diagram for observed, true, and error variance $(s_x^{\;2} = s_t^{\;2} + s_e^{\;2})$.

of values for the three variances. The true variance and the error variance are indicated, one on the abscissa, the other on the ordinate. The set of diagonal lines indicates points such that the sum of the true and the error variance is constant; hence each diagonal line can be marked with the appropriate value of $s_x{}^2$.

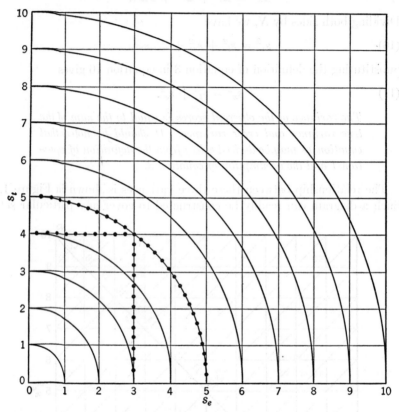

FIGURE 2. Computing diagram for observed, true, and error standard deviations

$$(s_x = \sqrt{s_t{}^2 + s_e{}^2}).$$

The computing diagram of Figure 1 is the basic one for addition of two quantities. The x and y scales should be set up to cover the appropriate range of values. If the two scales are the same, a set of 45-degree lines can be marked to indicate the sum of the x and y values. If it is not feasible to use the same units on the x and y scales, the slope of the "sum" lines must be different from 45 degrees.

The error variance ($s_e{}^2$) or the error of measurement (s_e) is a fundamental and important characteristic of any test. If the error of meas-

say, "It makes no difference which test is used." Also it is
able, in the light of what has been said previously, to require
$g = E_{ih}$. This statement would contradict the definition of
n 4, which says that the errors on one test correlate zero with
rors on another test. If for each person (i) the error score on one
equaled the error score on another test, the correlation between
s would be 1.00 and not zero. The closest we can reasonably come
defining the errors to be alike on parallel tests is to require that the
andard deviation of the errors on one test equal the standard devia-
on of errors on the other test. Since this can be true when the correlation is zero, it does not violate any other assumption that has been
made. Thus we may write the second equation defining parallel tests,

(20)
$$s_{e_g} = s_{e_h}.$$

This equation may be stated in the definition:

For two parallel tests, the errors of measurement are equal.

Equations 19 and 20 will serve to define parallel tests.

It will be noted that both equations 19 and 20 are stated in terms of
hypothetical quantities. In other words, these equations do not pro-
vide for testing the actual means, standard deviations, or intercorrelations of a set of tests and for determining whether or not they are parallel tests. Let us see what can be determined from equations 19 and 20
regarding the parameters of the *observed* scores.

If all true scores are identical, it follows that the means and standard
deviations of true scores are also identical for parallel tests. We may
write

(21)
$$M_{T_o} = M_{T_h} \quad \text{or} \quad \bar{T}_g = \bar{T}_h$$

and

(22)
$$s_{T_g} = s_{T_h}.$$

The correlation between two sets of identical scores is unity; therefore,

(23)
$$r_{T_g T_h} = 1.00.$$

Applying equation 17 to tests g and h, we see that

(24)
$$s_{X_g}{}^2 = s_{T_g}{}^2 + s_{E_g}{}^2,$$

and correspondingly for test h

(25)
$$s_{X_h}{}^2 = s_{T_h}{}^2 + s_{E_h}{}^2.$$

urement can be reduced, the test b*
operate to increase the error of m*
poorer. Much of the effort in test
analysis, and the precautions of test ad*
of decreasing the value of s_e.

Taking the square root of both sides of eq

$$(18) \qquad\qquad s_x = \sqrt{s_t{}^2 + s_e{}^2}.$$

This is the familiar Pythagorean theorem: "The hy*
triangle is equal to the square root of the sum of the s*
sides." s_t and s_e could be diagramed as the sides of a rig*
s_x would be the hypotenuse.

This relationship can be utilized to construct a simple *
diagram for the foregoing equation. Draw a series of concentric
circles, as illustrated in Figure 2, including the range of values of *
s_e likely to be found in the data being considered. Find s_t and s_e
the vertical and horizontal axes. From the point of intersection follo*
the circle to either axis and read off s_x. For example, the dotted lines
show that if $s_t = 4$ and $s_e = 3$, then $s_x = 5$.

7. Definition of parallel tests in terms of true score and error variance

From a common sense point of view, it may be said that two tests
are "parallel" when "it makes no difference which test you use." It is
certainly clear that, if for some reason one test is better than the other
for certain purposes, it does make a difference which test is used, and
the tests could not be termed parallel. However, this simple statement,
"it makes no difference which test is used," must be cast in mathematical form before we can use it in any derivations.

It would seem to be clear that if the true score of a given person (i)
on one test is *different* from his true score on a second test, we cannot
say that the two tests are parallel. In other words, if we designate the
person by the subscript i and the two tests by the subscripts g and h,
we can say that two tests are parallel only if

$$(19) \qquad\qquad T_{ig} = T_{ih}.$$

*The true score of any person on one test must equal the true
score of that person on the other parallel test.*

Equation 19, however, is not the only requirement for parallel tests.
If the difference between observed score and true score is in general
much greater for one test, it is clearly better to use the other test. And

From equations 20 and 22 we see that

$$(26) \qquad\qquad s_{X_g}{}^2 = s_{X_h}{}^2.$$

From equations 21 and 9 it follows that

$$(27) \qquad\qquad M_{X_g} = M_{X_h} \quad \text{or} \quad \overline{X}_g = \overline{X}_h.$$

The means and standard deviations of parallel tests are equal. [1]

We turn next to consideration of the problem of the *correlation* between parallel forms of a test.

8. Correlation between parallel forms of a test

For the present we shall define reliability as the correlation between two parallel forms of a test. The problem of determining whether or not two forms are parallel and of the best method of estimating the correlation between the two forms will be considered later.

The correlation between two parallel forms of a test may readily be found by using the deviation score formula for correlation:

$$(28) \qquad\qquad r_{x_g x_h} = \frac{\Sigma x_g x_h}{N s_g s_h}.$$

From equation 14 we may express the *numerator* of the right side of equation 28 as follows:

$$(29) \qquad\qquad \Sigma x_g x_h = \Sigma (t_g + e_g)(t_h + e_h).$$

Expanding and removing the parentheses gives

$$(30) \qquad\qquad \Sigma x_g x_h = \Sigma t_g t_h + \Sigma t_g e_h + \Sigma t_h e_g + \Sigma e_g e_h.$$

From the definitions of equations 3 and 4 we see that the last three terms in equation 30 are each zero. Since we are dealing with parallel tests, the true score on g equals the true score on h. Therefore, equation 30 may be rewritten as

$$(31) \qquad\qquad \Sigma x_g x_h = \Sigma t_g{}^2 = \Sigma t_h{}^2.$$

We may divide both sides of equation 31 by N, obtaining

$$(32) \qquad\qquad \frac{\Sigma x_g x_h}{N} = \frac{\Sigma t_g{}^2}{N}.$$

[1] It should be noted that equations 26 and 27 may be interpreted as applying either to gross scores or to scores after transformation by one of the methods discussed in Chapter 19. However, the set of scores (X_g) and the set of scores (X_h) are not parallel unless the means and standard deviations are about equal. Criteria of equality are discussed in Chapter 14.

From the definition of a standard deviation we see that

$$(33) \qquad \frac{\Sigma x_g x_h}{N} = s_t^2.$$

Substituting equations 26 and 33 in equation 28 gives

$$(34) \qquad r_{x_g x_h} = \frac{s_t^2}{s_{x_g}^2}.$$

We see from the reasoning used in developing equation 26 that, if we were dealing with several parallel forms, all the observed variances would be alike. That is, if we designate the forms by subscripts 1, 2, 3, and 4,

$$(35) \qquad s_{x_1} = s_{x_2} = s_{x_3} = s_{x_4}.$$

Also, by the reasoning used in developing equation 22, we see that

$$(36) \qquad s_{t_1} = s_{t_2} = s_{t_3} = s_{t_4}.$$

From equations 34, 35, and 36 we see that

$$(37) \qquad r_{x_1 x_2} = r_{x_1 x_3} = r_{x_2 x_3} = \cdots = r_{x_3 x_4}.$$

All intercorrelations of parallel tests are equal.

Equations 26, 27, and 37 show that parallel forms of a test should have approximately equal means, equal standard deviations, and equal intercorrelations.[1] These are objective quantitative criteria for which a statistical test will be presented in Chapter 14. In addition to satisfying these objective and quantitative criteria, parallel tests should also be similar with respect to test content, item types, instructions to students, etc. Similarity in these respects can as yet be determined only by the judgment of psychologists and of subject matter experts.

9. Equation for true variance

Multiplying equation 34 by s_x^2 gives

$$(38) \qquad s_t^2 = s_x^2 r_{x_g x_h} \qquad \text{(true variance)}.$$

Taking the square root of both sides, we have

$$(39) \qquad s_t = s_x \sqrt{r_{x_g x_h}} \qquad \text{(true standard deviation)}.$$

---

[1] Means and standard deviations may be equal for the raw scores or for scores transformed by one of the methods suggested in Chapter 19. For transformed scores, it is necessary to determine the transformation equation from one set of data and to test for equality of means and standard deviations after the same transformation has been applied to a *new set* of data.

*Equations 38 and 39 give the variance and standard devia-
tion of the distribution of true scores in terms of the test reliability and the standard deviation of the distribution of observed scores. These equations may be derived by assuming
only equations 1, 3, 20, and 26.*

10. Equation for error variance (the error of measurement)

We may solve for the error variance by substituting equation 38 in
equation 17, obtaining

$$(40) \qquad s_x{}^2 = s_x{}^2 r_{x_g x_h} + s_e{}^2.$$

Solving equation 40 for the error variance ($s_e{}^2$) gives

$$(41) \qquad s_e{}^2 = s_x{}^2 (1 - r_{x_g x_h})$$

(variance of the errors of measurement).

Taking the square root of both sides gives the equation for the standard
error of measurement,

$$(42) \qquad s_e = s_x \sqrt{1 - r_{x_g x_h}} \qquad \text{(error of measurement)}.$$

*Equations 41 and 42 give the variance of the errors of meas-
urement and the standard deviation of these errors. They
follow from the assumptions needed to derive equations 38
and 39. The error of measurement is a fundamental concept in test theory and an important characteristic of a test.*

It was suggested by Kelley (1921) and Otis (1922b) that the error of
measurement was an invariant of a test, that is, it did not vary with
changes in group heterogeneity. The equations given in Chapter 10
are based on this assumption.

The computing diagram used before to indicate the relationship
$s_x = \sqrt{s_t{}^2 + s_e{}^2}$ can also be used with some slight complication to
compute the true standard deviation and error of measurement, given
the standard deviation and reliability of the test. Figure 3 indicates
how this computation is done. Draw the series of circles, as before, to
indicate the relationship between true, error, and observed standard
deviation. Radial lines can then be drawn to indicate a given reliability.
Where each of the horizontal lines (indicating s_t) intersects the large
quadrant with radius 10, we have successively the points for which the
reliability is $.1^2$, $.2^2$, $\cdots$ $.9^2$. Still finer subdivisions can be drawn from
the general rule that the reliability coefficient is the ratio of the true
variance to the observed variance. By selecting the quadrant with

radius 10, the division consists in simply pointing over two places (standard deviation 10 gives variance of 100). For each point along this radius, the reliability coefficient is $s_t^2/100$.

In order to use the diagram, find the radius corresponding to the reliability coefficient and the circle corresponding to the observed

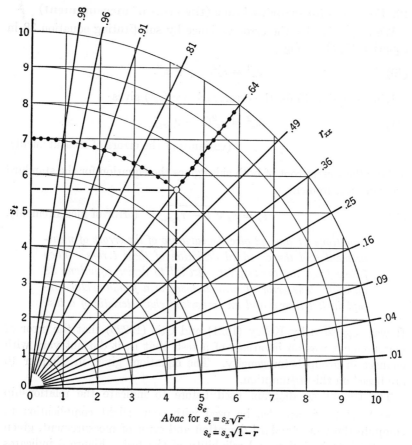

FIGURE 3. The true standard deviation, and error of measurement as functions of the test reliability and standard deviation.

standard deviation. Then note the intersection of this particular radius and circle. The y-coordinate of that point is the true standard deviation, the x-coordinate of that point is the error of measurement for that test.

For example, the point marked with a circle is where the reliability is .64, and the standard deviation of observed scores is 7. In this case the standard deviation of the true scores is 5.6 ($7 \times \sqrt{.64}$), and the error of measurement is the x-coordinate of the same point, 4.2 ($7 \times \sqrt{.36}$).

If we know the true and error standard deviations, it is possible to use the same diagram to read off the reliability and the observed standard deviation. In this case, look up the true standard deviation on the y-axis, the error of measurement on the x-axis, find the point with these two coordinates, and then read the value of the radius through this point to find the test reliability, and the value of the circle through this point to find the standard deviation of observed scores.

In general we may describe this graph by pointing out that it is a combination of rectangular and polar coordinate systems. Any point in it represents four quantities, one on the x-axis, one on the y-axis (the rectangular coordinate system), one on the radius, and one on the circle (the polar coordinate system). Each point, which represents four quantities, is determined by any two of these quantities. Therefore, generalizing, we may say that given any two of the four quantities involved, it is possible to determine the other two.

11. Use of the error of measurement

It should be noted that, in the development of the equations of this chapter, there is no reference to any particular type of frequency distribution. It is assumed that the average error is zero, and that errors are uncorrelated with each other or with true score. All the equations of this chapter follow from these assumptions, regardless of the frequency distribution of true scores, error scores, or observed scores. However, it is not possible to make use of the *error of measurement* without some assumption about its distribution. This quantity is usually assumed to be normally distributed. Figure 4 gives a concrete illustration for a particular test in which the error of measurement is assumed to be 5 score points. Observed scores are indicated on the base line. A is the distribution of observed scores for all persons whose true score is 50 points. It will be noted that the mean is at 50, the inflection points at 45 and 55 (50 plus and minus 5), and that all but a negligible part of the distribution lies between scores of 35 and 65 (50 plus and minus three times 5). That is to say, for the group of persons whose true score is 50, over 99 per cent of the observed scores will lie between 35 and 65.

We may also indicate a method for assigning a probability value to the statement: "If a person's observed score is 65, his true score probably lies between 50 and 80." Note that no probability value is given. We cannot say that for all persons whose observed score is

65, the probability is greater than .99 that the true score is between 50 and 80. However, consider the statement: "This person's true score lies between 50 and 80." If the person's true score were known, the statement could, for a given person, be classified as *true* or as *false*. It

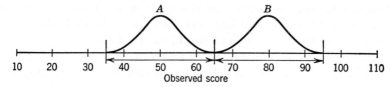

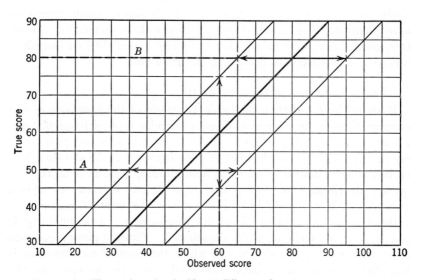

FIGURE 4. Illustration of a significant difference between two test scores.

would be possible to keep on following this rule of procedure. For each person (some with one observed score, and some with another), we could say: "This person's true score lies between T_L and T_U," where T_L, the lower limit for the true score, is found by subtracting three times the error of measurement from the observed score, and T_U, the upper limit for the true score, is found by adding three times the error of measurement to the observed score. For each of the persons whose observed score is known, such a statement can be made. In addition, the statement so made can be labeled *true* or *false*. For all the persons in the distribution, it will be found that the statement regarding limits is true over 99 per cent of the time and is false less than three times out of a thousand. In other words, if all the cases are considered, a probability can be attached to the truth or falsity of the statement that "true score is included within the specified limits." However, if we limit the statement to persons with any *given observed score*, no assertion regarding probability can be made.

The situation shown in the upper part of the diagram for persons with a true score of 50 and of 80 can be generalized if the correlation scatter plot is given. The lower part of the diagram shows the scatter plot of true score against observed score. The heavy line marks the cases in which observed score and true score are equal. Two lighter lines are drawn on each side of the heavy one to indicate those cases in which the observed score is equal to the true score minus three times the error of measurement, and in which the observed score is equal to the true score plus three times the error of measurement. For true scores of 50 and 80, again we can read the limits within which over 99 per cent of the observed scores will fall. We can also see that the observed score of 65 could reasonably be from any distribution where the true score was over 50 or under 80. Likewise, we may pick any observed score, such as 60 in the diagram, and see that such a score might have arisen from any true score over 45 and under 75. That is to say, take three times the error of measurement, or 15; then add 15 to 60 and subtract 15 from 60, obtaining the upper and lower limits of 75 and 45. Thus if we know the error of measurement of a test it is possible, for any given observed score, to specify limits within which the true score lies. We can also say that such a statement is true for 99.7 per cent of the cases (and false for 0.3 per cent of the cases) in the entire distribution. However, no such probability statement can be made which applies to the group of persons making any specified observed score. Distribution B shows the same information for persons whose true score is 80. Since it is assumed that the standard error of measurement is constant regardless of true score, distribution B also has a standard deviation of 5 points. For persons whose true score is 80, the observed scores, in over 99 per cent of the cases, will lie between 65 and 95 (80 plus and minus three times 5). It will be noted that if a person's observed score is 65, he might reasonably be either a top-scoring person from distribution A, or a very low-scoring person from distribution B. In other words, if a person's observed score is 65, his true score could reasonably be as low as 50 (65 minus three times 5), or as high as 80 (65 plus three times 5). His true score might also reasonably have been any value *between* 50 and 80. However, if a person's true score is below 50, there is considerably less than two chances in a thousand that his observed score would be 65 or higher. Conversely, if a person's true score is above 80, there is considerably less than two chances in a thousand that his observed score would be 65 or less. We say then that for a person whose observed score is 65, *reasonable limits* for his true score are 50 to 80.

It should be noted that, although we can assign reasonable limits for the true score, we cannot say that for all persons who score 65, over 99 per cent will have true scores between 50 and 80. In general no probability statements can be made to apply to all persons who make a given *observed* score. We can only make the statement the other way around. For all persons with a given *true* score, the probability is over .997 that the observed score will lie within plus or minus three times the error of measurement from that true score. Likewise, for all persons with a given true score, the probability is less than .003 that the observed score will lie outside the range given by the true score plus and minus three times the error of measurement.

For persons with any given observed score X_i, reasonable limits for the true score T_i may be taken as

$$(43) \qquad X_i + cs_e > T_i > X_i - cs_e,$$

where c is taken as equal to 2 or 3 and $s_e = s_x \sqrt{1 - r_{x_g x_h}}$.

The error of measurement may also be utilized to determine reasonable limits for the difference between the true scores of two persons. In this case we utilize the difference between two scores, $x_i - x_j$, and the standard error of that difference $s_{e_i - e_j}$. To write the formula for this error, we use equation 14 and write

$$(44) \qquad x_i - x_j = t_i - t_j + (e_i - e_j).$$

The terms in parentheses indicate the error. Thus the variation of the observed difference from the true difference is indicated by

$$(45) \qquad \Sigma(e_i - e_j)^2 = \Sigma e_i^2 + \Sigma e_j^2 - 2\Sigma e_i e_j.$$

From equation 4, we see that the last term of equation 45 is zero. Using equation 41 in equation 45, we have

$$(46) \qquad \Sigma(e_i - e_j)^2 = 2Ns_x^2(1 - r_{x_g x_h}).$$

Dividing by N and taking the square root, to get the standard error of the difference $s_{e_i - e_j}$, we have

$$(47) \qquad s_{e_i - e_j} = s_x \sqrt{2} \sqrt{1 - r_{x_g x_h}}.$$

Illustrating again, using the distribution of Figure 4, the standard error of which is 5, we have the standard error of the difference of two scores as $5\sqrt{2}$. Figure 5 illustrates the frequency distribution of observed score differences for persons with true score differences of -25, 0, and $+25$. In each case the distribution is shown as extending $3 \times 5\sqrt{2}$ above and below the true score difference.

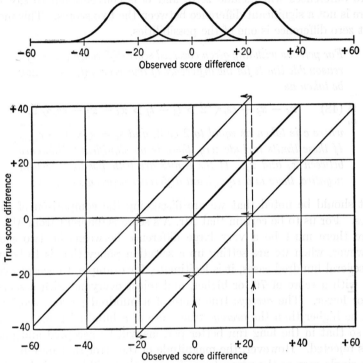

FIGURE 5.   Illustrating the standard error of a difference of observed scores.

Again it should be noted that in developing the equation for the standard error of a difference, no assumptions were made regarding the distribution of errors. However, in order to utilize this error to obtain reasonable limits for the value of the difference between true scores, some assumption regarding the frequency distribution of errors is needed. In Figure 5 the usual assumption of a normal distribution of errors is made.

As before, we may generalize for all possible distributions as shown in the lower part of Figure 5. It shows that if the observed score difference is zero, the true score difference may be as high as $+3 \times 5\sqrt{2}$ or as low as $-3 \times 5\sqrt{2}$. If the observed score difference is as large as 22, the entire range from $22 + 3 \times 5\sqrt{2}$ to $22 - 3 \times 5\sqrt{2}$ does not include zero. Hence it is not reasonable to assume that there is no difference between the two true scores represented by these observed scores. In such a case it has become customary to say that there is a significant difference between the two scores. When the difference between two scores is less than $3 \times 5\sqrt{2}$, the range of possible true score differences will include zero; and it is conventional to say that there is not a significant difference between the two scores. This means that zero difference is one of the possibilities.

> *For persons with any given observed score difference $(x_i - x_j)$,*
> *reasonable limits for the difference of true scores $(t_i - t_j)$ may*
> *be taken as*
>
> (48) $\qquad x_i - x_j + cs_e\sqrt{2} > t_i - t_j > x_i - x_j - cs_e\sqrt{2},$
>
> *where c is taken as equal to 2 or 3, and $s_e = s_x\sqrt{1 - r_{x_g x_h}}$.*
> *If these limits include zero, there is no significant difference*
> *between x_i and x_j. If the limits are both positive, or both*
> *negative, there is a significant difference between x_i and x_j.*

It should be noted that we are discussing the comparison of single cases. For us to be certain that Mr. A's score is different from Mr. B's score there must be a very large difference between the two scores. However, when we are setting up a selection policy that is to be used on several hundred cases, it is legitimate, for example, to accept everyone with a score of 76, or higher, and reject everyone with a score of 75 or lower. The *average* true score of a hundred persons scoring 76 will be higher than the *average* true score of a hundred persons scoring 75, so that in the long run better persons will be accepted and poorer ones rejected. However, the magnitude of the error that may be made in a single case or the percentage of errors that will be made in a large number of cases is indicated by the error of measurement.

12. Correlation of true and observed scores (index of reliability)

In order to obtain the correlation between true and observed scores we begin with the basic equation for correlation, writing the correlation of observed and true scores as

(49) $\qquad r_{xt} = \dfrac{\Sigma xt}{N s_x s_t}.$

Substituting equation 14 in equation 49 gives

(50) $\qquad r_{xt} = \dfrac{\Sigma(t + e)t}{N s_x s_t}.$

Removing parentheses, we have

(51)
$$r_{xt} = \frac{\Sigma t^2 + \Sigma te}{N s_x s_t}.$$

Dividing each of the terms in the numerator by the N in the denominator gives

(52)
$$r_{xt} = \frac{s_t^2 + r_{te} s_t s_e}{s_x s_t}.$$

Since the correlation between deviation scores is identical with the correlation between gross scores, we can see from equation 3 that the second term of the numerator in 52 vanishes. Dividing both numerator and denominator by s_t gives

(53)
$$r_{xt} = \frac{s_t}{s_x}.$$

Substituting equation 39 in equation 53 and canceling s_x from numerator and denominator gives

(54)
$$r_{xt} = \sqrt{r_{x_g x_h}} \qquad \text{(index of reliability)}.$$

The foregoing formula was given by Kelley (1916).

> *The correlation between observed scores and true scores as given by equation 54 is known as the index of reliability. The test validity* [1] *may not exceed the index of reliability.*

13. Correlation of observed scores and error scores

Just as in considering the correlation between observed and true scores we begin here with the basic deviation score formula for correlation,

(55)
$$r_{xe} = \frac{\Sigma xe}{N s_x s_e}.$$

As before, substituting equation 14 in equation 55 gives

(56)
$$r_{xe} = \frac{\Sigma (t + e)e}{N s_x s_e}.$$

Following the same procedure as in the preceding section, we remove parentheses, obtaining

(57)
$$r_{xe} = \frac{\Sigma te + \Sigma e^2}{N s_x s_e}.$$

---

[1] See definition and discussion of validity, Chapter 9.

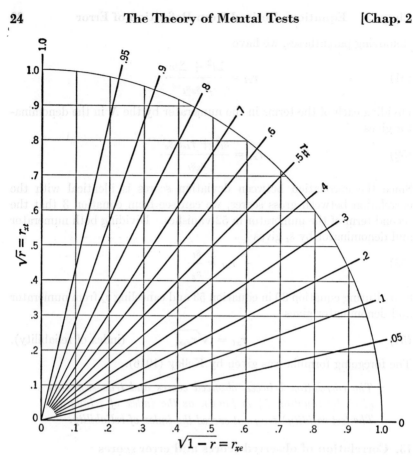

FIGURE 6.   Relationship between test reliability, index of reliability, and correlation of observed and error scores.

Dividing each of the terms in the numerator by the N in the denominator gives

(58) $$r_{xe} = \frac{r_{te}s_ts_e + s_e^2}{s_xs_e}.$$

Again from equation 3 we see that the first term in the numerator vanishes, and we may then divide numerator and denominator by s_e, obtaining

(59) $$r_{xe} = \frac{s_e}{s_x}.$$

Substituting equation 42 in equation 59 and dividing numerator and denominator by s_x gives

(60) $$r_{xe} = \sqrt{1 - r_{x_gx_h}}.$$

Equation 60 gives the correlation between observed scores and error scores as a function of the reliability coefficient. From equation 42, we see that r_{xe} is equal to the standard error of measurement when the test standard deviation is taken as unity. In Chapter 19 it is shown that the standard deviation of standard scores is equal to unity. Thus equation 60 gives the error of measurement for a standard score.

The relationship between the reliability coefficient, the index of reliability, and the quantity $\sqrt{1 - r_{x_g x_h}}$ is shown in Figure 6, which is similar to Figure 3 showing the relationship between reliability, standard deviation, and error of measurement.

The x- and y-axes are scaled by tenths, or finer, from zero to one. One of these axes gives the index of reliability, and the other the correlation between observed and error scores. A quadrant is drawn with radius unity, and is scaled in terms of the reliability coefficient. Any point on this quadrant then represents a given reliability, index of reliability, and correlation between observed and error scores. With any one of the values given, the other two can be read from the graph.

14. Summary

The material in this chapter has been based upon the following definitions:

1. Definitions, from elementary statistics, of the mean, standard deviation, and correlation,

$$M_X = \frac{\Sigma X}{N},$$

$$s_x = \frac{\Sigma x^2}{N},$$

$$r_{xy} = \frac{\Sigma xy}{N s_x s_y}.$$

2. Definition of the relationship between observed, true, and error score,

(1) $$X_i = T_i + E_i,$$

or its equivalent

(14) $$x = t + e.$$

3. Definition of random errors,

(2) $$M_E = 0,$$

(4) $$r_{E_1 E_2} = 0,$$

(3) $$r_{TE} = 0.$$

4. Definition of parallel tests,

(19) $$T_{ig} = T_{ih},$$

(20) $$s_{e_g} = s_{e_h}.$$

From these definitions the following equations have been derived:

1. Since the true score for each individual is the same on parallel tests, it follows that

(21) $$M_{T_g} = M_{T_h},$$

(22) $$s_{T_g} = s_{T_h},$$

(23) $$r_{T_g T_h} = 1.00.$$

2. From the two equations defining parallel tests, it is shown that the observed scores on parallel tests must satisfy the following characteristics:

(27) $$M_{X_g} = M_{X_h},$$

(35) $$s_{x_1} = s_{x_2},$$

(37) $$r_{x_1 x_2} = r_{x_3 x_4}.$$

3. The variance of true scores, observed and error scores are related by the equation

(17) $$s_x{}^2 = s_t{}^2 + s_e{}^2$$

or

(18) $$s_x = \sqrt{s_t{}^2 + s_e{}^2}.$$

4. It has been shown that the mean true score and the standard deviation of both true and error scores can be expressed in terms of observable quantities as follows:

(9) $$M_T = M_X,$$

(39) $$s_t = s_x \sqrt{r_{x_g x_h}},$$

(42) $$s_e = s_x \sqrt{1 - r_{x_g x_h}} \qquad \text{(error of measurement)}.$$

5. It has been shown that the correlation of observed scores with true and error scores can be expressed in terms of observable quantities as follows:

(54) $$r_{xt} = \sqrt{r_{x_g x_h}} \qquad \text{(index of reliability)},$$

(60) $$r_{xe} = \sqrt{1 - r_{x_g x_h}}.$$

Among the foregoing quantities, the error of measurement is the most significant and the most generally useful. Illustrations have been given of how the error of measurement can be used to assign limits between which the person's true score is very likely to be found.

Problems

1. Give the error of measurement, standard deviation of true scores, correlation between observed and error scores, and the index of reliability for each of the following tests:

Test	Number of Items	Means	Standard Deviation	Reliability
A	50	100	15	.91
B	100	211.6	25.7	.84
C	80	57.4	11.3	.78
D	700	361.9	76.5	.87
E	200	127.4	21.9	.76

2. Assume a normal distribution of error scores. Give the true score limits (approximately 0.3 per cent level) for persons making each of the following scores:

(a) A score of 115 on test A.
(b) A score of 211 on test B.
(c) A score of 31 on test C.
(d) A score of 500 on test D.
(e) A score of 100 on test E.

3. For each test A through E what is the minimum difference between the observed scores of two individuals that will give reasonable assurance that they do not have the same true scores?

3

Fundamental Equations Derived
from a Definition of True Score

1. Definition of true score

Again let us begin with basic equation 1 of Chapter 2 ($X = T + E$) and put it in the form

(1) $$E = X - T.$$

In other words, the error is defined as the difference between true score and observed score. Then, if "true score" is defined, the error can be determined. True score is defined as

(2) $$T_i = \lim_{K \to \infty} \frac{\sum_{g=1}^{K} X_{ig}}{K},$$

that is, the true score for a given person (i) is the limit that the average of his scores on a number of tests approaches, as the number of parallel tests (K) increases without limit. These tests are designated by the subscript g, which varies from 1 to K.

2. Definition of parallel tests

In addition to the definition of true score, a definition of parallel tests is needed. Instead of defining parallel tests in terms of true and error score (as we did in the chapter immediately preceding), and then deriving the observed score characteristics of parallel tests, we shall define parallel tests this time in terms of observable characteristics.

Again we may begin with the basic definition that tests are parallel if "it makes no difference which one is used." Clearly such a definition requires that the means and standard deviations of a given group of subjects be equal regardless of which test is used. Expressing this in equational form, we have

(3) $$\bar{X}_1 = \bar{X}_2 = \bar{X}_3 = \bar{X}_4 = \cdots = \bar{X}_k$$

and

(4)
$$s_1 = s_2 = s_3 = s_4 = \cdots = s_k.$$

Also it is clear that

(5)
$$r_{12} = r_{13} = r_{14} = r_{23} = r_{24} = r_{34},$$

since if one of these correlations were higher than the others, the "prediction" from one of these tests to the other would be higher than could be obtained by using other combinations of two tests. "It makes no difference" which test is used only if all the intercorrelations between parallel forms are equal. In order to be useful, this correlation must be high for parallel tests. That is, the standard deviation of the true scores must be considerably greater than the standard deviation of the error scores.

The basic definitions used in this chapter are given in equations 1 to 5, inclusive. From these equations we can, *without any further assumptions*, derive all the equations given in the preceding chapter.

3. Determination of mean true score

The mean true score is obtained by summing equation 2 over the number of cases (N) and dividing by N.

(6)
$$M_T = \frac{\sum\limits_{i=1}^{N} \sum\limits_{g=1}^{K} X_{ig}}{NK} \qquad (K \to \infty).$$

Since the order of summation makes no difference, we may substitute M_g for $\sum\limits_{i=1}^{N} X_i (1/N)$ and write

(7)
$$M_T = \frac{\sum\limits_{g=1}^{K} M_g}{K} \qquad (K \to \infty).$$

By the assumption of equation 3 all the means are equal for parallel tests. Therefore, in the summation, M_g or $\overline{X}_g$ may be treated as a constant, so that $\Sigma M_g = K M_g$. Substituting this value in equation 7 gives

(8)
$$M_T = M_g = \overline{X}_g.$$

The mean observed score is equal to the mean true score. Equation 8 is based only on the definition of equation 2 and the assumption of equation 3.

4. Determination of true score variance

From the definition of a standard deviation, we may write

$$(9) \qquad s_T{}^2 = \frac{\sum\limits_{i=1}^{N} (T_i - M_T)^2}{N}.$$

In order to simplify the term in parentheses, we can make use of equations 2 and 8, obtaining

$$(10) \qquad T_i - M_T = \frac{\sum\limits_{g=1}^{K} X_{ig}}{K} - M_g.$$

We omit here the proviso, stated in equation 2, that the true score is the limit of the average of a large number of tests as "K approaches infinity." This proviso is omitted for convenience in the following equations. It will be introduced explicitly again in equation 18. It should be noted that nothing is done in the meantime, in equations 11 through 17, to invalidate carrying the assumption through.

In order to simplify the notation, let us use t to designate a deviation score and put all the right-hand term over one denominator, obtaining

$$(11) \qquad t = \frac{\sum\limits_{g=1}^{K} X_{ig} - KM_g}{K}.$$

The numerator of equation 11 may be written as shown below and the equation expressed as follows:

$$(12) \qquad t = \frac{\sum\limits_{g=1}^{K} (X_{ig} - M_g)}{K}.$$

We may substitute x for $X - M$ and write out the numerator to avoid the summation sign, obtaining

$$(13) \qquad t = \frac{x_1 + x_2 + x_3 + \cdots + x_K}{K}.$$

The value of t in equation 13 may be substituted for $T - M$ in equation 9:

$$(14) \qquad s_t{}^2 = \frac{\sum\limits_{i=1}^{N} (x_{i1} + x_{i2} + x_{i3} + \cdots + x_{iK})^2}{NK^2}.$$

Expanding the numerator and omitting the limits on the summation sign, since all summations are over N, we can write

$$(15) \quad s_t^2 = \frac{\Sigma x_1^2 + \Sigma x_2^2 + \Sigma x_3^2 + \cdots + \Sigma x_K^2 + \Sigma x_1 x_2 + \Sigma x_1 x_3 + \cdots + \Sigma x_K x_{K-1}}{NK^2}.$$

We may substitute Ns^2 for Σx^2, and $Nr_{12}s_1 s_2$ for $\Sigma x_1 x_2$, and correspondingly for other products. This substitution gives

$$(16) \quad s_t^2 = \frac{Ns_1^2 + Ns_2^2 + Ns_3^2 + \cdots + Ns_K^2 + Nr_{12}s_1 s_2 + Nr_{13}s_1 s_3 + \cdots + Nr_{K(K-1)}s_K s_{K-1}}{NK^2}.$$

We may divide the numerator and the denominator by N. Since from equations 4 and 5 we see that, according to the definition of parallel tests, all standard deviations are equal and all intercorrelations are equal, we may substitute s_g^2 for each of the variances and r_{gh} for each of the intercorrelations.[1] These substitutions result in

$$(17) \quad s_t^2 = \frac{Ks_g^2 + K(K-1)r_{gh}s_g^2}{K^2}.$$

Dividing the numerator and the denominator through by K and separating terms gives

$$(18) \quad s_t^2 = \frac{s_g^2}{K} + \left(1 - \frac{1}{K}\right)r_{gh}s_g^2.$$

As was noted in equation 10, we neglected to specify that K should approach infinity, as was done in equation 2 defining the true score. If we now introduce this part of the definition of true score,

$$(19) \quad s_t^2 = r_{gh}s_g^2 \qquad \text{(true variance)}.$$

If we take the square root of both sides of equation 19, we have

$$(20) \quad s_t = s_g\sqrt{r_{gh}} \qquad \text{(true standard deviation)}.$$

Equations 19 and 20 give the variance and standard deviation of the distribution of true scores in terms of the test reliability and the standard deviation of the distribution of observed scores. These equations may be derived by assuming only equations 2, 4, and 5.

[1] Note that r_{gh} is the correlation between any two parallel tests (g and h), and therefore is a reliability coefficient. It is identical with $r_{x_g x_h}$, which was used for the reliability coefficient in Chapter 2.

It should be noted that equations 19 and 20 are the same as equations 38 and 39 given in Chapter 2 for true variance and true standard deviation. However, in the preceding chapter these theorems were derived from assumptions about "random errors" and a definition of "parallel tests" in terms of true and error scores. In this chapter the same theorems are derived from a definition of "true score" (equation 2) and from a definition of parallel tests that depends upon observed scores.

5. Correlation of true with observed scores (the index of reliability)

Using the usual formula for correlation and the definition of true score as the average of scores on a large number of parallel tests (see equation 2), we may write

$$(21) \qquad r_{xt} = \frac{\Sigma x_1(x_1 + x_2 + \cdots + x_K)}{NKs_1s_t} \qquad (K \to \infty).$$

Removing the parentheses gives

$$(22) \qquad r_{xt} = \frac{\Sigma x_1^2 + \Sigma x_1x_2 + \Sigma x_1x_3 + \cdots + \Sigma x_1x_K}{NKs_1s_t} \qquad (K \to \infty).$$

Dividing both numerator and denominator by N gives

$$(23) \qquad r_{xt} = \frac{s_1^2 + r_{12}s_1s_2 + r_{13}s_1s_3 + \cdots + r_{1K}s_1s_K}{Ks_1s_t} \qquad (K \to \infty).$$

Canceling s_1 from numerator and denominator, we have

$$(24) \qquad r_{xt} = \frac{s_1 + r_{12}s_2 + r_{13}s_3 + \cdots + r_{1K}s_K}{Ks_t} \qquad (K \to \infty).$$

It will be noted that there are $K - 1$ terms involving r. Since the sum of a series of terms is equal to the number of terms multiplied by the average term, we may write

$$(25) \qquad r_{xt} = \frac{s_1 + (K - 1)\overline{rs}}{Ks_t} \qquad (K \to \infty),$$

where $\overline{rs}$ equals the sum of the terms $r_{gh}s_g$ divided by $K - 1$. Substituting for s_t its value from equation 20, we have

$$(26) \qquad r_{xt} = \frac{s_g + (K - 1)\overline{r_{gh}s_g}}{Ks_g\sqrt{r_{gh}}} \qquad (K \to \infty).$$

According to equations 3, 4, and 5, one of the rs products may be substituted for the average of an infinite number.   Making this substitution, dividing numerator and denominator by s_g, and separating the terms gives

$$(27) \qquad r_{xt} = \frac{1}{K\sqrt{r_{gh}}} + \left(1 - \frac{1}{K}\right)\sqrt{r_{gh}} \qquad (K \to \infty).$$

If we let K approach infinity, equation 27 becomes

$$(28) \qquad r_{xt} = \sqrt{r_{gh}} \qquad \text{(index of reliability)},$$

where r_{gh} is the reliability of the test.

> *The test validity* [1] *may not exceed the correlation between observed scores and true scores, or the index of reliability as given by equation 28.*

Again it may be noted that this equation is identical with the equation given in the preceding chapter for the correlation between true and observed scores.   However, it is derived from one set of assumptions in Chapter 2 and from another set in Chapter 3.

6. Average error

Using equation 1 for errors, we may sum it over persons from 1 to N. Since all summations are over persons from 1 to N, no ambiguity will arise if subscripts are omitted and the limits of summation are not indicated.   We write

$$(29) \qquad \Sigma E = \Sigma X - \Sigma T.$$

Dividing equation 29 by N, we have

$$(30) \qquad M_E = M_X - M_T.$$

Substituting equation 8, we see that

$$(31) \qquad M_E = 0.$$

> *The average error is zero.*

7. The standard deviation of error scores (the error of measurement)

Using the usual formula for standard deviation, we may write from equation 1, noting that the differences of deviation scores equal the differences of gross score,

$$(32) \qquad s_e{}^2 = \frac{\Sigma(x - t)^2}{N}.$$

---

[1] See definition and discussion of validity, Chapter 9.

Expanding the numerator, we have

(33)
$$s_e^2 = \frac{\Sigma x^2 + \Sigma t^2 - 2\Sigma xt}{N}.$$

Dividing through by N gives

(34)
$$s_e^2 = s_x^2 + s_t^2 - 2r_{xt}s_xs_t.$$

Substituting equations 20 and 28 in equation 34 gives

(35)
$$s_e^2 = s_x^2 + s_g^2 r_{gh} - 2\sqrt{r_{gh}}s_xs_x\sqrt{r_{gh}}.$$

Combining terms in equation 35 and simplifying, we get [1]

(36)
$$s_e^2 = s_x^2 - s_x^2 r_{gh},$$

or

(37) $s_e^2 = s_x^2(1 - r_{gh})$ (variance of the errors of measurement).

Taking the square root of both sides of equation 37, we have the usual formula for the error of measurement,

(38)
$$s_e = s_x\sqrt{1 - r_{gh}}$$ (error of measurement).

where s_x is the standard deviation of the distribution of gross scores, and r_{gh} is the test reliability.

> *Equations 37 and 38 are the same as equations 41 and 42 in Chapter 2. In this chapter the error of measurement is derived from the assumptions of equations 1, 2, 4, and 5.*

8. Relationship between true and error variance

By adding equations 37 and 19 we obtain

(39)
$$s_t^2 + s_e^2 = r_{gh}s_g^2 + s_g^2(1 - r_{gh}).$$

If we factor out s_g^2, we have

(40)
$$s_t^2 + s_e^2 = s_g^2(r_{gh} + 1 - r_{gh}),$$

which equals

(41)
$$s_g^2 = s_t^2 + s_e^2.$$

> *The true variance plus the error variance is equal to the observed variance.*

[1] Note that for parallel tests s_x, s_g, and s_h may be used interchangeably.

Again it may be pointed out that the last three theorems involving error variance were proved from a different set of assumptions in Chapter 2.

9. Correlation of errors and observed scores

Using the usual formula for correlation, we can write—from equation 1,

$$(42) \qquad r_{ex} = \frac{\Sigma x(x - t)}{N s_x s_e}.$$

Expanding and factoring out N as before gives

$$(43) \qquad r_{ex} = \frac{s_g{}^2 - r_{gt} s_g s_t}{s_g s_e}.$$

Factoring out s_g and substituting from equations 20, 28, and 38 gives

$$(44) \qquad r_{ex} = \frac{s_g - \sqrt{r_{gh}} s_g \sqrt{r_{gh}}}{s_g \sqrt{1 - r_{gh}}}.$$

Dividing through by s_g again, we have

$$(45) \qquad r_{ex} = \frac{1 - r_{gh}}{\sqrt{1 - r_{gh}}},$$

which is equivalent to

$$(46) \qquad r_{ex} = \sqrt{1 - r_{gh}},$$

where r_{gh} is the test reliability.

Equation 46 is identical with equation 60 of Chapter 2. It is equal to the standard error of measurement when the test standard deviation is unity. Since the standard deviation of standard scores is equal to unity (see Chapter 19), equation 46 is sometimes referred to as the error of measurement for a standard score.

10. The correlation between true score and error score

This correlation is derived by exactly the same procedure as in the last section. We first write

$$(47) \qquad r_{et} = \frac{\Sigma t(x - t)}{N s_t s_e}.$$

Expanding equation 47 and dividing by N, we have

$$(48) \qquad r_{et} = \frac{r_{tx} s_t s_x - s_t{}^2}{s_t s_e}.$$

Substituting the values of r_{tx}, s_t, and s_t^2 from equations 19, 20, and 28, we have

(49)
$$r_{et} = \frac{s_g^2 \sqrt{r_{gh}} \sqrt{r_{gh}} - s_g^2 r_{gh}}{s_t s_e} \qquad (s_g \equiv s_x).$$

it can be seen that the numerator is equal to zero, and therefore

(50)
$$r_{et} = 0.$$

The correlation between error scores and true scores is zero.

This theorem, which is proved from the definitions of true score and parallel tests, is identical with one of the assumptions made in defining random error in Chapter 2.

11. Summary

In this chapter we began with a definition of true score and a definition of parallel tests in terms of observed scores. From these definitions the fundamental theorems of test theory were derived. By comparison we see that they are the same as those in Chapter 2, except that a different set of equations was chosen for the assumptions.

First error was defined as the difference between the observed and the true score:

(1)
$$E = X - T.$$

True score of a given person was defined as the average of his scores on a number of parallel tests, as this number increases without limit.

(2)
$$T_i = \lim_{K \to \infty} \frac{\sum\limits_{g=1}^{K} X_{ig}}{K}.$$

Parallel tests were defined as tests with equal means, standard deviations, and intercorrelations:

(3)
$$\overline{X}_1 = \overline{X}_2 = \cdots = \overline{X}_K,$$

(4)
$$s_1 = s_2 = \cdots = s_K,$$

(5)
$$r_{12} = r_{13} = \cdots = r_{K(K-1)}.$$

Another way to state the definitions of equations 3, 4, and 5 is to say that for a group of parallel tests we assume that a reasonable approximation is obtained if we substitute the mean of a single test for the mean of the mean of all tests. In like manner, the variance of a single test furnishes a reasonable approximation to the average of the variances of an infinite number of tests; and the covariance of a single pair of tests furnishes a reasonable approximation to the average of the covariances of an infinite number of parallel tests. This set of assumptions is necessary in order to enable us to substitute actual values in the formulas derived.

The true score mean, variance, and standard deviation were found to be

(8)
$$M_T = M_g,$$

(19)
$$s_t^2 = r_{gh}s_g^2,$$

(20)
$$s_t = s_g\sqrt{r_{gh}}.$$

It was proved that the error score mean, variance, and standard deviation were

(31)
$$M_E = 0,$$

(37)
$$s_e^2 = s_g^2(1 - r_{gh}),$$

(38)
$$s_e = s_g\sqrt{1 - r_{gh}} \qquad \text{(error of measurement)}.$$

The intercorrelations of observed, true, and error scores were shown to be

(50)
$$r_{te} = 0.$$

(46)
$$r_{ex} = \sqrt{1 - r_{gh}},$$

(28)
$$r_{tx} = \sqrt{r_{gh}} \qquad \text{(index of reliability)}.$$

It was also shown that

(41)
$$s_x^2 = s_e^2 + s_t^2.$$

From the definition of true score we see that the score is the same regardless of the particular few tests a person takes, and consequently the true variance for a number of parallel tests is the same. Since the observed and the true variances are the same for each of a set of parallel tests, it follows that the error variance of each of the tests should be the same. That is, we may write

$$T_{ig} = T_{ih},$$

$$s_{t_g} = s_{t_h},$$

$$s_{e_g} = s_{e_h}.$$

These characteristics of parallel tests were assumed in Chapter 2, and those given in equations 3, 4, and 5 were derived.

The set of equations derived in this chapter are identical with those derived in Chapter 2. It has been shown that the fundamental equations of test theory can be derived either from a definition of error and a definition of parallel tests in terms of true and error score or from a definition of true score and a definition of parallel tests in terms of observed scores.

Problems

1. Write the equation corresponding to each of the following assumptions:

A. The true score is the difference between observed score and error score.
B. The average error score for a large group of persons is zero.
C. True scores and error scores are uncorrelated.
D. Error scores on one form of a test are uncorrelated with those on another form.
E. Parallel tests have identical means.
F. Parallel tests have identical standard deviations.

2. Using only the necessary ones of the foregoing assumptions (and no additional assumptions), derive each of the following:

(*a*) What is the value of the average true score?
(*b*) The observed variance is the sum of true and error variance.
(*c*) Find the value of the true variance.
(*d*) Find the value of the error variance.
(*e*) Find the correlation between observed and error scores.
(*f*) Find the correlation between true and observed scores.

Note: Work each of the foregoing six derivations independently. At the beginning of each of the six derivations, give the assumptions from the list (*A–F*) that are *essential* for that particular derivation.

3. By using only equations 1, 20, and 28, prove that the correlation between errors on test *g* and errors on test *h* is zero if *g* and *h* are parallel tests.

4

Errors of Measurement,
Substitution, and Prediction

1. Introduction

The commonly used and most generally useful measure of "test error" is the "error of measurement" defined in Chapters 2 and 3. It is the standard deviation of the distribution of differences between observed score and true score. However, there are other possible measures of test error that are useful for certain purposes. These measures will be considered in this chapter. The four different types of error are defined as follows:

$$e = x - t,$$

$$\mathbf{e} = t - r_{xt}\left(\frac{s_t}{s_x}\right)x,$$

$$d = x_1 - x_2,$$

$$\mathbf{d} = x_1 - r_{12}\left(\frac{s_1}{s_2}\right)x_2.$$

Stated in words, these four types of error are:

The difference between true and observed score.
The error made in estimating true score from observed score.
The difference between two observed scores on parallel tests.
The error made in predicting one observed score from the score on a
    parallel test.

These different measures of error are presented by Kelley (1927).

The third type of error listed above is the simplest and most direct measure of error, so let us consider it first.

2. Error of substitution [1]

Here we define the error as the difference between two observed scores on parallel tests, that is,

$$(1) \qquad d = x_1 - x_2.$$

This definition of error applies if we are interested in considering the possible differences between the results of one investigator using a given test and another investigator using a parallel form of the same test.

In order to obtain the standard deviation of these difference scores, which is the standard error of substitution, we get the standard deviation in the usual way, by squaring, summing, and dividing by N. This gives

$$(2) \qquad \frac{\Sigma d^2}{N} = \frac{\Sigma(x_1 - x_2)^2}{N}.$$

We may substitute s_d^2 for the left-hand member and expand the right-hand member, obtaining

$$(3) \qquad s_d{}^2 = \frac{\Sigma x_1{}^2}{N} + \frac{\Sigma x_2{}^2}{N} - \frac{2\Sigma x_1 x_2}{N}.$$

Since the first two terms are variances and the last one a covariance, we may write

$$(4) \qquad s_d{}^2 = s_1{}^2 + s_2{}^2 - 2r_{12}s_1 s_2.$$

Since standard deviations of parallel tests are equal, we may write

$$(5) \qquad s_d{}^2 = 2s_1{}^2(1 - r_{12}),$$

where $s_d{}^2$ is the error of substitution or the error made in substituting a score on one test for a score on a parallel form,

$s_1{}^2$ is the observed variance of the test,

r_{12} is the test reliability, or the correlation of two parallel forms.

Taking the square root of both sides of equation 5 gives

$$(6) \qquad s_d = s_1 \sqrt{2(1 - r_{12})}$$

The error made in substituting a score on one test for a score on a parallel form is given by equation 6. This is also the standard error of a difference for the case in which the two standard deviations are alike.

---

[1] This term was introduced by M. W. Richardson while teaching at the University of Chicago.

3. Error in estimating observed score

Instead of saying that we substitute the score on one test for the score on a parallel form, we can use the ordinary "error of estimate" and compute the minimal error that can be made in predicting the score on one form from the other form by using the least squares regression equation. As indicated in the introduction to this chapter, we write

$$(7) \qquad \mathbf{d} = x_1 - r_{12}\left(\frac{s_1}{s_2}\right)x_2.$$

As before, we write the variance of $\mathbf{d}$, noting that since $s_1 = s_2$, the term in parentheses is unity and may be omitted.

$$(8) \qquad \frac{\Sigma \mathbf{d}^2}{N} = \frac{\Sigma(x_1 - r_{12}x_2)^2}{N}.$$

Expanding as before and substituting $s_\mathbf{d}^2$ for the left-hand term, we have

$$(9) \qquad s_\mathbf{d}^2 = \frac{\Sigma x_1^2}{N} + \frac{r_{12}^2 \Sigma x_2^2}{N} - \frac{2r_{12}\Sigma x_1 x_2}{N}.$$

Equation 9 can be rewritten as

$$(10) \qquad s_\mathbf{d}^2 = s_1^2 + r_{12}^2 s_2^2 - 2r_{12}^2 s_1 s_2.$$

Since the variances of parallel tests are equal we may write

$$(11) \qquad s_\mathbf{d}^2 = s_1^2(1 - r_{12}^2).$$

Taking the square root, we have the final equation

$$(12) \qquad s_\mathbf{d} = s_1\sqrt{1 - r_{12}^2},$$

which is the usual standard error of *estimate*.

> *Equation 12 gives the error made when the regression equation is used to estimate the scores on one test from scores on a parallel test.*

It should be noted that equation 12 is the correct one to use if the regression equation has been used to estimate scores on a parallel form and we wish to determine the error involved. Equation 6 is the correct one to use if scores on one test are assumed to be equal to those on a parallel test without use of any regression equation.

4. The error of measurement

The error of measurement can be interpreted in several ways, which will be considered in the next chapter. We shall consider here only one interpretation, namely, the error of measurement is the error made in substituting the observed score for the true score. We wish to assign each person a true score, and instead we assign the observed score. The difference between these two scores is the error of measurement. Derivations of this error of measurement have been given in preceding chapters; however, one will be repeated here.

One of the basic assumptions of test theory is that

(13) $$x = t + e.$$

Squaring and summing both sides gives

(14) $$\Sigma x^2 = \Sigma(t + e)^2.$$

Expanding the term in parentheses, we have

(15) $$\Sigma x^2 = \Sigma t^2 + \Sigma e^2 + 2\Sigma te.$$

Dividing through by N we can write this equation in terms of variances and covariances as follows:

(16) $$s_x{}^2 = s_t{}^2 + s_e{}^2 + 2r_{te}s_t s_e.$$

Since one of the fundamental assumptions in the definition of error is that it correlates zero with true score, we may omit the last term and write

(17) $$s_x{}^2 = s_t{}^2 + s_e{}^2.$$

From the previous discussion of true variance we see that $r_{xx}s_x{}^2$ is equal to the true variance.[1] Therefore, substituting this for $s_t{}^2$ and solving for $s_e{}^2$, we have

(18) $$s_e{}^2 = s_x{}^2 - s_x{}^2 r_{xx},$$

which may be written

(19) $$s_e{}^2 = s_x{}^2(1 - r_{xx}).$$

Taking the square root of both sides, we have

(20) $$s_e = s_x \sqrt{1 - r_{xx}},$$

which is the formula previously given for the error of measurement.

---

[1] In Chapter 2, the symbol $r_{x_g x_h}$ was used for the reliability coefficient to emphasize the fact that it was the correlation between forms g and h of a test. Similarly, in Chapter 3 the subscripts g and h were retained so that a sum of reliability coefficients could be indicated. When we are not emphasizing the correlation among various parallel forms, it is convenient to designate the reliability coefficient by repeating a subscript. Thus r_{xx} is the reliability of test x; r_{yy}, the reliability of test y; r_{11} and r_{22}, the reliability of tests 1 and 2, respectively; etc.

*The error of measurement is the error made in substituting
the observed score for the true score.*

5. Error in estimating true score

In this chapter we have considered the error made in substituting the
score on one test for the score on a parallel test. Also we have shown
that the error made is smaller if we use the score on the first test to
predict the score on the second test and then obtain the error of estimate. The error of measurement can be interpreted in several ways;
one way is to regard it as the error made in *substituting* the observed
score for the true score. Also it is possible to ask what error is made in
attempting to *predict* the true score from the observed score. In order
to obtain this error, we set up the usual prediction equation:

$$(21) \qquad \hat{t} = r_{xt}\left(\frac{s_t}{s_x}\right) x,$$

where $\hat{t}$ is the predicted value of the true score. The difference between
the actual and predicted true score is the error. This may be written

$$(22) \qquad \mathbf{e} = t - r_{xt}\left(\frac{s_t}{s_x}\right) x.$$

The standard deviation of $\mathbf{e}$ or the usual error of estimate then is

$$(23) \qquad s_{\mathbf{e}} = s_t\sqrt{1 - r_{xt}^2}.$$

Since $s_t = s_x\sqrt{r_{xx}}$ and $r_{xt} = \sqrt{r_{xx}}$, as was shown in Chapters 2 and 3,
we may write

$$(24) \qquad s_{\mathbf{e}} = s_x\sqrt{r_{xx}}\sqrt{1 - r_{xx}}.$$

*The error made in using the best fitting regression equation
to predict the true score from the observed score is given by
equation 24.*

It may seem paradoxical at first to note that $s_{\mathbf{e}} = 0$ if $r_{xx} = 0$. However, we see in equation 39 of Chapter 2 that $s_x\sqrt{r_{xx}}$ is the standard
deviation of the true scores. Thus $s_{\mathbf{e}}$ is always some fraction of the true
standard deviation. By inspection of the equation $s_t = s_x\sqrt{r_{xx}}$ we see
that if the reliability is zero, $s_t = 0$; hence any fraction of it also is zero.

6. Comparison of four errors

The relative magnitude of these four errors is shown in Figure 1.
The relationship can easily be seen if the expression $1 - r^2$ is factored

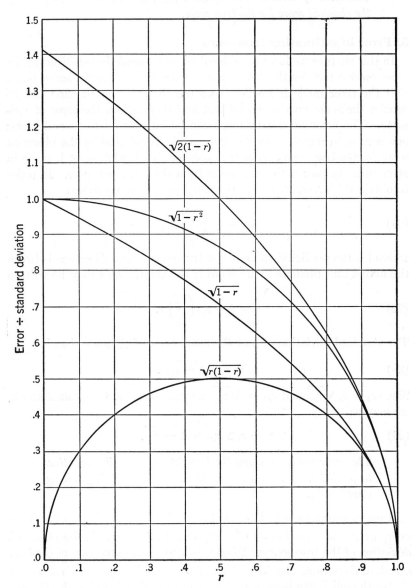

FIGURE 1. Comparison of errors of measurement, prediction, and substitution.

into $(1 - r)(1 + r)$. The four errors arranged in order from smallest to largest may be written as follows:

$$s_e = s_x\sqrt{1 - r_{xx}}\ \sqrt{r_{xx}},$$

$$s_e = s_x\sqrt{1 - r_{xx}}\ \sqrt{1},$$

$$s_d = s_x\sqrt{1 - r_{xx}}\ \sqrt{1 + r_{xx}},$$

$$s_d = s_x\sqrt{1 - r_{xx}}\ \sqrt{2}.$$

These terms are written so that they are identical except for the last factor. Since the reliability coefficient must be between zero and one, we shall always have $r_{xx} < 1 < 1 + r_{xx} < 2$. Thus for any given set of data we shall always find that $s_e < s_e < s_d < s_d$.

7. Summary

Four different sorts of test error have been considered. Two of them are what might be called "errors of substitution"; one is the error involved in substituting a score on one test for a score on a parallel test, the other is the error involved in substituting the observed score for the true score. This latter error is the most commonly used one and is termed the error of measurement.

Corresponding to each of these errors of substitution is an "error of estimate." One is the ordinary error of estimate, which is the error made in estimating score on one test from score on a parallel test. The other is the error made in estimating the true score from observed score. This latter one is almost never used, since no practical advantage is gained from using the regression equation to estimate true scores.

The equations for these four errors are

(1) $$d = x_1 - x_2,$$

(7) $$d = x_1 - rx_2,$$

(13) $$e = x - t,$$

(22) $$e = t - rx,$$

while the corresponding standard deviations are

(6) $$s_d = s_x\sqrt{2(1 - r_{xx})},$$

(12) $$s_d = s_x\sqrt{1 - r_{xx}^2},$$

(20) $$s_e = s_x\sqrt{1 - r_{xx}},$$

(24) $$s_e = s_x\sqrt{r_{xx}(1 - r_{xx})}.$$

Problems

1. Give each of the four error indices for each of the following five tests.

Test	Number of Items	Means	Standard Deviation	Reliability
A	70	40	10.0	.84
B	50	35	5.0	.72
C	400	251	55.7	.93
D	200	110	25.8	.89
E	150	60	15.2	.78

2. Read the Douglass (1934) and Monroe (1934) articles, and write a brief résumé and criticism of the material.

3. Forms M and L of the Stanford Binet are parallel forms. One investigator uses form M in a school, and later another investigator uses form L on the same group. An enterprising student calculates the score differences to verify the formula for the standard error of measurement $(1 - r)\sigma_x^2$.

(a) Will he verify this formula?

(b) What error measure would be verified for score differences?

(c) If the verification were not precise, what explanation would be reasonable?

4. One investigator used one form of an arithmetic test (a brief 5-minute form) in his investigation. Another investigator used another 2-hour arithmetic test and divided the total number solved by 24 to make results comparable with the 5-minute form. The standard deviation of the differences between these scores would be given by what formula?

5. Form M of the Binet test has been in constant use in a given clinic. The director orders that form L of the Binet test be used in the future. For uniformity all old M scores are to be expressed in terms of the new form.

(a) What method will accomplish this with minimum error?

(b) What formula gives this error?

6. Under what condition will the standard error of measurement equal zero?

7. Under what condition will the standard error of measurement equal the standard deviation of true scores?

8. Under what condition will the standard error of measurement equal the standard deviation of the test scores?

9. Under what condition is the standard error of estimate equal to zero?

10. Under what conditions is the standard error of estimate equal to the standard deviation of the variable being predicted?

11. Under what condition is the standard error of estimate equal to the standard deviation of the variable used for prediction?

12. Mr. A obtains a score of 117 on test E (problem 1) and Mr. B obtains a score of 95 on test E.

(a) What is the standard error of Mr. A's test score?
(b) What is the standard error of Mr. B's test score?
(c) What upper and lower limits would be assigned to Mr. A's true score at the 0.3 per cent level?
(d) What upper and lower limits would be assigned to Mr. B's true score at the 0.3 per cent level?

13. Study the material given by Bradford (1940).   Comment on his results.

14. Study the equation for the reliability of a standard score given by Dickey (1930), and comment on this concept of error.

5

Various Interpretations
of the Error of Measurement

1. Error of measurement and error of substitution

Having in the previous chapter shown the difference between several different types of "error," we shall now consider more intensively the "error of measurement." Several alternative derivations or "interpretations" of this quantity will be given in order to show more clearly its properties and its meaning.

The error of measurement has already been derived as the standard deviation of the difference between true and observed score. However, the fact that this formula $(s_1\sqrt{1-r})$ involves the expression $1 - r$ instead of $1 - r^2$, as does the error of estimate, usually provokes some inquiry such as, "Why don't you use $1 - r^2$ in the error of measurement?" It may be in order here to derive the error of measurement in some other ways to show the nature of the difference between it and the error of estimate. As shown in equation 7 of Chapter 4, the entire amount of the error made in predicting is called the "error of estimate." Also by inspecting equation 1 of Chapter 4, we see that the entire amount of the difference between the score on one test and on the other test is charged to the "error." Let us see what happens when this difference $(x_1 - x_2)$ is charged partly to one test and partly to the other.

If we assume that the error is partly in x and partly in y and that these two errors are uncorrelated, we obtain the following:

$$(1) \qquad e_1 + e_2 = d.$$

Summing and squaring, we find that

$$(2) \qquad \Sigma e_1^2 + \Sigma e_2^2 + 2\Sigma e_1 e_2 = \Sigma d^2.$$

If we divide by N,

$$(3) \qquad s_{e_1}^2 + s_{e_2}^2 + 2r_{e_1 e_2} s_{e_1} s_{e_2} = s_d^2,$$

and if we assume that the error variance for one test is equal to that for the other test and that errors correlate zero,

$$(4) \qquad\qquad 2s_{e_1}^{\,2} = s_d^{\,2}.$$

Substituting from equation 5 of Chapter 4, we obtain

$$(5) \qquad\qquad s_e^{\,2} = s_1^{\,2}(1 - r_{12}),$$

which is the error of measurement, as previously derived from the definition $e = x - t$.

> *If the difference between two parallel tests is assumed to be divided into two equal and uncorrelated parts, the standard deviation of each of these parts is given by the usual formula for the standard error of measurement.*

The error of estimate, which uses the term $(1 - r^2)$, is a measure of the total error made in predicting score on one test from score on another test by using the least squares regression line for prediction.

2. Error of measurement as an error of estimate

Let us consider another derivation of the error of measurement in order to aid in showing "why" we use $(1 - r)$ instead of $(1 - r^2)$. The error of measurement will be shown to be the error of estimate obtained from the regression of observed score on true score. We may begin with the ordinary regression equation,

$$(6) \qquad\qquad x = r_{xt}\left(\frac{s_x}{s_t}\right)t.$$

Obtaining the error of estimate in the usual way, we see that it may be written

$$(7) \qquad\qquad s_{e_{x}\cdot t} = s_x\sqrt{1 - r_{xt}^{\,2}}.$$

Since $r_{xt} = \sqrt{r_{xx}}$ (see Chapters 2 and 3), we may also write

$$(8) \qquad\qquad s_{e_{x}\cdot t} = s_x\sqrt{1 - r_{xx}},$$

which is the error of measurement.

> *The error of estimate derived from the regression of observed upon true score is the same as the error of measurement.*

3. Error of measurement as interaction between persons and tests

Those students who are acquainted with elementary analysis of variance methods, involving a first-order interaction—see Lindquist (1940) or Fisher (1946)—will find that the following material aids in understanding the error of measurement. Those unacquainted with analysis of variance should omit the remainder of this chapter. For additional material on the relation between analysis of variance and the error of measurement, see Hoyt (1941), Jackson (1939), (1940b), and Kaitz (1945a).

Let us consider first the case of two tests, designated as x and y. The average of the two scores $(x + y)/2$ is designated as a. We have thus the following matrix of scores for N persons:

x_1	x_2	x_3	$\cdots$	x_N	M_x	first score
y_1	y_2	y_3	$\cdots$	y_N	M_y	second score

$a_1 \quad a_2 \quad a_3 \quad \cdots \quad a_N$ average of first and second scores.

With no loss of generality, we can assume that the total mean $(\Sigma x + \Sigma y)$ is zero; then the sum of squares due to tests is

$$N(M_x^2 + M_y^2).$$

The sum of squares due to persons is

$$2\Sigma a^2,$$

and the total sum of squares is

$$\Sigma x^2 + \Sigma y^2.$$

Thus the sum of squares due to interaction is

$$\Sigma x^2 + \Sigma y^2 - 2\Sigma a^2 - N(M_x^2 + M_y^2).$$

If, in the foregoing expression, we substitute $(x + y)/2$ for a and write I^2 for the sum of squares due to interaction, we have

$$(9) \qquad I^2 = \Sigma x^2 + \Sigma y^2 - \frac{2\Sigma(x + y)^2}{4} - N(M_x^2 + M_y^2).$$

Expanding the third term gives

$$(10) \quad I^2 = \Sigma x^2 + \Sigma y^2 - \frac{\Sigma x^2}{2} - \frac{\Sigma y^2}{2} - \Sigma xy - N(M_x^2 + M_y^2).$$

Combining similar terms, and adding and subtracting NM_xM_y, we have Equation (11)

$$I^2 = \frac{\Sigma x^2}{2} + \frac{\Sigma y^2}{2} - \Sigma xy + NM_xM_y - N(M_x^2 + M_y^2) - NM_xM_y.$$

By dividing the term in parentheses into two equal parts and writing them separately, we have

(12) $I^2 = \dfrac{\Sigma x^2 - NM_x^2}{2} + \dfrac{\Sigma y^2 - NM_y^2}{2} - (\Sigma xy - NM_xM_y)$

$$- \frac{N}{2}(M_x^2 + M_y^2 + 2M_xM_y).$$

We obtain the variance due to interaction by dividing the sum of squares due to interaction by the degrees of freedom $(N - 1)$. Thus we obtain

(13) $\dfrac{I^2}{N-1} = \dfrac{\Sigma x^2 - NM_x^2}{2(N-1)} + \dfrac{\Sigma y^2 - NM_y^2}{2(N-1)} - \dfrac{\Sigma xy - NM_xM_y}{N-1}$

$$- \frac{N}{2(N-1)}(M_x + M_y)^2.$$

Since $M_x = -M_y$, the last term in equation 13 vanishes. The other terms are equal to variances and covariances so that we can rewrite the equation as follows:

(14) $$\frac{I^2}{N-1} = \frac{s_x^2}{2} + \frac{s_y^2}{2} - r_{xy}s_xs_y.$$

If $s_x = s_y$, we may put s_x in place of s_y and use r_{xx} instead of r_{xy}, obtaining

(15) $$\frac{I^2}{N-1} = s_x^2 - r_{xx}s_x^2,$$

which is equal to

(16) $$\frac{I^2}{N-1} = s_x^2(1 - r_{xx}).$$

The variance due to interaction between persons and tests is the square of the error of measurement.

Let us extend the demonstration of the relationship between interaction and error variance to the case of K tests, where K may be any number. We may begin with the matrix of scores

$$
\begin{array}{ccccccc}
x_{11} & x_{12} & x_{13} & \cdots & x_{1K} & a_1 \\
x_{21} & x_{22} & x_{23} & \cdots & x_{2K} & a_2 \\
x_{31} & x_{32} & x_{33} & \cdots & x_{3K} & a_3 \\
\cdot & \cdot & \cdot & & \cdot & \cdot \\
\cdot & \cdot & \cdot & & \cdot & \cdot \\
\cdot & \cdot & \cdot & & \cdot & \cdot \\
x_{N1} & x_{N2} & x_{N3} & \cdots & x_{NK} & a_N \\
M_1 & M_2 & M_3 & \cdots & M_K & 0.
\end{array}
$$

Again let us assume that the grand mean is zero since this will simplify the expressions without loss of generality. Let us use i and j (varying from 1 to N) as the subscripts representing persons, and g and h (varying from 1 to K) as the subscripts representing tests. We may then write the total sum of squares as

$$
\sum_{i=1}^{N} \sum_{g=1}^{K} x_{ig}^{2}.
$$

The sum of squares for tests would be

$$
N \sum_{g=1}^{K} M_g^{2},
$$

where

$$
M_g = \frac{\sum_{i=1}^{N} x_{ig}}{N}.
$$

Similarly the sum of squares due to persons would be

$$
K \sum_{i=1}^{N} a_i^{2},
$$

where

$$
a_i = \frac{\sum_{g=1}^{K} x_{ig}}{K}.
$$

The sum of squares due to interaction may be designated by I^2 and written as

$$
(17) \qquad I^2 = \sum_{i=1}^{N} \sum_{g=1}^{K} x_{ig}^{2} - K \sum_{i=1}^{N} a_i^{2} - N \sum_{g=1}^{K} M_g^{2}.
$$

Using the definition of a_i given above, we can write

$$(18) \qquad I^2 = \sum_{i=1}^{N} \sum_{g=1}^{K} x_{ig}^2 - \frac{K}{K^2} \sum_{i=1}^{N} \left[\sum_{g=1}^{K} x_{ig} \right]^2 - N \sum_{g=1}^{K} M_g^2.$$

This equation can be rewritten as

$$(19) \quad I^2 = \sum_{g=1}^{K} \left[\sum_{i=1}^{N} x_{ig}^2 \right] - \frac{1}{K} \sum_{g=1}^{K} \sum_{i=1}^{N} x_{ig}^2$$

$$- \frac{1}{K} \sum_{g \neq h=1}^{K^2-K} \sum_{i=1}^{N} x_{ig} x_{ih} - N \sum_{g=1}^{K} M_g^2.$$

The last term may be written in two parts, and $\sum_{g \neq h=1}^{K^2-K} NM_g M_h / K$ can be added and subtracted, giving terms that constitute variances and covariances as follows:

$$(20) \quad I^2 = \sum_{g=1}^{K} \left(1 - \frac{1}{K} \right) \left[\sum_{i=1}^{N} x_{ig}^2 - NM_g^2 \right]$$

$$- \frac{1}{K} \sum_{g \neq h=1}^{K^2-K} \left[\sum_{i=1}^{N} x_{ig} x_{ih} - NM_g M_h \right]$$

$$- \frac{1}{K} \sum_{g=1}^{K} NM_g^2 - \frac{1}{K} \sum_{g \neq h=1}^{K^2-K} NM_g M_h.$$

The last two terms can be combined into a squared term:

$$(21) \quad I^2 = \left(\frac{K-1}{K} \right) \sum_{g=1}^{K} \left[\sum_{i=1}^{N} x_{ig}^2 - NM_g^2 \right]$$

$$- \frac{1}{K} \sum_{g \neq h=1}^{K^2-K} \left[\sum_{i=1}^{N} x_{ig} x_{ih} - NM_g M_h \right] - \frac{N}{K} \left[\sum_{g=1}^{K} M_g \right]^2.$$

The last term can be omitted since ΣM_g is zero. We thus have the final expression for sum of squares due to interaction, as

$$(22) \quad I^2 = \left(\frac{K-1}{K} \right) \sum_{g=1}^{K} \left[\sum_{i=1}^{N} x_{ig}^2 - NM_g^2 \right]$$

$$- \frac{1}{K} \sum_{g \neq h=1}^{K^2-K} \left[\sum_{i=1}^{N} x_{ig} x_{ih} - NM_g M_h \right].$$

Dividing by the appropriate degrees of freedom $(K - 1)(N - 1)$, we obtain

$$(23) \quad \frac{I^2}{(K - 1)(N - 1)} = \frac{1}{K} \sum_{g=1}^{K} \left[\frac{\sum_{i=1}^{N} x_{ig}^2 - NM_g^2}{N - 1} \right]$$

$$- \frac{1}{K(K - 1)} \sum_{g \neq h=1}^{K^2-K} \left[\frac{\sum_{i=1}^{N} x_{ig}x_{ih} - NM_gM_h}{N - 1} \right],$$

which can be rewritten as an average variance and covariance.

$$(24) \quad \frac{I^2}{(K - 1)(N - 1)} = \frac{1}{K} \sum_{g=1}^{K} s_{x_g}^2 - \frac{1}{K^2 - K} \sum_{g \neq h=1}^{K^2-K} r_{gh}s_g s_h.$$

This gives the final expression for variance due to interaction:

$$(25) \quad \frac{I^2}{(K - 1)(N - 1)} = \overline{(s_{x_g}^2)} - \overline{r_{gh}s_g s_h}.$$

That is, the variance attributable to interaction between persons and tests is the average test variance, minus the average intertest covariance. Since we are dealing with parallel tests we may assume that the variances are equal and that the intercorrelations are equal, giving

$$(26) \quad \frac{I^2}{(K - 1)(N - 1)} = s_g^2(1 - r_{gh}).$$

> *For the general case of K parallel tests, the variance due to interaction between persons and tests is the square of the error of measurement.*

If the error of measurement is small as compared with the standard deviation of the test, the interaction variance is small (as compared with the true variance discussed in the next section), and the different tests are highly correlated. Correspondingly, if the interaction variance is large, as compared with variance due to persons, the error of measurement is large, relative to the standard deviation of the test, and the reliability of the test (the correlation between parallel forms) is low.

4. Relation between true variance and variance due to persons

In considering the relationship between test theory and analysis of variance, we have shown that interaction between persons and tests is identical with error of measurement. It is clear that if all the tests had the same mean, the variance due to tests would be zero. Thus the variance due to tests simply measures the extent to which the means of the different tests are identical.   If this difference is unduly large, the tests are not "parallel" in the sense of having equal means.

Since in test theory, the "true variance" represents a variance between persons, we should expect to find some relationship between true variance and "variance due to persons."   Referring to the previous section, we find an expression for the sum of squares due to persons. Designating this by P^2, we may write

$$(27) \qquad P^2 = K \sum_{i=1}^{N} a_i^2,$$

where

$$(28) \qquad a_i = \frac{\sum_{g=1}^{K} x_{ig}}{K}.$$

We may substitute equation 28 in equation 27, obtaining

$$(29) \qquad P^2 = \frac{K}{K^2} \sum_{i=1}^{N} \left[\sum_{g=1}^{K} x_{ig} \right]^2.$$

The square of a sum may also be written as a double summation, giving

$$(30) \qquad P^2 = \frac{1}{K} \sum_{i=1}^{N} \sum_{g=1}^{K} \sum_{h=1}^{K} x_{ig} x_{ih}.$$

Changing the order of summation, we obtain

$$(31) \qquad P^2 = \frac{1}{K} \sum_{g=1}^{K} \sum_{h=1}^{K} \sum_{i=1}^{N} x_{ig} x_{ih}.$$

Let us now explicitly separate the terms involving a sum of squares from those involving a cross product, obtaining

$$(32) \qquad P^2 = \frac{1}{K} \sum_{g=1}^{K} \sum_{i=1}^{N} x_{ig}^2 + \frac{1}{K} \sum_{\substack{g=1 \\ (g \neq h)}}^{K} \sum_{h=1}^{K} \sum_{i=1}^{N} x_{ig} x_{ih}.$$

We observe that, since all terms where $g = h$ are excluded from the second expression, it contains only $(K^2 - K)$ terms.   In order to have the upper limit of summation indicate the number of terms, we shall write equation 32 as follows:

$$(33) \qquad P^2 = \frac{1}{K} \sum_{g=1}^{K} \left[\sum_{i=1}^{N} x_{ig}^2 \right] + \frac{1}{K} \sum_{g \neq h=1}^{K^2-K} \left[\sum_{i=1}^{N} x_{ig} x_{ih} \right].$$

Referring to the preceding section, we note that we assumed the mean of all means to be zero, but did not specify that the mean of each test was zero. Therefore, in order to obtain deviations from the mean, it is necessary to rewrite equation 33 as

$$(34) \quad \frac{1}{K} \sum_{g=1}^{K} \left[\sum_{i=1}^{N} x_{ig}^2 - NM_g^2 \right] + \frac{1}{K} \sum_{g \neq h=1}^{K^2-K} \left[\sum_{i=1}^{N} x_{ig}x_{ih} - NM_gM_h \right].$$

This change, however, does not affect the value of P^2 since the terms added total to zero. We can see this by writing them explicitly:

$$(35) \quad \sum_{g=1}^{K} NM_g^2 + \sum_{g \neq h=1}^{K^2-K} NM_gM_h,$$

and then, expressing equation 35 as the square of a sum, we write

$$(36) \quad N \left[\sum_{g=1}^{K} M_g \right]^2.$$

Since the term in brackets is the grand mean, it equals zero, which shows that the value of equation 33 is equal to the value of equation 34. Hence we may write

Equation (37)

$$P^2 = \frac{1}{K} \sum_{g=1}^{K} \left[\sum_{i=1}^{N} x_{ig}^2 - NM_g^2 \right] + \frac{1}{K} \sum_{g \neq h=1}^{K^2-K} \left[\sum_{i=1}^{N} x_{ig}x_{ih} - NM_gM_h \right].$$

Dividing now by the appropriate degrees of freedom $(N - 1)$, we obtain

Equation (38)

$$\frac{P^2}{N-1} = \frac{1}{K} \sum_{g=1}^{K} \left[\frac{\sum_{i=1}^{N} x_{ig}^2 - NM_g^2}{N-1} \right] + \frac{1}{K} \sum_{g \neq h=1}^{K^2-K} \left[\frac{\sum_{i=1}^{N} x_{ig}x_{ih} - NM_gM_h}{N-1} \right].$$

This equation may be rewritten explicitly in terms of average variance and covariance, giving

$$(39) \quad \frac{P^2}{N-1} = \overline{(s_g^2)} + (K - 1)\overline{r_{gh}s_gs_h}.$$

Equation 39 gives the value of the variance due to persons. It is the average variance plus $(K - 1)$ times the average covariance.

We can see that, if we divide equation 39 by K, we obtain

$$(40) \qquad \frac{P^2}{K(N-1)} = \frac{\overline{(s_g{}^2)}}{K} + \left(1 - \frac{1}{K}\right)\overline{r_{gh}s_g s_h},$$

and that, if we let K approach infinity, we obtain

$$(41) \qquad \lim_{K \to \infty} \frac{P^2}{K(N-1)} = \overline{r_{gh}s_g s_h},$$

which is equivalent to true variance as discussed in Chapters 2 and 3.

> *For K parallel tests, one Kth of the value of the variance due to persons approaches the true variance as K approaches infinity.*

5. Summary

Several different interpretations of the error of measurement have been given.

1. The error of measurement is the standard deviation of the differences between the observed score and the true score.
2. If the difference between score on two parallel tests is regarded as being made up of two equal and uncorrelated components, the standard deviation of the distribution of these components is the error of measurement.
3. The error of measurement is identical with the error of *estimate* based on the regression of observed on true scores.
4. The error of measurement is the square root of the variance due to interaction between persons and tests, provided one assumes a set of parallel tests.

In addition to these interpretations of error variance, we have also seen that the true variance is the limit, as K approaches infinity, of $1/K$th of the variance due to persons.

Problems

1. Show that, if $x_1 - x_2$ is regarded as divided into two *equal* and *uncorrelated* parts, the standard deviation of one of these parts is the error of measurement.

2. Show that the error made in estimating observed score from true score is the error of measurement.

3. Show that the standard deviation of the difference between observed and true score is the error of measurement.

4. Derive the equation for predicting scores in X_1 from scores in X_2, where X_1 and X_2 are two different forms of a test whose reliability and validity are both known. Derive the equation for predicting the true score Y from Y_1, where Y_1 is a test whose reliability and validity are known.

5. (a) Describe the correct experimental method for checking the applicability of the equation

$$\sigma_e = \sigma_y \sqrt{1 - r_{xy}^2},$$

where σ_e is the standard error of estimate made in estimating y from x,
σ_y is the standard deviation of the observed y distribution; and
r_{xy} is the correlation between x and y.

(b) Would the method you suggest be expected to give an *exact* agreement, or only an *approximate* agreement?

(c) What explanations would you offer for a failure to check the equation?

6

Effect of Doubling Test Length
on Other Test Parameters

1. Introduction

We have now considered in some detail the parameters used to describe a test. They are the mean, the three variances (observed, true, and error), the reliability coefficient, or self-correlation, and the correlation with true score (or "index of reliability").

We have also considered the interrelationships of these parameters. The *number of items* in a test is another important parameter of a test. It is the one characteristic of a test which can be most readily controlled. If there is a good supply of items, it is relatively easy to decide to use 30 or 100 or 200 items in a test. What is the best number of items to use? The decision depends in part upon limitations of testing time available, but the number of items should also be sufficiently great to insure for the test a sufficiently high reliability and a sufficiently low error of measurement. How many items are necessary to give a reliability of, let us say, .95? In order to answer such questions, it is necessary to know the relationship between test length and the other parameters. Let us turn to a consideration of the effect of the length of a test upon its reliability, error of measurement, and other parameters.

2. Effect of doubling a test on the mean

First let us consider merely doubling the length of the test, after which we shall take up the more general case of increasing the length any number of times.

Let us consider the effect of doubling a test upon its *mean* and *standard deviation*. If we designate the original test by the subscript 1 and the added portion by the subscript 2, the "composite" score of the ith person (X_{ic}) may be written

(1) $$X_{ic} = X_{i1} + X_{i2}.$$

The average may be found by summing and dividing by N, obtaining

(2)
$$\frac{\sum\limits_{i=1}^{N} X_{ic}}{N} = \frac{\sum\limits_{i=1}^{N} X_{i1}}{N} + \frac{\sum\limits_{i=1}^{N} X_{i2}}{N}.$$

Since the mean equals the sum of scores divided by N, we have

(3)
$$M_c = M_1 + M_2.$$

Since the two tests are parallel, the mean of test 2 will be equal to the mean of test 1, and we have

(4)
$$M_c = 2M_1.$$

> *Doubling the length of a test doubles the mean, provided the original part and the added part are parallel tests.*

3. Effect of doubling a test on the variance of gross scores

We shall next observe what happens to the *variance* of a test when its length is doubled. Again we begin with the gross score

(5)
$$X_c = X_1 + X_2.$$

Since the mean of the combined tests equals the sum of the two part means, we may convert to deviation scores by writing

(6)
$$X_c - M_c = (X_1 - M_1) + (X_2 - M_2),$$

which may be written

(7)
$$x_c = x_1 + x_2.$$

Squaring both sides, summing, and dividing by N, we have

(8)
$$\frac{\Sigma x_c{}^2}{N} = \frac{\Sigma x_1{}^2}{N} + \frac{\Sigma x_2{}^2}{N} + \frac{2\Sigma x_1 x_2}{N}.$$

Expressing this in terms of variances and covariances, we have

(9)
$$s_c{}^2 = s_1{}^2 + s_2{}^2 + 2r_{12}s_1 s_2.$$

Since the tests are parallel, $s_1 = s_2$, and we may write

(10)
$$s_c{}^2 = 2s_1{}^2(1 + r_{12}).$$

We may take the square root of both sides in order to obtain the standard deviation. This gives

(11)
$$s_c = s_1\sqrt{2(1 + r_{12})}.$$

Doubling the length of a test increases its standard deviation as indicated in equation 11, provided that the original part and the added part are parallel tests.

4. Effect of doubling a test on true variance

Since the "true score" of a given person is the same on the original and on the new part of the test, his true score on the combined tests is double the original true score:

$$\text{(12)} \qquad\qquad T_c = T_1 + T_2 = 2T_1.$$

Since the mean true score is likewise doubled, we may also write the same equation in deviation score form as

$$\text{(13)} \qquad\qquad t_c = 2t_1.$$

Squaring, summing, and dividing by N gives

$$\text{(14)} \qquad\qquad \frac{\Sigma t_c^2}{N} = \frac{4\Sigma t_1^2}{N},$$

which may also be written

$$\text{(15)} \qquad\qquad s_{t_c}^2 = 4s_{t_1}^2.$$

Taking the square root of both sides gives

$$\text{(16)} \qquad\qquad s_{t_c} = 2s_{t_1}.$$

Doubling the length of the test doubles the true standard deviation, or quadruples the true variance, when the original part and the added part are parallel tests.

5. Effect of doubling a test on error variance

From equations 5 and 12, we may write

$$\text{(17)} \qquad\qquad X_c - T_c = (X_1 - T_1) + (X_2 - T_2).$$

This expression is clearly the "error score" for each of the part tests and the composite; therefore we may write

$$\text{(18)} \qquad\qquad e_c = e_1 + e_2.$$

Squaring both sides, summing, and dividing by N gives

$$\text{(19)} \qquad\qquad \frac{\Sigma e_c^2}{N} = \frac{\Sigma e_1^2}{N} + \frac{\Sigma e_2^2}{N} + \frac{2\Sigma e_1 e_2}{N},$$

which may also be written

$$\text{(20)} \qquad\qquad s_{e_c}^2 = s_{e_1}^2 + s_{e_2}^2 + 2r_{e_1 e_2} s_{e_1} s_{e_2}.$$

Since by the definition of random error the correlational term vanishes, and the error of measurement in 1 is equal to that in 2 because the tests are parallel, we may write

(21) $$s_{e_c}^2 = 2s_{e_1}^2.$$

Taking the square root of both sides gives

(22) $$s_{e_c} = s_{e_1}\sqrt{2}.$$

> *When a test is doubled in length the error variance is doubled or the error of measurement is multiplied by the square root of two, if the original part and the added part are parallel tests.*

6. Relation of true, error, and observed variance

Let us check to see if equation 18 of Chapter 2 (the true variance plus error variance equals the observed variance) holds for the double-length test. Equations 10, 15, and 21 give the value of the observed, true, and error variance for the double-length test. Let us set equation 10 equal to the sum of equations 15 and 21 and see if this gives an identity. We have

(23) $$2s_1^2(1 + r_{12}) = 4s_{t_1}^2 + 2s_{e_1}^2.$$

As has been shown previously, in equation 38 of Chapter 2, $r_{12}s_1^2 = s_t^2$, and $s_e^2 = s_1^2(1 - r)$; see equation 41, Chapter 2. Substituting these values in equation 23, we have

(24) $$2s_1^2(1 + r) = 4rs_1^2 + 2s_1^2(1 - r).$$

Since this expression is an identity, the relationship previously established for the single-length test still holds for the double-length test, so that the equations developed are not inconsistent among themselves.

> *Observed variance is equal to true variance plus error variance for the double-length test.*

7. Effect of doubling the length of a test on its reliability (Spearman-Brown formula for double length)

Since the reliability of a test means its correlation with a parallel form, we shall assume four unit parallel tests designated by the subscripts 1, 2, 3, and 4, and then determine the reliability of a test of double length by obtaining the correlation of 1 + 2 and 3 + 4. Substituting in the deviation score formula for correlation, we may write

$$(25) \qquad r_{(1+2)(3+4)} = \frac{\Sigma(x_1 + x_2)(x_3 + x_4)}{\sqrt{\Sigma(x_1 + x_2)^2} \; \sqrt{\Sigma(x_3 + x_4)^2}}.$$

This equation can be expanded into

Equation (26)

$$r_{(1+2)(3+4)} = \frac{\Sigma x_1 x_3 + \Sigma x_1 x_4 + \Sigma x_2 x_3 + \Sigma x_2 x_4}{\sqrt{\Sigma x_1^2 + \Sigma x_2^2 + 2\Sigma x_1 x_2} \; \sqrt{\Sigma x_3^2 + \Sigma x_4^2 + 2\Sigma x_3 x_4}}.$$

Dividing the numerator and the denominator each by N, we can write the result in terms of variances and covariances. We may also simplify the denominator by noting that, since we are dealing with parallel tests, the variance of $1 + 2$ will equal that of $3 + 4$. Making these changes gives

$$(27) \qquad r_{(1+2)(3+4)} = \frac{r_{13}s_1 s_3 + r_{23}s_2 s_3 + r_{14}s_1 s_4 + r_{24}s_2 s_4}{s_1^2 + s_2^2 + 2r_{12}s_1 s_2}.$$

We may write this result in terms of average variance and average covariance:

$$(28) \qquad r_{(1+2)(3+4)} = \frac{2\overline{(r_{gh}s_g s_h)}}{\overline{s_g^2} + r_{12}s_1 s_2}.$$

Since we have parallel tests, the variance of the first test and the covariance of the first two can be used in place of the average, giving

$$(29) \qquad r_{(1+2)(3+4)} = \frac{2r_{12}s_1 s_2}{s_1^2 + r_{12}s_1 s_2}.$$

Since the standard deviations are equal we can divide numerator and denominator by s_1^2. Let r_c stand for $r_{(1+2)(3+4)}$, the reliability of the composite test.

$$(30) \qquad r_c = \frac{2r_{12}}{1 + r_{12}} \qquad \text{(Spearman-Brown formula for double length).}$$

If the length of a test is doubled by adding a parallel form, the reliability is increased as indicated by equation 30.

This is the conventional Spearman-Brown formula for double length. It gives an estimate of the reliability of a test if the test is doubled in length. Equation 30 is probably more commonly used than any of the other equations in this chapter. Whenever the reliability of a test is computed by correlating odd with even items, or some other split-half method, the correlation between the halves is substituted (as r_{12}) in equation 30 to give the reliability coefficient for the total test. In this manner we have an estimate of the correlation of the test with a parallel form. Equation 30 is, of course, not used when reliability is determined by correlating two full-length parallel forms of a test.

By checking back over the derivation, we note that *nothing has been assumed except that the tests in question are parallel.* More explicitly, equality of standard deviations and of intercorrelations has been assumed, but *nothing else.* In other words, it has been assumed that $s_1 = s_2 = s_3 = s_4$ and that $r_{12} = r_{13} = r_{14} = r_{23} = r_{24} = r_{34}$. If these two sets of equalities hold, then the Spearman-Brown formula is simply a computational short cut for figuring the reliability of the double-length test. By the device of using average variance and average covariance, as in equation 28, we see that, if the variance s_1^2 and the covariance $r_{12}s_1s_2$ differ only slightly from the average variance and covariance in equation 28, then equation 30 gives a good approximation to the reliability that will be found for the doubled test.

The application of formulas for a double-length test may be illustrated by the following example. A 50-item test has a mean of 42.0, a standard deviation of 5.3, and a reliability of .85. By the use of equation 38, Chapter 2, or equation 19, Chapter 3, the true variance of this test is 23.88; and from equation 41, Chapter 2, or equation 37, Chapter 3, the square of the error of measurement is 4.21. If this test is increased to 100 items by adding another 50 items *that are parallel to the first set of 50*, we should find the following statistics for the 100-item test:

Mean	84.0	(from equation 4);
Standard deviation	10.2	(from equation 11);
Variance of the errors of measurement	8.42	(from equation 21);
True variance	95.52	(from equation 15);
Reliability	.92	(from equation 30).

The important thing to emphasize here is that to the extent to which we are able to construct *parallel* tests we do not have a "prophecy" formula, but simply a computing formula. If the Spearman-Brown formula fails to "work" or predicts "inaccurately" in any case, this simply means that the correlation used (for example, the correlation r_{12}) was larger or smaller than the average of the intercorrelations r_{gh}. There have been several "empirical studies" of the accuracy of the Spearman-Brown formula. Strictly speaking, it needs no verification, and cannot be verified. It is possible, however, to intercorrelate the four halves of the two parallel tests and to see if the tests are really parallel in the sense that $r_{12} = r_{13} = r_{14} = \cdots = r_{34}$, and in the sense that the four variances are equal.   If so, the Spearman-Brown formula cannot fail to "work" except through arithmetical error; and, if these assumptions are not verified, the Spearman-Brown formula does not apply, since the tests are not parallel.   It is possible to investigate empirically the extent to which the amount of departure from "strict parallelness" that is usually found affects the applicability of the Spearman-Brown formula.

The foregoing remarks apply to a test that is primarily a power test. If a test is a pure speed test, the equations showing the effect of test length will apply only if the test is administered on a work limit basis (each person finishes the test and his time is recorded), and no serious warm-up or fatigue effects result from doubling the number of items and allowing each person whatever time is needed to just complete the lengthened test.   For the more usual group speed test we have a time-limit method.   In this method a fixed time is allowed, and the number of items completed is recorded.   Ideally, there should be so many items that only the fastest person would complete the test in the time allowed. Then doubling the "test length" would mean doubling the number of items and allowing double the original time.   The formulas for the effect of doubling test length would then apply, if there were no serious warm-up or fatigue effects during the second half of the longer time limit.   The only general rule that can be given is to point out that the added portion of the test must be *parallel* to the old portion; and that the criterion of whether or not the two parts are parallel is the equality of means, variances, and errors of measurement for the two parts.   To the extent to which these equalities do not hold, the formulas for the effect of doubling the length of the test will not apply, and cannot be expected to apply.   A statistical criterion for parallel tests is given in Chapter 14.

8. Experimental work on the Spearman-Brown formula

It is interesting to note that the formula for the reliability of a double-length test (equation 30) and its generalization to K-parallel tests, equation 10 of Chapter 8, were first derived in 1910 in the *British Journal of Psychology*, Volume 3.   Spearman presented it on page 290, and William Brown presented it in the succeeding article (see page 299 of the same volume).   It is therefore referred to as the Spearman-Brown formula.

The earlier articles on the Spearman-Brown formula were vigorously adversely critical; see Holzinger (1923b) and Crum (1923).   Holzinger concluded that if we lengthened the test beyond five times its original length, the Spearman-Brown formula gave an overestimate of the reliability.   No mention was made of the decreasing likelihood that the first correlation would be equal to the average of all correlations or the decreasing likelihood that the first variance would equal the average of all variances.

Subsequent studies have led to the conclusion that the results obtained from the Spearman-Brown formula are reasonably accurate; see Kelley (1924), which is a reply to Crum's criticism, Kelley (1925), Holzinger and Clayton (1925), Ruch, Ackerson, and Jackson (1926), and Wood (1926c). Thurstone (1931a) has reviewed and summarized much of this material on the empirical verification of the Spearman-Brown formula.

Slocombe (1927a, 1927b) reviewed several studies. He pointed out that it was assumed that the coefficient substituted in the formula was "representative" of the group so that this coefficient must be selected with care.

Dunlap (1933) in discussing the problem of test reliability suggested that a tetrad technique should be used to determine whether or not split fourths of a test are measuring the same thing. It should be noted that a different assumption is made in the actual derivation of the Spearman-Brown formula.

It has also been suggested that the Spearman-Brown formula applies to rating scales and judgments and that it may be used in predicting the reliability to be expected by increasing the number of judges or raters; see Gordon (1924), Furfey (1926), Remmers, Shock, and Kelly (1927), and Remmers (1931). In general, this suggestion has been found to be correct. By considering the only assumption made in the development of the Spearman-Brown formula, we see that, if the variance and reliability for the first rater are equal to the average variance and inter-correlation for all raters used, the Spearman-Brown formula must give the correct result. If the formula does not give the correct result, it is because the variances from rater to rater or the covariances for various pairs of raters differ markedly. In other words, the problem here is not "Does the Spearman-Brown formula work?" but is "Do the *ratings* from the different raters satisfy the criterion for *parallel* tests?"

Lanier (1927) interpreted the work of Gordon (1924) and Kelley (1925) to mean that correlations increased as the number of cases increased. He showed that this was not true. Thurstone (1928a) points out clearly the difference between number of judges making a rating and number of cases in a correlation scatter plot.

It has also been suggested that increasing the number of choices in a scale might increase the reliability according to the Spearman-Brown formula (see Remmers and Ewart, 1941); and that increasing the number of alternatives in a multiple-choice test will increase reliability in the same way (Remmers, Karslake, and Gage, 1940, and Denney and Remmers, 1940).

Denney and Remmers reported that random elimination of incorrect alternatives from a five-alternative multiple-choice test resulted in a reduction of reliability that agreed with the Spearman-Brown formula. However, we see that there is no reason to expect the formula to work in this case, since it is meaningless to think of equality of variances or covariances for alternatives on a multiple-choice test. The logic relating number of alternatives to test reliability has been given by Carroll (1945) (see formula 30, page 11). An empirical study of this formula is being undertaken by Mrs. Plumlee, assistant director of Test Development for the Educational Testing Service.

Nomographs or tables for the Spearman-Brown formula are given by Arnold and Dunlap (1936), Cureton and Dunlap (1930), Dunlap and Kurtz (1932), and Edgerton and Toops (1928b).

In general, therefore, the work on the Spearman-Brown formula shows that even when relatively little effort is made to obtain parallel tests (or ratings) the formula gives reasonably good results. From the derivation it is clear that, if we are dealing with tests or ratings *known to be parallel*, the formula must give correct results.

9. Summary

For the double-length test it has been shown that:

$$(4) \qquad\qquad M_c = 2M_1,$$

$$(11) \qquad\qquad s_c = s_1\sqrt{2(1 + r_{12})},$$

$$(16) \qquad\qquad s_{t_c} = 2s_{t_1},$$

$$(22) \qquad\qquad s_{e_c} = s_{e_1}\sqrt{2},$$

$$(30) \qquad\qquad r_c = \frac{2r_{12}}{1 + r_{12}}.$$

For these equations the subscript c is used to denote the value for the composite or double-length test, the subscript 1 designates the mean or standard deviation of the unit-length test, and r_{12} is the reliability of the unit-length test.

Problems

1. Prove that the correlation between true and observed score for a test of double length is $\sqrt{2r/(1 + r)}$, where r is the reliability of the original test. List the assumptions used in making this derivation.

2. Prove that each of the other basic relations derived in Chapter 2 (or Chapter 3) holds for the augmented test.

3.

Test	Number of Items	Mean	Standard Deviation	Relia- bility
A	250	186.1	30.0	.96
B	30	20.0	4.5	.72
C	100	69.3	12.4	.87
D	200	83.7	22.8	.91
E	50	37.4	7.4	.83

Estimate the reliability of each of the foregoing tests if it is doubled in length.

4. Read the last section of the article by Lanier (1927) and comment on this application of the Spearman-Brown formula. Refer also to Thurstone (1928a).

7

Effect of Test Length
on Mean and Variance (General Case)

1. Effect of test length on mean

We shall now extend the discussion to consider the general case, the effect of test length on mean, variance (true, error and observed), and on reliability and index of reliability.

If we designate the composite score of the ith person by X_{ic}, we may write

$$(1) \qquad X_{ic} = X_{i1} + X_{i2} + \cdots + X_{iK}.$$

Summing and dividing by N to obtain the mean, we have

$$(2) \qquad \frac{\Sigma X_{ic}}{N} = \frac{\Sigma X_{i1}}{N} + \frac{\Sigma X_{i2}}{N} + \cdots + \frac{\Sigma X_{iK}}{N}.$$

Substituting the mean for the sum of scores divided by N, we have

$$(3) \qquad M_c = M_1 + M_2 + \cdots + M_K.$$

Since all the tests are parallel, the mean of each of the component tests will be equal. M_1 can be substituted for each of the means, giving

$$(4) \qquad M_c = KM_1.$$

Increasing the length of a test K times multiplies the mean by K, provided that each of the new parts is parallel to the original.

2. Effect of test length on variance of gross scores

As before, we can begin with the expression for the composite gross score,

$$(5) \qquad X_c = X_1 + X_2 + \cdots + X_K.$$

Since the mean of the combined tests equals the sum of the part means (see equation 3), we may convert to deviation scores by writing

(6) $X_c - M_c = (X_1 - M_1) + (X_2 - M_2) + \cdots + (X_K - M_K)$.

Using lower case x for a deviation score, we may write

(7) $$x_c = x_1 + x_2 + \cdots + x_K.$$

In order to obtain the standard deviation, we square both sides, sum, and divide by N, obtaining

(8) $$\frac{\Sigma x_c^2}{N} = \frac{\Sigma(x_1 + x_2 + \cdots + x_K)^2}{N}.$$

If we expand the numerator of the right-hand side of the equation, it will equal the sum of all the terms in the following matrix.

$$
\begin{matrix}
\Sigma x_1^2 & \Sigma x_1 x_2 & \Sigma x_1 x_3 & \cdots & \Sigma x_1 x_K \\
\Sigma x_1 x_2 & \Sigma x_2^2 & \Sigma x_2 x_3 & \cdots & \Sigma x_2 x_K \\
\Sigma x_1 x_3 & \Sigma x_2 x_3 & \Sigma x_3^2 & \cdots & \Sigma x_3 x_K \\
\cdot & \cdot & \cdot & & \cdot \\
\cdot & \cdot & \cdot & & \cdot \\
\cdot & \cdot & \cdot & & \cdot \\
\Sigma x_1 x_K & \Sigma x_2 x_K & \Sigma x_3 x_K & \cdots & \Sigma x_K^2.
\end{matrix}
$$

Dividing through by N, we have the sum of all the terms in the variance-covariance matrix that can be written

$$
\begin{matrix}
s_1^2 & r_{12}s_1s_2 & r_{13}s_1s_3 & \cdots & r_{1K}s_1s_K \\
r_{12}s_1s_2 & s_2^2 & r_{23}s_2s_3 & \cdots & r_{2K}s_2s_K \\
r_{13}s_1s_3 & r_{23}s_2s_3 & s_3^2 & & r_{3K}s_3s_K \\
\cdot & \cdot & \cdot & & \cdot \\
\cdot & \cdot & \cdot & & \cdot \\
\cdot & \cdot & \cdot & & \cdot \\
r_{1K}s_1s_K & r_{2K}s_2s_K & r_{3K}s_3s_K & \cdots & s_K^2.
\end{matrix}
$$

The sum of all these terms is the variance of the composite test composed of the sum of all the tests from 1 to K.

(9) $$s_c^2 = \sum_{g=1}^{K} s_g^2 + \sum_{g=1}^{K} \sum_{h=1}^{K} r_{gh}s_g s_h \qquad (g \neq h).$$

The variance of the composite test may be expressed in terms of the average variance and the average covariance as follows:

(10) $$s_c^2 = K\overline{(s_g^2)} + K(K - 1)\overline{(r_{gh}s_g s_h)}.$$

If the tests are parallel, the average s_g may be replaced by s_1, and the average covariance by $r_{12}s_1s_2$. If we factor out the s_1^2K, we have

$$(11) \qquad s_c^2 = s_1^2K[1 + (K - 1)r_{12}].$$

Lengthening a test K times increases the variance, as indicated in equation 11.

Taking the square root of both sides and writing r_{11} for the reliability coefficient, we have

$$(12) \qquad s_c = s_1\sqrt{K + K(K - 1)r_{11}},$$

where s_1 is the standard deviation of the unit length test,

   r_{11} is the reliability of the unit length test,

   K is the ratio of the number of items in the new test to the number in the unit length test, and

   s_c is the standard deviation of the lengthened test.

Multiplying the length of a test by K increases the standard deviation, as indicated in equation 12.

3. Effect of test length on true variance

Since the "true score" of a given person is the same on each of the part tests, we may write the true score on the composite test as

$$(13) \qquad T_c = KT_1.$$

Since the mean true score is likewise multiplied by K, we may write this same equation in deviation form,

$$(14) \qquad t_c = Kt_1.$$

Squaring, summing, and dividing by N, we obtain

$$(15) \qquad \frac{\sum\limits_{i=1}^{N} t_{ic}^2}{N} = \frac{K^2 \sum\limits_{i=1}^{N} t_{i1}^2}{N},$$

which is equivalent to

$$(16) \qquad s_{t_c}^2 = K^2 s_{t_1}^2.$$

Taking the square root of both sides, we have

$$(17) \qquad s_{t_c} = Ks_{t_1}.$$

Multiplying the length of a test by K multiplies the true standard deviation by K.

4. Effect of test length on error variance

From the equations developed in the preceding sections (see equations 5 and 13), we may write

$$(18) \quad X_c - T_c = (X_1 - T_1) + (X_2 - T_2) + \cdots + (X_K - T_K).$$

We may use e to represent the error score and write

$$(19) \qquad\qquad e_c = e_1 + e_2 + e_3 + \cdots + e_K.$$

Squaring both sides, summing, and dividing by N, we obtain

$$(20) \qquad \frac{\Sigma e_c{}^2}{N} = \frac{\Sigma(e_1 + e_2 + \cdots + e_K)^2}{N}.$$

This expression may be set up as the sum of all the terms in the following matrix:

$$
\begin{matrix}
\Sigma e_1{}^2 & \Sigma e_1 e_2 & \Sigma e_1 e_3 & \cdots & \Sigma e_1 e_K \\
\Sigma e_1 e_2 & \Sigma e_2{}^2 & \Sigma e_2 e_3 & \cdots & \Sigma e_2 e_K \\
\Sigma e_1 e_3 & \Sigma e_2 e_3 & \Sigma e_3{}^2 & \cdots & \Sigma e_3 e_K \\
\cdot & \cdot & \cdot & & \cdot \\
\cdot & \cdot & \cdot & & \cdot \\
\cdot & \cdot & \cdot & & \cdot \\
\Sigma e_1 e_K & \Sigma e_2 e_K & \Sigma e_3 e_K & \cdots & \Sigma e_K{}^2.
\end{matrix}
$$

Dividing by N, we have

$$(21) \quad s_{e_c}{}^2 = s_{e_1}{}^2 + s_{e_2}{}^2 + \cdots + s_{e_K}{}^2 + r_{e_1 e_2} s_{e_1} s_{e_2}$$
$$+ r_{e_1 e_3} s_{e_1} s_{e_3} + \cdots + r_{e_K - 1 e_K} s_{e_K - 1} s_{e_K}.$$

Since, by the definition of random error, the correlational terms vanish, we can write

$$(22) \qquad\qquad s_{e_c}{}^2 = \sum_{g=1}^{K} s_{e_g}{}^2.$$

This may also be written in terms of the average error variance as follows:

$$(23) \qquad\qquad s_{e_c}{}^2 = K(\overline{s_{e_g}{}^2}).$$

If we assume that the error variance of the first test is equal to the average error variance, we may write

$$(24) \qquad\qquad s_{e_c}{}^2 = K s_{e_1}{}^2.$$

Taking the square root of both sides gives

$$(25) \qquad\qquad s_{e_c} = s_{e_1} \sqrt{K}.$$

> *Multiplying the length of a test by K multiplies the error vari-*
> *ance by K or the error of measurement by the square root of K.*

5. Summary

For the general case of lengthening a test to K times its original length, the effect on the mean and the different variances has been shown. We have

(4) $$M_c = KM_1,$$

(12) $$s_c = s_1\sqrt{K + K(K - 1)r_{11}},$$

(17) $$s_{t_c} = Ks_{t_1},$$

(25) $$s_{e_c} = s_{e_1}\sqrt{K}.$$

As in Chapter 6, the subscript c is used to designate the composite score. In this case, however, it is the composite score formed by adding scores on K parallel forms. The subscript 1 is used to designate a mean or standard deviation of the original unit test, and r_{11} is the reliability of the original unit test.

Problems

1. Prove that the observed variance of an augmented test is equal to the sum of its true and error variance.

2. Prove for the other basic relationships established in Chapter 2 and Chapter 3 that they still hold for the test augmented K times.

3.

Test	Mean	Standard Deviation	Number of Items	Reliability	Number of Subjects
A	73.2	12.7	120	.92	300
B	17.3	3.8	25	.86	250
C	21.3	7.1	50	.80	430
D	29.3	7.9	75	.84	150
E	56.5	13.7	100	.89	200

(a) Estimate the variance of test A if it is increased to 240 items.
(b) Estimate the true variance of test B if 75 items are added.
(c) What is the error of measurement for test C?
(d) What will the error of measurement be if test C is lengthened to 150 items?
(e) How many items would need to be added to test D to double the true variance?
(f) How many items would need to be added to test E to double the error of measurement?
(g) You would like to increase the standard deviation of test B to 7.6. How many items would it be necessary to add to the test?

8

Effect of Test Length
on Reliability (General Case)

1. Introduction

The equation for the relationship between test length and test reliability will be developed from the usual formula for the correlation between any two sums. No assumptions will be used in the derivation until the last step. There it will be assumed that the variance of the unit test can be taken as a fair approximation to the average variance of all the unit parallel forms, and the reliability of the unit test times its variance can be taken as a reasonable approximation to the average covariance among all the unit parallel forms.

2. The correlation between any two sums

First let us write the formula for the correlation between any two sums. One series will be designated by the subscripts 1, 2, $\cdots$ K, and the other by the subscripts I, II, $\cdots$ L. From the usual formula for correlation, we have then

$$(1) \quad r_{(x_1+\cdots+x_K)(x_I+\cdots+x_L)}$$

$$= \frac{\Sigma(x_1 + x_2 + \cdots + x_K)(x_I + x_{II} + \cdots + x_L)}{\sqrt{\Sigma(x_1 + x_2 + \cdots + x_K)^2}\ \sqrt{\Sigma(x_I + x_{II} + \cdots + x_L)^2}}.$$

The terms involved in the expansion of the numerator can be systematically set down in the following rectangular matrix:

$$\begin{array}{ccccc}
\Sigma x_1 x_I & \Sigma x_1 x_{II} & \Sigma x_1 x_{III} & \cdots & \Sigma x_1 x_L \\
\Sigma x_2 x_I & \Sigma x_2 x_{II} & \Sigma x_2 x_{III} & \cdots & \Sigma x_2 x_L \\
\Sigma x_3 x_I & \Sigma x_3 x_{II} & \Sigma x_3 x_{III} & \cdots & \Sigma x_3 x_L \\
\cdot & \cdot & \cdot & & \cdot \\
\cdot & \cdot & \cdot & & \cdot \\
\cdot & \cdot & \cdot & & \cdot \\
\Sigma x_K x_I & \Sigma x_K x_{II} & \Sigma x_K x_{III} & \cdots & \Sigma x_K x_L.
\end{array}$$

First, x_1 is multiplied by $x_I, x_{II}, \cdots x_L$; the same is done for x_2, giving the second row; and so on to x_K. The sum of all these LK terms is equal to

$$\Sigma(x_1 + x_2 + \cdots + x_K)(x_I + x_{II} + \cdots + x_L).$$

Each of the terms in this matrix may also be written as a covariance, giving

$$
\begin{array}{cccc}
Nr_{1,I}s_1s_I & Nr_{1,II}s_1s_{II} & \cdots & Nr_{1,L}s_1s_L \\
Nr_{2,I}s_2s_I & Nr_{2,II}s_2s_{II} & \cdots & Nr_{2,L}s_2s_L \\
\cdot & \cdot & & \cdot \\
\cdot & \cdot & & \cdot \\
\cdot & \cdot & & \cdot \\
Nr_{K,I}s_Ks_I & Nr_{K,II}s_Ks_{II} & \cdots & Nr_{K,L}s_Ks_L.
\end{array}
$$

Using g and G as the general subscripts designating tests, where g varies from 1 to K and G varies from I to L, we can write the sum of all the terms in the foregoing matrix as follows:

$$\sum_{g=1}^{K} \sum_{G=I}^{L} Nr_{gG}s_gs_G.$$

Since the N is a constant for all terms, we may take it outside, writing the following equation for the numerator term of equation 1.

Equation (2)

$$\Sigma(x_1 + x_2 + \cdots + x_K)(x_I + x_{II} + \cdots + x_L) = N \sum_{g=1}^{K} \sum_{G=I}^{L} r_{gG}s_gs_G.$$

We also follow the same procedure for the denominator. The terms in the expansion of

$$\Sigma(x_1 + x_2 + \cdots + x_K)^2$$

may be set down in a square matrix as follows:

$$
\begin{array}{ccccc}
\Sigma x_1{}^2 & \Sigma x_1x_2 & \Sigma x_1x_3 & \cdots & \Sigma x_1x_K \\
\Sigma x_1x_2 & \Sigma x_2{}^2 & \Sigma x_2x_3 & \cdots & \Sigma x_2x_K \\
\Sigma x_1x_3 & \Sigma x_2x_3 & \Sigma x_3{}^2 & \cdots & \Sigma x_3x_K \\
\cdot & \cdot & \cdot & & \cdot \\
\cdot & \cdot & \cdot & & \cdot \\
\cdot & \cdot & \cdot & & \cdot \\
\Sigma x_1x_K & \Sigma x_2x_K & \Sigma x_3x_K & \cdots & \Sigma x_K{}^2.
\end{array}
$$

This matrix may also be rewritten in terms of variances and covariances as follows:

$$
\begin{matrix}
Ns_1{}^2 & Nr_{12}s_1s_2 & Nr_{13}s_1s_3 & \cdots & Nr_{1K}s_1s_K \\
Nr_{12}s_1s_2 & Ns_2{}^2 & Nr_{23}s_2s_3 & \cdots & Nr_{2K}s_2s_K \\
Nr_{13}s_1s_3 & Nr_{23}s_2s_3 & Ns_3{}^2 & \cdots & Nr_{3K}s_3s_K \\
\cdot & \cdot & \cdot & & \cdot \\
\cdot & \cdot & \cdot & & \cdot \\
\cdot & \cdot & \cdot & & \cdot \\
Nr_{1K}s_1s_K & Nr_{2K}s_2s_K & Nr_{3K}s_3s_K & \cdots & Ns_K{}^2.
\end{matrix}
$$

Again the sum of all the terms in this matrix may be written in a double subscript notation by using the subscripts g and h to designate the tests, having the limits for both g and h be from 1 to K. We may thus write

Equation (3)

$$
\Sigma(x_1 + x_2 + x_3 + \cdots + x_K)^2 = N \sum_{g=1}^{K} \sum_{h=1}^{K} r_{gh}s_gs_h \qquad \text{(where } r_{gg} = 1\text{)}.
$$

However, it will be noticed that the terms along the principal diagonal of the matrix are variances, while the non-diagonal terms are covariances. It is sometimes better to use a notation that keeps the variances and covariances separate and to write

$$
(4) \quad \Sigma(x_1 + x_2 + x_3 + \cdots + x_K)^2 = N \sum_{g=1}^{K} s_g{}^2 + N \sum_{g=1}^{K} \sum_{h=1}^{K} r_{gh}s_gs_h
$$
$$
(g \neq h).
$$

It is necessary to specify that "g does not equal h" since the cases where g does equal h have already been included in the sum of the variances.

By symmetry a term corresponding to equation 4 can be written for the second factor in the denominator of equation 1. For this case where the limits are I to L, let us substitute I for 1 and L for K in equation 4. Also let us change subscripts, using G instead of g and H instead of h. Making these substitutions, we have

$$
(5) \quad \Sigma(x_I + x_{II} + x_{III} + \cdots + x_L)^2 = N \sum_{G=I} s_G{}^2 + N \sum_{G=I}^{L} \sum_{H=I}^{L} r_{GH}s_Gs_H
$$
$$
(G \neq H).
$$

Using the double subscript notation indicated in equations 2 to 5, we can write the formula for the intercorrelation of any two sums in terms of the standard deviations and intercorrelations of the unit tests.

Substituting equations 2, 4, and 5 in equation 1, and dividing the numerator and denominator by N and using R_{KL} for $r_{(x_1+\cdots+x_K)(x_1+\cdots+x_L)}$ in equation 1, we have

Equation (6)

$$R_{KL} = \frac{\displaystyle\sum_{g=1}^{K}\sum_{G=I}^{L} r_{gG}s_g s_G}{\sqrt{\displaystyle\sum_{g=1}^{K} s_g^2 + \sum_{g=1}^{K}\sum_{\substack{h=1 \\ (g \neq h)}}^{K} r_{gh}s_g s_h}\ \sqrt{\displaystyle\sum_{G=I}^{L} s_G^2 + \sum_{G=I}^{L}\sum_{\substack{H=I \\ (G \neq H)}}^{L} r_{GH}s_G s_H}}\,.$$

This formula is found in Spearman (1913) and Kelley (1923c). We may also write the foregoing in terms of the average variance and the average covariance of the unit tests by substituting N times the average for the sum, and denoting the average by a bar above the term.

Equation (7)

$$R_{KL} = \frac{KL\overline{(r_{gG}s_g s_G)}}{\sqrt{K\overline{(s_g^2)} + K(K-1)\overline{(r_{gh}s_g s_h)}}\ \sqrt{L\overline{(s_G^2)} + L(L-1)\overline{(r_{GH}s_G s_H)}}}\,.$$

It should be noted that this equation is general and precise. It involves no assumptions whatever. It is based only on simple algebraic transformations, and it must be verified, barring arithmetical errors.

> *Equations 6 and 7 give the correlation of any two sums in terms of variances and covariances for the unit tests. These two equations form the basis for the derivations in this and the succeeding chapter.*

3. Effect of test length on reliability (Spearman-Brown formula)

However, in the usual case of trying to estimate the reliability of an augmented test, the average of the variances of the parallel unit tests that might be constructed is not available. Likewise the average covariance among these unit tests is not available. The only figure available is the variance of the first unit test and the reliability of this test. If we are willing to assume that the variance of the first unit test is a fair approximation to the average variance of all unit tests, and that the reliability coefficient times this variance is a fair approximation to the average covariance, we shall have some values to substitute in this formula. It should be noted that, unless we do this, the formula cannot be used at all. It should also be emphasized that, if the new unit tests have an average variance that is different from the variance of the first test, or an average covariance different from $r_{11}s_1^2$, the new tests are not parallel forms of the original unit test. In other words, if the new unit tests are parallel to the original one, the assumption is valid and the formula will hold. If the formula does not hold, the new tests are not parallel forms of the original one.

Making the substitution indicated in the foregoing paragraph, we shall set

$$s_1{}^2 = \overline{(s_g{}^2)} = \overline{(s_G{}^2)}$$

and

$$r_{11}s_1{}^2 = \overline{(r_{gh}s_gs_h)} = \overline{(r_{GH}s_Gs_H)} = \overline{(r_{gG}s_gs_G)}.$$

We may write the generalized formula giving the effect of increasing test length on reliability as follows:

$$(8) \quad R_{KL} = \frac{KLr_{11}s_1{}^2}{\sqrt{Ks_1{}^2 + K(K-1)r_{11}s_1{}^2}\;\sqrt{Ls_1{}^2 + L(L-1)r_{11}s_1{}^2}}.$$

This general formula may be simplified in several respects. For reliability, a test is assumed to be correlated with another form of the same length so that $K = L$. This means that the two expressions under the radicals in the denominator are identical so that the product of two square roots may be indicated by simply writing one of the expressions without the radical sign. These changes give

$$(9) \quad R_{KK} = \frac{K^2r_{11}s_1{}^2}{Ks_1{}^2 + K(K-1)r_{11}s_1{}^2}.$$

Dividing numerator and denominator by $Ks_1{}^2$, we have the final formula which is

$$(10) \quad R_{KK} = \frac{Kr_{11}}{1 + (K-1)r_{11}} \quad \text{(general Spearman-Brown formula)},$$

where r_{11} is the reliability of the unit test,

      K is the number of items in the lengthened test divided by the number of items in the unit test, and

R_{KK} is the reliability of the lengthened test.

Making a test K times as long increases the reliability as indicated in equation 10.

This is the generalized Spearman-Brown formula showing the relationship between test length (K) and reliability. As mentioned previously, derivations of this equation were published simultaneously by Spearman (1910) and Brown (1910). In view of the controversy waged around this equation, it should be emphasized again that no assumptions were made in deriving it, except that the variance and covariance figures obtained for the first unit test could be used in place of the average variance and the average covariance among the unit parallel tests. These assumptions are part of the definition of "parallel tests."

4. Graphing the relationships shown by the Spearman-Brown formula

By regarding R and r as the variables in equation 10 and K as a parameter, we can show that this is the equation of a rectangular hyperbola. In order to show this, let us first subtract each side of the equation from $1 + 1/(K - 1)$, giving

$$(11) \qquad 1 + \frac{1}{K-1} - R = 1 + \frac{1}{K-1} - \frac{Kr}{1+(K-1)r}.$$

We may rearrange terms in the left-hand member and simplify the first two terms in the right-hand member of equation 11 to give

$$(12) \qquad 1 - R + \frac{1}{K-1} = \frac{K}{K-1} - \frac{Kr}{1+(K-1)r}.$$

Putting the terms in the right member over a common denominator and simplifying gives

$$(13) \qquad 1 - R + \frac{1}{K-1} = \frac{K}{(K-1)[1+(K-1)r]}.$$

We may write the denominator of the right-hand term as $(K-1)^2$ $[r + 1/(K - 1)]$, and then multiply both sides by $r + 1/(K - 1)$, obtaining the usual form for the rectangular hyperbola $(xy = c)$.

$$(14) \qquad \left[1 - R + \frac{1}{K-1}\right]\left[r + \frac{1}{K-1}\right] = \frac{K}{(K-1)^2}.$$

This equation has been graphed in Figure 1. This figure shows the relationship between R and r for various values of K. It can be seen that for r-values of zero and unity, the value of R is the same as r for all values of K. For other values of r, R increases as K increases. It can be seen that these hyperbolas have a horizontal asymptote equal to $1 + 1/(K - 1)$. That is to say, as r approaches infinity, R approaches a horizontal line $1/(K - 1)$ units above one. Also as R approaches minus infinity, r approaches negative $1/(K - 1)$. Since r and R designate reliability coefficients, values outside the range zero to one are meaningless, and are not shown in the graph.

Equation 10 can also be graphed by regarding R and K as variables and r as a parameter. Such a graph will show how the reliability of

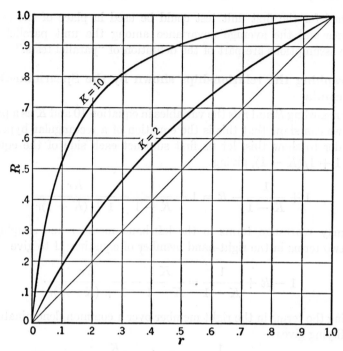

FIGURE 1.   Diagram for equation 14.   Shows the augmented reliability (R) as a
function of the original reliability (r) for various changes in test length (K).

the test increases as test length increases.   Dividing the numerator and
denominator of the right-hand side of equation 10 by r gives

$$(15) \qquad R = \cfrac{K}{K + \cfrac{1 - r}{r}}.$$

Subtracting each side from 1 and simplifying gives

$$(16) \qquad 1 - R = \cfrac{\cfrac{1 - r}{r}}{K + \cfrac{1 - r}{r}},$$

which can be converted readily into the form of the rectangular
hyperbola

$$(17) \qquad [1 - R]\left[K + \frac{1 - r}{r}\right] = \frac{1 - r}{r}.$$

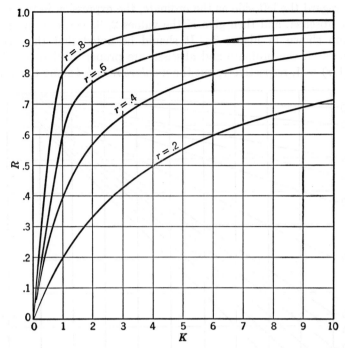

FIGURE 2.   Diagram for equation 17.   Shows the augmented reliability (R) as a function of the increase in test length (K) for different initial reliabilities (r).

It can be seen that as K approaches infinity, R approaches unity for all values of r. Also as R approaches negative infinity, K approaches the vertical asymptote $(1 - r)/r$. This equation is graphed in Figure 2. However, since negative test length and negative reliability coefficients have no meaning, this part of the graph is omitted.

For the purposes of preparing a computing diagram for equation 10, both equations 14 and 17 have the disadvantage of being composed of curved lines. This necessitates the computation of a great many points for each line and the use of an arbitrary smoothed curve for the intermediate points. If equation 10 can be changed into a straight-line form, it is necessary to have only two points for each line, which means that a practical computing diagram can be readily constructed by anyone who has occasion to compute a large number of values using equation 10.

If we take equation 10, take the reciprocal of both sides, divide the right-hand side by Kr, and then subtract unity from each side, we have

$$(18) \qquad \frac{1}{R} - 1 = \frac{1}{K}\left(\frac{1}{r} - 1\right).$$

If we regard the left side as the ordinate, the expression in parentheses as the abscissa, and then give K the values 2, 3, $\cdots$, etc., we get the diagram shown in Figure 3. It should be noted that the *measured* distances on the ordinate and abscissa are proportional to $(1/R) - 1$ and $(1/r) - 1$, respectively, but the *numbers recorded* along the ordinate

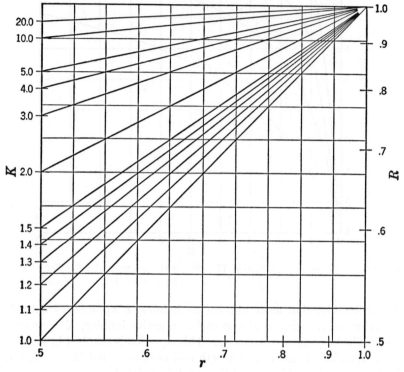

FIGURE 3. Diagram for equation 18. Gives a linear computing diagram for equation 10, the generalized Spearman-Brown formula $\dfrac{1}{R} - 1 = \dfrac{1}{K}\left(\dfrac{1}{r} - 1\right)$.

and abscissa are R and r, respectively. This graph shows the reliability obtained by increasing the length of the test, when the reliability of the unit test is .5 or greater.

5. Length of test necessary to attain a desired reliability

Equation 10 gives the reliability of the lengthened test as a function of the reliability of the unit test, and the length of the new test. However, the same equation also shows how long a test needs to be made in order to have a specified reliability. For example, on a trial run a given test has a reliability of .80, and we wish to construct a test with a reliability of .90 or slightly larger. If the increased reliability must be obtained solely by lengthening the test, is it necessary to double, treble, or quadruple the length of the test? We can answer this question by putting .80 for r, .90 for R, and solving for the one remaining unknown, K, in equation 10. If we follow this procedure, we find that the test must be slightly more than doubled to get a reliability of .90, whereas trebling the length of the test would give a reliability between .92 and .93.

Equation 10 can be changed to show the test length needed for any given reliability. An explicit solution for K can be obtained most readily from equation 18. If we divide through by the left-hand side and multiply both sides by K, we have

(19)
$$K = \frac{(1 - r_{11})R_{KK}}{(1 - R_{KK})r_{11}}.$$

The length of test needed for any specified reliability can be read from any of the graphs. Probably Figure 2 is best for this purpose since K appears here as one of the variables.

In order to increase the reliability of a test from r to R, the

number of items should be multiplied by $\dfrac{(1 - r)R}{(1 - R)r}$.

6. A function of test reliability that is invariant with respect to changes in test length

When we compare reliabilities for tests of different lengths, it is important to state clearly the precise question to be answered. We may ask: "Is this 20-item test (just as it stands) more or less reliable than this 100-item test?" In order to answer this question, the reliability coefficients of each of the tests should be compared. If the 20-item test has a reliability of .81, and the 100-item test a reliability of .87, the longer test is the more reliable test. However, we may wish to ask: "If the 20-item test could be lengthened to 100 items, how would it then probably compare with the 100-item test?" It should be carefully noted that this question implies that the test constructor can get 80 other items comparable with the 20 now in the test, and that the students can answer 100 items of this type with essentially the same sort of performance they are able to give for 20 items. Substituting $K = 5$ and $r = .81$ in the equation

$$R = \frac{Kr}{1 + (K - 1)r},$$

we have

$$R = \frac{4.05}{4.24} = .96.$$

That is to say, if the 20-item test can be lengthened to 100 items without undue fatigue for either the item writers or the test takers, it will have a reliability that is definitely greater than the .87 of the present competing 100-item test. However, it is still true that, as things stand, the short test has a reliability of .81 and the longer one a higher reliability of .87.

For some general comparison purposes, we may wish to compare test reliabilities, allowing for length of test, but may also feel that it is rather arbitrary to reduce all the tests to any specified length, such as 50, 100, or 200 items. Since all the reliabilities approach unity as the test length is increased, we easily see that, if we choose the 200-item test as the standard, all the reliabilities will be much closer together than if we choose the 50-item test as the standard. Also the statistical sampling problems become difficult to work out for various extrapolations of different amounts. It is possible to devise a quantity that depends on test reliability and number of items and is invariant for changes in test length, as long as the test reliability increases, with length, according to the Spearman-Brown formula.

Let us use the following notation:

R_{LL} designates the reliability of a test of length L,
R_{KK} designates the reliability of a test of length K.

The problem then is to find some function, F, such that $F(L, R_{LL}) = F(K, R_{KK})$. First let us express the reliabilities of each lengthened test in terms of the reliability of the unit test (r).

$$R_{LL} = \frac{Lr}{1 + (L - 1)r},$$

(20)

$$R_{KK} = \frac{Kr}{1 + (K - 1)r}.$$

Taking the reciprocal and deducting one from each of these equations, we have

$$\frac{1}{R_{LL}} - 1 = \frac{1 + (L - 1)r}{Lr} - 1,$$

(21)

$$\frac{1}{R_{KK}} - 1 = \frac{1 + (K - 1)r}{Kr} - 1.$$

Simplifying the right-hand member of each equation and multiplying through by the number of items, we have

$$(22) \qquad L\left(\frac{1}{R_{LL}} - 1\right) = K\left(\frac{1}{R_{KK}} - 1\right) = 1\left(\frac{1}{r} - 1\right).$$

The number of items multiplied by one less than the reciprocal of the reliability is invariant with respect to test length.

This, then, is the function mentioned at the beginning of this paragraph, a function of test length and reliability that is invariant with respect to test length, provided that test reliability increases with length according to the Spearman-Brown formula. It furnishes a method of comparing two tests without making any arbitrary decisions regarding the length of test at which the comparison is to be made. It may also be that the sampling theory for such a value can be worked out more readily than that for the reliabilities that have been increased by use of the Spearman-Brown formula.

7. Summary

The general formula for the correlation of any two sums may be expressed as follows:

Let one set of tests be designated by the subscripts g or h ($g = 1 \cdots K$, $h = 1 \cdots K$),

let the other set of tests be designated by the subscripts G or H ($G = I \cdots L, H = I \cdots L$),

s is a standard deviation of one of the unit tests,

r is the correlation between two of the unit tests,

R_{KL} is the correlation of the sum of K tests with the sum of L other tests.

R_{KL} can then be written as a function of the r's and s's,

$$(6) \quad R_{KL} = \frac{\sum\limits_{g=1}^{K} \sum\limits_{G=I}^{L} r_{gG} s_g s_G}{\sqrt{\sum\limits_{g=1}^{K} s_g^2 + \sum\limits_{\substack{g=1 \\ (g \neq h)}}^{K} \sum\limits_{h=1}^{K} r_{gh} s_g s_h} \sqrt{\sum\limits_{G=I}^{L} s_G^2 + \sum\limits_{\substack{G=I \\ (G \neq H)}}^{L} \sum\limits_{H=I}^{L} r_{GH} s_G s_H}}.$$

Writing the foregoing expression in terms of average variances and covariances and denoting the average by a bar over the term, we have

Equation (7)

$$R = \frac{KL\overline{(r_{gG} s_g s_G)}}{\sqrt{K\overline{(s_g^2)} + K(K-1)\overline{(r_{gh} s_g s_h)}} \sqrt{L\overline{(s_G^2)} + L(L-1)\overline{(r_{GH} s_G s_H)}}}.$$

It should be noted that equations 6 and 7 are general and precise. No assumptions regarding parallel tests or any other limitations on the nature of the tests were made in deriving them. They are based on simple algebraic transformations and will be verified, barring arithmetical errors in the work.

The relationship between test length and reliability has been shown. Solving explicitly for reliability as a function of test length, we have

$$(10) \qquad R_{KK} = \frac{Kr_{11}}{1 + (K - 1)r_{11}} \qquad \text{(the Spearman-Brown formula).}$$

Solving explicitly for test length as a function of reliability, we have

$$(19) \qquad K = \frac{(1 - r_{11})R_{KK}}{(1 - R_{KK})r_{11}}.$$

It was shown that

$$(22) \qquad K\left(\frac{1}{R_{KK}} - 1\right)$$

is a function of test length and reliability that can be expected to show no systematic changes in value as test length increases.

Problems

1. From the Spearman-Brown formula, write a formula that will show the test length necessary for any specified reliability.

2. There have been several articles dealing with the experimental verification of the Spearman-Brown formula. Study these articles; then summarize and comment on them. (See articles by Holzinger and Clayton, 1925; Ruch, Ackerson, and Jackson, 1926; Furfey, 1926c; Wood, 1926c; Remmers, Shock, and Kelly, 1927; Kelley, 1925; and Gordon, 1924.)

3. State clearly the assumptions made in deriving the Spearman-Brown formula.

4.

Test	Mean	Standard Deviation	Number of Items	Reliability
A	54.8	14.7	100	.92
B	27.9	10.6	50	.94
C	10.5	4.1	20	.83
D	33.4	10.1	60	.89
E	12.3	3.4	30	.53

(a) What will be the reliability of test A if it is lengthened to 300 items?

(b) Estimate the reliability of test B if 25 items are added, making a 75-item test.

(c) How long would test C need to be to have a reliability of .95?

(d) Suppose that for test A, we were satisfied with a reliability of .85. How many items would be required for this lower reliability?

(e) How many items would be required to give test D an index of reliability of .90?

(f) Estimate the index of reliability of test E for triple length.

(g) How many items would be required to give test E a reliability coefficient of .90?

5. Read and comment on the material in Guilford, *Psychometric Methods* (1936b), page 419, on the Spearman-Brown formula.

6. What is the reliability for a test of infinite length?

9

Effect of Test Length
on Validity (General Case)

1. Meaning of validity

Reliability has been regarded as the correlation of a given test with a parallel form. Correspondingly, the validity of a test is the correlation of the test with some criterion. In this sense a test has a great many different "validities." For example, the ACE Psychological Examination has one validity for predicting grades in English and a different validity for predicting grades in Latin. It is also found in studying various validity coefficients for a given test that they vary from school to school, and from time to time. In other words, validity cannot be regarded as a fixed or a unitary characteristic of a test. As new uses for a test are contemplated, new validity coefficients must be determined; and, when use of a test is continued, the validity coefficients must be redetermined at intervals. In the remainder of this chapter we shall refer to "test validity" only in the sense that we are considering the relationship between test length and its validity for predicting a specified criterion. In most practical investigations of a test, we should be comparing several different validity coefficients.

2. Effect of test length on validity

The general formula for the correlation of any two sums may also be utilized to determine the effect of test length upon test validity. We shall first consider the case in which the criterion variable is not altered. In this case L equals I, since we do not consider the effect of lengthening the criterion. Let $R_{(1 \cdot K)I}$ be used to designate the correlation between a test of length K and the original criterion variable. In this case the general formula (equation 6 of Chapter 8) for the correlation of any two sums becomes

(1)
$$R_{(1 \cdot K)I} = \frac{\sum_{g=1}^{K} r_{gI} s_g s_I}{\sqrt{\sum_{g=1}^{K} s_g^2 + \sum_{g=1}^{K} \sum_{\substack{h=1 \\ (g \neq h)}}^{K} r_{gh} s_g s_h} \sqrt{s_I^2}}.$$

The s_I in numerator and denominator cancel, and the expression remaining may be written in terms of averages as follows:

$$(2) \qquad R_{(1 \cdot K)\mathrm{I}} = \frac{K\overline{(r_{g\mathrm{I}}s_g)}}{\sqrt{K\overline{(s_g{}^2)} + K(K-1)\overline{(r_{gh}s_g s_h)}}}.$$

Again it should be noted that this expression is precise. It involves no assumptions whatever. The numerator is an average involving a number of validity coefficients. The denominator involves the reliabilities of the unit tests. However, when we have the data for this formula, we can actually compute the validity of the lengthened test. It is necessary to *estimate* the validity of the lengthened test only when the data necessary for equation 2 are not available. It is reasonable in such a case to assume that the values found for the first test are a reasonable approximation to the average values that would be found for all the unit tests. As indicated before, this assumption must be true if we succeed in making the new unit tests parallel to the original unit test. Setting these assumptions down explicitly, we have

$$r_{1\mathrm{I}}s_1 = \overline{(r_{g\mathrm{I}}s_g)},$$

$$(3) \qquad s_1{}^2 = \overline{(s_g{}^2)}, \quad \text{and}$$

$$r_{11}s_1{}^2 = \overline{(r_{gh}s_g s_h)}.$$

Substituting equations 3 in equation 2, we have

$$(4) \qquad R_{(1 \cdot K)\mathrm{I}} = \frac{Kr_{1\mathrm{I}}s_1}{\sqrt{Ks_1{}^2 + K(K-1)r_{11}s_1{}^2}}.$$

Dividing both numerator and denominator by $s_1\sqrt{K}$ and using $R_{K\mathrm{I}}$ to indicate the correlation of the new test (which is K times its original length) with the original unit criterion, we have

$$(5) \qquad R_{K\mathrm{I}} = \frac{r_{1\mathrm{I}}\sqrt{K}}{\sqrt{1 + (K-1)r_{11}}},$$

where $R_{K\mathrm{I}}$ is the augmented validity coefficient,

$r_{1\mathrm{I}}$ is the validity coefficient of the unit test,

r_{11} is the reliability coefficient of the unit test, and

K is the number of times the test is increased in length.

Multiplying the length of a test by K increases the validity coefficient as shown in equation 5.

By comparing the preceding equation (equation 5) with equation 10 of Chapter 8, we see that the multiplier for the validity coefficient is the square root of that for the reliability coefficient. That is, augmenting a test so that the reliability will be multiplied by 1.44 will only multiply the validity by 1.2. Since the validity coefficient is usually considerably smaller than the test reliability, this usually means that changing the length of a test can be expected to have only a very slight effect on the validity of the test.

In order to see readily the effect on validity to be expected from increasing test length, equation 5 can be simplified by dividing both sides of the equation by r_{1I} (the validity coefficient of the unit test) and then dividing both numerator and denominator of the right-hand side by $\sqrt{K}$. This procedure gives

$$(6) \qquad \frac{R_{KI}}{r_{1I}} = \frac{1}{\sqrt{1/K + (1 - 1/K)r_{11}}}.$$

Squaring both sides and taking reciprocals, we have

$$(7) \qquad \frac{r_{1I}{}^2}{R_{KI}{}^2} = \frac{1}{K} + \left(1 - \frac{1}{K}\right)r_{11}.$$

That is, the ratio of the squared validity coefficients is equal to a linear function of the reliability coefficient. It can be easily verified from equation 10 of Chapter 8 that the reliability of the unit test divided by the reliability of the augmented test equals this same linear function of the reliability coefficient. Equation 7 is graphed in Figure 1. The ratio of the squared validity coefficients is plotted as the ordinate, and the reliability as the abscissa. The appropriate straight line is shown for several selected values of K. The graph is read by entering at the bottom with the known reliability of the unit test and then moving up to the selected value of K, and then horizontally out to the right-hand margin. For example, as shown by the dotted lines in the figure, if a test with a reliability of .5 is doubled in length, the ratio of the squared validity coefficients is .75. That is, the squared validity for the doubled test will be one-third larger than the validity of the unit test. The validity coefficient will be increased by $\sqrt{1.3333}$, or 1.16; doubling a test with a reliability of .5 will increase the validity coefficient by 16 per cent.

By simply changing the scale markings to give the square root of the reciprocal, we can read directly the ratio of the augmented to the original validity coefficient. These values are indicated on the scale directly under the heading R_{KI}/r_{1I}. We see immediately from the graph, for example, that, if the test reliability is greater than .5, making the test infinitely long increases the validity by less than 41 per cent.

Since the same graph gives directly the ratio of the original to the augmented reliability coefficient, as can be seen from equation 10 of Chapter 8, an additional scale has been added at the extreme right giving the ratio of the augmented to the original reliability coefficient. This scale is given under the heading R_{KK}/r_{11}. By comparing the scale

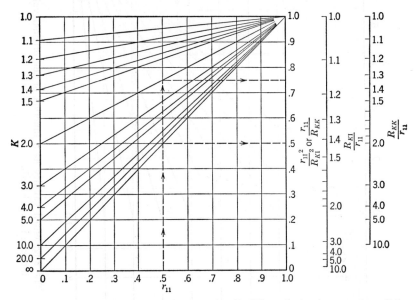

FIGURE 1. Computing diagram for equation 7. The relative increase in validity or reliability as a function of the original reliability and the amount of increase in test length.

for the reliability and validity coefficients, we see that an increase in test length that doubles the reliability coefficient increases the validity coefficient by only 41 per cent.

It is also possible to add another portion to the graph of Figure 1 in order to include the original and augmented reliability coefficients instead of merely their ratios. Such a diagram is Figure 2. The easiest way to read this graph is first to find the validity coefficient of the unit test (r_{1I}) in the scale at the extreme right and then to place a ruler on the horizontal line for r_{1I}. Next enter the bottom left-hand scale with the value of the reliability coefficient for the unit test, go up to the radiating line appropriate for K, right to the heavy vertical center line, down to the ruler (previously placed to indicate r_{1I}), and then up to the value of the augmented validity coefficient. In the illustration shown

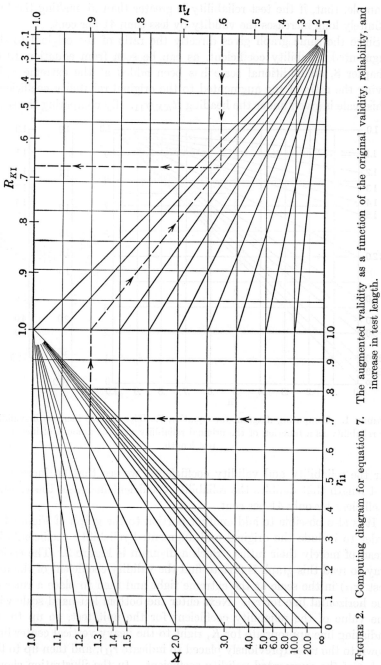

FIGURE 2. Computing diagram for equation 7. The augmented validity as a function of the original validity, reliability, and increase in test length.

(Figure 2), the validity of the unit test is .6, and the reliability of the unit test is .7. If this test is trebled in length, its new validity will be between .70 and .65 (about .67).

3. Length necessary for a given validity

Sometimes in planning new tests it is desirable to know how much a test must be lengthened in order to achieve a specified validity coefficient. It might be noted parenthetically here that, before inquiring how much the test must be lengthened to achieve a given validity, we might investigate the effect of making the test infinite in length. We do this simply by using the lowest of the radiating lines (marked $K = \infty$) in the left half of Figure 2. This topic is also discussed in a later section of this chapter, Section 5 (validity for a test of infinite length). If making a test infinitely long will not achieve the desired validity, we know that simply increasing test length will never achieve the desired validity. However, if the test of infinite length has a validity higher than desired, we see what would happen if the test were only 20, 10, 5, or 3 times as long. Again Figure 2 can be used entering it with the known validity and reliability coefficients for the unit test and the desired augmented validity. Then the K-value necessary for such an augmented validity can be determined.

In order to check the approximate result obtained with the graph, and also for more precise calculation, it is desirable to have an equation that gives K as a function of R_{KI}, r_{1I}, and r_{11}. Such a formula can readily be obtained from equation 5. Squaring and multiplying through by the denominator, we have

$$(8) \qquad R_{KI}^2 + Kr_{11}R_{KI}^2 - r_{11}R_{KI}^2 = Kr_{11}^2.$$

Solving equation 8 for K gives

$$(9) \qquad K = \frac{R_{KI}^2(1 - r_{11})}{r_{1I}^2 - r_{11}R_{KI}^2},$$

where the terms have the same meaning as in equation 5.

> *Equation 9 gives the test length (K), necessary for a specified validity (R_{KI}).*

The graphical representation of equation 7 given in Figures 1 and 2 also holds for equation 9. Since equation 9 is written explicitly for K, it is more convenient to use if we wish to know the length necessary for a desired augmented validity coefficient. A zero value for the denominator of equation 9 indicates that the test must be made infinite in length in order to achieve the desired R_{KI}. A negative value for the denominator indicates that the desired validity cannot be achieved by lengthening the test.

4. A function of validity that is invariant with respect to changes in test length

In the preceding chapter, which treated the effect of test length on reliability, we found one function that did not change with test length; see equation 22 of Chapter 8. Similarly, if we wish to compare different length tests with respect to validity for predicting a given criterion, it is desirable to have some function involving validity that does not vary with test length. Dividing equation 10 of Chapter 8 by r_{11} and taking the square root, we have

$$(10) \qquad \sqrt{\frac{R_{KK}}{r_{11}}} = \sqrt{\frac{K}{1 + (K - 1)r_{11}}}.$$

Substituting the left side of equation 10 for the radical in equation 5, we have

$$(11) \qquad R_{KI} = r_{1I} \sqrt{\frac{R_{KK}}{r_{11}}}.$$

Similarly, by analogy, if the test had been lengthened L times, we should have

$$(12) \qquad R_{LI} = r_{1I} \frac{\sqrt{R_{LL}}}{\sqrt{r_{11}}},$$

from which it follows that

$$(13) \qquad \frac{R_{KI}}{\sqrt{R_{KK}}} = \frac{R_{LI}}{\sqrt{R_{LL}}} = \frac{r_{1I}}{\sqrt{r_{11}}}.$$

The ratio of the validity coefficient to the index of reliability does not change with increase in test length.

It should be carefully noted that the foregoing relationship between validity and reliability holds only when validity and reliability are altered by changing the *length* of the *test*, without varying the nature of the items in the test. There must be no change in the *variability* of the *group* taking the test. For a discussion of the changes in reliability and validity with changes in the group heterogeneity, see Chapters 10, 11, and 12. Chapter 11 includes a discussion of the *relationship* between validity and reliability as the standard deviation of the group changes.

5. Validity of a perfect test for predicting the original criterion

We can extend equation 5 to estimate what would happen to the validity coefficient of a test if it were made infinitely long while the criterion measure remained the same. We shall need to assume, of course, that in lengthening the test each of the new unit tests is parallel to the original one. That is to say, they each have the same mean and standard deviation as the original test, and the same reliability and validity.

If we let K become infinite in equation 5, it gives the indeterminate form ∞/∞. However, if we first divide the numerator and denominator by $\sqrt{K}$, we have

$$(14) \qquad R_{KI} = \frac{r_{1I}}{\sqrt{\frac{1}{K} + \left(1 - \frac{1}{K}\right) r_{11}}}.$$

If we let K approach infinity, equation 14 simplifies to

$$(15) \qquad R_{\infty I} = \frac{r_{1I}}{\sqrt{r_{11}}}.$$

If a test is made infinitely long and hence perfectly reliable, its validity for predicting the original criterion measure will be the original validity coefficient divided by the index of reliability for the original test.

That is to say, if it is possible to increase a test in length without limit, and to do so by adding only parallel forms of the original test, the augmented validity can never be higher than indicated in equation 15. This equation is a convenient one to use where we desire to know if it is worth while to attempt to improve the validity of a test by simply increasing its length. This equation is much easier to apply than equation 5, and, if the test has a fair reliability, equation 15 will show that increasing the length of the test (even to infinite length) will not appreciably affect its validity. If the reliability of the test is reasonably low, we find that a reasonable increase in validity can be made by lengthening the test. Then it is relevant to ask how much longer the test should be made. Will doubling or trebling the length of the test probably give a sufficient increase in validity to be worth the effort? Equation 5 can be used with K, taking various values, such as 2, 3, 4, to see if a practicable increase in test length would change the validity sufficiently to be worth while. It may be remarked here parenthetically that the usual conclusion from equation 5 is that the increased validity obtained from increasing the length of a test is negligible.

Equation 15, showing the effect on the validity of making a test infinitely long, has been graphed in Figure 3. By looking up the validity at the bottom of the graph, and then moving up to the diagonal line

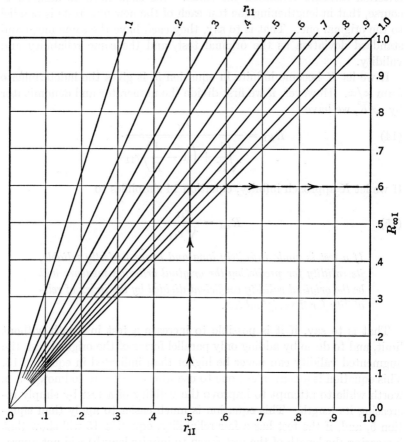

FIGURE 3. Computing diagram for equation 15 or equation 17. Correlation between two measures when one is increased to infinite length, while the other remains unaltered.

$$(15) \quad R_{\infty\,I} = \frac{r_{1I}}{\sqrt{r_{11}}} \quad \text{or} \quad (17) \quad R_{1\infty} = \frac{r_{1I}}{\sqrt{r_{I\,I}}}$$

for the appropriate reliability, we can read from the column at the right the expected validity of an infinitely long test. We see from this graph that, if the validity of a test is greater than the square root of its reliability, the expected validity for infinite length is greater than unity. This is an unreasonable situation. If any actual figures show a validity greater than the square root of the reliability, the result may be regarded as a fluke of some sort that cannot be relied on to repeat itself. Such a result should lead us to check computations very carefully to see if any error has been made, even though such results can arise without errors in arithmetic. Indeed, in general the reliability of a test should not merely be greater than the square of the validity coefficient but should also be greater than the validity coefficient. In most practical situations the validities of a test run much lower than its reliability. Tests with reliabilities in the nineties, have validity coefficients that might range from .70 to .30 or lower. The dotted lines in Figure 3 show that if the reliability and validity of the unit test are .7 and .5, respectively, lengthening the test cannot increase the validity above .6.

As remarked previously, application of the equations showing the probable effect of lengthening a test upon its reliability and validity will indicate that not much improvement is to be expected from increasing the length of the test somewhat. However, since altering length does not have much effect on reliability and validity, this frequently means that if we have a very good test, it is possible to shorten it considerably without seriously damaging its validity or reliability. Equation 5 may also be used with fractional values for K to determine the effect of cutting a test to one-third or one-half its present length. It can be seen that shortening a reliable test by one-third its present length will have little effect on reliability and validity and may well be considered if the reliability is already over .95.

6. Validity of the original unit length test for predicting a perfect criterion

Equation 14 may be regarded as showing what happens to the correlation between two measures when one of them is increased to infinite length and the other remains unaltered. It was indicated that the test length was increased, while the criterion measure remained unaltered. The same formal relationships would hold if the test remained the same, while the criterion measure were increased in length. Thus by symmetry we can use R_{1K} to represent the augmented validity coefficient and r_{II} to represent the reliability of the original criterion measure, and write

$$(16) \qquad R_{1K} = \frac{r_{1\text{I}}}{\sqrt{\dfrac{1}{K} + \left(1 - \dfrac{1}{K}\right) r_{\text{II}}}}.$$

Equation 16 shows the increase in test validity as the criterion measure is increased in length.

If K approaches infinity in equation 16, we have in the limit

(17)
$$R_{1\infty} = \frac{r_{1\mathrm{I}}}{\sqrt{r_{\mathrm{II}}}}.$$

> *If the criterion measure is made perfectly reliable by being made infinitely long, the validity of the original test for predicting this criterion measure will be the original validity coefficient divided by the index of reliability for the original criterion measure.*

7. Effect of altering length of both test and criterion

If we wish to consider the effect of lengthening both the test measure and the criterion measure, the general formula for the correlation of any two sums applies with very little alteration. We may begin with equation 7 of Chapter 8,

$$R_{KL} = \frac{KL(\overline{r_{gG}s_g s_G})}{\sqrt{K(\overline{s_g}^2) + K(K-1)(\overline{r_{gh}s_g s_h})}\ \sqrt{L(\overline{s_G}^2) + L(L-1)(\overline{r_{GH}s_G s_H})}},$$

and make the following assumptions:

1. Since the various forms of the test are parallel, $s_g = s_h$.
2. Since the various criterion units are parallel, $s_G = s_H$.
3. The average validity coefficient $r_{gG} = r_{1\mathrm{I}}$ (the validity of the original unit test).
4. The average test reliability r_{gh} equals the reliability of the original unit test (r_{11}).
5. The average criterion reliability $r_{GH} = r_{\mathrm{I\,I}}$ (the reliability of the original unit criterion measure).

Making these substitutions and simplifying gives

(18)
$$R_{KL} = \frac{KLr_{1\mathrm{I}}}{\sqrt{K + K(K-1)r_{11}}\ \sqrt{L + L(L-1)r_{\mathrm{II}}}}.$$

Dividing the numerator and denominator through by KL gives

(19)
$$R_{KL} = \frac{r_{1\mathrm{I}}}{\sqrt{\dfrac{1}{K} + \left(1 - \dfrac{1}{K}\right)r_{11}}\ \sqrt{\dfrac{1}{L} + \left(1 - \dfrac{1}{L}\right)r_{\mathrm{II}}}},$$

where R_{KL} = the validity of the test augmented K times for predicting the criterion augmented L times,

$r_{1\mathrm{I}}$ = the validity of the unit test for predicting the unit criterion measure,

r_{11} = the reliability of the unit test, and

r_{II} = the reliability of the unit criterion measure.

This formula and many variants of it were given by Spearman (1910).

*Equation 19 is the general equation showing the correlation
of a test K times as long as the original test with a criterion
measure L times as long as the original one. Equations 10,
Chapter 8, and 5, 15, 17, and 21 of Chapter 9 are special
cases of equation 19.*

135380

If we begin with equation 19 and set $L = K$, we obtain equation 10
of Chapter 8; set $L = \mathrm{I}$, we obtain equation 5 of Chapter 9; set $L = \mathrm{I}$
and $K = \infty$, we obtain equation 15 of Chapter 9; set $K = 1$ and $L = \infty$,
we obtain equation 17 of Chapter 9; and finally, by setting $L = K = \infty$,
we obtain equation 21 of Chapter 9.

If in equation 19 we divide by $r_{1\mathrm{I}}$, square both sides, and take the
reciprocal, we have

$$(20) \qquad \frac{r_{1\mathrm{I}}{}^2}{R_{KL}{}^2} = \left[\frac{1}{K} + \left(1 - \frac{1}{K}\right)r_{11}\right]\left[\frac{1}{L} + \left(1 - \frac{1}{L}\right)r_{\mathrm{II}}\right].$$

We see that equation 20 is essentially the same as equation 7, except
that the right side of equation 7 is one linear function, whereas the right
side of equation 20 is the product of two linear functions. This means
that the graph of Figure 1 can be complicated somewhat to serve for
equation 20. In Figure 4 the lower left-hand section gives the value
for the left-hand bracket of equation 20; the upper right-hand section
gives the value for the right-hand bracket of equation 20; and the
lower right-hand section gives the product of these two. For example,
if the criterion reliability is .6 and L is 2.0, we enter the upper right
section of the graph with these two values, as shown by the dotted lines,
and mark with a ruler the appropriate radiating line in the lower right
section of the graph. For the foregoing values of .6 and 2.0, this line is
the dashed line PO. Leaving the ruler here for a marker, we enter the
lower left graph with the values of K and the test reliability. The
dotted lines illustrate this procedure for the case in which the test reliability is .7, and K is 3.0. Thus we see that, if the criterion reliability
is .6 and the test reliability is .7, then if the criterion measure were
doubled and the test were tripled, the new validity coefficient would be
slightly more than 20 per cent above the old one.

Again, as was emphasized in Chapter 6, we must note that, in order to increase the "test length" effectively both the number of items and the test time limits must usually be altered. Also there must be no

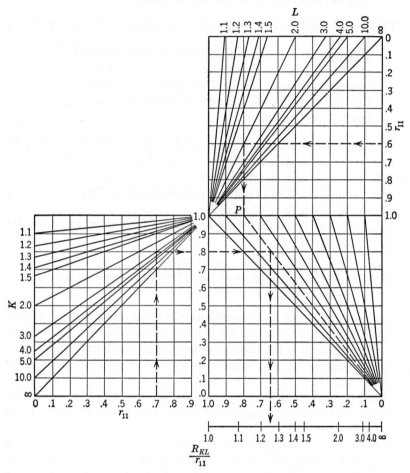

FIGURE 4. Computing diagram for equation 19 or equation 20. The relative increase in validity due to lengthening both measures by any specified amount.

serious fatigue or practice effects with the longer working period. In each case the objective criterion that must be satisfied before the equations of Chapters 6, 7, 8, and 9 apply is that each of the unit tests must have the same mean, standard deviation, and error of measurement and that all the intercorrelations of the unit tests must be the same. If these criteria are met, the tests satisfy the quantitative criteria for parallel tests, and the equations for the effect of test length apply. A statistical criterion for parallel tests is given in Chapter 14.

The problem of how to adjust the *relative* lengths of several tests to maximize the validity of the composite has been solved; see Horst (1948) and (1949), and Taylor (1950).

8. Validity of a perfect test for predicting a perfect criterion (the correction for attenuation)

If both K and L are allowed to approach infinity, several of the terms will vanish, giving the formula for the correlation of a test of infinite length (or unit reliability) with a criterion of infinite length (and hence of unit reliability). This equation is

$$(21) \qquad\qquad R_{\infty\infty} = \frac{r_{1\mathrm{I}}}{\sqrt{r_{11}r_{\mathrm{II}}}}.$$

This is the well-known correction for attenuation. It is not properly called a "correction." Rather it is an estimate of the correlation between a perfect test and a perfect criterion.

This formula was given by Spearman (1904a), (1907), (1910), and (1913).

> A correlation coefficient "corrected for attenuation" $(R_{\infty\infty})$ may be regarded as (a) the correlation between true scores in each of the two measures and (b) the correlation between the two measures when each is increased to infinite length (and hence given a reliability of 1.00). This correlation is equal to the correlation between the original measures divided by the geometric mean of the two reliability coefficients.

Initial interest in the correction for attenuation rose from the belief that it gave the "true" correlation between two variables, unattenuated because of the use of fallible (unreliable) measuring instruments. It was thought that one of the sources of variation in observed coefficients of correlation was variation in reliability of tests used. Therefore, if coefficients were corrected for attenuation, there would be greater agreement between different experiments. With the development of factor theory, it became clear that, although variation in reliability was one source of disagreement between the results of different experimenters, there were many other important sources. In particular, each test has a fairly high specific factor which is not duplicated in other similar tests, and therefore would be a source of variation in the results of different investigators. Also the factor composition of many, if not most, tests is complex, and the variation in factor structure from one test to another is another possible source of variation in results of different investigations. Although the notion that the correction for attenuation would give invariant results despite fallible tests does not seem to have been borne out, the equation is still valuable in giving a quick indication of the worth-whileness of attempting to increase validity by increasing test length.

It will be noted that equations 21 and 15 are analogous. In equation 15 the validity is divided by the square root of one reliability coefficient. If the result is divided by the square root of a second reliability coefficient, we have equation 21. Thus two graphs like that of Figure 3 will give a computing diagram for equation 21. These two graphs are shown in Figure 5. Enter the graph with the correlation of the two tests on the scale at the lower left, move up to the diagonal representing one of the reliability coefficients, then to the right to the diagonal representing the other reliability coefficient, and then up to read the result from the scale at the upper right. The dotted lines represent this procedure for the case in which the correlation between the two tests is .5, while the reliability coefficients are .8 and .9. In this case the correlation between true scores is about .59.

We should note carefully just what we are doing when using this equation. It is an estimate of the correlation between test and criterion if both could be made perfectly reliable by lengthening the test and the criterion measure indefinitely. Just because we might get a validity of .90, for example, by lengthening the test and criterion does not mean that we *have* such a validity coefficient with the original test. However, if the coefficient of validity "corrected for attenuation" is near unity, it does show that the major problem to work on for better prediction is the most appropriate means of increasing reliability of test and criterion measures. If (when corrected for "attenuation") the validity coefficient is still in the neighborhood of some reasonably low value, such as .6 or .7, we can conclude that further work in that particular field should take two directions. First, it is desirable to try to improve the reliability of both criterion and test measures. The coefficient corrected for attenuation shows the maximum validity we can reasonably hope for by such efforts. If this validity is still a considerable distance from unity, we can also look for new tests to add to the prediction battery. If used in this way, to determine what work should be done next—whether to search for new tests and also to improve the reliability of tests already in use, or only to improve reliability of tests now in use—the correction for attenuation is a valuable tool in directing future research. However, the use of this correction for the sole purpose of being able to report a higher validity coefficient—accom-

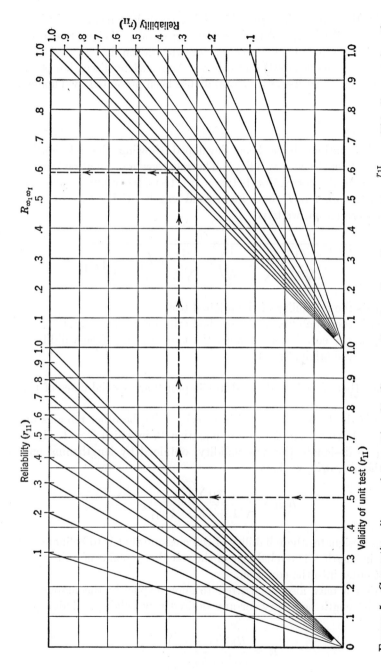

FIGURE 5. Computing diagram for equation 21, the correction for attenuation: $r_{\infty\infty} = \dfrac{r_{\mathrm{II}}}{\sqrt{r_{\mathrm{II}'\mathrm{II}}\, r_{\mathrm{II}}}}$.   This diagram gives the correlation between true scores as a function of the correlation and reliabilities of the original tests.

panied by the implication that this higher coefficient has already been achieved—is distinctly misleading and erroneous. When Spearman (1904a) first presented the correction for attenuation, it was vigorously criticized by Pearson (1904) and others. An excellent discussion of the correct and incorrect use of this formula has been presented by Thouless (1939).

9. Summary

Several equations have been developed showing the relationship between test length and validity. The most general equation enables us to estimate the correlation between two tests, when one is increased to K and the other to L times its original length. Using R_{KL} to designate this correlation, we have

$$(19) \qquad R_{KL} = \frac{r_{1\mathrm{I}}}{\sqrt{\dfrac{1}{K} + \left(1 - \dfrac{1}{K}\right) r_{11}} \; \sqrt{\dfrac{1}{L} + \left(1 - \dfrac{1}{L}\right) r_{\mathrm{II}}}},$$

where r_{11} is the reliability of the original test,
$\quad r_{\mathrm{I\,I}}$ is the reliability of the original criterion measure, and
$\quad r_{1\mathrm{I}}$ is the correlation between the two measures (the validity of the original test).

All the other equations derived in Chapter 9 are special cases of this one.

If one of the tests is increased in length, while the other remains unaltered, we have the special case of equation 19 in which $L = 1$. If we use R_{KI} to designate the new validity, obtained by lengthening only one of the measures, we have

$$(5) \qquad R_{KI} = \frac{r_{1\mathrm{I}}\sqrt{K}}{\sqrt{1 + (K - 1)r_{11}}},$$

where r_{11} designates the reliability of the measure that is to be increased K times in length. The reliability of the test that remains of unit length does not enter into the equation.

Equation 5 may also be written to show explicitly the amount of increase in length necessary for any desired new validity. This equation is

$$(9) \qquad K = \frac{R_{KI}{}^{2}(1 - r_{11})}{r_{1\mathrm{I}}{}^{2} - R_{KI}{}^{2}r_{11}}.$$

If the test denoted by subscript 1 becomes infinite in length, whereas the test denoted by I is unaltered, we have the special case of equation 19, in which K is ∞ and L is I. The resulting correlation $(R_{\infty\,\mathrm{I}})$ is given by

$$(15) \qquad\qquad R_{\infty\,\mathrm{I}} = \frac{r_{1\mathrm{I}}}{\sqrt{r_{11}}}.$$

If the test designated by I is made infinite in length, whereas the test designated by 1 is unchanged, we have the special case in which K is 1 and L is ∞. The corresponding equation is

$$(17) \qquad\qquad R_{1\,\infty} = \frac{r_{1\mathrm{I}}}{\sqrt{r_{\mathrm{I\,I}}}}.$$

It was also shown in developing equation 13 that the foregoing expressions, equations 15 and 17, do not change as the length of the test changes. Thus, for comparing the relative performance of tests that vary in length, the validity coefficient divided by the index of reliability may be used.

The correlation between true scores or between measures, each of which has been made infinitely long (and hence perfectly reliable), is the special case of equation 19, in which both K and L become infinite. This correlation $(R_{\infty\infty})$ is given by

$$(21) \qquad\qquad R_{\infty\infty} = \frac{r_{1\mathrm{I}}}{\sqrt{r_{11}r_{\mathrm{I\,I}}}} \qquad \text{(the correction for attenuation).}$$

Problems

1. Under what conditions can the validity of a test be equal to its reliability?

2. Prove that the validity of a test can never be greater than its reliability. What assumption was used?

3. From the equations showing the relationship of test length to validity and to reliability, determine the relationship between test reliability and validity as the length of the test is increased while the criterion is unchanged, that is, write

$$f(r_{11},\, r_{12},\, R_{KK},\, R_{K2}) = 0.$$

4. Fifty mathematics problems in free-answer form are rewritten as multiple-choice items. If the reliability of the free-answer form is .88 and the reliability of the multiple-choice form is .93, what correlation would be expected between the two forms?

5. If the reliability of a test is raised from .80 to .90 by lengthening the test, a validity coefficient of .60 for this test would be expected to increase to what value?

6.

Test	Mean	Standard Deviation	Number of Items	Relia-bility	Validity Criterion (School Grade Average)
A	16.5	4.4	30	.72	.68
B	12.6	3.5	20	.77	.50
C	53.2	10.7	100	.88	.68
D	32.3	8.8	50	.91	.71
E	66.3	17.2	120	.95	.75

(Criterion reliability = .70)

(a) If test A is lengthened to a 100-item test, what would you expect the new mean, standard deviation, reliability, and validity to be? (Assume that the criterion test has not been altered.)

(b) If test B is lengthened to increase its reliability to .90, how many new items will be needed? What will the new validity be, assuming that the criterion test remains unchanged?

(c) Which of the five tests is, *in its present form*, best for use in predicting school grade average?

(d) Which of the five tests seems to be intrinsically closest to this criterion?

(e) If there is time and material for a 200-item test in each case, which of the tests would probably perform best at the new length?

(f) If the reliability of the criterion is .70, what is the correlation between true criterion scores and true test scores for each of the tests?

(g) If it were possible to improve the criterion by methods analogous to increasing test length, so that the criterion reliability were raised from .70 to .90, what would be the new validity of test C in its present form?

(h) To raise the criterion reliability from .70 to .90 corresponds to an increase in criterion test length of about how many times?

(i) Give the true variance, and error variance for test C. Estimate the true and error variances for test C if it is increased to 300 items.

(j) If test D is increased to a 150-item test and the criterion test is doubled in length, estimate the new reliabilities and validity.

(k) What will be the validity of test E if its reliability is increased to unity?

7. Test X has a validity coefficient of .65 and reliability .75, whereas the validity of test Y is .67 and its reliability .95. Each of these tests is a 50-item test. Which type of item (that in test X or in test Y) would probably show the greater validity for a 200-item test?

8. Prove that, if a test of n items is a subtest of a test with m items $(n < m)$, the correlation r_{nm} is

$$r_{nm} = \sqrt{\frac{\dfrac{1-r}{m} + r}{\dfrac{1-r}{n} + r}},$$

where r is the reliability of a unit test.

9. Derive the equation for the correlation between *true* scores in two different tests. Use only the assumption that "true score plus error score equals gross score," that "all correlations with an error score are zero," and some appropriate definition of parallel tests.

10

Effect of Group Heterogeneity
on Test Reliability

1. Introduction

The correlation between two variables is markedly affected by the range of the variables. For example, if we correlated height and weight for a group of persons who ranged from 5 feet, 6 inches, to 5 feet, 8 inches in height, we should find that the correlation is very low, as illustrated in Figure 1. It is, of course, unlikely that we should make such a peculiar selection of persons for the purpose of correlating height and weight. However, the effect would be similar if, for example, we were to correlate height and weight for pupils in the fifth grade, as compared with correlating height and weight for pupils in grades one to twelve. The correlation between mental age and chronological age will be much greater for a school population than for a given grade.

In a similar manner, restriction of range lowers a reliability coefficient. If a mental test is given to a random sampling of children aged six to sixteen, the range of scores will be very great, and the reliability coefficient will be high. If, on the other hand, the test is given to a group of eighth-grade students who have a rather narrow mental ability range, the reliability coefficient will be much lower.

By making certain reasonable assumptions, it is possible to estimate the amount of change in reliability that will result from any given change in the group variance. Also by solving the equations for variance it is possible to estimate the amount of change in variability it would have taken to produce any given change in reliability.

First let us recall that the observed variance of a test has two components. It is the sum of the true variance and the error variance. It is possible to increase the observed variance by increasing either the true variance or the error variance. In all the illustrations given above, for example, it was the *true variance* that changed. That is to say, the *actual* mental ability range of a group of six- to sixteen-year-olds is greater than the mental ability range of a group of twelve-year-olds.

In general, when we give a test to *two different groups* and find that the standard deviation of one group is larger than that of the other group, we are dealing with a case where the true variance of one group is greater than that of the other group.   The only other event that could account for the difference in group standard deviations would be an alteration in the error variance.   This would mean that the test was

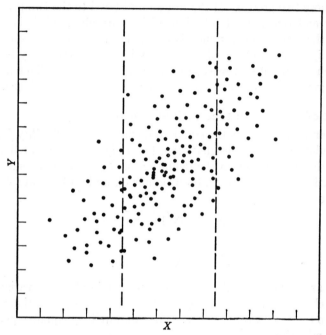

FIGURE 1.   Illustration of effect of changes in group heterogeneity on correlation.

given under good conditions in one group and under poor conditions in the other group.   It is to be noted that ordinary errors in test procedure, such as allowing too little time (erroneously calling time 10 minutes too soon, for example), would affect everyone's score in the same direction, and would not bring about an increase in the error *variance* of the test. An increase in error variance means that the scores of some persons were *raised* considerably above where the score should have been, while for other persons the score was considerably *lowered*.   This sort of effect might be produced, for example, if the room was large and the students in the first rows received good directions and some help in answering the questions, whereas the students in the last rows did not understand the directions and did not receive any special help so that their scores were lower than they would have been under the standard conditions for administering the test. Great *variability* in lighting conditions in different parts of the testing room might also produce the same effect. Poor *general* lighting could *not* produce such an effect. It can be seen that, although it is possible to have events that increase error variance, it is much more likely that a difference in *observed* variance of two groups is due to a difference in the true variance of the persons in those two groups. If the test administered to the two groups is the same and the same standard conditions are observed, it is highly unlikely that the error variance is affected. We shall first show the relationship between observed variance and observed reliability for two groups, on the usual and reasonable assumption that the differences in the two groups are to be attributed to differences in true variance.

2. Effect of changes in true variance on reliability

Let s_x and r_{xx} designate the standard deviation and reliability for one group, and S_X and R_{XX} designate the standard deviation and reliability for the other group. From the definition of the error of measurement (see equations 42 [Chapter 2], 38 [Chapter 3], and 20 [Chapter 4]), we may write

$$(1) \qquad\qquad s_{e_x} = s_x\sqrt{1 - r_{xx}}$$

and

$$(2) \qquad\qquad s_{e_X} = S_X\sqrt{1 - R_{XX}}.$$

Since we are assuming that the entire difference in observed variance is due to a change in true variance, it follows that the error variance of x is equal to the error variance of X. Therefore we may equate equations 1 and 2 and write

$$(3) \qquad\qquad s_x\sqrt{1 - r_{xx}} = S_X\sqrt{1 - R_{XX}}.$$

Equation 3 can readily be solved for either s_x or S_X to give an expression that will show the amount of change in standard deviation of observed scores required to account for any given change in reliability, solely on the basis of a group difference in true variance. Solving for S_X, we have

$$(4) \qquad\qquad S_X = s_x\sqrt{\frac{1 - r_{xx}}{1 - R_{XX}}},$$

where s_x is the standard deviation of group x on a given test,

$\quad$ r_{xx} is the test reliability for group x,

$\quad$ R_{XX} is the reliability of the same test for group X, and

$\quad$ S_X is the standard deviation of group X on the same test.

If r_{xx} is the reliability of a test for group x, R_{XX} is the reliability of the same test for group X, and this difference is attributed solely to a difference in the true variance of the two groups, the observed standard deviation of group X (S_X) is given by equation 4.

We may also determine the amount of change in reliability to be expected from any given change in observed variance, on the assumption that this change is due solely to a difference in true variance. Squaring equation 3 and solving for R_{XX} gives

(5)
$$R_{XX} = 1 - \frac{s_x^2}{S_X^2} (1 - r_{xx}),$$

where the terms have the same definitions as in equation 4.

If s_x^2 is the variance of group x on a given test, and S_X^2 is the variance of group X on the same test, and if this difference is attributed solely to a difference in true variance of the two groups, the reliability of the test for group X (R_{XX}) is given by equation 5.

Equations 4 and 5, or slight variants of them, have been presented by Kelley (1921), (1923c), (1927), by Otis (1922b), Holzinger (1921), Thurstone (1931a), Peters and Van Voorhis (1940), Crawford and Burnham (1946), and others. The only assumption used is that the error of measurement is invariant with respect to variations in range of ability of the group tested. This assumption was suggested by Kelley (1921), Otis (1922b), Nygaard (1923), and others. It was seriously questioned by Holzinger (1921). It seems reasonable to say that in some cases the error of measurement *is* the same for two groups, whereas in other cases the error of measurement for a given test may vary with the ability of the group. Equations 4 and 5 may be used if there is reason to believe that the error of measurement is about the same for the two groups under consideration, and may not be used if there is evidence to indicate that the error of measurement is radically different for the two groups.

A different formula based on explicit restriction in a correlated variable has been presented by Davis (1944) and Kaitz (1945b).

Wherever possible it is a good idea to test the basic assumption directly. Compute $s_x \sqrt{1 - r_{xx}}$ and $S_X \sqrt{1 - R_{XX}}$ to see if they are approximately alike for the two groups. In order to make a precise judgment about the similarity of two errors of measurement, appropriate statistical tests of significance of differences would need to be devised and used. A solution to this problem has been given by Green (1950b).

Otis and Knollin (1921) pointed out that the error of measurement was superior to reliability as a test statistic. Kelley (1921) also recognized some of the disadvantages of the reliability coefficient and the advantages of the error of measurement. He discussed, and suggested, some solutions for the problem of establishing a suitable unit for the error of measurement. Basic statistics on any test should include the error of measurement as well as the reliability.

It should be noted that learning can also have the effect of increasing or decreasing the test score variance for a given group. In general, if we began testing the group when they knew very little, all scores would be low, the mean would be low, and the variance would be low. We should say that the test was too *difficult* for this group. As the members of the group learned more, the average score and the score variance would increase for a time. Then as learning continued beyond this stage, we should eventually find that the test was too *easy* for the group. All persons would make perfect or near perfect scores; hence the mean score would be high, and the standard deviation of scores would be small again.

Copeland (1934) has pointed out that teaching a class so that the students begin to approach a perfect score will lower not only the test variance but also the test reliability. It is also clear that, if the test were initially too difficult for the group, so that the scores were uniformly near zero, we should expect the first effect of learning to be an increase in the test variance, and hence an increase in test reliability. It must be emphasized, however, that the effect of such changes in test variance are not related to the discussion presented in this chapter. There is no reason for believing that this effect is the equivalent of *selecting* the members of a group in such a way that the *true variance will be altered* and the *error variance unaffected*. As we approach the floor or the ceiling of a test, the error variance is clearly affected, but the theory presented in this chapter has nothing to do with such effects. The theory presented here is based on the assumption that we are working entirely within the appropriate range for the test and that no "floor" or "ceiling" effects are present.

Figure 2 is set up in terms of

$$(6) \qquad \frac{S_X}{s_x} = \sqrt{\frac{1 - r_{xx}}{1 - R_{XX}}}.$$

From it we can read the proportional change in standard deviation corresponding to a given change in reliability, or the change in reliability that corresponds to a given ratio of standard deviations.

For example, if r_{xx} is .64 and R_{XX} is .91, we locate .91 across the top of the graph, .64 along the left side, and note that these two lines inter-

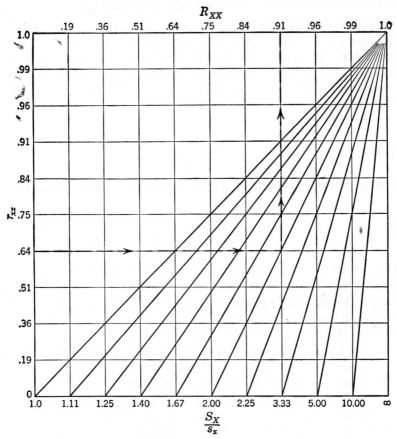

FIGURE 2.   Computing diagram for equations 5 and 6:

$$\frac{S_X^2}{s_x^2} = \frac{1 - r_{xx}}{1 - R_{XX}} \cdot$$

sect on the diagonal line labeled 2.0.   This means that a change in reliability of .64 to .91 would occur if the observed standard deviation were doubled and the entire increase were due to a change in *true* variance.   In a similar manner, we observe that an increase of 25 per cent in the standard deviation, if due entirely to a change in true variance, will be expected to raise the reliability coefficient from .75 to .84.

Graphs for computing the change in reliability with a change in group variance have also been presented by Rulon (1930), Cureton and Dunlap (1929), and Toops and Edgerton (1927).

3. Effect of changes in error variance on reliability

Occasionally students are confused by the fact that in the usual formulas for correlation, the standard deviation appears in the denominator. They point out that, if the denominator of a fraction is increased, the fraction is decreased; therefore, the argument runs, "an increase in standard deviation should be expected to lower the reliability." If we take the equation for the true variance (see equation 20 of Chapter 3),

$$(7) \qquad s_t^2 = s_x^2 r_{xx}$$

we may divide through by s_x^2 and write the reliability coefficient as

$$(8) \qquad r_{xx} = \frac{s_t^2}{s_x^2} = \frac{s_t^2}{s_t^2 + s_e^2}.$$

Thus we see that the only way for the denominator to increase *while the numerator remains constant* is for the true variance to remain constant. This necessarily means that the entire change must be due to an increase in the error variance. It is true that, if the observed variance of a test changes, owing solely to an increase in the *error variance*, the reliability of the test will decrease. It is possible to derive the equation showing the relationship between observed standard deviation and reliability on the assumption that the true variance is constant. No one, so far as I know, has ever reported a case where such an equation could reasonably be used. However, we may derive the equation here simply to emphasize the fact that an increase in observed standard deviation will have the effect of *increasing* reliability, if it is due to an increase in *true* variability, and will have the effect of *decreasing* the reliability if it is due to an increase in *error* variability.

If the true variance of the test for group x is equal to that for group X, we may write the two equations for true variance (see equations 39 of Chapter 2 or 20 of Chapter 3)

$$(9) \qquad s_{t_x} = s_x \sqrt{r_{xx}} \quad \text{and}$$

$$(10) \qquad S_{t_x} = S_X \sqrt{R_{XX}}.$$

Since the true variances are in this case assumed to be equal, we may write

(11) $$s_x \sqrt{r_{xx}} = S_X \sqrt{R_{XX}}.$$

Squaring both sides and dividing through by S_X^2 gives

(12) $$R_{XX} = r_{xx} \frac{s_x^2}{S_X^2},$$

where the terms have the same definition as in equation 4.

If s_x^2 is the variance of group x on a given test, and S_X^2 is the variance of group X on the same test, and if this difference is attributed **solely to a difference in error variance** *for the two groups, the reliability for group X (R_{XX}) is given by equation 12.*

From equation 12, we easily see that, as the variance (S_X^2) increases, the reliability (R_{XX}) decreases. The change is very drastic. For example, if the standard deviation (S_X) is double the standard deviation (s_x), the reliability (R_{XX}) is one-fourth the reliability (r_{xx}).

It should again be pointed out that the assumption that a change in observed variance is due entirely to a change in error variance is very unreasonable. It will not occur except with very peculiar and very careless testing methods.

4. Conditions under which the error of measurement is invariant with respect to test score

The derivations presented in this chapter have depended in general on the assumption that the error of measurement is constant for a given test regardless of the variability of the group to which the test is given. This assumption will be true in general only if the error of measurement is the same regardless of the magnitude of the test score. Does the error of measurement change in some systematic fashion as the magnitude of the test score changes? To study this problem analytically, we may proceed by expressing the error of measurement as a function of test score. The solution presented in this section is the one given by Mollenkopf (1948), (1949).

Let us regard the score for individual i as made up of two equivalent parts, for example,

(13) $$x_i = x_{i1} + x_{i2}.$$

The subscripts 1 and 2 designate equivalent halves which are such that

(14) $$s_1 = s_2,$$

where

$$s_g = \sqrt{\frac{\sum\limits_{i=1}^{N} x_{ig}^2}{N}} \qquad (g = 1, 2);$$

(15) $$\alpha' = \alpha''$$

and

(16) $$\beta' = \beta'',$$

where

$$\alpha' = \frac{\sum\limits_{i=1}^{N} x_{i1}^3}{N s_1^3}$$

(17)

$$\alpha'' = \frac{\sum\limits_{i=1}^{N} x_{i2}^3}{N s_2^3}$$

and

$$\beta' = \frac{\sum\limits_{i=1}^{N} x_{i1}^4}{N s_1^4}$$

(18)

$$\beta'' = \frac{\sum\limits_{i=1}^{N} x_{i2}^4}{N s_2^4}.$$

Using the relationship shown in equation 10, Chapter 6, we may write the standard deviation of the total test (S_x) as follows:

(19) $$S_x^2 = 2s_1^2(1 + r),$$

where

$$r = \frac{\sum\limits_{i=1}^{N} x_{i1} x_{i2}}{N s_1 s_2}.$$

From equation 30, Chapter 6, the reliability of the total test (R) may be written as

(20)
$$R = \frac{2r}{1 + r}.$$

From equation 37, Chapter 3, the error of measurement (S_e) may be written as

(21)
$$S_e^2 = S_x^2(1 - R).$$

To express S_e in terms of s_1 and r, we substitute equations 19 and 20 in equation 21 and simplify, obtaining

(22)
$$S_e^2 = 2s_1^2(1 - r).$$

Using equation 14, we may write the standard deviation of the differences $(x_{i1} - x_{i2})$ as

(23)
$$\frac{\sum\limits_{i=1}^{N} (x_{i1} - x_{i2})^2}{N} = 2s_1^2(1 - r).$$

Thus we see that

(24)
$$S_e^2 = \frac{\sum\limits_{i=1}^{N} (x_{i1} - x_{i2})^2}{N}.$$

The square of the error of measurement for the total test is equal to the standard deviation of the differences of parallel halves. Thus we may regard the squared difference $(x_{i1} - x_{i2})^2$ as the "error" for individual i, and the sum of these errors as the error of measurement for the test. Let us define this error for individual i by

(25)
$$y_i = (x_{i1} - x_{i2})^2.$$

Let us now approximate y_i as closely as possible by a second-degree function of x, designated

(26)
$$\dot{y}_i = ax_i^2 + bx_i + c,$$

where a, b, and c are chosen so that

(27)
$$\sum_{i=1}^{N} (y_i - \dot{y}_i)^2 = \sum_{i=1}^{N} (y_i - ax_i^2 - bx_i - c)^2$$

is a minimum.

To minimize this expression, differentiate successively with respect to a, b, and c, and set the derivatives equal to zero. This procedure gives the equations

$$a \sum_{i=1}^{N} x_i^4 + b \sum_{i=1}^{N} x_i^3 + c \sum_{i=1}^{N} x_i^2 = \sum_{i=1}^{N} x_i^2 y_i,$$

(28)
$$a \sum_{i=1}^{N} x_i^3 + b \sum_{i=1}^{N} x_i^2 + c \sum_{i=1}^{N} x_i = \sum_{i=1}^{N} x_i y_i,$$

$$a \sum_{i=1}^{N} x_i^2 + b \sum_{i=1}^{N} x_i + cN = \sum_{i=1}^{N} y_i.$$

The solution for a, b, and c in determinantal form is

$$a = \frac{\begin{vmatrix} \Sigma x^2 y & \Sigma x^3 & \Sigma x^2 \\ \Sigma xy & \Sigma x^2 & \Sigma x \\ \Sigma y & \Sigma x & N \end{vmatrix}}{\begin{vmatrix} \Sigma x^4 & \Sigma x^3 & \Sigma x^2 \\ \Sigma x^3 & \Sigma x^2 & \Sigma x \\ \Sigma x^2 & \Sigma x & N \end{vmatrix}}$$

(29)
$$b = \frac{\begin{vmatrix} \Sigma x^4 & \Sigma x^2 y & \Sigma x^2 \\ \Sigma x^3 & \Sigma xy & \Sigma x \\ \Sigma x^2 & \Sigma y & N \end{vmatrix}}{\begin{vmatrix} \Sigma x^4 & \Sigma x^3 & \Sigma x^2 \\ \Sigma x^3 & \Sigma x^2 & \Sigma x \\ \Sigma x^2 & \Sigma x & N \end{vmatrix}}$$

$$c = \frac{\begin{vmatrix} \Sigma x^4 & \Sigma x^3 & \Sigma x^2 y \\ \Sigma x^3 & \Sigma x^2 & \Sigma xy \\ \Sigma x^2 & \Sigma x & \Sigma y \end{vmatrix}}{\begin{vmatrix} \Sigma x^4 & \Sigma x^3 & \Sigma x^2 \\ \Sigma x^3 & \Sigma x^2 & \Sigma x \\ \Sigma x^2 & \Sigma x & N \end{vmatrix}}.$$

The problem now is to express a, b, and c in terms of the moments of the x-score distribution. The terms Σx, Σx^2, Σx^3, Σx^4, and Σy can be expressed readily as follows:

$$(30) \qquad\qquad \Sigma x = 0,$$

$$(31) \qquad\qquad \Sigma x^2 = NS_x^2,$$

$$(32) \qquad\qquad \Sigma x^3 = NS_x^3 \alpha_x,$$

$$(33) \qquad\qquad \Sigma x^4 = NS_x^4 \beta_x,$$

and

$$(34) \qquad\qquad \Sigma y = NS_x^2(1 - R),$$

where

$$(35) \qquad\qquad \alpha_x = \frac{\displaystyle\sum_{i=1}^{N} x_i^3}{NS_x^3},$$

$$(36) \qquad\qquad \beta_x = \frac{\displaystyle\sum_{i=1}^{N} x_i^4}{NS_x^4}.$$

This completes the solution, except for the expressions Σxy and $\Sigma x^2 y$. We must now find expressions for these terms as functions of the moments of the x-score distribution.

In order to do this, it is necessary first to find the value of the third- and fourth-degree product moments, $\Sigma x_1^2 x_2$ (or $\Sigma x_1 x_2^2$), $\Sigma x_1^3 x_2$ (or $\Sigma x_1 x_2^3$), and $\Sigma x_1^2 x_2^2$.

To simplify $\Sigma x_1^2 x_2$, we proceed as follows. We consider the regression of x_2 on x_1, and write x_2 as the sum of the score predicted from x_1 and the residual error designated e_2. This gives

$$(37) \qquad\qquad x_2 = r\left(\frac{s_2}{s_1}\right) x_1 + e_2.$$

Substituting this value for x_2 in $\Sigma x_1^2 x_2$, and noting that $s_1 = s_2$, we have

$$(38) \qquad\qquad \Sigma x_1^2 x_2 = r\Sigma x_1^3 + \Sigma e_2 x_1^2.$$

Let us assume that

$$(39) \qquad\qquad r_{e_2 x_1^2} = 0.$$

From the gross score formula for correlation,

$$r_{xy} = \frac{\Sigma XY - N\bar{X}\bar{Y}}{\sqrt{(\Sigma X^2 - N\bar{X}^2)(\Sigma Y^2 - N\bar{Y}^2)}} \, ,$$

we note that if $r_{xy} = 0$, then $\Sigma XY = N\bar{X}\bar{Y}$. Thus, if $r_{e_2x_1{}^2} = 0$,

$$\Sigma e_2 x_1{}^2 = N \left[\frac{\Sigma e_2}{N}\right] \left[\frac{\Sigma x_1{}^2}{N}\right].$$

Since Σe_2 is zero, it follows that

(40) $\Sigma e_2 x_1{}^2 = 0.$

Substituting equations 17 and 40 in equation 38, we have

(41) $\Sigma x_1{}^2 x_2 = N r s_1{}^3 \alpha'.$

To evaluate $\Sigma x_1 x_2{}^2$, we assume that

(42) $r_{e_1 x_2{}^2} = 0,$

and by a corresponding procedure find that

(43) $\Sigma x_1 x_2{}^2 = N r s_1{}^3 \alpha'.$

To simplify $\Sigma x_1{}^3 x_2$, we proceed by substituting for x_2 from equation 37, noting that $s_1 = s_2$, and writing

(44) $\Sigma x_1{}^3 x_2 = r \Sigma x_1{}^4 + \Sigma e_2 x_1{}^3.$

As before, if we assume that

(45) $r_{e_2 x_1{}^3} = 0,$

it follows that

$$\Sigma e_2 x_1{}^3 = N \left[\frac{\Sigma e_2}{N}\right] \left[\frac{\Sigma x_1{}^3}{N}\right].$$

Since Σe_2 is zero, it follows that

(46) $\Sigma e_2 x_1{}^3 = 0;$

hence, substituting equations 18 and 46 in equation 44, we have

(47) $\Sigma x_1{}^3 x_2 = N r s_1{}^4 \beta'.$

In like manner, by assuming that

(48) $r_{e_1 x_2{}^3} = 0$

we may show that

(49) $\Sigma x_1 x_2{}^3 = N r s_1{}^4 \beta'.$

To simplify $\Sigma x_1^2 x_2^2$, we again use equation 37, note that $(s_2/s_1 = 1)$, and write

(50) $$\Sigma x_1^2 x_2^2 = \Sigma x_1^2 (rx_1 + e_2)^2.$$

Expanding and taking the constants outside the summation, we have

(51) $$\Sigma x_1^2 x_2^2 = r^2 \Sigma x_1^4 + \Sigma x_1^2 e_2^2 + 2r\Sigma x_1^3 e_2.$$

If we assume that

(52) $$r_{x_1^2 e_2^2} = 0,$$

then

$$\Sigma x_1^2 e_2^2 = N \left[\frac{\Sigma x_1^2}{N} \right] \left[\frac{\Sigma e_2^2}{N} \right].$$

We see that the first term in brackets is the variance of x_1 and the second is the variance of the error made in estimating x_2 from x_1. Thus we may write

(53) $$\Sigma x_1^2 e_2^2 = N s_1^2 s_2^2 (1 - r^2).$$

Substituting equations 18, 46, and 53 in equation 51, noting that $s_1 = s_2$, and simplifying, we have

(54) $$\Sigma x_1^2 x_2^2 = N s_1^4 (r^2 \beta' + 1 - r^2).$$

Let us now write the skewness index for the half test (α') as a function of that for the total test (α_x). From equation 13,

(55) $$\Sigma x^3 = \Sigma(x_1 + x_2)^3.$$

Using equation 35 and expanding equation 55, we have

(56) $$N S_x^3 \alpha_x = \Sigma x_1^3 + 3\Sigma x_1^2 x_2 + 3\Sigma x_1 x_2^2 + \Sigma x_2^3.$$

Substituting equations 15, 17, 41, and 43 in equation 56 and simplifying, we have

(57) $$S_x^3 \alpha_x = 2s_1^3 \alpha'(1 + 3r).$$

Solving equation 20 explicitly for r, we have

(58) $$r = \frac{R}{2 - R}.$$

Solving equation 19 for s_1 and substituting from equation 58, we have

(59) $$s_1^2 = \frac{S_x^2 (2 - R)}{4}.$$

Substituting equations 58 and 59 in equation 57 and simplifying, we have

(60)
$$\alpha_x = \alpha' \frac{(1+R)\sqrt{2-R}}{2},$$

from which we may write

(61)
$$\alpha' = \frac{2\alpha_x}{(1+R)\sqrt{2-R}}.$$

To write the kurtosis index for the half test β' as a function of the corresponding index for the total test β_x, we use equation 13, and write

(62)
$$\Sigma x^4 = \Sigma(x_1 + x_2)^4.$$

Using equation 36 and expanding equation 62, we have

(63)
$$NS_x^4\beta_x = \Sigma x_1^4 + 4\Sigma x_1^3 x_2 + 6\Sigma x_1^2 x_2^2 + 4\Sigma x_1 x_2^3 + \Sigma x_2^4.$$

Substituting equations 16, 18, 47, 49, and 54 in equation 63 and simplifying, we have

(64)
$$S_x^4\beta_x = 2s_1^4[\beta'(1 + 4r + 3r^2) + 3(1 - r^2)].$$

Substituting equations 58 and 59 in equation 64 and simplifying, we have

(65)
$$\beta_x = \beta'\left(\frac{1+R}{2}\right) + \frac{3(1-R)}{2}.$$

Solving explicitly for β' gives

(66)
$$\beta' = \beta_x\left(\frac{2}{1+R}\right) - \frac{3(1-R)}{1+R}.$$

We now have all the equations needed to solve for Σxy and $\Sigma x^2 y$ so that equation 29 can be expressed entirely in terms of moments of the total score distribution and the reliability of the test. Multiplying equation 13 by 25, we have

(67)
$$\Sigma xy = \Sigma(x_1 + x_2)(x_1 - x_2)^2,$$

which expands to give

(68)
$$\Sigma xy = \Sigma x_1^3 + \Sigma x_2^3 - \Sigma x_1^2 x_2 - \Sigma x_1 x_2^2.$$

Substituting equations 15, 17, 41, and 43 in equation 68 and simplifying gives

(69)
$$\Sigma xy = 2Ns_1^3\alpha'(1 - r).$$

Substituting equations 58, 59, and 61 in equation 69 and simplifying, we have

$$(70) \qquad \Sigma xy = NS_x{}^3 \alpha_x \left(\frac{1 - R}{1 + R} \right).$$

To express $\Sigma x^2 y$ in terms of moments of the total score distribution, we use equations 13 and 25 to give

$$(71) \qquad \Sigma x^2 y = \Sigma (x_1 + x_2)^2 (x_1 - x_2)^2.$$

Expanding, we have

$$(72) \qquad \Sigma x^2 y = \Sigma x_1{}^4 + \Sigma x_2{}^4 - 2\Sigma x_1{}^2 x_2{}^2.$$

Substituting equations 16, 18, and 54 in equation 72 and simplifying, we have

$$(73) \qquad \Sigma x^2 y = 2N s_1{}^4 (\beta' - 1)(1 - r^2).$$

Substituting equations 58, 59, and 66 in equation 73 and simplifying, we have

$$(74) \qquad \Sigma x^2 y = NS_x{}^4 \left(\frac{1 - R}{1 + R} \right) (\beta_x - 2 + R).$$

Substituting equations 70, 74, and 30 to 34 in equations 29 and simplifying, we have

$$(75) \qquad
\begin{aligned}
a &= \frac{(1 - R)(\beta_x - 3 - \alpha_x{}^2)}{(1 + R)(\beta_x - 1 - \alpha_x{}^2)} \\[2mm]
b &= \frac{(1 - R)2S_x \alpha_x}{(1 + R)(\beta_x - 1 - \alpha_x{}^2)} \\[2mm]
c &= \frac{(1 - R)S_x{}^2(\beta_x R - \alpha_x{}^2 R + 2 - R)}{(1 + R)(\beta_x - 1 - \alpha_x{}^2)}.
\end{aligned}$$

Using these values for a, b, and c in equation 26, we have

$$(76) \quad \dot{y} = \frac{(1 - R)}{(1 + R)(\beta_x - 1 - \alpha_x{}^2)} [(\beta_x - 3 - \alpha_x{}^2)x^2$$
$$+ 2S_x \alpha_x x + (\beta_x R - \alpha_x{}^2 R + 2 - R)S_x{}^2].$$

When α_x is zero, that is, in a symmetrical distribution, we have

$$(77) \quad \dot{y} = \frac{(1 - R)}{(1 + R)(\beta_x - 1)} \{(\beta_x - 3)x^2 + (\beta_x R + 2 - R)S_x{}^2\}.$$

When kurtosis is equal to that of the normal curve, that is, $\beta_x = 3$, we have

Equation (78)

$$\dot{y} = \frac{(1 - R)}{(1 + R)(2 - \alpha_x{}^2)} \{-\alpha_x{}^2 x^2 + 2S_x \alpha_x x + (2R - \alpha_x{}^2 R + 2)S_x{}^2\}.$$

For a symmetrical ($\alpha_x = 0$), mesokurtic ($\beta_x = 3$) distribution, we have

(79) $$\dot{y} = S_x{}^2(1 - R).$$

In this case the error of measurement is constant as test score varies.

   We see from these equations that for the case of zero skewness and kurtosis of 3, the average error of measurement is the same regardless of the score. However, for distributions that are positively or negatively skewed, or for a kurtosis greater or less than three, we should expect the error of measurement to vary with the magnitude of the test score. In addition to presenting the theoretical derivation given above, Mollenkopf (1948), (1949) has presented empirical verification to show that the error of measurement does vary in general in accordance with the indications of equation 76.

5. Summary

   The effect of group heterogeneity on test reliability has been derived on the assumption that the error variance is the same for the two groups, the entire difference in *observed* variance being attributed to a difference in *true variance* of the two groups.

   Solving explicitly for one of the standard deviations, we have

(4) $$S_X = s_x \sqrt{\frac{1 - r_{xx}}{1 - R_{XX}}}.$$

Solving explicitly for one of the reliability coefficients gives

(5) $$R_{XX} = 1 - \frac{s_x{}^2}{S_X{}^2}(1 - r_{xx}).$$

In these equations $s_x{}^2$ is the variance of group x on a given test,
r_{xx} is the reliability of the same test for group x,
$S_X{}^2$ is the variance of group X on the same test, and
R_{XX} is the reliability of the same test for group X.

   A computing diagram for these equations is shown in Figure 2.

Mollenkopf (1948), (1949) has shown that, if we assume the test has been divided into two parallel halves so that

(14) $$s_1 = s_2,$$

(15) $$\alpha' = \alpha'',$$

(16) $$\beta' = \beta'';$$

and if the errors of estimate are unrelated to the independent variable so that

(39) $$r_{e_2 x_1{}^2} = 0,$$

(42) $$r_{e_1 x_2{}^2} = 0,$$

(45) $$r_{e_2 x_1{}^3} = 0,$$

(48) $$r_{e_1 x_2{}^3} = 0,$$

(52) $$r_{x_1{}^2 e_2{}^2} = 0;$$

then the best fitting quadratic to express the error of measurement as a function of test score is

(76) $$\dot{y} = \frac{(1 - R)}{(1 + R)(\beta_x - 1 - \alpha_x{}^2)} [(\beta_x - 3 - \alpha_x{}^2)x^2 + 2S_x\alpha_x x + (\beta_x R - \alpha_x{}^2 R + 2 - R)S_x{}^2],$$

where R is the corrected parallel halves reliability,

S_x is the standard deviation of the distribution of test scores,

α_x is the skewness of the distribution of test scores, and

β_x is the kurtosis of the distribution of test scores.

According to this derivation the error of measurement is constant with respect to variation in test score if and only if the test score distribution has a skewness of zero and a kurtosis of three. The error of measurement has a minimum for a leptokurtic and a maximum for a platykurtic distribution of test scores.

It should be noted particularly that equation 76 follows from the assumption that the two halves used for computing reliability were *parallel* halves (that is, from equations 14, 15, and 16, and from the assumptions of equations 39, 42, 45, 48, and 52). It also should be noted that, if the conclusions of equation 76 do not apply in any given case, it must follow that one or more of the foregoing eight assumptions do not hold for that case. That is, either the halves used for computing reliability were not parallel, the errors of estimate correlated with the squares or cubes of the independent variable, or the squares of the errors of estimate correlated with the squares of the independent variable.

According to Mollenkopf's derivation, if the distribution of test scores has zero skewness and kurtosis of three, the error of measurement is invariant with respect to changes in magnitude of test score. The error of measurement has a minimum for a leptokurtic and a maximum for a platykurtic distribution of test scores.

Problems

1. Assume a set of test scores each of which has been divided into comparable halves for purposes of obtaining a split-half reliability. Designate these halves by x_a and x_b, $d = x_a - x_b$ (the difference between a person's score on part a and part b). The total score on the test is the sum of the halves ($s = x_a + x_b$). Assume that the halves are comparable so that their means and standard deviations are identical.

(a) Write $r_{x_a x_b}$ in terms of the standard deviations of s and d.
(b) Write the reliability of the *total test* in terms of the standard deviations of s and d.
(c) Express the variance of d in terms of the reliability coefficient and the variance of test scores.
(d) Assume that selection of cases occurs by rejecting persons with high or low *total* scores, which would have the effect of changing the variance of s without altering the variance of d. Write the new reliability coefficient in terms of the old reliability coefficient and the two total score variances.
(e) Show that the standard deviation of d is the error of measurement of the test.

2. In one study of tests, A, B, C, D, and E, the following results are obtained:

Test	Mean	Standard Deviation	Number of Items	Reliability
A	18.4	4.2	30	.72
B	28.9	9.8	60	.96
C	37.2	8.1	50	.90
D	63.7	10.4	100	.86
E	39.2	11.5	75	.92

(a) Another investigator reports administering test A to a new group and finding a mean of 25.3 and a standard deviation of 8.4. About what reliability would you expect the test to have for this new group?
(b) It is reported that test B has been administered to a new group and the reliability coefficient is only .90. What would account satisfactorily for this lowered reliability without indicating any faults of test administration or scoring?

(c) Test C is administered to a new group with the following results: mean 31.9, standard deviation 12.7, reliability .96. Are these results in reasonable agreement with those reported in the table for test C?

(d) Test D is reported as having a mean of 68.2, a standard deviation of 14.6, and a reliability of .98. Are these results in reasonable agreement with those reported in the table for test D?

(e) If the report on test D also stated that the reliability was based on a corrected odd-even correlation and that the time allowance for the test had been changed, would you infer that the time allowance had been increased or decreased? (A brief survey of the chapters on experimental methods of determining reliability and on speed versus power tests may help answer this question.)

(f) A teacher wishes to use test E for sectioning a class, and finds a mean score of 45.3 and a standard deviation of 3.9. What comment would you make on this proposal?

3. Study the equation for estimating a change in reliability due to a change in group variance given by Dickey (1934). Comment on this equation.

4. Write Davis' (1944) equations for the special case in which the "restricting variable "is "true score."

11

Effect of Group Heterogeneity
on Validity (Bivariate Case)

1. Illustrations of selection

In addition to affecting the reliability coefficient of a test, the heterogeneity of the group tested will also affect the validity coefficient. For example, if in Figure 1 the abscissa represents a test and the ordinate a criterion, the validity coefficient for the total group will be much greater than the validity coefficient for the restricted portion of the group included between the two dotted lines. The validity coefficient would be lowered in a similar manner if the selection were made upon the basis of the criterion variable.

It should be noted that here again we are assuming that the change in variability is due mainly to a change in true variance. The *actual persons* at the upper or the lower end of the scale are removed, which means that the true variance is lowered. In this section we shall not consider the case in which there are changes in observed variance due to changes in error variance. As pointed out in Chapter 10, such an assumption is quite unreasonable.

In considering the effect of selection of cases upon the intercorrelation between two tests it is important to note that this effect will vary with the nature of the selection procedure. In any practical situation the actual selection procedures are usually complex, and to a great degree unknown. We can only investigate the situation and make the most reasonable guesses possible regarding the selection procedure operative in any particular instance.

For example, if an intelligence test is given to all applicants for admission to a college, and only those with a score greater than 0.5 sigma are accepted, we have a clear case of selection on the basis of the test. Similarly, if a business concern uses a selection test and accepts only the upper 60 per cent, we have a clear-cut case of selection on the basis of the test. Usually such clear cases do not occur. The college admits all students with a score over 0.5 sigma, provided they do not have poor grades or a bad recommendation from their high school principal.

Likewise, the college may reject all applicants with a score of less than 0.5 sigma unless they have an exceptionally good high school record and excellent recommendations.   In most if not all practical situations it is impossible to find out just what weighted combination of the available variables was used for selection.   In many cases, however, it is

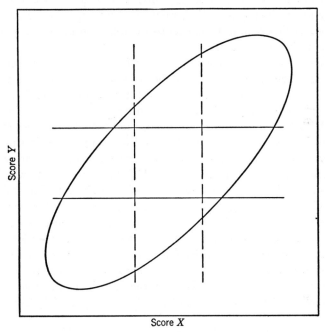

FIGURE 1.   A diagrammatic illustration of the change in correlation with a change in standard deviation.

clear that a given selection test was one of the *major* items in the selection procedure so that the results found by assuming that selection was *solely* on the basis of the test will not be far from the correct estimate.

There may also be times when the criterion itself is the selective device.   For example, if we are using a given test to predict college grades, it may be that students with a grade less than C or less than D are dropped.   Then selection is clearly on the basis of the criterion. Likewise if a manufacturing concern wishes to develop a test that will predict a given production record, and dismisses employees if the production record falls below a given minimum standard, we have a clear case of selection on the basis of the criterion.

In any practical situation there are usually several selection devices at work.   This fact may suggest that, if we considered the case of selection on the basis of two or more variables (multivariate selection), we should have equations that would be more applicable to practical situations.[1] Careful investigation of selection procedures show, however, that there are numerous extenuating circumstances that *sometimes* override the strict selection rules. In other words, the equations given to "correct for selection," whether univariate or multivariate selection, are only approximations to the practical situation. The equation that will give the closest approximation to the selection facts of a particular situation is the one to use.

In short, there is no completely satisfactory substitute for a well set-up experiment, in which a number of selection tests are given to a group. *All of the group* without any selection are then admitted to the training program and given the criterion measure *under identical conditions*. If these conditions are observed, the necessity of "correcting for homogeneity" is completely avoided, and we can make very simple and straightforward comparisons of the relative merit of different selection procedures. However, many practical situations arise in which it is not possible to have such complete control over the experimental conditions. If we are dealing with such situations and wish, for example, to compare the validities of two tests, one of which was used for selection and the other was given after selection, the simple zero-order validity coefficients are definitely misleading. *It is necessary either to make a correction for the results of selection*, taking care to select the equations that are most nearly appropriate for the case in hand or *to use some index, such as the error of estimate, that is not affected by the selection procedure.*

In the material that follows we shall consider only the case of univariate selection. We shall consider first the bivariate case, in which we are interested in the correlation between two variables (X and Y) and selection has been on the basis of one of these variables. Next we shall consider the trivariate case, where we are interested in the correlation between Y and Z, when selection has been on the basis of a third variable (X).

2. The distinction between explicit and incidental selection

Considerable confusion and error have been caused by the failure to distinguish carefully between two types of selection. We have first the direct selection of cases on the basis of a given variable. Those who are above the critical score are admitted, and those below the critical score are rejected. This selection is referred to as *explicit* selection. Second, we have an indirect selection effect on one variable brought about by

---

[1] Multivariate selection is discussed in Chapter 13.

explicit selection on another correlated variable. For example, if a given college rejects all applicants who are below the 50 percentile score on the ACE Psychological Examination, the result will be the selection of a group of persons who would score high on the Ohio Psychological Examination, even though the Ohio Psychological is never given to that group. This occurs because scores on the two examinations are positively correlated. We shall refer to the selection effect on the Ohio Psychological in this case as *incidental* selection. Explicit selection on a given examination results in *incidental* selection on all tests correlated with that examination.

In order to avoid the confusion that has appeared in much of the literature on correction for the effects of selection, we shall treat the two cases separately. First, however, we shall consider the basic assumptions common to both types of selection for the bivariate case.

3. Basic assumptions for the bivariate case

Figure 1 illustrates this case. Our problem is to find what parameters are invariant from the curtailed to the extended distribution. These parameters can then be used to bridge the gap from one distribution to the other. If selection is on the basis of the x variable, the regression line *of y on x* will not be systematically affected, and can be assumed to be the same for the curtailed and extended distribution. In Figure 1 we see that the *mean y* for a *given x* is not altered by explicit selection on x. Since the regression of y on x is the line through these means, we see that, if the regression is perfectly linear, the assumption will hold exactly. Also, from inspecting the diagram, we see that explicit selection on x will markedly alter the *mean x* for a *given y* and hence will alter the regression of x on y. If we designate the curtailed group by x and y and the extended group by X and Y, the foregoing assumption may be written by putting down the equation of the regression line of y on x for each group:

$$(1) \qquad \dot{y} = r_{xy} \frac{s_y}{s_x} x,$$

$$(2) \qquad \dot{Y} = R_{XY} \frac{S_Y}{S_X} X.$$

Since it is assumed that the predicted or average y (Y) for a given x (X) is the same in both cases, the slopes of the two regression lines are equal, and we may write

$$(3) \qquad r_{xy} \left(\frac{s_y}{s_x} \right) = R_{XY} \left(\frac{S_Y}{S_X} \right).$$

From inspection of Figure 1, we see that the *dispersion* about the regression line of y (Y) on x (X) will not be affected. That is to say, not only is the mean y for a given x the same, but the dispersion of y's for a given x is the same in both groups.[1] A little geometric consideration will show that, if the selection is explicitly on x as shown in the diagram, the dispersion of the x's for a given y cannot remain the same for all values of y. In fact for each and every value of y (Y) in the middle range, the dispersion of x for the curtailed group is much less than the dispersion for the complete group. From the foregoing considerations, we see that, when there is explicit selection on x, the error made in estimating y from x is the same for both the complete and the curtailed group. We may thus write the expressions for the two errors of estimate and set them equal to each other as follows:

$$(4) \qquad\qquad s_{y \cdot x} = s_y \sqrt{1 - r_{xy}^2},$$

$$(5) \qquad\qquad S_{Y \cdot X} = S_Y \sqrt{1 - R_{XY}^2},$$

$$(6) \qquad\qquad s_y \sqrt{1 - r_{xy}^2} = S_Y \sqrt{1 - R_{XY}^2}.$$

4. Variance known for both groups on variable subject to incidental selection

In the usual case of correction for restriction of range, we have complete information on one group (usually the curtailed group) and we have, or can estimate to a reasonable accuracy, one of the variances for the other group (usually the more heterogeneous group). That is to say, in the typical case we have values for r_{xy}, s_y, s_x, and one standard deviation for the other group, either S_X or S_Y. Unless we know these four values, the problem cannot be solved.

Let us use the subscript x to designate the variable subjected to *explicit* selection and y to designate the variable subjected to *incidental* selection, as indicated in Figure 1. First we shall consider the case in which both variances are known for y, the variable subject to incidental selection. Here we have given r_{xy}, s_x, s_y, and S_Y. The problem is to express S_X and R_{XY} in terms of these four given values.

The solution for R_{XY} can be obtained directly from equation 6. Squaring both sides and dividing by S_Y^2 gives

$$(7) \qquad\qquad 1 - R_{XY}^2 = (1 - r_{xy}^2) \frac{s_y^2}{S_Y^2}.$$

[1] This assumption follows from the usual assumption of homoscedasticity. This is the assumption that the dispersion of y for a given x is the same regardless of the value of x, and is basic to many of the theorems of statistics.

Solving equation 7 explicitly for R_{XY} gives the final result

$$(8) \qquad R_{XY} = \sqrt{1 - (1 - r_{xy}^2)\frac{s_y^2}{S_Y^2}},$$

where r_{xy} is the correlation between x and y for one group,

s_y is the standard deviation of the variable subjected to incidental selection for the same group, and

S_Y is the standard deviation of the same variable for the other group—the group for which an estimate of the correlation (R_{XY}) is desired.

If the variance of a variable subject to incidental selection is known for two groups (s_y^2 and S_Y^2 are known), and the correlation between the incidental and explicit selection variables is known for one group (r_{xy} is known), equation 8 should be used to estimate the correlation between these two variables for the second group.

Equation 8 or slight variants of it has been presented by Kelley (1923c), Garrett (1947), Guilford (1942), Crawford and Burnham (1946), Thorndike (1947), and others.

It should be noted that nowhere in the previous derivations has it been assumed that S_Y was greater than s_y. In a broader sense the lower-case subscripts (x and y), which were originally assigned to the "curtailed group" as shown in Figure 1, may be taken to designate the group for which *complete information is available*. Then the upper-case subscripts (X and Y) designate the group for which only one standard deviation is available and for which additional information is sought. Usually we shall have complete information on the group with the smaller variance and shall wish to estimate the correlation for the unrestricted group, the one with the larger variance. The equations, however, are equally applicable if we have complete information for the unrestricted group and wish to estimate the correlation for various sorts of restriction. For example, we may know the validity of a given test in an unrestricted group and may wish to estimate the validity of that same test for use in a second university that has higher entrance standards, and hence gets a group of students with a larger mean and smaller standard deviation.

A computing diagram for equation 8 is shown in Figure 2. This diagram is set up in terms of equation 7. It shows the value of the ratio of the standard deviations (S_Y/s_y) and the values of the two correlation coefficients. In order to use this diagram, we find the diagonal line corresponding to the standard deviation of Y divided by the standard deviation of y; then we locate the correlation (r_{xy}) at the bottom of the diagram, follow up to the appropriate diagonal line, and then to the right to read the value of R_{XY}. For example, if the ratio S_Y/s_y is 1.2, and r_{xy} is .45, the expected value of R_{XY} is .64. It is also possible to

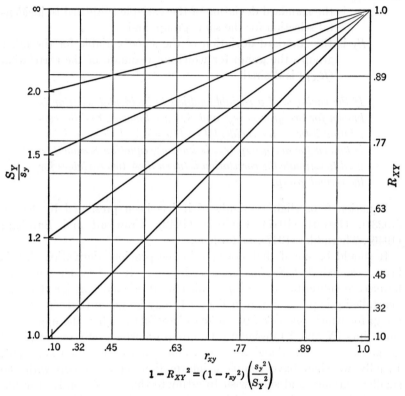

$$1 - R_{XY}^2 = (1 - r_{xy}^2)\left(\frac{s_y^2}{s_Y^2}\right)$$

FIGURE 2.   Showing the change in correlation as a function of change in variance of the incidental selection variable.

use this chart to find the ratio of standard deviations needed to account for a given difference in the correlation between x (X) and y (Y). Locate the value of the smaller correlation on the abscissa, and the larger correlation on the ordinate, and note the diagonal line that corresponds to the intersection of these two lines.

In constructing Figure 2, we *measure* the ordinate and the abscissa in terms of $1 - r_{xy}^2$, $1 - R_{XY}^2$ (from the upper right-hand corner). However, the ordinate (on the right) and the base line are *labeled* in terms of r_{xy} and R_{XY}. The diagonal lines have been *drawn* to correspond to the variance ratio but have been *labeled* in terms of the ratio of standard deviations.

In addition to estimating the correlation for the XY group, it is sometimes also desirable to estimate the standard deviation of the variable subjected to explicit selection. In our present notation, this is the standard deviation of X. It can be estimated readily by solving equation 3 for S_X, obtaining

$$(9) \qquad S_X = \frac{R_{XY}S_Y s_x}{r_{xy}s_y}.$$

If we square the foregoing equation and substitute the value of R_{XY} from equation 8, we have

$$(10) \qquad S_X{}^2 = \left[1 - (1 - r_{xy}{}^2)\frac{s_y{}^2}{S_Y{}^2}\right]\frac{S_Y{}^2}{s_y{}^2}\frac{s_x{}^2}{r_{xy}{}^2},$$

which simplifies to

$$(11) \qquad S_X{}^2 = s_x{}^2\left[1 - \frac{1}{r_{xy}{}^2} + \frac{1}{r_{xy}{}^2}\frac{S_Y{}^2}{s_y{}^2}\right].$$

The terms in the brackets may be combined and the square root taken, giving

$$(12) \qquad S_X = \frac{s_x\sqrt{S_Y{}^2 - s_y{}^2 + r_{xy}{}^2 s_y{}^2}}{r_{xy}s_y},$$

where s_x is the standard deviation of the variable subjected to explicit selection in the group for which complete information is available,

S_X is the estimate of the standard deviation of the same variable in the group for which only S_Y is available, and the other variables have the same definitions as for equation 8.

If complete information (s_x, s_y, and r_{xy}) is available for one group, and only the variance of Y (the variable subject to incidental selection) is known for a second group, equation 12 should be used to estimate the variance of X (the explicit selection variable) in the second group.

5. Variance of both groups known for variable subject to explicit selection

Let us turn now to the situation where we know the variance for both groups for the *explicit* selection variable. This case is much more common than the one previously discussed. For example, if we give a selection test to a group of applicants, use this test score to select the upper K per cent of applicants, and then admit this upper K per cent to college or to an industry so that performance records can be secured for the upper K per cent, we should then have the variance of the selection test for both the applicant and the selected group. That is to say, the variance of both groups would be known for the explicit selection variable. This case occurs frequently so that the equations developed in this section will be the ones that are most generally useful in estimating the effects of selection on validity coefficients.

As before, we shall use x or X to represent the explicit selection variable, and y or Y to represent the incidental selection variable, in accordance with the symbols of Figure 1. In the previous notation we have values for r_{xy}, s_x, s_y, and S_X. The problem is to solve for R_{XY} and S_Y in terms of these four known values.

As before, it must be remembered that we are not assuming that s_x is smaller than S_X. The equations developed will apply when s_x is smaller than S_X and will also apply when s_x is larger than S_X. In the notation used here, the lower-case subscripts designate the group for which we have complete information (two variances and the correlation), whereas the upper-case subscript designates the group for which we know only the variance of the explicit selection variable.

In order to obtain the equation for R_{XY}, we may first solve equation 3 for S_Y, obtaining

$$(13) \qquad S_Y = \frac{r_{xy}s_y S_X}{R_{XY}s_x},$$

and then substitute this value for S_Y in equation 6, obtaining

$$(14) \qquad s_y\sqrt{1 - r_{xy}{}^2} = \frac{r_{xy}s_y S_X}{R_{XY}s_x}\sqrt{1 - R_{XY}{}^2}.$$

Dividing both sides by s_y, squaring both sides, and segregating R_{XY} on one side of the equation gives

$$(15) \qquad \frac{1 - R_{XY}{}^2}{R_{XY}{}^2} = \frac{s_x{}^2(1 - r_{xy}{}^2)}{S_X{}^2 r_{xy}{}^2}.$$

The simplest way to graph this function is to divide both numerator and denominator on the right side by r^2, obtaining

$$(16) \qquad \frac{1}{R_{XY}{}^2} - 1 = \frac{s_x{}^2}{S_X{}^2}\left(\frac{1}{r_{xy}{}^2} - 1\right).$$

Thus we may express the two standard deviations as a ratio and graph the function as indicated in Figure 3. Solving explicitly for R_{XY} gives

(17)
$$R_{XY}^2 = \frac{1}{1 + \dfrac{s_x^2}{S_X^2}\left(\dfrac{1}{r_{xy}^2} - 1\right)}.$$

$$\left(\frac{1}{R_{XY}^2} - 1\right) = \frac{s_x^2}{S_X^2}\left(\frac{1}{r_{xy}^2} - 1\right)$$

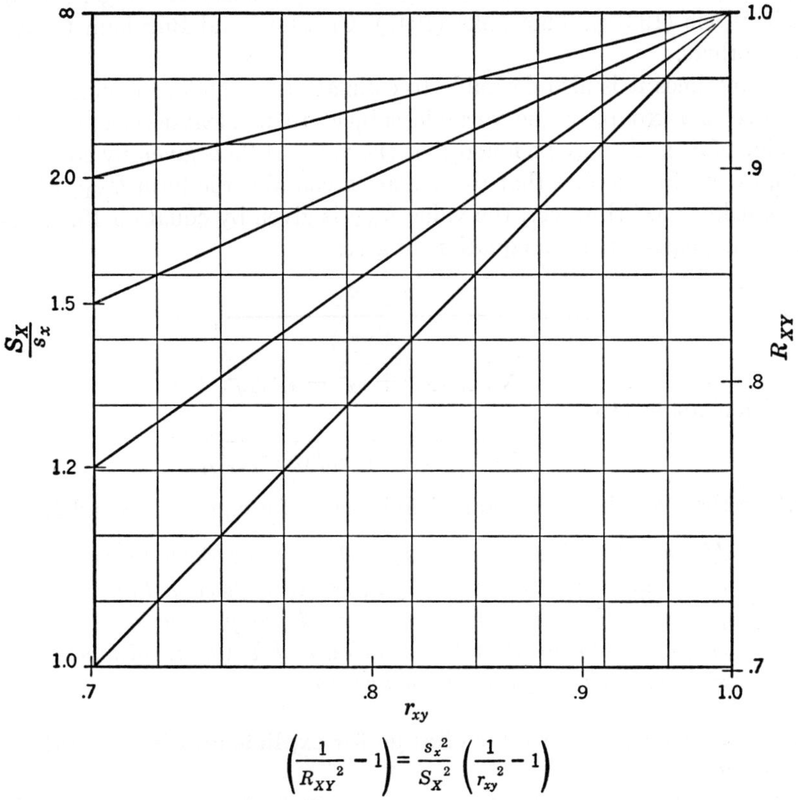

FIGURE 3.   Showing the change in correlation as a function of the change in variance of the explicit selection variable.

Putting all the denominator over $S_X^2 r_{xy}^2$, inverting, and taking the square root gives

(18)
$$R_{XY} = \frac{S_X r_{xy}}{\sqrt{S_X^2 r_{xy}^2 + s_x^2 - s_x^2 r_{xy}^2}},$$

where the terms have the same definitions as for equations 8 and 12.

If complete information (s_x, s_y, and r_{xy}) is available for one group, and only the variance of X (the variable subject to explicit selection) is known for a second group, equation 18 should be used to estimate the correlation between X and Y for the second group (R_{XY}).

Equation 18, or slight variants of it, was first derived by Pearson (1903a). It has also been presented by Kelley (1923c), Holzinger (1928), Thurstone (1931a), Thorndike (1947), Crawford and Burnham (1932), and others.

Sometimes it is also desirable to estimate the standard deviation for the second group, of the variable subject to incidental selection (the value of S_Y). It may be noted that the value of S_Y is given by equation 13, except for the fact that this equation contains the term R_{XY}, which is not known. However, the value R_{XY} is given by equation 18. Substituting equation 18 in equation 13 gives

$$(19) \qquad S_Y = \frac{r_{xy} s_y S_X}{\dfrac{s_x S_X r_{xy}}{\sqrt{S_X^2 r_{xy}^2 + s_x^2 - s_x^2 r_{xy}^2}}},$$

which simplifies to

$$(20) \qquad S_Y = s_y \sqrt{1 - r_{xy}^2 + r_{xy}^2 (S_X^2 / s_x^2)},$$

where the terms have the same definitions as for equations 8 and 12.

If complete information (s_x, s_y, and r_{xy}) is available for one group, and only the variance of X (the variable subject to explicit selection) is known for a second group, equation 20 should be used to estimate the variance of Y (the incidental selection variable) for the second group.

6. Comparison of variance change for explicit and incidental selection

In order to compare the change in variability of the variable on which there is explicit selection with the change in variability of the variable on which there is incidental selection, we can rewrite equation 20 as follows:

$$(21) \qquad \left(\frac{S_Y^2}{s_y^2} - 1 \right) = r_{xy}^2 \left(\frac{S_X^2}{s_x^2} - 1 \right).$$

The percentage of change in variance of the variable subject to incidental selection is equal to r_{xy}^2 times the percentage change in the variance of the variable subjected to explicit selection.

It should be noted that, if both S_Y and S_X are available, it is possible to check by means of equation 21 to see if the proper relationship holds. If this relationship does not hold, the selection probably was not entirely and consistently made on variable x.

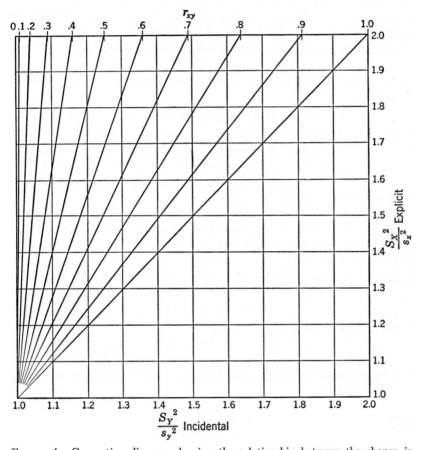

FIGURE 4. Computing diagram showing the relationship between the change in variance ratios for the explicit selection variable (designated by X and x) and the incidental selection variable (designated by Y and y).

Figure 4 gives the relationships of equation 21. From this graph it is possible to determine the variance ratios of the explicit and incidental selection variables that correspond to any given correlation r_{xy}. The diagram indicates, for example, that, if the variance ratio for the explicit selection variable is 1.6 and the correlation r_{xy} is .90, the variance ratio for the incidental selection variable is 1.49.

It should be noted that there is no need to rework the foregoing derivations for the case where variable y was subjected to explicit selection. Simply let x (X) in the foregoing equations stand for the variable on which explicit selection occurred. It may be either the criterion or the test. Then note whether the variance of the complete group is known for the variable on which *explicit* selection occurred (S_X^2), or for the variable on which incidental selection occurred (S_Y^2), and use the equations appropriate to the information available.

7. Relationship between reliability and validity for incidental selection

In Chapter 9 we saw that the ratio of the validity coefficient to the index of reliability does not change with increases (or decreases) in test length (see equation 13 of Chapter 9). Similarly, when considering the effect of changes in group heterogeneity, it is possible to find a relationship between validity and reliability that does not change as the heterogeneity of the group changes.

First let us consider this effect for the variable subject to incidental selection. As before, we shall use y to designate this variable and x to designate the variable subject to explicit selection. As noted in equation 6, when y is subject to incidental and x to explicit selection, the quantity $s_y\sqrt{1 - r_{xy}^2}$ is invariant with respect to explicit selection on variable x. As indicated in Chapter 10, equation 3, the quantity $s_y\sqrt{1 - r_{yy}}$ (the error of measurement) for y does not change as the heterogeneity of the group changes.

Since each of these quantities is invariant with respect to changes in group heterogeneity, their ratio is also invariant. Dividing one quantity by the other, canceling the term s_y, and squaring the remaining fraction, we have

$$(22) \qquad C = \frac{1 - r_{yy}}{1 - r_{xy}^2},$$

where C is arbitrarily used to designate this constant,

   r_{yy} is the reliability of the test y, and

   r_{xy} is the correlation between y and the explicit selection variable (x).

   If x is subject to explicit and y to incidental selection, then for any type of explicit selection on x the ratio $\dfrac{1 - r_{yy}}{1 - r_{xy}^2}$ is constant.

8. Relationship between reliability and validity for explicit selection

In order to obtain a relationship between r_{xx} (the reliability of x) and r_{xy} (the correlation between x and y) that does not change with explicit selection on x, we make use of the following assumptions:

1. The error of measurement for x is invariant with respect to explicit selection on x (equation 3, Chapter 10),

$$s_x \sqrt{1 - r_{xx}} = c_1.$$

2. The error made in estimating y from x does not change (equation 6),

$$s_y \sqrt{1 - r_{xy}^2} = c_2.$$

3. The slope of the regression of y on x does not change (equation 3),

$$\left(\frac{s_y}{s_x}\right) r_{xy} = c_3.$$

These three equations can readily be combined so as to eliminate the standard deviations of x and of y. The first equation multiplied by the third and divided by the second gives an expression in which the standard deviations cancel out, leaving a constant that we may designate as C'.

$$(23) \qquad C' = \frac{r_{xy}\sqrt{1 - r_{xx}}}{\sqrt{1 - r_{xy}^2}},$$

where r_{xx} is the reliability of the variable subject to explicit selection, and r_{xy} is the correlation of this variable with any other variable.

If x is subject to explicit and y to incidental selection, then for any type of explicit selection on x the quantity $\dfrac{r_{xy}\sqrt{1 - r_{xx}}}{\sqrt{1 - r_{xy}^2}}$ *is constant.*

9. Summary

The variable directly used for selection has been termed the *explicit* selection variable and designated by x or X. The correlated variable, which is affected only indirectly because of its relationship with the explicit selection variable, has been termed the *incidental* selection variable and designated by y or Y.

The basic assumptions for the bivariate case are first that the slope of the regression of y on x is equal to the slope of the regression of Y

on X, which is given in equation

(3)
$$r_{xy}\left(\frac{s_y}{s_x}\right) = R_{XY}\left(\frac{S_Y}{S_X}\right),$$

and second that the error made in estimating y from x is the same as that made in estimating Y from X, which is given in equation

(6)
$$s_y\sqrt{1 - r_{xy}^2} = S_Y\sqrt{1 - R_{XY}^2}.$$

There is no need to specify that one group is the extended and the other the curtailed group. The same equations apply either for estimation from a restricted to an extended range or from an extended to a restricted range. The convention was adopted that the lower-case letters should stand for the group on which complete information was available. In other words, it was assumed that r_{xy}, s_x, and s_y were known. We then have two types of cases.

First we considered the case in which the variance of both groups is known for the incidental selection variable (S_Y is known). For this case, we have

(8)
$$R_{XY} = \sqrt{1 - (1 - r_{xy}^2)\frac{s_y^2}{S_Y^2}}$$

and

(12)
$$S_X = \frac{s_x\sqrt{S_Y^2 - s_y^2 + r_{xy}^2 s_y^2}}{r_{xy}s_y}.$$

Second we considered the case in which the variance of both groups is known for the explicit selection variable (S_X is known). For this case we have

(18)
$$R_{XY} = \frac{S_X r_{xy}}{\sqrt{S_X^2 r_{xy}^2 + s_x^2 - s_x^2 r_{xy}^2}}$$

and

(20)
$$S_Y = s_y\sqrt{1 - r_{xy}^2 + r_{xy}^2(S_X^2/s_x^2)}.$$

Two computing diagrams were presented for these selection equations, Figure 2 for equation 8 and Figure 3 for equation 18.

In order to demonstrate that the effect on the standard deviation of the explicit selection variable (x or X) was greater than the effect on the standard deviation of the incidental selection variable, this relationship was shown in

(21)
$$\left(\frac{S_Y^2}{s_y^2} - 1\right) = r_{xy}^2\left(\frac{S_X^2}{s_x^2} - 1\right).$$

Figure 4 was presented to illustrate this equation.

Just as there is a relationship between validity and reliability of a test that is maintained as the *length of the test* is varied (see equation 13, Chapter 9), there is a different relationship between reliability and validity as the *heterogeneity of the group* is varied. The relationship between the reliability of the incidental selection variable and its validity for predicting the explicit selection variable is given by

(22) $$\frac{1 - r_{yy}}{1 - r_{xy}^{2}} \text{ equals a constant.}$$

The relationship between the reliability of the explicit selection variable and its validity for predicting the incidental selection variable is given by

(23) $$\frac{r_{xy}\sqrt{1 - r_{xx}}}{\sqrt{1 - r_{xy}^{2}}} \text{ equals a constant.}$$

Problems

Assume that a population is selected on the basis of test scores in such a way as to change the variance of test scores.

1. Write the equation for estimating reliability in the new population as a function of test variance in the new population, and the test variance and reliability for the old population.

2. Write the corresponding equation showing the relationship between the test variances and validities for both populations. (The criterion is subject only to incidental selection.)

3. Write the equation showing the relationship between test reliability and test validity for a given test, as the population is subject to selection on the basis of test score. (*Suggestion:* Eliminate variances in the two preceding equations.)

4. Compare this relationship with the expected relationship between reliability and validity when test *length* is varied for a fixed population.

DATA FOR PROBLEMS 5–10

Test	Mean	Standard Deviation	Number of Items	Reliability	Correlation of Each Test with the Same Criterion
A	19.3	4.1	30	.74	.69
B	10.2	4.2	20	.87	.70
C	58.3	13.8	100	.92	.77
D	27.8	9.7	50	.95	.74
E	68.1	24.8	130	.97	.75
Criterion	117.8	20.1	200	.90	

5. Assume that selection has occurred on the basis of test A.

(a) Estimate the validity that test A would have in an unselected group for which the standard deviation of test A was 6.7.

(b) Estimate the standard deviation of the criterion for this unselected group.

6. Assume that only persons with criterion scores over 90.0 were included in this sample, and that otherwise there has been no selection of cases. It is also known that for an unselected group the standard deviation of test A is 6.7.

(a) Estimate the validity of test A for the unselected group.

(b) Estimate the standard deviation of the criterion for the unselected group.

7. A group of high-scoring persons on test B are selected, and it is found that the standard deviation of test B for this limited group is 3.2.

(a) What validity would test B probably have for this restricted group?

(b) What would be the variance of the criterion for this restricted group?

8. Compare tests C and D on the assumptions that the data are from the same subjects, that no selection occurred on test C, whereas subjects were screened on the basis of test D scores from an unselected group with a standard deviation of 12.0 on test D.

9. What is the standard deviation of the difference between actual criterion scores and criterion scores predicted from scores on test E?

10. If we screen a group using test E scores and obtain a selected subgroup with standard deviation 15.0 on test E, what will (a) the validity and (b) the error of estimate be for test E in this subgroup?

12

Correction for Univariate Selection
in the Three-Variable Case

1. Introduction

Let us consider the three-variable case. If there is explicit selection on test X, what effect will this have upon the correlation between two variables (Y and Z) subject to incidental selection because they each correlate with X? It may be noted that insofar as we are interested in the correlation between X and Y, or between X and Z, the equations for the bivariate case given in Chapter 11 will apply directly. Also, if we are given the variance of X and wish to obtain that of Y or Z and, conversely, if we are given the variance of Y or Z and wish to obtain that of X, the bivariate equations given in Chapter 11 may also be used. There is only one problem regarding variances that is unique to the three-variable situation: given the variance of Y, solve for that of Z, or vice versa. That is, we have the problem of how to express the variance of one incidental selection variable in terms of the other incidental selection variable. The other problem that occurs in the three-variable but not in the two-variable case is determining the correlation between two incidental selection variables (the correlation R_{YZ}).

2. Practical importance of the three-variable case in univariate selection

Let us consider a practical illustration of three variables with univariate selection. Suppose we are trying out a new test for the selection of college students. Let us call this new test, *test Y*. The students available for a validation study have already been admitted to college on the basis of selection on *test X*. Test Y is then administered to the freshman class, and the new test is correlated with college grades. College grades is the criterion score which for present purposes we may designate as *variable Z*. Since tests X and Y do not correlate perfectly, it is evident that all the freshman class will have passed test X (since it was used for admission), but some of the freshman class will *fail* *test Y*. That is, the range of scores on Y will be greater than the range of scores on test X, since X is subject to explicit selection and Y only to incidental selection. Equation 21 of Chapter 11 and Figure 4 of that chapter show that the variance of the explicit selection variable is reduced more than the variance of the incidental selection variable. We are interested in comparing the validity of text X and test Y under similar sampling procedures. If an unselected group had been admitted to college, would the validity of test X have been higher or lower than the validity of test Y?

To illustrate the importance of this problem, let us consider a hypothetical case in which two admissions tests (X and Y) have the *same* validity, the same correlation with grades (Z). That is, both tests have the same validity for an *unrestricted* group. Then for the restricted group, the validity of the test actually *used* for selection (the explicit selection variable) would always be lower than the validity of the test *not* used for selection (the incidental selection variable). In other words, if we considered only the zero-order uncorrected correlation coefficients, we should always reach the conclusion that the test not being used for selection was better than the one being used. When X was used for selection, Y would have the higher validity (uncorrected); and, when Y was used for selection, X would have the higher validity.

It follows that, whenever a test is already being used for selection, it is relatively easy to try out another test *on the selected group* and find that it is better than the test already in use. Evidence that a selection program already in use is not as good as a new one proposed is not convincing if we use only the uncorrected validity coefficients. It is necessary to use validity coefficients that have been adjusted for the effects of selection. Some of the appropriate equations were presented in Chapter 11; the others will be given here.

3. Basic assumptions for univariate selection in the three-variable case

Let us designate these three variables as X, Y, and Z and find out how selection on the basis of variable X will affect the correlation between and the variance of Y and Z. Since selection was on the basis of test X, the regression of Y on X and also the regression of Z on X will not be altered. In order to state this, we shall designate one group by capital letters, the other group by lower-case letters, and write

$$(1) \qquad r_{xy}\left(\frac{s_y}{s_x}\right) = R_{XY}\left(\frac{S_Y}{S_X}\right),$$

$$(2) \qquad r_{xz}\left(\frac{s_z}{s_x}\right) = R_{XZ}\left(\frac{S_Z}{S_X}\right).$$

Also, as before, it is reasonable to assume that the variance of Y about the regression of Y on X will be about the same for both groups. Similarly, the variance of Z about the regression of Z on X will be about the same for both groups. Again using capital letters for one group and small letters for the other, we can write

(3) $$s_y^2(1 - r_{xy}^2) = S_Y^2(1 - R_{XY}^2),$$

(4) $$s_z^2(1 - r_{xz}^2) = S_Z^2(1 - R_{XZ}^2).$$

In addition to the foregoing assumptions, which are identical with those that were used in the bivariate case, it is also necessary to make one other assumption for the three-variable case. This assumption is that the correlation between Y and Z *for a constant* X is the same for both groups. It can be seen that holding X constant by the statistical device of partial correlation should give about the same results, regardless of whether or not there is selection on X. Holding X constant is the most extreme form of selection possible so that the resulting partial correlation between Y and Z will be about the same both for the entire group and the curtailed group. Using the conventional notation, we may write

Equation (5)

$$r_{yz \cdot x} = \frac{r_{yz} - r_{xy}r_{xz}}{\sqrt{(1 - r_{xy}^2)(1 - r_{xz}^2)}} = R_{YZ \cdot X} = \frac{R_{YZ} - R_{XY}R_{XZ}}{\sqrt{(1 - R_{XY}^2)(1 - R_{XZ}^2)}}.$$

All the assumptions necessary for the three-variable problem in univariate selection are given in equations 1 to 5. It should be noted that the equations are perfectly symmetrical so that any solution obtained for estimating a correlation in a group with a larger variance will apply equally well for estimating the correlation in a group with a smaller variance. Therefore, instead of saying that the lower-case letters stand for the restricted group and the upper-case letters for the unrestricted group, we shall adopt the convention that the lower-case letters designate values for the group *on which complete information is available.* For one of the groups involved it is necessary to have the complete information, consisting of three correlations (r_{xy}, r_{xz}, and r_{yz}) and three standard deviations (s_x, s_y, and s_z). We shall use the lower-case letters to designate this group, regardless of whether it is the restricted or the unrestricted group.

The upper-case letters will be used to designate the group for which only one standard deviation is known. The equations developed will hold regardless of whether this group is the restricted or the unrestricted group. We shall consider first the case where only the standard deviation of the explicit selection variable is known for the second group (only S_X is known). We shall consider second the case where only the standard deviation of one of the incidental selection variables is known for the second group (only S_Y is known).

4. Variance of both groups known for the explicit selection variable

Let us proceed as before to solve equation 1 for R_{XY}, obtaining

$$(6) \qquad R_{XY} = r_{xy} \frac{s_y S_X}{S_Y s_x}.$$

Next this value for R_{XY} is substituted in equation 3, giving

$$(7) \qquad s_y^2(1 - r_{xy}^2) = S_Y^2 \left(1 - r_{xy}^2 \frac{s_y^2 S_X^2}{S_Y^2 s_x^2} \right).$$

Multiplying the right side through by S_Y^2 in order to remove parentheses gives

$$(8) \qquad s_y^2(1 - r_{xy}^2) = S_Y^2 - r_{xy}^2 s_y^2 \frac{S_X^2}{s_x^2}.$$

This equation can readily be solved for S_Y^2:

$$(9) \qquad S_Y^2 = s_y^2 \left[1 - r_{xy}^2 + r_{xy}^2 \frac{S_X^2}{s_x^2} \right].$$

This value for S_Y is then substituted in equation 6, H_X being substituted for the ratio S_X/s_x, giving the following value for R_{XY}:

$$(10) \qquad R_{XY} = \frac{r_{xy} H_X}{\sqrt{1 - r_{xy}^2 + r_{xy}^2 H_X^2}}.$$

It will be noted by way of check that these values of S_Y and R_{XY} are the same as the results previously obtained in Chapter 11 for S_Y and R_{XY} on the basis of the assumption of selection on X. Similarly, we may write by analogy the results for S_Z and R_{XZ} in the present case. The solutions already obtained for S_Y and R_{XY} will give S_Z and R_{XZ} if Z is substituted for Y as follows: [1]

$$(11) \qquad S_Z^2 = s_z^2[1 - r_{xz}^2 + r_{xz}^2 H_X^2],$$

$$(12) \qquad R_{XZ} = \frac{r_{xz} H_X}{\sqrt{1 - r_{xz}^2 + r_{xz}^2 H_X^2}}.$$

---

[1] Students who do not yet feel at home with this device of substituting subscripts should solve independently for S_Z and R_{XZ} by following the general plan of equations 6 to 10. It will be seen that equations 11 and 12 must be the result of this procedure.

The only remaining task is to solve for R_{YZ}. It involves solving equation 5 for R_{YZ} and substituting the known values of R_{XY} and R_{XZ}. A rather simple algebraic routine for doing this is to note from equations 3 and 4 that we may write

$$(13) \qquad \sqrt{1 - R_{XY}^2} = \frac{s_y}{S_Y} \sqrt{(1 - r_{xy}^2)}$$

and

$$(14) \qquad \sqrt{1 - R_{XZ}^2} = \frac{s_z}{S_Z} \sqrt{(1 - r_{xz}^2)}.$$

These values may then be substituted for the denominator of the right-hand term in equation 5, giving

$$(15) \qquad \frac{r_{yz} - r_{xy}r_{xz}}{\sqrt{1 - r_{xy}^2}\sqrt{1 - r_{xz}^2}} = \frac{(R_{YZ} - R_{XY}R_{XZ})S_Y S_Z}{\sqrt{1 - r_{xy}^2}\sqrt{1 - r_{xz}^2}\, s_y s_z}.$$

Solving for R_{YZ}, we have

$$(16) \qquad R_{YZ} = \frac{(r_{yz} - r_{xy}r_{xz})s_y s_z}{S_Y S_Z} + R_{XY}R_{XZ}.$$

From equations 1 and 2 we can write

$$(17) \qquad R_{XY}R_{XZ} = r_{xy}r_{xz}\frac{s_y s_z S_X^2}{s_x^2 S_Y S_Z}.$$

Substituting equation 17 in equation 16 and factoring out $s_y s_z / S_Y S_Z$, we have

$$(18) \qquad R_{YZ} = \frac{s_y s_z}{S_Y S_Z}\left[r_{yz} - r_{xy}r_{xz} + r_{xy}r_{xz}\frac{S_X^2}{s_x^2} \right],$$

which expresses R_{YZ} in terms of given quantities and of the two values (S_Y and S_Z) for which solutions have already been obtained. Substituting equations 9 and 11 in equation 18 and simplifying, we have

$$(19) \qquad R_{YZ} = \frac{\left[r_{yz} - r_{xy}r_{xz} + r_{xy}r_{xz}\dfrac{S_X^2}{s_x^2} \right]}{\sqrt{\left[1 - r_{xy}^2 + r_{xy}^2\dfrac{S_X^2}{s_x^2} \right]\left[1 - r_{xz}^2 + r_{xz}^2\dfrac{S_X^2}{s_x^2} \right]}},$$

where R_{YZ} is the correlation between two incidental selection variables for one group, and

S_X is the standard deviation of the explicit selection variable in the same group.

For the other group involved, *complete* information is available as follows:

r_{yz} is the correlation between two incidental selection variables,

r_{xy} and r_{xz} are the correlation of the explicit selection variable with each of the incidental selection variables,

s_x is the standard deviation of the explicit selection variable, and

s_y and s_z are the standard deviations of the two incidental selection variables.

If there is explicit selection on variable x, the variance of x, and three correlations (r_{xy}, r_{xz}, and r_{yz}) are available for one group, and only the variance of X ($S_X{}^2$) is available for a second group, then the correlation of the two incidental selection variables (R_{YZ}) for the second group may be estimated by equation 19.

It should be noted that where the variance of the explicit selection variable is known for both groups, it is necessary to present only the equation for the correlation between the two incidental selection variables. All other values (the variance of the two incidental selection variables and their correlation with the explicit selection variable) are given by the bivariate equations 18 and 20, presented in Chapter 11.

Equation 19, or slight variants of it, has been given by Pearson (1903a) and Thorndike (1947).

5. Variance of both groups known for one of the incidental selection variables

We now turn to the final case for univariate selection with three variables. Again we designate the explicit selection variable as x and assume that the standard deviation for both groups is known on one of the other variables.

Since both Y and Z are variables that have been subject only to incidental selection, it makes no difference whether S_Y is assumed known and S_Z unknown, or vice versa. We shall assume S_Y known, and solve for S_Z. The equations derived can be applied generally by designating as Y the variable subject to incidental selection for which both variances are known. The incidental selection variable for which only one variance is known will be designated as variable Z.

Without loss of generality then, we may say that selection is on variable X and that the standard deviations of both groups are available on variable Y. For this case the known values are r_{xy}, r_{xz}, r_{yz}, s_x, s_y,

s_z, and S_Y. Knowing these values enables us immediately to solve for R_{XY}^2 by equation 3, giving

$$(20) \qquad R_{XY}^2 = 1 - \left(\frac{s_y^2}{S_Y^2}\right)(1 - r_{xy}^2),$$

which is the same as equation 8 of Chapter 11. Rearranging the terms in equation 1, we find that

$$(21) \qquad \frac{S_X}{s_x} = \frac{R_{XY}S_Y}{r_{xy}s_y}.$$

Substituting the value for R_{XY} found in equation 20 and solving for S_X, we have

$$(22) \qquad S_X = s_x \frac{\sqrt{S_Y^2 - s_y^2(1 - r_{xy}^2)}}{s_y r_{xy}}.$$

Equation 22 is essentially the same as equation 12 of Chapter 11.

Next let us solve for S_Z. One way of doing this is to write equation 2 explicitly for R_{XZ}:

$$(23) \qquad R_{XZ} = r_{xz} \frac{s_z S_X}{s_x S_Z}.$$

This value for R_{XZ} is then substituted in equation 4, giving

$$(24) \qquad s_z^2(1 - r_{xz}^2) = S_Z^2 \left[1 - r_{xz}^2 \frac{s_z^2 S_X^2}{s_x^2 S_Z^2}\right].$$

Removing the brackets on the right-hand side of equation 24, we obtain

$$(25) \qquad s_z^2(1 - r_{xz}^2) = S_Z^2 - r_{xz}^2 \frac{s_z^2 S_X^2}{s_x^2}.$$

Solving this equation for S_Z^2, we have

$$(26) \qquad S_Z^2 = s_z^2 \left[1 - r_{xz}^2 + r_{xz}^2 \frac{S_X^2}{s_x^2}\right].$$

Substituting equation 22 in equation 26 and simplifying gives

$$(27) \qquad S_Z^2 = s_z^2 \left[1 - r_{xz}^2 + r_{xz}^2 \frac{S_Y^2 - s_y^2(1 - r_{xy}^2)}{s_y^2 r_{xy}^2}\right].$$

Expanding and simplifying, we have

$$(28) \qquad S_Z^2 = s_z^2 \left[\frac{s_y^2 r_{xy}^2 - s_y^2 r_{xz}^2 + S_Y^2 r_{xz}^2}{s_y^2 r_{xy}^2}\right],$$

where $S_Z{}^2$ is the unknown variance of Z, expressed in terms of the
known quantities,

$S_Y{}^2$ is the variance of one of the incidental selection variables
for the second group,

$s_y{}^2$ is the variance of y for the first group,

$s_z{}^2$ is the variance of z for the first group, and

r_{xy} and r_{xz} are the correlation of the explicit selection variable with
each of the other variables for the first group.

If selection is explicitly based on variable x, complete infor-
mation is available for one group, and the variance of one of
the incidental selection variables (y) is known for another
group, then equation 28 may be used to estimate the vari-
ance of the other incidental selection variable (Z) for the sec-
ond group.

In order to obtain a value for R_{XZ}, let us use equation 4 and solve
for $R_{XZ}{}^2$, obtaining

(29) $$R_{XZ}{}^2 = 1 - \frac{s_z{}^2(1 - r_{xz}{}^2)}{S_Z{}^2}.$$

Substituting the value of $S_Z{}^2$ from equation 28, we obtain

(30) $$R_{XZ}{}^2 = 1 - \frac{s_y{}^2 r_{xy}{}^2(1 - r_{xz}{}^2)}{S_Y{}^2 r_{xz}{}^2 - s_y{}^2 r_{xz}{}^2 + s_y{}^2 r_{xy}{}^2}.$$

This solution expresses R_{XZ} entirely in terms of known quantities. We
may put this in another form by multiplying and simplifying, obtaining

(31) $$R_{XZ} = r_{xz} \sqrt{\frac{S_Y{}^2 - s_y{}^2 + s_y{}^2 r_{xy}{}^2}{S_Y{}^2 r_{xz}{}^2 - s_y{}^2 r_{xz}{}^2 + s_y{}^2 r_{xy}{}^2}}.$$

This form, it will be noted, could also have been readily obtained by
substituting equations 22 and 28 in equation 23.

In equation 31 R_{XZ} is the unknown, the correlation between the
explicit selection variable and the other incidental selection variable,
and all other terms have the same definition as in equation 28.

If selection is explicitly based on variable x, complete infor-
mation is available for one group, and the variance of one
of the incidental selection variables (y) is known for another
group, then equation 31 should be used to estimate the cor-
relation between the explicit selection variable and the other
incidental selection variable for the second group.

Let us now turn to the problem of solving for R_{YZ}. First let us note that from equations 3 and 4 we may write

$$(32) \quad \sqrt{(1 - R_{XY}^2)(1 - R_{XZ}^2)} = \frac{\sqrt{(1 - r_{xy}^2)(1 - r_{xz}^2)}(s_y s_z)}{S_Y S_Z}.$$

Substituting this value in equation 5 gives

$$(33) \quad \frac{r_{yz} - r_{xy} r_{xz}}{\sqrt{(1 - r_{xy}^2)(1 - r_{xz}^2)}} = \frac{(R_{YZ} - R_{XY} R_{XZ}) S_Y S_Z}{\sqrt{(1 - r_{xy}^2)(1 - r_{xz}^2)} \, s_y s_z}.$$

Solving this equation for R_{YZ}, we have

$$(34) \quad R_{YZ} = \frac{s_y s_z}{S_Y S_Z}(r_{yz} - r_{xy} r_{xz}) + R_{XY} R_{XZ}.$$

From equations 1 and 2 we obtain the following expression for $R_{XY} R_{XZ}$:

$$(35) \quad R_{XY} R_{XZ} = r_{xy} r_{xz} \frac{s_y s_z S_X^2}{s_x^2 S_Y S_Z}.$$

If this value for the product $R_{XY} R_{XZ}$ is substituted in equation 34 and the common terms $(s_y s_z / S_Y S_Z)$ factored out, we have

$$(36) \quad R_{YZ} = \frac{s_y s_z}{S_Y S_Z}\left[r_{yz} - r_{xy} r_{xz} + r_{xy} r_{xz} \frac{S_X^2}{s_x^2} \right].$$

This equation expresses R_{YZ} in terms of known quantities, and the values S_X and S_Z for which equations have already been given. If we substitute equations 22 and 28 in equation 36 and simplify, we get

$$(37) \quad R_{YZ} = \frac{r_{xz}(S_Y^2 - s_y^2) + r_{xy} r_{yz} s_y^2}{S_Y \sqrt{r_{xz}^2 (S_Y^2 - s_y^2) + s_y^2 r_{xy}^2}},$$

where r_{yz} is the correlation between the two incidental selection variables
for the first group,

R_{YZ} is the correlation between the two incidental selection variables
for the second group, and the other terms have the same
definitions as for equation 28.

*If selection is explicitly based on variable x, complete infor-
mation is available for one group, and the variance of one of
the incidental selection variables (y) is known for another
group, then equation 37 should be used to estimate the correlation between the two incidental selection variables for the
second group.*

This completes the consideration of the second case considered under the three-variable problem, the case in which selection was on one variable (X), and the standard deviation of the variable that was subject to incidental selection was known for both groups. This variable was designated Y, and equations were derived to express S_X, S_Z, R_{XZ}, and R_{YZ}, and R_{XY} in terms of the known quantities r_{xz}, r_{yz}, r_{xy}, s_x, s_y, s_z, and S_Y. The equations for S_X and R_{XY} were similar to those derived for the corresponding bivariate case in Chapter 11. However, the equations (involving variable Z) for S_Z, R_{YZ}, and R_{XZ} were different from those previously derived for the bivariate case.

One general caution must be noted in the application of the selection equations presented in Chapters 11 and 12. They are applicable only when the selection is made on the basis of *one* variable, and is made in such a way as not to alter the regression line of other variables on the explicit selection variable or the error made in estimating other variables from the explicit selection variable. If these assumptions hold, then the equations are perfect. However, as noted at the beginning of Chapter 11, in most practical situations the equations are likely not to apply.

We should inspect the frequency distribution of the uncurtailed distribution and of the curtailed distribution for the variables involved before deciding upon the equations to use. If there is a sharp cut-off point, and every person above was accepted while every one below was rejected, it is clear that the variable in question may be regarded as the explicit selection variable, and the equations of Chapters 11 and 12 used with confidence. If there is not a sharp cut-off point or a reasonably sharp cut-off point on one variable, the exact selection procedure must be more carefully investigated to determine if the type of selection used can reasonably be assumed not to have altered certain of the errors of estimate and regression slopes involved. If we can justify the assumptions indicated in equations 1 to 5, the selection equations apply. If, after study, we feel that the assumptions of equations 1 to 5 do not apply, there is no way of estimating the probable effects of selection.

As mentioned in Chapter 11, there is no adequate substitute for a well-designed experiment that makes the proper comparisons without any selection procedure. If we must work in a practical situation where selection is essential, every effort must be made to have the selection proceed in a specified manner, using definite critical score points, and rejecting every one below and accepting every one above these points. If such procedures are instituted and actually followed, the selection formulas can be used. If the selection procedure varies in accordance with "numerous practical considerations," it is impossible to estimate the effect of selection.

6. Summary

These are the basic assumptions for the three-variable case.

1. The slopes of the regressions of the incidental on the explicit selection variable are not altered by selection. This assumption is given in equations

(1)
$$r_{xy}\left(\frac{s_y}{s_x}\right) = R_{XY}\left(\frac{S_Y}{S_X}\right)$$

and

(2)
$$r_{xz}\left(\frac{s_z}{s_x}\right) = R_{XZ}\left(\frac{S_Z}{S_X}\right).$$

2. The error made in estimating either of the incidental selection variables from the explicit selection variable is not altered by selection. This assumption is given in equations

(3)
$$s_y^2(1 - r_{xy}^2) = S_Y^2(1 - R_{XY}^2)$$

and

(4)
$$s_z^2(1 - r_{xz}^2) = S_Z^2(1 - R_{XZ}^2).$$

3. The partial correlation between the two incidental selection variables is not altered by selection. This assumption is given in equation

(5)
$$\frac{r_{yz} - r_{xy}r_{xz}}{\sqrt{(1 - r_{xy}^2)(1 - r_{xz}^2)}} = \frac{R_{YZ} - R_{XY}R_{XZ}}{\sqrt{(1 - R_{XY}^2)(1 - R_{XZ}^2)}}.$$

It was assumed that we were always given complete information on one of the groups, and the convention that this group was represented by lower-case letters was adopted. That is, it was assumed that r_{xy}, r_{xz}, r_{yz}, s_x, s_y, and s_z were always known. Unless complete information is available on one group, it is not possible to solve the problem. Two cases were then considered.

1. The case was considered in which the standard deviation of the explicit selection variable (S_X) is known for the second group. The value of S_Y was given in equation 9, and the value of S_Z in equation 11. These equations are not repeated here because they are formally identical with equation 20 of Chapter 11 (on bivariate selection). Similarly, the value of R_{XY} was given in equation 10, and of R_{XZ} in equation 12. These equations are formally identical with equation 18, Chapter 11. The only new problem posed by the three-variable problem for this first

case is estimating the correlation between the two incidental selection variables for the second group. This value is given by equation

$$(19) \quad R_{YZ} = \frac{\left[r_{yz} - r_{xy}r_{xz} + r_{xy}r_{xz}\dfrac{S_x^2}{s_x^2} \right]}{\sqrt{\left[1 - r_{xy}^2 + r_{xy}^2\dfrac{S_x^2}{s_x^2} \right]\left[1 - r_{xz}^2 + r_{xz}^2\dfrac{S_x^2}{s_x^2} \right]}}.$$

2. The case was also considered in which the standard deviation of one of the incidental selection variables was known for both groups. Without loss of generality, we may designate the known standard deviation S_Y and use S_Z for the unknown standard deviation of the other selection variable. The formula for S_X is given in equation 22, which is not repeated since it is identical with equation 12, Chapter 11. The variance of the other incidental selection variable (S_Z^2) is given by equation

$$(28) \quad S_Z^2 = s_z^2 \left[\frac{s_y^2 r_{xy}^2 - s_y^2 r_{xz}^2 + S_Y^2 r_{xz}^2}{s_y^2 r_{xy}^2} \right].$$

The value of R_{XY} is given in equation 20, which is identical with equation 8, Chapter 11, and is not repeated here. The correlation R_{XZ} is given by equation

$$(31) \quad R_{XZ} = r_{xz} \sqrt{\frac{S_Y^2 - s_y^2 + s_y^2 r_{xy}^2}{S_Y^2 r_{xz}^2 - s_y^2 r_{xz}^2 + s_y^2 r_{xy}^2}}.$$

The correlation between the two incidental selection variables is given by equation

$$(37) \quad R_{YZ} = \frac{r_{xz}(S_Y^2 - s_y^2) + r_{xy}r_{yz}s_y^2}{S_Y\sqrt{r_{xz}^2(S_Y^2 - s_y^2) + s_y^2 r_{xy}^2}}.$$

These equations (31 and 37) have no counterpart in the bivariate case.

Problems

1. Assume that we are dealing with a case in which explicit selection occurs on the criterion, and the test is subject only to incidental selection (such as would occur if everyone taking the entrance test were admitted, but only those who received "passing" scores on the criterion were included in the selected group).

    (a) Write the equation showing the relationship between the entrance test variances and validities for the curtailed and the complete group.

    (b) Write the equation showing the relationship between the entrance test variances and reliabilities for both groups.

2. Compare, from information in previous chapters and problems, the relationship between reliability and validity:

(a) When the change is due to alteration of test length.
(b) When the change is due to explicit curtailment of test variability.
(c) When the change is due to explicit selection on the criterion resulting in incidental selection on the test in question.

3. Test X is given to a group of applicants for admission to a certain college. The mean score for all applicants is 150, and the standard deviation is 30. After the students have been selected on the basis of this test and admitted to college, test Y is given. The two tests, X and Y, are correlated with grade average, which is used as a criterion, with the following results:

Test X; mean 170 standard deviation 20; validity .63.
Test Y; mean 160 standard deviation 25; validity .68.
The correlation of X and Y is .80.

According to these data, which test would be better to use for college admission?

4. Prove that, if $r_{yz} = r_{xz}$ and $S_X < s_x$, $R_{YZ} > R_{XZ}$.

5. Prove that, if $r_{yz} = r_{xz}$ and $S_X > s_x$, $R_{YZ} < R_{XZ}$.

6. Study this reference: G. G. Thompson and S. L. Witryol (1946), "The relationship between intelligence and motor learning ability as measured by a high relief finger maze," *J. Psychol.*, **22**, pages 237–246.

(a) Comment on the use of the correction for restriction of range.
(b) Present a correction for homogeneity which you consider appropriate for these data.
(c) Give both the calculations and the argument for the correction you select.

13

Correction for Multivariate Selection
in the General Case

1. Basic definitions and assumptions

The equations for multivariate selection in the general case become almost prohibitively complex unless matrix algebra is used. Since only a few theorems of matrix algebra are used in this derivation, these theorems will be summarized here. Any set of numbers arranged in rows and columns is termed a matrix, and is designated by a single letter, such as **M, N, A, B**. In the derivations of this chapter four basic matrices are necessary. We have the matrix of test scores for the variables subject to explicit selection. For N individuals and A tests we may define

$$(1) \qquad \mathbf{X}_{NA} = \left\| \begin{array}{ccc} X_{11} & \cdots & X_{1A} \\ \vdots & & \vdots \\ X_{N1} & \cdots & X_{NA} \end{array} \right\|.$$

The X's on the right-hand side of this equation are defined as deviation scores to simplify the formulas for variances and covariances. In defining the score matrix we may let each individual represent a row and each test a column, or vice versa. In the score matrices used here we shall arbitrarily let each row represent an individual, and each column a test. The matrix of test scores for the variables subject to incidental selection is defined by

$$(2) \qquad \mathbf{Y}_{NB} = \left\| \begin{array}{ccc} Y_{11} & \cdots & Y_{1B} \\ \vdots & & \vdots \\ Y_{N1} & \cdots & Y_{NB} \end{array} \right\|$$

for N individuals and B tests. Again the Y's on the right-hand side of the equation designate deviation scores. The X's are regarded as independent variables, and the Y's as dependent variables, which may be estimated by a weighted sum of the X's. Let us use $W_{X_g Y_b}$ to designate the weight to be applied to X_g to predict Y_b. The complete matrix of weights will be defined by

$$(3) \qquad \mathbf{W}_{XY} = \left\| \begin{array}{ccc} W_{X_1 Y_1} & \cdots & W_{X_1 Y_B} \\ \cdot & & \cdot \\ \cdot & & \cdot \\ \cdot & & \cdot \\ W_{X_A Y_1} & \cdots & W_{X_A Y_B} \end{array} \right\| .$$

The first column contains the weights to be applied to the independent variables X_1 to X_A to predict Y_1. In general any column (which may be designated b) gives the weights to apply to the independent variables X_1 to X_A to predict Y_b. If the predicted Y_b is indicated by $\dot{Y}_b$, we have

$$\dot{Y}_{ib} = W_{X_1 Y_b} X_{i1} + W_{X_2 Y_b} X_{i2} + \cdots + W_{X_A Y_b} X_{iA} \qquad (b = 1 \cdots B).$$

The weights are to be chosen so that $\displaystyle\sum_{i=1}^{N} (Y_{ib} - \dot{Y}_{ib})^2$ is a minimum. It is also necessary to introduce a diagonal matrix with the terms along the principal diagonal, each equal to $1/N$, and all other terms equal to zero. Thus we have the square matrix

$$(4) \qquad \mathbf{D}_{GG} = \left\| \begin{array}{ccccc} 1/N & 0 & \cdots & 0 & 0 \\ 0 & 1/N & \cdots & 0 & 0 \\ \cdot & \cdot & & \cdot & \cdot \\ \cdot & \cdot & & \cdot & \cdot \\ \cdot & \cdot & & \cdot & \cdot \\ 0 & 0 & \cdots & 1/N & 0 \\ 0 & 0 & \cdots & 0 & 1/N \end{array} \right\| ,$$

where the subscript G designates the number of rows (columns) in the matrix and may equal either A or B.

It should be noted that $\mathbf{D}$ is a scalar; hence for any two matrices $\mathbf{P}$ and $\mathbf{Q}$ for which $\mathbf{PQ}$ exists,

$$\mathbf{DPQ} = \mathbf{PDQ} = \mathbf{PQD}.$$

Persons not acquainted with matrix algebra will need to study a text—the first four chapters of Bôcher's *Higher Algebra* (1907), for instance, or the first chapter of Thurstone (1935a) or (1947b). Those who have not worked recently with matrix algebra may find the following ten principles helpful in studying the derivations given here.

1. The matrix sum $\mathbf{M} + \mathbf{N}$ exists only if the number of rows in $\mathbf{M}$ is equal to the number of rows in $\mathbf{N}$, and the number of columns in $\mathbf{M}$ is equal to the number of columns in $\mathbf{N}$.

2. Matrix addition follows the associative and the commutative laws.

(A)
$$\mathbf{M} + (\mathbf{N} + \mathbf{O}) = (\mathbf{M} + \mathbf{N}) + \mathbf{O}$$

and

(B)
$$\mathbf{M} + \mathbf{N} = \mathbf{N} + \mathbf{M}.$$

3. The matrix product $\mathbf{MN}$ exists only if the number of columns in $\mathbf{M}$ is equal to the number of rows in $\mathbf{N}$. Matrix multiplication is associative but not commutative.

(C)
$$\mathbf{M}(\mathbf{NO}) = (\mathbf{MN})\mathbf{O},$$

(D)
$$\mathbf{MN} \neq \mathbf{NM}.$$

4. Matrix multiplication satisfies the distributive law for both pre-multiplication and postmultiplication.

(E)
$$\mathbf{M}(\mathbf{N} + \mathbf{O}) = \mathbf{MN} + \mathbf{MO}, \text{ and}$$
$$(\mathbf{N} + \mathbf{O})\mathbf{M} = \mathbf{NM} + \mathbf{OM}.$$

5. Any square matrix $\mathbf{M}$ with a non-vanishing determinant $(|\mathbf{M}| \neq 0)$ has an inverse, $\mathbf{M}^{-1}$. A matrix premultiplied or post-multiplied by its inverse gives the identity matrix, $\mathbf{I}$.

(F)
$$\mathbf{M}^{-1}\mathbf{M} = \mathbf{MM}^{-1} = \mathbf{I}.$$

6. The inverse of a transpose is equal to the transpose of the inverse.

(G)
$$(\mathbf{M}^{-1})' = (\mathbf{M}')^{-1}.$$

7. The transpose of a product is the product of transposes taken in reverse order.

(H)
$$(\mathbf{MNO})' = \mathbf{O}'\mathbf{N}'\mathbf{M}'.$$

8. The transpose of a sum is the sum of the transposes.

(I)
$$(\mathbf{M} + \mathbf{N})' = \mathbf{M}' + \mathbf{N}'.$$

9. The inverse of a product is the product of the inverses taken in reverse order.

(J)
$$(\mathbf{MNO})^{-1} = \mathbf{O}^{-1}\mathbf{N}^{-1}\mathbf{M}^{-1}.$$

10. The inverse of a sum $(\mathbf{M} + \mathbf{N})^{-1}$ cannot in general be simplified.

The solutions given in this chapter will be stated in terms of matrices of variances and covariances so that no explicit expressions for the correlation matrices will be needed. The variance-covariance matrix for the explicit selection variables, designated as C_{XX}, is given by

$$(5) \qquad C_{XX} = X'_{AN}X_{NA}D_{AA}.$$

In like manner, we may write C_{YY}, the variance-covariance matrix for the variables subject to incidental selection, as

$$(6) \qquad C_{YY} = Y'_{BN}Y_{NB}D_{BB}.$$

The (XY) covariance matrix is designated by C_{XY} and written

$$(7) \qquad C_{XY} = X'_{AN}Y_{NB}D_{BB}.$$

The variables subject to incidental selection (Y-variables) are regarded as being estimated by linear combinations of the explicit selection variables (X-variables). We designate the matrix of predicted Y-values by $\dot{Y}_{NB}$ and write

$$(8) \qquad \dot{Y}_{NB} = X_{NA}W_{XY}.$$

The matrix of errors of prediction is given by the difference between the actual Y-values and the predicted Y-values. This matrix is designated E and written

$$(9) \qquad E = Y_{NB} - \dot{Y}_{NB}.$$

The variance-covariance matrix of the errors of prediction, designated C_{EE}, is given by

$$(10) \qquad C_{EE} = E'ED_{BB}.$$

Equations 1 to 10, written in upper-case letters, will be used to designate the group for which complete information is *not* available on all variables. Corresponding equations with lower-case letters will be used to designate the group for which complete information *is* available. We have, corresponding to equations 5 to 10, for the group on which complete information is available,

$$(11) \qquad c_{xx} = x'_{an}x_{na}d_{aa},$$

$$(12) \qquad c_{yy} = y'_{bn}y_{nb}d_{bb},$$

$$(13) \qquad c_{xy} = x'_{an}y_{nb}d_{bb},$$

$$(14) \qquad \dot{y}_{nb} = x_{na}w_{xy},$$

$$(15) \qquad e = y_{nb} - \dot{y}_{nb},$$

and

$$(16) \qquad c_{ee} = e'ed_{bb}.$$

It should be noted that the number of cases in the two groups need not be the same so that, in general, $n \neq N$, $d_{aa} \neq D_{AA}$, and $d_{bb} \neq D_{BB}$. However, the *number* of explicit selection variables must be the same in both groups, and the *number* of incidental selection variables must be the same, so that $a = A$ and $b = B$.

The group designated by upper-case letters is assumed to be similar to the one designated by lower-case letters in that the gross score weights applied to the explicit selection variables to predict the incidental selection variables are the same for both groups. This assumption is the generalization of the assumption of equal slopes given in equations 1 and 2 of Chapter 12 for the three-variable case in univariate selection. In matrix notation this assumption is written

$$(17) \qquad\qquad \mathbf{W}_{XY} = \mathbf{w}_{xy}.$$

In addition, it is assumed that the errors of estimate are the same for both groups. (See equations 3 and 4, Chapter 12.) It is also assumed, as in equation 5 of Chapter 12, that the correlations among the Y's when the X's are partialled out is the same as the correlation among the y's when the x's are partialled out. These two assumptions are written in the matrix equation

$$(18) \qquad\qquad \mathbf{C}_{EE} = \mathbf{c}_{ee}.$$

The diagonal terms of these matrices are the squares of the errors of estimate; assuming them equal corresponds to the generalization of assumptions of equations 3 and 4 of Chapter 12. The non-diagonal terms of equation 18 are the partial covariances. Assuming them equal corresponds to the generalization of equation 5, Chapter 12.

Since the basic assumptions given in equations 17 and 18 involve $\mathbf{W}_{XY}$ and $\mathbf{C}_{EE}$, we shall turn to the problem of expressing these matrices in terms of the basic variance-covariance matrices $\mathbf{C}_{XX}$, $\mathbf{C}_{YY}$, and $\mathbf{C}_{XY}$.

The error made in predicting any given set of Y-values, such as Y_{ib} (where $i = 1 \cdots N$, and b is some specified value that may be any one of the values from 1 to B), is indicated by subtracting the summed product $(\sum\limits_{g=1}^{A} W_{gb}X_{ig})$ from Y_{ib}, squaring these differences, summing over i for a given value of b, and dividing by N. This gives an error variance term that is one of the diagonal terms of the matrix $\mathbf{C}_{EE}$. In order to deal solely with these diagonal terms, equations 19 to 21, inclusive, are in the usual algebraic summation notation; equation 22 returns to matrix notation. Let us designate a typical diagonal term by $E_b{}^2$ (where

$b = 1 \cdots B$). We then have

$$(19) \qquad E_b^2 = \sum_{i=1}^{N} (Y_{ib} - \sum_{g=1}^{A} W_{gb}X_{ig})^2 \frac{1}{N} \qquad (b = 1\cdots B).$$

The multiple correlation problem is to select the weights (W_{gb}) so as to minimize the value of the error variance E_b^2. For a given value of E_b^2, we differentiate with respect to W_{hb} ($h = 1 \cdots A$) and set the derivative equal to zero, obtaining

$$(20) \qquad \frac{dE_b^2}{dW_{hb}} = \frac{2}{N} \sum_{i=1}^{N} (Y_{ib} - \sum_{g=1}^{A} W_{gb}X_{ig})X_{ih} = 0.$$

Removing parentheses and changing the order of summation in the second term, we have

$$(21) \qquad \frac{dE_b^2}{dW_{hb}} = \frac{2}{N}\left[\sum_{i=1}^{N} Y_{ib}X_{ih} - \sum_{g=1}^{A} W_{gb} \sum_{i=1}^{N} X_{ig}X_{ih} \right] = 0.$$

For a single value of h, equation 21 states a single condition for minimizing a given term in the diagonal of $\mathbf{C}_{EE}$. If we let h take in turn each of the values from 1 to A, while b remains fixed, equation 21 indicates a *set* of A equations which specifies the weights necessary to minimize a given term (E_b^2) in the diagonal of $\mathbf{C}_{EE}$. If b now takes in turn each of the values from 1 to B equation 21 indicates a set of AB equations which specifies the weights necessary to minimize in turn each of the terms (E_b^2) ($b = 1 \cdots B$) in the diagonal of $\mathbf{C}_{EE}$. When $h = 1 \cdots A$ and $b = 1 \cdots B$, the first term of equation 21 is identical with the matrix given in equation 7. The last term is in the general case identical with the product of equations 5 and 3, or $\mathbf{C}_{XX}\mathbf{W}_{XY}$. Putting equations 21 into matrix notation, we have

$$(22) \qquad \mathbf{C}_{XY} - \mathbf{C}_{XX}\mathbf{W}_{XY} = 0.$$

From equation 22 we obtain the solution for the matrix of weights ($\mathbf{W}_{XY}$). Transferring $\mathbf{C}_{XX}\mathbf{W}_{XY}$ to the other side of the equation, and premultiplying both sides by the inverse of $\mathbf{C}_{XX}$, we have

$$(23) \qquad \mathbf{C}^{-1}_{XX}\mathbf{C}_{XY} = \mathbf{C}^{-1}_{XX}\mathbf{C}_{XX}\mathbf{W}_{XY} = \mathbf{W}_{XY}.$$

A corresponding equation can be derived for the group on which complete information is available. Substituting lower-case letters in equation 23 gives this equation,

$$(24) \qquad \mathbf{w}_{xy} = \mathbf{c}^{-1}_{xx}\mathbf{c}_{xy}.$$

Since the transpose of both equations 23 and 24 will also be needed, we shall write these explicitly as

$$(25) \qquad \mathbf{W}'_{YX} = \mathbf{C}'_{YX}\mathbf{C}^{-1}_{XX}$$

and

$$(26) \qquad \mathbf{w}'_{yx} = \mathbf{c}'_{yx}\mathbf{c}^{-1}_{xx}.$$

Since $\mathbf{C}_{XX}$ is a symmetric matrix, its inverse is also symmetric; hence $(\mathbf{C}^{-1}_{XX})' = \mathbf{C}^{-1}_{XX}$, and correspondingly, since $\mathbf{c}_{xx}$ is symmetric, $(\mathbf{c}^{-1}_{xx})' = \mathbf{c}^{-1}_{xx}$.

Equations 23 and 24 or equations 25 and 26 give the best weights to use for the X's (or for the x's) to predict the Y's (y's). These equations are identical with the equations for the best weights used in multiple correlation. (See Chapter 20, equations 52 and 53.)

We now turn to the evaluation of the variance-covariance matrix of the errors of prediction ($\mathbf{C}_{EE}$) in terms of the matrices $\mathbf{C}_{XX}$, $\mathbf{C}_{YY}$, and $\mathbf{C}_{XY}$, which can be obtained from the data on observed scores. Substituting equation 9 in equation 10 gives

$$(27) \qquad \mathbf{C}_{EE} = (\mathbf{Y}_{NB} - \dot{\mathbf{Y}}_{NB})'(\mathbf{Y}_{NB} - \dot{\mathbf{Y}}_{NB})\mathbf{D}_{BB}.$$

Removing parentheses and expanding, we have

$$(28) \quad \mathbf{C}_{EE} = \mathbf{Y}'_{BN}\mathbf{Y}_{NB}\mathbf{D}_{BB} - \mathbf{Y}'_{BN}\dot{\mathbf{Y}}_{NB}\mathbf{D}_{BB}$$
$$- \dot{\mathbf{Y}}'_{BN}\mathbf{Y}_{NB}\mathbf{D}_{BB} + \dot{\mathbf{Y}}'_{BN}\dot{\mathbf{Y}}_{NB}\mathbf{D}_{BB}.$$

Substituting equations 6 and 8 in equation 28, we have

$$(29) \quad \mathbf{C}_{EE} = \mathbf{C}_{YY} - \mathbf{Y}'_{BN}\mathbf{X}_{NA}\mathbf{W}_{XY}\mathbf{D}_{BB} - \mathbf{W}'_{YX}\mathbf{X}'_{AN}\mathbf{Y}_{NB}\mathbf{D}_{BB}$$
$$+ \mathbf{W}'_{YX}\mathbf{X}'_{AN}\mathbf{X}_{NA}\mathbf{W}_{XY}\mathbf{D}_{BB}.$$

Substituting equations 5, 7, 23, and 25 in equation 29, and noting that $\mathbf{D}$ is a scalar, we obtain

$$(30) \quad \mathbf{C}_{EE} = \mathbf{C}_{YY} - \mathbf{C}'_{YX}\mathbf{C}^{-1}_{XX}\mathbf{C}_{XY} - \mathbf{C}'_{YX}\mathbf{C}^{-1}_{XX}\mathbf{C}_{XY}$$
$$+ \mathbf{C}'_{YX}\mathbf{C}^{-1}_{XX}\mathbf{C}_{XX}\mathbf{C}^{-1}_{XX}\mathbf{C}_{XY}.$$

Since a matrix times its inverse is the identity matrix, the last two terms cancel each other, leaving

$$(31) \qquad \mathbf{C}_{EE} = \mathbf{C}_{YY} - \mathbf{C}'_{YX}\mathbf{C}^{-1}_{XX}\mathbf{C}_{XY}.$$

Equation 31 may be written in another form by substituting equation 23 in it. Alternatively, equation 25 may be substituted in equation 31. Making these substitutions gives

$$(32) \qquad \mathbf{C}_{EE} = \mathbf{C}_{YY} - \mathbf{C}'_{YX}\mathbf{W}_{XY} = \mathbf{C}_{YY} - \mathbf{W}'_{YX}\mathbf{C}_{XY}.$$

A corresponding set of equations can be derived for the group on which complete information is available. Substituting lower-case letters in equations 31 and 32 gives these equations as

$$(33) \qquad \mathbf{c}_{ee} = \mathbf{c}_{yy} - \mathbf{c}'_{yx}\mathbf{c}^{-1}_{xx}\mathbf{c}_{xy}$$

and

$$(34) \qquad \mathbf{c}_{ee} = \mathbf{c}_{yy} - \mathbf{c}'_{yx}\mathbf{w}_{xy} = \mathbf{c}_{yy} - \mathbf{w}'_{yx}\mathbf{c}_{xy}.$$

2. Complete information available for all the explicit selection variables

We now consider the case in which the variance-covariance matrix of both groups is known for the variables subject to explicit selection. In this case $\mathbf{C}_{XX}$ is given. In general it is assumed that $\mathbf{c}_{xx}$, $\mathbf{c}_{yy}$, and $\mathbf{c}_{xy}$ are known. The problem of this section, then, is to express the unknown variance-covariance matrix for the incidental selection variables $\mathbf{C}_{YY}$ and the covariance matrix $\mathbf{C}_{XY}$ as functions of the known terms $\mathbf{C}_{XX}$, $\mathbf{c}_{xx}$, $\mathbf{c}_{yy}$, and $\mathbf{c}_{xy}$. Substituting equations 23 and 24 in equation 17 gives

$$(35) \qquad \mathbf{C}^{-1}_{XX}\mathbf{C}_{XY} = \mathbf{c}^{-1}_{xx}\mathbf{c}_{xy}.$$

Premultiplying both sides by $\mathbf{C}_{XX}$ and noting that a matrix times its inverse is equal to the identity matrix, we have

$$(36) \qquad \mathbf{C}_{XY} = \mathbf{C}_{XX}\mathbf{c}^{-1}_{xx}\mathbf{c}_{xy}.$$

Using equation 24, we may write equation 36 in the alternative form,

$$(37) \qquad \mathbf{C}_{XY} = \mathbf{C}_{XX}\mathbf{w}_{xy}.$$

Since the transpose of $\mathbf{C}_{XY}$ will be needed in solving for $\mathbf{C}_{YY}$, we may write it from equations 36 and 37 as

$$(38) \qquad \mathbf{C}'_{YX} = \mathbf{c}'_{yx}\mathbf{c}^{-1}_{xx}\mathbf{C}_{XX} = \mathbf{w}'_{yx}\mathbf{C}_{XX}.$$

Equation 36 or 37 gives $\mathbf{C}_{XY}$ entirely in terms of known quantities when complete information is available for the explicit selection variable (X).

This solution for $\mathbf{C}_{XY}$ in terms of the explicit selection variables is given by Pearson (1903a), Aitken (1934), and Burt (1943) and (1944).

To solve for $\mathbf{C}_{YY}$, substitute equations 32 and 34 in equation 18, obtaining

$$(39) \qquad \mathbf{C}_{YY} - \mathbf{C}'_{YX}\mathbf{W}_{XY} = \mathbf{c}_{yy} - \mathbf{c}'_{yx}\mathbf{w}_{xy}.$$

Using equation 17 and solving explicitly for C_{YY}, we obtain

(40) $$C_{YY} = c_{yy} + (C'_{YX} - c'_{yx})w_{xy}.$$

Substituting equations 24 and 38 in equation 40, we have

(41) $$C_{YY} = c_{yy} + c'_{yx}c^{-1}{}_{xx}C_{XX}c^{-1}{}_{xx}c_{xy} - c'_{yx}c^{-1}{}_{xx}c_{xy}.$$

Since C_{YY} is symmetric, it is equal to its transpose. Thus, from equation 40, we have an alternative form,

(42) $$C_{YY} = c_{yy} + w'_{yx}(C_{XY} - c_{xy}).$$

This equation is also given by Pearson (1903a), Aitken (1934), and Burt (1943) and (1944).

> *Equation 41 gives C_{YY} entirely in terms of known quantities.*
> *Equation 40 or 42 gives C_{YY} if C_{XY} is taken from equation 36 or 38.*

These equations complete the solution for the case in which complete information is available for the variables subject to explicit selection. Equations 36, 37, and 38 are generalizations of equation 18, Chapter 11, and equations 10 and 12 of Chapter 12. Equations 40, 41, and 42 are generalizations of equation 20, Chapter 11, and equations 9 and 11 of Chapter 12.

3. Complete information available for some of the incidental selection variables

For the generalized treatment of this case, it is necessary to distinguish between two categories of variables subject to incidental selection. We will let Y (or y) designate only those incidental selection variables for which complete information is available. That is, C_{YY} is known in addition to c_{yy}. Incidental selection variables for which incomplete information is available will be designated by Z (or z). For these only c_{zz} is known. It thus becomes necessary to express five unknowns, C_{XX}, C_{XY}, C_{ZZ}, C_{XZ}, and C_{YZ} in terms of the known quantities C_{YY}, c_{yy}, c_{xx}, c_{zz}, c_{xy}, c_{xz}, and c_{yz}.

The solution for all terms involving Z will be postponed. Let us first consider the solution for C_{XX} and C_{XY} in terms of the known quantities c_{yy}, c_{xx}, c_{xy}, and c_{YY}.

Substituting equations 32, 34, and 17 in equation 18, we have

(43) $$C_{YY} - C'_{YX}w_{xy} = c_{yy} - c'_{yx}w_{xy}.$$

Transferring the known terms to one side of the equation, we have

(44) $$C'_{YX}w_{xy} = C_{YY} - c_{yy} + c'_{yx}w_{xy}.$$

Postmultiplying both sides by $\mathbf{w}^{-1}{}_{yx}$ gives the solution for the transpose of $\mathbf{C}_{XY}$ as

$$(45) \qquad \mathbf{C}'_{YX} = (\mathbf{C}_{YY} - \mathbf{c}_{yy})\mathbf{w}^{-1}{}_{yx} + \mathbf{c}'_{yx}.$$

Taking the transpose of both sides gives

$$(46) \qquad \mathbf{C}_{XY} = \mathbf{w}'^{-1}{}_{xy}(\mathbf{C}_{YY} - \mathbf{c}_{yy}) + \mathbf{c}_{xy}.$$

> *Equation 46 gives $\mathbf{C}_{XY}$ in terms of known quantities, if information on both groups is available for the incidental selection variables (Y).*

Equation 46 is a generalization of the solution for R_{XY} given in equation 8, Chapter 11, and equation 20, Chapter 12.

It should be noticed that this solution assumes that the inverse of $\mathbf{w}_{xy}$ exists. Since the inverse of a product is the product of the inverses taken in the reverse order, equation 24 gives

$$(47) \qquad \mathbf{w}^{-1}{}_{yx} = \mathbf{c}^{-1}{}_{yx}\mathbf{c}_{xx}.$$

That is, $\mathbf{w}_{xy}$ has an inverse if $\mathbf{c}_{xy}$ has an inverse. In other words, the variables y for which complete information is available must be at least equal in number to the explicit selection variables, and must *not* be linearly dependent on the explicit selection variables (x). If these two conditions are met, $\mathbf{c}^{-1}{}_{yx}$ will exist, $\mathbf{w}^{-1}{}_{yx}$ will exist, and the solution given by equation 46 will be meaningful. If the number of incidental selection variables for which complete information is available is less than the number of explicit selection variables, or if these incidental selection variables are linearly dependent on the explicit selection variables, the information available is not sufficient for an exact solution of the problem. Given such conditions, various sets of values for $\mathbf{C}_{XY}$ would be possible solutions. If the number of incidental selection variables for which complete information is available is greater than the number of explicit selection variables, $\mathbf{C}_{XY}$ is overdetermined. The solution for $\mathbf{C}_{XY}$ would be in terms of least squares or some other maximum likelihood procedure. It would also be desirable to devise some method for assessing variation of the individual solutions from the least squares solution. If this variation is small, the least squares solution could be accepted. If this variation is large, it probably indicates that unknown factors are entering into the selection procedures so that a further effort must be made to secure a more accurate description of selection procedures before proceeding with any corrections for selection.

In this book we shall consider only the case in which adequate information is available, and the solution is exact. That is, the number of incidental selection variables for which complete information is available (Y) is equal to and not linearly dependent on the explicit selection variables. In this case equation 46 is the solution for $\mathbf{C}_{XY}$.

The solution for $\mathbf{C}_{XX}$ may be obtained by postmultiplying both sides of equation 37 by $\mathbf{w}^{-1}{}_{yx}$, obtaining

$$(48) \qquad \mathbf{C}_{XX} = \mathbf{C}_{XY}\mathbf{w}^{-1}{}_{yx}.$$

Using equations 46 and 24, we may write $\mathbf{C}_{XX}$ as

$$(49) \qquad \mathbf{C}_{XX} = \mathbf{w}'^{-1}{}_{xy}(\mathbf{C}_{YY} - \mathbf{c}_{yy})\mathbf{w}^{-1}{}_{yx} + \mathbf{c}_{xx}.$$

Equation 49 gives $\mathbf{C}_{XX}$ in terms of known quantities when complete information is available for the incidental selection variables (Y).

It should be noticed that the solution for $\mathbf{C}_{XX}$ also involves only the assumption that the inverse of $\mathbf{w}_{xy}$ or of $\mathbf{c}_{xy}$ exists. Equation 48 or 49 is a generalization of the solution for S_X given in equation 12, Chapter 11, and in equation 22, Chapter 12.

Thus we have $\mathbf{C}_{XX}$ and $\mathbf{C}_{XY}$ in terms of known quantities. The equations of the preceding section can then be used to give $\mathbf{C}_{ZZ}$, $\mathbf{C}_{XZ}$, and $\mathbf{C}_{YZ}$. Substituting Z for Y and z for y in equation 37, we have

$$(50) \qquad \mathbf{C}_{XZ} = \mathbf{C}_{XX}\mathbf{w}_{xz}.$$

Substituting equation 49 in equation 50, we have

$$(51) \qquad \mathbf{C}_{XZ} = \mathbf{w}'^{-1}{}_{xy}(\mathbf{C}_{YY} - \mathbf{c}_{yy})\mathbf{w}^{-1}{}_{yx}\mathbf{w}_{xz} + \mathbf{c}_{xx}\mathbf{w}_{xz}.$$

Using equations 24 and 47, we have

$$(52) \qquad \mathbf{C}_{XZ} = \mathbf{w}'^{-1}{}_{xy}(\mathbf{C}_{YY} - \mathbf{c}_{yy})\mathbf{c}^{-1}{}_{yx}\mathbf{c}_{xz} + \mathbf{c}_{xz}.$$

Equation 52 gives the solution for $\mathbf{C}_{XZ}$ in terms of known quantities when complete information is available for the incidental selection variables (Y).

Equation 52 is a generalization of equation 31 of Chapter 12.

In a corresponding manner we may write the solution for $\mathbf{C}_{ZZ}$ by substituting Z for Y and z for y in equation 42, obtaining

$$(53) \qquad \mathbf{C}_{ZZ} = \mathbf{c}_{zz} + \mathbf{w}'_{zx}(\mathbf{C}_{XZ} - \mathbf{c}_{xz}).$$

Substituting equation 52 in equation 53, we have

$$(54) \qquad \mathbf{C}_{ZZ} = \mathbf{c}_{zz} + \mathbf{w}'_{zx}\mathbf{w}'^{-1}{}_{xy}(\mathbf{C}_{YY} - \mathbf{c}_{yy})\mathbf{c}^{-1}{}_{yx}\mathbf{c}_{xz}.$$

Using equation 26 and the rule that the inverse of a product is the product of the inverses in reverse order, we may write equation 54 in an alternative form as

$$(55) \qquad \mathbf{C}_{ZZ} = \mathbf{c}_{zz} + \mathbf{c'}_{zx}\mathbf{c'}^{-1}{}_{xy}(\mathbf{C}_{YY} - \mathbf{c}_{yy})\mathbf{c}^{-1}{}_{yx}\mathbf{c}_{xz}.$$

Equations 54 and 55 give $\mathbf{C}_{ZZ}$ in terms of known quantities when complete information is available on some of the incidental selection variables.

Equation 55 is the generalization of equation 28, Chapter 12.

The value of $\mathbf{C}_{YZ}$ may be found from the assumption that the partial correlations between Y and Z (X held constant) are equal to the partial correlations between y and z (x held constant). This matrix may be written by substituting Z for the *second* Y in equations 32, giving

$$(56) \qquad \mathbf{C}_{E_Y E_Z} = \mathbf{C}_{YZ} - \mathbf{C'}_{YX}\mathbf{W}_{XZ} = \mathbf{C}_{YZ} - \mathbf{W'}_{YX}\mathbf{C}_{XZ}.$$

In like manner, using the lower-case letters, we have

$$(57) \qquad \mathbf{c}_{e_y e_z} = \mathbf{c}_{yz} - \mathbf{c'}_{yx}\mathbf{w}_{xz} = \mathbf{c}_{yz} - \mathbf{w'}_{yx}\mathbf{c}_{xz}.$$

If we assume that $\mathbf{C}_{E_Y E_Z} = \mathbf{c}_{e_y e_z}$, use assumption equation 17, and solve for $\mathbf{C}_{YZ}$ from equations 56 and 57, we have

$$(58) \qquad \mathbf{C}_{YZ} = \mathbf{c}_{yz} + \mathbf{w'}_{yx}(\mathbf{C}_{XZ} - \mathbf{c}_{xz}).$$

Substituting equation 52 in equation 58, we have

$$(59) \qquad \mathbf{C}_{YZ} = \mathbf{c}_{yz} + \mathbf{w'}_{yx}\mathbf{w'}^{-1}{}_{xy}(\mathbf{C}_{YY} - \mathbf{c}_{yy})\mathbf{c}^{-1}{}_{yx}\mathbf{c}_{xz},$$

which simplifies to

$$(60) \qquad \mathbf{C}_{YZ} = \mathbf{c}_{yz} + (\mathbf{C}_{YY} - \mathbf{c}_{yy})\mathbf{c}^{-1}{}_{yx}\mathbf{c}_{xz}.$$

Equation 60 gives $\mathbf{C}_{YZ}$ in terms of known quantities.

Equation 60 is a generalization of the expression for R_{YZ} given in equation 37 of Chapter 12.

This completes the solution for the general case in which complete information is available for some of the variables subject to incidental selection. An exact solution is possible only when the number of incidental selection variables for which complete information is available is at least equal to the number of explicit selection variables, and when there is not complete linear dependence between these incidental selection variables and the explicit selection variables. The solution has been given for the five matrices $\mathbf{C}_{XX}$, $\mathbf{C}_{ZZ}$, $\mathbf{C}_{XZ}$, $\mathbf{C}_{XY}$, and $\mathbf{C}_{YZ}$ in terms of the known quantities $\mathbf{C}_{YY}$, $\mathbf{c}_{yy}$, $\mathbf{c}_{xx}$, $\mathbf{c}_{zz}$, $\mathbf{c}_{xy}$, $\mathbf{c}_{xz}$, and $\mathbf{c}_{yz}$.

It is also possible to solve a more general case in which complete information is assumed to be available for *some* of the incidental selection variables and *some* of the explicit selection variables. The detailed solution for this case will not be given. It can be solved by using the methods of this section to solve for the remaining explicit selection variables, and then using the methods in this and the preceding section to complete the solution.

4. Summary

In dealing with the general case of multivariate selection, X (or x) was used to designate the variables subject to explicit selection, and Y (or y) to designate the variables subject to incidental selection. Lower-case letters are used to designate the group for which complete information is available. Thus the variance-covariance matrices c_{xx} and c_{yy} are known, as well as the covariance matrix c_{xy}. Upper-case letters are used to designate the group for which only one variance-covariance matrix is known. That is, either C_{XX} or C_{YY} is known. The problem is to solve for the unknown variance-covariance matrix and for the covariance matrix C_{XY}.

It is assumed that the properties of the regression of Y on X are identical with the properties of the regression of y on x. This means that the gross score weights are equal for both groups, that is,

$$(17) \qquad\qquad \mathbf{W}_{XY} = \mathbf{w}_{xy}.$$

Since these are the least square weights, equation 17 may be rewritten as

$$(35) \qquad\qquad \mathbf{C}^{-1}{}_{XX}\mathbf{C}_{XY} = \mathbf{c}^{-1}{}_{xx}\mathbf{c}_{xy}.$$

The assumption of identical properties of the two regressions also means that the error made in estimating Y from X is the same as the error made in estimating y from x; and that the correlations among the Y's with the X's partialled out are the same as the correlations among the y's with the x's partialled out. These assumptions are given in the equation

$$(18) \qquad\qquad \mathbf{C}_{EE} = \mathbf{c}_{ee}.$$

Rewriting equation 18 explicitly for the least squares case, we have

$$(39) \qquad \mathbf{C}_{YY} - \mathbf{C}'_{YX}\mathbf{W}_{XY} = \mathbf{c}_{yy} - \mathbf{c}'_{yx}\mathbf{w}_{xy}.$$

For the case in which complete information is available on all the explicit selection variables, $\mathbf{C}_{XX}$ is known. The two unknowns $\mathbf{C}_{XY}$ and $\mathbf{C}_{YY}$ are given by

$$(37) \qquad\qquad \mathbf{C}_{XY} = \mathbf{C}_{XX}\mathbf{w}_{xy},$$

where

(24) $$\mathbf{w}_{xy} = \mathbf{c}^{-1}{}_{xx}\mathbf{c}_{xy},$$

and by

(42) $$\mathbf{C}_{YY} = \mathbf{c}_{yy} + \mathbf{w}'_{yx}(\mathbf{C}_{XY} - \mathbf{c}_{xy}).$$

For the case in which complete information is available on some of the incidental selection variables, it is necessary to distinguish between the incidental selection variables for which complete information is available (designated by Y or y) and the incidental selection variables that are known for only one group (designated by Z or z). The solution for the unknowns ($\mathbf{C}_{XY}$, $\mathbf{C}_{XX}$, $\mathbf{C}_{XZ}$, $\mathbf{C}_{ZZ}$, and $\mathbf{C}_{YZ}$) can be indicated in terms of the known quantities ($\mathbf{C}_{YY}$, $\mathbf{c}_{yy}$, $\mathbf{c}_{xx}$, $\mathbf{c}_{zz}$, $\mathbf{c}_{xy}$, $\mathbf{c}_{xz}$, and $\mathbf{c}_{yz}$). It should be noted that all these solutions are dependent upon the existence of the inverse of $\mathbf{w}_{xy}$ that is equivalent to the existence of the inverse of $\mathbf{c}_{xy}$, since

(47) $$\mathbf{w}^{-1}{}_{yx} = \mathbf{c}^{-1}{}_{yx}\mathbf{c}_{xx}.$$

That is, we are not considering the cases in which the number of y's is greater or less than the number of x's; nor are we considering the case in which the y's are linearly dependent upon the x's. For all the following solutions, it is assumed that the $\mathbf{c}_{xy}$ or $\mathbf{w}_{xy}$ is a square matrix with its rank equal to its order.

For this case we have

(46) $$\mathbf{C}_{XY} = \mathbf{w}'^{-1}{}_{xy}(\mathbf{C}_{YY} - \mathbf{c}_{yy}) + \mathbf{c}_{xy},$$

where $\mathbf{w}'^{-1}{}_{xy}$ is given as the transpose of equation 47. Using equations 46 and 47, we may write

(48) $$\mathbf{C}_{XX} = \mathbf{C}_{XY}\mathbf{w}^{-1}{}_{yx},$$

(50) $$\mathbf{C}_{XZ} = \mathbf{C}_{XX}\mathbf{w}_{xz},$$

(53) $$\mathbf{C}_{ZZ} = \mathbf{c}_{zz} + \mathbf{w}'_{zx}(\mathbf{C}_{XZ} - \mathbf{c}_{xz}),$$

and

(58) $$\mathbf{C}_{YZ} = \mathbf{c}_{yz} + \mathbf{w}'_{yx}(\mathbf{C}_{XZ} - \mathbf{c}_{xz})$$

or

(60) $$\mathbf{C}_{YZ} = \mathbf{c}_{yz} + (\mathbf{C}_{YY} - \mathbf{c}_{yy})\mathbf{c}^{-1}{}_{yx}\mathbf{c}_{xz}.$$

For these equations the value of $\mathbf{w}_{xz}$ may be found by substituting z for y in equation 24.

Problems

1. Express the weights (W_{XY}) of equation 3 as functions of the correlation matrices R_{XY} and R_{XX}. Show all steps in the derivation and all the necessary assumptions and definitions.

2. For the case in which complete information is available on the variables (x) subject to explicit selection, express the correlation matrices R_{XY} and R_{YY} as functions of the correlation matrices R_{XX}, r_{xx}, r_{yy}, and r_{xy}. Show all the steps in the derivation and all the necessary assumptions and definitions.

3. For the case in which complete information is available on the variables (Y), subject to incidental selection, express the correlation matrices R_{XY} and R_{XX} as functions of the correlation matrices R_{YY}, r_{xx}, r_{yy}, and r_{xy}. Show all the steps in the derivation and all the necessary assumptions and definitions.

14

A Statistical Criterion
for Parallel Tests

1. Introduction

As indicated in Chapters 2, 3, 6, 7, 8, and 9, parallel tests are tests that have equal means, equal variances, and equal intercorrelations. For any given set of experimental data, where the parallel forms of a test are given to a single group, there will be, even under the best conditions, some small sampling differences. To be certain that the tests may be regarded as parallel, it is necessary to have some statistical criterion that will show whether or not the means may be regarded as samples from a population in which the means are identical, the variances may be regarded as samples from a population in which variances are identical, and the intercorrelations may be regarded as samples from a population in which the correlations are identical. Such a test has recently been provided by Dr. S. S. Wilks (Wilks, 1946). Since two parallel forms have only one intercorrelation, it is possible in this case to check only for equality of means and of variances; hence we must consider the case of three or more parallel tests in order to demonstrate the statistical criterion for parallel tests.

We shall not give the derivation of this statistical criterion, which may be found in the foregoing reference but shall simply indicate the proper statistic to compute, and give the table for evaluating the significance of this statistic in the large sample case.[1]

In addition to equal means, variances, and reliabilities, parallel tests should have approximately equal validities for any given criterion. David Votaw has recently solved this problem as a part of his PhD dissertation in mathematical statistics at Princeton University (Votaw, 1947, 1948).

It should also be noted that, in addition to satisfying statistical criteria for being parallel, the tests should contain items dealing with the

---

[1] This material on tests of compound symmetry is given here with acknowledgements to and the permission of the editors of *The Annals of Mathematical Statistics*.

same subject matter, items of the same format, etc. In other words, the tests should be parallel as far as psychological judgment is concerned. At present, this criterion of psychological judgment is usually the only one used. The emphasis in this chapter is on the statistical criteria that the tests must satisfy in addition to the psychological criteria.

2. Basic statistics needed to compute the statistical criterion for parallel tests

Let us assume that k parallel forms of a test have been given to a population of N individuals. Assume further that the usual statistics have been obtained for such a set of data. These statistics are the mean of each test (M_g), the variance of each test $(s_g{}^2)$, and the co-variances for each pair of tests (c_{gh}).

It is then necessary to compute the following four quantities:

D, the determinant of the variance, covariance matrix,[1]

$$(1) \quad s^2 = \frac{\displaystyle\sum_{g=1}^{k} s_g{}^2}{k} \text{ , the average variance,}$$

$$(2) \quad r = \frac{\displaystyle\sum_{g \neq h=1}^{k} c_{gh}}{k(k-1)s^2} \text{ , the average correlation, computed as the average covariance divided by the average variance,}$$

and

$$(3) \quad v = \frac{\displaystyle\sum_{g=1}^{k} (M_g - M)^2}{k-1} \text{ , the variance of the means,}$$

where

$$(4) \quad M = \frac{\displaystyle\sum_{g=1}^{k} M_g}{k} \text{ , the mean of the test means.}$$

3. Statistical criterion for equality of means, equality of variances, and equality of covariances

Following Wilks' notation, we shall use L_{mvc} to designate the statistic appropriate for testing simultaneously the hypothesis that all means are equal, all variances are equal, and all covariances are equal.

[1] For the case of three parallel tests, the formulas are given without the use of determinantal notation. In order to deal with four or more parallel tests, it is necessary to know how to compute the value of determinants of order 4 or higher.

(5) $$L_{mvc} = \frac{D}{s^2[1 + (k - 1)r][s^2(1 - r) + v]^{k-1}}.$$

In the simplest case of three tests, this reduces to

(6) $$L_{mvc} = \frac{s_1^2 s_2^2 s_3^2[1 + 2r_{12}r_{13}r_{23} - r_{12}^2 - r_{13}^2 - r_{23}^2]}{s^2(1 + 2r)(s^2 - s^2 r + v)^2}.$$

Small sample tables for evaluating this statistic are given by Wilks (1946). In the large sample case, according to Wilks, the statistic $-N \log_e L_{mvc}$ is approximately distributed as chi-square with $(k/2)(k + 3) - 3$ degrees of freedom when the hypothesis of equal means, equal variances, and equal covariances is true. We are comparing an hypothesis using k means, k variances, and $(k/2)(k - 1)$ covariances, a total of $2k + (k/2)(k - 1)$ parameters, with an hypothesis using only three parameters; hence the degrees of freedom will be

$$2k + (k/2)(k - 1) - 3 = (k/2)(k + 3) - 3.$$

For three tests, this reduces to $9 - 3 = 6$ degrees of freedom. The statistic L_{mvc} varies between zero and unity. If the means are identical in the sample, the variances identical, and the covariances identical, L_{mvc} equals one. As L_{mvc} approaches one, the quantity $-N \log L_{mvc}$ approaches zero. The accompanying table gives the 5 per cent and 1 per cent points so that, if the quantity $-N \log_{10} L_{mvc}$ calculated from a given set of data is less than the value given in the 5 per cent column for the appropriate number of tests (k), we may consider that the tests are parallel.[1] If the value of $-N \log_{10} L_{mvc}$ from the data is greater than that in the 1 per cent column for appropriate k, there is less than one chance in a hundred that such a sample would be drawn from a population in which means were equal, variances were equal, and covariances were equal. Under such circumstances we should conclude that the tests were not parallel in all respects.

If L_{mvc} is sufficiently near unity to support the hypothesis that the means are identical, the variances are identical, and the covariances are identical, the population is characterized by one common mean, one common variance, and a common correlation (in this case reliability)

---

[1] Table 1 is given in terms of common logarithms (that is, to the base 10) instead of in terms of the natural logarithms (to the base e), since extensive tables of common logarithms are more generally available than tables of the natural logarithms.

coefficient. Using the subscript zero to indicate the best estimates of these parameters, we have

(7) $$M_0 = M,$$

(8) $$s_0{}^2 = s^2 + \frac{v(k-1)}{k},$$

and

(9) $$r_0 = \frac{s^2 r - \dfrac{v}{k}}{s_0{}^2},$$

where k is the number of parallel tests and the other terms are defined by equations 1, 2, 3, and 4.

It should be noted that the use commonly made of chi-square and other significance tests is to test an hypothesis that the experimenter hopes is incorrect. The term "significant difference" means that the data diverge significantly from what would be expected in view of the hypothesis being tested. In other words, the experimenter tests the hypothesis that "$A = B$" while arranging the experimental conditions to the best of his ability so that $A \neq B$. The use of the criterion for parallel tests is an instance of testing an hypothesis that the investigator hopes will be verified. Since considerable effort has been expended to select items and establish norms so that the tests will be parallel, we hope that the means, variances, and covariances will be about equal. Therefore what we hope to find in this test is what would commonly be called an "insignificant difference."

Whenever the ideational structure of any scientific field has developed sufficiently, investigators will be testing hypotheses that they believe are true; hence they will be hoping to find insignificant differences between the data they get and those to be expected from the hypothesis. The current search by psychologists for significant differences is merely a concomitant of the fact that they have no precise hypotheses that can be tested; hence typically the investigator does his best to shape conditions so that groups A and B will be different, and yet tests the hypothesis that "$A = B$" hoping to find that it is not adequate for the data. Only rarely do we find the next step, of devising an hypothesis that presumably fits the data, testing this hypothesis, and finding a "nonsignificant difference," which indicates that an acceptable hypothesis has been found.

4. Criterion for equality of variances and equality of covariances

If, on testing for the hypothesis that means, variances, and covariances are equal, we find a significant difference (a small value of L_{mvc} or a relatively large value of $-N \log_e L_{mvc}$), there would then be some interest in determining whether or not that difference is attributable solely to differences in means. If it can be shown that the variances are equal and that the covariances are equal, while the means are different, it is easy to adjust test scores (by adding or subtracting a suitable constant) so that the means of the adjusted scores will be equal. It should be noted that a test for equality of means cannot be made on data from the group of subjects used to compute the adjustment. However, if the norms established from one group are used to adjust test scores for a second group, the test for equality of means of these converted scores could be made on the second group. In order to determine whether the difficulty is with the means alone or with variances and covariances, or both, two other statistics are of interest, one for testing equality of variances and equality of covariances and another for testing equality of means. The statistic (L_{vc}) for testing equality of variances and equality of covariances is like (L_{mvc}) given in section 3 except that the term v is omitted from the denominator:

(10) $$L_{vc} = \frac{D}{s^2[1 + (k - 1)r][s^2(1 - r)]^{k-1}}.$$

When there are three tests, we have

(11) $$L_{vc} = \frac{s_1^2 s_2^2 s_3^2 [1 + 2r_{12}r_{13}r_{23} - r_{12}^2 - r_{13}^2 - r_{23}^2]}{s^6(1 + 2r)(1 - r)^2}.$$

The quantity $-N \log_e L_{vc}$ is approximately distributed for large samples according to the chi-square law with $(k/2)(k + 1) - 2$ degrees of freedom, when the hypothesis is true. For three tests, $-N \log_e L_{vc}$ is approximately distributed for large samples according to the chi-square law with *four* degrees of freedom. L_{vc} varies between zero and one. As the variances become more alike and the covariances become more alike, the value of L_{vc} approaches unity, or the value of $-N \log L_{vc}$ approaches zero. If the value of $-N \log_{10} L_{vc}$ is smaller than that indicated in the 5 per cent column for appropriate k, we may conclude that the tests are parallel except possibly for differences in means. If the value of $-N \log_{10} L_{vc}$ is larger than that indicated in the 1 per cent column for appropriate k, the tests are not parallel as far as variances and covariances are concerned.

If the test with L_{mvc} indicated that the tests could not be regarded as parallel, whereas the test with L_{vc} showed that the tests were parallel as far as variances and covariances were concerned, the population represented by the data is characterized by $k + 2$ parameters. These are the k means, one variance, and one reliability coefficient. The best estimates of these parameters are, respectively, the test means (M_g), the average variance, s^2 (see equation 1), and the average correlation r, as given in equation 2.

If, after finding a "significant" L_{mvc}, we also find a significant L_{vc}, this shows that equating the means still would not make the tests parallel. Either the variances, the covariances, or both are significantly different. It would be desirable next to test covariances and variances separately for significance, for, if the covariances are not significantly different, both means and variances can be brought into line by an appropriate linear transformation. However, if the covariances are significantly different, it is not possible to set up norms that will "equate" the tests. Unfortunately, since it is not yet possible to test the significance of the difference of covariances independently of similarities or differences in variances, for the present this step must be omitted. If we have two samples to which the tests have been given, it is possible to make the equivalent of a test of covariances independently of variances by the following procedure. Compute the standard deviations of both forms (s_x and s_y) for the first sample. If the y-scores are multiplied by s_x/s_y, the standard deviation of the y-scores will be identical with that of the x-scores for that same sample. Now regardless of the standard deviations of x and y in the second sample, multiply all the y-scores by the multiplier (s_x/s_y) *determined from the first sample*. The test with L_{vc} may then be made, using the x-scores and the transformed y-scores *both from the second sample*. If the test L_{vc} indicates that the forms are parallel, we may conclude that, if the multiplier s_x/s_y is used for the y-scores, the forms are parallel. If the test with L_{vc} shows that the forms are not parallel, the difficulty probably lies with the covariances, since standard deviations were equated.

Suppose, on the other hand, that, after finding a significant L_{mvc}, we find homogeneity when testing with L_{vc}. It is then reasonable to suppose that the difference in means was responsible for the heterogeneity shown by the test L_{mvc}. If subsequently the test by L_m shows that the means are heterogeneous, we have a consistent set of results and can conclude that the variances and covariances are equal, and that the heterogeneity of the means is the reason for failure to show homogeneity when testing with L_m or L_{mvc}. If after failing to find a sufficiently large value of L_{mvc}, we find large values for both L_{vc} and L_m, the results are inconsistent. In this sort of instance (which is not impossible) we are dealing with some peculiar borderline case in which the means alone or the variances and covariances alone show homogeneity. With the increased degrees of freedom for testing the more comprehensive hypothesis, however, we find a significant difference. In such a case the only conclusion we can reach is that the tests are not parallel tests, but that the difficulty is not clearly indicated as due to mean differences or to variance, covariance differences.

5. Statistical criterion for equality of means

For testing equality of means (if L_{vc} is nonsignificant), we use

$$(12) \qquad L_m = \frac{s^2(1-r)}{s^2(1-r)+v}.$$

The quantity $-N\,(k-1)\log_e L_m$ is distributed approximately as chi-square with $k-1$ degrees of freedom for large samples when the hypothesis is true. The value of L_m is unity if the sample means are identical, and approaches zero as the sample means diverge. The quantity $-N(k-1)\log L_m$ is zero if the sample means are identical, and increases as the sample means diverge. The 5 per cent and 1 per cent points for $-N(k-1)\log_{10} L_m$ are given in the last two columns of Table 1.

Wilks (1946) has shown that

$$(13) \qquad L_{mvc} = L_{vc} \cdot L_m{}^{k-1}.$$

This relationship may be used as a partial arithmetical check when all three values are computed.

We can also conclude from equation 13 and from Table 1 that, if L_{vc} and L_m are *each* small enough to give $-N\log_{10} L$ values above the 5 per cent or the 1 per cent points, the value of L_{mvc} will be small enough to give a value of $-N\log_{10} L_{mvc}$ that will be above the 5 per cent or 1 per cent point, as the case may be. It will be noted that the 5 per cent and 1 per cent points for $-N\log_{10} L_{mvc}$ are in each case less than the sum of the two corresponding values for $-N\log_{10} L_{vc}$ and $-N(k-1)\log_{10} L_m$. That is, if the means tested by themselves are significantly different and if also the variance-covariance matrix tested by itself shows a significant difference at the 1 per cent or 5 per cent level, the test with L_{mvc} must show a significant difference unless errors were made in the computations.

If L_{mvc} shows that the tests may be regarded as parallel, whereas one and only one of the other tests (either L_{vc} or L_m) indicates a significant difference, again we are dealing with a perfectly possible but borderline case, and must conclude that the tests are not parallel either with respect to means or with respect to variances and covariances.

TABLE 1

Approximate 5 per Cent and 1 per Cent Points for $-N \log_{10} L_{mvc}$, $-N \log_{10} L_{vc}$, and $-N (k-1) \log_{10} L_m$ for $k = 2, 3, 4, 5, 6$

k	d.f.	$-N \log_{10} L_{mvc}$		d.f.	$-N \log_{10} L_{vc}$		d.f.	$-N (k-1) \log_{10} L_m$	
		5 per cent	1 per cent		5 per cent	1 per cent		5 per cent	1 per cent
2	2	2.60206	4.00000	1	1.66832	2.88150	1	1.66832	2.88150
3	6	5.4685	7.3013	4	4.12047	5.7660	2	2.60206	4.00000
4	11	8.5448	10.7379	8	6.7347	8.7251	3	3.39389	4.9270
5	17	11.9809	14.5092	13	9.7117	12.0249	4	4.12047	5.7660
6	24	15.8149	18.6659	19	13.0912	15.7175	5	4.8079	6.5519

Adapted from Wilks (1946), page 266.

If $N \geqq 100$, this table is sufficiently accurate. If $N < 100$, see Wilks (1946) for a detailed statement of the accuracy of this table, and for small sample methods.

Note that the entries in this table are given in terms of logarithms to the base 10. Hence these entries are 0.43429 times the entries in Wilks (1946), page 266.

6. Illustrative problem for hypotheses H_{mvc}, H_{vc}, and H_m

The computation of the three criteria is illustrated in the following example. Three parallel tests (1, 2, and 3) are given to 130 subjects.

			1		2		3
Mean			27.8		28.3		27.9
Standard Deviation			9.9		10.1		10.4
		r_{12}	.93	r_{13}	.92	r_{23}	.90

M_g		$(M_g - M)^2$	s_g	s_g^2	$r_{gh}s_g s_h$
	27.8	.04	9.9	98.01	92.9907
	28.3	.09	10.1	102.01	94.7232
	27.9	.01	10.4	108.16	94.5360
Σ	84.0	.14		308.18	282.2499
M	28.0	(.07) * $= v$		$s^2 = 102.73$	$94.0833 = s^2 r$

* Divided by 2. The other sums are divided by 3.

$$D = s_1{}^2 s_2{}^2 s_3{}^2 (1 + 2r_{12}r_{13}r_{23} - r_{12}{}^2 - r_{13}{}^2 - r_{23}{}^2) = 20{,}308.3859.$$

$$s^2(1 - r) = 8.6467 \qquad [s^2(1 - r)]^2 = 74.7654 \qquad s^2(1 + 2r) = 290.8967.$$

$$s^2(1 - r) + v = 8.7167 \qquad [s^2(1 - r) + v]^2 = 75.9809.$$

$$L_{mvc} = \frac{D}{s^2(1 + 2r)[s^2(1 - r) + v]^2} = .9188.$$

$$-N \log_{10} L_{mvc} = 4.78.$$

$$L_{vc} = \frac{D}{s^2(1 + 2r)[s^2(1 - r)]^2} = .9338.$$

$$-N \log_{10} L_{vc} = 3.87.$$

$$L_m = \frac{s^2(1 - r)}{s^2(1 - r) + v} = .9920.$$

$$-N(k - 1) \log_{10} L_m = 0.91.$$

By reference to Table 1 it is clear that all three criteria show the three tests to be parallel. The data are in agreement with the hypothesis that the means are equal, the variances are equal, and the covariances are equal.

7. Hypotheses of compound symmetry

The criterion devised by Wilks (1946) applies only to means, variances, and covariances of parallel tests. In addition, parallel tests should have equal validities for predicting any criterion. The statistical criteria for "compound symmetry" presented by Votaw (1948) include a statistical test for equal validities of a set of parallel tests. We shall present here only a restricted case of one form of compound symmetry, the case where we are interested in two sets of parallel tests (x_g and z_g) and the criteria y_g. Let us say that there are k parallel tests in the x-set, f parallel tests in the z-set, and b *different* criteria to be predicted. This set of $b + k + f$ tests given to N persons results in a variance-covariance matrix and its determinant $\hat{D}$ given in equation 14.

Equation (14)

$$
\hat{D} =
\begin{vmatrix}
s_{y_1}^2 & c_{y_1 y_2} & \cdots & c_{y_1 y_b} & c_{y_1 x_1} & c_{y_1 x_2} & \cdots & c_{y_1 x_k} & c_{y_1 z_1} & c_{y_1 z_2} & \cdots & c_{y_1 z_f} \\
c_{y_2 y_1} & s_{y_2}^2 & \cdots & c_{y_2 y_b} & c_{y_2 x_1} & c_{y_2 x_2} & \cdots & c_{y_2 x_k} & c_{y_2 z_1} & c_{y_2 z_2} & \cdots & c_{y_2 z_f} \\
\vdots & \vdots & & \vdots & \vdots & \vdots & & \vdots & \vdots & \vdots & & \vdots \\
c_{y_b y_1} & c_{y_b y_2} & \cdots & s_{y_b}^2 & c_{y_b x_1} & c_{y_b x_2} & \cdots & c_{y_b x_k} & c_{y_b z_1} & c_{y_b z_2} & \cdots & c_{y_b z_f} \\
c_{x_1 y_1} & c_{x_1 y_2} & \cdots & c_{x_1 y_b} & s_{x_1}^2 & c_{x_1 x_2} & \cdots & c_{x_1 x_k} & c_{x_1 z_1} & c_{x_1 z_2} & \cdots & c_{x_1 z_f} \\
c_{x_2 y_1} & c_{x_2 y_2} & \cdots & c_{x_2 y_b} & c_{x_2 x_1} & s_{x_2}^2 & \cdots & c_{x_2 x_k} & c_{x_2 z_1} & c_{x_2 z_2} & \cdots & c_{x_2 z_f} \\
\vdots & \vdots & & \vdots & \vdots & \vdots & & \vdots & \vdots & \vdots & & \vdots \\
c_{x_k y_1} & c_{x_k y_2} & \cdots & c_{x_k y_b} & c_{x_k x_1} & c_{x_k x_2} & \cdots & s_{x_k}^2 & c_{x_k z_1} & c_{x_k z_2} & \cdots & c_{x_k z_f} \\
c_{z_1 y_1} & c_{z_1 y_2} & \cdots & c_{z_1 y_b} & c_{z_1 x_1} & c_{z_1 x_2} & \cdots & c_{z_1 x_k} & s_{z_1}^2 & c_{z_1 z_2} & \cdots & c_{z_1 z_f} \\
c_{z_2 y_1} & c_{z_2 y_2} & \cdots & c_{z_2 y_b} & c_{z_2 x_1} & c_{z_2 x_2} & \cdots & c_{z_2 x_k} & c_{z_2 z_1} & s_{z_2}^2 & \cdots & c_{z_2 z_f} \\
\vdots & \vdots & & \vdots & \vdots & \vdots & & \vdots & \vdots & \vdots & & \vdots \\
c_{z_f y_1} & c_{z_f y_2} & \cdots & c_{z_f y_b} & c_{z_f x_1} & c_{z_f x_2} & \cdots & c_{z_f x_k} & c_{z_f z_1} & c_{z_f z_2} & \cdots & s_{z_f}^2
\end{vmatrix},
$$

where y_g, y_h $(g, h = 1, 2, \cdots b)$ designates the criterion variables,

 x_g, x_h $(g, h = 1, 2, \cdots k)$ designates the parallel tests of the x-set,

 z_g, z_h $(g, h = 1, 2, \cdots f)$ designates the parallel tests of the z-set,

 s designates a standard deviation,

 c designates a covariance term,

 b designates the number of criterion variables,

 k designates the number of parallel tests in the x-set,

 f designates the number of parallel tests in the z-set.

We shall consider three hypotheses ($\hat{H}_{mvc}$, $\hat{H}_{vc}$, and $\hat{H}_m$) regarding the relationships among the set of tests designated in equation 14.

Let $\hat{H}_{mvc}$ designate the hypothesis that, for each set of parallel tests, the population means are equal, the population variances are equal, the population covariances are equal, and the population covariances with any single criterion variable are equal; between any two sets of parallel tests, the population covariances are equal. For the case of two sets of parallel tests and b different criterion variables that is indicated in equation 14, let μ_{y_g}, μ_{x_g}, and μ_{z_g} designate population means, $\sigma_{y_g}^2$, $\sigma_{x_g}^2$, and $\sigma_{z_g}^2$ designate population variances, and let ζ with appropriate subscripts designate a population covariance. In terms of this notation, hypothesis $\hat{H}_{mvc}$ asserts that:

1. All μ_{x_g} $(g = 1, 2, \cdots k)$ are equal.

2. All μ_{z_g} ($g = 1, 2, \cdots f$) are equal.
3. All $\sigma_{x_g}^2$ ($g = 1, 2, \cdots k$) are equal.
4. All $\sigma_{z_g}^2$ ($g = 1, 2, \cdots f$) are equal.
5. All $\zeta_{x_g x_h}$ ($g \neq h = 1, 2, \cdots k$) are equal.
6. All $\zeta_{z_g z_h}$ ($g \neq h = 1, 2, \cdots f$) are equal.
7. All $\zeta_{x_g z_h}$ ($g = 1, 2, \cdots k; h = 1, 2, \cdots f$) are equal.
8. For any fixed value of h ($h = 1, 2, \cdots b$), all $\zeta_{x_g y_h}$ ($g = 1, 2, \cdots k$) are equal.
9. For any fixed value of h ($h = 1, 2, \cdots b$), all $\zeta_{z_g y_h}$ ($g = 1, 2, \cdots f$) are equal.

Let $\hat{H}_{vc}$ designate the hypothesis that, for each set of parallel tests, the population variances are equal, the population covariances are equal, and the population covariances with any single criterion variable are equal; between any two sets of parallel tests, the population covariances are equal. This hypothesis is identical with $\hat{H}_{mvc}$, except that no restrictions are imposed on the means.

Let $\hat{H}_m$ designate the hypothesis that, for each set of parallel tests, the population means are equal, given that $\hat{H}_{vc}$ is true.

8. Basic statistics needed for tests of compound symmetry

In addition to the determinant of equation 14, and the variances and covariances indicated in its elements, the following quantities are needed for the tests of compound symmetry represented by hypotheses $\hat{H}_{mvc}$, $\hat{H}_{vc}$, and $\hat{H}_m$.

The mean for each of the $k + f$ predictor tests and the grand mean for each of the two sets is needed as follows:

$$(15) \qquad \overline{X}_{\cdot g} = \frac{\sum\limits_{i=1}^{N} X_{ig}}{N},$$

$$(16) \qquad \overline{X}_{\cdot\cdot} = \frac{\sum\limits_{g=1}^{k} \sum\limits_{i=1}^{N} X_{ig}}{kN},$$

$$(17) \qquad \overline{Z}_{\cdot g} = \frac{\sum\limits_{i=1}^{N} Z_{ig}}{N},$$

$$(18) \qquad \overline{Z}_{\cdot\cdot} = \frac{\sum\limits_{g=1}^{f} \sum\limits_{i=1}^{N} Z_{ig}}{fN}.$$

The variance of each set of means is also needed:

$$(19) \qquad v_x = \frac{\sum\limits_{g=1}^{k} (\overline{X}_{\cdot g} - \overline{X}_{\cdot\cdot})^2}{k - 1},$$

$$(20) \qquad v_z = \frac{\sum\limits_{g=1}^{f} (\overline{Z}_{\cdot g} - \overline{Z}_{\cdot\cdot})^2}{f - 1}.$$

The averages for certain sets of variances and covariances are needed, as follows:

$$(21) \qquad \bar{c}_{y_g \bar{x}} = \frac{\sum\limits_{h=1}^{k} c_{y_g x_h}}{k},$$

$$(22) \qquad \bar{c}_{y_g \bar{z}} = \frac{\sum\limits_{h=1}^{f} c_{y_g z_h}}{f},$$

$$(23) \qquad u_x = \frac{\sum\limits_{h=1}^{k} s_{x_h}^{\,2}}{k},$$

$$(24) \qquad u_z = \frac{\sum\limits_{h=1}^{f} s_{z_h}^{\,2}}{f},$$

$$(25) \qquad w_x = \frac{\sum\limits_{g \neq h=1}^{k} c_{x_g x_h}}{k(k - 1)},$$

$$(26) \qquad w_z = \frac{\sum\limits_{g \neq h=1}^{f} c_{z_g z_h}}{f(f - 1)},$$

$$(27) \qquad \bar{c}_{\overline{xz}} = \frac{\sum\limits_{g=1}^{k} \sum\limits_{h=1}^{f} c_{x_g z_h}}{kf}.$$

Using the matrix of *criterion* intercorrelations from equation 14, and the averages defined in equations 21 to 27, we define the determinant $\hat{B}$, of order $b + 2$, as follows:

Equation (28)

$$
\hat{B} = \begin{vmatrix}
s_{y_1}^2 & c_{y_1y_2} & \cdots & c_{y_1y_b} & \bar{c}_{y_1\bar{x}}\sqrt{k} & \bar{c}_{y_1\bar{z}}\sqrt{f} \\
c_{y_2y_1} & s_{y_2}^2 & \cdots & c_{y_2y_b} & \bar{c}_{y_2\bar{x}}\sqrt{k} & \bar{c}_{y_2\bar{z}}\sqrt{f} \\
\vdots & \vdots & & \vdots & \vdots & \vdots \\
c_{y_by_1} & c_{y_by_2} & \cdots & s_{y_b}^2 & \bar{c}_{y_b\bar{x}}\sqrt{k} & \bar{c}_{y_b\bar{z}}\sqrt{f} \\
\bar{c}_{y_1\bar{x}}\sqrt{k} & \bar{c}_{y_2\bar{x}}\sqrt{k} & \cdots & \bar{c}_{y_b\bar{x}}\sqrt{k} & [u_x + (k-1)w_x] & \bar{c}_{\bar{x}\bar{z}}\sqrt{kf} \\
\bar{c}_{y_1\bar{z}}\sqrt{f} & \bar{c}_{y_2\bar{z}}\sqrt{f} & \cdots & \bar{c}_{y_b\bar{z}}\sqrt{f} & \bar{c}_{\bar{x}\bar{z}}\sqrt{kf} & u_z + (f-1)w_z
\end{vmatrix}.
$$

9. The criterion for hypothesis $\hat{H}_{mvc}$

The sample criterion for $\hat{H}_{mvc}$ is given by

$$
(29) \qquad \hat{L}_{mvc} = \frac{\hat{D}}{\hat{B}[u_x - w_x + v_x]^{k-1}[u_z - w_z + v_z]^{f-1}}.
$$

If N is large and $\hat{H}_{mvc}$ is true, the quantity $-N \log_e \hat{L}_{mvc}$ is distributed approximately as chi-square with $\dfrac{k+f}{2}(k+f+3) + b(k+f-2) - 7$ degrees of freedom. If only one set of parallel tests is available, for the test with $\hat{L}_{mvc}$ we have $(k/2)(k+3) + b(k-1) - 3$ degrees of freedom. The general formulation for any number of sets of parallel tests with N large is given by Votaw (1948), page 467.

For the special case of two parallel tests designated by subscripts 1 and 2 and a single criterion variable (y), we have

$$
(30) \qquad \hat{L}_{mvc} = \frac{s_y^2 s_1^2 s_2^2 (1 + 2r_{y1}r_{y2}r_{12} - r_{y1}^2 - r_{y2}^2 - r_{12}^2)}{[s_y^2(u+w) - 2\bar{c}_{y\bar{x}}^2][u - w + v]},
$$

where $u = (s_1^2 + s_2^2)/2$,

$\qquad w = r_{12}s_1s_2$,

$$
v = \frac{(\bar{X}_1 - \bar{X}_2)^2}{2},
$$

$$
\bar{c}_{y\bar{x}} = \frac{c_{yx_1} + c_{yx_2}}{2}.
$$

If N is large and $\hat{H}_{mvc}$ is true, the quantity $-N \log_e \hat{L}_{mvc}$ is distributed approximately as chi-square with $5 + 1 - 3 = 3$ degrees of freedom.

When $\hat{L}_{mvc}$ is sufficiently near unity to support the hypothesis $\hat{H}_{mvc}$, the best estimates (shown below by 0 subscripts) of the common parameters indicated in conditions 1 to 9 for $\hat{H}_{mvc}$, are as follows.

(31) $$\overline{X}_0 = \overline{X}..$$ (see equation 16),

(32) $$\overline{Z}_0 = \overline{Z}..$$ (see equation 18),

(33) $$s_{x_0}^2 = u_x + \frac{v_x(k-1)}{k}$$ (see equations 19 and 23),

(34) $$s_{z_0}^2 = u_z + \frac{v_z(f-1)}{f}$$ (see equations 20 and 24),

(35) $$r_{x_0 x_0} = \frac{(w_x - v_x/k)}{s_{x_0}^2}$$ (see equations 19 and 25),

(36) $$r_{z_0 z_0} = \frac{(w_z - v_z/f)}{s_{z_0}^2}$$ (see equations 20 and 26),

(37) $$r_{x_0 z_0} = \frac{\bar{c}_{\bar{x}\bar{z}}}{s_{x_0} s_{z_0}}$$ (see equation 27),

(38) $$r_{x_0 y_g} = \frac{\bar{c}_{y_g \bar{x}}}{s_{y_g} s_{x_0}}$$ (see equation 21),

(39) $$r_{z_0 y_g} = \frac{\bar{c}_{y_g \bar{z}}}{s_{y_g} s_{z_0}}$$ (see equation 22).

10. The criterion for hypothesis $\hat{H}_{vc}$

If the value of $\hat{L}_{mvc}$ is small (that is, the value of $-N \log_e \hat{L}_{mvc}$ is large), $\hat{H}_{mvc}$ cannot be accepted. In this case we may wish to see if the differences in *means* of the parallel tests account for the failure to satisfy $\hat{H}_{mvc}$. In order to do this we next investigate hypothesis $\hat{H}_{vc}$. For this test the sample criterion is taken as

(40) $$\hat{L}_{vc} = \frac{\hat{D}}{\hat{B}[u_x - w_x]^{k-1}[u_z - w_z]^{f-1}}.$$

If N is large and $\hat{H}_{vc}$ is true, the quantity $-N \log_e \hat{L}_{vc}$ is distributed approximately as chi-square with $\dfrac{k+f}{2}(k+f+1) + b(k+f-2) - 5$ degrees of freedom. If only one set of parallel tests is available, for the test with $\hat{L}_{vc}$ we have $(k/2)(k+1) + b(k-1) - 2$ degrees of freedom. The general formulation for any number of tests with N large is given by Votaw (1948), page 467.

For the special case of one criterion variable (y) and two parallel tests (designated by subscripts 1 and 2), we have

$$(41) \qquad \hat{L}_{vc} = \frac{s_y^2 s_1^2 s_2^2 [1 + 2r_{y1}r_{y2}r_{12} - r_{y1}^2 - r_{y2}^2 - r_{12}^2]}{[s_y^2(u_x + w_x) - 2\bar{c}_{y\bar{x}}^2][u_x - w_x]},$$

where $u_x = (s_{x_1}^2 + s_{x_2}^2)/2$ (see equation 23),

$\qquad\quad w_x = c_{x_1 x_2}$ (see equation 25), and

$\qquad\quad \bar{c}_{y\bar{x}} = (c_{yx_1} + c_{yx_2})/2$ (see equation 21).

In this case, when N is large and $\hat{H}_{vc}$ is true, the quantity $-N \log_e \hat{L}_{vc}$ is distributed approximately as chi-square with $3 + 1 - 2 = 2$ degrees of freedom.

If the test with $\hat{L}_{mvc}$ indicated that the tests could *not* be regarded as parallel, whereas the test with $\hat{L}_{vc}$ indicated that the tests could be regarded as parallel as far as variances and covariances were concerned, the population represented by the data is characterized by:

1. A mean for each test, giving $k + f + b$ means, represented by $\overline{X}_g$, $\overline{Z}_g$, and $\overline{Y}_g$.
2. A variance for each criterion variable $(s_{y_g}^2)$ and the two variances u_x and u_z, given by equations 23 and 24.
3. Two reliability coefficients given by w_x/u_x and w_z/u_z (see equations 23 to 26).
4. The intercorrelation r_{xz} given by $\bar{c}_{\overline{xz}}/\sqrt{u_x u_z}$ (see equations 23, 24, and 27).
5. Two validity coefficients for each y_g given by $\bar{c}_{y_g\bar{x}}/(s_{y_g}\sqrt{u_x})$ and $\bar{c}_{y_g\bar{z}}/(s_{y_g}\sqrt{u_z})$ (see equations 21 and 22).

11. The criterion for hypothesis $\hat{H}_m$

If the test with $\hat{L}_{mvc}$ has shown "significant" differences, whereas the test with $\hat{L}_{vc}$ substantiates hypothesis $\hat{H}_{vc}$, the presumption would be that the tests might be regarded as parallel except for the values of the means. *If $\hat{H}_{vc}$ is true*, it is possible to test the means directly. The criterion for hypothesis $\hat{H}_m$ (assuming $\hat{H}_{vc}$) is

$$(42) \qquad \hat{L}_m = \frac{(u_x - w_x)^{k-1}(u_z - w_z)^{f-1}}{(u_x - w_x + v_x)^{k-1}(u_z - w_z + v_z)^{f-1}}.$$

If N is large and $\hat{H}_m$ is true, the quantity $-N \log_e \hat{L}_m$ is distributed approximately as chi-square with $k + f - 2$ degrees of freedom.

If only one set of parallel tests is used, for the test with $\hat{L}_m$ we have $k - 1$ degrees of freedom. The general formulation for any number of sets of parallel tests with N large is given by Votaw (1948), page 467.

As an arithmetical check it should be noted that

(43) $$\hat{L}_m \cdot \hat{L}_{vc} = \hat{L}_{mvc}.$$

12. Illustrative problem for compound symmetry

The computation of the three criteria for compound symmetry is illustrated in the following example. Information is available on three parallel tests (1, 2, and 3) and a criterion (y) for 100 subjects. The correlations, means, and standard deviations are:

	y	1	2	3
y	1.00	.64	.66	.65
1	.64	1.00	.88	.92
2	.66	.88	1.00	.90
3	.65	.92	.90	1.00
Standard deviation	21.	10.	9.	12.
Mean	191.	118.	117.	119.

The determinant of the correlation matrix is .014 420 64. Multiplying this by the product of the four variances gives the determinant of the variance-covariance matrix (D),

$$D = 144 \times 441 \times 81 \times 100 \times .01442064 = 7,417,723.$$

The determinant $B = (441)(299.5) - (141\sqrt{3})^2 = 72,436.5,$

$(u_x - w_x + v_x)^{k-1} = (108.3 - 95.6 + 1)^2 = 187.69,$

$(u_x - w_x)^{k-1} = (108.3 - 95.6)^2 = 161.29.$

From the foregoing results, we have

$$\hat{L}_{mvc} = \frac{7,417,723}{(72,436.5)(187.69)} = .5456,$$

$$\hat{L}_{vc} = \frac{7,417,723}{(72,436.5)(161.29)} = .6349,$$

$$\hat{L}_m = \frac{161.29}{187.69} = .8593.$$

Table 2 shows the 5 per cent and 1 per cent points for $-N \log_e \hat{L}$, which is chi-square, and also the corresponding 5 per cent and 1 per cent

TABLE 2

APPROXIMATE 5 PER CENT AND 1 PER CENT POINTS FOR $-N \log_e L$, AND ALSO FOR
$-N \log_{10} L$ FOR DEGREES OF FREEDOM 1 TO 30

	$-N \log_e L$		$-N \log_{10} L$	
d.f.	5 per cent	1 per cent	5 per cent	1 per cent
1	3.84	6.64	1.67	2.88
2	5.99	9.21	2.60	4.00
3	7.82	11.34	3.39	4.93
4	9.49	13.28	4.12	5.77
5	11.07	15.09	4.81	6.55
6	12.59	16.81	5.47	7.30
7	14.07	18.48	6.11	8.02
8	15.51	20.09	6.73	8.72
9	16.92	21.67	7.35	9.41
10	18.31	23.21	7.95	10.08
11	19.68	24.72	8.54	10.74
12	21.03	26.22	9.13	11.39
13	22.36	27.69	9.71	12.03
14	23.68	29.14	10.28	12.66
15	25.00	30.58	10.86	13.28
16	26.30	32.00	11.42	13.90
17	27.59	33.41	11.98	14.51
18	28.87	34.80	12.54	15.11
19	30.14	36.19	13.09	15.72
20	31.41	37.57	13.64	16.32
21	32.67	38.93	14.19	16.91
22	33.92	40.29	14.73	17.50
23	35.17	41.64	15.27	18.08
24	36.42	42.98	15.82	18.67
25	37.65	44.31	16.35	19.24
26	38.88	45.64	16.89	19.82
27	40.11	46.96	17.42	20.39
28	41.34	48.28	17.95	20.97
29	42.56	49.59	18.48	21.54
30	43.77	50.89	19.01	22.10

For d.f. larger than 30,

$$x = \sqrt{2\chi^2} - \sqrt{2(\text{d.f.}) - 1}$$

is distributed approximately as the unit normal curve. For x the 5 per cent point is 1.645, and the 1 per cent point is 2.326.

The values in columns 2 and 3 are chi-square values; those in columns 4 and 5 are 0.43429 times the corresponding chi-square value.

points for $-N \log_{10} \hat{L}$, which is 0.43429 times the corresponding chi-square value. These values in terms of logarithms to the base 10 are given because such tables are usually more readily available; hence some workers may prefer to use these values. For this illustrative problem, we have

$$-N \log_e \hat{L}_{mvc} = 60.7 \qquad -N \log_{10} \hat{L}_{mvc} = 26.3 \qquad \text{d.f.} = 8,$$

$$-N \log_e \hat{L}_{vc} = 45.4 \qquad -N \log_{10} \hat{L}_{vc} = 19.7 \qquad \text{d.f.} = 6,$$

$$-N \log_e \hat{L}_{m} = 15.2 \qquad -N \log_{10} \hat{L}_{m} = 6.59 \qquad \text{d.f.} = 2.$$

By reference to Table 2 we see that these values are considerably larger than the 1 per cent point values for the corresponding degrees of freedom. The values are clearly significant at the 1 per cent level, that is, these three tests cannot be regarded as parallel tests for predicting criterion y.

13. Summary

The statistic L_{mvc} given in equations 5 and 6 is used to test simultaneously for equality of means, variances, and covariances. If they are equal, the best estimate of each is given in equations 7, 8, and 9.

The statistic L_{vc} given in equations 10 and 11 is used to test simultaneously for equality of variances and covariances. If these are equal the best estimate of each is given by equations 1 and 2.

The statistic L_m given in equation 12 is used to test for equality of means (assuming equality of variances and covariances).

The tables of the 5 per cent and 1 per cent points are given in terms of $-N \log_{10} L_{mvc}$, $-N \log_{10} L_{vc}$, and $-N(k-1) \log_{10} L_m$. If the value computed from the data is greater than the one found in the table, the tests cannot be regarded as parallel. If it is less than the one found in the table, the indication is that the tests may be regarded as parallel.

If one or more of the three statistics L_{mvc}, L_{vc}, and L_m show a significant difference, we must conclude that the tests are not strictly parallel. There is only one combination of results that is impossible. It is not possible that L_{mvc} indicates a non-significant difference when L_{vc} and L_m *each* indicate a significant difference at the 1 per cent or 5 per cent level. The tests can be regarded as parallel only when each of the three statistics considered separately shows a non-significant difference.

The more general case of compound symmetry that includes equality of validity coefficients and equality of correlations between two sets of parallel tests was also presented. Equations for the three criteria $\hat{L}_{mvc}$, $\hat{L}_{vc}$, and $\hat{L}_m$ are presented in equations 29, 40, and 42, respectively.

Problems

1. Three comparable forms of a test are given to 200 persons with the following results:

$$M_1 = 54.0 \qquad M_2 = 55.5 \qquad M_3 = 56.6,$$

$$s_1 = 13.9 \qquad s_2 = 13.5 \qquad s_3 = 14.4,$$

$$r_{12} = .90 \qquad r_{13} = .88 \qquad r_{23} = .86.$$

Do these data indicate that the tests are parallel?

2. The following table gives means, standard deviations, and correlations for four of the subtests of the College Entrance Examination Board Comprehensive Mathematics Test, Form WCM-1, April 1948. (These data were supplied by Mr. Richard Pearson and Dr. Ledyard Tucker of the Educational Testing Service.)

	Subtest 3	Subtest 4	Subtest 5	Subtest 6
Subtest 3		.7350	.5983	.6203
Subtest 4	.7350		.6049	.6357
Subtest 5	.5983	.6049		.5515
Subtest 6	.6203	.6357	.5515	
Means	9.0983	9.5817	3.0417	2.4483
Standard deviations	3.9411	4.4291	1.7569	1.9330

(The foregoing data are based on a sample of 600.)

(a) Can these four subtests be regarded as parallel tests?

(b) Would additive adjustments to equate the means be sufficient to make the tests parallel?

(c) Can subtests 3 and 4 be regarded as parallel tests with respect to means? With respect to variances and covariances? With respect to all three?

(d) Can subtests 5 and 6 be regarded as parallel tests with respect to means? With respect to variances and covariances? With respect to all three?

3. The following table gives means, variances, and covariances for various grades on the College Entrance Examination Board English Composition Test, December 1946. (These data were supplied by Dr. Ledyard Tucker of the Educational Testing Service.)

	A	B	C	D	E
A	25.0704	12.4363	11.7257	20.7510	20.9425
B	12.4363	28.2021	9.2281	11.9732	23.4544
C	11.7257	9.2281	22.7390	12.0692	18.0384
D	20.7510	11.9732	12.0692	21.8707	19.8371
E	20.9425	23.4544	18.0384	19.8371	77.8976
Means	14.9048	15.4841	14.4444	14.3810	28.0556

$(N = 126)$

A = reader's grade on original theme, question 1.
B = a different reader's grade on a hand copy of the original theme, question 1. (The second reader would not know that the theme had been read before.)
C = Carbon copy of B. (With this copy the reader would know that he was reading a theme already graded by someone else as check on the accuracy of reading.)
D = Table leader's check on the grade assigned in A. He might either let the grade stand, or alter it as a result of his check reading.
E = Sum of reader's scores on questions 2 and 3.

(a) Can the four grades assigned to question 1 (A, B, C, and D) be regarded as parallel grades?
(b) Can the three grades that were assigned *independently* (that is, without knowledge of previous grades), A, B, and C, be regarded as parallel grades?
(c) Can A and B be regarded as parallel grades?
(d) Can C and D be regarded as parallel grades?
(e) From these results, what conclusions can be drawn regarding the precautions necessary in checking on the reliability of reading English themes?
(f) Can B, C, and D be regarded as parallel tests for predicting a criterion E?
(g) Can A, B, and C be regarded as parallel tests for predicting criterion E?

4. Given the following table showing means, standard deviations, and intercorrelations for a criterion y, and three tests x_1, x_2, and x_3, on a group of 50 persons can the three tests be regarded as parallel tests for the purpose of predicting the criterion y?

	y	x_1	x_2	x_3
y	1.00	.52	.56	.53
x_1	.52	1.00	.94	.91
x_2	.56	.94	1.00	.89
x_3	.53	.91	.89	1.00
Means	45.0	29.0	30.0	31.0
Standard deviations	24.0	9.0	8.0	7.0

15

Experimental Methods
of Obtaining Test Reliability

1. Introduction

In previous chapters (see Chapters 2, 3, 6, and 8) reliability was defined as the "correlation between parallel tests." In Chapters 2 and 3 a definition of parallel tests was given, in terms of equality of means, standard deviations, and intercorrelations. Chapter 14 presented a statistical test for equality of a set of means, a set of variances, and a set of covariances. In this chapter we shall consider the different possible ways of obtaining parallel test scores.

The term reliability was introduced by Spearman in his basic papers on test theory; see Spearman (1904a), (1904b), (1907), (1910), and (1913). Since then there have been many discussions of the various factors influencing reliability in relation to the different methods of measuring reliability. For an introduction to these discussions see, for example, Kelley (1921), Muenzinger (1927), Symonds (1928), Anastasi (1934), Adams (1936), Kuder and Richardson (1937), Kelley (1942), Guttman (1945), Cronbach (1947), and Thorndike (1947). There are many different ways of classifying the factors influencing reliability and the methods of measuring reliability. Here we shall consider the following major methods.

The use of parallel forms.
Retesting with the same test form.
Various split-half methods, such as first versus second halves, odd versus even items, and the method of matched random subtests (either halves or thirds).

Recently methods of assessing test reliability or homogeneity have been devised that do not make use of correlation of parallel scores. Instead, these methods use item analysis data to assess the homogeneity of the group of items in the test. One of these methods will be considered in the next chapter.

Although the error of measurement, discussed in Chapters 2, 3, 4, and 5, is a more basic concept in test theory than the reliability coefficient, it has become customary during the last forty years to assess tests in terms of the reliability coefficient rather than in terms of the error of measurement. Since there are advantages and disadvantages for each of these measures, it is urged here that *both must always be given* in order to make possible a complete assessment of any test. Otis and Knollin (1921) pointed out that the error of measurement is superior to the reliability coefficient, in that it does not vary with changes in the heterogeneity of the group. This property of the error of measurement and its effect on the reliability coefficient were discussed in Chapter 10. Kelley (1921) and Franzen and Derryberry (1932a) indicated that, although the error of measurement did not vary with group heterogeneity, nevertheless the unit in which the error of measurement was expressed did vary from one test to another. They suggested several ways of overcoming this disadvantage. Lincoln (1932) and (1933) pointed out that reliability could be very high even when the differences between two sets of measures were very large. This point was also amplified and clarified by Ackerson (1933).

The tests or subtests that are correlated to determine test reliability should be parallel both in the sense that they satisfy the statistical criteria for parallel tests presented in Chapter 14 and in the sense that the items appear to require the same psychological processes and the same type of learning on the part of the subjects. This latter criterion depends on the judgment of the test technician and the subject matter expert, and it will be different for each different type of aptitude and achievement test. We shall consider here only general methods of setting up parallel tests or subtests, which are common to all types of material.

2. Use of parallel forms

For most sorts of situations, it will be found that the best method of obtaining a test reliability is to construct parallel forms of the test and administer them on different days to the same group of subjects. The method usually used would be to construct *two* parallel forms for this purpose. However, from the discussion presented in Chapter 14, we see that with *three* parallel forms it is possible to make a more complete check and to be certain that the forms are parallel, not only with respect to means and variances but also with respect to correlations.

There is only one situation in which the use of parallel forms administered on different days is not advisable. This is when the ability that is being tested changes markedly in the interval between the tests.

For example, if we wish to determine the reliability of a typewriting test by administering one form to a group on Monday and another form on Friday, the method would not work if the group was practicing (and hence improving rapidly in typewriting ability) during the intervening time. Likewise the method is not good if the first test is given when the subjects are in excellent "form" and the second test is given when the subject's ability has decreased, for lack of practice during the intervening week.

The same sort of consideration applies, for example, to any test of physical fitness or muscular skill. The two administrations of the test cannot be used to estimate the reliability of the test if there is good reason for believing that the subjects have either improved or declined in the ability that is being tested.

For most tests of scholastic achievement and mental ability, it is reasonably easy to be sure that the subjects have not actually changed markedly during the period intervening between two tests. For other types of performance, of which athletic skills of various types are a good example, it is very difficult to maintain a group at a state of uniform excellence. The skill is likely to deteriorate with lack of practice, and may either improve or the person may "go stale" with practice. In such cases all the "error of measurement" cannot be attributed to the test. Much of what shows up in the statistical check as error of measurement is actually true variation in ability. However, from another point of view we must perhaps recognize that measurement of some skills is extremely unreliable (regardless of the cause of this unreliability); hence in using any such measures we must for many purposes treat them just as we would treat very unreliable measures.

However, if we are dealing with a period of time during which the ability measured will not change systematically for different members of the group, and are dealing with a group of subjects under conditions such that it is not likely that the ability will change, the use of different forms of the test is the most realistic method of indicating reliability.

It should be noted that as tests are actually used, if several forms of a test are available, we are likely to use any of the forms somewhat indifferently. Likewise, if we are testing a freshman class, the test is likely to come on different days in different institutions, or in different years. We can thus see that any form of the test may be given, and it may be given on any day, so that variability introduced by change of form and change of day would normally enter into the error of measurement of a test.

It should also be pointed out that the error possibilities noted above can be easily detected. If the group has improved or deteriorated, the mean will be higher or lower the second time. If some persons have improved and others deteriorated, the standard deviation will in all likelihood have changed. A complicated set of influences in which some persons improve and others deteriorate in such a way that the mean and standard deviation of the group remain the same is a possibility, but would doubtless be very rare.

In summary, the method of testing with parallel forms given several days apart is a method that allows the relevant sources of error to influence the reliability coefficient. If the statistical tests for equal means and standard deviations are used, and satisfied, the method is one that may be used routinely with relatively little fear that undetected and irrelevant factors are rendering the obtained reliability coefficient either spuriously high or spuriously low.

It should be noted, since speed tests will enter prominently into some of the later discussion, that the parallel forms method is valid for speed tests. A speed test is a test composed of very easy items—items so simple that everyone could answer them if given time. For example, a set of two-digit additions given to eighth-grade students would approach being a "speed test." If we are to get a good range of scores on such a test, it is necessary to have a large number of items, and to set a time limit so short that only the best people in the class finish, if at all. In such a test, practice effect from one time to the next is important. Unless such conditions as amount of practice and use of "fore exercise" were very carefully standardized, it would not be possible to have the mean and variance of the parallel forms the same for the group. However, if means and variances are the same one can be reasonably certain that the intercorrelation between the two parallel forms is a reasonable approximation to the reliability coefficient that the test should have.

A parallel form reliability may also be secured by administering both forms at the same session. In some tests there may again be a marked difference of performance due to the fact that the giving of the first test influenced the second test. For example, if it is a speed test of two-digit additions, it is likely that for many persons, particularly the poorer ones, the score on the second test will be much better because of the practice on the first test. Of course this could easily be detected in the results because the mean would be larger on the second form. There are also other tests for which the performance on the second form is likely to be much worse than the performance on the first form. Any test that is fatiguing to the subjects would clearly fall in this category, and again such fatigue could easily be detected from the results. The average would be lower for the second test than for the first.

If the foregoing rather obvious and easily detected difficulties were not present, the major difficulty with reliability obtained by the successive administration of parallel forms is that it is too high. This is because there is no possibility for the variation due to normal daily variability to lower the correlation between parallel forms. Woodrow (1932) in his study of quotidian variability gathered evidence to show that there are day-to-day variations in test performance.

Several other writers have pointed out that sometimes a low correlation between two parallel forms of a test indicates that the test is an unstable measure of a stable trait; at other times such a low correlation may arise from a stable measurement of an unstable trait. Instability in *either* the test or the trait would result in a low correlation between parallel forms. Methods of determining the instability of a trait as distinguished from the instability of a test have been suggested by Paulsen (1931), Thouless (1936) and (1939), Preston (1940), and Jackson and Ferguson (1941). We can conclude then that, if parallel forms of a test are given on the same day and if the statistical criterion for parallel forms is satisfied—namely, equal means and standard deviations—the reliability obtained is likely to be higher than that which would be obtained if day-to-day variability had also been allowed to affect the reliability.

Generally speaking then, the use of two or three parallel forms administered on different days is the best method of determining reliability of a test. However, since several parallel forms are frequently not available, and since it is sometimes difficult to secure cooperation from subjects for an extended period, we shall consider the possibilities of obtaining an indication of reliability when only one form of a test is available.

3. Retesting with the same form

Sometimes, when two parallel forms of a test are not available, it is possible to get an estimate of the reliability by administering the same test twice. Usually it is preferable to do this at rather widely separated times. Again with this method we should watch out for a practice or a fatigue effect that would be readily detectable in most instances by observing the distributions of test scores for the first and second administrations. Aside from such an effect, the major danger in such a technique is that the reliability will be too high because there will be a tendency for the subject to duplicate his former performance. That is, if the subject does not know the answer to an item, but makes a lucky guess and gets it right, he is likely to make the same guess next time and again secure credit for the item which he really does not know. Likewise, if he makes some minor mistake, and as a result answers incorrectly an item that he normally would answer correctly, he is more likely to repeat this performance when the same test is regiven. Such an effect could not occur if the person were taking a parallel form that would not contain the same items. In other words, the performance on a repetition of a test is likely to be much closer to the original score than the performance on a parallel form of the same test. This method of repetition of the same test at a different time should in general not be used, since it will give a spuriously high coefficient, and the amount of error is not easy to determine.

The major exception is probably some simple perceptual discrimina-tions for which parallel forms cannot be devised. For example, a test of pitch discrimination or a test of auditory threshold for different pure tones can probably be regiven without such an effect. The person sim-ply judges each time whether he hears a tone or whether he does not hear a tone. In such a test there does not seem to be a ready way in which the person could spuriously duplicate his errors and successes of the previous set of trials. However, even in such simple tasks, it is fre-quently desirable to devise several different measuring techniques and correlate them, as well as to get the reliability for a repeat test by the use of each method. In general we may say that, even where it seems that a repetition of the same form is all that can be done, it is well for the test constructor to use some ingenuity and to get at the given factor in several different ways that he believes are roughly comparable, and then to see how well the different tests agree. New light will frequently be cast on the function being measured in this way. See, for example, the tests of auditory discrimination used by Karlin (1942). Studies of performance on retesting with the same form have been made by Wood-row (1932), Jackson and Ferguson (1941), and Greene (1943).

4. General considerations in split-half methods

Usually, when only one form of a test is available, reliability is deter-mined by a "split-half" method. This means that the items of the one form are divided into two forms, each with half the number of items of the original form. Typically, the subjects do not know that the test is to be scored in two parts, and do not know which items are in which of the halves. The experimenter need not, and frequently does not, decide how the items are to be divided until he sees the test results. However, from the viewpoint of setting up efficient scoring procedures, it is desir-able to decide on the division into two subtests before the test is set up for printing.

The methods discussed in previous sections (either the parallel forms method or retesting with the same form), provided the experimenter with two scores. In such a case the reliability is given directly by the Pearson product moment correlation between the two scores. A slightly modified method is necessary when reliability is to be obtained from two subtest scores obtained from a single test. One method is to correlate the two half scores, and then substitute this correlation in the Spearman-Brown formula for double length (formula 30, Chapter 6). We may write

(1)
$$r'_{xx} = \frac{2r_{12}}{1 + r_{12}},$$

where r'_{xx} designates the reliability of the total test as estimated by correcting the split-half correlation to double length, and

r_{12} designates the correlation between the two halves of the test.

Another method of obtaining the reliability of the total test from information contained in two subtest scores is to use the formula presented by Rulon (1939),

(2)
$$r''_{xx} = 1 - \frac{s_d^2}{s_x^2},$$

where s_d^2 is the variance of $x_1 - x_2$, the difference of scores on the two halves of the test,

s_x^2 is the variance of scores on the total test, the sum of the scores on the two halves of the test ($x = x_1 + x_2$), and

r''_{xx} is used to designate the test reliability as given by equation 2.

Flanagan (1937b) has suggested that the use of this formula in conjunction with a test-scoring machine provides a rapid and efficient method of obtaining test reliability.

If it is easier to calculate the variance of x_1 and the variance of x_2 than it is to calculate the variance of the difference ($x_1 - x_2$), r''_{xx} may be written as

(3)
$$r''_{xx} = 2 \left[1 - \frac{s_{x_1}^2 + s_{x_2}^2}{s_x^2} \right],$$

where $s_{x_1}^2$ is the variance of the x_1 subtest scores,

$s_{x_2}^2$ is the variance of the x_2 subtest scores, and the other terms are as defined in equation 2.

Guttman (1945) derived this equation as lower bound (L_4). He showed that, under the assumption that $s_1 = s_2$, this formula is identical with equation 1. Guttman also points out that, since this formula gives a lower bound, it may be that in some cases the reliability coefficient of a test has been underestimated, and that this fact may explain why correlations corrected for attenuation are sometimes above unity.

In order to prove that equation 2 is equal to equation 3 we note that the variance of a sum is equal to $s_1{}^2 + s_2{}^2 + 2r_{12}s_1s_2$, and that the variance of a difference is equal to $s_1{}^2 + s_2{}^2 - 2r_{12}s_1s_2$. Substituting these expressions in equation 2 gives

(4) $$r''_{xx} = 1 - \frac{s_1{}^2 + s_2{}^2 - 2r_{12}s_1s_2}{s_1{}^2 + s_2{}^2 + 2r_{12}s_1s_2}.$$

Putting this over a least common denominator and simplifying, we have

(5) $$r''_{xx} = \frac{4r_{12}s_1s_2}{s_1{}^2 + s_2{}^2 + 2r_{12}s_1s_2}.$$

If we put equation 3 over a common denominator in the same way we obtain

(6) $$r''_{xx} = 2 \left[\frac{2r_{12}s_1s_2}{s_x{}^2} \right],$$

which is identical with equation 5 derived from equation 2; hence the two formulas (2 and 3) for r''_{xx} are identical.

Rulon (1939) has shown that r'_{xx} given by equation 1 and r''_{xx} given by equations 2 or 3 are identical if the standard deviation of subtest 1 is equal to the standard deviation of subtest 2. It may also be shown that, whenever $s_1 \neq s_2$, $r''_{xx} < r'_{xx}$. If we divide the numerator and denominator of equation 4 by $s_2{}^2$, and write h for the ratio s_1/s_2, we have

(7) $$r''_{xx} = 1 - \frac{h^2 + 1 - 2r_{12}h}{h^2 + 1 + 2r_{12}h}.$$

By taking the derivative of r''_{xx} with respect to h, and setting it equal to zero, we can show that, for all positive values of h, r''_{xx} is a minimum if $h = 1$. For students not acquainted with the calculus, we may indicate the condition for a minimum value of r''_{xx} by the following algebraic transformations. If we put equation 7 over a common denominator, simplify, and divide the numerator and denominator by h, we obtain

(8) $$r''_{xx} = \frac{4r_{12}}{h + \dfrac{1}{h} + 2r_{12}}.$$

By adding and subtracting 2 in the denominator, we may write

(9) $$r''_{xx} = \frac{4r_{12}}{\dfrac{(h-1)^2}{h} + 2 + 2r_{12}}.$$

We can see by inspection that, if $h = 1$, $r''_{xx} = r'_{xx}$; and, if h has any positive value other than unity, $r''_{xx} < r'_{xx}$. Since the ratio of two standard deviations is always positive, it follows that $r'_{xx} \geqq r''_{xx}$.

> *The corrected split-half correlation (as indicated in equation 1) is identical with the reliability as computed by equations 2 or 3 if the variances of the two halves are equal. If the variances of the two halves are unequal, the corrected split-half estimate of reliability will be larger than the value given by equations 2 or 3.*

It should also be pointed out that the statistical tests of Chapter 14 make it desirable not to use the correlation between two subtest scores for the estimation of reliability, but to divide the total test into three or possibly four parts, and to test the similarity of these parts as well as to obtain the correlation between them. These correlations can then be used in the generalized Spearman-Brown formula (see equation 10, Chapter 8), with K set equal to three or to four and the reliability of the total test estimated. By using this method we know that we are using a correlation between *parallel* subtests as the basis for obtaining reliability. This means that the reliability found will not be too low because non-parallel subtests were chosen as the basis for estimating reliability. It is interesting to note that the use of more than two subtests in determining reliability has been suggested by Cureton (1931), Dunlap (1933), and Stephenson (1934).

The major problem in using subtest scores for the purpose of estimating reliability is dividing the original test into equivalent subtests. We shall next consider some of the methods of dividing a test into subtests, and the advantages and disadvantages of each.

5. Successive halves or thirds

Dividing a test into comparable halves or thirds is not a simple matter. For example, the easiest way to divide the test is to take the first half of the test against the second half of the test. Often such a method will not result in parallel tests at all. For example, if the test is given in one session and is a timed test, any items that are not answered for lack of time will be in the second half of the test. The score on the second half will be lower than on the first half. For a speed test composed of easy items the results of plotting score on first half against score on second half are very peculiar. All subjects who did not reach the second half would score zero on it, regardless of what their score was on the first half. If the test is a pure speed test, in the sense that the vast majority of subjects get the item correct if they try it, so that the only *errors* are "items not yet attempted," everyone who finishes the first half gets a perfect or near-perfect score on it, regardless of his score on the second half. Figure 1 is such a scatter diagram. Clearly any correlation worked on such a diagram could not be interpreted as a reliability coefficient. Probably such a pure case will rarely be found. But wherever the score is in *large part* determined by the fact that time is called before many subjects have finished, this situation will be approximated, and the first versus the second half will not be "comparable halves" suitable for obtaining an estimate of the reliability coefficient.

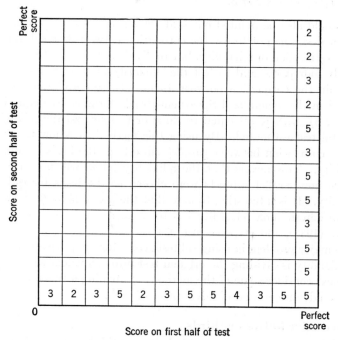

FIGURE 1.   Showing the relationship between scores on the first and last halves of a test for a pure speed test.

It might be thought that, if all subjects finished two-thirds of the test, we could correlate the first third with the second third of the test, and correct this coefficient to triple length. However, such a method is valid only if the last third is parallel to the two matching halves secured from the first two-thirds. If the difficult items are at the end of the test, it is impossible to make any plausible guesses regarding what would happen if the time limit were increased so that everyone could finish the test. Furthermore, such a method does *not* give the reliability of the test *with the shorter time limit*. It estimates what the reliability might be if the time limit were such that practically everyone finished the test.   If the time limit is important, we must use a parallel form method of estimating reliability.   If the time limit is generous so that most subjects finish the test, it may be possible to estimate reliability from subtest scores.

In addition to the problem of time limits on a test, the problem of item difficulty must also be considered.   Many tests are constructed with the easy items first, the items of average difficulty next, and the most difficult items at the end of the test.   Clearly, if the items in the test are in difficulty order, the first and second halves will not be comparable halves.

It can be seen that, if a test contains a number of items of average difficulty, and is then lengthened by adding more very difficult items, the reliability of the test will decrease, despite increased test length and the increased testing time.   The new added items will be answered on a chance basis by most of the persons; hence it will be a matter of accident whether they get the new items right or wrong.   As a larger number of very difficult items are added, a larger component of the score will be due to guessing, and this component will decrease the reliability of the score on the augmented test.   This in no way contradicts the Spearman-Brown formulation on the relation of test length to test reliability, since in this formulation it was assumed that the new set of items was parallel to the old ones.   This means that the items were of similar mean, standard deviation, and reliability.   The new items supposedly added here would be difficult items with a lower mean; and, since they would be answered on the basis of chance, the reliability of this new portion and its correlation with the easier part of the test would each be near zero.

From considerations such as these, we see that the effect of *increasing the time limit* on a test is difficult to predict.   Increasing the time limit will permit subjects to answer more items; hence it may be thought of as increasing the effective length of a test.   However, many of the subjects will not know the answers to the more difficult items at the end of the test; hence they will guess about these items and add a chance increment to their score.   This increment will not remain stable from form to form; hence it will lower the reliability of the test.

If we wish to use the first and second halves (or the successive thirds) of a test for computing reliability, it is possible to plan the test to overcome both the problems raised by time limits and by the difficulty ordering of items.   For the first versus the second halves method, for example, we arrange the test items so that the item difficulty range in the first half of the test is duplicated in the second half of the test.

Then, if sufficient time is given so that everyone, or practically everyone, has a chance to finish the test, the first and second halves will be comparable unless there is either a *practice* or a *fatigue* effect as a subject goes through the test. If a test is given in two sessions, with time out between for rest and relaxation, if item difficulty is equated between the two sessions, and comparable time allowances are given for each session, it is probable that a good estimate of reliability can be obtained by correlating the first session with the second.

For example, the University of Chicago comprehensive examinations are six-hour examinations given in two three-hour sessions, with two hours elapsing between sessions. It was found feasible to construct the examinations so that the subjects or topics covered in the morning session were dealt with again in the afternoon session, and consequently the morning and afternoon sessions were roughly comparable in length, in item difficulty (as judged by the committee constructing the examination), and in topics covered. When the examinations were set up in this way, the correlation between morning and afternoon sessions was found to be about the same as for other selections of comparable halves.

Likewise, for radio code receiving tests, use has been made of a correlation between errors on first versus second halves of the test. In this case the material received by the students is of about comparable difficulty all the way through, since the same characters (letters of the alphabet) are used, and they are sent at the same speed throughout the test. Also there is no question of a differential time limit. All subjects must keep up with the rate of sending, or skip characters and start afresh at all times. Furthermore, these particular tests are short, only about three minutes in length, so that there is relatively little opportunity for a fatigue effect. The tests are preceded by about ten minutes of warming-up practice by the students so that there is probably little consistent improvement from the early to the later parts of the test. It should be noted that for these radio code receiving tests the best method of testing reliability is provided by a parallel form, but it should be given very shortly after the first form in order to avoid the effects of practice. The method of using errors in odd versus even words would in this case result in a spuriously high reliability, since the making of an error in one word is likely to throw the student off a little, and he is also likely to miss the next word or two before he gets "back into stride" again. Thus it is likely that the correlation between errors made on odd- versus even-numbered words would be considerably higher (and spuriously higher) than the correlation between parallel forms of the test administered under comparable conditions with a relatively brief period between the two tests. Also each test should be given with suitable provision for a warming-up period that is not counted on the test score.

6. Odd versus even items or every nth item

By far the commonest form of comparable halves is the odd-even items division. It is probable that this method never gives too low a value for the reliability coefficient. If there is an error it is always in the direction of a reliability that is spuriously high. Sometimes, as will be shown, the odd-even reliability seriously overestimates the test reliability as indicated by parallel forms.

It can readily be seen that, if the items are in difficulty order, the odd items will have about the same average difficulty and spread of difficulty as the even items. If there is any bias, it is likely to be that the odd items will be on the average very slightly easier than the even items.

In using this method, however, we must be certain that there is no dependence of one item on another. For example, in the radio code tests just mentioned, success or failure on one item—particularly failure—is very likely to influence the performance on the next item. In some tests we find a series of questions on a given topic, and it is sometimes difficult to decide whether the items are independent, in the sense that knowing the answer depends primarily upon whether or not we have studied the topic or whether there is a spurious dependence, as in the case of errors in radio code. In performance tests, where the subject is to assemble or disassemble a mechanism, and is graded on the various steps, there is very likely to be a spurious relationship, in the sense that the subject learns or does not learn a certain set of acts as a unit while the examiner, in order to grade the performance objectively, sets up numerous rather artificial divisions. In such cases as these, it seems that the fair test to apply is: "Would you as an examination constructor set up such halves as separate tests?" In performance on assembly of apparatus, it is doubtful if the test constructor would want the students to go through the *entire* performance, as would be necessary, and grade them on only half the points that it was possible to observe. In a set of statements describing the characteristics of rods and cones in the eye, for example, it is rather likely that the test constructor *would* assent to using half the statements for a shortened form of the test. It might readily be, however, that the odd items would not constitute a satisfactory parallel form for the even items. The items should be inspected to insure that the type of subject matter and the difficulty distribution for one of the halves are roughly paralleled in the other half.

Odd-even correlation is also spuriously high on a test with a rather stringent time limit so that a large number of subjects do not finish the test. If a subject fails to answer the last ten items in the test, obviously he "misses" all of them. Thus he gets five points more on his *"odds"* error score, and likewise five points more on his *"even"* error score. It is highly probable that careful observation will show that many of the published reliabilities are spuriously high because of this factor. Again this type of error can be strikingly illustrated in the "pure speed" test to which previous reference has been made. If every subject gets all items correct as far as he goes, one who finishes ten items will have an odds score of five and an evens score of five. If he finishes eleven items, he will have an evens score of five and an odds score of six, and then at twelve items the score will be six and six. That is, the odds and evens scores will either be identical, or the odds score will be one point greater than the evens score. The correlation scatter plot will appear as in Figure 2, and the correlation will be well over .99. Again such a pure case probably never occurs, but an approximation to it (coupled with a spuriously high reliability) occurs whenever the odd-even method is used, and not *all* the subjects *finish the test.*

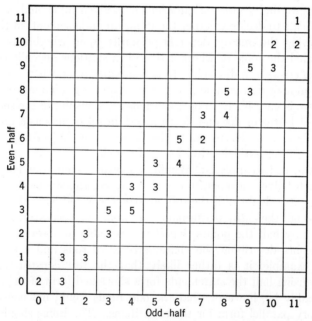

FIGURE 2. Showing the plot of odd versus even items for a pure speed test.

It should be noted that the odd-even reliability is probably still too high, even when the items are in order of difficulty, and all persons are allowed to finish the test, and the items are independent of one another (in the sense that making a mistake on one item does not of itself increase the probability of making a mistake on another item). Any variability due to day-to-day variations in ability is ruled out, and even the variation that might be caused by a slight practice or fatigue effect as we progress through the test is ruled out. If we use the parallel forms as a standard, the odd-even reliability, as generally applied to most tests, probably gives a result that is too high, owing to the careful control of various other sources of variation and also to the fact that most tests are timed tests having a fair proportion of the score dependent upon most of the subjects not getting a chance to try the last items. To the extent that a test is a speed test, the score depending on how rapidly a subject works in the given time limit, there is *no way of estimating the reliability* except by testing a second time with a *parallel form*.

There have been several studies comparing the *odd-even* with parallel form reliability and with the correlation between test and retest (with the same test). See Foran (1931), Jordan (1935), Goodenough (1936), Remmers and Whisler (1938), Ferguson (1941*b*), Greene (1943), and Jackson and Ferguson (1941). These experiments show clearly that different methods of measuring reliability give different results. In general, the parallel form reliability is lowest, and the odd-even (corrected) is the highest.

It might be thought that, if everyone finished *two-thirds* of the test, we could use an odd-even reliability on the first two-thirds, get the correlation between these two thirds, and then correct to triple length. However, this gives an estimate of the reliability of the total test on the assumption that *everyone finishes* the test. It does not give any estimate of the extent to which a given subject will hit the *same speed rate* on different administrations of the test; and hence will get to the same point in the test. There is no possible way to estimate this factor accurately except by giving *parallel* forms with *comparable time limits* and under *standard directions*, and then observe the extent to which the score is the same.

7. Matched random subtests

If a single test score for each subject is to be used in estimating test reliability, it is necessary to regard this single score as divided into two, three, or four equivalent subtest scores. In the preceding sections we have seen that under certain conditions successive halves or thirds of a test can reasonably be regarded as parallel forms, whereas under other conditions the successive segments of a test are clearly not parallel forms. Similarly, assigning every second or every third item to one of two or three subtests is sometimes a good method for obtaining parallel subtests, and sometimes a poor method.

If a test is composed of a large number of independent items and is administered with a liberal time limit, it can usually be divided into parallel subtests. If the test has only a few item groups in it, as, for example, in most mechanical assembly tests or in tests involving the writing of a paragraph in English, it may or may not be possible to devise a test that is composed of parallel subtests. If a single time limit that is short is used, there is no possibility at present of getting any valid estimate of the reliability of such a test by using subtest scores of any sort.

If item analysis data are available on a test (that has a large number of independent items and a liberal time limit), items may be matched on such item analysis data and assigned to the subtests. This is an excellent method of insuring that the subtests will be parallel. For example, suppose that the percentage of persons answering the item correctly (p) and a biserial or point biserial correlation with total test score (r) are available for each item. The best procedure for constructing parallel subtests is to represent each item by a point on a scatter diagram, the abscissa of which represents p and the ordinate r. In order subsequently to identify the items, each point should be numbered with the item number, as shown in Figure 3. Items may then be simultaneously matched on p and r, and a ring drawn around the matched pairs, triples, or quadruples, as shown in the diagram. It is important to note that, if the test is heterogeneous with respect to item type or with respect to type of subject matter covered, it is important to match items for subject matter, item type, etc., as well as for p and r.

One member of each group should then be *randomly* assigned to a given subtest. For example, if only two subtests are to be formed, the assignment could be made by tossing a coin, and assigning the lower numbered item of the pair to form A if the coin showed heads and to form B for tails. In constructing three parallel subtests, it is necessary to assign each triple of items to the three parallel subtests by a somewhat more complicated procedure. For example, the items in each triple may be identified by item number, as low, medium, and high (L, M, and H). There are then six possible ways of assigning these three items, one to each of three subtests. Each such order may then be assigned a number from 1 to 6 (1 = LMH, 2 = LHM, etc.), and each triple assigned according to the throw of a die.

If such item analysis information is available before the test is assembled, scoring routines are much simplified if the items of one subtest are put first, another second, etc., or else if items from the different subtests are distributed successively through the test.   For example for three subtests, A, B, and C, the items might be arranged ABCABC, etc.

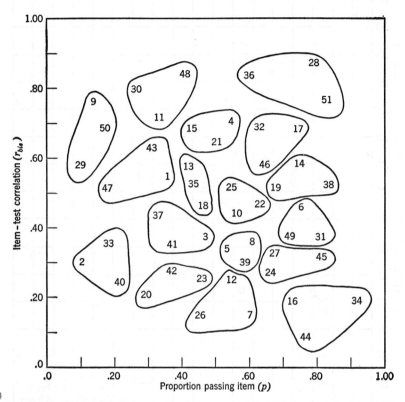

FIGURE 3.   Showing how to construct three parallel subtests or tests by simultaneously matching items on a difficulty and reliability index.

It must again be emphasized that no matter which order of items is used, it is necessary to allow time for almost all students to finish almost all items.   It is not possible to estimate test reliability from parallel subtests if the test score is markedly influenced by the time limit.

An analogous method may also be used in attempting to build a second test to match a first one already in use.   Figure 4 illustrates the use of such a procedure in developing an aptitude test for the U. S. Navy. In this case the items for form 1 were already in use when form 2 was constructed, so that the two forms could not be matched as well as if it had been possible to set up two forms simultaneously.

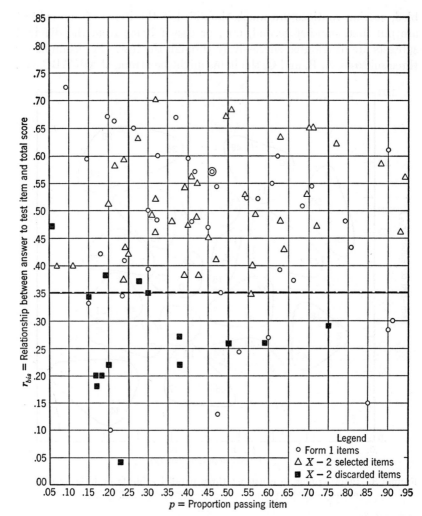

FIGURE 4. Selecting items for a second form of a test to match items previously selected for a first form. Item analysis data used in the selection of items for GCT Form 2 Analogies. [From Satter (1944), OSRD Report 3756; Applied Psychology Panel, NDRC.]

In conclusion, it should be pointed out that a statistical criterion for parallel tests is now available. We should use it on the subtest scores to find out whether or not the precautions used in constructing the subtests resulted in parallel sets of scores. In order to make complete use of the methods of Chapter 14 in testing covariances as well as variances, it is necessary to have three subtest scores.

8. Reliability of essay examinations

In dealing with the reliability of essay examinations, we encounter certain special considerations that are not involved when determining the reliability of objective examinations.

One major problem in essay examinations is the accuracy with which the same (or different) readers will grade the examinations. The usual method of checking on the accuracy of reading is to have two or three different readers assign a mark to the examination independently of each other. This means that the readers will agree before hand on the different marks to be assigned, and on the type of papers to which each mark is to be given, and then each reader will record his marks on some sort of master list of students. It is necessary to be certain that one reader does not see any of the marks assigned by another reader, and that an earlier reader does not make any marks on the paper, since these could be seen by and perhaps influence a later reader.

These marks, independently assigned to each of a set of papers by different readers are then correlated. This correlation between the marks of two readers is known as "the reader reliability" of the examination. It should be noted that the *correlation* between marks of two readers may be high, even though the means and standard deviations of the marks may be radically different. If the mean of reader A is higher than the mean of reader B for a given set of papers, it indicates that A is an "easier grader" than B. Such a difference can be adequately taken care of by adding a constant to each grade assigned by B, or subtracting a constant from each grade assigned by reader A. Correspondingly, if reader A has a larger standard deviation for his marks on a set of papers than reader B, this can be corrected by multiplying B's marks by an appropriate constant, or dividing A's marks by some constant. A difference in mean and standard deviation is not serious provided the correlation between the marks is high. That is, the papers need not be regraded by the readers, but it is essential, in order to have a fair marking system, that the marks of the different readers be equated in mean and standard deviation before being used further. If the reader *reliability* is low, there is no way of equating marks; it is necessary for the readers to discuss their differences of opinion and to regrade the papers before the marks can be used.

A more precise method of handling the problem of comparability among readers is to use the methods of Chapter 14 to analyze the results of several different readers. The test with L_{mvc} will indicate immediately whether or not the means, variances, and correlations among the set of readers may be regarded as identical or not. If L_{mvc} is near unity, we have only to inspect the magnitude of the correlations to see if they are high enough to be satisfactory. In general, we should strive for a reader reliability over .90 if it is possible to achieve this level. It would seem that a reader reliability of less than .80 is so low as to necessitate further discussion and alteration in methods of reading. It should be remembered that the reader reliability is an upper bound for the test reliability. If two readers looking at the same paper agree to the extent of .80, for example, then if different questions (parallel questions) on the same material were read by different readers, the agreement is practically certain to be much less than .80.

In order to make clear the method of comparing reliability of essay examinations with that of objective examinations, we shall consider what has been termed "content reliability" (see Gulliksen, 1936). In an objective examination scored with a key that has previously been agreed on by all persons concerned, the equivalent of "reader reliability" is unity. Any difference in scores between parallel tests is due to differences in sampling of subject matter content in the two tests, and to possible changes in the subject between the time of administration of the two tests. If two parallel essay examinations are matched just as successfully with respect to content as are two parallel objective examinations, the correlation between the two parallel essay forms will practically always be lower than between the two objective forms, owing to the fact that the unreliability of reading will still further lower the correlation between the two essay forms. In order to determine the extent to which the low reliability of an essay examination is due to poor agreement among readers or to poor matching of questions in parallel forms, it is necessary to determine the content reliability of the essay examination.

For one form of an examination, let us use:

x'_1 to indicate the score assigned by reader 1,

x'_2 to indicate the score assigned by reader 2, and

x'_c to designate the correct score that the student should have received on the content of his paper, if it had not been for reader errors. It should be noted that x'_c is not the "true score." It is comparable to the score on an objective examination and like such a score has a true component, and an error due to the unreliability of sampling, unreliability of student performance, etc.

e'_1 designates the error made by reader 1, and

e'_2 designates the error made by reader 2.

For the parallel form we shall use x''_1, x''_2, x''_c, e''_1, and e''_2, all defined as above, but for the second form of the test. It is assumed that

(10)
$$x'_1 = x'_c + e'_1,$$

(11)
$$x'_2 = x'_c + e'_2,$$

(12)
$$x''_1 = x''_c + e''_1,$$

and

(13)
$$x''_2 = x''_c + e''_2.$$

It is possible to compute the correlations $r_{x'_1x'_2}$ and $r_{x''_1x''_2}$, which are reader reliabilities, and also to compute the four correlations of the form $r_{x'_ax''_b}$, where $a = 1$ or 2 and $b = 1$ or 2. These are test reliabilities, attenuated by the inaccuracy of reading. The problem is to express $r_{x'_cx''_c}$ (the content reliability of the test) as some function of the known correlations.

First we may obtain the relationship of the reader reliability to the variance of x'_1, and x'_c.

(14)
$$r_{x'_1x'_2} = \frac{\Sigma x'_1 x'_2}{N s_{x'_1} s_{x'_2}}.$$

If we assume that the two readers are reading with equal accuracy, we may substitute $s_{x'_1}$ for $s_{x'_2}$. Also for x'_1 and x'_2 let us substitute their values as given in equations 10 and 11, obtaining

(15)
$$r_{x'_1x'_2} = \frac{\Sigma(x'_c + e'_1)(x'_c + e'_2)}{N s^2_{x'_1}}.$$

If we expand the numerator and assume that the correlations $e'_1 e'_2$, $e'_1 x'_c$, and $e'_2 x'_c$ are equal to zero, we have

(16)
$$r_{x'_1x'_2} = \frac{\Sigma(x'_c)^2}{N s^2_{x'_1}}.$$

If we write $s^2_{x'_c}$ for $\Sigma(x'_c)^2/N$ and take the square root, we have

(17)
$$\sqrt{r_{x'_1x'_2}} = \frac{s_{x'_c}}{s_{x'_1}}.$$

By a similar procedure for the other test, and the other reader, we have

(18)
$$\sqrt{r_{x''_1x''_2}} = \frac{s_{x''_c}}{s_{x''_2}}.$$

The correlation between the two forms is $r_{x'_ax''_b}$. There are four such correlations for different values of a and b. Let us assume that all may be regarded as equal, that is, that the tests are parallel and that the error variance due to reader is equal for each reader and each form; then one of the four correlations, say $r_{x'_1 x''_2}$ may be taken as typical of the group. We have then

$$(19) \qquad r_{x'_1 x''_2} = \frac{\Sigma x'_1 x''_2}{N s_{x'_1} s_{x''_2}}.$$

Substituting equations 10 and 13 in the numerator gives

$$(20) \qquad r_{x'_1 x''_2} = \frac{\Sigma (x'_c + e'_1)(x''_c + e''_2)}{N s_{x'_1} s_{x''_2}}.$$

Expanding the numerator and noting that the correlations of reader errors with each other and with test score (x_c) is zero, we have

$$(21) \qquad r_{x'_1 x''_2} = \frac{\Sigma x'_c x''_c}{N s_{x'_1} s_{x''_2}}.$$

By the usual definition for correlation this becomes

$$(22) \qquad r_{x'_1 x''_2} = \frac{r_{x'_c x''_c} s_{x'_c} s_{x''_c}}{s_{x'_1} s_{x''_2}}.$$

Substituting from equations 17 and 18, we have

$$(23) \qquad r_{x'_1 x''_2} = r_{x'_c x''_c} \sqrt{r_{x'_1 x'_2}} \sqrt{r_{x''_1 x''_2}}.$$

Solving for $r_{x'_c x''_c}$, the content reliability, we have

$$(24) \qquad r_{x'_c x''_c} = \frac{r_{x'_1 x''_2}}{\sqrt{r_{x'_1 x'_2} r_{x''_1 x''_2}}}.$$

It will be noted that equation 24 is identical in form with the correction for attenuation, equation 21, Chapter 9. It gives the correction for the "attenuation due to inaccuracy of reading."

> *The reliability of an essay test corrected for attenuation due to the inaccuracy of reading has been termed the content reliability of the essay test. The content reliability is equal to the correlation between parallel forms divided by the geometric mean of the reader reliabilities of the two forms.* (See equation 24.)

9. Summary

Three main methods of determining reliability have been considered.

1. *Parallel forms.* Generally speaking, this method is best, provided that we can regulate the interval between the two tests and the activity

of the subjects during that interval so that the influence of practice, fatigue, and other similar effects will be negligible. If three parallel forms are used, and the statistical criterion for parallel tests given in Chapter 14 is applied, score changes due to practice, fatigue, etc., are detected immediately and routinely.

It should be especially noted that, if the score variance depends in any large part on unanswered items at the end of the test (for example, if speed is an important factor in test score), it is necessary to use the parallel forms method. Neither of the other two methods is satisfactory in this case.

2. *Retesting with the same test.* This can be done particularly well in such tests as sensory limen or discrimination tests, in which it is not likely that the subject will remember and recognize the individual items. As with parallel forms, it is necessary for the experimenter to control both the length of time between tests and the activity of the subjects during the interval so as to rule out practice, fatigue, and similar effects. If the test has a distinct speed component, it is very unlikely that the same form can be repeated with no score change such as those produced by either practice or fatigue. However, if the statistical criterion for parallel tests is routinely applied, such score changes are detected immediately.

3. *Some variant of the split-half or parallel subtests method.* If only one form of the test is available, and it is not possible or desirable to repeat the test with the same group of subjects, it is possible to consider using one of these methods. Such methods cannot be used unless the test has a liberal time limit. It is also desirable, but not always essential, that the test have a large number of independent items. If three or more parallel subtests are used, then again the criteria presented in Chapter 14 will show whether or not parallel subtests were obtained. In many instances, first versus second halves or odds versus evens will form satisfactory parallel subtests. The most certain method, however, is to match groups of items on statistical and other criteria available, and then to assign randomly each member of a group to a different parallel form. This matching and randomizing method gives excellent results. If information is available for such matching before the items are arranged in the test, it is possible to be certain that either the successive halves (thirds) of a test or the alternate items will be parallel subtests of representative items from the total test.

In studies comparing these three methods of obtaining test reliability, it is generally found that the parallel forms correlation is the lowest and the "corrected odd-even" reliability is the highest.

When either of the first two methods is used, the correlation between two sets of scores is the reliability coefficient of the test. When the split-half method is used, it is necessary to substitute the obtained correlation (r_{12}) in the formula

$$(1) \qquad\qquad r'_{xx} = \frac{2r_{12}}{1 + r_{12}},$$

in order to obtain the test reliability; or to obtain the variance of the difference scores $(x_1 - x_2)$ and use the formula

$$(2) \qquad\qquad r''_{xx} = 1 - \frac{s_d^2}{s_x^2};$$

or to obtain the variance of each half and use the formula

$$(3) \qquad\qquad r''_{xx} = 2\left[1 - \frac{s_{x_1}^2 + s_{x_2}^2}{s_x^2}\right],$$

which is identical with equation 2.

It was shown that, if $s_1 = s_2$, then $r'_{xx} = r''_{xx}$; whereas, if $s_1 \neq s_2$, then $r'_{xx} > r''_{xx}$. If three parallel subtests are used, the obtained correlation is substituted in the formula $3r/(1 + 2r)$ to obtain the reliability; and correspondingly, for greater numbers of subtests, equation 10, Chapter 8, should be used with K set equal to the number of subtest scores.

The last section presents some special considerations related to the reliability of essay examinations. In addition to the usual sources of error in objective examinations, inaccuracy of reading contributes to lowering the reliability of essay examinations. The correlation between scores assigned to the same set of papers by two different readers is known as reader reliability. The agreement in means and variances, as well as in correlations, can also be assessed by the methods of Chapter 14, provided the examinations are read by three or more readers.

The correlation between two parallel forms of an essay examination, when corrected for the attenuation due to inaccuracy of reading, was called the content reliability $(r_{x'_c x''_c})$ of the essay examination. It is given by

$$(24) \qquad\qquad r_{x'_c x''_c} = \frac{r_{x'_1 x''_2}}{\sqrt{r_{x'_1 x'_2} r_{x''_1 x''_2}}},$$

where $r_{x'_1 x''_2}$ is the correlation between assigned scores on the parallel forms,

$r_{x'_1 x'_2}$ is the reader reliability for the x' scores, and

$r_{x''_1 x''_2}$ is the reader reliability for the x'' scores.

Problems

1. If the correlation between the first and second halves of a test is .70, what is the reliability of the test?

2. If the odd-even correlation for a test is .83, what is the reliability of the test?

3. If the reliability of a test is .92, what should be the correlation between two parallel halves?

4. If the reliability of a test is .97, what should be the correlation:

(*a*) Between two parallel thirds?
(*b*) Between two parallel fourths?

5. If the standard deviation of the total scores is 45.3 and the standard deviation of the "odds minus evens" score is 12.1, what is the test reliability on the assumption that odds and evens are parallel subtests?

6. If x and y are parallel tests, the variance of $x - y$ is 73.28, and the variance of $x + y$ is 841.56.

(*a*) What is the reliability of the $x + y$ score?
(*b*) What is the reliability of the x score?
(*c*) What is the reliability of the y score?

7. Consider each of the following tests that are to be administered to a group of high school seniors. For each test, three methods of estimating reliability are being considered: (*a*) the parallel form method, (*b*) the odd-even method, and (*c*) the first-second halves method. For each test indicate whether each of the methods is suitable or not, and explain why.

Test A. Two-digit additions, 100 items 2-minute time limit.

Test B. Current events information questions, 50 items 25-minute time limit. Each item answered correctly by 65 to 75 per cent of students. They are not arranged in order of difficulty, but in a random order.

Test C. A series of 30 mathematical reasoning problems, ranging in difficulty from some that are answered correctly by 90 per cent of the students to others answered correctly by 20 per cent. The problems are arranged in order of difficulty; one hour is allowed for the test.

Test D. A test of differential brightness acuity. Two lights are flashed simultaneously, and the task is to indicate which is brighter. The items have a large difficulty range and are presented more or less in order of increasing difficulty. The test contains 50 items presented at the rate of one every 5 seconds.

Test E. A shorthand dictation test, a 1600-word passage read at the rate of 80 words per minute.

8. An examination has an objective section (*o*) and an essay section (*e*). The split-half correlation of scores for section *o* is .80. The corresponding correlation for section *e* is .60. On section *e* the correlation between the total score given by reader A and reader B is .78. Estimate the content reliability:

(*a*) For section *o*?
(*b*) For section *e*?

9. The following data on 52 students taking the composition section of the French 104–5–6 in June 1940 at the University of Chicago were made available by Dr. Lawrence Andrus.

I	II	III	IV	I	II	III	IV
1	41	24	17	27	58	32	26
2	40	22	18	28	35	24	11
3	73	40	33	29	55	31	24
4	39	20	19	30	62	32	30
5	74	37	37	31	68	32	36
6	49	31	18	32	55	30	25
7	35	20	15	33	62	29	33
8	59	33	26	34	67	36	31
9	44	28	16	35	53	30	23
10	51	25	26	36	54	29	25
11	55	26	29	37	61	32	29
12	54	31	23	38	68	31	37
13	36	25	11	39	58	30	28
14	74	35	39	40	60	29	31
15	48	29	19	41	84	43	41
16	52	28	24	42	39	20	19
17	66	42	24	43	37	22	15
18	73	39	34	44	56	28	28
19	59	33	26	45	56	31	25
20	50	26	24	46	25	15	10
21	25	18	7	47	72	36	36
22	60	31	29	48	33	24	9
23	60	34	26	49	41	26	15
24	65	34	31	50	66	35	31
25	41	18	23	51	38	27	11
26	65	35	30	52	84	41	43

Column I gives the code number of each student.
Column II gives the total score for each student.
Column III gives the score on the first fifty items for each student.
Column IV gives the score on the second fifty items for each student.

Number of items = 100
Maximum number of score points = 100
Mean raw score = 54.52
Standard deviation = 13.98
Number of students = 52

From the foregoing data calculate:

(a) The reliability coefficient for the total test by the split-half method using the Spearman-Brown correction.

(b) The reliability coefficient of the total test from the variance of the total score, and the variance of the difference between scores on the two halves.

(c) The reliability coefficient of the total test from the variance of the total score, the variance of score on the first fifty items, and the variance of scores on the second fifty items.

(d) The standard error of measurement for this test.

(e) What are reasonable limits for the true score of a person who scores 51 on the total test? One who scores 73 on the total test?

(f) Estimate the reliability for a comparable test, twice as long as this one, four times as long, seven times as long, ten times as long. (See table for Spearman-Brown formula in Dunlap and Kurtz, 1932.)

(g) If one wished this test to have a reliability of .97, how long would it be necessary to make it?

(h) Graph the results of problems f and g.

(i) Estimate the reliability this test would have if it were applied to a group whose scores had a standard deviation half that of the original group.

(j) Estimate the reliability this test would have if it were applied to a group whose scores had a standard deviation twice that of the original group.

16

Reliability Estimated
from Item Homogeneity

1. Introduction

As previously indicated, the original approach to the problem of reliability by Spearman was based on the correlation of parallel tests. Kelley (1942) has pointed out that, according to this concept, the major function of the reliability coefficient is to evaluate the *judgment* of the test constructor, to indicate whether or not two forms *thought* to measure the same thing do in fact measure approximately the same thing. Recently there have been several other approaches designed to measure the homogeneity of the items in a test. It should be noted that, if two tests have each a high "homogeneity index" while the correlation between them is low, we have a distinctly disturbing situation. The indication would perhaps be that a homogeneous field existed but that the test constructor did not know enough about that field to construct two parallel tests, clearly an unsatisfactory situation. Likewise, suppose the "homogeneity index" is very low, but the test constructor is able to set up a different form, a parallel test that correlates highly with the first form. Here it would seem that the situation is satisfactory. The field is not unitary, but the test constructor knows the field well enough to set up different tests and have them agree. In short, if a parallel form reliability is high, the situation is satisfactory; if the parallel form reliability is low, the situation is unsatisfactory, regardless of what happens to the index of homogeneity.

One approach to the problem of item homogeneity is to make a factor analysis of the inter-item correlations for a test. If there is only one common factor, the items are homogeneous. If the analysis reveals more than one common factor, it might be desirable to consider dividing the test into parts, each of which represented a single common factor. Such a method would be extremely laborious for any very long test. Carroll (1945) has shown that the point biserial correlation cannot give

220

a one-factor solution if the items differ in difficulty. He has suggested that the two-by-two scatter plot for each pair of items be corrected for the effect of guessing and that the tetrachoric correlation coefficients then be used for a factor analysis. Such a suggestion will probably not be widely adopted until very much more rapid methods of obtaining correlations and factor analyses are available.

The use of methods of analysis of variance for the solution of the problem of reliability has been suggested by many writers; see Johnson and Neyman (1936), Jackson (1939), (1940b), and (1942), Hoyt (1941), and Alexander (1947). Jackson and Ferguson (1941) show how the analysis of variance can aid in separating out and assessing the various sources of unreliability in a test. The consideration of such methods and such a detailed analysis of sources of unreliability are beyond the scope of an elementary discussion.

It has also been shown that the homogeneity of a set of items may be assessed by comparing the standard deviation of the test with the standard deviation to be expected from items of the same difficulty that are correlated zero, or correlated perfectly with each other. This approach has been developed by Loevinger (1947).

Kuder and Richardson (1937) developed several methods of assessing the homogeneity of a set of items without the use of a parallel test. Further studies of these methods have been presented by Richardson and Kuder (1939), Dressel (1940), and Kaitz (1945a). The use of the Lexian ratio in measuring reliability was suggested by Edgerton and Thomson (1942).

Guttman (1945) and (1946) has presented a theory of reliability in terms of estimation of lower bounds for reliability. His view is that the upper bound for reliability of any test is always unity, and that frequently a lower bound can be determined that is far enough from zero and near enough to unity to be of use. He has presented a number of different lower bound estimates for both quantitative and qualitative data.

In this chapter, we shall present only two of these alternative methods of estimating reliability by means of an index of item homogeneity which does not require the division of a test into parallel subtests. Both methods require the number of test items (K) and the standard deviation of the test (s_x). One method requires, in addition, the average item variance; the other requires the test mean.

2. Reliability estimated from item difficulty and test variance

If we assume two tests that are parallel item for item, the intercorrelation (reliability) of these tests may be written as follows. Let us use x

for one test and y for the other test. The items are designated by subscripts from 1 to K.

Equation (1)

$$r_{\Sigma x \Sigma y} = \frac{\sum\limits_{i=1}^{N} (x_{1i} + x_{2i} + \cdots + x_{Ki})(y_{1i} + y_{2i} + \cdots + y_{Ki})}{\sqrt{\sum\limits_{i=1}^{N} (x_{1i} + x_{2i} + \cdots + x_{Ki})^2} \sqrt{\sum\limits_{i=1}^{N} (y_{1i} + y_{2i} + \cdots + y_{Ki})^2}}.$$

Expanding and collecting terms in the numerator, and noting that since we are dealing with parallel tests the two factors in the denominator are equal, we have

$$(2) \qquad r_{\Sigma x \Sigma y} = \frac{\sum\limits_{g=1}^{K} \sum\limits_{i=1}^{N} x_{gi} y_{gi} + \sum\limits_{i=1}^{N} \sum\limits_{g=1}^{K} \sum\limits_{h=1}^{K} x_{gi} y_{hi} \qquad (g \neq h)}{\sum\limits_{i=1}^{N} \sum\limits_{g=1}^{K} x_{gi}^2 + \sum\limits_{i=1}^{N} \sum\limits_{g=1}^{K} \sum\limits_{h=1}^{K} x_{gi} x_{hi} \qquad (g \neq h)}.$$

Dividing through by N and writing the results in terms of correlation and standard deviations, we have

$$(3) \qquad r_{\Sigma x \Sigma y} = \frac{\sum\limits_{g=1}^{K} r_{x_g y_g} s_{x_g} s_{y_g} + \sum\limits_{g=1}^{K} \sum\limits_{h=1}^{K} r_{x_g y_h} s_{x_g} s_{y_h} \qquad (g \neq h)}{\sum\limits_{g=1}^{K} s_{x_g}^2 + \sum\limits_{g=1}^{K} \sum\limits_{h=1}^{K} r_{x_g x_h} s_{x_g} s_{x_h} \qquad (g \neq h)}.$$

Since s_{x_g} and s_{y_g} are standard deviations of parallel items in two forms of the test, we may assume that they are equal. Likewise, since $r_{x_g y_g}$ is the correlation between two parallel items, it is a reliability coefficient, and may be written r_{gg}. In general, we may now drop the distinction between x and y and retain only the subscripts that denote whether we have the same or a different item. This change gives

$$(4) \qquad r_{\Sigma x \Sigma y} = \frac{\sum\limits_{g=1}^{K} r_{gg} s_g^2 + \sum\limits_{g=1}^{K} \sum\limits_{h=1}^{K} r_{gh} s_g s_h \qquad (g \neq h)}{\sum\limits_{g=1}^{K} s_g^2 + \sum\limits_{g=1}^{K} \sum\limits_{h=1}^{K} r_{gh} s_g s_h \qquad (g \neq h)}.$$

It will be noted that the denominator is the variance of the total test. Since the numerator and denominator are alike except for the first term, we may designate the total test variance by s_x^2 and write

$$(5) \qquad r_{\Sigma x \Sigma x} = \frac{s_x^2 - \sum_{g=1}^{K} s_g^2 + \sum_{g=1}^{K} r_{gg} s_g^2}{s_x^2}.$$

Since we do not actually have two tests that parallel each other item for item, it is necessary to make some assumption in order to have a value for r_{gg}. The simplest and most direct assumption is that the average $r_{gg} s_g^2$, which is the covariance between parallel items, is equal to the average $(r_{gh} s_g s_h)$, which is the covariance between non-parallel items. That is,

$$(6) \qquad \sum_{g=1}^{K} r_{gg} s_g^2 = \frac{\sum_{g=1}^{K} \sum_{h=1}^{K} r_{gh} s_g s_h}{K-1} \qquad (g \neq h).$$

Since

$$(7) \qquad s_x^2 = \sum_{g=1}^{K} s_g^2 + \sum_{g=1}^{K} \sum_{h=1}^{K} r_{gh} s_g s_h,$$

we may write

$$(8) \qquad \sum_{g=1}^{K} r_{gg} s_g^2 = \frac{s_x^2 - \sum_{g=1}^{K} s_g^2}{K-1}.$$

Substituting this value in equation 5 gives

$$(9) \qquad r_{\Sigma x \Sigma x} = \frac{s_x^2 - \sum_{g=1}^{K} s_g^2 + \dfrac{s_x^2 - \sum_{g=1}^{K} s_g^2}{K-1}}{s_x^2}.$$

We may write r_{xx} for the reliability of the test and simplify equation 9 to

$$(10) \qquad r_{xx} = \left[\frac{K}{K-1} \right] \left[1 - \frac{\sum_{g=1}^{K} s_g^2}{s_x^2} \right],$$

where r_{xx} is the reliability coefficient of the test,

   K is the number of items in the test,

   s_g^2 is the variance of item g (equals $p_g(1 - p_g)$, where p is the percentage getting the item correct), and

   s_x^2 is the test variance.

It should again be noted that the only assumption made in deriving this equation was that the average covariance among *non-parallel* items was equal to the average covariance among *parallel* items.

In terms of item difficulties or percentage passing a given item, we may write

$$(11) \qquad r_{xx} = \left(\frac{K}{K-1}\right)\left[1 - \frac{\sum\limits_{g=1}^{K}(p_g - p_g{}^2)}{s_x{}^2}\right],$$

where p_g is the proportion passing a given item, and all other terms are defined as in the preceding equation.

> *If the test variance, the number of items in a test, and the percentage of persons correctly answering each item are known, and if the test score is the number of items answered correctly, a lower bound for the reliability coefficient of the test is given by equation 10 or equation 11. These equations are based on only one assumption, that the average covariance between non-parallel items is equal to the average covariance between parallel items.*

It should be noted that formulas 10 and 11 are identical with "formula 20," derived by Kuder and Richardson (1937), with formula 29, in Chapter V of Jackson and Ferguson (1941), and the formula for L_3 given by Guttman (1945). However, the assumptions used for the derivation were radically different in these three papers. Kuder and Richardson assumed that all inter-item correlations were equal. Jackson and Ferguson, however, showed that it is necessary only to assume that the average covariance between parallel items is equal to the average covariance between non-parallel items. They also showed that the assumptions made by Kuder and Richardson (1937) were not only unnecessarily restrictive, but were in some cases internally inconsistent. Guttman demonstrated that the value given by equation 10 is a lower bound to the reliability coefficient.

If the item-test correlations or the inter-item correlations are known, it is possible to use this information in more complex formulas to obtain better estimates of the test reliability. Such formulas have been given by Kuder and Richardson (1937) and by Guttman (1945). These formulas are not given here since it seems that formula 10 is usually quite satisfactory. As a result of some empirical studies, Richardson and Kuder (1939) recommended their "formula 20" as the best one to use.

3. Reliability estimated from test mean and variance

Let us consider the simplified Kuder-Richardson formulation that is obtained by assuming that all items are of the same difficulty. In this case it is possible to estimate Σs_g^2 or $\Sigma(pq)$ from the mean of the test. The number of subjects getting item g correct is Np_g. The sum of these terms over all the items is the total number of correct answers, $N \sum_{g=1}^{K} p_g$. Since the total number of correct answers divided by the number of subjects is the mean of the test, we have

$$(12) \qquad M_x = \sum_{g=1}^{K} p_g,$$

or using $\bar{p}$ to designate the average item difficulty, we may write

$$(13) \qquad M_x = K\bar{p}.$$

Likewise the sum of the variances (Σs^2) may be written

$$(14) \qquad \Sigma p - \Sigma p^2 = K\bar{p} - K\overline{p^2}.$$

If all items are the same difficulty, the average of the squares will be equal to the square of the average, and we may write

$$(15) \qquad \Sigma p - \Sigma p^2 = M_x - \frac{M_x^2}{K}.$$

If we substitute this equation in the numerator of equation 11, we have

$$(16) \qquad r_{xx} = \frac{K}{K-1} \left[1 - \frac{M_x - \dfrac{M_x^2}{K}}{s_x^2} \right],$$

where r_{xx} is the reliability of the test,
   K is the number of items in the test,
   M_x is the test mean, and
   s_x^2 is the variance of raw scores on the test.

This formula is identical with the Kuder-Richardson "formula 21." The derivation given here uses the same assumption as equation 10 or equation 11 plus the assumption that all item difficulties are equal. Formula 16 has the advantage of being very simple to calculate, since it uses only the mean, variance, and number of items. Also it has the advantage of being a lower bound so that we can by the use of this formula quickly satisfy ourselves that a given test is performing fairly well. This formula gives an exact figure for the reliability if all items are of the same difficulty level. If the items in an examination have a wide difficulty range, formula 16 gives an unsatisfactorily low figure for the reliability.

> *If only the mean, standard deviation, and number of items in a test are known, and if the test score is the number of items answered correctly, a lower bound for the reliability co-efficient of the test is given by formula 16. If all the test items are of equal difficulty, this value will be identical with that given by formulas 10 and 11; otherwise it will be smaller.*

4. Summary

If score on a test is the number of items correctly answered, and if we know the number of items in the test, the test variance, and the percentage of persons answering each item correctly, the test reliability may be calculated by

$$(10) \qquad r_{xx} = \left(\frac{K}{K-1}\right)\left[1 - \frac{\sum_{g=1}^{K} s_g^2}{s_x^2}\right],$$

where r_{xx} is the reliability coefficient of the test,
  K is the number of items in the test,
  s_x^2 is the test variance, and
  s_g^2 is the variance of item g, which equals $p_g(1 - p_g)$, where p
   is the percentage of persons answering the item correctly.

Substituting for s_g its value in terms of p_g, we have

$$(11) \qquad r_{xx} = \left(\frac{K}{K-1}\right)\left[1 - \frac{\sum_{g=1}^{K} (p_g - p_g^2)}{s_x^2}\right].$$

These formulas are based on the assumption that the average covariance between non-parallel items is equal to the average covariance between parallel items. Since, in general, the former is smaller than the latter, the values given by equations 10 and 11 will, in general, be underestimates of the reliability.

Using only the test mean, variance, and number of items, we may estimate the test reliability by

$$(16) \qquad r_{xx} = \left(\frac{K}{K-1}\right)\left[1 - \frac{M_x - (M_x^2/K)}{s_x^2}\right]$$

where M_x is the test mean and the other terms have the same definitions as in equation 10. If all the test items are of equal difficulty, equation 16 will be identical with equations 10 and 11. Usually equation 16 gives values that are considerably less than the values given by equations 10 and 11. Like equations 10 and 11, equation 16 may be used only when the score on a test is a linear function of the number of items answered correctly.

Problems

1. We have the following information on a test. Find the reliability by using formulas 11 and 16.

Item	p		
1	70		
2	90		
3	88		
4	94		
5	77		
6	86		
7	69		
8	85		
9	46		
10	77		
11	74		
12	60		
13	30	$M = 15.5$	
14	50		
15	85	$s = 5.6$	
16	90		
17	35		
18	25		
19	47		
20	91		
21	27		
22	23		
23	34		
24	32		
25	65		
	———		
	15.50		

p is the percentage of persons answering each item correctly. (Ample time was allowed for this test so that all 500 persons attempted each item.) The score was number of items answered correctly.

2. Use the following information to obtain the test reliability by formulas 11 and 16.

Item	p	N_a	
1	73	500	
2	68	500	
3	90	500	
4	91	500	
5	70	500	
6	80	500	
7	77	500	
8	39	500	
9	61	500	
10	72	500	
11	71	500	
12	66	500	
13	37	500	
14	50	500	
15	85	500	$M_x = 15.3$
16	49	500	$s_x = 5.1$
17	70	496	
18	65	495	
19	57	490	
20	54	488	
21	16	475	
22	15	465	
23	15	455	
24	20	450	
25	23	440	
26	35	420	
27	34	410	
28	30	400	
29	28	400	
30	33	390	

Use the item analysis data to determine the reliability of the test. (Note that p is not percentage of *total* group answering item correctly.)

Score is number of items answered correctly.

N_a is number of persons attempting each item.

p is percentage of persons *attempting the item* who answer it correctly.

3. The following data on 52 students taking the composition section of the French 104–5–6 in June 1940 were made available by Dr. Lawrence Andrus of the University of Chicago.

Column A gives the item number.

Column B gives the proportion of entire group passing.

A	B	A	B	A	B	A	B
1	.13	26	.42	51	.04	76	.56
2	.54	27	.56	52	.69	77	.25
3	.42	28	.83	53	.44	78	.38
4	.56	29	.50	54	.79	79	.25
5	.73	30	.79	55	.25	80	.44
6	.27	31	.69	56	.19	81	.75
7	.65	32	.27	57	.52	82	.29
8	1.00	33	.52	58	.52	83	.33
9	.25	34	.62	59	.19	84	.37
10	.21	35	.75	60	.77	85	.71
11	.54	36	.81	61	.60	86	.62
12	.38	37	.75	62	.54	87	.69
13	.60	38	.44	63	.58	88	.25
14	.60	39	.44	64	.92	89	.67
15	.77	40	1.00	65	.56	90	.58
16	.62	41	.98	66	.42	91	.08
17	.60	42	.71	67	.38	92	.90
18	.62	43	.67	68	.35	93	.52
19	.88	44	.63	69	.44	94	.81
20	.42	45	.79	70	.27	95	.83
21	.83	46	.77	71	.56	96	.81
22	.62	47	.58	72	.52	97	.44
23	.60	48	.63	73	.56	98	.08
24	.77	49	.17	74	.23	99	.79
25	.63	50	.06	75	.65	100	.56

$N = 52.$ $M = 54.52.$ $s = 13.98.$

From the foregoing data:

(a) Estimate the reliability of the test from the test variance and average item variance.

(b) Estimate the reliability from the test mean and variance.

(c) Compare these values with those found for the same set of test papers in problem 9, Chapter 15.

17

Speed versus Power Tests

1. Definition of speed and power tests

In this chapter the problem of distinguishing between speed and power tests will be considered, and a criterion will be proposed for determining the extent to which a given test approaches a "pure speed" or a "pure power" test. This material is presented as a suggestion toward a differential rationale for speed and power tests. Relatively little has been written on this subject, despite the fact that the problems of item analysis, test length, item difficulty distribution, determination of reliability, and error of measurement are all quite different for the two types of tests. At present most tests are a composite in unknown proportions of speed and power, which makes the development of appropriate theorems in test theory more difficult than for the pure type tests.

First let us define what is meant by a pure speed and a pure power test. A pure speed test is a test composed of items so easy that the subjects never give the wrong answer to any of them. The answers are correct as far as the subject has gone in the test. However, the test contains so many items that no one finishes it in the time allowed. The subject's score, therefore, depends entirely on how far he is able to go in the time allowed. (We shall assume here that the subjects are instructed not to skip any of the items, and that they follow that instruction.)

In order to discuss the speed-power problem symbolically we shall distinguish between two types of "errors." We let

W designate the number of items for which the subject gives an incorrect answer,

U designate the number of items that the subject does not reach, and

X designate the total error score on the test.

That is, $X = W + U$.

In a "pure speed" test W will be zero for each subject; hence both the mean and the standard deviation of W will equal zero. Also $X = U$, that is, the subject's entire score is determined by the number of items that he does not attempt; hence the mean of X equals the mean of U, and the variance of X equals the variance of U.

These are the characteristics of a pure speed test. Any actual test then may be said to approach being a pure speed test to the extent that M_W, the mean, and s_W, the standard deviation of the W's approach zero, and the mean and the standard deviation of the U's approach the mean and standard deviation of the total number of errors $(W + U)$.

In a "pure power" test all the items are attempted so that the score on the test depends entirely upon the number of items that are answered, and answered incorrectly. (Again we assume that by careful directions none of the items is skipped.) In the pure power test, U will be zero for each person; hence the mean and standard deviation of U will be zero. Since for each subject $X = W$, the mean and standard deviation of X equal the mean and standard deviation of W. Again we should note that these characteristics hold strictly only for the pure power test. To the extent that these conditions are approximated, the test approaches a power test.

As has already been pointed out, the split-half (especially the odd-even) reliability cannot be used for any test except a pure power test. As the speed factor enters more and more into the determination of test score, the higher the odd-even reliability will become. Let us now consider a criterion that will indicate when a test is sufficiently close to a pure power test so that we may be relatively certain that the odd-even reliability or some other split-half reliability will not be spuriously high or low. Likewise a criterion for a pure speed test should indicate when a test is primarily a speed test so that the variability due to item difficulty or to carelessness in answering items is negligible. Depending on whether speed and power are positively or negatively correlated, the test-retest reliability of a test that involves both elements is likely to be higher or lower than the reliability of a test that involves only one element. Therefore, if we wish to measure speed in a given function it is important to make certain that we are dealing only to a negligible extent with a test involving power.

2. Effect of unattempted items (or wrong items) on the standard deviation

First let us consider the problem of determining whether the standard deviation of a test is influenced mainly by the speed or the power factor in the test. As in previous derivations, $M_X = M_W + M_U$ so that we may designate the deviation scores by lower-case letters, and write

$$x = w + u.$$

Taking the standard deviation, we square, sum, and divide by N, obtaining

(1)
$$\frac{\Sigma x^2}{N} = \frac{\Sigma(w + u)^2}{N}.$$

Expanding, we have

(2)
$$\frac{\Sigma x^2}{N} = \frac{\Sigma w^2}{N} + \frac{\Sigma u^2}{N} + \frac{2\Sigma wu}{N}.$$

This may also be written

(3)
$$s_x^2 = s_w^2 + s_u^2 + 2r_{wu}s_w s_u.$$

In a pure power test, all subjects will finish, the variance of u will be zero; hence the last two terms will be zero. In a pure speed test there will be no errors made by one who attempts an item; hence the first and the last terms of the right-hand expression will be zero.

In a pure speed test, $s_w = 0$ and $s_u = s_x$. In a pure power test, $s_u = 0$ and $s_w = s_x$.

It should be noted that r_{wu} may well be negative. The subject who omits the fewest items will have answered the most items. Therefore, he may well have a great many errors, thus tending to make the subject with many actual errors (w) the one with the fewest unattempted items (u). For this reason, if we do not wish to calculate both s_u and s_w, it is necessary to rely on the one likely to be zero, or near zero.

For example, if r_{wu} is -1, $s_x = s_w - s_u$ or else $s_x = s_u - s_w$. In either case it is possible that both s_w and s_u would be larger than s_x, thus making the use of either one alone unsuitable as an indication of the magnitude of the other variance.

On the other hand, if either s_w or s_u is zero, or very nearly zero, the other component must be very nearly equal to s_x. The two extreme cases occur when $r_{wu} = +1$ or -1. In the former case $s_x = s_w + s_u$; in the latter $| s_x | = | s_w - s_u |$. If $s_u/s_x = 0.1$, s_w/s_x must lie between 0.9 and 1.1. If $s_u/s_x = 0.01$, the ratio s_w/s_x cannot be less than 0.99 nor more than 1.01. In such a case we have a test that is primarily a power test, in the sense that the test variance would not be changed much if the subjects were allowed to finish the test. At one extreme possibility, if they were allowed to finish, they would all get all the unfinished items wrong, in which event the new s_x would equal the old one. At the other extreme no one would get any of the items wrong, in which case the new s_x would be equal to the present s_w, which, as we have seen above, must be within 10 per cent of s_x if the ratio $s_u/s_x = 0.1$.

Thus from the viewpoint of effect upon the standard deviation of a test, we may say that a test is essentially a speed test if s_w/s_x is very small; and that a test is essentially a power test if s_u/s_x is very small.

For a speed test s_w/s_x is small and

$$(4) \qquad 1 + \frac{s_w}{s_x} > \frac{s_u}{s_x} > 1 - \frac{s_w}{s_x}.$$

A lower bound for the standard deviation is indicated by

$$(5) \qquad s_{u'} = s_x - s_w;$$

an upper bound indicated by

$$(6) \qquad s_{u''} = s_x + s_w.$$

For a power test s_u/s_x is small and

$$(7) \qquad 1 + \frac{s_u}{s_x} > \frac{s_w}{s_x} > 1 - \frac{s_u}{s_x}.$$

From which we have a lower bound for the standard deviation indicated by

$$(8) \qquad s_{w'} = s_x - s_u;$$

and an upper bound indicated by

$$(9) \qquad s_{w''} = s_x + s_u.$$

It should be noted that, although statements identical to the foregoing ones can be made for a large ratio, they are in that case not very helpful. For example, if $s_u/s_x = 0.75$, then

$$1 + 0.75 > \frac{s_w}{s_x} > 1 - 0.75.$$

In other words, s_w/s_x may be as small as 0.25, which is one-third of the ratio s_u/s_x, or it may be equal to 1.75, which is more than double the ratio s_u/s_x.

3. Effect of unattempted items on the error of measurement

The error of measurement for the total score x is equal to the standard deviation times the quantity $\sqrt{(1 - r)}$. Since we have already considered the standard deviation let us consider the other quantity, $\sqrt{(1 - r)}$. Again we define the reliability as the correlation between two parallel forms, designated 1 and 2:

$$(10) \qquad r_{x_1 x_2} = \frac{\Sigma x_1 x_2}{N s_{x_1} s_{x_2}}.$$

Let us first write out the numerator in terms of the component scores w and u:

(11) $$\Sigma x_1 x_2 = \Sigma(w_1 + u_1)(w_2 + u_2).$$

Expanding, we have

(12) $$\Sigma x_1 x_2 = \Sigma w_1 w_2 + \Sigma u_1 u_2 + \Sigma w_2 u_1 + \Sigma w_1 u_2.$$

Using reliabilities and intercorrelations, and noting that variances of parallel forms are equal, we have

(13) $$\Sigma x_1 x_2 = N r_{w_1 w_2} s_w^2 + N r_{u_1 u_2} s_u^2 + 2N r_{wu} s_w s_u.$$

Substituting equation 13 in equation 10, and setting the two variances in the denominator equal to each other, we have

(14) $$r_{x_1 x_2} = \frac{r_{w_1 w_2} s_w^2 + r_{u_1 u_2} s_u^2 + 2r_{wu} s_w s_u}{s_x^2}.$$

Substituting equation 3 in equation 14, we have

(15) $$r_{x_1 x_2} = \frac{r_{w_1 w_2} s_w^2 + r_{u_1 u_2} s_u^2 + 2r_{wu} s_w s_u}{s_w^2 + s_u^2 + 2r_{wu} s_w s_u}.$$

Using equation 15, we may write

(16) $$1 - r_{x_1 x_2} = \frac{s_w^2(1 - r_{w_1 w_2}) + s_u^2(1 - r_{u_1 u_2})}{s_w^2 + s_u^2 + 2r_{wu} s_w s_u}.$$

From equation 3 we see that the denominator of equation 16 is s_x^2. Making this substitution gives

(17) $$s_x^2(1 - r_{xx}) = s_w^2(1 - r_{ww}) + s_u^2(1 - r_{uu}),$$

where s_w^2 is the variance of the w-score (number of items answered incorrectly),

s_u^2 is the variance of the u-score (number of items unattempted at the end of the test),

s_x^2 is the variance of x, which equals $w + u$,

$r_{ww}, r_{uu},$ and r_{xx} represent the reliabilities of these scores. The formula is correct for either split-half or alternate form estimates of reliability.

If x is defined as $w + u$, the error variance for the x-score is equal to the error variance of the w-score plus the error variance of the u-score.

It should be noted that in any test that has both the w and u components, the split-half reliability of u is unity; hence the last term of equation 17 is zero for any split-half reliability. A valid estimate of this second term is given only by a test-retest reliability. For a pure power test, the variance of u is zero; hence a stepped-up split-half correlation is a valid estimate of its reliability. If a test is primarily a power test, that is, if the variance of u is negligible, the stepped-up split-half correlation is still a reasonable estimate of the test reliability. However, when a test is partly speed as well as power so that the second term of equation 17 is not negligible, or when a test is primarily a speed test so that this second term is the major component of the error of measurement, the error of measurement obtained from a split-half reliability is too low. In such a case a test-retest or a parallel form reliability must be used. Whenever the standard deviation of u is much greater than two or three tenths of the standard deviation of w, a split-half correlation is an unsafe basis for estimating the test reliability.

If a test is primarily a power test, it is possible to use the split-half reliability to estimate a range for the error of measurement. Setting r_{uu} equal to zero in equation 17 will give an upper bound for the error of measurement; setting it equal to unity (as is done in the split-half reliability coefficient) will give a lower bound for the error of measurement. For any split-half reliability in which the untried items are divided equally between the halves it is necessarily true that

$$(18) \qquad s_x{}^2(1 - r_{xx}) = s_w{}^2(1 - r_{ww}).$$

Since the error of measurement would be larger if the subjects had been allowed to finish the test, but could not increase by more than the value of $s_u{}^2(1 - r_{uu})$ when $r_{uu} = 0$, we may use $s^2{}_{\text{meas.}}$ to represent the error variance of the test and write

$$(19) \qquad s_x{}^2(1 - r_{xx}) + s_u{}^2 > s^2{}_{\text{meas.}} > s_x{}^2(1 - r_{xx}),$$

where the terms have the same definition as in equation 17. However equation 19 applies only in the case of a split-half reliability estimate for a test that is primarily a power test so that $s_u{}^2$ will be a relatively small possible addition to the error of measurement.

If a test is primarily a *speed test*, a *test-retest* or an *alternate form* reliability must be used. The error of measurement calculated from this reliability will have the two components indicated by equation 17. For a pure speed test, the first of these components would be zero because s_w is zero for a speed test. Regardless of the magnitude of s_w, the error of measurement calculated from a test-retest or an alternate form reliability correctly represents the functioning error of measurement of the test. If the directions for the test and the attitude of the subjects were changed so that no errors (w-score) were made, the new error of measurement would be different from the old one. It does not seem feasible at present to try to estimate the possible magnitude of this change.

4. Effect of unattempted items on the reliability

Equation 18 of Chapter 4 may be rewritten

$$(20) \qquad s^2{}_{meas.} = s_x{}^2(1 - r_{xx}).$$

Solving equation 20 explicitly for the reliability coefficient, we have

$$(21) \qquad r_{xx} = 1 - \frac{s^2{}_{meas.}}{s_x{}^2}.$$

If we use equation 21 and substitute various values of the error of measurement and the standard deviation as indicated in the two preceding sections, we shall obtain some possible upper and lower bounds for the reliability coefficient of power tests that are partially speeded and speed tests that are in part power tests.

For a test that is primarily a power test, a possible estimate of a lower bound for the reliability coefficient may be found by using a small estimate of the standard deviation as given in equation 8 and a large value for the error of measurement as indicated in the first expression of equation 19. Substituting these two values in equation 21 gives

$$(22) \qquad r'_{xx} = 1 - \frac{s_x{}^2(1 - r_{xx}) + s_u{}^2}{(s_x - s_u)^2}.$$

Dividing through by $s_x{}^2$, setting H for s_u/s_x, and writing the expression with a common denominator gives

$$(23) \qquad r'_{xx} = \frac{1 - 2H + H^2 - 1 + r_{xx} - H^2}{1 - 2H + H^2}.$$

Simplifying and ignoring the term H^2, we have

$$(24) \qquad r'_{xx} = \frac{r_{xx} - 2H}{1 - 2H}.$$

Using a stepped-up split-half correlation for the reliability of a partially speeded power test will certainly give a figure higher than the actual reliability of the test so that the obtained reliability coefficient that has been designated by r_{xx} may be regarded as an upper bound for the reliability coefficient. We may use equation 24 as a lower bound and designate the correct reliability by R, obtaining

$$(25) \qquad r_{xx} > R > \frac{r_{xx} - 2H}{1 - 2H},$$

where r_{xx} is the stepped-up split-half correlation,

H is s_u/s_x, the ratio of the standard deviation of the "number unattempted score" to the standard deviation of the number not answered correctly $(u + w)$, and

R is the reliability of the test.

It should be noted that for many tests the right-hand term of equation 25 will give a lower bound that is distressingly low, and may well be far lower than an alternate form reliability for the test. However, it seems probable that, if this lower bound turns out to be satisfactorily high, there can be little doubt that the reliability of the test will be satisfactory. Beginning with equation 15, there are various other assumptions that may be made regarding what might happen if a parallel form instead of a split-half reliability had been used. An experimental investigation of the typical behavior of the various terms in equation 15 is probably needed in order to determine which assumptions are most appropriate.

Another possible lower bound for the reliability of a somewhat speeded power test can be illustrated with equation 15. We may assume that for a split-half reliability all the terms on the right-hand side of equation 15 are correct except for $r_{uu}s_u{}^2$. In a split-half correlation, this term is clearly too large, since r_{uu} is necessarily unity. If the term $s_u{}^2$ is subtracted from the numerator of equation 15 this will have the effect of assuming that r_{uu} is zero, and may well give a good lower bound for the reliability of the test. Let us refer to equation 14. The numerator may be expressed as $r_{xx}s_x{}^2$. If we subtract $s_u{}^2$ from this, and divide by the variance of x, we shall have a reliability figure under the assumption that r_{uu} is zero instead of unity. Thus we have

$$(26) \qquad r''_{xx} = \frac{r_{xx}s_x{}^2 - s_u{}^2}{s_x{}^2}.$$

Writing H for s_u/s_x, we have

$$(27) \qquad r''_{xx} = r_{xx} - H^2,$$

where the terms have the same definition as in equation 25. For this new lower bound we may write

$$(28) \qquad r_{xx} > R' > r_{xx} - H^2.$$

If a power test is partially speeded, and a split-half reliability (r_{xx}) has been calculated, equation 25 or 28 may be used to give some idea of the extent to which r_{xx} is an overestimate of the test reliability.

Some evidence has been presented (see Gulliksen, 1950) indicating that equation 28 may be satisfactory provided H^2 is less than 0.2.

If a test is primarily a speeded test, an alternate form or a test-retest reliability must be used. Such a reliability correctly represents the functioning reliability of the test. If only the number of items unattempted is used as the score, we have a relatively pure measure of speed; if the number correct is used, both speed and accuracy enter into the score. By using both these scores, we can determine the relative reliability of speed alone and of speed together with accuracy. Since this problem is purely experimental, no further theoretical discussion will be given here.

5. Estimation of the variance of the number-unattempted score from item analysis data

The preceding discussion has been in terms of the number of unattempted items because it is possible to obtain the variance of this score from item analysis data which gives number answered correctly, number answered incorrectly, and number of persons not reaching the item. Thus, if item analysis data are available, the variance of the "number-unattempted score," hence the ratio H, can be calculated without rescoring of the papers.

Let us use K to designate the number of items in the test and y_g to designate the number of persons who did not reach item g. It is clear then that $y_{g+1} \geq y_g$, since all persons who did not reach item g did not reach any subsequent item. We shall also assume that $y_g = 0$ for the items near the beginning of the test. It is clear that

$$(29) \qquad \sum_{i=1}^{N} U_i = \sum_{g=1}^{K} y_g.$$

That is, the sum of all the unattempted scores may be obtained by summing over persons or over items. Therefore,

$$(30) \qquad M_U = \frac{\sum_{i=1}^{N} U_i}{N} = \frac{\sum_{g=1}^{K} y_g}{N}.$$

That is, the average unattempted score is equal to the sum of the number unattempted from item 1 to item K, divided by the *number of persons* taking the test.

In order to obtain the standard deviation of the number-unattempted score, we shall use the usual formula for standard deviation written as follows:

$$(31) \qquad s_u{}^2 = \frac{\sum\limits_{i=1}^{N} U_i{}^2}{N} - M_U{}^2.$$

Since M_U is given by formula 30, we know all the terms in this equation except ΣU^2. Let us use n_u to indicate the number of persons making an unattempted score of U; then

$$
\begin{aligned}
n_1 &= y_K & &- y_{K-1} \\
n_2 &= y_{K-1} & &- y_{K-2} \\
n_3 &= y_{K-2} & &- y_{K-3} \\
&\ \ \vdots & &\ \ \vdots \\
(32) \qquad n_u &= y_{K-u+1} & &- y_{K-u} \\
&\ \ \vdots & &\ \ \vdots \\
n_{K-2} &= y_3 & &- y_2 \\
n_{K-1} &= y_2 & &- y_1 \\
n_K &= y_1.
\end{aligned}
$$

Many of the terms in equation 32 will be zero, since all the subjects will presumably attempt many of the earlier items in the test.

In order to obtain ΣU^2 it is necessary to multiply the first frequency by 1^2, the second by 2^2, and so on. The sum of the resulting products is ΣU^2. Using equations 32 to write this sum of products, we obtain

$$(33) \quad \Sigma U^2 = 1^2(y_K - y_{K-1}) + 2^2(y_{K-1} - y_{K-2})$$
$$+ 3^2(y_{K-2} - y_{K-3}) + \cdots + u^2(y_{K-u+1} - y_{K-u})$$
$$+ \cdots + (K-2)^2(y_3 - y_2) + (K-1)^2(y_2 - y_1) + K^2 y_1.$$

As pointed out in connection with equations 32, when one of the y-terms is zero, all subsequent terms are zero and may be omitted from the summation.

Removing the parentheses in equation 33 and performing the subtractions gives

$$(34) \quad \Sigma U^2 = y_K(1^2) + y_{K-1}(2^2 - 1^2) + y_{K-2}(3^2 - 2^2) + \cdots +$$
$$y_{K-u+1}[u^2 - (u-1)^2] + y_{K-u}[(u+1)^2 - u^2]$$
$$+ \cdots + y_3[(K-2)^2 - (K-3)^2]$$
$$+ y_2[(K-1)^2 - (K-2)^2] + y_1[K^2 - (K-1)^2].$$

As before, this series is continued until all subsequent y's are zero.

Since the difference of successive squares constitutes a series of consecutive odd numbers, equation 34 can be written as

$$(35) \quad \Sigma U^2 = 1y_K + 3y_{K-1} + 5y_{K-2} + \cdots + (2u-1)y_{K-u+1} +$$
$$(2u+1)y_{K-u} + \cdots + (2K-5)y_3 + (2K-3)y_2 + (2K-1)y_1.$$

The sum of this series may be written

$$(36) \qquad \sum_{i=1}^{N} U_i^2 = 2 \sum_{u=0}^{K-1} uy_{K-u} + \sum_{u=0}^{K-1} y_{K-u}.$$

The summation begins with $u = 0$ because the first term is y_K, that is, y_{K-u}, where $u = 0$. For the sake of completeness, the summation is indicated as extending to $(K-1)$, but in any computational problem many terms will be zero and can be omitted. From equation 30 we see that the last term of equation 36 is equal to NM_U. Substituting equation 36 in equation 31, we have the solution,

$$(37) \qquad s_u^2 = \left(\frac{1}{N}\right) 2 \sum_{u=0}^{K-1} uy_{K-u} + M_U - M_U^2,$$

where s_u is the standard deviation of the number-unattempted score,
$\quad y_{K-u}$ is the number of persons not reaching the $(K-u)$th item,
$\quad N$ is the number of persons, and
$\quad M_U$ is given by equation 30.

By using equations 30 and 37, s_u, and hence H (for use in equations 24, 25, and 28), may be calculated directly from item analysis data showing the number of persons not reaching each item. These equations will enable us to avoid the labor of rescoring the answer sheets in order to obtain s_u.

6. Summary

In discussing the speed-power problem, the following symbols were used:

W (wrongs), the number of items for which the subject gives an incorrect answer,

U (unattempted), the number of items not reached at the end of the test, and

X the total error score ($X = U + W$).

It is assumed that there are no skipped items.

In a pure speed test M_W and s_w are zero. If s_w/s_x is small (0.1 or less), the test may be regarded as primarily a speed test. In this case

$$(4) \qquad 1 + \frac{s_w}{s_x} > \frac{s_u}{s_x} > 1 - \frac{s_w}{s_x},$$

a lower bound for the standard deviation is indicated by

$$(5) \qquad s_{u'} = s_x - s_w,$$

and an upper bound for the standard deviation by

$$(6) \qquad s_{u''} = s_x + s_w,$$

where s_w is the standard deviation of the W-score,
s_u is the standard deviation of the U-score, and
s_x is the standard deviation of the X-score.

If a test is primarily a speed test, the reliability and the error of measurement must be estimated by means of a test-retest or an alternate form reliability coefficient. The reliability and the error of measurement so computed will correctly represent the functioning reliability of the test under the test directions and administrative conditions that were used. If the test conditions are changed in an effort to eliminate the W-score, it does not seem possible to make reasonable estimates regarding what will happen to the error of measurement and the reliability.

In a pure power test, M_U and s_u are zero. If s_u/s_x is small (0.1 or less), the test may be regarded as primarily a power test. In this case

$$(7) \qquad 1 + \frac{s_u}{s_x} > \frac{s_w}{s_x} > 1 - \frac{s_u}{s_x},$$

a lower bound for the standard deviation is indicated by

$$(8) \qquad s_{w'} = s_x - s_u;$$

and an upper bound for the standard deviation by

$$(9) \qquad\qquad s_{w''} = s_x + s_u.$$

For any split-half reliability that divides the U-score equally between the two halves, it is necessarily true that

$$(18) \qquad\qquad s_x^2(1 - r_{xx}) = s_w^2(1 - r_{ww}).$$

If $s^2_{\text{meas.}}$ is used to designate the error variance as obtained from an alternate form reliability or from allowing the subjects to finish the test,

$$(19) \qquad s_x^2(1 - r_{xx}) + s_u^2 > s^2_{\text{meas.}} > s_x^2(1 - r_{xx}).$$

Two different methods were suggested for estimating a lower bound for the reliability coefficient that would be obtained if the students were allowed to finish the test, or if an alternate form reliability had been calculated. It was found that

$$(25) \qquad\qquad r_{xx} > R > \frac{r_{xx} - 2H}{1 - 2H}$$

or that

$$(28) \qquad\qquad r_{xx} > R' > r_{xx} - H^2.$$

It should be noted that both these estimates are highly tentative and that more experimental work on the relation between speed and power needs to be done before we can know which assumptions are the best ones to make. It seems now that R' is better than R.

In the four preceding equations:

r_{xx} is the split-half reliability for the X-score,
r_{ww} is the split-half reliability for the W-score, and
  H is s_u/s_x.

In order to guard against the possibility of spuriously high split-half reliabilities being reported for partly speeded tests, it would seem desirable to present routinely the coefficient H or the lower bound of formula 28 whenever a split-half reliability is reported.

It was also shown that the variance of the U-score could be calculated from item analysis data showing the number of persons who did not reach each item. If y_g designates the number of persons who did not reach item g,

$$(30) \qquad\qquad M_U = \left(\frac{1}{N}\right) \sum_{g=1}^{K} y_g,$$

and

$$(37) \qquad\qquad s_u^2 = \left(\frac{1}{N}\right) 2 \sum_{u=0}^{K-1} u y_{K-u} + M_U - M_U^2,$$

where M_U is the mean U-score,

    $s_u{}^2$ is the variance of the U-score,

    N is the number of persons taking the test, and

    y_{K-u} is the number of persons not reaching the $(K - u)$th item.

Problems

DATA FOR PROBLEMS 1–3

Item	p	N_a	
1	96	500	
2	94	500	
3	90	500	
4	87	500	
5	92	500	
6	82	500	
7	84	500	
8	87	500	
9	80	500	
10	60	500	
11	68	500	
12	63	498	
13	45	497	
14	55	497	$M = 15.9$
15	50	495	$s = 8.3$
			$r = .97$
16	40	493	corrected odd-
17	62	490	even correlation.
18	50	487	
19	65	485	
20	30	480	
21	20	470	
22	23	465	
23	25	460	
24	40	450	
25	30	441	
26	22	432	
27	26	417	
28	36	406	
29	48	393	
30	21	372	

N_a = number of persons who attempted, that is, indicated some answer (right or wrong) for each item.

p = percentage of those attempting the item who answered it correctly.

1. Calculate the standard deviation of the number-unattempted score from the item analysis data given.

2. Using the data given, plot the frequency distribution of the number-unattempted score, calculate the mean and standard deviation of this distribution to verify the calculation in problem 1.

3. How seriously might the reliability of this test be affected by the speeded nature of the test score?

DATA FOR PROBLEMS 4–6

Test	Number of Items	Gross Score		R	s_u
		Mean	Standard Deviation		
A	180	73.6	27.4	.97	2.1
B	150	93.7	16.3	.93	7.6
C	90	55.1	14.5	.95	6.3
D	70	30.2	8.4	.85	0.5
E	100	53.6	11.2	.82	5.4

$R = 2r/(1 + r)$, where $r =$ the odd-even correlation.

4. Give a lower bound for the reliability coefficient of each of the tests A to E.

5. Give the error of measurement for each test, and also an upper bound for this error.

6. (*a*) For which tests is an odd-even reliability justified?
(*b*) Which tests require an alternate form or a test-retest reliability?

18

Methods of Scoring Tests

1. Introduction

In this chapter we shall consider two basically different types of scoring problems. One type includes the problems in scoring tests where each item has one or possibly more answers that are correct (hence are scored one point) and other answers that are incorrect (hence receive zero credit). The other type of test question is the one for which there is no generally "correct" answer. Items used in attitude, interest, or personality schedules are of this type, and they present special scoring problems.

Only the simpler methods of scoring tests, based on *time* or on *item count*, will be considered here. Scoring methods that attempt to determine "level reached," such as used in the Binet test, demand a different type of theoretical approach, and will not be considered here. The more precise absolute scaling methods presented by Thurstone (1925 and 1927b) also require a different theoretical approach, and are beyond the scope of this book.

For purposes of this discussion, we shall consider that the items of a test can be divided into four categories, designated as follows:

R (rights), the number of items marked correctly,

W (wrongs), the number of items *marked* incorrectly,

S (skips), the number of items that have not been marked, but are followed by items that have been answered (R or W). It looks as if the subject attempted to work the item, and then decided to skip it and move on to a later item.

U (unattempted), the number of consecutive items at the end of the test that are not marked. It looks as if the subject did not have a chance to attempt these items before time was called.

There is a possibility that the number of items skipped (S) or the number at the end of the test that are unattempted (U) would be useful scores. Such scores, coupled with careful test directions, may indicate "cautiousness" or some other similar personality characteristic of the subjects. Some subjects may show a consistent tendency to mark items and to get them wrong; others may hesitate and skip items, hence have a much larger S or U score. No one seems to have investigated such possibilities.

2. Number of correct answers usually a good score

The way tests are usually handled at present is to frame the directions to emphasize that the subjects should answer the items consecutively. This means that the number skipped (S) will be zero or negligibly small. In a power test an effort is made to allow sufficient time for nearly all the questions to be answered by nearly everyone. This means that the number of items unattempted (U) will be small, and the score can be regarded as depending primarily on the number of items marked incorrectly (W). In a speed test an effort is made to have no items answered incorrectly ($W = 0$). The score in this case can be regarded as depending primarily on the number of items unattempted (U).

If a test is primarily a power test, that is, if S and U are each negligible, the score may be the number marked correctly (R) or its complement (W), the number marked incorrectly. If a test is primarily a speed test, as is the case if W and S are each negligible, the score should be the number marked correctly (R) or its complement (U), the number of items unattempted. We shall now consider the cases in which S or U (the number of unmarked items) is not negligible for a test that is designed as a power test, and in which S or W, the number of items marked incorrectly or skipped, is not negligible for a test that is designed as a speed test.

3. The problem of guessing in a power test

Under ordinary examining conditions, even if S and U, the number of unmarked items, are fairly large, the number of items marked correctly (R) will turn out to be a suitable score for the examination. This will be the case if each student reads each item and honestly tries to solve the problem before marking an answer. In general, the student who knows the material will solve the problems correctly and more quickly; hence he will have more correctly marked answers than the student who does not know the material. However, the test constructor and the test scorer must bear in mind that it is possible for a student who does not know the answer to an item to mark it correctly by chance in an objective examination. If practically all items are marked by each of the students, this effect is not a serious one and can be ignored. However, sometimes a student may observe that he has only two minutes left and may feel that it is good policy to mark quickly the last twenty or thirty items that he does not have time to read in order to get the benefit of a chance score. If the score is taken as number marked correctly, this student is likely to add more to his score in the last two minutes than another equally good student who spent the last two minutes attempting to solve one item.

It should be possible to detect such cases by plotting the number of the last item attempted as the abscissa, against R, the number marked correctly as the ordinate. On such a plot, the line $y = x$ would indicate the locus of scores that were perfect as far as the items were marked, and the line $y = (1/A)x$, where A is the number of alternatives for each item, would indicate the locus of the average chance score. For example, if the test is composed of five-choice items, the average score from pure guessing would be one-fifth of the items correct, and the line $y = (1/5)x$ would be the locus of such scores. If some points with a relatively high R, number of correct answers, are near this line, they show that a relatively good R score is made by some persons who are apparently guessing the answers to a large number of items.

A more accurate plot to indicate the presence of good scores made by guessing would be to plot the number correct (R) as the ordinate against the number attempted $(R + W)$ as the abscissa. In the plot previously mentioned, the number of the last item attempted is equal to $(R + W + S)$. In the new plot the points would be moved to the left, and therefore away from the chance line. That is, if the first plot of R against number of last item attempted shows no points near the chance line, there are no scores that are chance scores. If the first plot shows points near the chance line, it may be desirable to make the second plot, which is more time consuming, in order to see if we still have a clear indication that good R scores can be made near the level of an average chance score.

If we have a test in which some persons are making high R scores on the basis of a chance ratio between number right and number attempted, the situation is unsatisfactory, and steps must be taken to alter it. If the test is a trial run, it may be possible to shorten the test by eliminating some of the items, so that more people will finish the test, or it may be possible to lengthen the time allowed for the test so that more persons can finish. If either of these changes can be made, we may still retain the simple number right score. This score has the advantage of being quick to obtain, and of allowing relatively little opportunity for clerical errors. However, if the test scores must be used as is, or if it is not possible for other reasons to shorten the test or lengthen the time, it is possible to consider more complicated scoring formulas that attempt to take account of some of the possible effects of guessing. It must be emphasized again that there is no reason for considering any of these formulas if, for most of the people, $R + W$ is essentially equal to the total number of items in the test. Such formulas are to be used if, and only if, the number of unmarked items $(S + U)$ is fairly large for some persons, and fairly small for others.

Let B = the number of items left blank. This includes those left blank because they were skipped and those not attempted at the end of the test. That is,

$$B = S + U.$$

Using K to designate the total number of items in the test, we have

$$K = R + W + B.$$

One method of dealing with the problem of variation in amount of "guessing" from one person to another is to assume that, if there are A alternative choices for each item, then if each person had answered every item he would have answered $1/A$-th of them correctly by chance. Let X_B designate the score (number right) that would probably have been made if every item had been attempted; then

$$(1) \qquad\qquad X_B = R + \left(\frac{1}{A}\right)B.$$

It should be noted that, if any of the items in an examination are so difficult and have such plausible distractors that less than $1/A$-th of the persons attempting the item get it correct, equation 1 cannot be used. Using it would have the peculiar result that persons not attempting an item would get a higher score than those who thought about the item and answered it. Items of such a high level of difficulty should not be used unless there is some special reason that demands their use. For example a test of "common fallacies" or "popular superstitions" would necessarily contain items that often might be answered correctly by less than the expected chance percentage of those attempting the item. In such a case, however, it is necessary to allow time for *every person to answer each of the items* so that *no correction for effects of guessing will be necessary.*

Instead of estimating how many items would have been marked correctly if all items had been marked, it is also plausible to approach this problem of correction for guessing by attempting to estimate the number of items for which the person knew the correct answer. In this approach it is assumed that the items left blank are not known so that nothing need be added for them. It is also assumed that of the items that the person guessed, $1/A$-th were (by chance) answered correctly and are included in the group of items (R) answered correctly. The remaining fraction of the items answered by guessing, $(A - 1)/A$, represents the items answered incorrectly or the group of items previously designated W. It follows then that $W/(A - 1)$ is equal to the number of items in the R group that were lucky guesses. This number should be subtracted from the number answered correctly to give an estimate of the number of items for which the answer is known. Let X_W designate the number of items for which the answer is known: then

$$(2) \qquad X_W = R - \frac{W}{A - 1}.$$

Again it should be noted that, like equation 1, equation 2 cannot be used when items are so difficult that less than a chance proportion of those attempting the item get it correct. Hamilton (1950) has utilized the regression line to give a more accurate treatment of the problem of chance success.

Equation 1 will always give higher numerical scores than equation 2, except for persons making a perfect score. From the viewpoint of checking against norms, for example, the two equations are not interchangeable. However, from the viewpoint of ranking the students or of making correlational studies, the two scores will give exactly the same results, since they are perfectly correlated. To show this, we shall write the functional relationship between X_B and X_W.

Since $K = R + W + B$, we may write

$$(3) \qquad B = K - W - R.$$

Substitute this value in equation 1 and rearrange terms, obtaining

$$(4) \qquad X_B = \frac{A - 1}{A} R - \frac{1}{A} W + \frac{1}{A} K.$$

If we multiply both sides by $A/(A - 1)$ and subtract the constant $K/(A - 1)$, we have

$$(5) \qquad \frac{A}{A - 1} X_B - \frac{K}{A - 1} = R - \frac{W}{A - 1}.$$

Since the right side of equation 5 is identical with equation 2, we have expressed X_W as a linear function of X_B.

There is another method of dealing with the problem of correcting scores on a primarily power test for the effects of possible guessing. The method to be proposed guards against the practice of quickly answering all unfinished items just before time is called. The suggestion is to use the score

(6)
$$X_U = R + \frac{U}{A}.$$

To the number right (R), add $1/A$-th of the number of items at the end of the test that were unattempted by the subject. This differs from equation 1 in that no partial credit is given for skipping an item. If a subject studies an item, it is desirable to encourage him to give his most considered response to that item. Under equation 6 the subject would have everything to gain and nothing to lose by marking each item that he had time to study. However, there would be no point to rushing through during the last minute of the examination and marking all remaining items since he would get credit for a chance proportion of them anyway. Even the last minute of the examination would, under such a system, best be spent in attempting to give a correct answer to one more item.

As far as the writer knows, equation 6 has not been suggested previously or studied, especially with respect to its effect on the attitude of students taking an examination. Perhaps it would avoid some of the undesirable examination attitudes that are sometimes engendered by objective examinations. It must again be stressed that equations 1, 2, and 6 are suggested only when it is not feasible to allow the students to finish the examination. The best policy is to insure that practically all items are attempted by practically all the students, and then simply score number right (R).

If we depend on IBM machine scoring of tests, the possibility that a student will mark several answers to one item must be considered. Multiple marks on a single item may occur either because the student has misunderstood the directions or because of a belief that the "machine will just sense the correct marks." By ordinary scanning procedures it is difficult to be sure of detecting all multiple marking. An easy method of dealing with this possibility, and also with the possibility that some students will mark items without reading them in order to finish the test, is to score the test rights minus an appropriate fraction of the wrongs. For hand scoring, this equation is considerably more labor than the number right score. For machine scoring, the papers are scored in the same time regardless of the scoring formula. For the rights minus wrongs scoring, it takes a little longer to make the preliminary adjustments on the machine.

When marking papers by hand, scoring solely on the basis of number correct is usually perfectly satisfactory and considerably more rapid and accurate than using any of the foregoing scoring formulas. However, if the test has a short time limit so that many persons do not finish it, the scorers must note, and call to the attention of the supervisor, any cases in which an unusually large number of items have been answered and an unusually large number of errors occur toward the end of the test paper. If a moderately high score is made in this way it may be desirable to rescore the papers using one of the scoring formulas given in this section.

4. The problem of careless errors in a speed test

In a speed test none of the equations given in the preceding section is appropriate. Giving credit for $1/A$-th of the unfinished items (equations 1 or 6) is inappropriate because the score in a speed test should represent the number of items the student is able to do in the allotted time. Deducting for items answered correctly by chance (equation 2) is inappropriate because in a properly constructed speed test the items should not be difficult. Each student should be able to answer each item if he studies the item. Thus there is no problem of estimating how many items the student knows, as distinct from how many lucky guesses he made. The problem is simply, how many items can be solved in the allotted time? If time were increased sufficiently each student would receive a perfect score. If a speed test is properly constructed, and if the students respond properly, the number of skips (S) and the number answered incorrectly (W) will be zero. The test can be scored either in terms of number right (R) or number unattempted at the end of the test (U).

However, if a test is designed as a relatively pure speed test, and we observe papers in which all the items are marked and the number of errors near the end of the paper is much greater than the number near the beginning, it may be well to suspect that those students are answering the items without studying them in order to capitalize on a possible chance score. It is then necessary to rescore the papers using some sort of penalty for items marked incorrectly.

In order to motivate the students to answer each item correctly (not to mark items carelessly), and not to skip items, it is desirable to stress both these points in the instructions. It may also be well to have a small penalty for skips and a larger penalty for errors. This formula would be

$$(7) \qquad X_S = R - \frac{W}{C} - \frac{S}{D},$$

where C and D are arbitrary constants, $C < D$. In order to motivate the students properly, it perhaps is appropriate to make D slightly larger than the number of alternatives (A), and C slightly smaller than $A - 1$. For example, in a five-alternative multiple-choice test the formula might be chosen as

$$R - \frac{W}{3} - \frac{S}{6}.$$

Perhaps such a device would encourage the student to mark the item, but to be careful to mark it correctly.

If the penalty for errors or omissions in a speed test is to be used, it is probably desirable to study the effect of different penalties on the performance of the students. For example, the penalty for errors in a typing test is arbitrarily set at ten words per error. What would be the effect on student performance if he knew that the penalty would be twenty words, or if he knew that it would be five words per error?

It should also be noted that, if we have a criterion to predict, it is unnecessary to bother with these arbitrary scoring formulas. Multiple correlation methods will give the best weights to use.

It is important to adjust the instructions and the motivation of the students so that all items are answered, and are answered honestly, after some study and thought by the student. If such an attitude is secured from all students, then either number right (R), number wrong (W), or number not attempted (U) could readily be used as the score without troubling about any scoring formula. It would be desirable to choose the one of the three that had the largest variance for that particular test as the final score. Every effort should be made to design the examination, the instructions, and the motivation of the students to discourage the use of various irrelevant tricks that are frequently applied in connection with objective examinations. For example, students often inquire if there is a "penalty for guessing." If the answer is "no," they will mark a great many items without bothering to read them if time seems short, with the expectation that some will be correct by chance; if the answer is "yes," they will skip items rather than imperil their score by guessing. Either attitude is to be avoided since both introduce considerations that are probably irrelevant to the student's knowledge and understanding of the field, and these are the things that should be measured by the examination.

5. Time scores for a speed test

Sometimes the *time* taken to perform a standard task is the score assigned to a test. The larger the score, the poorer the performance. In this respect the time score has one property of an error score. It should be noted that in general a time score is not especially suitable for group testing. When testing individuals or small groups of three to five, the examiner can easily hold a stop watch and mark the time when each person finishes. If we wish to secure more uniform timing and are satisfied with relatively coarse groupings, such as half-minute or one-minute groupings, it is possible to have a single time-keeper for a large group of proctors, each of whom is responsible for a small group of students. The time-keeper displays a card with a number on it or writes a number on the blackboard at stated intervals. This digit indicates the number of minutes or half minutes since the test started, or the number until the conclusion of the test (if we wish to have a score such that higher numbers indicate better performance). The proctor then writes this number on the student's answer blank when the student has finished the task. If we are willing to rely on the students, it is possible to have the student write the number on his own answer blank. It is probable that this method should not be used if only one time limit is being taken, since it would be relatively simple for the student to write a different number from the one that was actually being shown. However, if the test is long and keeps the students working for the entire time, it is probably all right to have the student indicate the time of finishing each of a number of subsections, if such a time score is desired.

It should also be noted that time scores could readily have many of the properties of number-correct scores. For example, doubling the test would give two time scores for each person, and the total score on the test would be the sum of the two time scores. If the means, variances, and covariances satisfied the criterion for parallel tests (see Chapter 14), the theorems regarding effect of increased length would hold. In applying the theorems previously established to time scores, it is essential to see that differential fatigue is not a serious factor. For example, the time taken to run a hundred-yard dash is a perfectly good score for the hundred-yard dash "test." It does not follow that the test becomes more reliable as it is lengthened. We cannot use four one-hundred-yard dashes in succession and then perhaps decide to use a five-hundred-yard dash as our final test in order to secure adequate reliability. The same consideration applies in lesser degree to any test. To a considerable extent the nature of a fifteen-minute test cannot be the same as a six-hour test. There are added factors of fatigue, etc., entering in; and we usually find six-hour tests divided into two three-hour sessions. In other words, when equations on test length are used for timed tests, the same precautions previously mentioned apply. Each of the new "unit" tests must be "parallel" to each other. This means that the test average, the standard deviation, and all intercorrelations must be the same. If this is not found to be true as we lengthen either a power or a speed test, the equations relating test length to other parameters no longer hold.

6. Weighting of time and error scores

Sometimes the question of weighting time and error scores to get a single composite score is raised. Again, in general, the best thing to do

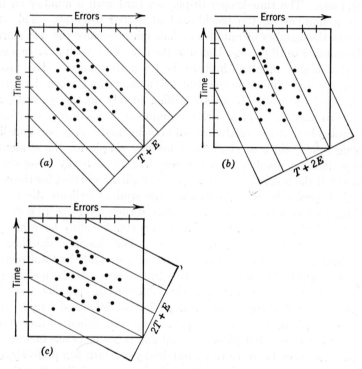

FIGURE 1. Illustrating different weightings of time and errors: (a) Equal weights for time and errors. (b) Errors receive twice as much weight as time. (c) Time receives twice as much weight as errors.

is to have a criterion and to use the weights that best enable us to predict the criterion. The multiple correlation approach is the best one for the problem of weighting when an outside criterion is available.

Often, however, no outside criterion is available. Then the only recourse is to fall back upon judgment. A detailed technical method for securing and dealing with such judgments is given by Thurstone (1931b) in his article "The Indifference Function." If a sufficient amount of time and number of judges are available, this method should be used. However, a very crude approach can also be used that utilizes a correlation scatter plot of time against errors. This scatter plot may be a plot of actual cases or simply an imaginary one where the instructor is asked to suppose that cases of various types occurred.

The instructor in the course, or a group of instructors, or some other authority is then asked to judge "which is better" for various pairs of students. In this way we can rapidly and crudely determine a family of lines that will divide the scatter plot into appropriate zones of increasing ability. Usually these zones can be approximated closely enough by a series of parallel straight lines. This fact indicates that a linear combination of time and errors is adequate. The relative weights of the two factors are proportional to the slopes of the lines. For Figure 1a time and errors are equally weighted, for Figure 1b errors have twice the weight of time, and for Figure 1c time has double the weight of errors.

A similar graphic system can be used for determining rapidly the opinion of an expert judge in the field regarding the appropriate weighting of any two subtests in a composite score.

7. Weighting with a criterion available

When a definite criterion score is available, we should always use the multiple correlation to determine the relative weighting of time and errors, of rights and wrongs, or of rights, wrongs, and skips, or any other set of subscores that can be obtained from a test.

If the test score is used to predict a definite criterion, the scoring method should be based on multiple-correlation methods to secure maximum prediction of the criterion. In principle it is possible to determine a separate weight for each item in the test, and to do this in such a way as to maximize the correlation of total test score with the criterion. In practice, however, this procedure is not usually followed, partly because of the very great amount of calculation involved and partly because the individual item weights are likely to be very unstable unless based on large numbers of cases. For example, Guttman reports a study in which a sample was divided into two random halves; the first half was scored on the basis of multiple-correlation weights assigned to each item, with a resulting multiple correlation of .73. When these same weights were used on the second sample the correlation was .04. (See Horst, 1941, page 360.)

It is often, however, both feasible and desirable to determine the multiple correlation and corresponding weights for a few subscores. For example, instead of being weighted on the basis of average chance success, the wrongs can be weighted to secure maximum prediction of the criterion. This method was given by Thurstone (1919). If the rights are to be weighted unity, the best formula is [1]

$$(8) \qquad X_{W'} = R - \frac{s_R}{s_W} \frac{r_{YW} - r_{YR}r_{RW}}{r_{YR} - r_{YW}r_{RW}} W,$$

where s_R is the standard deviation of the rights score,

s_W is the standard deviation of the wrongs score,

r_{RW} is the correlation between "number right" and "number wrong,"

r_{YR} is the validity coefficient for number right, and

r_{YW} is the validity coefficient for number wrong.

When the weights of equation 8 are used, the correlation between $X_{W'}$ and Y will be the multiple correlation given by

$$(9) \qquad R_{YX_{W'}} = \sqrt{\frac{r_{YR}^2 + r_{YW}^2 - 2r_{YR}r_{YW}r_{RW}}{1 - r_{RW}^2}}.$$

The same type of weighting scheme can be used for any two variables that are being used to predict a third. For example, if Y is the criterion, W is the number of errors, and T is the time score, the best weighting of errors in relation to time will also be given by formula 8 if T is substituted for R. Formula 9 also gives the multiple correlation of this weighted time and errors score with the criterion, if correlations involving time are substituted for those involving number right in the formula.

8. Scoring items that have no correct answer

The items in tests of personality characteristics, attitudes, and interests frequently do not have clear-cut "correct" and "incorrect" answers. Then it is necessary to have a criterion that we wish to predict in order to set up the scoring key for the test. The simplest scoring key is one in which each alternative answer is to be scored either 1 or 0. If there are only two alternatives, say A and B, we obtain the average criterion score for those choosing the A alternative, and the average criterion score for those choosing the B alternative, and assign the score 1 to the alternative having the higher and zero to the alternative having the lower criterion score. If there are many items, and we desire to eliminate some of them, a measure of the significance of the difference, such as $(M_A - M_B)/s_{A-B}$ may be obtained, and items with a low value for this critical ratio may be discarded.

[1] Formulas 8 and 9 are derived in Chapter 20. See equations 56 and 58 of Chapter 20.

If there are several alternative responses for an item, it may still be well to stick to a simple 1 or 0 scoring key. Then the procedure would be to compute the mean criterion score for each of the alternatives, to arrange them in order of magnitude, and to observe where the greatest difference occurred between successive means. The ones above this dividing point are scored 1, and those below are scored 0. A somewhat more elaborate procedure would be to use a measure of the significance of the difference for each of the possible cutting points, and to choose that which gave the largest critical ratio.

If a very large number of cases are available for standardization, so that we can have confidence in the stability of the results, it may be reasonable to consider a more complex scoring key that would assign a different weight to each possible alternative. A procedure is given by Guttman (see Horst, 1941, page 341). In order to maximize the correlation between the score and the criterion, it is necessary to obtain the mean criterion score for those selecting each alternative, and then to assign weights such that the *differences* in weights are proportional to the *differences* in mean criterion scores. A simple method of doing this is to assign the value 0 to the alternative with the lowest mean criterion score, and then to subtract this mean from each of the others, and assign a rounded fraction of this difference in means as the weight for the alternative. For example, in weighting it is probably desirable to limit the weights to the integers from 0 to 5, or from 0 to 10. Wilks (1938) has shown that under certain fairly general sets of assumptions, the correlation between one linear composite and another composite using different weights will differ from unity by about $1/n$, where n is the number of different elements entering into each weighted composite (see equation 47, Chapter 20). That is, elaborate weighting systems with fractional or negative weights probably should be avoided. The use of 0 and 1 or of 0, 1, and 2 is enough for most situations.

It is also possible to score a five-alternative multiple choice item by assigning a different weight to each alternative. The usual procedure is to select one of the alternatives as correct, and to score any one of the other four zero. Sometimes item analysis data indicate clearly that the persons selecting one wrong answer are much better or poorer than those selecting another wrong answer. If it is possible to standardize a test on five or ten thousand cases, it might be worth while to consider the possibility of differential weighting for each alternative. The most common plan at present is to use such detailed item analysis data only for the purpose of discarding the poorer distractors, since it is felt that scoring items either 1 or 0 is highly desirable.

9. Scoring of rank-order items

In testing for certain types of knowledge it is frequently convenient to require the student to arrange the alternative answers in order with respect to some characteristic. If we wish to test for knowledge of chronology without the use of dates, a series of three to ten events can be listed and the student required to number them in order from the earliest to the latest. In testing for the student's appreciation of a given philosophical or political viewpoint, it is possible to present three to five arguments for a given line of action, and require the student to mark 1 for the argument most likely to be used by a socialist (for example), 2 for the argument next most likely to be used, and so on to 5 for the argument that is least likely to be used by a person with such a viewpoint. In order to test for very fine discrimination in any field, it is possible to ask a question, and then present the student with three to five answers. The task is for the student to grade these answers, just as if he were the instructor in the course, by ranking them in order from best to worst. In all cases like the foregoing, we have a problem of how to grade rank-order items.

To simply prepare a key giving the correct order and then give one point for each agreement between the key and the student's ranking is clearly a poor method. For example, if the correct order is 1, 2, 3, 4, the answer 2, 1, 4, 3 shows zero agreement with the key, and so does the answer 4, 3, 2, 1. Yet the first is clearly better than the second. One easy method for scoring such items is to insist that every item be correct in order for credit to be given; any error regardless of how many is given zero credit. Usually the subject matter expert deems such a method unsatisfactory. The person who makes only one inversion (hence has two disagreements with the key) is clearly better than the person who has things mixed up all along the line. A better method is to secure the differences between the rank order given by the subject and the rank order given by the key. For an elaborate scoring procedure we should square these differences, sum them, and compute the rank correlation by the formula

$$(10) \qquad R = 1 - \frac{6\Sigma d^2}{n^3 - n},$$

where Σd^2 is the sum of the squares of rank differences and n is the number of items ranked. However, the computation of a correlation coefficient for each such item on each paper introduces both considerable labor and considerable probability of error.

A simple and satisfactory method for scoring such items is to use the sum of the absolute differences. If the rest of the examination is scored in number of errors, this sum can be added directly in with the errors. If the rest of the examination is scored in terms of number correct, this sum can be subtracted from some constant to give zero disagreement the highest score and great disagreement the lowest score. The formula would be

$$(11) \qquad \text{Score} = C - \Sigma |d|,$$

where $\Sigma |d|$ is the sum of differences ignoring sign, and
C is a constant larger than the greatest $\Sigma |d|$ we are likely to find. (If in scoring we find a few negative differences, these may be counted as zero.)

In ranking three items a still simpler method is available. Ask the student to mark $+$ for the best of the three, 0 for the poorest, and to leave the middle one blank. For all students who have marked the item with one $+$, one 0, and one blank, the papers can be scored by matching the key against the student's item and scoring only the alternative keyed $+$ and the alternative keyed 0. The student gets one point for each of these, which means that he receives two points for perfect agreement with the key, one point if either the best or the poorest alternative has been confused with the middle one, and zero for all more serious confusions. In order to secure more different scores, it is possible to assign two points for agreement with the key on $+$ and two points for agreement on 0; one point for leaving either the $+$ or the zero alternative blank; and no credit for marking with the wrong symbol. Such a scoring system gives four points for perfect agreement; three points if the only error is a confusion of either the best or worst alternative with the middle one; zero for a complete reversal of the correct order; and one point for only one inversion from this worst order. It is not possible to get two points with this system if the student follows the directions. Such a scoring plan makes possible the rapid scoring of rank-order items, and has given scores correlating highly with total score in many instances.

It should be noted that with rank-order items theorems involving K (number of items) cannot be applied except for parallel tests that contain matched rank-order type items.

10. Summary

For most tests in the aptitude and achievement field, it has been found that the number of items answered correctly, or the number of errors, is an eminently satisfactory score. The added labor of using a weighted composite of errors and correct responses is worth while only in certain special cases.

The notation used in the special scoring formulas is:

R (rights), the number of items marked correctly.

W (wrongs), the number of items marked incorrectly.

S (skips), the number of items that have not been marked but are followed by marked items.

U (unattempted), the number of consecutive items at the end of the test that are not marked.

B (blank), the number of unmarked items $(S + U)$.

A (alternatives), the number of possible answers listed for each question. It is assumed here that the same number of alternatives are presented for each question.

If a test that has been designed primarily as a power test turns out to have a large number of unattempted (U) items on some papers, and a small number on others, it may be that some students are using the last two minutes of testing time to mark answers without reading items in order to get the benefit of a chance score. In order to score the examination fairly, in spite of considerable variation in guessing from one person to another, one of the following weighted composites should be used.

$$(1) \qquad X_B = R + \left(\frac{1}{A}\right) B$$

or

$$(2) \qquad X_W = R - \frac{W}{A - 1}$$

or

$$(6) \qquad X_U = R + \frac{U}{A}.$$

Equations 1 and 2 correlate perfectly but do not give identical scores.

If a test is designed primarily as a speed test, and we find that there has been a considerable number of items skipped (S-score) or answered incorrectly (W-score), it may be desirable to introduce a small penalty for skips and a larger penalty for errors. The formula suggested was

$$(7) \qquad X_S = R - \frac{W}{C} - \frac{S}{D},$$

where C and D are arbitrary constants, $C < D$, in order to penalize errors (W) more than skips (S). It is perhaps appropriate to make D slightly larger than the number of alternatives A, and C slightly smaller than $A - 1$.

If time and error scores are to be weighted in determining a composite score, and if no criterion is available, judgments must be relied on to determine relative weights. Such problems may be handled by the "indifference function" technique, or by a rapid and crude graphic method as illustrated in Figure 1. If a criterion is available, multiple correlation methods can be used as indicated by formulas 8 and 9.

If we are dealing with items that do not have a clear-cut correct answer, such as items in a personality questionnaire, it is necessary to have a criterion in order to set up the scoring key. In order to maximize the correlation between score and criterion, weights should be assigned the different alternatives so that the *differences* in weights will be proportional to the *differences* in mean criterion score for the persons choosing each alternative. See the procedure given by Guttman in Horst (1941, page 341).

Rank-order items may be quickly scored by an approximation to a correlation coefficient given by

$$(11) \qquad\qquad \text{Score} = C - \Sigma|\,d\,|,$$

where $\Sigma|\,d\,|$ is the sum of absolute differences in rank between the correct order and the order assigned by the student, and

C is any arbitrary constant, larger than the greatest possible $\Sigma|\,d\,|$.

A still simpler system suitable only for the ranking of three items is also described in section 9.

Problems

1. Derive the formula for the correlation between number correct and number incorrect for an objective test, assuming that there are no omissions.

2. Derive the formula for the correlation between number correct and number incorrect for an objective test. Assume that there *are* omissions and express the results in terms of the *variances* of number *right* and number *omitted* and the *correlation* between these two variables.

3. Derive the formula for correction for chance success in a test each item of which has one correct and six incorrect choices. State clearly each assumption used in the derivation.

4. Comment briefly on the material in Moore's 1940 article.

19

Methods of Standardizing
and Equating Scores

1. Introduction

After having decided on an appropriate scoring system for the test, as indicated in the preceding chapter, we must make some decisions with reference to the distribution of gross scores obtained. In a scholarship examination some are awarded the scholarships, and the rest are not. For Civil Service Examinations, certain persons are placed on the eligible list, while others are considered ineligible for certain types of jobs. In the examinations given by the College Entrance Examination Board the scores are converted to a certain standard form and reported to college admissions officers, who use these scores along with other information in deciding which applicants to accept and which to reject. In a college achievement test, given by an instructor in his course, it is necessary to decide which students failed the examination, which ones made an A grade, which ones made a B grade, etc. In general, we may say that, in using the scores from an examination, it is necessary to determine one or more "critical scores" or to report the results in some standardized form to persons who will make such decisions, and possibly study the relationship of these scores to other variables. We shall now consider various factors in, and the different methods available for, determining critical scores and for standardizing test scores.

2. Assessing the gross score distribution

For every test, regardless of the standardizing system to be used, it is desirable to make a frequency distribution of the gross, or raw, scores and to inspect this distribution carefully. If the test is an achievement test, it is desirable for a test technician to discuss the various points with a subject matter expert, since either one alone might overlook important points.

The first points to note about any test are the number of items (K) and the number of alternative answers (A) presented for each item. From this information we can determine three quantities very important in evaluating any distribution of scores. These quantities are:

1. The perfect score, which is usually equal to K, the number of items in the test.
2. The average chance score M_c, which is usually equal to K/A.
3. The variance of a distribution of chance scores, which is $Kp(1 - p)$, where K is the number of items and p is the probability of answering an item correctly. If p is taken as $1/A$, the variance of a distribution of chance scores becomes $K(A - 1)/A^2$, and the standard deviation of the distribution of chance scores is

$$(1) \qquad s_c = \frac{\sqrt{K(A - 1)}}{A}.$$

It should be noted that these considerations regarding the magnitude of a chance score apply only to power tests or to tests that are primarily power tests. In speed tests it is necessary to be certain that the number of errors made is negligible; methods for determining this have been discussed in Chapters 17 and 18. These three quantities (K, K/A, and s_c) will show the possible meaningful score range for the test. A score that is within one or two standard deviations (s_c) of a chance score should not be interpreted as signifying any knowledge of the subject matter of the examination. For example, if we take the standard that the score must exceed the average chance score by more than $2s_c$, then, for a 25-item test of 5-choice items, we should have a perfect score of 25, an average chance score of 5, and, since s_c is 2, a reasonable upper limit for chance scores may be set at $5 + 2 \times 2 = 9$. That is, this examination has only 16 possible scores (10 to 25 inclusive) that could indicate varying degrees of achievement in the field. On the same basis, we see that a 10-item true-false quiz has only two possible scores (9 and 10) that could indicate varying degrees of achievement in the field. As a first check on any examination, it is well to be certain that the lowest score that is taken as indicative of knowledge is well above the average chance score, and to be certain that the number of possible scores between this lowest score and the highest score is considerably greater than the number of subgroups we wish to determine from the test.

Having obtained the lowest non-chance score and the perfect score from knowing only the number of items, and the number of choices per item, we next make a frequency distribution of scores and find the mean and standard deviation of this distribution. It is also necessary to use some method of determining the reliability of the test and the error of measurement in order to compare the error of measurement with the score range between the upper and lower bound of any given subgroup. For example, if an achievement examination is being used to divide students into A's, B's, C's, and D's, it would seem desirable to have the score range of about three or four times the error of measurement from the lowest B to the highest B. We can readily see that, if this score range is equal only to the error of measurement, then through examination error alone quite a few students who should receive A's will receive C's, and vice versa. Errors in classification of students at the borderline between A and B, between B and C, etc., cannot be avoided under any circumstances. It is possible, however, by making the distance between the upper and lower bound of any one subclass large, in comparison with the error of measurement, to be relatively certain that errors of classification of *two* or more groups will be avoided.

In general the significant or important distances on the scale, such as the distances between different critical scores or the differences between successive school grades or successive years, should be very large in comparison with the error of measurement of the test. A difference as large as this is necessary in order to insure that important decisions are not made on the basis of accidental fluctuations.

It should be noted that nothing has been said about "per cent of a perfect score" as one of the criteria for judging the distribution of raw scores. Unless we have very thorough procedures for pretesting items so that item difficulty and test reliability are equated from one examination to another, the amount of knowledge indicated by a given per cent of perfect score will vary tremendously from one examination to another. If an examination is composed of items that are answered correctly on the average by 80 per cent of the students, the *average* student will make 80 per cent of a perfect score, and the upper half of the class will be grouped in the narrow score range between 80 per cent of perfect and perfect. Compare such an examination with one which attempts to discriminate between the good student and the very superior student. This latter examination would probably be composed of items answered correctly on the average by 50 per cent of the students so that the average student would make 50 per cent of a perfect score, and the wide score range from 50 per cent correct to perfect would be available for distinguishing between various degrees of ability in the upper half of the class. Scoring these two examinations on the basis of per cent of a perfect score would not give satisfactory results. Each distribution must be inspected to determine where the average score and scores one, two, and three standard deviations above and below average lie with respect to the perfect score and the lowest non-chance score. The judges should then select the various critical score points, taking care to make the distance between these points reasonably greater than the error of measurement of the test.

The effect on standards of requiring "successive hurdles" versus permitting multiple attempts to pass the examination must be considered in setting any critical score. The term successive hurdles is used to designate a procedure whereby the successful candidate must have passed each of several tests; failure on *any one* disqualifies the person. If such an administrative procedure is being followed, it is essential to pass many more at any given step than are desired to pass the total procedure. On the other hand, the effect of permitting multiple attempts is to lower standards, particularly if the examination is unreliable. In effect this is the opposite of the successive hurdles procedure in which a single failure disqualifies the candidate. If many trials are allowed, the candidate is usually passed if he succeeds in *any one attempt*. In order not to be accepted the candidate must fail in every attempt. It is clear then that, if multiple trials are permitted, it is well to err on the side of fixing the lowest passing score too high; whereas, if a successive hurdles procedure is followed, it is well to err on the side of fixing the lowest passing score too low.

3. Standardizing by expert judgment, using an arbitrary scale

In some cases the major interest of the subject matter expert lies in one or two critical scores; yet it is desirable, or required by some regulation, that many different score values be reported. For example, in some colleges it is conventional to grade on a scale from 100 (representing a perfect score) to 65 or 70 (representing the failure line). In Navy schools it is conventional to grade on a scale from 4.0 (representing a perfect score) to 1.0, or possibly lower, for the poorest possible performance. On this scale 2.5 is a critical score (the lowest passing grade). In Civil Service ratings 70 is defined by regulations as the mark to be assigned the lowest acceptable performance, and 100 is the highest mark to be assigned.

In making any transformation from a given raw score scale to some conventional scale with critical limiting values, the simplest and best procedure is to determine the limiting values carefully and then to make a linear interpolation between these values. Such a procedure is described for use in Navy schools by Stuit (1947), pages 485–487. A similar procedure for converting raw scores into Civil Service ratings is described by Adkins *et al.* (1947), pages 194–202. The simplest method is a graphic one.

1. Prepare a graph in which the various possible raw score values are indicated on one axis, and the various possible values of the desired arbitrary scale are indicated on the other axis.

2. Prepare a frequency distribution of the raw score values with the various key points such as the mean, standard deviation, standard error of measurement, perfect score, average chance score, and average chance score plus one or two times the standard deviation of such scores (see equation 1) indicated.

3. Determine the raw score corresponding to some critical level, such as the lowest passing mark. In determining this point all relevant factors must be considered, such as the probable difficulty level of the examination, the standards it is necessary to maintain, and the number and per cent of candidates above or below this critical point. Parenthetically, it may be remarked that sometimes a committee will feel that it is desirable to look for gaps in the score distribution, and to set the lowest passing mark just above such a gap. As pointed out by Adkins *et al.* (1947), pages 197–198, such gaps are purely accidental and should be ignored in favor of more rational considerations in determining the critical points.

4. Determine the raw score corresponding to another fixed point, such as the highest score to be assigned. The top score of 100, 99, or 4.0 need not be assigned to a raw score that corresponds to a perfect paper. If the examination is very difficult, it might be desirable to take a raw score considerably lower than the perfect one to correspond to the highest assigned score. At the other extreme, if the examination is very easy so that, for instance, 5 or 10 per cent of the persons made a perfect raw score, it might be desirable to assign a score below the highest allowable (such as 80 or 3.5) to the perfect raw score.

5. Plot the points determined in steps 3 and 4 on the graph, and connect them with a straight line. From this line it is possible to read off the transformed score corresponding to each raw score.

By repeating steps analogous to 3 and 4 for other critical points it is possible to set up several different linear transformations in different parts of the scale, should that appear desirable.

4. Transformations to indicate the individual's standing in his group—general considerations

In many testing situations it is not possible or desirable or necessary to make immediate decisions for action on the basis of the gross score distribution. In such situations it is conventional to transform the gross scores into some uniform set of numbers that indicates the relative standing of the individual in his group.   For example, transformed scores on the tests of the College Entrance Examination Board are reported to the designated colleges.   The admissions officer of each college determines which scores will be regarded as critical for purposes of admission to his institution.   In the aptitude testing programs of the Army, Navy, and Air Forces, during the second World War, the tests were given and the transformed scores made a part of the man's permanent record.   As experience accumulated regarding the performance of men in different schools and jobs or as the relative needs in the different schools changed, the critical score requirements could be specified and altered.

Four different gross score transformations that indicate the relative standing of the individual in his group will be considered: (1) linear transformations, including (a) standard score and (b) linear derived scores; (2) non-linear transformations, including (a) percentile score and (b) normalized score.

In using standard, linear derived, percentile, or normalized scores, we should bear in mind that such scores indicate only the relationship of the individual to a given group.   They indicate nothing about the general level of knowledge or attainment of the group or its members.   For example, a set of percentile or standard scores on a test in American history would not indicate whether the students had a comprehensive grasp of the major items in American history or only a very meager knowledge.   Such an assessment must be based on the judgment of subject matter experts, and can never be determined by clever quantitative scoring devices.   In setting up the test, the judgment of the subject matter expert is used to include a good sampling of items from the field, and as indicated in section 2 of this chapter the subject matter expert must assess the gross score distribution, with the help of a test technician, in order to determine critical scores between the chance score and the perfect score.   From this point of view the most satisfactory testing programs are those closely related to training programs so that the subject matter expert may, for instance, judge: "The performance of these students is unsatisfactory; I will step up the quality and quantity of work demanded in the training program so that the next class will make a higher average gross score than this one has made."   By using the same or parallel tests, it is then possible to see whether or not the altered training program has produced the desired result of a higher test score.   For an illustration of such a use of testing in conjunction with training programs, see Stuit (1947), pages 303–313.   The blind use of group norms, such as the standard, percentile, or normalized scores, without any assessment of the absolute level of achievement in terms of judgments of subject matter experts, may serve to conceal marked inadequacy of training standards.

5. Linear transformations—standard score

The basic linear transformation of gross scores is known as the "standard score." The individual's score is expressed as a deviation from the mean of the distribution (that is, the mean is taken as the origin or zero point). The score unit is taken as the standard deviation of the gross score distribution. Standard scores will thus have a mean of zero and a standard deviation of unity. Using z_i to designate the standard score of the ith individual, we may write

$$(2) \qquad z_i = \frac{X_i - \mu}{\sigma},$$

where X_i is the gross score of the ith individual,

    μ is the population mean, and

    σ is the standard deviation of the population.

Since the mean and standard deviation of the population are usually unknown, it is conventional to have a large sample and to use the mean and standard deviation of this sample in computing standard scores. The formula may be written

$$(3) \qquad z_i = \frac{X_i - M_X}{s_X},$$

where M_X and s_X are the mean and standard deviation of the distribution of gross scores (X). The numerator of equation 3 is frequently designated by the lower case x $(x_i = X_i - M_X)$, and is referred to as a *deviation* score. The term "deviation score" usually refers to scores expressed in terms of deviations from the mean of the distribution. Since the population mean and standard deviation, as indicated in equation 2, are usually unknown, it is usually necessary to use equation 3 instead of equation 2 in calculating standard scores. However, the general problem of standardizing several different forms of a test or of using standard scores when several different groups are involved becomes clearer if the problem is considered in terms of equation 2. This equation indicates that the problem is to define clearly the population in terms of which the standard scores are to be computed, and then to use maximum likelihood estimates of the gross score mean and standard deviation of this population.

From equations 2 or 3, we see that a standard score is a score in which the mean of the distribution is zero and its standard deviation is unity. All standard scores above the mean will be positive, and all below the mean will be negative. A person whose raw score is at the mean of the distribution will have a standard score of zero, since for that person

$$\frac{M_X - M_X}{s_X} = 0.$$

A person whose score is one standard deviation above the mean will have a standard score of 1.00, since $X_i - M_X = s_X$; hence equation 3 equals 1.00.

In order to use equation 3 for computing the standard score equivalent to each gross score, it is convenient to rewrite it in the form

(4)
$$z_i = \left(\frac{1}{s_X}\right) X_i - \frac{M_X}{s_X}.$$

In computing z-scores when $X_i > M_X$, enter $-M_X/s_X$ in the computing machine, clear the keyboard, put the quantity $(1/s_X)$ in the keyboard,

TABLE 1

FREQUENCY DISTRIBUTION

Score	Frequency	v	fv	fv^2	
120–129	2	−5	−10	50	Assumed mean 174.5
130–139	3	−4	−12	48	plus
140–149	12	−3	−36	108	correction term −1.0
150–159	23	−2	−46	92	equals
160–169	37	−1	−37	37	gross score mean 173.5
170–179	51	0			
180–189	39	+1	+39	39	$\frac{\Sigma fv^2}{N} - \bar{v}^2 = 2.98 - 0.01 = 2.97$
190–199	21	+2	+42	84	
200–209	9	+3	+27	81	
210–219	2	+4	+8	32	Gross score variance = $2.97(CI)^2$
220–229	1	+5	+5	25	= 297.0
Column sums	200		−20	596	Gross score standard deviation
Sums/N			−0.1	2.98	$= \sqrt{297} = 17.234$
Correction term		$\bar{v}(CI) = -1.0$			Class Interval (CI) = 10

and add it in X_b times, where X_b is the gross score value just above the mean score. Record the z-value corresponding to this X-score, and then add in $(1/s_X)$ once more for the next higher score, and so on until the z-value for the highest attained or the highest possible X-score has been found. When $X_i < M_X$, the procedure is similar, except that all the signs of the quantities must be reversed. Enter $+(M_X/s_X)$ in the machine, put in the quantity $(1/s_X)$, and subtract it once to give the z-score corresponding to a gross score of 1, twice to give the value corresponding to a gross score of 2, and so on until the value X_a is reached, where X_a is the gross score value just below the mean. All the z-scores corresponding to X-scores below the mean must be given negative signs.

This computing procedure is illustrated with the frequency distribution of 200 cases shown in Table 1 on the preceding page. This frequency distribution has a mean of 173.5, a variance of 297.0, and a standard deviation of 17.234. Substituting these values in equation 3 gives

$$z_i = \frac{X_i - 173.5}{17.234}.$$

The computation equation 4 thus becomes

$$z_i = \frac{1}{17.234} X_i - \frac{173.5}{17.234}$$

or

$$z_i = 0.058025X_i - 10.067309.$$

This equation is used directly in the computing machine for computing the standard score equivalent of all gross scores above the mean. Table 2 illustrates a worksheet used to compute a standard score equivalent for the *midpoint of each class interval*.[1] The entries *below* the horizontal line in Table 2, where X_i takes in succession the values from 174.5 to 224.5, correspond to scores *higher* than the mean of the distribution. Since the class interval in Table 1 is 10, the coefficient in the computing equation is multiplied by $10X$ at each step, instead of by X. For the negative entries *above* the horizontal line in Table 2 the equation used in the computing machine is

$$-z_i = 10.067309 - 0.058025X_i,$$

where X_i takes in succession the values from 124.5 to 164.5 shown in the column labeled X in Table 2. Column z gives the standard scores

---

[1] For linear derived scores to be discussed in the next section, a convenient worksheet will be shown that gives a derived score equivalent for each different gross score. This procedure, illustrated in Table 3, may be adapted to z-scores if a standard score equivalent is desired for each gross score.

to six decimal places. However, standard scores of psychological tests should at most be given to two decimal places, as shown in column z'. It may be noted that, even with a test reliability as high as .99, the error of measurement is

$$s_x\sqrt{1 - .99} = s_x\sqrt{.01} = .1s_x,$$

so that the error of measurement is greater than one-tenth the standard deviation for practically all tests.

TABLE 2

COMPUTING FORM FOR STANDARD SCORES

X	z	z'	
124.5	-2.843196	-2.84	
134.5	-2.262946	-2.26	
144.5	-1.682696	-1.68	$-z_i = 10.067309 - 0.058025X_i$
154.5	-1.102446	-1.10	
164.5	-0.522196	-0.52	
174.5	$+0.058054$	$+0.06$	
184.5	$+0.638304$	$+0.64$	
194.5	$+1.218554$	$+1.22$	$z_i = 0.058025X_i - 10.067309$
204.5	$+1.798804$	$+1.80$	
214.5	$+2.379054$	$+2.38$	
224.5	$+2.959304$	$+2.96$	

In order to check the entries in Table 2, the differences between adjacent entries should be computed. In this table these differences are each equal to .58, which is ten times the multiplying coefficient in the computing equation. It is also desirable to recompute the entries for about three selected points, one near the middle and one near each end of the scale. Gross errors may also be detected by computing the gross score equivalents for -3, -2, -1, 0, $+1$, $+2$, and $+3$ standard deviations from the mean to see that these scores fall in the proper intervals.

If a graphic method of setting up the transformation from X-scores to z-scores is preferred, the simplest method is to set up appropriate coordinates on a graph, including the range of X-scores on one axis and z-scores from about -3.0 to $+3.0$ on the other axis. Select one X-score approximately -2 or -3 standard deviations below the mean, and calculate the corresponding z-score. Do the same for a high X-score approximately $+2$ or $+3$ standard deviations above the mean. Plot these two points on the graph, and connect them with a straight line. Several check points may then be selected. For example, a z-score of zero should correspond exactly to M_X on the X-scale, and scores that are one standard deviation above and below the mean on the X-scale should correspond to z-values of plus one and minus one, respectively.

The standard score is primarily useful for theoretical purposes. For example, it simplifies algebraic derivations involving variances and covariances; and tables of the normal curve have z-scores as one of their entries. However, it has marked disadvantages as a method of reporting scores for the individuals of a group. The range from -3 to $+3$ is awkward since it necessitates the use of negative and positive numbers. Also, in order to have a sufficient number of different scores, it is necessary to use decimals. It is conventional, therefore, to use some more convenient linear transformation of standard scores for reporting purposes. These, termed linear derived scores, will be considered in the next section.

6. Linear transformations—linear derived scores

Since the standard score (z-score) with a mean of zero and a standard deviation of unity necessitates using negative and decimal scores, it is usual to report scores in terms of some arbitrary distribution that has a standard deviation considerably greater than unity and a mean that is four or five times the standard deviation. Such a set of units, called here linear derived scores, avoids both negative and fractional scores.

Several different transformations of this type have been found useful in different circumstances. For example, the Board of Examinations at the University of Chicago has used a linear derived score with a mean of 20 and a standard deviation of 4. Most scores would thus lie between 8 and 32; and, even if an occasional score of plus or minus five standard deviations were found, we should still have scores ranging only from 0 to 40. Such scores would not be confused easily with percentile scores that were used in reporting some of the entrance tests, and a class interval of one-fourth standard deviation is convenient for computing variances and correlations so that decimal scores need not be used. The College Entrance Examination Board adopted a linear derived score system for reporting scores on its examinations to the colleges. These scores have a mean of 500 and a standard deviation of 100. They range from a lower limit of 200 to an upper limit of 800, and cannot possibly be confused with percentile ratings, grade ratings (with 100 as perfect and 60 or 65 as failure), mental age ratings (in the 10 to 20 range), or I.Q. ratings (in the 100 to 150 range) that may appear on the applicant's secondary school record. Because such scores would be unwieldy to record or to use in IBM card operations, the College Entrance Examination Board also adopted another linear derived score system for use within the office for keeping certain records, computing correlations, making item analyses, etc. This system uses a mean of 13 and a standard deviation of 4. The particular advantage of this scale is that the scores can be recorded in two columns of an IBM card, and the squares of the scores can be recorded in three columns. A score as large as 4.5σ would be 31, and the square of 31 is 961. Using five columns of the card to record the score and the square of the score facilitates many operations that require computing sums and sums of squares.

During the second World War, the United States Navy used a basic aptitude test battery and reported scores in terms of a linear derived scale with a mean of 50 and a standard deviation of 10. Such a scale could be reported in two columns of an IBM card. Moreover, as long as operations requiring sums of squares were not used to a great extent, maximum use was made of the IBM cards, and a scale had reasonably fine subdivisions. The United States Army used an aptitude test battery and reported the scores on a linear derived scale with a mean of 100 and a standard deviation of 20. This made the scale somewhat comparable to the I.Q. scale so that not too much change in habits regarding meaning of the numbers was required to make reasonable judgments for the new test scores. These examples illustrate some of the types of linear derived scores in use, and indicate some of the reasons for selecting given arbitrary values for the mean and standard deviation of the derived score scale.

In order to determine the formula for computing any of these linear derived scores, let us use w_i to designate the linear derived score of the ith individual and write

$$(5) \qquad w_i = s_w z_i + M_w,$$

where M_w is the value that has been selected as convenient for the mean of the linear derived scores, and

s_w is the value that has been selected as convenient for the standard deviation of these scores.

Since the standard deviation of the z-scores is unity, multiplying each z-score by s_w will give a set of scores with a standard deviation equal to s_w. Also, since the mean z-score is zero, adding M_w to each score will give a set of scores with a mean equal to M_w. Thus the transformation of equation 5 insures that the new scores will have the desired mean and standard deviation.

To express the w-scores directly in terms of the gross scores, substitute equation 4 in equation 5 and write

$$(6) \qquad w_i = \left(\frac{s_w}{s_X}\right) X_i + M_w - \left(\frac{s_w}{s_X}\right) M_X,$$

where the terms have the same definitions as in equations 3 and 5. The computing procedure is similar to that for equation 4, except that no provision need be made for negative scores, since M_w and s_w are selected so that all scores are positive. The procedure is to enter $M_w - (s_w/s_X)M_X$ in the keyboard, put it into the machine, clear the keyboard, and enter (s_w/s_X). Add this quantity once to obtain the w-score equivalent to an X-score of one, twice for the equivalent of an X-score of two, and so on until the highest X-score has been reached. Again a graphic check can be made by computing the w-score equal to a very low X-score, and to a very high X-score, plotting these two points on a graph, connecting them with a straight line, and then computing several intermediate check points.

Linear derived scores (including, of course, standard scores) have this very valuable property: the characteristics of the original distribution of gross scores are duplicated in the transformed scores. The indices of skewness and kurtosis for the distribution of gross scores are identical with the indices for the distribution of linear derived scores, and both sets of scores will have the same correlation with any other variable. Non-linear transformations of gross scores will in general have indices of skewness, kurtosis, and correlation that are different from those of the original gross scores.

The data of Table 1 are used to illustrate the computation of linear derived scores with a mean of 500 and a standard deviation of 100. Substituting these values for M_w and s_w, and the mean and standard deviation of Table 1 for M_X and s_X in equation 6, gives the equation

$$w_i = \frac{100}{17.234} X_i + 500 - \frac{100}{17.234} 173.5,$$

which may be written as the computing equation

$$w_i = 5.8025 X_i - 506.7309.$$

The rectangular layout of Table 3 furnishes a convenient method of recording a linear derived score equivalent for each gross score of 120 to 229. The computing procedure is to enter the additive term (-506.7309) in the keyboard and into the machine, then to clear the keyboard and to enter the coefficient $(+5.8025)$. This coefficient is then multiplied by 120 to give the first entry (190).   One additional rotation of the machine is needed ⸝to give each of the remaining 109 entries in Table 3.   The results are recorded to only three digits, which corresponds to units of one-hundredth of a standard deviation.   The best method for checking a table like Table 3 is first to compute successive differences.   These differences should each be equal to the constant term, which in the present illustration is about 5.8, so that⸝to the

TABLE 3

COMPUTING FORM FOR LINEAR DERIVED SCORES

$$w_i = \frac{100}{17.234} X_i + 500 - \frac{100}{17.234} 173.5$$

or

$$w_i = 5.8025 X_i - 506.7309$$

	0	1	2	3	4	5	6	7	8	9
12–	190	195	201	207	213	219	224	230	236	242
13–	248	253	259	265	271	277	282	288	294	300
14–	306	311	317	323	329	335	340	346	352	358
15–	364	369	375	381	387	393	398	404	410	416
16–	422	427	433	439	445	451	456	462	468	474
17–	480	485	491	497	503	509	515	520	526	532
18–	538	544	549	555	561	567	573	578	584	590
19–	596	602	607	613	619	625	631	636	642	648
20–	654	660	665	671	677	683	689	694	700	706
21–	712	718	723	729	735	741	747	752	758	764
22–	770	776	781	787	793	799	805	810	816	822

nearest unit the difference is usually 6, with an occasional 5.   Second, to check for gross errors, it is desirable to determine the gross score points corresponding to -3, -2, -1, 0, $+1$, $+2$, and $+3$ standard deviations from the mean and to see that these are, respectively, 200, 300, 400, 500, 600, 700, and 800.

Linear derived scores, like standard scores, may also be obtained graphically.   The best procedure is to set up the gross score and the derived score scale in suitable units on graph paper.   The gross score and corresponding linear derived score are then found for three points, such as -3, 0, and $+3$ standard deviations from the mean.   These three points are plotted; they should lie in a straight line.   This line is the transformation line from which the derived score equivalent for a given gross score, or the reverse, may be read.

Let us contrast the properties of *linear* transformations of gross scores (such as standard and other derived scores) with the properties of *non-linear* transformations (percentile and normalized scores) to be considered next.

1. The linear transformation involves no assumptions about the distribution of the population or the sample. It has third and fourth moments identical with those of the raw score distribution. This fact has several important consequences.
2. It is possible to tell from the distribution of transformed scores whether the test was too easy, too difficult, or about the correct difficulty level for the group.
3. Since the correlation between gross scores is identical with the correlation between linear transformations of gross scores, the equations dealing with the effect of test length and group heterogeneity on reliability and validity (see Chapters 6 to 13) hold for gross scores and for any linear transformation of gross scores. The equations developed in Chapters 6 to 13 do not necessarily hold for non-linear transformations of gross scores.
4. Equating various forms of tests is simpler if some linear transformation is used, since such a transformation depends only on estimating two parameters, the mean and the variance. The theory for equating when transformations are non-linear is more difficult to develop, and probably will give results with greater sampling errors.

7. Non-linear transformations—percentile ranks

We shall consider only the two most commonly used non-linear transformations, namely, percentile scores and normalized scores.

A given individual's percentile score indicates the percentage of persons in the distribution who score less than that individual. Consider a distribution of ten cases, each of which makes a different gross score. Each person is considered to occupy one-tenth of the entire percentile range from 0 to 100, as illustrated:

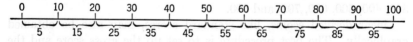

The score assigned to each person is the midpoint of the range occupied by that person so that, for a distribution of ten persons, the percentile scores will be 5, 15, $\cdots$, 95, as indicated above. If several different persons make the same score, each person's score is the midpoint of the range occupied by all of them. In terms of the foregoing illustration, assume that the lowest three persons made the same score and that the second and third from the top made the same score. In such a case we should have

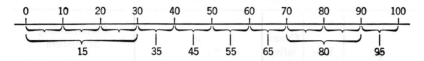

three percentile scores of 15 and two of 80, as illustrated. For a distribution of 100 cases, each person having a different score, the percentile scores would begin with 0.5 and proceed by unit steps to 99.5.

Let us use the data of Table 1 to illustrate the general procedure for calculating a percentile equivalent for the midpoint of each class interval. Table 4 illustrates the computation of a percentile corresponding to the midpoint of each class interval and to the boundary between the class intervals. The midpercentile for a given interval is assigned to all the cases in that interval. The procedure is to compute $100/2N$, enter this figure in the calculating machine keyboard, and multiply by the number of cases in the lowest class interval to obtain the midpercentile for that interval. Multiplying a second time by the number of cases in the lowest class interval gives the percentile corresponding to the upper bound of the lowest, and the lower bound of the next class interval. We then multiply twice by the frequency in the next class interval, and so on until the percentile score 100 is reached.

In Table 4 this procedure is illustrated for a distribution of 200 cases. The quantity $100/2N$ is 0.25. This quantity is entered in the machine and multiplied by 2, giving 0.50, then by 2 again, giving 1.00. Thus the percentile score assigned to the lowest two persons is 0.5. Next multiply by 3, the frequency in the next class interval, and enter 1.75, the percentile score for the three persons scoring in the 130's; then by 3 again, obtaining 2.50 for the boundary between the second and third class intervals. This procedure is continued until the final check percentile is obtained. The percentile equivalent of the upper bound of the highest class interval must be $100.000 \cdots$ to as many decimal places as are being recorded. In Table 4 the percentile corresponding to the upper and lower bound of each class interval has been recorded (the upper bound of one class interval being identical with the lower bound of the next higher class interval). Since only the midpercentile is used, it is better procedure to record only the midpercentile and omit the upper and lower bounds. They were included to make the computational procedure clear. Also for a check on the number of revolutions that should be recorded in the calculating machine at each step, the last three columns of Table 4 are given. The speediest method of calculating percentiles is

TABLE 4

Computing Form for Percentile Scores

X	Frequency	Cumulative Frequency	p			Corresponding Multipliers		
			Lower	Mid	Upper	Lower	Mid	Upper
120–129	2	2	0.00	0.50	1.00	0	2	4
130–139	3	5	1.00	1.75	2.50	4	7	10
140–149	12	17	2.50	5.50	8.50	10	22	34
150–159	23	40	8.50	14.25	20.00	34	57	80
160–169	37	77	20.00	29.25	38.50	80	117	154
170–179	51	128	38.50	51.25	64.00	154	205	256
180–189	39	167	64.00	73.75	83.50	256	295	334
190–199	21	188	83.50	88.75	94.00	334	355	376
200–209	9	197	94.00	96.25	98.50	376	385	394
210–219	2	199	98.50	99.00	99.50	394	396	398
220–229	1	200	99.50	99.75	100.00	398	399	400
N =	200							

$$\frac{100}{2N} = \frac{100}{400} = 0.25$$

to follow the procedure indicated in Table 4, recording only the midpercentiles and the final check percentile of 100.00 · · ·.

A routine for computing percentiles that gives a check on the number of revolutions in the machine at each step and records only midpercentiles is shown in Table 5. The columns X and f give scores and frequencies as before. A zero frequency is added for a hypothetical class interval below the lowest and above the highest. Column f' gives the sums of *adjacent* entries in column f. The column labeled $\Sigma f'$ is a cumulative frequency of the f' column. The entries in column $\Sigma f'$ are identical with those in the next to the last column in Table 4, except that the check multiplier of 400 (2N) has been added. The quantity 100/2N (0.25) is multiplied in turn by each of the entries in column $\Sigma f'$, giving the percentiles in the column labeled p. These are identical with the midpercentiles of Table 4, except that the final check percentile appears at the bottom.

Regardless of the original shape of the distribution of gross scores, the distribution of percentile scores will be rectangular. Percentile scores furnish a convenient method of indicating a person's standing relative to a specified group. Such scores are easy to explain to other persons, and are felt to be readily understood. Here, however, the advantages of percentile scores end. Such scores cannot legitimately be subjected

TABLE 5

COMPUTING FORM FOR PERCENTILE SCORES

X	f	f'	$\Sigma f'$	p
	0		0	0.00
		2		
120–129	2		2	0.50
		5		
130–139	3		7	1.75
		15		
140–149	12		22	5.50
		35		
150–159	23		57	14.25
		60		
160–169	37		117	29.25
		88		
170–179	51		205	51.25
		90		
180–189	39		295	73.75
		60		
190–199	21		355	88.75
		30		
200–209	9		385	96.25
		11		
210–219	2		396	99.00
		3		
220–229	1		399	99.75
		1		
	0		400	100.00

$$N = \Sigma f = 200$$

$$\frac{100}{2N} = \frac{100}{400} = 0.25$$

Enter 100/2N in the machine. Multiply cumulatively by the entries in f'. The dial indicating number of revolutions will show successively the entries in $\Sigma f'$. *Check:* The last product should be unity to as many decimals as are being recorded.

to the usual arithmetical operations. For example, if two tests are involved, and Mr. A has a percentile rating of 60 in one and 70 in the other, whereas Mr. B has ratings of 50 and 80, the procedure of averaging the percentiles would give 65 in both tests. Mr. B, however, probably would have a higher average if the original gross scores were used. Just as average percentiles are misleading, so the correlation coefficients found from using percentiles are different (usually smaller) from those found with gross scores. The amount of drop in correlation brought about by changing from gross scores to percentile scores in a normal distribution has been discussed by Karl Pearson (1907). Pearson indicates that at most the correlation between normalized scores is .0180 greater than the correlation between percentile scores.

From the illustrations given, we see that the maximum possible and the minimum possible percentile scores are functions of the size of the group taking the test. For a distribution of ten cases, these limits are 95 and 5. For a distribution of a hundred cases, these limits are 99.5 and 0.5. For distributions of a hundred cases or over, the effect of N on percentile scores can usually be ignored. However, *normalized* scores of the very high-scoring and the very low-scoring persons are markedly affected by the number of cases in the distribution and by slight differences in the extremes of the distribution. These effects will be illustrated in the discussion of normalized scores in section 8.

The most striking defect of percentile scores appears, however, when we consider the problems of making norms comparable from group to group or test to test. Each percentile score is sensitive to any local change in its part of the distribution. Unlike the standard scores, the percentile score does not depend upon certain constants characteristic of the distribution as a whole. Standard scores, as indicated in equation 2, depend upon only two parameters, a mean and a standard deviation.

In the equating of percentile scores, no such simple parameters exist. Thus we see why it is that, with the growth of testing techniques, the percentile score has gradually been abandoned as a basic type of score, despite its seeming ease of interpretation. It is frequently convenient, however, to supplement linear derived scores with a table of percentiles expressed with reference to some specified group to aid in the initial interpretation of these scores.

8. Non-linear transformations—normalized scores

Since the normal distribution has many convenient properties, and since many distributions have been found to be normal or Gaussian distributions, another type of score is used in which the frequency distribution has been distorted from its original shape into a normal distribution.

After percentile scores are obtained, the normalized scores are obtained from tables of the normal curve. The base line (usually listed in the tables as x or z) value corresponding to each percentile is found.

Such a set of scores would range from -3 to $+3$, which is sometimes regarded as an undesirable score range. So again, as in the change from standard scores to the more general linear derived scores, we may multiply the normalized scores by any suitable value to give a standard deviation greater than unity, and we may add any suitable value to avoid negative scores.

Like percentile scores, the normalized scores do not duplicate the properties of the original gross score distribution. Regardless of the skewness and kurtosis of the original distribution, the skewness of the normalized scores will be zero and the kurtosis three. However, the usual arithmetic operations with scores, such as averaging and calculating correlations, are probably legitimate operations to perform with normalized scores, as they are not with percentile scores. The problem of comparability from test to test and group to group is more difficult with normalized than with standard or linear derived scores. Thurstone (1925 and 1927b), however, has presented a method for dealing with this problem. Flanagan (1939b) has described the use of a system of normalized scores by the Cooperative Test Service.

As in the case of percentile scores, the range of normalized scores varies with the number of cases in the distribution. With normalized scores this difference is very marked at the extremes of the distribution. For a distribution of 10 cases, the percentile score limits are 95 and 5. The corresponding normalized score limits are ∓ 1.64. For a distribution of 100 cases, the percentile score limits of 99.5 and 0.5 correspond to normalized score limits of ∓ 2.58. Also slight differences in grouping in the extremes of a distribution, such as might be brought about by varying degrees of skewness or kurtosis, will have a very pronounced effect upon the extreme normalized scores. For example, in a distribution of 200 cases, if *one* person makes the highest raw score his percentile score is 99.75, and his normalized score is 2.81, as shown in Table 6. If *five* persons of the 200 tie for top score, the percentile score for this group is 98.75, which is only one point lower than the score obtained by the top one person. However, the normalized score equivalent is 2.24, or more than half a standard deviation less than 2.81—the normalized score for the top ranking *one*. Such apparently slight differences in groupings can make very serious differences in reported test results. If normalized scores on different tests are to be compared, it is important to be sure that slight differences in groupings in extreme cases do not occur, and also to be certain that the groups are similar in size; otherwise the results reported for normalized scores will be influenced more by the size of the group and by slight differences in grouping in the extremes than by the abilities of the students.

The computation of normalized scores is illustrated in Table 6. First, we compute the percentile score equivalents as illustrated in Table 5. Then from a table of the normal curve we read the base line values (normalized scores) that correspond to the various areas under the curve (that is, the percentile scores).

TABLE 6

A WORKSHEET FOR RECORDING NORMALIZED SCORES

X	f	p	n
120–129	2	0.50	−2.58
130–139	3	1.75	−2.11
140–149	12	5.50	−1.60
150–159	23	14.25	−1.07
160–169	37	29.25	−0.55
170–179	51	51.25	+0.03
180–189	39	73.75	+0.64
190–199	21	88.75	+1.21
200–209	9	96.25	+1.78
210–219	2	99.00	+2.33
220–229	1	99.75	+2.81

Columns X, f, and p are taken from Table 5. Column n gives the normalized score. n is read from a table of the normal curve by entering it with the values p or $1 - p$.

The use of normalized scores is indicated if there is reason to believe that the ability measured by the test is normally distributed and that defects in the test make the distribution of gross scores non-normal. Normalized scores on different tests are not comparable unless the groups are of similar size, and the distribution of extreme scores is similar in both distributions.

9. Standardizing to indicate relation to a selected standard group—McCall's T-score; Cooperative Test Scaled Scores

In order to give a common reference point for various scores, it has been suggested that some standard group be chosen and carefully defined, and that then the scores of all individuals be referred to that group regardless of whether or not the individual is a member of that group.

For example, McCall (1922) suggested that a normalized scale for general use in standardized tests be based on scores of 12-year-old children. He suggested that the mean normalized score for 12-year-olds be called 50, and the standard deviation of the normalized scores for 12-year-olds be fixed at 10. He suggested that such scores might be called T-scores (in honor of Thorndike and Terman), and that all individuals might be scored on this scale regardless of whether or not they were 12 years old. McCall suggests the use of normalized scores, but he does not explain how we are to find out what gross score corresponds to very extreme normalized scores, such, for example, as plus or minus five or six standard deviations away from the mean. This difficulty in extrapolation has been overcome in subsequent expositions of the T-score by making it a standardized score or a linear derived score with mean 50 and standard deviation 10 based on a group of 12-year-old children. Although this change in McCall's original idea (see Hull, 1928, pages 166–171, for example) makes it possible to extend the scale somewhat farther than the range of the original group, it still is rather a meaningless standardization to include in a test for 12-year-olds items suitable for first-grade children that will be answered correctly by all the 12-year-old group, and items suitable for college students that will be answered correctly by essentially none of the 12-year-old group. The only usable type of solution for such a problem seems to lie in the devising of methods for putting several different groups on the same scale. Thurstone's absolute scaling methods and the Cooperative Test Service system of Scaled Scores illustrate such methods.

Thorndike suggested that successive groups be normalized on the same scale. He suggested making allowance only for differences in the means of the various groups. If the normalized score of one group is designated by X and the normalized score of another group by Y, Thorndike's method amounts to equating the groups by using only the assumption that $X = Y + C$. The score when related to the X-group will differ by a constant from the score related to the Y-group. He assumed that the means of the groups differed but that the different groups each had the same standard deviation. In using this method to standardize items, it was found that scale values of items varied systematically from one group to another. Thurstone suggested that more freedom be allowed in equating the groups. His suggestion was that all the groups be assumed to be normally distributed on the same base line, but that it be assumed that the *means and standard deviations* of the different distributions might be different. Thurstone's method of absolute scaling based on this assumption has been found to give consistent results in several instances in which it has been used. Gardner (1947), working with Rulon and Kelley at Harvard, has suggested that another degree of freedom be allowed in trying to match several different distributions to the same base line. He has assumed that the groups may differ in mean, in standard deviation, *and in skewness*. That is, the distributions need not have the *zero* skew characteristic of the normal distribution. Gardner has used this method in analyzing score distributions for tests given at various grade levels, and has found definite skewness differences from grade to grade.

The Scaled Scores of the Cooperative Test Service are similar to the absolute scaling units Thurstone has suggested, in that the different groups used are assumed to be normally distributed with different means and standard deviations, on the same basic scale. The Cooperative Test Service Scaled Scores are based on the performance of a group of average white children in the United States at the completion of a particular course in a typical school with the usual instruction in that subject. Such a group is assumed to be normally distributed with a mean of 50 and a standard deviation of 10. It is clear that, in selecting cases for such a standardization, there must be a number of somewhat arbitrary decisions and assumptions. Thurstone made no suggestions regarding any arbitrary value for a mean and a standard deviation. He pointed out that the standard deviation of some selected group could be termed unity or ten, and that a zero point could be chosen three to five standard deviations below the mean of the lowest group.

A system for normalizing several distributions on the same base line that is rigorous and complete with significance tests and confidence intervals has not yet been devised. The procedure described by Flanagan (1939b) is an iterative one and uses only the points corresponding to the median score of each of the distributions considered. Since Thurstone's procedure is simple and direct, requiring no successive approximations, we shall describe it here. Flanagan (1939b) has described the Cooperative test procedure and has worked out an illustrative example with both his own and Thurstone's method.

In his bulletin on Scaled Scores, Flanagan (1939b) indicates that it was Kelley who suggested 50 as the mean for the average child, subject to the average training. The concept was developed in connection with Kelley's unpublished Universal Grading System.

10. Thurstone's absolute scaling methods for gross scores

Thurstone's absolute scaling procedure as applied to test scores involves the following steps.

1. Give the test to two or more groups, so that there will be a marked overlap in the distributions of adjacent groups. We shall illustrate with two such groups, a and b.
2. Select ten or twenty gross score points (X_i), so that percentile scores (and hence normalized scores) can be determined for both groups a and b.
3. Determine the normalized scores $(Y_{ia}$ and $Y_{ib})$ for groups a and b corresponding to each of the selected gross score points X_i.

4. Plot Y_{ia} on the ordinate against Y_{ib} on the abscissa for these selected points.

5. If the two groups can each be normalized on the same base line, this plot will be linear.

In order to show this, let us assume a basic scale of values V_i, in terms of which both groups are measured. If M_{Va}, and s_{Va} designate the mean and the standard deviation of the a-group in these standard units, any given score V_i may be expressed in terms of this mean and standard deviation as

(7) $$V_i = M_{Va} + Y_{ia}s_{Va},$$

where Y_{ia}, the normalized score with respect to the a-distribution, indicates the number of standard deviation steps between the mean (M_{Va}) and the score (V_i). Such an equation, with a different value of V_i and Y_{ia}, and the same value of M_{Va} and s_{Va}, applies for each of the gross score points selected for the comparison. Similarly, each of these points may be referred to distribution b instead of distribution a, and another set of equations written. These equations are

(8) $$V_i = M_{Vb} + Y_{ib}s_{Vb}.$$

Equating these for successive values of V_i, we have

(9) $$M_{Va} + Y_{ia}s_{Va} = M_{Vb} + Y_{ib}s_{Vb},$$

where M_{Va} and M_{Vb} are the means in hypothetical absolute units for distributions a and b,

s_{Va} and s_{Vb} are the standard deviations in hypothetical absolute units for distributions a and b, and

Y_{ia} and Y_{ib} are the normalized scores for distributions a and b, respectively.

This fundamental equation as applied to test scores is given by Thurstone (1938). Since the M's and s's are constant regardless of the varying values of the Y's, we have a linear relationship between Y_{ia} and Y_{ib} that may be written

(10) $$Y_{ia} = \left(\frac{s_{Vb}}{s_{Va}}\right) Y_{ib} + \frac{M_{Vb} - M_{Va}}{s_{Va}}.$$

That is, if it is possible to normalize both the a and the b distributions on the same base line, by assuming only different means and standard deviations, the plot of the normalized scores (Y_{ia}) against the normalized scores (Y_{ib}) will be linear with a slope equal to the ratio of the standard deviations, and an intercept equal to the difference of means divided by one of the standard deviations. If one mean and one standard deviation are known, it is possible to solve for the other mean and standard deviation. Thus, by assuming a mean and standard deviation for the a group, the mean and standard deviation of the b group can be computed. Then this computed mean and standard deviation for the b group can be used in the b-c comparison to solve for the mean and the standard deviation of c.

It must be noted, however, that the entire process of equating the scores of the various distributions is dependent upon the linearity of the plot Y_{ia} against Y_{ib}. If this plot deviates markedly from the linear, we must conclude that both these groups cannot be normal on the same base line. The equating procedure is indicated to be impossible on these assumptions, and cannot be carried out legitimately. At present we do not have significance tests to determine when the procedure is legitimate, and when not. It is necessary to use judgment regarding the seriousness of deviation from linearity until significance tests are developed.

Thurstone (1938) has applied this method and has shown that a national distribution of 40,229 A.C.E. scores, the distribution of 646 University of Chicago freshmen, and of 113 test subjects volunteering for the primary mental abilities battery may all be regarded as normal on the same base line.

The absolute scaling technique makes it possible to plot the frequency distributions of many different groups on the same base line. With units so established, it would be possible to indicate something about the nature of the mental growth curve for different types of mental functions. Thurstone has applied such scaling methods to Binet test items from different ages, and he finds a mental growth curve that is slightly negatively accelerated although it is still rising rapidly at age 14; see Thurstone (1925). He also applied the same absolute scaling method to the completion test data collected by Trabue (Thurstone, 1927b), and he found a growth curve with only a very slight negative acceleration that was still rising very rapidly at grade 12.

11. Standardizing to indicate age or grade placement

One of the methods currently much in use for scaling of test scores is to express the results in terms of the subject's standing with respect to one of several possible standard groups. Mental Age units and Educational Age units are examples of this type of scaling. In the case of Mental Age units, the individual is given a score that represents the "age group to which he belongs on account of his test score." Similarly, the Educational Age units are used to indicate the grade group that the individual resembles. Thurstone (1926) has shown the unsatisfactory nature of the Mental Age unit as well as the ambiguity of definition of such a unit.

An Educational Age of 8, for example, may be assigned to the average score made by all eighth-grade students; or it may be assigned to a score X_i, which is selected so that the eighth grade is the *average grade* of persons who make that score. These two definitions will not lead to the same set of norms. The first definition corresponds to the regression of test score on grade placement, and the second corresponds to the regression of grade placement on test score.

In order to interpret such age or grade norms, we must know which regression line has been used, and we must also know the amount of variation about that regression line. For example, suppose that grade norms are established on the basis of the regression of score on grade. Then a person who has a grade placement score of 8, for example, has made a score equal to the average of scores made by a representative group of eighth-grade students. Suppose we know that this student is in the sixth grade; it is then possible to say that he is two years advanced, in the sense that if he were put with a group of eighth graders he would score at the average of that group. However, we do not learn from such information alone how usual or unusual such a performance is. If such a student is a 95 percentile on sixth-grade norms, we know that only 5 per cent of sixth-grade students are two years or more advanced. However, if this point is an 80 percentile on the sixth-grade norms, we know that there is a great deal of overlap between the successive grades, so much in fact that 20 per cent of students in the sixth grade are at or above the score made by the average eighth grader.

The same type of remarks apply to any other set of norms based on successive groups, whether they are age groups, grade groups, height groups, or some other type of grouping. To know that a person is two or three years advanced or retarded in a given characteristic becomes much more meaningful if we also know the percentage of his group that is advanced or retarded an equal or greater amount.

Similar considerations apply if the other regression line is used. Suppose, for example, that we are using the regression of chronological age on test score. Then the age equivalent would be the average age of persons making the same score. Suppose that the average age of persons making a given score is ten, and that the student whose score is being interpreted is eight years old. We know that he is with a group that is on the average two years older than he is. Again if only 5 per cent of the students making that score are under eight years of age, we are dealing with a relatively unusual degree of advancement. However, if 20 or 25 per cent of students making that score are under eight, we are dealing with a somewhat more common degree of advancement.

Figure 1 illustrates the difference between these two modes of procedure. Line A is the regression of score on age—the average score made by persons of each chronological age. According to this line a score of X_1 is equivalent to an age level of b years, whereas a score of X_2 is equivalent to an age level of c years. On the other hand, the line B is the regression of age on score—the average age of those persons making a given score. According to this line, the age level corresponding to a

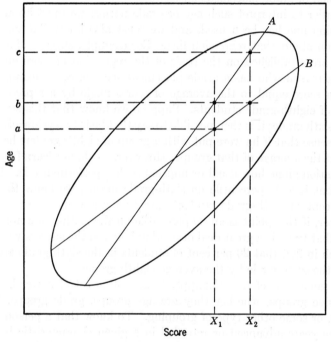

FIGURE 1. Illustrating the difference between the regression of score on age, and age on score.

score of X_1 is a years, and the age level corresponding to a score of X_2 is b years. It will be noticed that, for all scores above the mean, the regression of age on score will give lower age equivalents for any gross score level than will the regression of score on age. For scores below the mean, the regression of age on score gives higher age equivalents than does the regression of score on age. It will also be noticed that the "age difference" corresponding to any two scores is very large if the regression of score on age is used, and it is small if the regression of age on score is used.

It is interesting to note that, if the regression of age on score is used, as tests become more unreliable children above the average will be reported as less advanced than they are, and children below the average will be reported as less retarded than they are. If the regression of score on age is used, children who are above average are reported as very remarkably advanced, and children below average are reported as very markedly retarded.

This effect is demonstrated in Figure 2. Line *A* is the regression of test score on age, and line *B* the regression of age on test score for a very

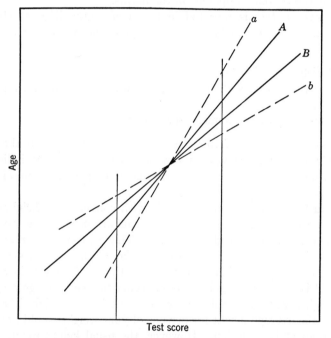

FIGURE 2.   Showing the effect of test unreliability and regression line used, upon norms.

reliable test that correlates highly with age. Since lines *A* and *B* are close together, it makes little difference which regression line is used when the correlation between score and age is high. If the test is shortened and becomes unreliable, line *A* will tend to move into a position such as line *a*, and *B* will move toward line *b*. Line *a* then represents the regression of score on age for a relatively unreliable test, one that does not correlate very high with age. Line *b* represents the regression of age on score for such a test.

By taking any illustrative score level above the mean, we see that such a child will appear more advanced if the regression of score on age is used, and less advanced if the regression of age on score is used. In a similar manner, for any score less than average, the unreliable test will minimize the degree of retardation if the regression of age on score is used, and exaggerate it if the regression of score on age is used. The only method of taking account of such effects is to report the error of measurement of the test and the variability about the regression line which is used. Once this is done, the difference between the test represented by lines A and B and the unreliable test represented by the dotted lines a and b becomes apparent in the norms.

Whenever a test is reported in terms of many different standard groups, as in the case of age norms or grade norms, it is essential to know:

1. Which regression line is used.
2. The variability of the standardization group about that regression line.
3. The error of measurement of the test.

Unless we have this information it is impossible to estimate the degree to which two or three years retardation or advancement indicates a marked deviation from normal performance or a marked unreliability in the test.

To illustrate the same sort of logic with conventional height-weight norms, we may point out that such norms are usually constructed to give the regression of weight on height. That is, to use the norms, *first* find your height, and then note the average weight for persons of your height. Such information is of value in that it tells you how many pounds it is necessary to gain or lose in order to be of average weight for your height. Since it is not as easy to alter height as weight, the norms showing the average height for persons of your weight would not give a useful item of information. However, the usual height-weight norms do not tell anything about how usual or unusual your particular weight is for your height. Some percentile tables would be useful in indicating to each person that he was within the weight range of 50 per cent of persons of his height, or was heavier or lighter than all but 5 per cent of persons of his height. Such added information would be of value in indicating whether the person was unusually over- or underweight. In reporting norms on older tests, various types of quotients became popular. Not only was the test scored, for example, in terms of Mental Age, with no reference to variability of Mental Age attaching to a given chronological age, but the child's Mental Age was divided by the chronological age to obtain a quotient, known as the Intelligence

Quotient or the I.Q. Similarly, the grade placement indicated by the test score was called Educational Age; and the Educational Age was divided by chronological age to obtain an educational quotient or E.Q. It was also suggested that one of these quotients be divided by the other to determine an accomplishment quotient or A.Q.

Since we need the error of estimate and the error of measurement in order to make any reasonable interpretation of norms such as Mental Age or Educational Age, it would seem clear that further routine division would only make the scores more and more difficult to interpret. As Thurstone (1926) has pointed out, the best procedure is to abandon the various quotient type units, as well as the Mental or Educational Age units, and to use normalized or standard score type units referring a given case to several different sets of norms if necessary. We could then say that this eight-year-old child has a percentile score of 92 on eight-year norms, and one of 50 on the eleven-year norms. Such a system would reflect both the typicality or atypicality of the child, and the rate of advancement of the group in the trait or skill in question.

It should also be noted that the relationship between different norms is changed by social customs. For example, the relationship between age and grade norms is affected by changes in the educational customs regarding promotion from grade to grade. In the early 1900's promotion was based primarily on achievement. The pupil who did not learn as rapidly as the average was not promoted. Such an educational system would give rise to a marked difference between age and grade norms, and also lead to a smaller dispersion of scores within each grade, accompanied by less overlap in the scores of adjacent grades. The present custom of promoting a pupil primarily on the basis of age will increase the resemblance between age and grade norms, increase the dispersion of scores within a given grade, and produce a marked overlap in the scores of adjacent grades. Norms that were determined under the former system of promotion cannot be compared with norms established under the present system of promotion primarily on the basis of age. Similarly, norms that have been established under limited educational opportunities, and when the illiteracy rate is high, cannot be expected to resemble norms established when the educational level of the population is increased, and the illiteracy rate is low.

12. Standardizing to predict criterion performance

If we are dealing with a situation where predicting a criterion performance is desired, the proper regression line is readily indicated. For this purpose the regression of criterion score on test score is the correct one to use and will give the best predictions in the sense that this line

gives the average criterion score obtained by the persons making each
given test score. The regression of test on criterion score will systematically give overpredictions of the performance of those scoring
above the mean, and underpredictions of the performance of those
scoring below the mean.

In using either regression line, we must note the possible effects of a
change in the population. For example, if we have established a re-

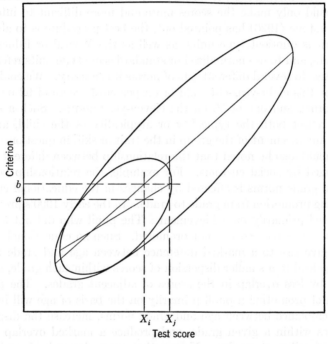

FIGURE 3. Showing the effect on regression line of selection of the group on some
variable related to criterion performance.

gression line and a cutting score at level X_i on Figure 3, and we find that
the high-level applicants are attracted to other types of jobs, the new
group of applicants will be in general considerably lower than the
standardization group. If this selection is made in terms of variables
that are correlated with criterion score more than with test score, the
effect will be to lower the regression line as indicated in Figure 3 so
that, in order to have as good a quality of selected persons it would be
necessary to raise the cutting score to some such point as X_j. Conversely, if a depression throws a large number of highly qualified persons
on the market, we should be dealing with a higher regression line; and,

if the old cutting score (X_i) were maintained, it would be expected that the quality of work obtained from the selected applicants would be increased.

In summary, then, if we are using test scores to predict a criterion score, and wish to set a cutting score such that the average criterion score of those at the cutting score will be some fixed value, then if there is a shortage of high scoring and a surplus of low scoring persons, it is necessary to raise the cutting score. Whereas, if there is a surplus of high-scoring persons, or a shortage of low-scoring persons, it is necessary to lower the cutting score in order to have the average criterion performance of those at the cutting score remain at a specified level. That is, the adjustment required to maintain a given level of performance at the cutting score is the opposite of what we should wish.

In part the decision for the use of the regression of x on y or of y on x may depend upon which variable is made the basis of selection of cases for the standardization group. For example, if there is reason to believe that we have a representative sample of eight-year-old children or nine-year-old, ten-year-old, etc., we might use the regression of score on age and expect the regression of score on age found for that group to be duplicated in future samples. The regression of age on score (average age of those making a given score) is indicated if we feel that the sample drawn is representative of all ages making a given score. That is, if there have been no influences at work that would select with respect to age of the population, the regression of age on score is indicated.

If we wish to use the regression of criterion on test score, the group may be selected explicitly on the basis of test score without biassing the regression line, but within the test score range selected there must be no selection on the basis of criterion score. For example, if workers who do not show a certain minimum production record are dismissed, and hence not included in the standardization group, the regression of criterion on test score will not be correct. We may select on the basis of the independent variable without biassing the regression of the dependent on the independent variable. There must be no selection on the basis of scores on the dependent variable or the regression line will not be correct.

13. Marginal performance as a guide in determining cutting score

In determining cutting score or in deciding on possible changes in a cutting score, it is sometimes helpful to consider the performance of the "marginal" student—the student immediately above or below the proposed cutting score. Figure 4 illustrates a correlation scatter plot of criterion versus test score, with the regression of criterion on test score ($Y = aX + \overline{Y} - a\overline{X}$), and a critical level (L) for the criterion score. Let us consider any given test score array (C') as illustrated in

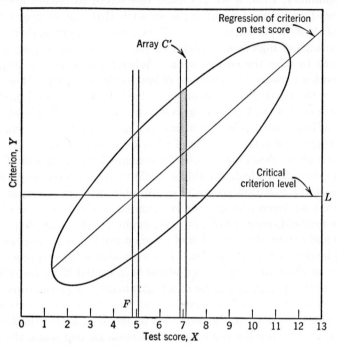

FIGURE 4. Critical criterion level and regression of criterion on test score.

Figure 4. The mean criterion score of this array is on the regression line, and it may be written as

$$aX_i + \overline{Y} - a\overline{X}.$$

The standard deviation of this array—of any array—is the standard error of estimate,

$$s_y\sqrt{1 - r_{xy}{}^2}.$$

For any given x-array, the critical criterion level L may be written as the deviation score,

$$L - aX_i - \overline{Y} + a\overline{X}.$$

Or, written as a standard score, we have

$$z_{L_i} = \frac{L - aX_i - \overline{Y} + a\overline{X}}{s_y\sqrt{1 - r_{xy}{}^2}},$$

where z_{L_i} is the deviation of the cutting score (L) from the mean of array (i), using the standard deviation of the array or the error of estimate as the standard unit.

This quantity z_{L_i} may be computed for each of the possible test score values (X_i). These values may be converted into percentages by the use of a table of the normal curve. This series of percentages will show the percentage of persons that will be above (or below) the critical criterion level for each test score (X_i). Figure 5 is such a graph, showing p, the percentage above the critical criterion score for each value of X_i. A cutting score just below F would mean that the lowest persons accepted would have a 50-50 chance of being above the critical criterion level (see F in Figure 4 or 5). As the cutting score is moved below this point, the lowest persons accepted have a better than even chance of being below the critical criterion level. If the cutting score is fixed at a level considerably above F, persons with a better than even chance of being above the critical criterion level are being rejected. The decision to move the cutting score away from the point F depends on judging either that the need for additional persons is sufficiently urgent to justify accepting those who are more likely to fail than to qualify, or that we can afford to reject a group that has a better than even chance of success in order to reduce the total number of failures.

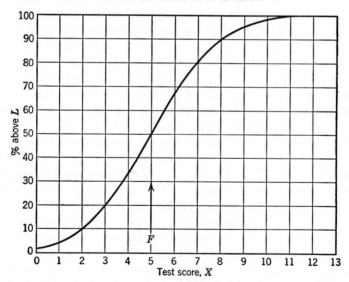

FIGURE 5.   Percentage above critical criterion level as a function of test score.

This approach to selecting a cutting score can be quantified if it is possible to determine or estimate the ratio of the two quantities: H, the

cost of selecting a person who will fail, and G, the net gain from selecting a person who will qualify. The cutting score should be at the point
where for the marginal group the total gain from the successes will
equal the total cost from the failures, or where

$$pG = (1 - p)H.$$

Solving for p, we find that

$$p = \frac{H}{G + H}.$$

For example, if $G = H$, then, according to this equation, $p = \frac{1}{2}$. In
such a case, the cutting score would be at the point F in Figures 4 and 5,
where the probability of success or failure is $\frac{1}{2}$. If the ratio $R = H/G$
can be approximated, we have a solution as

$$p = \frac{R}{R + 1}.$$

14. Equating two forms of a test by giving them to the same group

It is usually thought that when two forms of a test are given to the
same group, no special equating problems arise. The procedure is to
convert each form directly to standard, normalized, or percentile scores,
and to assume that such scores are comparable since they were obtained
on the same group for both forms of the test. It should be noted however that a conversion to standard score makes adjustments only for
differences in the mean and the standard deviation of the two forms.
If the skewness or the kurtosis of the two forms differs, this difference
will be reflected in the standard scores and will also be reflected in most
cases in percentile or in normalized scores.

For example, if a distribution of scores is negatively skewed, there
will be some very low scores, but there will not be corresponding very
high scores. This will be true of percentile or normalized scores just as
it will be true of standard scores. With a positively skewed distribution, the reverse will be true. We shall get a few scores that are very
far above the mean, and no scores that are correspondingly far below the
mean. If a distribution is markedly leptokurtic, some scores will be
extremely low and others extremely high; whereas for a platykurtic distribution the extremely low and high scores will be missing, and instead
there will be a grouping of the subjects at mediumly low and mediumly
high scores.

This effect of grouping subjects may be illustrated concretely by
considering the five top ones in a distribution of 200 cases. If all these

subjects make different scores, they will have percentile scores of 99.75, 99.25, 98.75, 98.25, and 97.75. If all these subjects make the same score, all of them will get a percentile score of 98.75. Such a test cannot discriminate between the 97.75 and the 99.75 performance. There is no opportunity for even the best person to score higher than 98.75. With normalized scores this difference is even greater, since in the first instance the highest possible percentile score of 99.75 corresponds to a highest possible normalized score of 2.81, whereas, in the second case, the highest possible percentile score of 98.75 corresponds to a normalized score of 2.24. This is a normalized score difference of 0.57. In the central part of the distribution it would take a very much larger percentile difference to correspond to a normalized score difference of 0.57. For example, a percentile score of 50.00 corresponds to a normalized score of 0.00, and a percentile score of 71.57 to a normalized score of 0.57. The difference between having one or five persons grouped at the highest score changes the highest possible normalized score by as much as the difference between the fiftieth and the seventy-first percentile.

If two tests have skewness and/or kurtosis coefficients that are radically different, it is difficult to define the meaning of parallel scores on the two tests. No set of standard, linear derived scores, percentile, or normalized scores will be parallel.

As yet there is no statistical test available for equality of skewness and kurtosis. However, by inspecting the cases at the extremes of the distributions involved, it is possible to compare the highest possible and the lowest possible scores in two distributions, and to judge whether or not the difference is serious in terms of the decisions that are being made on the basis of the scores. In particular it is necessary to be careful when special action is being taken on the basis of extremely high or extremely low scores, as, for instance, if the best student is awarded a scholarship or if a few especially low students are dismissed.

If three or more parallel forms are being standardized on the same group of persons, Wilks' test for equality of variances and covariances given in Chapter 14 may be used. If the tests are not homogeneous with respect to covariances, no adjustment of norms can make the forms parallel in this respect.

A second type of case arises if we are standardizing two forms of a test on the same group, and a criterion, which the test is to predict, is also available. In such a case, we may define the problem of equating test scores as matching the regression line of criterion on test for the two tests. Let us use the subscript c to designate the criterion, and x and y to designate the two tests. Then the problem of equating x and y for the purpose of predicting criterion c may be stated as follows.

Step 1. Check to see that $r_{yc} = r_{xc}$ or that $(1 - r_{yc}^2)s_c^2 = (1 - r_{xc}^2)s_c^2$. This check may be made on an approximate judgmental basis or by using the extension of Wilks' criterion given by Votaw (1947) or (1948). If the criterion correlations of the two tests (or what is the same thing, the criterion errors of estimate) are essentially the same, it is possible to equate scores on the two tests, x and y. If the criterion correlations are different, equating scores *for the purpose of predicting the criterion* is not possible.

Step 2. Express both x and y in terms of standard scores or linear derived scores, using the same mean and standard deviation. If there are slight differences in the criterion correlations of x and y, which may be attributed to sampling errors, it is possible to match the regression lines *exactly* by setting the mean of x equal to the mean of y, and making the ratio of the standard deviations equal to the ratio of the criterion correlations (that is, $s_x/s_y = r_{xc}/r_{yc}$).

Kelley (1947), pages 364–365, describes a method of establishing norms for a new test (X_0) in terms of an "anchor test" (X_1) that is based on the use of the regression of X_0 on X_1. If this method is used to determine equivalent scores for two parallel forms of a test, a systematic bias will result. As compared with the anchor test, the new test will have a smaller unit of measurement, and hence the numerical value of its standard deviation will necessarily be larger than that of the anchor test.

In summary, when two forms of a test are given to the same group, converting each form directly to standard, normalized, or percentile scores does not necessarily and automatically result in comparable scores for the two forms. It is necessary first to see that the skewness and kurtosis coefficients are similar for the two tests. If the skewness and kurtosis are similar, standard, normalized, or percentile scores are comparable. If either or both of these coefficients are different, standard scores will certainly not be comparable, and because of the possibilities of different groupings of scores at the extremes of the distribution, percentile or normalized scores are also likely not to be comparable.

If in addition to the two forms of the test, criterion scores are available on the standardization group, and the purpose of the test is to predict the criterion, it is necessary first to be certain that the criterion correlations of the two forms are similar, and then to use standard scores or some linear derived score for the two forms. Means and standard deviations or else means and regression slopes should be equated for the two forms.

15. Equating two forms of a test given to different groups

A more complex and also more usual case of equating arises when form Y (given to group A) is to be equated to form Z (given to group B). This is usually done by means of another test or segment of a test that will be designated X, which is administered to both groups. The theory for equating test Y given to group A with test Z given to group B by means of test X given to both groups has been developed by Ledyard Tucker (unpublished manuscript) for the case of standardized or linear derived scores.

The equating "test" X mentioned above may be a single test or subtest, yielding only one score, or it may be that several equating variables $(X_g, g = 1 \cdots K)$ will be available. We shall first consider the case where only one equating variable is available $(g = 1)$, and then the more general case where K equating variables are available.

Since standard scores or linear derived scores are dependent entirely on mean and variance, the problem may be stated as that of estimating the mean and variance of test Y for group B. This mean and variance would then be arbitrarily assigned to the new test Z that was given to group B. The Z-norms would thus be comparable to the Y-norms in the sense that the mean and variance of the transformed Z-scores for group B would be the same as they would have been if test Y had been used on group B.

Let us use a subscript set in roman type to designate the group, a bar over the variable to designate the mean, and a wavy line to designate the standard deviation. In this notation, we may say that the problem is to estimate $\overline{Y}_\mathrm{B}$ and $\tilde{Y}_\mathrm{B}$ (the mean and standard deviation of Y for group B) from the known items of information, $\overline{X}_\mathrm{A}$, $\tilde{X}_\mathrm{A}$, $\overline{X}_\mathrm{B}$, $\tilde{X}_\mathrm{B}$, $\overline{Y}_\mathrm{A}$, and $\tilde{Y}_\mathrm{A}$ (the mean and standard deviation of Y for group A and of X for groups A and B).

Making use of the equation of the regression line and the deviation score notation, we may say that

$$(11) \qquad\qquad y_i = ax_i + e_i.$$

The score of the ith person on test y is equal to a times his deviation score on test x plus an error, e_i. We may change to gross scores by substituting $Y_i - \overline{Y}$ for y_i, $X_i - \overline{X}$ for x_i, and write equation 11 explicitly for each of the groups A and B, as follows:

$$(12) \qquad\qquad Y_{\mathrm{A}i} = a_\mathrm{A} X_{\mathrm{A}i} + \overline{Y}_\mathrm{A} - a_\mathrm{A}\overline{X}_\mathrm{A} + e_{\mathrm{A}i}$$

and

$$(13) \qquad\qquad Y_{\mathrm{B}i} = a_\mathrm{B} X_{\mathrm{B}i} + \overline{Y}_\mathrm{B} - a_\mathrm{B}\overline{X}_\mathrm{B} + e_{\mathrm{B}i}.$$

Since complete information is available on group A, equation 12 presents no problem. However, for group B only the X-scores are available; hence some estimates must be made regarding the constants in equation 13. It seems reasonable to assume that the slope and intercept of the regression of Y on X for group B are equal, respectively, to the slope and intercept of the same regression for group A, that is,

$$(14) \qquad a_A = a_B$$

and

$$(15) \qquad \overline{Y}_A - a_A \overline{X}_A = \overline{Y}_B - a_B \overline{X}_B.$$

Summing equation 13 and dividing by N_B to obtain the mean of Y_{Bi}, we have

$$(16) \qquad \overline{Y}_B = a_B \overline{X}_B + \overline{Y}_B - a_B \overline{X}_B + \bar{e}_B.$$

If we assume that

$$(17) \qquad \bar{e}_A = \bar{e}_B = 0,$$

and substitute equations 14, 15, and 17 in equation 16, we obtain

$$(18) \qquad \overline{Y}_B = \overline{Y}_A + a_A(\overline{X}_B - \overline{X}_A).$$

Equation 18 expresses the Y-mean for group B in terms of known quantities.

> *The value $\overline{Y}_B$ given by equation 18 is the arbitrary mean to be assigned to the B-group in order to have the scores comparable with the Y-scores of the A-group. This is the value to be used as M_w in equation 6. Equation 18 is derived from assumptions that are the same as those used in the equations for group heterogeneity in Chapters 10 to 13.*

To obtain the variance of Y_{Bi}, we write equation 13 in deviation score form as in equation 11, and take the sum of the squares of the deviations over N_B, obtaining

$$(19) \qquad \frac{\sum\limits_{i=1}^{N} y_{Bi}{}^2}{N} = \frac{\sum\limits_{i=1}^{N} (a_B x_{Bi} + e_{Bi})^2}{N}.$$

Since the correlation between x and e is zero, Σxe is zero. Expanding the right side of the equation, and writing $\breve{Y}_B{}^2$ for the variance of Y and $\tilde{E}^2$ for the error variance, we obtain

(20)
$$\breve{Y}_B{}^2 = \frac{a_B{}^2 \sum\limits_{i=1}^{N} x_{Bi}{}^2}{N} + \frac{\sum\limits_{i=1}^{N} e_{Bi}{}^2}{N}$$

or

(21)
$$\breve{Y}_B{}^2 = a_B{}^2 \breve{X}_B{}^2 + \tilde{E}_B{}^2.$$

Likewise, for the A group we have

(22)
$$\breve{Y}_A{}^2 = a_A{}^2 \breve{X}_A{}^2 + \tilde{E}_A{}^2.$$

From equation 22 we can solve for $\tilde{E}_A{}^2$ in terms of $\breve{Y}_A$ and $\breve{X}_A$. If we make the assumption that

(23)
$$\tilde{E}_A{}^2 = \tilde{E}_B{}^2,$$

we may write $\breve{Y}_B{}^2$ entirely in terms of known quantities as

(24)
$$\breve{Y}_B{}^2 = \breve{Y}_A{}^2 + a_A{}^2(\breve{X}_B{}^2 - \breve{X}_A{}^2).$$

Equation 24 expresses the y-variance for group B in terms of known quantities.

> The value $\breve{Y}_B$ given by equation 24 is the arbitrary standard deviation to be assigned to the B-group in order to have the scores comparable with the Y-scores of the A-group. This is the value to be used as s_w in equation 6. Equation 24 is derived from assumptions that are the same as those used in the equations for group heterogeneity in Chapters 10 to 13.

Equation 24 is identical with equation 20 of Chapter 11.

If K equating variables are available, the derivation of the Y mean and variance for group B follows the same general pattern, except that a multiple regression equation is used instead of the regression line of equation 11. To correspond to equation 11 for the multiple-regression case, we write

(25)
$$y_i = \sum_{g=1}^{K} a_g x_{ig} + e_i.$$

From equation 25, the equations corresponding to equations 12 and 13 are written as

(26)
$$Y_{Ai} = \sum_{g=1}^{K} a_{Ag} X_{Aig} + \overline{Y}_A - \sum_{g=1}^{K} a_{Ag} \overline{X}_{A \cdot g} + e_{Ai}$$

and

(27)
$$Y_{Bi} = \sum_{g=1}^{K} a_{Bg} X_{Big} + \overline{Y}_B - \sum_{g=1}^{K} a_{Bg} \overline{X}_{B \cdot g} + e_{Bi}.$$

To obtain the mean $\overline{Y}_B$, sum equation 27 and divide by N_B, obtaining

$$(28) \qquad \overline{Y}_B = \sum_{g=1}^{K} a_{Bg}\overline{X}_{B \cdot g} - \sum_{g=1}^{K} a_{Bg}\overline{X}_{B \cdot g} + \overline{Y}_B + \overline{e}_B.$$

To correspond to equations 14 and 15, we assume that the regression coefficients, a_g, for group B are equal to those for group A, and that the constant term for group A is equal to that for group B. These assumptions give the $K + 1$ equalities,

$$(29) \qquad a_{Ag} = a_{Bg} \qquad\qquad (g = 1 \cdots K)$$

and

$$(30) \qquad \overline{Y}_A - \sum_{g=1}^{K} a_{Ag}\overline{X}_{A \cdot g} = \overline{Y}_B - \sum_{g=1}^{K} a_{Bg}\overline{X}_{B \cdot g}.$$

Substituting equations 17, 29, and 30 in equation 28 gives

$$(31) \qquad \overline{Y}_B = \overline{Y}_A + \sum_{g=1}^{K} a_{Ag}(\overline{X}_{B \cdot g} - \overline{X}_{A \cdot g}).$$

For the general case of K equating variables, equation 31 gives the Y-mean for group B. This is the value to be used for M_w in equation 6. The derivation uses the same assumptions as those of Chapters 10 to 13.

In order to obtain the Y-variance for group B, write equation 27 in deviation score form as

$$(32) \qquad Y_{Bi} - \overline{Y}_B = \sum_{g=1}^{K} a_{Bg}(X_{Big} - \overline{X}_{B \cdot g}) + e_{Bi}.$$

Using the lower-case symbols to designate deviation scores gives

$$(33) \qquad y_{Bi} = \sum_{g=1}^{K} a_{Bg}x_{Big} + e_{Bi}.$$

To obtain N times the variance of y, square both sides of equation 33, and sum. Noting that all terms of the form $\sum_{i=1}^{N} x_{ig}e_i$ are zero, we may write

$$(34) \qquad \sum_{i=1}^{N} y_{Bi}^2 = \sum_{i=1}^{N} \left[\sum_{g=1}^{K} a_{Bg}x_{Big} \right]^2 + \sum_{i=1}^{N} e_{Bi}^2.$$

The first term on the right side of the equation may be expressed as a triple summation, and the order of summation may be altered, giving

$$(35) \qquad \sum_{i=1}^{N} y_{Bi}^{2} = \sum_{g=1}^{K} \sum_{h=1}^{K} \sum_{i=1}^{N} a_{Bg} a_{Bh} x_{Big} x_{Bih} + \sum_{i=1}^{N} e_{Bi}^{2}.$$

Equation 35 may be simplified by the notation

$$(36) \qquad \sum_{i=1}^{N} x_{ig} x_{ih} = N c_{gh}.$$

If $g \neq h$, c is a covariance. If $g = h$, c is a variance. For variables y and e, the sum of squares will be designated by $N\tilde{Y}^2$ and $N\tilde{E}^2$, respectively. Introducing these notational changes in equation 35 and dividing by N gives

$$(37) \qquad \tilde{Y}_{B}^{2} = \sum_{g=1}^{K} \sum_{h=1}^{K} a_{Bg} a_{Bh} c_{Bgh} + \tilde{E}_{B}^{2}.$$

Likewise, for group A, we have

$$(38) \qquad \tilde{Y}_{A}^{2} = \sum_{g=1}^{K} \sum_{h=1}^{K} a_{Ag} a_{Ah} c_{Agh} + \tilde{E}_{A}^{2},$$

from which the variance of E_A may be written as

$$(39) \qquad \tilde{E}_{A}^{2} = \tilde{Y}_{A}^{2} - \sum_{g=1}^{K} \sum_{h=1}^{K} a_{Ag} a_{Ah} c_{Agh}.$$

Using the assumption of equation 23, we may substitute equation 39 in equation 37; then using the assumptions of equation 29 and simplifying the result, we find the solution

$$(40) \qquad \tilde{Y}_{B}^{2} = \tilde{Y}_{A}^{2} + \sum_{g=1}^{K} \sum_{h=1}^{K} a_{Ag} a_{Ah} (c_{Bgh} - c_{Agh}),$$

where $\tilde{Y}_{B}^{2}$ is the variance of variable Y for group B,

$\tilde{Y}_{A}^{2}$ is the variance of variable Y for group A,

a_{Ag} is the regression weight for variable X_g in predicting Y in group A, and

c_{Agh} is the covariance $(1/N) \sum\limits_{i=1}^{N} x_{Aig} x_{Aih}$.

For the general case of K equating variables, equation 40 gives the Y-variance for group B. This is the value to be used for s_w in equation 6. The derivation uses the same assumptions as those of Chapters 10 to 13.

The problem discussed in this section is equating test Z, given to group B, to test Y, given to group A by means of an equating test X or a set of K equating tests X_g. The solution is to estimate the mean of Y

for group B by equations 18 or 31; and to estimate the variance of Y for group B by equations 24 or 40. These estimated values are then used as the arbitrary mean and variance (M_w and $s_w{}^2$) to be assigned to the new test Z (see equations 5 and 6). This equating procedure is appropriate for any linear derived scores.

For non-linear transformations of gross scores no appropriate procedure has yet been suggested. For percentile scores, it may well be impossible to develop a rigorous equating method. For normalized scores, it may be that some adaptation of Thurstone's absolute scaling methods will give a satisfactory solution. These normalized scores might then furnish a satisfactory basis for equating percentile scores. If and when a solution for the equating problem is developed for normalized and percentile scores, it is highly likely that the sampling errors involved will be very much greater than those found in equating on the basis of linear derived scores. If the magnitude of sampling errors involved in equating tests from one group to another are considered, it seems likely that linear derived scores have a distinct advantage over the non-linear transformations.

16. Summary

After the test papers have been scored, the next step is to assess the gross score distribution in terms of the average chance score K/A, and the variability of chance scores

$$(1) \qquad\qquad s_c = \left(\frac{1}{A}\right) \sqrt{K(A - 1)},$$

where K is the number of items in the test and A is the number of alternatives per item. The lowest score taken as indicating knowledge of the subject should be greater than $K/A + 2s_c$.

Whenever the distribution is divided into groups, the distance from the lower bound to the upper bound of a group should be large with respect to the error of measurement of the test.

It should be noted that, whenever several tests are used, the principle of successive hurdles makes for raising of passing standards, whereas permitting multiple trials lowers standards, particularly with unreliable tests.

In converting gross scores to an arbitrarily specified scale, as in Navy grades, Civil Service ratings, and some college grading systems, a good procedure is to determine certain critical points (such as the lowest passing grade and the lowest honors grade) by expert judgment, and then use linear interpolation between these points.

In most large-scale testing programs, the procedure is to convert gross scores to some predetermined scale that indicates the relative standing of the individual in his group, and to report scores in terms of this scale. The transformations usually considered are:

1. Linear transformations, termed standard scores, or linear derived scores.
2. Non-linear transformations, of which the commonest are the percentile score, and the normalized score.

Percentile scores represent the percentage of persons in a typical group scoring less than the person in question. Such scores are very easy to explain to persons unacquainted with testing, but they have so many disadvantages that percentile scores are not generally used except as auxiliary scores. Percentile differences or averages are not constant in meaning from the middle to the extreme of the scale, and the equating of different groups is difficult if not impossible. Normalized scores should in general not be used unless there is some good reason for believing that the underlying distribution of ability is normal and is misrepresented by the distribution of gross scores. Thurstone's Absolute Scaling Methods furnish one way of checking on this belief for two partly overlapping groups given the same test. The range of possible normalized scores is also sensitive to the number of cases in the group, and to the grouping of the extreme cases. This effect must be watched carefully if comparisons are to be made from group to group or from test to test.

The various disadvantages of percentile and normalized scores has led to the general use of some linear transformation of gross scores, with a convenient scale specified by an arbitrary mean and standard deviation. For standard scores the computation equation is

$$(4) \qquad z_i = \left(\frac{1}{s_X}\right) X_i - \frac{M_X}{s_X},$$

where z_i is the standard score of the ith individual,
$\quad\quad X_i$ is the gross score of the same individual, and
M_X and s_X are the mean and standard deviation of the gross score distribution.

For other types of linear derived scores the computing equation is

$$(6) \qquad w_i = \left(\frac{s_w}{s_x}\right) X_i + M_w - \left(\frac{s_w}{s_x}\right) M_X,$$

where w_i is the linear derived score of individual i, and
M_w and s_w are the arbitrarily specified mean and standard deviation of the linear derived scores.

The other terms have the definitions given for equation 4.

The use of normalized scores referred to some standard group has been suggested by McCall (the T-score), by Flanagan (the Cooperative Test Scaled Scores), and by Thurstone (absolute scaling methods). Thurstone gives the fundamental scaling equation as

$$(9) \qquad M_{Va} + Y_{ia} s_{Va} = M_{Vb} + Y_{ib} s_{Vb}$$

or

$$(10) \qquad Y_{ia} = \left(\frac{s_{Vb}}{s_{Va}}\right) Y_{ib} + \frac{M_{Vb} - M_{Va}}{s_{Va}},$$

where M_{Va} and M_{Vb} are the means in hypothetical absolute units for distributions a and b,

s_{Va} and s_{Vb} are the standard deviations in hypothetical absolute units for distributions a and b, and

Y_{ia} and Y_{ib} are the normalized scores for distributions a and b, respectively.

Equation 10 demonstrates that the normalized scores for two distributions will be linearly related to each other, if both distributions can be regarded as normal on the same scale.

In standardizing to predict a criterion performance it is necessary to use the regression of criterion on test score and to give the corresponding error of estimate in order to use the norms properly.

If, in addition to the regression of criterion on test score, we have a specified critical criterion level, it is possible from these two items of information to draw a curve showing the percentage of persons (p) above the critical level at each test score range. This graph can be used for determining the cutting score. If the ratio of H, the cost of selecting a potential failure, to G, the net gain due to selecting a successful person, can be determined or estimated, the cutting score can be fixed at the test score level, where $p = R/(R + 1)$, $R = H/G$.

Another type of standardization seeks to indicate the age or grade placement of the person. In such norms it is necessary to know which regression line has been used, and to know the nature of the sampling used for selecting the standardization group. It is also important to know the size of the error of measurement in relation to the size of the crucial steps in the norms. Without such facts as these, the degree of over- or underachievement of a person can easily be markedly exaggerated or minimized.

If two forms of a test to be equated have been given to the same group, it is possible to make two independent transformations to some linear or non-linear scores. Such scores for the two forms, however, will not be comparable unless the skewness and kurtosis coefficients for the gross score distributions are similar. Also if we are standardizing in terms of a criterion, two forms cannot be regarded as parallel unless the correlation with the criterion is approximately the same for the two forms.

In standardizing two forms of a test, each given to a separate group, it is necessary to use some form of linear derived scores and to have a matching test. When linear derived scores are used, the only problem is to determine an appropriate mean and standard deviation for the second group. For a single equating variable, we have

$$(18) \qquad \overline{Y}_{\mathrm{B}} = \overline{Y}_{\mathrm{A}} + a_{\mathrm{A}}(\overline{X}_{\mathrm{B}} - \overline{X}_{\mathrm{A}})$$

and

$$(24) \qquad \check{Y}_{\mathrm{B}}^{2} = \check{Y}_{\mathrm{A}}^{2} + a_{\mathrm{A}}^{2}(\check{X}_{\mathrm{B}}^{2} - \check{X}_{\mathrm{A}}^{2}).$$

For K equating variables $X_g (g = 1 \cdots K)$, we have

$$(31) \qquad \overline{Y}_{\mathrm{B}} = \overline{Y}_{\mathrm{A}} + \sum_{g=1}^{K} a_{\mathrm{A}g}(\overline{X}_{\mathrm{B}\cdot g} - \overline{X}_{\mathrm{A}\cdot g})$$

and

$$(40) \qquad \check{Y}_{\mathrm{B}}^{2} = \check{Y}_{\mathrm{A}}^{2} + \sum_{g=1}^{K} \sum_{h=1}^{K} a_{\mathrm{A}g} a_{\mathrm{A}h}(c_{\mathrm{B}gh} - c_{\mathrm{A}gh}),$$

where $\overline{Y}_{\mathrm{A}}$ and $\check{Y}_{\mathrm{A}}^{2}$ are the mean and variance of Y for group A. (These are the original scores to which the B-group scores are to be matched.)

$\overline{X}_{\mathrm{A}}, \check{X}_{\mathrm{A}}^{2}, \overline{X}_{\mathrm{B}},$ and $\check{X}_{\mathrm{B}}^{2}$ are the mean and variance of X for groups A and B, respectively. (X is the matching test that has been given to both groups A and B. Also $X_g, g = 1 \cdots K$ indicates K matching tests.)

$a_{\mathrm{A}g}$ is the regression weight for variable X_g in predicting Y in group A.

$c_{\mathrm{A}gh}$ is $(1/N) \sum_{i=1}^{N} x_{\mathrm{A}ig} x_{\mathrm{A}ih}$ $(x_{ig} = X_{ig} - \overline{X}_g)$. (If $g \neq h$, this term is a covariance; if $g = h$, this term is a variance.)

TABLE FOR USE IN CONNECTION WITH PROBLEMS 3 TO 7

The following scores were made by 68,899 students in 323 colleges on the 1937 edition of the American Council on Education Psychological Examination for College Freshmen.

Scores	Men	Women	Total *
		Frequency	
0–9		2	4
10–19	5	3	12
20–29	27	22	58
30–39	85	50	170
40–49	169	112	329
50–59	329	225	626
60–69	471	358	943
70–79	667	479	1,314
80–89	923	769	1,915
90–99	1,108	892	2,264
100–109	1,387	1,171	2,897
110–119	1,669	1,376	3,429
120–129	1,768	1,529	3,764
130–139	2,064	1,768	4,348
140–149	2,113	1,793	4,471
150–159	2,188	1,830	4,650
160–169	2,220	1,748	4,600
170–179	2,128	1,798	4,583
180–189	1,990	1,610	4,207
190–199	1,823	1,479	3,904
200–209	1,639	1,351	3,593
210–219	1,488	1,251	3,281
220–229	1,234	996	2,686
230–239	1,097	906	2,441
240–249	893	748	2,025
250–259	750	596	1,630
260–269	584	488	1,309
270–279	474	329	998
280–289	358	273	772
290–299	284	187	580
300–309	184	122	387
310–319	153	74	286
320–329	96	52	181
330–339	70	38	133
340–349	29	13	51
350–359	24	9	40
360–369	6	3	14
370–379	2		2
380–389	1		2
Total	32,500	26,450	68,899
Lower quartile	127.27	127.54	128.67
Median	165.75	164.84	167.08
Upper quartile	207.57	206.10	208.87

$$M = 170.0214$$
$$s = 57.7012$$

* The total includes the scores of 9949 students not classified according to sex.

Data taken from L. L. Thurstone and T. G. Thurstone, The 1937 Psychological Examination for College Freshmen, *The Educational Record*, April, 1938, pages 209–234.

Problems

1. Draw a graph corresponding to the following transformation. The distribution of Table 1 is to be linearly transformed to a scale 00–99, such that a gross score of 150 equals 70 (the lowest passing mark) and a gross score of 210 equals 90 (the lowest honors mark).

2. Give the average chance score ($\bar{c}$), the variance of scores due to chance ($\bar{c}^2$), and the lowest gross score exceeding $\bar{c} + 2\bar{c}$ for each of the following tests:

(a) A 20-item true-false test.
(b) A 100-item true-false test.
(c) A 20-item multiple-choice test that has one correct and four incorrect alternatives for each item.
(d) A 100-item multiple-choice test, with 5 alternatives per item, as in c.
(e) A 10-item test, with 10 alternatives for each item.

3. Using only the total distribution given in the right-hand column of the foregoing table, compute the table, and draw the graph for transforming raw scores of the foregoing frequency distribution to (a) standard scores (z-scores), (b) linear derived scores, with a mean of 50 and a standard deviation of 10 (w-scores), (c) percentile scores (p-scores), (d) normalized scores (n-scores).

4. From the information in the preceding problem, draw the graphs showing the relationship between (a) z-scores and w-scores, (b) z-scores and p-scores, (c) z-scores and n-scores, (d) w-scores and p-scores, (e) w-scores and n-scores, (f) p-scores and n-scores.
Write a brief paragraph stating the relationships shown in the foregoing six graphs.

5. As a check on normality use arithmetic probability paper and plot (a) p-scores against n-scores, (b) p-scores against w-scores.

6. Using the distribution for men only as given in the foregoing frequency distribution, compute the table and draw the graph for transforming raw scores of men to (a) z-scores, (b) w-scores, with mean 50 and standard deviation 10, (c) p-scores, (d) n-scores.

7. Using the distribution for women only as given in the foregoing frequency distribution, compute the table and draw the graph for transforming raw scores of women to (a) z-scores, (b) w-scores, with a mean of 50 and standard deviation 10, (c) p-scores, (d) n-scores.
Write a brief paragraph comparing the norms for men with those for women.

8. Below is given the frequency distribution of A.C.E. scores for 113 students taking the 56 tests used in Dr. Thurstone's first large study of primary mental abilities. (Thurstone, 1938, page 19.) This distribution is given in terms of percentile points on the national norms for the A.C.E. test. The table shows that there was one student between the 35 and 40 percentile points on the national norms; two students between the 45 and 50 percentile points; and so forth. It will be noticed that over 25 per cent of the students are above the 98 percentile point on the national norms. Can this distribution of 113 cases be regarded as a normal distribution, granted the assumption of a Gaussian distribution of intelligence in the 40,000 students on whom the national norms were based? Use the absolute scaling methods to answer this question.

Scores *	Frequency	Cumulative Frequency
35–40	1	1
40–45	1	2
45–50	2	4
50–55	2	6
55–60	4	10
60–65	6	16
65–70	2	18
70–75	4	22
75–80	10	32
80–85	6	38
85–90	10	48
90–95	25	73
95–96	3	76
96–97	4	80
97–98	3	83
98–99	6	89
99–99.9	23	112
99.9–100.0	1	113

* National norms (1933), 40,229 cases, 203 colleges.

9.

Set	Criterion (y)		Selection Test (x)		r_{xy}	Minimum Acceptable y-score
	Mean	Standard Deviation	Mean	Standard Deviation		
A	9.11	2.95	9.78	3.12	.74	6.00
B	30.42	9.25	20.48	6.75	.55	20.00

For each of the foregoing sets of data, graph p, the percentage of acceptable y-scores, as a function of x, the selection test score. Determine the cutting score appropriate for each set of data on the assumption that:

(a) The net gain due to selecting an acceptable student is equal to the loss incurred by selecting one who will fail.

(b) The gain is double the loss.

(c) The loss is double the gain.

10. Form A of a spelling test was given to a sample of 1000 eighth-grade students in 1942. The mean number correct was 49.1, and the standard deviation was 13.6. This test was standardized in terms of derived scores with a mean of 500 and a standard deviation of 100. In 1946, form B of the spelling test was given to a sample of 1000 eighth-grade students. The mean was 61.3, and the standard deviation 14.8.

An equating test, form C, had been given to both groups of students when tests A and B were given, with the following results. For the second group, the mean was 23.4, and the standard deviation 6.8; for the first group, the mean was 21.3, the standard deviation 6.2, and the correlation r_{AC} was .75. It is desired to use linear derived scores for form B that will give scores directly comparable with the derived scores (mean = 500, standard deviation = 100), used for form A.

(a) Write the transformation equation used on the 1942 group for form A.
(b) Write the transformation equation that should be used with the 1946 group for form B.

11. In 1944 a group of 1000 college freshmen were given two mathematics and one vocabulary test with the following results:

	Mean	Standard Deviation	Correlations
Math. A	137.6	15.8	$r_{AC} = .81$
Math. C	48.1	7.3	$r_{AD} = .63$
Voc. D	206.4	25.7	$r_{CD} = .51$

In 1947 another group of 1000 college freshmen were given two mathematics tests and one vocabulary test. The vocabulary test and the mathematics test C were identical with the tests given to the 1944 group. For the 1947 group, the results were as follows:

	Mean	Standard Deviation	Correlations
Math. B	172.7	21.4	$r_{BC} = .85$
Math. C	53.6	8.5	$r_{BD} = .61$
Voc. D	213.2	28.9	$r_{CD} = .49$

Test A has been converted to a linear derived score with a mean of 100 and a standard deviation of 20.

(a) In order to make scores on test B comparable with the linear derived scores for test A, what arbitrary mean and standard deviation should be used for transforming test B? Use both tests C and D for equating.
(b) Write the transformation for test A.
(c) Write the appropriate computing equation to use for transforming scores on test B.

12. One of the equations presented in connection with the discussion of the influence of group heterogeneity (see Chapters 10, 11, and 12) is analogous to one of the equations in this chapter. Find and compare these two equations.

20

Problems of Weighting
and Differential Prediction

1. General considerations in determining weights

When several test scores are available, on the basis of which a decision is to be made, we have the problem of the appropriate method of combining these scores. When a single total score is to be derived from a number of measures, this score should represent the standing of the candidates with respect to something. The type of judgment involved in determining what this something should be and various methods of combining scores will be considered in this chapter.

It should be noted that it is not possible to dodge the weighting problem if any decisions are to be made. Occasionally we hear the suggestion that scores simply be added together without bothering about problems of weighting. No matter what scores we add, the weighting problem is not avoided. Adding the gross scores on a series of tests gives relative weights of one sort, adding standard scores gives relative weights of a different type. What information must be obtained, and what major questions must be answered in order to secure reasonable composite scores from pooling the components?

It has also been suggested that a separate cutting score may be determined for each test so that we should use a combination of cutting scores instead of a weighted score. Franzen (1943) has presented a type of "multiple chi" procedure for determining the best combination of cutting scores. This procedure consists essentially in trying all possible combinations of various cutting scores, and then using the one that turns out to be best for the set of data in hand. Systematic short-cut computational procedures are also presented by Franzen.

In connection with multiple-cutting scores, it must be noted that policy changes that seem slight may in effect produce a marked difference in standards. In Figure 1 we see that, if a person must pass *both* tests to be accepted, only group 2 will be accepted. If passing *either* test is acceptable, groups 1, 2, and 3 will be accepted. It should also be noted that, if those who fail the first time are allowed to try a second and a third time, this policy is equivalent to saying that the person is acceptable if he passes *either* test; hence many more will pass.

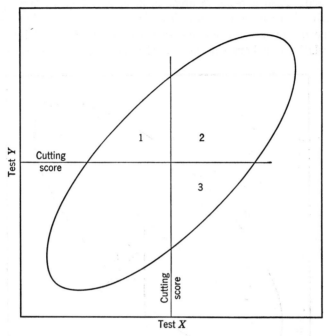

FIGURE 1.   Illustrating the difference between passing *both* and passing *either* test.

The difference between multiple-cutting scores and a weighted composite may be seen by referring to Figure 2. In this figure the cutting scores are adjusted so that the same number will be passed by each policy. If *both* tests must be passed, we accept those above and to the right of line *abc*. If passing *either* test is acceptable, the person must be above *or* to the right of line *def*. In the first case, persons in areas 1, 4, and 5 are accepted; those in areas 2, 3, 6, 7, and 8 are rejected. In the second case those in areas 1, 2, 3, 6, and 7 are accepted; those in areas 4, 5, and 8 are rejected. If the number of persons in area 4, plus the number in area 5, is equal to the total number in areas 2, 3, 6, and 7, the same number will be accepted by either system. Likewise, the number rejected will be the same for either system. The use of a weighted score is illustrated by the line *gh*. In using this line we accept those in areas 1, 2, 4, and 6, while rejecting those in areas 3, 5, 7, and 8. By all three methods everyone in area 1 is accepted, and everyone in area 8 is rejected. The methods differ only in the disposition of persons

with closely similar scores in the areas 2, 3, 4, 5, 6, and 7. It may be
noted that the use of multiple-cutting scores results in putting areas
4 and 5 (with difference scores near zero) together as either accepted
or rejected. Also persons in areas 2, 3, 6, and 7 (with large positive
or negative difference scores) are classed together as rejected or accepted.
Thus the use of multiple-cutting scores would be justified by a curvilinear relationship between the criterion and the difference score. If

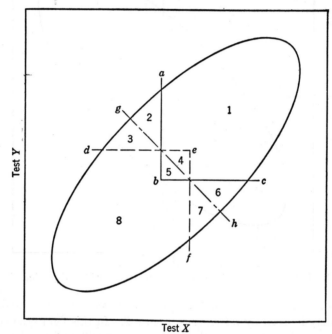

FIGURE 2.   Illustrating the difference between multiple cutting scores and a weighted
composite.

this relationship is linear rather than curvilinear, the use of a straight
line such as *gh* would be more appropriate than a multiple-cutting score.
Since in general linear relationships have been found adequate for most
test work, we shall limit ourselves in this chapter to a discussion of
weighting in terms of various linear combinations of scores.

The first problem is to find the best way of describing a set of weights.
It will be found that the ratio of the standard deviation of the distribution of weights to the mean of the distribution is the best single number
for characterizing a set of weights. The relationship between two sets
of weights is represented by their covariance or correlation. It is important first to note that, if the two sets of weights being considered are

similar to each other, the two weighted composites will correlate highly with each other. For example, if tests A, B, and C receive weights 1, 2, and 3, respectively, or 1, 2, and 4, respectively, the resulting composite scores will be very similar. The weights 3, 4, and 5 will give essentially the same results as 2, 4, and 6. Unless we are considering radically different sets of weights, the resulting scores cannot be altered much by changing from one set of weights to the other. If the two sets of weights have a low intercorrelation, the correlation between the composites will be determined by the ratio of the standard deviation of the distribution of the weights to the mean of the distribution, and also by the properties of the test battery, such as the number of tests combined and the correlation between these tests.

It will be found that, if the standard deviation of the set of weights is very large in comparison to the mean, changes in weights used can produce great changes in scores regardless of the number of variables to be combined, and regardless of their intercorrelation. For example, if both positive and negative weights are permitted, the mean of the distribution of weights will be near zero, while the standard deviation will be very large. If freedom of this type is allowed in weighting, two composites may have very low correlations regardless of the number of variables combined and regardless of the intercorrelation of these variables. However, if the mean of the distribution of weights is about equal to or larger than the standard deviation of the distribution of weights and if the correlation between the two sets of weights is low, the correlation between the two composites will depend largely upon the number of variables involved and upon the intercorrelations of these variables. This case is important, since it is the usual one found in the weighting of items to give a total test score, and of tests in an aptitude battery to give a composite score. Limiting our consideration to sets of positive weights with low intercorrelations, we find that the composites will not be different unless there are relatively *few* variables to be combined and a *low* correlation among these variables.

Thus we have seen that in considering the effect of weighting on a composite the test battery may be characterized by two variables: (1) the average intercorrelation between the tests and (2) the number of tests. The weights likewise may be characterized by two variables: (1) the ratio of the standard deviation to the mean of the distribution of weights and (2) the correlation between the two sets of weights. In order to demonstrate the effect of each of these factors on the correlation between the two composites, it is necessary to write an expression for the correlation between two weighted sums.

Let us consider a set of standard scores z and two different sets of weights designated by V and W. We have

$$(1) \qquad X_{Vi} = V_1 z_{1i} + V_2 z_{2i} + \cdots + V_K z_{Ki} = \sum_{g=1}^{K} V_g z_{gi}.$$

The composite score (X_V) for individual i is equal to the sum of the products of z-scores for that individual, each multiplied by the assigned weight (V_g). In like manner we may write another composite X_W, obtained by applying a difference set of weights (W_g) to the same set of standard scores, namely,

$$(2) \qquad X_{Wi} = W_1 z_{1i} + W_2 z_{2i} + \cdots + W_K z_{Ki} = \sum_{g=1}^{K} W_g z_{gi}.$$

The composite score (X_W) for individual i is the sum from $g = 1$ to K of the products of the z-scores for that individual, each multiplied by the assigned weight (W_g). In order to indicate the influence of two different sets of weights, we shall write the correlation between X_V and X_W,

$$(3) \qquad R_{X_V X_W} = \frac{\displaystyle\sum_{i=1}^{N} X_{Vi} X_{Wi}}{\sqrt{\displaystyle\sum_{i=1}^{N} X_{Vi}{}^2} \sqrt{\displaystyle\sum_{i=1}^{N} X_{Wi}{}^2}}.$$

It should be noted that, since the z-scores have a zero mean, the X-scores will also have a zero mean; hence the gross score formula for correlation need not be used.

Substituting equations 1 and 2 in the numerator of equation 3 and expanding, we have

$$(4) \quad \Sigma X_V X_W = V_1 W_1 \Sigma z_1{}^2 \quad + V_2 W_1 \Sigma z_1 z_2 \quad + \cdots + V_K W_1 \Sigma z_1 z_K$$
$$+ V_1 W_2 \Sigma z_1 z_2 \quad + V_2 W_2 \Sigma z_2{}^2 \quad + \cdots + V_K W_2 \Sigma z_2 z_K +$$
$$\vdots \qquad\qquad \vdots \qquad\qquad \vdots$$
$$+ V_1 W_K \Sigma z_1 z_K + V_2 W_K \Sigma z_2 z_K + \cdots + V_K W_K \Sigma z_K{}^2,$$

where it is understood that all summations are over individuals $(i = 1 \cdots N)$. Since the z's are standard scores, $\Sigma z_g{}^2 = N$ and $\Sigma z_g z_h = N r_{gh}$, $(g \neq h)$. If we make these substitutions, indicating first the sum of the K diagonal terms and then the $K^2 - K$ non-diagonal terms, we have

$$(5) \qquad \sum_{i=1}^{N} X_{Vi} X_{Wi} = \sum_{g=1}^{K} V_g W_g N + \sum_{g \neq h=1}^{K} V_g W_h r_{gh} N.$$

It must be noted that there are K terms in the first summation and $K^2 - K$ terms in the second summation. By substituting V for W in equation 5, we may write the first factor in the denominator of equation 3 as follows:

$$(6) \qquad \sum_{i=1}^{N} X_{Vi}^2 = \sum_{g=1}^{K} V_g^2 N + \sum_{g \neq h=1}^{K} V_g V_h r_{gh} N.$$

By substituting W for V in equation 6, we may obtain an expression for the second factor in the denominator of equation 3. Substituting equations 5 and 6 in equation 3 and factoring N out of both numerator and denominator, we have

Equation (7)

$$R_{X_V X_W} = \frac{\displaystyle\sum_{g=1}^{K} V_g W_g + \sum_{g \neq h=1}^{K} V_g W_h r_{gh}}{\sqrt{\displaystyle\sum_{g=1}^{K} V_g^2 + \sum_{g \neq h=1}^{K} V_g V_h r_{gh}} \sqrt{\displaystyle\sum_{g=1}^{K} W_g^2 + \sum_{g \neq h=1}^{K} W_g W_h r_{gh}}}.$$

Again it must be remembered that the single-subscript summations contain K terms, whereas the summations involving both g and h contain the $K^2 - K$ non-diagonal terms. Let us now consider the numerator term of equation 7. We may use C_{VW} to designate the covariance between the two sets of weights and write

$$(8) \qquad C_{VW} = \left(\frac{1}{K}\right) \sum_{g=1}^{K} V_g W_g - \overline{V}\overline{W},$$

where $\overline{V}$ is the mean of the V's and $\overline{W}$ is the mean of the W's. Solving equation 8 for ΣVW, we have

$$(9) \qquad \Sigma V_g W_g = K(C_{VW} + \overline{V}\overline{W}).$$

We may also introduce the concept of the covariance of r_{gh} with the product $V_g W_h$, designated by $C_{(VW)r}$. This term will in general have a lower bound of zero and an upper bound equal to the product of the standard deviation of r and the standard deviation of VW. We are limiting outselves here to the conventional case in which highly intercorrelated parts are given more weight than those with low intercorrelations.

Following the form of equation 9, we may write

$$(10) \qquad \sum_{g \neq h=1}^{K} V_g W_h r_{gh} = (K^2 - K)(C_{(VW)r} + \overline{(VW)}\bar{r}).$$

Referring to equation 4, we see that the term $\overline{(VW)}$ is the mean of only the non-diagonal product terms of the form $V_g W_h$. Summing the VW terms by columns gives

$$V_1 \Sigma W + V_2 \Sigma W + \cdots + V_K \Sigma W = (\Sigma V)(\Sigma W) = K\overline{V}K\overline{W}.$$

To obtain $\overline{(VW)}$ we deduct the sum of the terms in the principal diagonal and divide by $K^2 - K$, obtaining

$$(11) \qquad \overline{(VW)} = \frac{K\overline{V}K\overline{W} - \Sigma V_g W_g}{K^2 - K}.$$

Substituting equation 9 in equation 11, and then the rewritten equation 11 in equation 10 and rearranging terms, we have

$$(12) \qquad \sum_{g \neq h=1}^{K} V_g W_h r_{gh} = (K^2 - K)(C_{(VW)_r} + \overline{V}\,\overline{W}\overline{r}) - KC_{VW}\overline{r}.$$

Combining equations 9 and 12, we may write the numerator of equation 7 as follows:

$$(13) \qquad \sum_{g=1}^{K} V_g W_g + \sum_{g \neq h=1}^{K} V_g W_h r_{gh} = K(1 - \overline{r})(C_{VW} + \overline{V}\,\overline{W})$$
$$+ (K^2 - K)C_{(VW)_r} + K^2 \overline{V}\,\overline{W}\overline{r},$$

where $\overline{r}$ is the average intercorrelation of the subtests,
$\ \ \overline{V}$ is the average of the V-weights,
$\ \ \overline{W}$ is the average of the W-weights,
$\ \ K$ is the number of scores to be combined,
$\ \ C_{VW}$ is the covariance between the two sets of weights, and
$C_{(VW)_r}$ is the covariance between r_{gh} and the product $V_g W_h$.

By substituting V for W in equation 13, we may write the first factor in the denominator of equation 7 as follows:

$$(14) \qquad \sum_{g=1}^{K} V_g{}^2 + \sum_{g \neq h=1}^{K} V_g V_h r_{gh} = K(1 - \overline{r})(\tilde{V}^2 + \overline{V}^2)$$
$$+ (K^2 - K)C_{(VV)_r} + K^2 \overline{V}^2 \overline{r}.$$

The covariance term C_{VW}, it should be noted, changes into the variance of V, which has been designated by the symbol $\tilde{V}^2$. By substituting W for V in equation 14, an expression can be written for the second term in the denominator of equation 7. Substituting equations 13 and 14 in equation 7, we obtain the final expression for the correlation between the two weighted sums,

Equation (15)

$$R_{X_V X_W} = \frac{K(1 - \bar{r})(C_{VW} + \bar{V}\bar{W}) + (K^2 - K)C_{(VW)r} + K^2\bar{V}\bar{W}\bar{r}}{\sqrt{\begin{matrix} K(1 - \bar{r})(\tilde{V}^2 + \bar{V}^2) \\ + (K^2 - K)C_{(VV)r} \\ + K^2\bar{V}^2\bar{r} \end{matrix}} \sqrt{\begin{matrix} K(1 - \bar{r})(\tilde{W}^2 + \bar{W}^2) \\ + (K^2 - K)C_{(WW)r} \\ + K^2\bar{W}^2\bar{r} \end{matrix}}}.$$

This equation expresses the correlation between two composites obtained by using different weights, in terms of

K, the number of scores to be combined,
$\bar{W}$ and $\bar{V}$, the averages of the W and V weights,
$\tilde{W}$ and $\tilde{V}$, the standard deviations of the two sets of weights,
$\bar{r}$, the average intercorrelation of the scores to be combined,
C_{VW}, the covariance between the two sets of weights used, and three
    terms of the form
$C_{(VW)r}$, the covariance of a product of weights with r_{gh}.

Horst (1941), pages 379–401, contains a discussion by M. W. Richardson of the principles to be followed and the precautions to be observed in deciding upon a set of weights. Richardson presents an equation analogous to equation 15, but derived from more restrictive assumptions.

To see what happens as K increases, we may divide the numerator and denominator by K^2 and omit all terms which have $(1/K)$ as a factor. This gives

$$(16) \qquad R_{X_V X_W} \rightarrow \frac{C_{(VW)r} + \bar{V}\bar{W}\bar{r}}{\sqrt{C_{(VV)r} + \bar{V}^2\bar{r}} \sqrt{C_{(WW)r} + \bar{W}^2\bar{r}}},$$

which is equal to unity if the covariance terms are equal and the mean V-weight equals the mean W-weight. In particular, if the covariance terms are near zero they may be ignored; and in this case $R_{X_V X_W}$ approaches unity regardless of the value of the mean weights.

Also we learn from equation 15 that, if the average intercorrelation of the items ($\bar{r}$) is near unity, the factor $(1 - \bar{r})$ approaches zero, and equation 15 approaches an expression similar to that given in equation 16. That is, when $\bar{r}$ in equation 15 approaches unity, $R_{X_V X_W}$ approaches unity if the covariance terms are equal and if $\bar{V} = \bar{W}$. It is also true in this case that $R_{X_V X_W}$ approaches unity if $\bar{r}$ approaches unity and the covariance terms approach zero, regardless of the values of $\bar{V}$ and $\bar{W}$.

It should also be noted that, if positive, zero, and negative weights in any combination are allowed, either or both $\bar{V}$ and $\bar{W}$ may be zero, and $\tilde{V}$ and $\tilde{W}$ may be either large or small in relation to finite values of $\bar{V}$ and $\bar{W}$. If such freedom in selection of weights is allowed, we can learn from equation 15 and from the limit given in equation 16 that $R_{X_V X_W}$ may assume any value, regardless of the intercorrelation of the weights, the number of variables, or the average intercorrelation of these variables.

If all the weights cannot be positive, we are considering the situation in which $\overline{V}$ and $\overline{W}$ are small in relation to $\tilde{V}$ and $\tilde{W}$. Assuming that the terms containing $\overline{V}$ or $\overline{W}$ may be ignored as being small, we see that $R_{X_V X_W}$ depends primarily on the four covariance terms C_{VW}, $C_{(VW)r}$, $C_{(VV)r}$, and $C_{(WW)r}$. The number of variables to be combined (K) and the average intercorrelation of these variables ($\bar{r}$) are of only minor importance in determining $R_{X_V X_W}$ when $\overline{V}$ and $\overline{W}$ are both small.

Let us examine equation 15 to see what happens as the correlation between the two sets of weights increases. Under this condition, the term C_{VW} approaches $\tilde{V}\tilde{W}$, and the covariance $C_{(VW)r}$ becomes similar to $C_{(VV)r}$ and $C_{(WW)r}$ so that, as r_{VW} approaches unity, the value of $R_{X_V X_W}$ is dependent upon the value of $\overline{V}$ and $\overline{W}$. Thus we see that as r_{VW} approaches unity, $R_{X_V X_W}$ also approaches unity, *provided that* $\overline{V} = \overline{W}$.

We may also see that, as the standard deviations of V and of W are decreased, the covariance and variance terms in equation 15 decrease. In the limit these terms will vanish. Dividing the numerator and the denominator of the remaining terms by $\overline{V}\overline{W}$, we find that $R_{X_V X_W}$ approaches unity as the variance of the weights is decreased, provided that the terms $\overline{V}$ and $\overline{W}$ do not approach zero.

Summarizing the information furnished by equation 15 and the limit given in equation 16, we see that:

    A. If either or both $\overline{V}$ and $\overline{W}$ may be zero, $R_{X_V X_W}$ may assume any value regardless of the value of $\bar{r}$, K, or the various covariance terms involving the weights.

    B. If $\overline{V}$ and $\overline{W}$ are small in relation to $\tilde{V}$ and $\tilde{W}$, $R_{X_V X_W}$ depends primarily on the four covariance terms C_{VW}, $C_{(VW)r}$, $C_{(VV)r}$, and $C_{(WW)r}$, and is relatively insensitive to changes in the values of $\bar{r}$ and K.

    C. If we consider only positive weights so that $\tilde{V}/\overline{V}$ and $\tilde{W}/\overline{W}$ are less than unity, the correlation between the two composites obtained by using two different sets of weights approaches unity as (a) the correlation between the two sets of weights is increased, (b) the average intercorrelation of the part scores is increased, and (c) the number of scores *to be combined is increased. It should be particularly noted that this last effect holds, even if the correlation between the two sets of weights (r_{VW}) is zero, but that $\bar{r}$ must be greater than zero. (d) As the standard deviation of the weights ($\tilde{V}$ and $\tilde{W}$) is decreased in proportion to the mean weights ($\overline{V}$ and $\overline{W}$), $R_{X_V X_W}$ approaches unity regardless of the values of $\bar{r}$, $\overline{V}$, and $\overline{W}$.*

From the practical point of view, we may say that, if a large number of scores are to be combined (of the order of 50 to 100) or if the scores have high intercorrelations, it makes relatively little difference what sets of positive weights are assigned. The computationally simplest set would probably be the best one to use. If, however, we are combining only a few scores (for example, three to ten), and the average intercorrelation is low (.5 or less), differential weighting equations may profitably be considered. However, the set of weights must have a large standard deviation if it is to give results appreciably different from the set 1, 1, $\cdots$, 1; also if two sets of weights have a high intercorrelation it makes little or no difference which set is used.

Wilks (1938) has dealt with the special case in which the weights are distributed so that $\tilde{V}/\overline{V} \lessgtr 1$ and $\tilde{W}/\overline{W} \lessgtr 1$, and the weights are independent of each other and of the correlations between the variables to be weighted. It should be noted that the usual practice in weighting items in a test is to use positive weights so distributed that the standard deviation will not be large relative to the mean weight. Furthermore, in considering alternative sets of weights, the two sets considered are *usually positively* correlated so that the case dealing with weights independent of each other, which is considered by Wilks, will give composites that correlate *less* than the alternative composites usually considered in practice. It is also important to remember that, if we are willing to consider two sets of positive weights that are *negatively correlated* with each other, the correlation between the resulting composites will be lower than that indicated by Wilks' formula, given as equation 47 in this chapter. This formula may be derived in the following manner.

If a sample of K-weights (V_i) are drawn from an infinite population with mean a_v and standard deviation σ_v, the variable

$$e_v = \frac{(\overline{V} - a_v)\sqrt{K}}{\sigma_v}$$

has a zero mean and unit variance regardless of the magnitude of K

(the number in the sample). (See Wilks, 1943, page 81.) The mean of a given sample may thus be expressed as

$$\bar{V} = a_v + \frac{e_v \sigma_v}{\sqrt{K}}.$$

The sample mean is thus expressed as a function of the population mean, and standard deviation, the number of cases in the sample, and a variable (e_v) with zero mean and unit standard deviation. The standard deviation is thus independent of the number of cases in the sample.

Since we have limited the treatment to the case in which the weights V are independent of W, the mean of the distribution of products VW for the entire population sampled will be equal to the product of the means of the two populations $(a_v a_w)$. Hence we may write

$$(17) \qquad \frac{\displaystyle\sum_{g=1}^{K} V_g W_g}{K} = a_v a_w + \frac{e_1}{\sqrt{K}},$$

where e_1 is a random variable with zero mean and a constant standard deviation independent of $\sqrt{K}$.

Likewise the mean of the distribution of products VWr for the entire population of weights and correlations will be equal to the product of the means $(a_v a_w \bar{r})$. Thus we have

$$(18) \qquad \frac{\displaystyle\sum_{g \neq h=1}^{K} V_g W_h r_{gh}}{K^2 - K} = a_v a_w \bar{r} + \frac{e_2}{\sqrt{K^2 - K}},$$

where e_2 is a random variable with zero mean and a standard deviation independent of K.

Similarly, if we use b_v to designate the second moment *about the origin* for the population of weights V,

$$(19) \qquad \frac{\displaystyle\sum_{g=1}^{K} V_g{}^2}{K} = b_v + \frac{e_3}{\sqrt{K}}.$$

Correspondingly, the mean of the product $V_g V_h r_{gh}$ may be written

$$(20) \qquad \frac{\displaystyle\sum_{g \neq h=1}^{K} V_g V_h r_{gh}}{K^2 - K} = a_v{}^2 \bar{r} + \frac{e_4}{\sqrt{K^2 - K}}.$$

Substituting W for V in the two foregoing equations, we obtain appropriate expressions for the W-weights.

Substituting equations 17, 18, 19, 20, and analogous equations for the weights W in equation 7, we have

Equation (21)

$$R_{X_V X_W} = \frac{K\left[a_v a_w + \dfrac{e_1}{\sqrt{K}}\right] + (K^2 - K)\left[a_v a_w \bar{r} + \dfrac{e_2}{\sqrt{K^2 - K}}\right]}{\sqrt{\left\{K\left[b_v + \dfrac{e_3}{\sqrt{K}}\right] + (K^2 - K)\left[a_v^2 \bar{r} + \dfrac{e_4}{\sqrt{K^2 - K}}\right]\right\} \times \left\{K\left[b_w + \dfrac{e_5}{\sqrt{K}}\right] + (K^2 - K)\left[a_w^2 \bar{r} + \dfrac{e_6}{\sqrt{K^2 - K}}\right]\right\}}}.$$

In order to determine the factors influencing the composite as K becomes large, we shall define a new variable,

$$y = \frac{1}{\sqrt{K}}.$$

R may then be regarded as a function of y and expanded in Taylor's series about $y = 0$. If we set $\sqrt{K} = 1/y$ in equation 21, multiply numerator and denominator by y^4, and define three new functions, $G(y)$, $H(y)$, and $F(y)$, we obtain

$$(22) \qquad R_{X_V X_W} = G(y) = \frac{H(y)}{\sqrt{F_v(y)}\,\sqrt{F_w(y)}}$$

where

$$(23) \quad H(y) = a_v a_w y^2 + e_1 y^3 + a_v a_w \bar{r}(1 - y^2) + e_2 y^2 \sqrt{1 - y^2},$$

$$(24) \quad F_v(y) = b_v y^2 + e_3 y^3 + a_v^2 \bar{r}(1 - y^2) + e_4 y^2 \sqrt{1 - y^2},$$

and

$$(25) \quad F_w(y) = b_w y^2 + e_5 y^3 + a_w^2 \bar{r}(1 - y^2) + e_6 y^2 \sqrt{1 - y^2}.$$

We are now regarding $R_{X_V X_W}$ as a function of the variable y, and the parameters a, b, and $\bar{r}$. The problem is to evaluate this function in the vicinity of $y = 0$. Using Taylor's theorem for small values of y, we may write

$$(26) \qquad G(y) = G(0) + y G'(0) + \left(\frac{y^2}{2}\right) G''(0).$$

Setting $y = 0$ in equation 22, we see that

(27) $$G(0) = 1.$$

The problem is now to evaluate $G'(0)$ and $G''(0)$.

To evaluate $G'(0)$, we differentiate equation 22, obtaining

(28) $$G'(y) = \frac{H'(y)}{\sqrt{F_v(y)}\,\sqrt{F_w(y)}} - \frac{G(y)}{2}\left[\frac{F'_v(y)}{F_v(y)} + \frac{F'_w(y)}{F_w(y)}\right].$$

To determine the value of equation 28, when $y = 0$, we need the derivatives of equations 23, 24, and 25. These derivatives are

(29) $$H'(y) = 2a_v a_w y + 3e_1 y^2 - 2a_v a_w \bar{r}y - e_2 \frac{3y^3 - 2y}{\sqrt{1 - y^2}},$$

(30) $$F'_v(y) = 2b_v y + 3e_3 y^2 - 2a_v{}^2 \bar{r}y - e_4 \frac{3y^3 - 2y}{\sqrt{1 - y^2}},$$

and

(31) $$F'_w(y) = 2b_w y + 3e_5 y^2 - 2a_w{}^2 \bar{r}y - e_6 \frac{3y^3 - 2y}{\sqrt{1 - y^2}}.$$

Setting $y = 0$ in equations 28 to 31 inclusive, we find that

(32) $$F'_v(0) = F'_w(0) = H'(0) = G'(0) = 0.$$

To evaluate $G''(y)$, when $y = 0$, we differentiate equation 28, obtaining

(33) $$G''(y) = \frac{H''(y)}{\sqrt{F_v(y)F_w(y)}} - \frac{H'(y)}{2\sqrt{F_v(y)F_w(y)}}\left[\frac{F'_v(y)}{F_v(y)} + \frac{F'_w(y)}{F_w(y)}\right]$$
$$- \frac{G'(y)}{2}\left[\frac{F'_v(y)}{F_v(y)} + \frac{F'_w(y)}{F_w(y)}\right]$$
$$- \frac{G(y)}{2}\left[\frac{F''_v(y)}{F_v(y)} - \left(\frac{F'_v(y)}{F_v(y)}\right)^2 + \frac{F''_w(y)}{F_w(y)} - \left(\frac{F'_w(y)}{F_w(y)}\right)^2\right].$$

Let us set $y = 0$ and substitute equations 27 and 32 in equation 33, obtaining

(34) $$G''(0) = \frac{H''(0)}{\sqrt{F_v(0)F_w(0)}} - \frac{F''_v(0)}{2F_v(0)} - \frac{F''_w(0)}{2F_w(0)}.$$

The terms in the denominator of equation 34 may be evaluated from equations 24 and 25. The terms of the numerator, however, require the derivatives of equations 29, 30, and 31. These derivatives are

$$(35) \qquad H''(y) = 2a_v a_w + 6e_1 y - 2a_v a_w \bar{r} + e_2 \frac{6y^4 - 9y^2 + 2}{(1 - y^2)^{3/2}},$$

$$(36) \qquad F''_v(y) = 2b_v + 6e_3 y - 2a_v{}^2 \bar{r} + e_4 \frac{6y^4 - 9y^2 + 2}{(1 - y^2)^{3/2}},$$

$$(37) \qquad F''_w(y) = 2b_w + 6e_5 y - 2a_w{}^2 \bar{r} + e_6 \frac{6y^4 - 9y^2 + 2}{(1 - y^2)^{3/2}}.$$

Setting $y = 0$, we have

$$(38) \qquad\qquad H''(0) = 2a_v a_w - 2a_v a_w \bar{r} + 2e_2,$$

$$(39) \qquad\qquad F''_v(0) = 2b_v - 2a_v{}^2 \bar{r} + 2e_4,$$

$$(40) \qquad\qquad F''_w(0) = 2b_w - 2a_w{}^2 \bar{r} + 2e_6.$$

Substituting equations 38, 39, and 40, as well as equations 24 and 25 in equation 34, we have

$$(41) \qquad G''(0) = \frac{2}{\bar{r}} - 2 + \frac{2e_2}{a_v a_w \bar{r}} - \left[\frac{b_v + e_4}{a_v{}^2 \bar{r}} + \frac{b_w + e_6}{a_w{}^2 \bar{r}} - 2 \right].$$

If we factor out $-1/\bar{r}$ in equation 41, and rearrange the terms, we have

$$(42) \quad G''(0) = -\left(\frac{1}{\bar{r}}\right)\left[\frac{b_v}{a_v{}^2} - 1 + \frac{b_w}{a_w{}^2} - 1 - \frac{2e_2}{a_v a_w} + \frac{e_4}{a_v{}^2} + \frac{e_6}{a_w{}^2} \right].$$

From the gross score formula for variance, we see that

$$(43) \qquad\qquad \sigma_v{}^2 = b_v - a_v{}^2$$

and

$$(44) \qquad\qquad \sigma_w{}^2 = b_w - a_w{}^2.$$

Substituting equations 43 and 44 in equation 42, we have

$$(45) \qquad G''(0) = -\left(\frac{1}{\bar{r}}\right)\left[\frac{\sigma_v{}^2}{a_v{}^2} + \frac{\sigma_w{}^2}{a_w{}^2} - \frac{2e_2}{a_v a_w} + \frac{e_4}{a_v{}^2} + \frac{e_6}{a_w{}^2} \right].$$

Substituting equations 27, 32, and 45 in equation 26 and setting $y^2 = 1/K$, we have

$$(46) \qquad R_{X_V X_W} = 1 - \frac{1}{2\bar{r}K}\left[\frac{\sigma_v{}^2}{a_v{}^2} + \frac{\sigma_w{}^2}{a_w{}^2} - \frac{2e_2}{a_v a_w} + \frac{e_4}{a_v{}^2} + \frac{e_6}{a_w{}^2} \right].$$

If we consider the expectation of R, the variables designated by e_i will vanish, since each of these variables was defined in such a way as to have a mean of zero and a constant standard deviation. Designating the mean value of R by $\bar{R}$, we have the final formula given by Wilks (1938), page 26:

Equation (47)

$$\bar{R}_{X_V X_W} = 1 - \frac{1}{2\bar{r}K}\left[\frac{\sigma_v^{\,2}}{a_v^{\,2}} + \frac{\sigma_w^{\,2}}{a_w^{\,2}}\right] \quad \text{or} \quad 1 - \frac{1}{2\bar{r}K}\left[\left(\frac{\tilde{V}}{\overline{V}}\right)^2 + \left(\frac{\tilde{W}}{\overline{W}}\right)^2\right],$$

where $\bar{R}$ is an approximation to the mean value of the correlation between two weighted composites,

$\bar{r}$ is the average intercorrelation between the variables being combined,

K is the number of variables being combined,

σ_v and σ_w are the standard deviations of the two populations of weights being considered, and

a_v and a_w are the means of the two populations of weights being considered.

In the absence of information on the mean and the standard deviation of the population of weights being sampled, the values for the sample ($\tilde{V}$, $\tilde{W}$, $\overline{V}$, and $\overline{W}$) may be used instead. The variance of R is given by terms of the order

$$(R - \bar{R})^2 = \frac{1}{4\bar{r}^2 K^2}\left[\frac{2e_2}{a_v a_w} - \frac{e_4}{a_v^{\,2}} - \frac{e_6}{a_w^{\,2}}\right]^2.$$

Since each term e_i has a constant variance independent of K, we see that the variance of R is of the order $(1/K)^2$ so that the individual R terms will vary from $\bar{R}$ by terms of the order $1/K$.

> *Equation 47 may be used as an approximation of the correlation between two weighted composites. It should be noted that the equation does not apply if (a) the average intercorrelation of the variables ($\bar{r}$) is near zero or is negative, or (b) negative and positive weights are used so that a is near zero and small in relation to σ, or (c) the correlation between the two sets of weights (r_{vw}) is negative. Under any one or more of these conditions, a more general equation such as equation 15 must be used.*

For example, equation 47 indicates that, if the quantity $2K\bar{r}$ is thirty or larger, there is no point to bothering with different weighting systems, unless we are prepared to consider negatively correlated weights or weights some of which are positive and some negative.

In arriving at equation 47, Wilks assumed that there was no probability dependence between the V's and W's. There might or might not be such dependence between r and V or r and W. He also assumed that $\bar{r}$ was greater than zero, and that the number of r_{gh} values greater than zero was of the order of K^2. The use of generally positive weights was also assumed, that is, $\overline{V}$ and $\overline{W}$ were assumed to be larger than $\tilde{V}$ and $\tilde{W}$, respectively.

2. Predicting an external criterion by multiple correlation

If an external criterion is available, and we desire to weight the sub-scores in such a manner that the composite score will have the highest possible correlation with the criterion, the method of multiple correlation is the one to use. Again it must be remembered, as pointed out in the preceding section, that the precise method of weighting is not important unless we are dealing with relatively few tests that are not highly correlated with each other.

We will present the proof, using calculus and the solution of linear equations by determinants.

In the multiple correlation problem we have one criterion or dependent variable, which is to be approximated as closely as possible by a weighted sum of the independent variables. We may write

$$(48) \qquad \dot{x}_{i0} = b_1 x_{i1} + b_2 x_{i2} + \cdots + b_K x_{iK} = \sum_{g=1}^{K} b_g x_{ig},$$

where $\dot{x}_{i0}$ is the predicted criterion score of the ith individual,

b_g, $(g = 1 \cdots K)$ is the weight assigned to the gth test, and

x_{ig}, $(i = 1 \cdots N; g = 1 \cdots K)$ is the deviation score of the ith individual on the gth test.

The multiple correlation problem is to choose the values of b_g so that the correlation of the *criterion* scores (x_0) with the *predicted* criterion scores $(\dot{x}_0)$ will be as large as possible. This is the same as making the sum of the squares of the differences between x_0 and $\dot{x}_0$ as small as possible. We may write

$$(49) \qquad E = \sum_{i=1}^{N} (x_{i0} - \dot{x}_{i0})^2,$$

where x_{i0} is the criterion score of the ith individual, and E is the error of prediction. The multiple correlation problem is to select the b's that will minimize the value of E.

If we substitute equation 48 in equation 49, and set each of the derivatives (dE/db_g) equal to zero, we have

$$\Sigma x_0 x_1 - b_1 \Sigma x_1{}^2 - b_2 \Sigma x_2 x_1 - \cdots - b_K \Sigma x_K x_1 = 0$$

$$\Sigma x_0 x_2 - b_1 \Sigma x_1 x_2 - b_2 \Sigma x_2{}^2 - \cdots - b_K \Sigma x_K x_2 = 0$$

(50)

$$\Sigma x_0 x_K - b_1 \Sigma x_1 x_K - b_2 \Sigma x_2 x_K - \cdots - b_K \Sigma x_K{}^2 = 0.$$

From equations 50 one may express the b's in terms of the variances and covariances of the independent variables, and the covariances of the dependent with each of the independent variables.

The solution of equations 50 can be expressed in determinantal form. Let the determinant

(51)
$$\Delta = \begin{vmatrix} 1 & r_{10} & r_{20} & r_{30} & \cdots & r_{K0} \\ r_{01} & 1 & r_{21} & r_{31} & \cdots & r_{K1} \\ r_{02} & r_{12} & 1 & r_{32} & \cdots & r_{K2} \\ r_{03} & r_{13} & r_{23} & 1 & \cdots & r_{K3} \\ \cdot & \cdot & \cdot & \cdot & & \cdot \\ \cdot & \cdot & \cdot & \cdot & & \cdot \\ \cdot & \cdot & \cdot & \cdot & & \cdot \\ r_{0K} & r_{1K} & r_{2K} & r_{3K} & \cdots & 1 \end{vmatrix}.$$

Let Δ_{00} be the determinant formed by deleting the first row and the first column of Δ, Δ_{01} be the determinant formed by deleting the first row and second column of Δ, Δ_{02} be the determinant formed by deleting the first row and third column of Δ, and in general let Δ_{0g} be the determinant formed by deleting the first row and the $(g + 1)$-th column of Δ. Then the solution of equations 50 is given by

$$b_{01.234 \cdots K} = (-1)^0 \frac{\Delta_{01} s_0}{\Delta_{00} s_1}$$

$$b_{02.134 \cdots K} = (-1)^1 \frac{\Delta_{02} s_0}{\Delta_{00} s_2}$$

(52)
$$b_{03.124 \cdots K} = (-1)^2 \frac{\Delta_{03} s_0}{\Delta_{00} s_3}$$

$$\cdot \qquad \cdot \qquad \cdot$$
$$\cdot \qquad \cdot \qquad \cdot$$
$$\cdot \qquad \cdot \qquad \cdot$$

$$b_{0K.1234 \cdots (K-1)} = (-1)^{(K-1)} \frac{\Delta_{0K} s_0}{\Delta_{00} s_K}.$$

In general, we may write

$$(53) \qquad b_{0g.12 \cdots (g-1)(g+1) \cdots K} = (-1)^{(g-1)} \frac{\Delta_{0g} s_0}{\Delta_{00} s_g}.$$

When the multiple regression weights have been determined accurately for a set of variables, it is well to remember the proof given in the preceding section that two sets of highly correlated weights will give highly correlated composites. This means that, instead of using the awkward fractional weights indicated by the multiple correlation solution, we approximate them by a set of simple integral weights.

The weights indicated in equations 52 when used in equation 48 will give the best estimate of x_0 in the sense that the error (E) indicated in equation 49 will be a minimum. Dividing E by N, the number of cases, and taking the square root gives the error of estimate, which may be written

$$(54) \qquad \sqrt{\frac{E}{N}} = s_{0.123 \cdots K} = s_0 \sqrt{\frac{\Delta}{\Delta_{00}}}.$$

The weighted sum $\dot{x}_0$ given by equation 48, using the weights of equations 52, correlates higher with x_0 than any other possible weighted sum of the independent variables $x_1 \cdots x_K$. This correlation is the multiple correlation, and its value is given by

$$(55) \qquad R_{0.123 \cdots K} = \sqrt{1 - \frac{\Delta}{\Delta_{00}}}.$$

For the simplest possible case of multiple correlation, that of predicting one criterion (x_0) from two independent variables $(x_1$ and $x_2)$, these equations may be written very much more simply. Equations 52 for the weights of x_1 and x_2 become

$$(56) \qquad \begin{aligned} b_{01.2} &= \frac{s_0(r_{01} - r_{02}r_{12})}{s_1(1 - r_{12}^2)}, \\[2mm] b_{02.1} &= \frac{s_0(r_{02} - r_{01}r_{12})}{s_2(1 - r_{12}^2)}. \end{aligned}$$

The error of estimate of equation 54 becomes

$$(57) \qquad s_{0.12} = s_0 \sqrt{\frac{1 + 2r_{01}r_{02}r_{12} - r_{01}^2 - r_{02}^2 - r_{12}^2}{1 - r_{12}^2}}.$$

The multiple correlation given in equation 55 becomes

$$(58) \qquad R_{0.12} = \sqrt{\frac{r_{01}^2 + r_{02}^2 - 2r_{01}r_{02}r_{12}}{1 - r_{12}^2}}.$$

The equations 56 to 58 give the weights, error of estimate, and multiple correlation for the three-variable case in terms of the three intercorrelations and three standard deviations of the original variables.

It should be noted that it may readily happen in multiple correlation methods that a given test is assigned a negative weight. This means that the better a person does on that test, the poorer will be his composite score, and vice versa. Such weights should lead to a careful scrutiny of the test and a consideration of the reasonableness of such a finding. Many situations arise where a negative weight is plausible. However, it should be noted that in a test which is to be given repeatedly, and for which the scoring method may become known to the candidates, it would be very unwise to retain a test with negative weight, since it is very easy for the subjects who know the scoring method to attempt to obtain, and succeed in getting, a low score. Such a change in motivating conditions would destroy any predictive value that the test might have had previously when the subjects were all attempting to obtain a high score. Adkins *et al.* (1947), page 170, indicates that negative weights are not used in civil service tests.

In dealing with more than three variables, it is necessary to use special computational methods, such as those described in Guilford (1936*b*), pages 390–404.

> *If a criterion is available, multiple correlation methods give the best weights for predicting that criterion. Simple integral approximations to these weights will usually give a composite score that correlates almost as well with the criterion.*

3. Selecting tests for a battery by approximations to multiple correlation

In addition to specifying the best set of weights to use for each of the tests in a battery, it is frequently desirable to eliminate some of the tests as well. For example, we might use *six* subtests in an experimental battery, and wish to know which *three* would give the highest multiple correlation. It would also be desirable to know what the multiple correlation was for all six tests, as well as for the best set of three, in order to see how much was lost in predictive accuracy by eliminating the poorest half of the tests.

The only certain method of obtaining an exact answer to such questions is to work the zero-order correlations, the multiple correlations for all possible combinations of two tests, for all possible combinations of three, or four, or five, and the multiple correlation using all six tests. This would mean, for six predictor tests and one criterion, computing $15 + 20 + 15 + 6 + 1$, or 57 multiple correlations. We could then easily pick the best combination of tests at each stage and decide whether the additional testing time was adequately repaid in terms of higher validity coefficients. With the ordinary computing methods in use at present, the labor of such computations makes such analyses prohibitive. It may well be that, with the development of high-speed electronic computing machines, the exact solution of such a problem would be more economical than many of the approximation methods now in use.

Frisch (1934) described a method of dealing with what he termed "complete regression systems" by "confluence analysis." This method essentially involved computing multiple correlations and multiple regression weights for all combinations of the variables involved in order to understand thoroughly the relationships among these variables.

One very good approximation method is to look first at the zero-order correlation coefficients, and select the one best test. This test is then tried out with each of the $K - 1$ remaining tests to see which two (including the one best) will give the highest multiple. These two best are then combined in turn with each of the $K - 2$ remaining tests to pick the "best" combination of three. With this method we should select three tests out of a set of six by working multiples for only 5 two-test composites and 4 three-test composites, that is, 9 instead of 57 multiple correlations. Such a method has been described by Toops (1923). Other closely similar procedures have been described by Wherry (see Stead, Shartle, and associates, 1940, Appendix V), by Toops (1941), and by Wherry and Gaylord (1946), and Horst (1934*b*).

If we are willing to assume that the best set of two tests includes the best one, the best set of three includes the two previously indicated, and so on, and in addition to assume that the *relative weights determined for the best two also hold when these two are combined with a third*, and so on up, a very quick and easy graphic approximation method has been provided by Jenkins (1946).

4. Weighting according to test reliability or inversely as the error variance

Giving the more reliable tests greater weight in a composite has been suggested by Kelley (1927), pages 211–213, Thurstone (1931*a*), pages

88–90, and Richardson [see Appendix D, pages 392–396, in Horst (1941)]. Kelley and Richardson give the gross score weight of any test (g) as $r_{gg}/(1 - r_{gg})$, that is, the weight is the ratio of the reliability coefficient to the error variance of the standard scores. Thurstone follows a slightly different procedure and finds the gross score weights to be $\sqrt{r_{gg}}/(1 - r_{gg})$. The former formula can readily be derived from multiple correlation theory with two assumptions. The first is that all the tests are measures of the same true score, except for the fact that they contain different proportions of random error. This assumption means that the intercorrelations will be unity, when corrected for attenuation. The second assumption is that we wish to maximize the correlation between this common true score and the weighted composite.

Stated in mathematical terms, these assumptions mean that

$$(59) \qquad r_{gh} = \sqrt{r_{gg}r_{hh}} \qquad (g \neq h = 1 \cdots K),$$

the intercorrelation between any two tests is equal to the geometric mean of the reliability coefficients. The criterion may be assumed to be the true score, in which case the validity coefficient of each test is given by

$$(60) \qquad r_{tg} = \sqrt{r_{gg}},$$

or it may be assumed that the criterion is another test x_0, which also has the same true score, in which case the validity coefficient of each test is given by

$$(61) \qquad r_{0g} = \sqrt{r_{00}r_{gg}}.$$

Identical relative weights are given by either assumption. In the following derivation we shall use equations 59 and 61. We see that the criterion reliability (r_{00}) is a factor common to all the weights, hence may be ignored if we are interested only in relative weights. Substituting equations 59 and 61 in equation 51, we have

$$(62) \quad \Delta = \begin{vmatrix} 1 & \sqrt{r_{00}r_{11}} & \sqrt{r_{00}r_{22}} & \cdots & \sqrt{r_{00}r_{KK}} \\ \sqrt{r_{00}r_{11}} & 1 & \sqrt{r_{11}r_{22}} & \cdots & \sqrt{r_{11}r_{KK}} \\ \sqrt{r_{00}r_{22}} & \sqrt{r_{11}r_{22}} & 1 & \cdots & \sqrt{r_{22}r_{KK}} \\ \vdots & \vdots & \vdots & & \vdots \\ \sqrt{r_{00}r_{KK}} & \sqrt{r_{11}r_{KK}} & \sqrt{r_{22}r_{KK}} & \cdots & 1 \end{vmatrix}.$$

Since the factor s_0/Δ_{00} is common to all the weights in equations 52, we may ignore it and evaluate terms of the form Δ_{0g}/s_g to determine the relative weights for the variables. We may form Δ_{01} by deleting the first row and second column of equation 62 and then transform the determinant Δ_{01} by multiplying the first column by $\sqrt{r_{22}}/\sqrt{r_{00}}$ and deducting the product from the second column. In general multiply the first column by $\sqrt{r_{gg}}/\sqrt{r_{00}}$ and deduct the product from column g. These transformations do not alter the value of the determinant, so we have

$$(63) \quad \Delta_{01} = \begin{vmatrix} \sqrt{r_{00}r_{11}} & 0 & 0 & \cdots & 0 \\ \sqrt{r_{00}r_{22}} & 1 - r_{22} & 0 & \cdots & 0 \\ \sqrt{r_{00}r_{33}} & 0 & 1 - r_{33} & \cdots & 0 \\ \cdot & \cdot & \cdot & & \cdot \\ \cdot & \cdot & \cdot & & \cdot \\ \sqrt{r_{00}r_{KK}} & 0 & 0 & \cdots & 1 - r_{KK} \end{vmatrix}.$$

Expanding equation 63 in terms of minors of the first row, we have

$$(64) \quad \Delta_{01} = \sqrt{r_{00}r_{11}}\,(1 - r_{22})(1 - r_{33}) \cdots (1 - r_{KK}).$$

If we multiply and divide the right side of equation 64 by $(1 - r_{11})$ and let

$$P = \sqrt{r_{00}}\,(1 - r_{11})(1 - r_{22})(1 - r_{33}) \cdots (1 - r_{KK}),$$

we have

$$\Delta_{01} = \frac{P\sqrt{r_{11}}}{1 - r_{11}}.$$

We may write all the other terms of the form Δ_{0g} similarly, omitting the common factor P in order to deal only with relative weights. If the factors common to all the weights are designated by C, and the standard score weight for test g is indicated by $\beta_{0g.12\ldots K}$, we have equations of the form

$$(65) \quad C\beta_{0g.12\ldots K} = \frac{\sqrt{r_{gg}}}{1 - r_{gg}}.$$

From equations 53 of this chapter and 20 of Chapter 3, we obtain the weights appropriate for use with *gross* scores.   These weights, designated by $b_{0g.12 \ldots K}$, are

$$(66) \qquad\qquad C'b_{0g.12 \ldots K} = \frac{r_{gg}}{1 - r_{gg}}, \qquad\qquad (g = 1 \cdots K)$$

where C' designates the factors common to all the weights. Weighting formulas 65 and 66 were presented by Kelley (1927), pages 211–213. The detailed derivation has been given by Richardson in Appendix D, see Horst (1941, pages 392–396). Thurstone (1931a) has suggested the use of weights dependent on reliability, which differ from these by a factor of $\sqrt{r_{gg}}$.

The use of the weights of equation 66 depends upon the assumptions indicated in equations 59 and 61. Whenever several tests and their reliabilities are available so that the weights of equation 66 may be used, it is also always possible to calculate the intercorrelations among these tests in order to verify the assumption in equation 59. It is probably only in exceptional cases that this assumption would be verified. Constructing a set of tests that satisfy a single factor solution is a fairly difficult job. Equation 59 is a far more stringent requirement than a single factor battery. Tests may have one common factor, and differ both in error and in factors specific to each test. Equation 59 does not allow for any possibility of a factor specific to each test.

In summary, we may say that, while it is usually desirable to give greater weight to the more reliable test, there is usually no special justification for the particular weights indicated by equations 66.

5. Weighting inversely as the standard deviation

Weighting gross scores in tests by the reciprocal of the standard deviation has also been frequently given as one method of combining tests. See Kelley (1927), page 66, Thurstone (1931a), pages 83–87, and others. It should be noted that such a weighting principle is justified only in highly specialized and unusual cases. For example, if the true variance of the group tested is large, this will contribute to making the standard deviation of the test large, and would seem to be no valid reason for decreasing the weight of the test. On the other hand, test score variance may be increased by increasing the error variance of a test. If such is the case, a decreased weight for the test is plausible; however, there is no reason for making this weight proportional to the total standard deviation, which is the square root of the *sum* of true and error variance. The third factor that may influence the standard deviation of a test is its length. A 100-item test will have a much larger standard deviation than a 10-item test. Clearly on a common-sense basis, we should not increase the accuracy of a test by lengthening it from 10 to 100 items, and then reduce the weight of the better test by weighting it inversely as its standard deviation. A detailed criticism of the method of weighting inversely as the standard deviations is given by Richardson. See Horst (1941), Appendix D, pages 385–388.

It is interesting to note that under certain highly specialized conditions the multiple correlation weights of equation 53 become equal to the reciprocal of the standard deviation of the test. If it is assumed that all the test intercorrelations are equal to some value, r, for instance, and that all the validity coefficients (r_{0g}) are equal to some value, for example, v, then $\Delta_{01} = \Delta_{02} = \cdots = \Delta_{0K}$, so that all the weights indicated in equations 52 are identical except for the standard deviation appearing in the denominator. In other words, if all the independent variables in a set are identical with respect to validity, and have identical intercorrelations, so that no special test clusters are formed, and if in spite of such remarkable similarity the tests still differ in variability, the *multiple correlation weights* are inversely proportional to the *standard deviations* of the tests.

It should also be noted that various methods of scoring a test may also have an effect on its standard deviation. For example, if two 100-item tests are scored differently, test a receiving one point per item and test b ten points per item, then if the tests are reasonably similar the standard deviation of b and its influence in any composite would be very much greater than that of a. Similarly, tests scored number right will have a different standard deviation if the scoring system is changed to $R - cW$.

The standard deviation of a test is an important factor in determining the influence of that test on any composite. However, it is not possible to set up any sensible routine method for using the standard deviation in determining the weight of a test. If one test has a larger standard deviation than another test, and this difference seems to be due to factors that are largely irrelevant to the reliability and validity of the test, weighting inversely as the standard deviation is probably reasonable. If the test with the larger standard deviation is more valid or reliable, or if it seems to be reasonable to assume that it would be more valid and reliable because it is a longer or a better test, then simply adding in the gross scores of the two tests would be a reasonable procedure, and weighting inversely as the standard deviations would only help to decrease the influence of the best test. On the other hand, if it seems that the test with the larger standard deviation owes this extra variability to error variance, some still different weighting scheme that would decrease the weight of or eliminate the poorer test would seem reasonable.

Weighting inversely as the standard deviation is to be avoided as a routine procedure. Other factors being approximately equal, a composite will be influenced more by a test with a large standard deviation than by one with a small standard deviation. This higher weight is probably desirable if the greater standard deviation is due to such factors as greater test length or reliability that contribute to true variance. The higher weight is probably undesirable if it seems that the greater standard deviation is due to irrelevant multiplying factors in the scoring key or to any factors that would increase the error variance.

6. Weighting inversely as the error of measurement

Weighting each test by the factor $1/(s_g\sqrt{1 - r_{gg}})$ is a method that would be free of the obvious objections that apply to weighting either inversely as the standard deviations or inversely as the square of the error of measurement. For example, such a weighting would automatically correct for any arbitrary change in scoring that affected the standard deviation of the test without altering its reliability. As the true variance increased, or the error variance decreased, there would be an appropriate *direction* of adjustment of the weights. If the test length were altered so as to raise the reliability, the weight would be increased. As an arbitrary rule of thumb method for use when no criterion is available and the tests seem indifferent as far as judgment of content is concerned, it would seem that such a system would be appropriate.

Weighting inversely, as the error of measurement automatically corrects for any arbitrary multiplying factors introduced in the scoring system, increases the weight of a test as true variance or reliability is increased, and decreases the weight of a test as the error variance is increased. Although no rationale has been suggested for this method, it has excellent properties from a common-sense point of view, and is probably the safest arbitrary rule of thumb method to recommend for general use, when no criterion is available and when test intercorrelations are not computed.

7. Irrelevance of test mean, number of items, or perfect score

In most amateur discussions of weighting of tests the first factors considered are the number of items in the test and the average magnitude of the score. It is believed, for example, that if gross scores are added, the effect will be to give a 100-item test twice the weight of a 50-item test. That such is not the case can be seen for example by assuming that the 100-item test was a very easy one on which everyone obtained scores ranging from 95 to 100. Adding scores on this test to a student's record would then, at the most, make a 5-point difference in the total score. If, on the other hand, the 50-item test were composed of fairly difficult items and were fairly reliable, it could easily be that scores on it would range from 20 to 50. In other words, adding this test would make a 30-point difference in extreme cases, and a 10- or 20-point difference in the majority of cases, so that the total score would agree rather closely with the score on the 50-item test and not correlate with the score on the 100-item test.

From the illustration just given, we also see that the weight a test exerts is not related to the magnitude of the average score either. The 100-item test in the illustration would have a mean of 97 or 98 correct answers, and the 50-item test would have a mean in the 30's. The initial amateur reaction on seeing two sets of test scores, one set mostly in the 30's and the other all in the high 90's, would be to feel that, if the two sets were added, the first would have approximately one-third the weight of the second. As we have just seen, the total range of scores for a test is the important factor in determining its effect on a composite.

It can be seen that, of themselves, the test mean, and number of items have no effect whatever on the relationship between a test and the composite of which it is a part. *Both factors should be completely ignored in considering weighting problems.*

It might be noted that, if all students do not have the same series of tests, the mean score is an important factor. Suppose, for example, that the students have the choice of answering questions X or Y, or of submitting answers on the X-test or, alternatively, on the Y-test. If the X-scores range from 30 to 50 with an average around 40, and the Y-scores range from 70 to 90 with an average around 80, clearly the students who have chosen Y and not X will get in general 40 more points in their total than those who have chosen X and not Y. In such a case it is possible to "adjust" by adding 40 points to each person's X-score or subtracting 40 points from each person's Y-score. However, another complication arises here. Can it correctly be assumed that the students who submitted X are on the average identical with those who submitted Y? Frequently when alternative choices are given it happens that better students tend to pick one and poorer students the other, so that equating the average scores is not an appropriate procedure. Neither is it correct simply to add the gross scores, which means assuming that these correctly represent the difference between the two groups. In general, it is impossible to determine the appropriate adjustment without an inordinate amount of effort. Alternative questions should always be avoided. The only possible rational solution is in the type of methods suggested in the chapter on standardizing tests. A common section must be used as the basis for equating the alternate parts. In order to use these equating procedures, both the common parts and the alternate parts need to be of a reasonable length to secure reliability, so that the equating will be reasonably stable for similar groups. In the conventional examination, where the student is asked to answer any six of nine questions, we are really setting nine different examinations. If the examination were given to 150 students, there would be only 100 per examination on the average, which would mean that many of the combinations would be taken by very few students. The data would be inadequate for equating, and the labor would be great. The alternative questions should in general not be used. If some choice seems unavoidable, the choice should be set up systematically by requiring a given set of items to be answered by everyone, and then reducing the number of possible combinations that can be submitted by requiring that the student answer *one* question from this set, or that he answer *one* of the following three sets of questions.

> *The number of items in a test (the perfect score) and the test mean have no effect in determining the test's influence in a composite and should be ignored when considering the appropriate weight for a test. The only exception arises when alternative questions (or tests) are used, in which case we must allow not only for the test mean but also for ability differences in the groups making the different choices.*

8. Effect of a subtest on a composite score

Having considered the effects of alternate sets of weights used on the same set of subtests, we may turn to the problem of the effect of a subtest on a composite score.

Most of the discussions of this topic attempt to regard the composite as broken up into parts, and then assess the percentage contribution of each of the parts to the total. In general, such a solution is impossible, and will not be given here.

A simple, direct, and meaningful way to think of the contribution of a part to the total is to use the correlation between the part and the total as an index of the contribution of the part. Wilks (1938) has suggested this method, pointing out that, if each part has the same correlation with the total, in one sense each part has the same weight in determining total score. It should be noted that using the correlation coefficient as an index enables us to define the "same" weight of two tests and to define "greater" weight and "less" weight. However, it is not possible to say that one test has two or three times the weight of another test.

Using the part-total correlation as an index of relative weights, we are able to speak in terms of equal, greater, or less weight. It does not enable us to divide the total into a given number of parts, one for each subtest, totaling to 100 per cent; nor does it enable us to speak of double or triple weights. However of the various methods that have been proposed of assessing the relationship or the "contribution" of the part to the total, it is the most generally useful and intelligible.

The correlation between any part X_g and the total X_C, which is a weighted sum of the parts, may be expressed as follows. Let

$$(67) \quad X_{iC} = W_1 X_{i1} + W_2 X_{i2} + \cdots + W_K X_{iK} = \sum_{g=1}^{K} W_g X_{ig}.$$

The composite score (X_{iC}) for individual i is the weighted sum of his scores on the individual tests. If the X's are regarded as deviation scores, we may write the correlation of part X_g with X_C as follows:

$$(68) \quad r_{gC} = \frac{\sum_{i=1}^{N} X_{ig} X_{iC}}{N s_g s_C}.$$

Expanding and summing the terms in X_{iC}, we have

$$(69) \quad r_{gC} = \frac{\sum_{i=1}^{N} \sum_{h=1}^{K} W_h X_{ig} X_{ih}}{N s_g s_C}.$$

Reversing the order of summation and writing $\sum_{i=1}^{N} X_{ig} X_{ih}$ as a covariance or a variance term gives

$$(70) \quad r_{gC} = \frac{\sum_{h=1}^{K} W_h r_{gh} s_g s_h}{s_g s_C} \qquad (r_{gg} = 1).$$

If we separate the one variance term from the $K - 1$ covariance terms, and divide numerator and denominator by s_g, we have

$$(71) \quad r_{gC} = \frac{W_g s_g + \sum_{h=1}^{K} W_h r_{gh} s_h}{s_C} \qquad (h \neq g),$$

where r_{gC} is the correlation between test g and the weighted composite,

W_g (or W_h) is the weight assigned to any test,

s_g (or s_h) is the standard deviation of the test,

r_{gh} is the intercorrelation between two tests, and

s_C is the standard deviation of the composite.

Since s_C is identical for each of the tests, it may be ignored. We see then that the correlation between the composite and any test is determined by the weight assigned that test, the standard deviation of that test, and the weighted sum of the correlations between that test and each of the other tests.

In particular it should be noted that the test mean M_X and the number of items K (that is, the perfect score) have nothing whatever to do with determining the correlation of any test with the total composite. This correlation is determined by the test standard deviations, the intercorrelations, and the weights assigned. If the weighting factor for a test is increased, the correlation of that test with the composite will be increased. If the average correlation of a test with the other tests is increased, its correlation with the composite will be increased. If the standard deviation of a test is increased, its correlation with the composite will be increased.

If all the tests in a set have zero intercorrelations, the correlation of any test with the composite will be proportional to the product of its assigned weight and its standard deviation. However, in the usual case this term will be small in proportion to the weighted sum of the correlations of that test with all the other tests.

To show that the factors of test variance and intercorrelations are crucial and must be considered, we may cite an illustration reported in Stuit (1947), pages 305–306. In one basic engineering school the students' time was divided as follows: about four-sevenths in shop work, one-seventh classroom work in mathematics, and two-sevenths classroom work in mechanical drawing and shop theory. The weights (W) were assigned to the part grades in proportion to the time spent on the subject, and the weighted sum taken as the total grade. For one class of 350 the correlation of total score with mathematics was .86, with mechanical drawing was .74, and shop work, .48. The final grades were determined primarily by the one-seventh classroom work in mathematics, and only to a slight extent by the four-sevenths spent in shop work. The explanation is found in the standard deviations of the three sets of part grades. The standard deviation of the mathematics grades was 7.7, of mechanical drawing, 4.1, and of shop work 2.5. It is also interesting to note the means of the three sets of part grades. These were, for mathematics, 83.6, mechanical drawing 89.1, and shop 84.0. The mathematics part, with the lowest assigned weight and lowest mean score, had the highest actual weight in determining total score because of its very high standard deviation. In shop, as the standard deviation shows, the vast majority of men received grades in the 80 to 88 range so that these grades had little influence on the total, even though they were weighted nominally four times as much as the mathematics score. Here the problem was to secure a greater spread of grades in shop work. Since the grades of different instructors for the students' shop work correlated from −.11 to .55, it was clearly desirable to secure more uniform grading methods rather than simply to multiply such apparently inaccurate ratings by a factor such as ten or twenty in order to have them exert a predominant influence on final grades. Various gages were devised to measure the products of shop work quickly and accurately. Such increased accuracy in grading the shop work increased the variability of shop grades, and thus these grades legitimately contributed more to the total score of the students than the classroom work in mathematics. (See Chapter 7, equation 9.)

It is hoped that this illustration will demonstrate that both the correlation and the standard deviation, as well as the nominal weight, must be taken into consideration when making combinations of scores. It also shows that it may not be possible to reach an adequate solution of the problem simply by altering the weights of the different part scores. It may be necessary to devise new and better tests for certain aspects of the work before it is possible to give these aspects their desired weight in the total score.

> *Equation 71 shows that the correlation between a composite (C) and any one of its parts (g) is completely determined by the weights, standard deviations, and intercorrelations of the subtests. The test mean and the number of items (or perfect score) have no effect on the correlation between part and total, unless they influence the standard deviations and intercorrelations.*

9. Use of judgment in weighting tests if no criterion is available

If several part scores are to be combined to determine a total score and no criterion is available, so that multiple correlation methods cannot be used, one method is to use judgment regarding the relative magnitude of the correlation desired between the total and the different part scores. Before such judgments can be meaningfully made, it is necessary to have considerable information on the interrelationships of the part scores. First we note that the total number of items in each test and the mean of each test are irrelevant, *provided all the students have taken each test.* The necessary information includes the standard deviation, reliability, and error of measurement for each test and the intercorrelations between the tests so that we may see the kinds of relationships already existing in the part scores. With this information at hand, we decide on a judgmental basis which of the parts should be weighted equal, which higher, and which lower. Wilks (1938) has proposed that one definition of "equal" weights be equal correlations with the composite score. Higher weight means a higher correlation between composite and the part; lower weight, a lower correlation. In terms of such a definition, we should then decide the relative magnitude of the correlations on a judgmental basis. In general, if a test is long and reliable, it probably should have a higher correlation with the final composite than a test that is short and unreliable. Furthermore, it must be noted that, if certain subtests intercorrelate highly with each other, these tests will *necessarily* have *similar* correlations with the composite. It is possible to decide that they will *all* correlate *high* with the composite or that they will *all* correlate *low* with the composite; but it is not possible to decide that one member of the set will correlate high and the others low with the composite. Roughly speaking, it is necessary that a set of highly intercorrelated subtests all "weight" high, or all "weight" low in the sense of correlating high or low with the composite score. When these decisions are made, the weights are found by solving a set of equations of the form

$$(72) \qquad r_{gC}s_C = \sum_{h=1}^{K} W_h r_{gh}s_h \qquad (r_{gg} = 1),$$

in which r_{gC} are the desired correlations determined by judgment, and the W's are the unknown weights.

> *If in a problem of weighting tests in a battery no criterion is available, but the test intercorrelations and standard deviations are available, it is possible to define relative weights in terms of relative magnitude of the correlation of the part with the composite. Then we judge what the relative magnitudes of the various part-total correlations should be, enter these values in equation 72 and solve for the relative weights. It is also desirable to check the composite to see that the different subtests have approximately the desired correlation with the composite.*

10. Use of factor analysis methods in determining weights of subtests

As a general method for combining subtests we can see that, if the battery of tests is factored and a score set up for each factor, we have represented a maximum of material in the tests with the minimum number of scores. Such methods are dealt with in textbooks on factor analysis, and they are beyond the scope of this book. Usually such methods are too laborious and time consuming to be adopted for ordinary weighting problems.

It should also be noted that this recommendation results in several different scores for each person. If a single grade is to be given or a single pass-fail line is to be drawn, the problem of how to combine these several factor scores into such a single total score still remains. It is of course possible to use judgment in assigning relative weights to the different factor scores. However, if judgment is to be used at this stage in determining the nature of the composite, it may be almost as good to use judgment directly on the subtest scores and avoid the work of the factor analysis. In a complex set of tests, however, it is likely that the groupings revealed by the factor analysis will make our judgments simpler and more meaningful.

In determining a single score for a set of tests, it has been suggested that a particular factor score be used as the single score to represent the battery. There are several possibilities for selecting this factor score.

The first principal axis has been suggested by Wilks (1938), Horst (1936a), and by Edgerton and Kolbe (1936). Computationally this method is quite laborious. It requires a successive approximations procedure with even as few as four or five variables. It must also be noted that this method is directly sensitive to arbitrary changes in score variance. For example, if scores on one test are multiplied by ten, the principal axis will swing in the direction of that test. Furthermore, as previously indicated, it is of no help to adopt a device such as standard scores. Such a procedure would give great weight to short unreliable tests in the composite and relatively little weight to a test that was very long and accurate. However, provided we are able to fix arbitrarily on the appropriate units for each of the subtests, this method has some interesting properties.

Horst derived this method by determining the set of weights that would maximize the variance of the composite scores (given a fixed value for the sum of squares of the weights). Edgerton and Kolbe derived the same method by determining the set of weights that would minimize the variance of the set of scores assigned to a given individual. Wilks derived the same method in seeking to minimize the "generalized variance" for all individuals receiving the same score. The fact that these three different approaches resulted in the same method is interesting. It shows that, provided we fix the units for each test, the largest principal axis score maximizes the variance of the composite score, minimizes the variance of scores for a given individual, and minimizes the generalized variance for all persons receiving the same score.

Use of the first centroid axis was suggested by Horst (1936a) as an approximation procedure. He derived the principal axis solution as indicated above but, recognizing its laboriousness, suggested that the first centroid axis be used instead as an approximation to the principal axis. Using the first centroid axis means making the weights for test g proportional to $\sum_{h=1}^{K} r_{gh}$. This term is easily obtained. There is, however, the usual problem in factor analysis regarding the selection of an appropriate value for the term r_{gg}. In some solutions this term is given the value unity; in other solutions it is set equal to zero, equal to the reliability coefficient, or equal to some estimate of the communality of the test. From the initial discussion of the effects of weighting, we see that, if there are few small correlations, the decision on the appropriate value for r_{gg} will make a great difference in the composite score. If the correlations are many and large, the resulting composite score will be only negligibly affected by this decision.

Horst, in recommending the use of the first centroid axis, felt that it was an approximation to the longest principal axis. Edgerton and Kolbe, however, gave an illustration in which the two were quite different. The amount of difference between these two solutions will depend on the nature of interrelationships in the battery.

Using a single common factor as a guide to the weighting of tests in a battery was suggested by Spearman (1927, Appendix, page xix). This method would apply only to a battery of tests that satisfied Spearman's original two-factor theory, which means that one factor is common to all the tests in the battery, and in addition each test has its own specific factor which is uncorrelated with the general factor and with the specific factor in each of the other tests. The correlation between the factor specific to x and that specific to y may be regarded as the correlation between x and y with the general factor partialled out. Since the specifics correlate zero, we have from the formula for partial correlation

$$0 = r_{xy} - r_{gx}r_{gy}$$

or

$$r_{xy} = r_{gx}r_{gy}.$$

That is, if the battery is explained entirely by one common factor, the correlation between any two tests is the product of the correlation of each of those tests with the general factor. By methods formally identical with those of section 4 on weighting by reliabilities, we can show that the multiple correlation weights to use in predicting the general factor from the tests in a one-factor battery are proportional to

$$(73) \qquad \frac{r_{gx}}{1 - r_{gx}^2}$$

for any test (x), where r_{gx} is the factor loading of test x or its correlation with the one common factor. The methods of determining whether or not a given set of tests is adequately represented by one common factor and the methods of determining the correlation with this factor are discussed in the various textbooks on factor analysis; see Spearman (1927), Thurstone (1935a), (1947b), and others.

These various solutions based essentially on factor theory are interesting. The principal axis solution is especially interesting since it both maximizes interindividual differences and minimizes intraindividual differences. It is, however, markedly influenced by arbitrary decisions made on test scoring. Similar remarks apply to the centroid solution. Where only one factor is necessary to account for the correlations, this system will give a unique solution. It should be noted that, from one point of view, only tests that form a one-factor system should be combined into a single score. Where several factors are present, several scores should result.

The results of any one-factor solution to the weighting problem should still be inspected to determine the correlation between the composite and the individual tests to be certain that, from a judgmental point of view, there is nothing obviously peculiar or undesirable about the solution.

> *If no criterion is available and the battery of tests turns out to have only one common factor, the tests may be weighted to give the best prediction of this factor. If the battery is a multifactor one, it is possible arbitrarily to select the longest principal axis or the first centroid axis as the best one to represent the entire battery.*

11. Weighting to equalize marginal contribution to total variance

Wilks (1938) has suggested another method of defining and determining "equal" weights. He points out that the variance of the weighted sum of $K - 1$ tests will be less than that of the K tests, and suggests that in one sense all the tests are equally weighted if the variance of any combination of $K - 1$ tests is equal. That is, the variance of the total test would be equally affected no matter which *one* of the K constituent tests was removed from the composite. This method again is computationally complex and seems also to have little in its favor.

12. Weighting to maximize the reliability of the composite

If no external criterion is available, we may wish to assign weights so that the reliability of the weighted composite will be a maximum. The solution to this problem has been given for a special case by Mosier (1943), and for the general case by Thomson (1940) and Peel (1948). The solution given by Thomson can be shown to be equivalent to that given by Peel, and since that given by Peel is much simpler we shall use it.

Let the matrix of intercorrelations for the test battery be designated

$$\mathbf{R} = \begin{Vmatrix} 1 & r_{12} & r_{13} & \cdots & r_{1K} \\ r_{12} & 1 & r_{23} & \cdots & r_{2K} \\ r_{13} & r_{23} & 1 & \cdots & r_{3K} \\ \cdot & \cdot & \cdot & & \cdot \\ \cdot & \cdot & \cdot & & \cdot \\ \cdot & \cdot & \cdot & & \cdot \\ r_{1K} & r_{2K} & r_{3K} & \cdots & 1 \end{Vmatrix}.$$

Let the matrix of intercorrelations between the tests of the two parallel batteries be designated

$$\mathbf{C} = \begin{Vmatrix} r_{11} & r_{12} & r_{13} & \cdots & r_{1K} \\ r_{12} & r_{22} & r_{23} & \cdots & r_{2K} \\ r_{13} & r_{23} & r_{33} & \cdots & r_{3K} \\ \cdot & \cdot & \cdot & & \cdot \\ \cdot & \cdot & \cdot & & \cdot \\ \cdot & \cdot & \cdot & & \cdot \\ r_{1K} & r_{2K} & r_{3K} & \cdots & r_{KK} \end{Vmatrix}.$$

The off-diagonal entries of $\mathbf{C}$ are identical with the corresponding entries of $\mathbf{R}$. The two matrices differ only in that one has reliability coefficients, and the other has unity in the diagonals.

Let us also define the row vector of weights,

$$\mathbf{W} = W_1 \quad W_2 \quad W_3 \quad \cdots \quad W_K.$$

Since the second battery is assumed to be parallel to the first, the matrix of intercorrelations ($\mathbf{R}$) for this battery is assumed to be identical with that for the first battery. Equation 7, the general expression for the correlation of two weighted sums, is given in matrix notation by

$$R_{X_V X_W} = \frac{\mathbf{WCW'}}{\sqrt{\mathbf{WRW'}}\ \sqrt{\mathbf{WRW'}}}.$$

Since we are dealing with a reliability coefficient, the two batteries of tests and two sets of weights are identical. Thus the two factors in the denominator are identical, giving

$$(74) \qquad\qquad R_{X_W X_W} = \frac{\mathbf{WCW'}}{\mathbf{WRW'}}.$$

Since the reliability of the composite will remain the same if all the weights are multiplied or divided by any arbitrary factor, another condition is needed to determine the weights. We may say that the weights shall be chosen to make the variance of the composite unity, that is,

$$(75) \qquad\qquad\qquad \mathbf{WRW'} = 1.$$

In order to select weights that maximize equation 74 subject to the condition given in equation 75, we define a new function, using the Lagrange multiplier (λ) as follows:

$$(76) \qquad\qquad R_{X_W X_W} = \mathbf{WCW'} - \lambda(\mathbf{WRW'} - 1).$$

Differentiating equation 76 with respect to each of the W's in turn, setting each derivative equal to zero, and dividing by 2 gives the set of equations

$$(77) \qquad\qquad\qquad \mathbf{WC} - \lambda\mathbf{WR} = 0.$$

Postmultiplying both matrices by $\mathbf{W'}$ and solving for λ gives

$$(78) \qquad\qquad \lambda = \frac{\mathbf{WCW'}}{\mathbf{WRW'}} = R_{X_W X_W}.$$

Since λ is a scalar, it may occupy any position in a product. Thus the solution of equation 77 for $\mathbf{W}$ gives

$$(79) \qquad\qquad\qquad \mathbf{W(C} - \lambda\mathbf{R)} = 0.$$

Equations 79 have a solution other than $\mathbf{W} = 0$ only if the determinant of the coefficients of $\mathbf{W}$ equals zero; thus

$$(80) \qquad\qquad\qquad |\mathbf{C} - \lambda\mathbf{R}| = 0.$$

Equation 80 is a Kth degree equation in λ. Since, from equation 78, $\lambda = R_{X_W X_W}$, and we are seeking the maximum reliability, we choose λ as the largest root of equation 80, substitute this value in equation 79, and solve for the relative weights. Using the condition given by equation 75 completes the solution for the weights that will maximize the reliability of the weighted composite.

A simplified formula that gives a principal axis solution has been given by Green (1950a).

13. The most predictable criterion

By methods analogous to those used in equations 74 to 80, two *different* batteries may be weighted in such a fashion that the correlation between the two composites will be maximized. This is the problem of the "most predictable criterion" solved by Hotelling (1935, 1936).

Let us define the following matrices:

R is the matrix of intercorrelations of tests in the first battery.
S is the matrix of intercorrelations of tests in the second battery.
C is the matrix of correlations of the tests of the first battery with those of the second.
V is the row vector of weights (V) to be used for the first battery.
W is the row vector of weights (W) to be used for the second battery.

Writing equation 7 for the correlation of two weighted sums in matrix notation, we have

$$(81) \qquad R_{X_V X_W} = \frac{\mathbf{VCW'}}{\sqrt{\mathbf{VRV'}} \sqrt{\mathbf{WSW'}}}.$$

In order to avoid multiple solutions, some other restriction on the weights is necessary, such as adjusting the weights to make the variance of each composite unity. This corresponds to the restriction that

$$(82) \qquad \mathbf{VRV'} = \mathbf{WSW'} = 1.$$

Thus we may define a new function using two Lagrange multipliers, λ and γ, as

$$(83) \qquad \mathbf{R} = \mathbf{VCW'} - \frac{\lambda}{2}(\mathbf{VRV'} - 1) - \frac{\gamma}{2}(\mathbf{WSW'} - 1).$$

Differentiating with respect to the V's and the W's and setting the derivatives equal to zero, we have

$$(84) \qquad \mathbf{CW'} - \lambda\mathbf{RV'} = 0$$

and

$$(85) \qquad \mathbf{VC} - \gamma\mathbf{WS} = 0.$$

Premultiplying the first equation by V and solving for λ, and post-multiplying the second equation by W' and solving for γ, we find that

$$(86) \qquad \gamma = \lambda = \frac{VCW'}{VRV'} = \frac{VCW'}{WSW'} = R_{X_V X_W}.$$

Postmultiplying both terms of equation 85 by S^{-1} and solving for W, we obtain

$$(87) \qquad W = \frac{1}{\gamma} VCS^{-1}.$$

Substituting equation 87 in the transpose of equation 84 factoring out V, and writing λ^2 for the product $\gamma\lambda$, we have

$$(88) \qquad V(CS^{-1}C' - \lambda^2 R) = 0.$$

By a corresponding procedure we find the solution for W as

$$(89) \qquad W(C'R^{-1}C - \lambda^2 S) = 0.$$

Equations 88 and 89 have a solution for the weights other than zero only if the determinant of the coefficients of V and of W equals zero. We may write

$$(90) \qquad \begin{aligned} |\, CS^{-1}C' - \lambda^2 R \,| = 0 \\[6pt] |\, C'R^{-1}C - \lambda^2 S \,| = 0. \end{aligned}$$

Equations 90 are polynomials in λ^2. Since equation 86 shows $\lambda^2 = R^2_{X_V X_W}$ and we are seeking the maximum correlation between the weighted composites, we choose the largest root of equation 90, and use this value in equations 88 and 89 and the conditions given by equation 82. This procedure completes the solution for the weights that will maximize the correlation between the two weighted composites.

Setting $C = C'$, $R = S$, and $W = V$ in equations 88 and 89 gives the solution for maximizing battery reliability given by Thomson (1940). Such a solution of the problem of maximizing battery reliability is equivalent to the much simpler solution of equation 79. The following procedure for demonstrating this equivalence was suggested by Dr. L. R. Tucker of the Educational Testing Service.

Postmultiplying both terms of equation 77 by $R^{-1}C$ gives

$$WCR^{-1}C = \lambda WC.$$

Multiplying both sides of equation 77 by λ gives

$$\lambda WC = \lambda^2 WR.$$

Thus we have the solution derived from simplifying equations 88 and 89,

$$\mathbf{W(CR^{-1}C - \lambda^2 R)} = 0,$$

where λ^2 equals $R^2{}_{X_W X_W}$. Since the two solutions are equivalent, the simpler one indicated in equation 79 is to be preferred.

The weights given by equations 88 and 89 constitute a mathematically very elegant method of weighting to secure a maximum correlation. However, it should be noted that, unless used with discretion, the procedure of determining the most predictable criterion has certain dangers. For example, if one of the criterion measures and one of the predictor measures happen to be tests of the same factor, both batteries are likely to be weighted to correspond with that factor. That is, if one test of spatial visualization is used in the prediction battery, and another test of spatial visualization in the criterion, while verbal and quantitative factors are represented in only one of the batteries, the most predictable criterion procedure is likely to result in warping the criterion to represent primarily spatial visualization. The blind acceptance of such a result would mean that there would be no effort to represent the other factors, such as, for example, verbal and quantitative in the predicting battery. In an extreme case such a procedure could mean that all factors in the criterion that were *initially* omitted from the prediction battery would *always* be omitted since they would receive very little weight in the criterion.

The remedy here, as in all other uses of mathematical procedures, is to inspect the results to see if they have any peculiar characteristics. Any set of tests that have low weight for the criterion should be inspected to see if they would be regarded by experts in the field as being important and deserving of an important place in determining the total criterion. The prediction battery should be inspected to see if an attempt has been made to include the type of ability required by the criterion variables that received low weight in determining the composite. In general we should alter the variables entering into the two batteries if the results do not seem to be appropriate.

Another way of stating the caution given in the foregoing paragraphs is to say that a mathematical method should be adopted only to choose between alternatives that are judgmentally very similar. For example, if all the criterion variables are indifferent so that the expert would accept any set of weights positive or negative, the most predictable criterion results need not be questioned. However, if the expert judgment is that any set of *positive* weights are acceptable, it would seem proper to use the most predictable criterion only if all weights were positive. The expert judgment might be even more restrictive. For example, if the criterion measures were grades and tests in college, and if these measures appeared to involve three types of abilities—verbal, quantitative, and spatial—the faculty might judge that any composite was acceptable as long as the verbal and quantitative factors had weights distinctly higher than those of the spatial factor. Given this judgment, we could use the most predictable criterion if the weights fell in the area indicated. Otherwise the problem for the technician would be to alter the criterion or predictor variables in some reasonable and acceptable fashion so that the weights would have reasonably appropriate relative values. In general, we may say that mathematical procedures are appropriately used when they serve to *guide* thought. If an attempt is made to utilize such routines as a *substitute* for thought, we may unwittingly arrive at and accept absurd conclusions.

14. Differential tests

Sometimes when a battery of tests is given, the problem is to obtain a single score from the battery. This implies that the battery is a one-factor battery or is to be treated as a one-factor battery. Sometimes it is desired to obtain several different scores from the battery. This implies that the battery represents several different factors, and a score is to be obtained for each of the factors. In this latter case the best procedure is to determine the factors present in the battery, and then to use the scores that best predict the factor scores of each individual.

It may happen when this procedure is followed that the factor scores finally obtained still intercorrelate rather high so that, instead of having a set of differential scores, we have scores that in large part give different *patterns* of ability only through incidental errors of measurement. Whenever a set of supposedly differential scores are set up by factor analysis or other methods, it is desirable to make a check on the scores finally proposed to determine the extent to which such scores will give valid differentiation of different scores for the same individual.

When the accomplishment quotient (A.Q.) was introduced, Kelley pointed out that the problem involved was to obtain reliable measures of each variable. Clearly these measures would be correlated, so that the accomplishment quotient might reflect only errors of measurement.

Kelley (1923a) proposed a method for testing the extent to which two tests are giving differential scores to a set of persons. This method makes use of both test reliability and intercorrelation to determine the percentage of scores that will show a reasonable difference and the percentage that will show such a difference solely through errors of measurement. The first percentage should be considerably larger than the second if the scores are to be used for their differential value.

If we use x and y to designate deviation scores in the two tests under consideration and the subscript t to designate the true scores in these variables, the difference between the observed score difference and the true score difference constitutes the error with which a difference in scores is measured.

$$(91) \qquad e_d = (x - y) - (x_t - y_t).$$

By rearranging terms, the error of the difference may be written in terms of the error in x and in y, as follows:

$$(92) \qquad e_d = (x - x_t) - (y - y_t) = e_x - e_y.$$

Since the errors in x are independent of the errors in y, the sum of squares may be written

$$(93) \qquad \Sigma e_d^2 = \Sigma e_x^2 + \Sigma e_y^2.$$

Expressing the error in x and y in terms of the test reliability and standard deviation, we have

$$(94) \qquad s_{e_d}^2 = \Sigma e_d^2/N = s_x^2(1 - r_{xx}) + s_y^2(1 - r_{yy}).$$

The magnitude of this term which is the variability of difference due to error may be compared with the total variability of differences.

$$(95) \qquad s^2_{x-y} = \frac{\Sigma(x - y)^2}{N} = \frac{\Sigma x^2}{N} + \frac{\Sigma y^2}{N} - \frac{2\Sigma xy}{N}.$$

From the equations for variance and correlation, we have

$$(96) \qquad s^2_{x-y} = s_x^2 + s_y^2 - 2r_{xy}s_xs_y.$$

If the tests x and y are expressed in standard score, the standard deviations and variances become unity, and equations 94 and 96 become, respectively,

$$(97) \qquad s_{e_d}^2 = 2 - r_{xx} - r_{yy} = 2(1 - \bar{r})$$

and

$$(98) \qquad s^2_{x-y} = 2(1 - r_{xy}),$$

where $\bar{r}$ is the average reliability of the two tests.

As the average reliability becomes markedly larger than the intercorrelation of the tests, the dispersion of obtained differences becomes greater than that obtained by chance.

Kelley (1923a) proposed using normal curve proportions derived from equations 97 and 98 to find the percentage of observed differences in excess of that which could be expected to occur by chance because of the error of measurement.

To put this material in more familiar form, equation 21, Chapter 17, shows us the reliability expressed as a function of the error variance and total variance. Equations 97 and 98 in this chapter and 21 of Chapter 17 give

$$(99) \qquad r_{x-y} = 1 - \frac{2(1 - \bar{r})}{2(1 - r_{xy})}.$$

Simplifying, we have

$$(100) \qquad r_{x-y} = \frac{\bar{r} - r_{xy}}{1 - r_{xy}},$$

where r_{x-y} is the reliability of the difference between x and y,

r_{xy} is the correlation between tests x and y, and

$\bar{r}$ is one-half the sum of the reliabilities of tests x and y.

A similar equation is given by Conrad (1944b), page 7.

> *For any pair of tests, equation 100 gives the reliability of the difference as a function of the intercorrelation of the two tests (r_{xy}) and the average of the two reliability coefficients ($\bar{r}$).*

Figure 3 is a linear graph showing the nature of this relationship. To use this computing diagram, mark the diagonal line corresponding to the intercorrelation of the two tests (r_{xy}). Locate the average reliability at the bottom of the chart, then move up to the diagonal line and over to the scale at the right showing the reliability of the difference. In the illustrative problem (shown by the heavy dashed line in Figure 3), if the average reliability is .6 and the intercorrelation is .5, the reliability of the difference is only .2. It should be noted that, if the average reliability of the two tests is about the same as their intercorrelation, the reliability of the difference is approximately zero. In order for the reliability of the difference to be .8, when r_{xy} is .5, the average reliability of the tests must be .9.

In setting up a profile type of battery in which differences in a given person's score on different tests is important, we must be certain that the reliability of the difference in scores is fairly high before giving this difference much weight in the interpretation. Kelley (1923a) suggested that this reliability figure be interpreted in terms of the percentage of observed difference scores in excess of that which could be expected to occur by chance because of the errors of measurement. If this percentage were very small, the difference score would not be very useful. The interpretation in terms of reliability is more conventional; also the error of measurement can be obtained so that differences less than one or

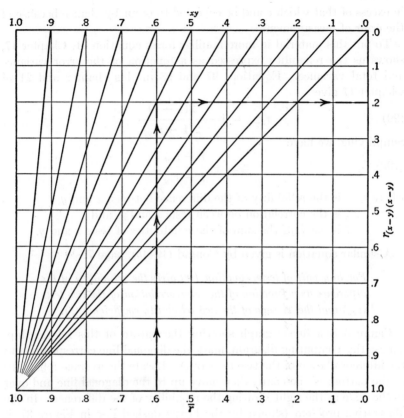

FIGURE 3. Showing the relationship between the average reliability of two tests, their intercorrelation, and the reliability of the difference between the two tests.

Equation (100)
$$r_{x-y} = \frac{\bar{r} - r_{xy}}{1 - r_{xy}} \text{ or}$$

$$1 - r_{x-y} = \frac{1 - \bar{r}}{1 - r_{xy}}$$

two errors of measurement will not be interpreted as indicating a real difference in ability in the two tests.

Many profile tests furnish no information on the reliability of the *differences* in scores. Such information should be required as a routine part of the validation and standardization of any battery to be used as a profile.

The Differential Aptitude Battery of the Psychological Corporation has been set up in this manner; see Bennett (1947) or Bennett and Doppelt (1948).

Brogden (1946a) has presented a method for determining cutting scores in connection with the problem of differential prediction. A more complete analysis of the problems of differential prediction is given by Tucker (1948), Thorndike (1949), and Mollenkopf (1950).

15. Summary

Whenever a single total score is to be derived from a number of separate scores, the weighting problem cannot be avoided. However, if *many* different scores with reasonably *high* intercorrelations are being combined, the resulting composite will be fairly similar for a large variety of weights. If, however, relatively *few* items are to be combined, there is a *low* correlation among these items, the standard deviation of the distribution of weights being considered is fairly *large*, and the correlation between two sets of weights is *low*, the two resulting composites will be different. The correlation between two composites obtained by using *different* weights on the *same* set of scores is given by

Equation (15)

$$R_{X_V X_W} = \frac{K(1 - \bar{r})(C_{VW} + \overline{V}\,\overline{W}) + (K^2 - K)C_{(VW)r} + K^2 \overline{V}\,\overline{W}\bar{r}}{\sqrt{\begin{matrix} K(1 - \bar{r})(\tilde{V}^2 + \overline{V}^2) \\ + (K^2 - K)C_{(VV)r} \\ + K^2 \overline{V}^2 \bar{r} \end{matrix}} \sqrt{\begin{matrix} K(1 - \bar{r})(\tilde{W}^2 + \overline{W}^2) \\ + (K^2 - K)C_{(WW)r} \\ + K^2 \overline{W}^2 \bar{r} \end{matrix}}},$$

where

K is the number of scores to be combined,

$\overline{W}$ and $\overline{V}$ are the averages of the W and V weights,

$\tilde{W}$ and $\tilde{V}$ are the standard deviations of the two sets of weights,

$\bar{r}$ is the average intercorrelation of the scores to be combined,

C_{VW} is the covariance between the two sets of weights used,

$C_{(VW)r}$, $C_{(VV)r}$, and $C_{(WW)r}$, represent the covariance of a product of weights with the corresponding correlation r_{gh}, and

$R_{X_V X_W}$ is the correlation between the composite obtained using the V-weights and that obtained using the W-weights.

Equation 15 shows us that, if $\bar{r}$, $\overline{V}$, and $\overline{W}$ are positive, the correlation $R_{X_V X_W}$ approaches unity: (*a*) as the correlation between the two sets of weights is increased or (*b*) as the standard deviation of the weights

$(\tilde{V}, \tilde{W})$ is decreased in proportion to the mean weights $(\overline{V}$ and $\overline{W})$. Also, if the covariance terms of the form $C_{(VW)_r}$ may be ignored, $R_{X_V X_W}$ approaches unity: (c) as K approaches infinity or (d) as $\bar{r}$ approaches unity.

Some appraisal of the magnitude of $R_{X_V X_W}$ for positive weights may be obtained from

$$(47) \qquad \overline{R}_{X_V X_W} = 1 - \frac{1}{2K\bar{r}}\left[\left(\frac{\tilde{V}}{\overline{V}}\right)^2 + \left(\frac{\tilde{W}}{\overline{W}}\right)^2\right],$$

where $\overline{R}$ is an approximation to the mean value of the correlation between two weighted composites, and the other terms have the definitions indicated for equation 15.

Equations 15 and 47 show us that, if a *few* scores with *low* intercorrelations are involved, and if also we are considering alternative sets of weights with *large* variance and *low* intercorrelation, weighting will make an appreciable difference, and the selection of a "best" set of weights is important. For such a case we may say:

1. If a criterion is available, the multiple correlation weights indicated by equations 52 and 53 for the general case and by equation 56 for the three-variable case will give the best results, in the sense that the correlation between the weighted composite and the criterion will be a maximum (see equation 55 for the general case and 58 for the three-variable case). For practical purposes, simple integral approximations to the exact multiple weights will usually give a satisfactory composite score.

2. If many variables are involved, and particularly if a selection is to be made among these variables, some approximation to multiple correlation as indicated in section 3 is to be preferred to the exact method.

3. Where no criterion is available, various weighting methods have been adopted:

(a) Weighting in terms of the *average* score or the *perfect* score, which is usually equal to the *number of items* in an objective test, is always to be avoided. There is no justification for the belief that these factors have or should have any effect on the weight of an item in a composite.

(b) Weighting inversely as the standard deviation $(1/s_x)$ or inversely as the error variance, that is, by the factor $r/(1 - r)$ has been suggested in the literature on testing. Both these methods depend on a rationale involving assumptions that are probably never satisfied in practice. Also there are many situations in which either method will give results clearly inappropriate.

(c) Weighting to equalize "marginal" contributions to total variance has been suggested (see section 11). This method also has peculiar properties.

(d) Weighting inversely as the error of measurement was discussed in section 6. No rationale is at present available for this method, and it seems not to have been used or suggested before. From a common-sense point of view, this method has a valuable set of properties; and, of the different rule-of-thumb methods presented in this chapter, it is the one that would seem to be most generally acceptable.

4. Where no criterion is available, it is probably best not to use any rule-of-thumb method. Two alternatives are suggested here.

(a) We may weight the items so as to maximize the reliability of the composite by using the matrix formula

$$(79) \qquad\qquad \mathbf{W}(\mathbf{C} - \lambda\mathbf{R}) = 0,$$

where $\mathbf{R}$ is the matrix of intercorrelations among the variables (with unity in the diagonals),

$\mathbf{C}$ is the same matrix with the substitution of reliabilities for unity in the diagonals,

$\mathbf{W}$ is the vector of weights, and

λ is chosen as the largest root of

$$(80) \qquad\qquad |\, \mathbf{C} - \lambda\mathbf{R} \,| = 0.$$

(b) We may depend on expert judgment for the determination of weights. For a system of correlated variables there is no satisfactory method of assessing the *proportional* contribution of each component to the total. The best guide is the correlation of each part with the composite. The correlation of any part (g) with the composite (C) is given by

$$(71) \qquad\qquad r_{gC} = \frac{W_g s_g + \displaystyle\sum_{h=1}^{K} W_h r_{gh} s_h}{s_C} \qquad (g \neq h),$$

where r_{gC} is the correlation between part g and the weighted composite (C),

W_g (or W_h) is the weight assigned to any part (g or h),

s_g (or s_h) is the standard deviation of that part,

r_{gh} is the correlation between two parts, and

s_C is the standard deviation of the composite.

In equation 71 the correlation between part g and the composite is shown to depend entirely upon (a) the weight of that part (W_g), (b) the standard deviation of that part (s_g), and (c) the sum of products $W_h r_{gh} s_h$ for all other parts entering into the composite.

In judging what weights are to be assigned to the different parts, we must understand clearly that these are the only factors determining the "weight" of the part in the composite, and that the correlation between the part and the composite is the best criterion to use in judging the effective weights of each part in the composite. If the judges will assign certain relative values to the correlations r_{gC}, the solution of equation 72 for W_h will give the relative weights for the different parts.

5. If multiple criterion and predictor measures are available, we may select weights so that the correlation between the two composites will be maximized. These weights are given by the matrix equations,

$$(88) \qquad \mathbf{V}(\mathbf{CS^{-1}C'} - \lambda^2\mathbf{R}) = 0$$

and

$$(89) \qquad \mathbf{W}(\mathbf{C'R^{-1}C} - \lambda^2\mathbf{S}) = 0,$$

where **R** and **S** are the matrix of intercorrelations among the variables of each set,

   C is the matrix of correlations of variables in one set with those in the other set,

   V is the set of weights to be applied to the variables of the R-matrix,

   W is the set of weights to be applied to the variables of the S-matrix, and

   λ^2 is chosen as the largest root of

$$(90) \qquad \begin{aligned} |\,\mathbf{CS^{-1}C'} - \lambda^2\mathbf{R}\,| &= 0 \\ |\,\mathbf{C'R^{-1}C} - \lambda^2\mathbf{S}\,| &= 0. \end{aligned}$$

The weights given by this system are so flexible that we may easily be led to a composite criterion that is undesirable from a judgmental point of view. When using "the most predictable criterion" it is necessary to inspect the weights carefully from the point of view of the expert judge in order to avoid accepting an unreasonable criterion.

6. It has been suggested that the methods of factor analysis may aid in solving the weighting problem. Where a *single score* is to be determined, it has been suggested:

(a) That the first principal axis be used as the best representative of the set of scores. This method has a number of very interesting properties. It maximizes the interindividual differences, minimizes the differences between the various scores obtained by a given person, and minimizes the "generalized variance" for all individuals receiving the same score. Despite such a set of properties, however, it has two serious disadvantages. It is laborious to compute, since it necessitates a successive approximations procedure, and it is sensitive to the units in which the various tests are measured.

(b) That the first centroid axis be used. It may be a good possibility if some one score is desired to represent a set of scores.

(c) That, if the set of scores is actually a one-factor system, the one common factor would seem to be a very good choice for the composite score. Spearman suggested this solution, and gave the equations for it. However, a set of tests must be very carefully selected if it is to contain only one factor. This rule, therefore, could be applied in only a very few cases.

If several scores are to be derived from a set of tests, the best procedure would be a factor analysis procedure. The battery should be factored, and a score assigned for each principal factor that is determined. It should also be noted that, whenever several different scores are assigned to each person in a group, and differential use is made of these scores, it is necessary to assess the reliability of the score differences. This reliability is given by

$$(100) \qquad\qquad r_{x-y} = \frac{\bar{r} - r_{xy}}{1 - r_{xy}},$$

where r_{x-y} is the reliability of the difference score,
$\quad\quad r_{xy}$ is the correlation between the two tests, and
$\quad\quad \bar{r}$ is half the sum of the two reliabilities.

A computing diagram for this equation is given in Figure 3. Equation 100 shows that, unless the average reliability of two tests is considerably higher than the correlation between them, the differences will be very unreliable. This means that in making differential predictions, or in interpreting profiles, judgments will usually be made on the basis of accidental score differences. Unless r_{x-y} is .80 or larger, valid judgments of individuals cannot be made on the basis of score differences between tests x and y. All differential prediction batteries or batteries that are to be used as profiles should give information on the reliability of the difference score for each pair of tests in the battery.

Problems

1. What is the expected value of the correlation between any two composites from a battery of forty tests, with an average intercorrelation of .30? Assume that only positive weights are used and that the average weight is about equal to the standard deviation of the weights.

2. On the foregoing assumption regarding weights, what is the expected value of the correlation between any two composites from a battery of five tests with an average intercorrelation of .20?

DATA FOR PROBLEMS 3 TO 7

Entering freshmen at the University of Chicago are given an A. C. E. Psychological Examination (a), a physical sciences aptitude test (s), an English placement test (e). A year later they are given the physical science comprehensive (p) and the humanities comprehensive (h).

The following zero-order correlations are obtained:

$$r_{as} = .50, \quad r_{ae} = .70, \quad r_{es} = .40,$$

$$r_{ap} = .50, \quad r_{sp} = .70, \quad r_{ep} = .40,$$

$$r_{ah} = .60, \quad r_{sh} = .20, \quad r_{eh} = .70, \quad r_{ph} = .60.$$

The following means and standard deviations are found:

	a	s	e	p	h
Mean	120	110	150	220	460
Standard deviation	30	20	25	30	40

3. Write the equation for making the best prediction of the humanities comprehensive score from the three placement tests.

4. What will be the correlation between the predicted humanities scores and the actual scores, using the prediction equation given in 3?

5. Which two placement tests will give the best prediction of scores in the physical-science comprehensive?

6. Write the equation for making the best prediction of the physical-science comprehensive score from the two tests mentioned in 5.

7. What is the correlation between the actual physical-science scores and the scores predicted by using the equation given in 6?

DATA FOR PROBLEMS 8 TO 17

	Number of Items	Mean	Std. Dev.	Formula for Transformed Scores	Reliability	Intercorrelations
	(K)	$(\overline{X})$	$(\tilde{X})$	(Y)	r_{xx}	
Test a	10	6.1	1.3	$Y = 10X$	.62	$r_{ab} = .36$
Test b	50	35.6	4.2	$Y = X$	.83	$r_{ac} = .42$
Test c	200	153.7	15.8	$Y = X/2$	.95	$r_{bc} = .65$

$$z = \frac{X - \overline{X}}{\tilde{X}}$$

X, Y, and z scores for the following problems are defined in the foregoing table.

8. For the data given in the table, discuss the desirable and undesirable characteristics of a composite score formed by weighting X_a, X_b, and X_c according to the reliability of each test as indicated in equation 66. Would the composite be the same or different if the Y-scores or the z-scores were weighted as indicated in equations 65 or 66?

9. Give the desirable and undesirable characteristics of a composite formed by weighting the X-scores inversely as the standard deviation of the test. Would the composite be the same, or different, if the Y-scores or the z-scores were weighted according to the same principle?

10. Give the desirable and undesirable characteristics of a composite formed by weighting the X-scores, Y-scores, and z-scores inversely as the error of measurement.

11. Give the desirable and undesirable characteristics of a composite formed by weighting the X-scores, Y-scores, and z-scores inversely as the error variance.

12. Give the desirable and undesirable characteristics of a composite formed by weighting the X-scores, Y-scores, and z-scores directly as K, the number of items in the test.

13. Give the desirable and undesirable characteristics of a composite formed by weighting the X-scores, Y-scores, and z-scores inversely as K.

14. Give the desirable and undesirable characteristics of a composite formed by weighting the X-scores, Y-scores, and z-scores inversely as the test mean.

15. Judging in terms of the correlation of the part with the composite (equations 71 or 72), how would a, b, and c be weighted by (a) adding X-scores; (b) adding Y-scores; (c) adding z-scores; (d) taking the composite, $T = 10X_a + 2X_b + X_c$.

16. What weighting factors should be assigned to the X-scores in order to obtain a composite t, such that r_{at}, r_{bt}, and r_{ct} are approximately in proportion to 2, 3, and 4, respectively (see equation 72).

17. What is the reliability (a) of the difference score $X_a - X_b$; (b) of the difference score $X_a - X_c$; (c) of the difference score $X_b - X_c$?

18. Prove that gross score weights that are inversely proportional to the error variance for gross scores are identical with the weights of equations 65 and 66.

19. (a) Find the standard score weights that are inversely proportional to the error variance of a standard score. Compare this weight with that of equation 65.

(b) Determine the gross score weights that will give results identical with these standard score weights, and compare these gross score weights with those of equation 66.

21

Item Analysis

1. Introduction

Basically, item analysis is concerned with the problem of selecting items for a test so that the resulting test will have certain specified characteristics. For example, we may wish to construct a test that is easy or one that is difficult. In either case it is desirable to develop a test that will correlate as high as possible with certain specified criteria and will have a satisfactory reliability. The index of skewness should be positive, negative, or zero for a specified population. If a battery of several tests is being constructed, it may be desirable to have the intercorrelations as low as possible. It is also of considerable interest to be able to construct a test so that the error of measurement is a minimum for a specified ability range or so that the error of measurement is constant over a wide ability range, as is assumed in the development of formulas for variation in reliability with variation in heterogeneity of the population (see Chapters 10, 11, and 12). In each of these situations it would be convenient to be able to write the prescription for item selection so that we should be able to subject a set of K items to an appropriate type of analysis, and then to select the subset of k items that would come nearest to satisfying the desired characteristics.

As yet the rationale of item analysis has been developed for only a few of the problems indicated. Numerous arbitrary indices have been devised and used. Twenty-three methods are listed and described by Long and Sandiford (1935). Nineteen methods are summarized by Guilford (1936b) in *Psychometric Methods*, pages 426–456. With one or two exceptions, these lists are essentially the same. For earlier surveys of item analysis methods, see Cook (1932) or Lentz, Hirshstein, and Finch (1932). The striking characteristic of nearly all the methods described is that no theory is presented showing the relationship between the validity or reliability of the total test and the method of item analysis suggested. The exceptions, which show a definite relationship between the item selection procedure and some important parameter of the test, are Richardson (1936a); the method of successive residuals, Horst (1934b); the use of a maximizing function, Horst (1936b); the L-method and its various modifications (see Toops, 1941, Adkins and Toops, 1937, and Richardson and Adkins, 1938).

In developing and investigating procedures of item analysis, it would seem appropriate, first, to establish the relationship between certain item parameters and the parameters of the total test; next, to consider the problem of obtaining the item parameters in such a way that they will, if possible, not change with changes in the ability level of the validating group; and, last, to consider the most efficient methods, from both a mathematical and a computational viewpoint, of estimating these parameters for the items.

The method of item selection used and the theory on which it is based must be directly related to the method of test scoring. For the usual aptitude or achievement test, the responses to each item may be classified as either correct or incorrect, and the item analysis procedures utilize this information. For items relating to personality, interests, attitudes, or biographical facts, the responses cannot be classified as either correct or incorrect. A set of such items demands a more complex type of item analysis procedure that not only gives information on item selection but also furnishes a scoring key. If an achievement or aptitude test is scored in terms of "level reached," it would seem appropriate to use the item analysis methods of absolute scaling (see Thurstone, 1925 and 1927b) or some other analogous scaling method. Such procedures do not seem appropriate for the usual test that is scored by counting the number of correct responses. In this chapter we shall consider only those item analysis procedures suitable for the case in which the item responses may be classified as correct or incorrect and in which the score is the number of correct responses.

Another consideration that will affect item analysis methods is the extent to which the group available for item analysis purposes is similar to or different from the prospective test group. For example, a group of students in a college with high admission standards might be the only group available for experimental purposes for a test that is to be generally used for college admission. In this case item information from a group of high ability is to be used in constructing a test to be used for a group with a lower average ability and a larger variance in ability. Other variants of this problem may arise. For example, considerable item analysis data may be available on a large population of applicants for college admission, and we may wish to use this information in selecting items suitable for a scholarship examination that is to be taken only by superior students. The item selection problem is clearly much simpler when the item analysis group and the prospective test group are similar in mean and variance on the particular ability to be tested.

It is important to note that, while the item analysis rationale and the quantitative item selection procedures are the same for aptitude and achievement tests, there is one important difference. In the construction of aptitude tests the item statistics may be allowed to control the rejection and selection of items more fully than in the construction of achievement tests. The judgment of the subject matter expert must always play an important part in the selection and rejection of items for an achievement test. If the item analysis results show that a given item should be used, and the expert finds that the item is incorrect, that item must be revised. If the item analysis results show that an item should be deleted, and the subject matter expert feels that essential knowledge is being tested in the item, then attempts must be made to discover the flaw in item construction and revise the item so that it will satisfy both the item analysis criteria and the judgment of the subject matter specialist. It may even be that the fault lies in the teaching methods used so that the item that is unsatisfactory from the viewpoint of item analysis statistics will show satisfactory item analysis results for a new class that has been taught differently. In an achievement test the goal should be to obtain items that are satisfactory from the viewpoint of both the item analysis results and the subject matter specialist. In order to do this, it may be necessary to revise the item, to revise the criterion against which the item is validated, to revise the methods of teaching, or the content of the course.

Relatively little of a precise nature is now known regarding the effect of item selection on test skewness, kurtosis, or on the constancy of the error of measurement throughout the test score range. It is possible, however, to select items in such a way as to influence the test mean, variance, reliability, and validity. We shall now consider item selection in relation to these four test parameters for tests that are scored by counting the number of correct responses and are composed of items the responses to which are either correct or incorrect. It will also be assumed that the item analysis group and the prospective test group have similar means and variances of the ability to be tested.

2. Item parameters related to the test mean

Let A_{ig} designate the score of the ith person on the gth item. As shown in Table 1, A_{ig} is unity if the ith person answered the gth item correctly, and zero if the answer was incorrect.
N be the number of persons taking the test, $(i = 1 \cdots N)$, and
K be the number of items in the test, $(g = 1 \cdots K)$.

Since each person's score is the number of items correctly answered, we may write

$$(1) \qquad X_i = \sum_{g=1}^{K} A_{ig}.$$

That is, each person's score is the sum of the entries in a *row*, as shown in Table 1.

TABLE 1

Items

$(g, h, = 1 \cdots K)$

		1	2	3	4	$\cdots$	K	
	1	1	1	0	0	$\cdots$	0	X_1
	2	1	0	1	1	$\cdots$	1	X_2
	3	0	1	1	1	$\cdots$	0	X_3
	4	0	0	0	1	$\cdots$	1	X_4
Individuals	$\cdot$	$\cdot$	$\cdot$	$\cdot$	$\cdot$		$\cdot$	$\cdot$
$(i, j, = 1 \cdots N)$	$\cdot$	$\cdot$	$\cdot$	$\cdot$	$\cdot$		$\cdot$	$\cdot$
	$\cdot$	$\cdot$	$\cdot$	$\cdot$	$\cdot$		$\cdot$	$\cdot$
	N	0	1	0	0	$\cdots$	0	X_N
	Sums	d_1	d_2	d_3	d_4	$\cdots$	d_K	$\Sigma d = \Sigma X$
	Sums $\div N$	p_1	p_2	p_3	p_4	$\cdots$	p_K	$\dfrac{\Sigma d}{N} = \dfrac{\Sigma X}{N} = M_X$

The test mean is given by

$$(2) \qquad M_X = \frac{\sum\limits_{i=1}^{N} X_i}{N}.$$

Substituting equation 1 in equation 2 and noting that the grand total given by adding the row sums is the same as that given by adding the column sums, we may write

$$(3) \qquad M_X = \frac{\sum\limits_{i=1}^{N} \sum\limits_{g=1}^{K} A_{ig}}{N} = \frac{\sum\limits_{g=1}^{K} \sum\limits_{i=1}^{N} A_{ig}}{N}.$$

For any given item g the item difficulty is defined as the proportion of correct responses. Designating the difficulty of item g by p_g, we have

$$(4) \qquad p_g = \frac{\sum\limits_{i=1}^{N} A_{ig}}{N}.$$

Substituting equation 4 in equation 3, we write

(5) $$\bar{X} \quad \text{or} \quad M_X = \sum_{g=1}^{K} p_g = K\bar{p},$$

where M_X is the test mean, also designated $\bar{X}$,

   p_g is the proportion of correct responses for the gth item $(g = 1 \cdots K)$,

   K is the number of items in the test, and

   $\bar{p}$ is $(1/N) \sum_{g=1}^{K} p_g$, the average item difficulty.

If test score is taken as the number of correct answers, the test mean is equal either to the number of items multiplied by the average item difficulty or to the sum of the item difficulties, when item difficulty is defined as the proportion of correct responses.

It should be noted that equation 5 holds only if "correct response" and "incorrect response" are defined in the same way for *both test scoring* and *item analysis* purposes. For example, if the score is "number right," items answered incorrectly, items skipped, and items omitted will each count zero in determining total score. They must then be *similarly counted when obtaining p_g*. Table 1 shows that we have assumed a matrix of "1's" and "0's." These terms are added by rows to determine the score of each person, and the *same terms* are added by columns to determine item difficulty. If the test is a power test, item difficulty defined as the proportion of correct responses will represent a characteristic of the item in relation to the ability of the group. If the test is a speed test, p_g is entirely or primarily a characteristic of the position of the item in the test and the timing of the total test. For a speed test, "proportion of correct responses" does not represent a characteristic of the item; hence this type of analysis is inappropriate insofar as a test is speeded.

3. Item difficulty parameters that compensate for changes in group ability

Several measures of item difficulty have been suggested that allow for the possibility that the item analysis group may be different from the prospective test group.

Thurstone's difficulty calibration method (Thurstone, 1947a), which he has used in the construction of the American Council on Education Psychological Examination, is the simplest and most direct method of compensating for possible changes in the ability level of the group whenever a new set of items is given to a new item analysis group. Consider the situation in which test Y given to group B is to be equated to test X, which has previously been given to group A. About twenty items from test X, which are well scattered over the total item difficulty range, are included in test Y. For these twenty items the percentage correct is known for both the original test group (A) and for the new item analysis group (B). These two sets of values for the twenty items are plotted on a graph, with, for example, the A-group difficulty values as abscissa and the B-group difficulty values as ordinate. A smooth line is drawn through these points and used for translating the difficulty values of all new items for the B-group into difficulty values for the original A-group. Thus changes in the general ability of the group used each year for testing new items will not affect the item difficulties in any systematic manner. It should be noted that the difficulties of the overlap items must show some sort of consistent trend line for this method to be used. Thurstone (1947a) points out that, if one item shows a markedly greater increase or decrease in difficulty than the other items, that item should be ignored in determining the trend. It is probable that some special conditions are affecting that item, and its behavior is not indicative of the group differences.

A *normal curve transformation* of percentage correct has been suggested by several authors, Ayres (1915), Thurstone (1925), Thorndike (1927), Bliss (1929), Symonds (1929), Horst (1933), and others. A variant of this method used by the College Entrance Examination Board was devised by Brolyer, and is described by Brigham (1932), page 356. Brolyer's index, called delta (Δ), was set up to take care of the problem posed by time limit tests in which only the superior students reach the items at the end of the test. As a result, we do not have direct information about the percentage of the slow students who would have answered the item correctly had they attempted it.

The College Entrance Examination Board procedure is to assign each person a linear derived score (w) on the total test. This score is used as the criterion against which each item is evaluated. For the group attempting an item, we find the mean (m) and the standard deviation (s) of the total test score in terms of the w-scale. The number of persons answering the item correctly is divided by the total number attempting that item to determine the percentage correct (p). This percentage is then converted into delta (Δ), a base line reading on the w-scale, by the equation,

(6) $$\Delta = m_w + s_w z_p,$$

where z_p is a base line normal deviate corresponding to p (if $p > .50$, $z_p < 0$; if $p < .50$, $z_p > 0$),

$\quad m_w$ is the mean w-score of the group attempting the item,

$\quad s_w$ is the standard deviation of w-scores for this group,

$\quad \Delta$ is the desired standard measure of item difficulty, and

$\quad p$ is the number answering the item correctly divided by the number attempting the item.

The most serious objection to this method of indicating item difficulty is that it takes no account of the correlation between the item and the total score. Given a certain set of values for m, s, and p, the value of Δ is the same regardless of whether the correlation between item and total score is .00, .30, or .60. Other writers have presented a method of transforming p to a linear scale that is influenced by the item criterion correlation.

A regression line transformation for p (percentage correct) has been suggested by Thorndike (1927), Bliss (1929), and others. The purpose of this method is to find the ability level at which half the persons will pass the item, and half will fail. It is analogous to the cutting score method described in Chapter 19, section 13. The regression of the normalized item score (designated z) on the criterion score (designated x) is used. This is written

$$(7) \qquad z = r_{xz} \left(\frac{\tilde{z}}{\tilde{x}} \right) x,$$

where r_{xz} is the biserial correlation between item and total test score or some other criterion,

$\quad \tilde{z}$ is the standard deviation of the normalized item score, which is taken as unity, and

$\quad \tilde{x}$ is the standard deviation of the criterion score.

It is desired to find the criterion score x_p, which corresponds to the point at which half the persons would fail and half pass the item. This is the point x_p, which corresponds to the line between those passing and those failing the item. This point on the z-scale will be designated z_p. It is equal to the normal base line equivalent of the percentage passing the item (p). If p is greater than .50, z_p is negative; if p is less than .50, z_p is positive. Substituting z_p and x_p in equation 7 and solving explicitly for x_p gives

$$(8) \qquad x_p = \left[\frac{\tilde{x}}{r_{xz}\tilde{z}} \right] z_p,$$

where x_p is the criterion score level at which half the persons will fail, and half pass the item,

z_p is a normal base line equivalent of p, the percentage correct for the item (if $p > .50$, $z_p < 0$; if $p < .50$, $z_p > 0$). The other terms have the same definition as in equation 7, $\bar{z}$ being taken as unity.

The item criterion curve has also been suggested as giving an indication of the ability level at which half the persons would fail and half pass the item. In this method the group taking the test is divided into five, ten, or twenty subgroups on the basis of some criterion, usually the total test score. These groups are taken as representing various ability levels. Then the percentage correct on a given item for *each of these subgroups* is computed. In general it is found that only a small percentage of the lowest group gets the item correct and that a larger and larger percentage of each succeeding ability group gets the item correct. From this information we can determine by interpolation (or extrapolation, in the case of very easy or very difficult items) the ability level at which half the persons would answer the item correctly and half incorrectly. This level then represents the criterion level at which half fail and half pass the item, and is taken as indicating the item difficulty. If the assumptions for a biserial correlation coefficient are met, this method will give results identical with those obtained by equation 8, since its purpose and method of procedure are essentially identical.

The four types of methods just discussed, Thurstone's method of calibrating item difficulty, the normal curve transformation as represented in equation 6, the transformation based on the regression line as shown in equation 8, or the use of the midpoint of the item curve, may all be regarded as attempts to find an item difficulty parameter that is invariant with respect to changes in the mean or dispersion of the ability of the group. As far as the author is aware, there is no published experimental evidence to show how well any of these methods succeeds in its purpose. The first and last methods are simple and direct, involving no assumptions such as those in equations 6 or 8. However, if the assumptions of biserial correlation are justified, it would seem that the method represented by equation 8 is best since it makes use of all the available data to determine the item difficulty level.

If the total test score is to be determined by counting the number of items answered correctly, it does not seem particularly appropriate to measure item difficulty in terms of criterion level, as is done in equations 6, 8, and the item curve method. Such measures of item difficulty would seem appropriate for a test that is to be scored in terms of "level reached" or for a test that is constructed by the absolute scaling principles (Thurstone, 1925 and 1927*b*). However, if these item difficulty measures in terms of criterion level turn out to be relatively invariant with respect to changes in group ability level, it should be possible to translate them into different "percentage correct" scores corresponding to the particular group to be tested.

4. Estimates of the percentage who know the answer to an item

Other measures of item difficulty have been devised to estimate the percentage of persons in the group that "know" the answer to the item, as distinct from those who guess, and guess correctly.

Guilford (1936a) has suggested that the usual method of correcting for chance be applied to items as well as test scores. This method involves two assumptions.

1. That the persons can be divided into two groups, (a) those who know the answer and (b) those who guess the answer.
2. Those who guess are equally likely to select any one of the alternatives given.

Let f designate the number of different answers given for an item, then $1/f$th of those who "guessed" would guess correctly, and $(f - 1)/f$ would guess incorrectly. Since this latter group includes *all* who answer incorrectly (by assumption 1 above there is no misinformation leading to the incorrect answer), $1/(f - 1)$ of those who answer incorrectly is equal to the number of lucky guessers; hence, subtracting (Number wrong)$/(f - 1)$ from the number right will give the number who got the right answer not by guessing but by knowledge. The percentage who know the answer (designated p') may be written

$$
(9) \qquad p' = \frac{R_i - \dfrac{W_i}{f - 1}}{T},
$$

where R_i is the number of correct answers to the item,

    W_i is the number of incorrect answers to the item,

    f is the number of possible answers given for each item,

    T is the total number who tried the item [T may be considered equal to rights plus wrongs $(R_i + W_i)$ or may also include those who skipped the item] and

    p' is an estimate of the percentage knowing the answer to that item.

It should be noted that one implication of this method is that the same number of persons will select each of the incorrect alternatives, and that some number greater than this will select the correct alternative. Investigation of any multiple choice test will show that rarely, if ever, are all the distractors equally attractive. Horst (1933) has suggested an item difficulty measure for multiple choice items that assumes that the different distractors are unequally attractive.

Horst (1933) makes the two assumptions indicated for equation 9, and in addition he assumes that those who do not know the correct answer fall into various subgroups. The first subgroup is composed of those who know nothing about the alternatives in question; hence the members of this group are distributed equally to all of the f possible answers. A second group is composed of those who know that one of the alternatives is wrong, hence distributes its answers uniformly over the remaining $f - 1$ choices, and so on. The next-to-the-best group knows that all but two of the alternatives are wrong, hence distributes its choices evenly between the correct answer and one of the incorrect choices. The best group is composed of those who know the right answer and those who know that each of the other choices is wrong, hence pick the right answer by elimination. According to this reasoning, the number of persons in this last group is equal to the number choosing the correct alternative minus the number who mark the most popular incorrect alternative.

Let us consider what would happen to a five-alternative item. Let $5a$ designate the number of persons knowing nothing. Since they distribute equally among the five alternatives, a persons will choose each of the five alternatives. Let $4b$ designate the number who know that one of the alternatives is wrong; b of them will choose each of the other four answers. The next group is designated by $3c$, c of whom will choose the correct answer and c of whom will choose each of the two most popular wrong answers. Assume that $2d$ persons know enough to avoid all but one of the distractors, hence divide equally between it and the correct answer. Finally we have e persons who know the right answer, or else know that all the others are wrong; hence all these e will pick the correct answer. Let us use W_1 to designate the number picking the poorest distractor, W_2 for the number picking the next most popular, and so on up to W_{f-1} for the number picking the most popular distractor. Then we may write

$$W_1 = a,$$
$$W_2 = a + b,$$
$$W_3 = a + b + c,$$
$$W_4 = a + b + c + d,$$
$$R = a + b + c + d + e.$$

Thus we have

$$e = R - W_4.$$

In general we see that the number of persons who *know* the correct answer is equal to the number *marking* the correct answer minus the largest number selecting any one of the incorrect answers. If we designate the corresponding estimate of the percentage knowing the correct answer by p'', we have

$$(10) \qquad p'' = \frac{R - W_{f-1}}{T},$$

where R is the number of persons selecting the correct answer,

W_{f-1} is the number selecting the most popular incorrect answer, and

T is the total number of persons responding to that item.

This method has the distinct advantage over equation 9 that it takes account of the fact that different numbers of persons will pick the different distractors in an item. It also furnishes a criterion for the possible presence of actual misinformation. According to the theory, more persons will select the correct alternative than will select any of the incorrect alternatives. This is a fact as a consequence of the assumption that any subgroup with a given amount of information will distribute equally among the alternatives they do not know to be false. In amplifying this theory, allowance should be made for chance variations from such a distribution. We may say, however, that, if a considerably greater number of persons select one distractor than select the correct answer, it is likely that some actual misinformation exists in the group, and the method indicated in equation 10 does not apply. A method of test scoring appropriate for the measures of item difficulty shown in equations 9 and 10 has not been suggested.

5. Item difficulty parameters—general considerations

Innumerable other measures of item difficulty have been suggested that are based on the percentage correct for the upper and lower K per cent of the population; see Cook (1932), Lentz, Hirshstein, and Finch (1932), Guilford (1936b), Kelley (1939), and Davis (1946). The upper and lower k per cent are chosen on the basis of total test score, and k has been given various values such as 10, 20, 25, 27, 33. Such difficulty measures are usually incidental to methods for obtaining a rapid approximation to the correlation between item and test score. Insofar as they are measures of item difficulty, they are regarded as approximations to the basic statistic of percentage of persons answering correctly. In general, the proper method of evaluating a statistic that is an economical approximation to some other statistic is

1. To determine the standard error or confidence interval for each of the statistics.

2. To determine how many cases must be used for each method in order to give statistics of equal precision.[1]

3. To determine the dollar cost of each method for the number of cases indicated in step 2.

Thus the expense of obtaining statistics of equal precision is determined, and the cheaper method may then be advocated. As far as the author is aware, none of the statistics indicating item difficulty or item-total correlation have been subjected to such theoretical and experimental comparisons. Thus we do not have the only type of information that is relevant for judging the relative merits of the different *short-cut* methods.

In summary, then, we may say that the methods of item analysis should be considered as a part of the total test theory problem. The theoretical relation between the item parameters and test parameters should be shown. In the test theory presented here the number correct is the score, and, since the mean test score is the sum of the proportion of correct responses for each item, there is a very simple relationship between item difficulty and test mean provided item difficulty is measured as the proportion of correct responses.

The only other difficulty measure that is consistently related to a method of test scoring is the median ability level for the item. This measure of item difficulty is appropriate for tests set up and scored by methods of absolute scaling.

The other measures of item difficulty have been set up to cope with special problems, such as change in ability level of the group, the problem of guessing, or the problem of inadequate clerical help, necessitating abbreviated methods. Theoretical and experimental information adequate for evaluating these methods is not yet available.

There have been several empirical studies that show that tests composed of items answered correctly by about 50 per cent of the group have a higher validity than tests composed of items that are easier or harder than 50 per cent, but otherwise of the same type. See, for example, Cook (1932), T. G. Thurstone (1932), and Richardson (1936a). In section 8 of this chapter, an equation showing the relationship between item parameters and test validity is developed (equation 24). This equation does not show any direct relationship between test validity and item difficulty. Test validity, however, does depend on the point-biserial item-criterion correlation. This correlation may increase rapidly, as items approach a 50 per cent difficulty level; see Carroll

---

[1] The paper by Mosteller (1946) illustrates a good theoretical comparison of several different methods of estimating a parameter.

(1945) and Gulliksen (1945). Hence it is suggested that the higher validity found for tests composed of items with 50 per cent difficulty may be due to and directly measured by the increase in item-criterion correlation.

6. Item parameters related to test variance

Another item analysis problem is selecting items in order to control the standard deviation of the total test score (s_x). We may, for example, wish to select a subset of k items out of a total of K items in such a way as to have a k-item test with the largest possible standard deviation, the smallest, or so that its standard deviation will equal as closely as possible that of another test.

Equation 9 of Chapter 7 gives the variance of a composite as the sum of all the terms in the variance-covariance matrix. If the complete variance-covariance matrix were available for a set of items, it would be possible to add the variances and covariances for different possible subsets of items and to find the variance of total test score for each possible subset of items. For any large number of items, however, the amount of labor required to do this is very great. The procedure usually seems impractical with present computational facilities.

We can obtain a reasonably useful result by working with the correlation between the item and total test score. From equations 3 to 7, Chapter 7, we learn that, if a composite gross score is formed by adding gross scores of parts, the deviation score for the composite is the sum of deviation scores for the parts; hence from equations 1 and 5 we have

$$(11) \qquad x_i = X_i - \overline{X} = \sum_{g=1}^{K} (A_{ig} - p_g) = \sum_{g=1}^{K} a_{ig},$$

where x_i designates the deviation score for the test, and

$\qquad a_{ig}$ designates the deviation score for the item.

Designating the standard deviation of item g by s_g, that of the total test by s_x, and the item-test correlation by r_{xg}, we may write

$$(12) \qquad N r_{xg} s_g s_x = \sum_{i=1}^{N} x_i a_{ig}.$$

Substituting equation 11 in equation 12 and reversing the order of summation gives

$$(13) \qquad N r_{xg} s_g s_x = \sum_{h=1}^{K} \sum_{i=1}^{N} a_{ih} a_{ig}.$$

Note that it is necessary to use two different subscripts (h and g) to indicate that, for a given item g, we take the cross products with all items ($h = 1$ to K, including g). Since the terms of the form $\Sigma a_h a_g / N$ indicate an interitem covariance, we may divide both sides by N and write

$$(14) \qquad\qquad r_{xg} s_g s_x = \sum_{h=1}^{K} r_{gh} s_g s_h \qquad\qquad (r_{gg} = 1).$$

Since g is a number from 1 to K, and h varies from 1 to K, there will be one term in the summation where $h = g$. This term will be a variance, and the other $K - 1$ terms will be covariances. To indicate this explicitly, we write

$$(15) \qquad\qquad r_{xg} s_g s_x = s_g{}^2 + \sum_{h=1}^{K} r_{gh} s_g s_h \qquad\qquad (h \neq g),$$

where s_g and s_h are item standard deviations, which may be written $\sqrt{p(1 - p)}$,

$\quad r_{gh}$ is the fourfold point correlation of items g and h,

$\quad r_{xg}$ is the point-biserial correlation of item g with the total test composite x, and

$\quad s_x$ is the standard deviation of total test score.

In other words, the sum of the terms in any one column (or row) of the interitem variance-covariance matrix is the covariance between that item and the total test score. By using the gross score formula for variance and covariance, these results may be expressed in terms of the proportion answering an item correctly and the proportion answering both items of a pair correctly. From equation 11 and the definition of covariance we have

$$N r_{gh} s_g s_h = \sum_{i=1}^{N} (A_{ig} - p_g)(A_{ih} - p_h) = \sum_{i=1}^{N} A_{ig} A_{ih} - N p_g p_h.$$

Since the term $\Sigma A_{ig} A_{ih}$ is zero if either factor is zero and is unity if both factors are unity, the summed products are equal to the number of persons answering *both* items g and h correctly. This may be verified with the help of the illustrative table of scores (Table 1). Dividing by N, we have the proportion of persons answering both g and h correctly, which will be designated p_{gh}. Thus the interitem covariance is

$$(16) \qquad\qquad r_{gh} s_g s_h = p_{gh} - p_g p_h.$$

For the variance of an item, we have the special case of equation 16 in which $h = g$. In this case p_{gh} becomes p_{gg}, which is identical with p_g; thus we have

$$(17) \qquad\qquad s_g{}^2 = p_g - p_g{}^2 = p_g(1 - p_g).$$

The item-test covariance shown in equations 14 and 15 may, by the use of equations 5 and 16, be written

$$(18) \qquad r_{xg}s_g s_x = \sum_{h=1}^{K} p_{gh} - M_X p_g \qquad (p_{gg} = p_g),$$

where p_g is the proportion of persons answering item g correctly,

$\qquad p_{gh}$ is the proportion of persons answering both item g and item h correctly,

$\qquad M_X$ is the mean of the total test score, and the other terms have the definitions indicated for equation 15.

Substituting equation 15 (Chapter 21) in equation 9 (Chapter 7) and designating the test variance by $s_x{}^2$, we have

$$(19) \qquad s_x{}^2 = \sum_{g=1}^{K} r_{xg}s_g s_x.$$

The sum of the item-test covariances is equal to the sum of the terms in the interitem variance-covariance matrix, which is equal to the test variance. Thus the test variance is expressed in terms of item parameters.

Since s_x is a constant when summing over g, the right-hand side of equation 19 may be written $s_x \Sigma r_{xg}s_g$. Dividing both sides by s_x gives

$$(20) \qquad \tilde{X} \quad \text{or} \quad s_x = \sum_{g=1}^{K} r_{xg}s_g = K\overline{(r_{xg}s_g)}.$$

Define the product $r_{xg}s_g$ as the "reliability index" for item g. Then the standard deviation of the total test score (designated s_x or $\tilde{X}$) is equal to the sum of the item reliability indices.

It should be noted particularly that no approximations were used in deriving equations 19 and 20. The only possible reason for either of these equations failing to work in any particular case is the occurrence of an arithmetical error in the calculations. It should also be noted that, in terms of the derivation, r_{xg} must be a point biserial correlation.

Unfortunately, however, these equations hold exactly only for the standard deviation of the total test. For a subtest made up of a subset of items, the sum of the item reliability indices based on correlation of item with *total* test score will not exactly equal the standard deviation of the subtest. For example, if the interitem correlations are nearly equal and all positive, the sum of the reliability indices for half the items in the test $\left(\sum_{g=1}^{K/2} r_{xg}s_g \right)$ will give a value larger than the standard deviation of the test composed of half the items because for approximately parallel items the correlation of an item with a longer test will be greater than its correlation with a shorter test. This may be seen from equation 5, Chapter 9.

However, a test composed of items with large reliability indices will probably have a greater standard deviation than one composed of items with small reliability indices. Also if the items in two tests are matched simultaneously with respect to two item parameters such as r_{xg} and p_g (since s_g is a function of p_g, see equation 17), the two tests will have closely comparable means and standard deviations. Refer to the method sketched in Chapter 15, section 7, and Figure 3 of Chapter 15. We shall see in the next section that the reliability of a test is determined by the item variances and interitem covariances, together with the number of items, so that matching two tests item for item with respect to both r_{xg} and p_g would give tests with similar reliabilities as well as similar variances.

7. Item parameters determining test reliability

The equation showing the relation between number of items, item variance, item reliability index, and test reliability may be written by substituting equation 20 (Chapter 21) in equation 10 (Chapter 16). This gives

$$(21) \qquad r_{xx} = \left(\frac{K}{K-1}\right)\left[1 - \frac{\sum\limits_{g=1}^{K} s_g^2}{\left(\sum\limits_{g=1}^{K} r_{xg}s_g\right)^2}\right],$$

where K is the number of items in the test,

s_g^2 is the item variance which equals $p_g - p_g^2$,

$r_{xg}s_g$ is the item reliability index, and

r_{xx} is the reliability of the total test.

If we write a sum of terms as K times the average, and divide numerator and denominator by K, we have

$$(22) \qquad r_{xx} = \left(\frac{K}{K-1}\right)\left[1 - \frac{\overline{(s_g^2)}}{K\overline{(r_{xg}s_g)}^2}\right],$$

where $\overline{s_g^2}$ is the average item variance, and

$\overline{r_{xg}s_g}$ is the average item reliability index, and the other terms have the same definitions as in equation 21.

The item variance $(s_g^2$ or $p_g - p_g^2)$ approaches zero as p_g approaches zero or unity, and is a maximum value of .25 when $p_g = .5$. Since the values of s_g^2 vary between zero and .25, the average item variance must also be between these limits. The value of s_g varies between 0 and .5, and the value of r_{xg} between 0 and 1. Thus the reliability index must lie between 0 and .5. That is, the average item variance and the average reliability index vary within narrow limits; hence these factors cannot have much influence on the test reliability unless r_{xg} is near zero, in which case the denominator will become small and the reliability will be low. On the other hand, K, the number of items, increases uniformly with the addition of new items. As can be seen from equation 22, the effect of this change in K is to move the reliability nearer to unity. The number of items is of itself an important determiner of reliability. As long as we avoid items that have a very low or negative correlation with total test score, the addition of items with low positive correlations will usually increase the reliability of the total test.

Equations 21 and 22 give the test reliability as functions of the item reliability index $(r_{xg}s_g)$, the item variance (s_g^2), and the number of items (K).

If the number of items composing the test is fixed, the reliability of the test can be increased only by making the average item variance smaller or the average item reliability index larger. To make such a selection of items graphically, each item is represented by a point, the ordinate of which is the item variance (s_g^2) and the abscissa of which is the reliability index $(r_{xg}s_g)$. In order to maximize the test reliability, we must select a subset of points such that the average ordinate is as small as possible and the average abscissa is as large as possible. This means that the points must be selected from the lower right-hand portion of the graph.

It should be noted that equations 21 and 22 are strictly accurate if all the points, that is, all the items in the test, are used. If we consider a subset of items that is only a half or a third of the original number of items, it is likely that the values of r_{xg} for the total test will be different from the values of r_{xg} for the subtest. Thus using equation 21 and the values of r_{xg} for the total test will give an over- or an underestimate of the reliability of the subtest. However, tests that are matched item for item on the basis of both item variance (s_g^2) and item reliability index $(r_{xg}s_g)$ will probably have closely similar reliabilities. A subset of a given number of items selected for large reliability index and small item variance will have a higher reliability than a test composed of the same number of items that have a small reliability index and a large item variance.

Note that, if we desire to select a subset of k items from a total group of K items, a completely accurate solution is obtained by using the inter-item variance-covariance matrix, computing the sum of the diagonal elements (Σs_g^2) and the sum of all the elements for various subsets of items, and selecting the one subset of size k that has the highest reliability. However, with current methods of computation, this method is considered too laborious to be of practical use. The approximation indicated by the use of equation 21 is, however, computationally feasible and reasonably accurate if the purpose is to eliminate the poorest 10 or 20 per cent of the items.

Numerous arbitrary indices of the relationship between item and test score have been developed. Adkins (1938) has pointed out that these indices may be classified as approximations to some one of three statistics:

1. The item-test correlation.
2. The slope of the regression of test on item.
3. The slope of the regression of item on test.

The first type would be illustrated by the use of various correlation coefficients, such as the biserial, the point biserial, or the tetrachoric; the second by the use of indices that depend on the mean difference in test score between those passing and failing the item; and the third by indices dependent on the slope of the item curve (see Ferguson, 1942, Finney, 1944, or Turnbull, 1946). Some of the suggested indices are attempts to decrease the clerical and machine costs of item analysis by using only a part of the data; see, for example, Kelley (1939), Flanagan (1939a), and Davis (1946).

8. Item parameters determining test validity

Having considered item selection in relation to test mean, variance, and reliability, we turn now to the problem of selecting items to maximize the validity of the total test score. It is not possible to do this directly unless we have information regarding the correlation of each item with the appropriate criterion score. In most practical cases it is probable that selecting items to increase the reliability of a test will also incidentally increase test validity. Equation 5, Chapter 9, shows that increasing test length increases the validity of the test. Increasing test length is also an effective means of increasing test reliability as shown in equation 22 (of this chapter) and equation 10 (Chapter 8). However, special cases have been demonstrated where it is possible to decrease validity while increasing reliability or to increase validity at the expense of reliability; see, for example, Cook (1932), Tucker (1946), or Brogden (1946b). In other words, if no criterion is available it is highly desirable to take steps to increase test reliability; however, in laying a theoretical foundation for improving test validity it is essential to consider the correlation of each item with a criterion.

Theoretically the problem of maximizing test validity for predicting any specified criterion has been solved. We have only to obtain the complete interitem variance-covariance matrix and the item-criterion covariances, and then solve all multiple correlations or all multiple correlations using a specified number of items (equation 55, Chapter 20). Frisch (1934) has described the method for dealing with "complete regression systems." Such methods, however, are generally regarded as too laborious for present computational procedures. Several approximation techniques have been devised as indicated in Chapter 20, section 3. All these methods have in common the assumption that the best single test (or item) is included in the best two; that the best two will be included in the best three, and so on. By such methods we work only $K - 1$ multiple correlations for K items, which is laborious but feasible. Such procedures have been described by Horst (1934b), Edgerton and Kolbe (1936), Adkins and Toops (1937), Wherry (1940), Toops (1941), and Jenkins (1946). However, it would seem that most test workers still consider the labor of these methods prohibitive, since they have not attained very wide use. It is possible by using additional assumptions to develop a less laborious method that makes use of only $2K$ item parameters, namely, a reliability index and a validity index for each of the K items of the original experimental test.

The general formula for the correlation of a criterion with a composite is given in equation 1, Chapter 9. Here we will use the subscript y to designate the criterion instead of I as in equation 1, Chapter 9. The formula for the variance of a sum is given in equation 9, Chapter 7. Here we shall use the subscript x to designate the total test, instead of c, as in equation 9, Chapter 7. If we change subscript c in equation 9, Chapter 7, to x, change subscript I of equation 1, Chapter 9, to y, and substitute equation 9, Chapter 7, in equation 1, Chapter 9, we have

$$(23) \qquad r_{xy} = \frac{\sum\limits_{g=1}^{K} r_{yg} s_g s_y}{s_x s_y}.$$

Since s_y is the same for all the terms in the summation, it may be factored out. If we divide numerator and denominator by s_y, and substitute equation 20 in equation 23, we have

$$(24) \qquad r_{xy} = \frac{\displaystyle\sum_{g=1}^{K} r_{yg}s_g}{\displaystyle\sum_{g=1}^{K} r_{xg}s_g}.$$

If we substitute K times the mean for the sums and divide numerator and denominator by K, we have

$$(25) \qquad r_{xy} = \frac{\overline{r_{yg}s_g}}{\overline{r_{xg}s_g}},$$

where the bar over a term indicates the average,

r_{xg} is the point biserial correlation of item g with the test x,

r_{yg} is the point biserial correlation of item g with the criterion y,

s_g is $\sqrt{p(1-p)}$, the standard deviation of item g,

r_{xy} is the correlation between the criterion and test, and

K is the number of items in the test.

> *If $r_{yg}s_g$ is defined as the "validity index" of item g and $r_{xg}s_g$ as the "reliability index" of item g, the test validity is the ratio of the sum of the validity indices to the sum of the reliability indices, or the ratio of the average validity index to the average reliability index.*

As a practical item selection procedure it is desirable to plot the item analysis results. For example, the reliability index may be plotted as the abscissa and the validity index as the ordinate (Figure 1); then the items should be selected as far as possible from the upper left-hand corner of the plot. This method was described and illustrated by Gulliksen (1944) and (1949a); see Figure 2.

This method of selecting items to give a valid test is similar to the one suggested by Horst (1936b). It is of particular interest to note that the number of items in the test has, of itself, no effect on validity. However, an increase in number of items will, except under unusual circumstances, increase the reliability of the test. If no validity index is available, increasing the number of items in a test may well contribute to lowering the test validity.

As mentioned in the introduction to this chapter, it should be noted that the methods presented here do not consider sampling errors nor the possibility of systematic variation in the item parameters. A subtest composed of only a *few* of the most valid items is probably less likely to maintain its high validity on a new sample of persons than a test composed of a large number of items. The chance and systematic fluctuations of the various item analysis parameters need to be studied and compared for various item analysis methods.

In using equations 24 or 25 for item selection, we should note that the validity index for an item is independent of the effects of item selection.

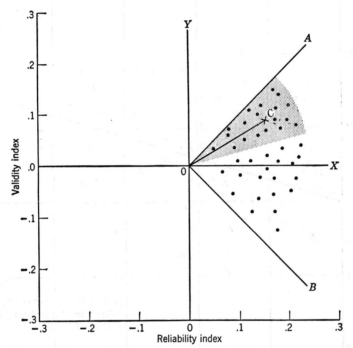

Figure 1. Illustrating plot of validity index and reliability index for item selection. (From Gulliksen, 1949a.)

On the other hand, the reliability index will change as the items composing the test are changed. This effect need cause no concern if only a few of the poorest items are eliminated from the test. However, if we wish, for example, to select a test of 100 items from an initial test of 500 items, it is well to make the selection in two or more stages, as suggested by Horst (1936b). If all the item-test correlations are positive and high, the selection is not so likely to change the reliability index as if there were quite a few items with negative reliability indices that were to be eliminated. In such a case the reliability indices should be recalculated after the first elimination of items with low and negative reliability indices.

As mentioned in conjunction with item selection to control test variance and test reliability, it should be noted that, if we consider the entire test, the ratio of the average validity index to the average reliability index must equal the test validity. No approximation is involved.

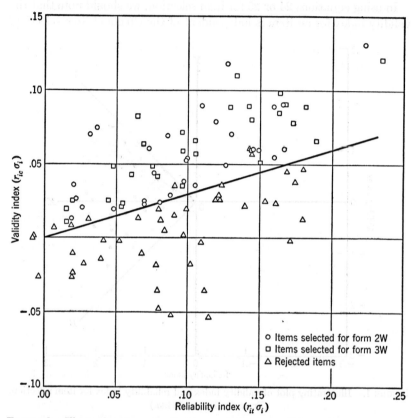

FIGURE 2. Illustrating item selection to maximize test validity. (From Gulliksen, 1944; OSRD Report 3187; Applied Psychology Panel, NDRC.)

However, as we make more and more stringent selection of test items, correlation of the item with the new subtest is increasingly likely to be different from the correlation of the item with the original total test. The item selection introduces no error whatever into the numerator term of equation 24. The error made in estimating the validity coefficient is due *solely* to the fact that the correlation of item with total test will vary as the test length changes. Hence, as mentioned before, if a computationally feasible method of utilizing the interitem variance-covariance matrix were developed, it would be possible to select any subset k from a larger set of K items and to determine precisely the variance, reliability, and validity of that subset of items.

9. Computing formulas for item parameters

From the theory given in the preceding sections, the essential item statistics are:

1. p_g, the proportion of persons answering each item correctly. This quantity is a measure of item difficulty. From it, the item variance $s_g^2 = p_g(1 - p_g)$ can readily be computed.

2. $r_{xg}s_g$, the reliability index, which is the point-biserial correlation between item and total score multiplied by the item standard deviation.

3. $r_{yg}s_g$, the validity index, which is the point-biserial correlation between item and criterion score multiplied by the item standard deviation.

Having determined the item parameters that are related to test mean, variance, reliability, and validity, we turn to the problem of computing these values.

We shall not consider here short-cut methods of estimating these parameters from a portion of the data. The principal purpose of these methods is to avoid the clerical labor involved in dealing with all the data; hence they can be compared only on the basis of computing costs and statistical precision. As yet such comparisons have not been made. For a description of such methods, see Kelley (1939), Flanagan (1939a), and Davis (1946).

The item difficulty measure requires simply a count of the number of correct answers to each item. This count may be made manually or, if punched-card equipment is available, the count may be made with the counting sorter or the tabulator. Usually the count is obtained incidentally in connection with the computation of the point-biserial correlation or the reliability index.

When some of the persons taking a test fail to answer certain items, we have the problem of how to treat such responses. As indicated in Chapter 17, if we are dealing with a speed test all the items must be easy so that the only purpose of an item analysis is to eliminate items with a significant proportion of errors. In a power test, the number of items left blank, either skipped or unattempted, should be negligible. An adequate theoretical analysis of a test that is a mixture of speed and power has not yet been presented. Such an analysis probably requires some information or assumptions about the correlation between speed and power.

The analysis given here applies strictly only to a power test that has an ample time limit so that practically all the items are attempted. The discussion of Chapter 17 indicates objective criteria for the possible influence of number of blank items. For analyzing a power test with a large number of unattempted items, some of the methods given in section 3 of this chapter should probably be used.

The derivation showing the relationship of item parameters to test reliability or validity, used the Pearson product-moment correlation of the item with the test or criterion score. The raw score for an item is *unity* if the item is answered correctly, and *zero* if the item is answered incorrectly. Let us begin with the formula for correlation in terms of summations and make the simplifications appropriate for this particular case. Since the formula for the item-criterion correlation is identical with that for the item-test correlation, we shall consider in detail only the correlation between a dichotomously scored item and the test score X.

Equation (26)

$$r_{xg} = \frac{N \sum_{i=1}^{N} A_{ig}X_i - \sum_{i=1}^{N} A_{ig} \sum_{i=1}^{N} X_i}{\sqrt{N \sum_{i=1}^{N} A_{ig}^2 - \left(\sum_{i=1}^{N} A_{ig}\right)^2} \sqrt{N \sum_{i=1}^{N} X_i^2 - \left(\sum_{i=1}^{N} X_i\right)^2}}.$$

$\sum_{i=1}^{N} A_{ig}X_i$ may be simplified by noting that A is either unity or zero; hence the sum of products is equal to the sum of the test scores for those who answer the item correctly. This sum may be designated as $\sum_{i=1}^{N_g} X_{ig}$. Let us define N_g as the number of persons answering item g correctly and $\overline{X}_g$ as the average test score for those who answer item g correctly. From these definitions and equation 4 we may write

(27) $$N_g = \sum_{i=1}^{N} A_{ig} = Np_g$$

and

(28) $$\sum_{i=1}^{N} A_{ig}X_i = \sum_{i=1}^{N_g} X_{ig} = N_g\overline{X}_g = Np_g\overline{X}_g.$$

From the definition of a standard deviation,

(29) $$Ns_g = \sqrt{N \sum_{i=1}^{N} A_{ig}^2 - \left(\sum_{i=1}^{N} A_{ig}\right)^2}.$$

Substituting equations 27, 28, and 29 in equation 26 and multiplying both sides by s_g gives the item reliability index in terms of gross score summations as

$$(30) \qquad r_{xg}s_g = \frac{N \sum_{i=1}^{N_g} X_{ig} - N_g \sum_{i=1}^{N} X_i}{N \sqrt{N \sum_{i=1}^{N} X_i^2 - \left(\sum_{i=1}^{N} X_i\right)^2}}.$$

The reliability index may also be written in terms of means, a proportion, and a standard deviation. From the definitions of a mean $(\overline{X})$ and a standard deviation $(\tilde{X})$ we have

$$(31) \qquad \sum_{i=1}^{N} X_i = N\overline{X}, \quad \text{and}$$

$$N\tilde{X} = Ns_x = \sqrt{N \sum_{i=1}^{N} X_i^2 - \left(\sum_{i=1}^{N} X_i\right)^2}.$$

Substituting equations 28 and 31 in equation 30, dividing numerator and denominator by N^2, and factoring out p_g, we have

$$(32) \qquad r_{xg}s_g = p_g\left(\frac{\overline{X}_g - \overline{X}}{\tilde{X}}\right).$$

If Y is used to designate gross scores on the criterion measure, by substituting Y for X in equations 30 and 32, we have the corresponding formulas for the item validity index.

$$(33) \qquad r_{yg}s_g = \frac{N \sum_{i=1}^{N_g} Y_{ig} - N_g \sum_{i=1}^{N} Y_i}{N \sqrt{N \sum_{i=1}^{N} Y_i^2 - \left(\sum_{i=1}^{N} Y_i\right)^2}}.$$

and|

$$(34) \qquad r_{yg}s_g = p_g\left(\frac{\overline{Y}_g - \overline{Y}}{\tilde{Y}}\right).$$

In equations 30, 32, 33, and 34:

N is the total number of persons taking the test,

N_g is the number of persons answering item g correctly $(g = 1 \cdots K)$,

p_g is N_g/N, the proportion of persons answering item g correctly,

X_i and Y_i designate, respectively, the test and criterion score for individual i $(i = 1 \cdots N)$,

$\overline{X}$ and $\breve{X}$ are, respectively, the mean and the standard deviation of the total distribution of test scores,

$\overline{Y}$ and $\breve{Y}$ are, respectively, the mean and the standard deviation of the distribution of criterion scores,

X_g and Y_g designate, respectively, the test and the criterion score for each person who answers item g correctly,

$\overline{X}_g$ and $\overline{Y}_g$ are the average test and criterion scores, respectively, for those answering item g correctly,

$r_{x_g s_g}$ is the reliability index for item g, and

$r_{y_g s_g}$ is the validity index for item g.

The reliability and validity index for each item can be computed if we have the mean and the standard deviation of all N persons for both the test and the criterion, p_g, the proportion of persons answering each item correctly, and the average test and average criterion score for those answering each item correctly.

The formulas given here for the point-biserial correlation are a slight variant of those presented by Richardson and Stalnaker (1933) and Stalnaker (1940).

Equations 30, 32, 33, and 34 are the basic computing formulas to be used in calculating the reliability index and the validity index for a group of items. They are analogous except for the factor $\breve{Y}$ or $\breve{X}$ to the formulas presented by Horst (1936b).

10. Summary of item selection theory

The basic theoretical problem for item analysis procedures is to find a functional relationship between the parameters of the total test and appropriately selected item parameters. Such a theory must take due account of important changes in methods of test scoring. It is then necessary to investigate various factors that produce variation in these item parameters, such as random sampling error and systematic variation produced by changes in such factors as the length of the test and the heterogeneity of the group. Various computational short-cut procedures utilizing only a portion of the data can also be studied to determine which method is most economical. In making such comparisons it is necessary to adjust the sample size so that the statistics compared will have the same sampling fluctuation.

In the foregoing sections an item analysis rationale has been proposed for the case in which the test score is the number of items answered correctly. It has been shown that the test mean, standard deviation, reliability, and validity may be estimated from three item parameters, a difficulty, reliability, and validity index. The equations are as follows:

$$(5) \qquad M_X \quad \text{or} \quad \overline{X} = \sum_{g=1}^{K} p_g = K\overline{p},$$

$$(20) \qquad s_x \quad \text{or} \quad \tilde{X} = \sum_{g=1}^{K} r_{xg}s_g = K(\overline{r_{xg}s_g}),$$

$$(21) \qquad r_{xx} = \left(\frac{K}{K-1}\right)\left[1 - \frac{\sum_{g=1}^{K} s_g^2}{\left(\sum_{g=1}^{K} r_{xg}s_g\right)^2}\right],$$

$$(22) \qquad r_{xx} = \left(\frac{K}{K-1}\right)\left[1 - \frac{\overline{(s_g^2)}}{K\overline{(r_{xg}s_g)}^2}\right],$$

$$(24 \text{ and } 25) \qquad r_{xy} = \frac{\sum_{g=1}^{K} r_{yg}s_g}{\sum_{g=1}^{K} r_{xg}s_g} = \frac{\overline{(r_{yg}s_g)}}{\overline{(r_{xg}s_g)}}.$$

In these equations:

K is the number of items in the test,

N is the total number of persons taking the test,

N_g is the number of persons answering item g correctly $(g = 1 \cdots K)$,

p_g is the proportion of persons answering item g correctly (that is, $p_g = N_g/N$),

s_g^2 is the variance of item g $[s_g^2 = p_g(1 - p_g)]$,

$r_{xg}s_g$, the item reliability index, is the point-biserial item-test correlation multiplied by the item standard deviation,

$r_{yg}s_g$, the item validity index, is the point-biserial item-criterion correlation multiplied by the item standard deviation,

M_X or $\overline{X}$ is the mean for all scores in the test distribution,

s_x or $\tilde{X}$ is the standard deviation of the distribution of test scores,

r_{xx} is the reliability of the test, and

r_{xy} is the test validity, the correlation of test (x) with the criterion (y).

Computing formulas for the item reliability and validity indices were given as

Equations (30 and 32)

$$r_{x_g s_g} = \frac{N \sum_{i=1}^{N_g} X_{ig} - N_g \sum_{i=1}^{N} X_i}{N \sqrt{N \sum_{i=1}^{N} X_i^2 - \left(\sum_{i=1}^{N} X_i\right)^2}} = p_g \left(\frac{\overline{X}_g - \overline{X}}{\tilde{X}}\right).$$

Equations (33 and 34)

$$r_{y_g s_g} = \frac{N \sum_{i=1}^{N_g} Y_{ig} - N_g \sum_{i=1}^{N} Y_i}{N \sqrt{N \sum_{i=1}^{N} Y_i^2 - \left(\sum_{i=1}^{N} Y_i\right)^2}} = p_g \left(\frac{\overline{Y}_g - \overline{Y}}{\tilde{Y}}\right).$$

In these formulas:

X or x designates the test,

Y or y designates the criterion,

$\overline{Y}$ and $\tilde{Y}$ are, respectively, the mean and the standard deviation of the criterion scores,

X_g designates the test score only for those persons who have answered item g correctly,

Y_g designates the criterion score only for those who have answered item g correctly, and

$\overline{X}_g$ and $\overline{Y}_g$ are the average test and criterion scores, respectively, for those answering item g correctly.

The other terms have the same definition as in equations 24 and 25.

One systematic error in the foregoing formulas arises from the fact that the item reliability index is not invariant with respect to test length. In most cases the item-test correlation will increase as the test length increases. The item difficulty and validity indices are not affected by test length. All three indices are affected by a change in the ability level of the group. This means that the item parameters must be obtained on a group similar to that for which the test is being constructed. The item parameters will be more generally useful if it is possible to discover parameters that do not vary systematically with changes in the mean or variance of group ability. If such parameters cannot be found, it may be possible to make some empirical estimations of the amount of change that may be expected in the item parameters as a result of a given change in the group.

In addition to *systematic* changes of item parameters with group ability and with test length, the item statistics are subject to *random* sampling variation. The magnitude of such fluctuations should be determined in order that we may estimate the change in test parameters to be expected when the test is used on a new sample. These sampling errors could also be used to determine the size for the item analysis sample that is necessary to give reasonable sampling stability in the test parameters.

Numerous arbitrary indices of item difficulty and reliability have been given in the item analysis literature. The attempts to express item difficulty in terms of an ability level at which the item will be answered correctly by half the persons are interesting in that one of them may give a difficulty index that does not vary systematically with changes in the ability level of the group. Horst's difficulty index, which estimates the number of persons knowing the answer to the item, may also offer some interesting possibilities for test construction and scoring.

A large number of arbitrary indices of item reliability or homogeneity have been reported in the literature. Adkins (1938) has shown that these indices may be classified as estimates of (1) the item-test correlation, (2) the regression of item on test, or (3) the regression of test on item. The regression of item on test should be invariant with respect to selection on the basis of test score.

Many of the item reliability indices make use of only a portion of the data and estimate a correlation or a slope from widespread classes. As far as the author is aware, the efficiency of these methods has not been compared with methods using the entire sample, when sample size is adjusted so as to secure equal sampling errors.

11. Prospective developments in item selection techniques

In considering the subsequent development of item analysis procedures, there are a number of problems to which special attention should be called. For the special case of tests for which the score is the number of correct answers we have several unsolved problems. What are the appropriate item selection procedures for controlling the skewness or the kurtosis of the distribution of total test scores? The development of such procedures will probably present more difficulties than the problem of maximizing reliability or validity, since we should usually be interested in arriving at some intermediate point, such as zero skew or normal kurtosis. This would require much more accurate estimation than obtaining the highest reliability or validity possible with a given set of items.

A basic assumption in developing the theory of the influence of group heterogeneity (see Chapters 10 and 11) is that the error of measurement does not vary systematically with test score. It is likely that this is true for some types of item selection and not for others. How can items be selected to keep the error of measurement constant at different points on the scale? How can items be selected to make the error of measurement smallest at a prospective cutting score? Since the variation of the error of measurement with test score depends on the third and fourth moments, Mollenkopf (1948, 1949), the theoretical analysis of the item selection procedures offers some difficulties that have not yet been surmounted. However, since the error of measurement is a fundamental statistic for a test, it will be a distinct advance when item selection techniques can selectively control the error of measurement for different test scores.

In this chapter the theoretical analysis of item analysis procedures has been presented only for the special case of the number right score. A corresponding analysis of the relationship between the item parameters and the test parameters is needed for other types of test scoring procedures. For example, a different type of item analysis is appropriate if the score is on the basis of level reached as in the absolute scaling methods (Thurstone, 1925 or 1927b), or as in the scaling methods developed by Guttman or the latent structure methods of Lazarsfeld; see Social Science Research Council (1950), Vol. IV.

As pointed out repeatedly in *Psychometric Methods* (Guilford, 1936b), the persons developing test theory have been for the most part unacquainted with, or have ignored, the work in psychophysics. There has been some attempt to develop a theory relating the two fields (Mosier, 1940 and 1941), but the psychophysical techniques, as developed by Thurstone (1925, 1927b), have not been systematically applied in the large-scale practical work in aptitude or achievement testing. Some exploratory work in this field has been done by Grossnickle (1942) and Lorr (1944). The integration of psychophysical theory and test theory would be a major achievement.

Another set of important item analysis problems deals with the nature of the changes in item parameters with changes in the test group. A significant contribution to item analysis theory would be the discovery of item parameters that remained relatively stable as the item analysis group changed; or the discovery of a law relating the changes in item parameters to changes in the group.

Relatively little experimental or theoretical work has been done on the effect of group changes on item parameters. If we assume that a given item requires a certain ability (A), the proportion of a group answering that item correctly will increase and decrease as the ability level of the group changes. The amount of this change will be greater for an item that is highly correlated with ability A than for one that correlates only moderately with ability A. If we have some standard measure of ability A, it may be that the ability level at which 50 per cent pass and 50 per cent fail would not be subject to as much fluctuation as the proportion of correct responses. As yet there has been no systematic theoretical treatment of measures of item difficulty directed particularly toward determining the nature of their variation with respect to changes in group ability. Neither has the experimental work on item analysis been directed toward determining the relative invariance of item parameters with systematic changes in the ability level of the group tested.

A similar problem of invariance is encountered in considering measures of the relationship between an item and the total test score or the criterion score. For example, the reliability index presented in this chapter involves the point biserial correlation. This coefficient varies systematically with item difficulty, Carroll (1945), Ferguson (1941a), and Gulliksen (1945), and consequently will vary with the ability level of the group tested. Theoretically there is no such systematic bias in biserial correlation. The biserial correlation *should not change* as the item difficulty changes with variations in group ability level. However, the data given by Richardson (1936a) showed *systematic changes* in biserial correlation with changes in *ability level* of the group. It might be found that some statistic related to the error of measurement or the slope of the regression line would turn out to be relatively stable despite changes in the mean and the standard deviation of ability in the group tested. If such a statistic were developed and used, then in constructing any test it would be necessary to have information on the ability range to be tested in order to construct a suitable test from the items available. As is true for item-difficulty parameters, we do not have the appropriate theoretical and experimental investigations showing how different item-test correlation measures vary with changes in the average and standard deviation of ability of the group tested.

The discussion in the foregoing paragraph applies both to item-test, and item-criterion correlations. There is one additional factor affecting item-test correlations that does not influence item-criterion correlations. The length of the test of which the item is a part will affect the item-test correlation but cannot influence the item-criterion correlation. For very short (two or three items) tests, the item score will form a considerable fraction of the test score; hence the item-test correlation will at first tend to decrease as items are added to the test. For tests larger than fifty or a hundred items, this effect is negligible; and, as the test length increases, a slight increase in item-test correlation could be expected because of the decrease in the error component of the total test score as test length is increased. Again the appropriate theoretical and experimental investigations are lacking. It is probable, however, that some conditions regarding a minimum number of items for a subset could be found so that we might say that neither of these factors is serious as long as we consider subsets of no less than, for instance, fifty items.

In addition to the problems of the relationship between item parameters and test parameters, and the nature of the variation of item parameters with changes in other factors such as the length of the test and the ability of the group, we have the problem of the most efficient statistics to use in estimating these parameters. A complete treatment of this problem would include both statistical efficiency in the sense of reducing the sampling error of the statistic, and cost efficiency in the sense of reducing the labor and machine costs of computation. In comparing different methods for an over-all determination of efficiency, it is necessary to adjust the number of cases for each method so as to equalize the sampling error, and then compare the costs of dealing with these appropriately adjusted numbers of cases.

Problems

1. Assume that published data give the biserial correlation between each item and the total test or the criterion score. Give the formula for changing biserial correlation into the reliability or the validity index discussed here.

2. Show the relationship between the method of improving test validity presented by Horst (1936b), "Item Selection by Means of a Maximizing Function" (*Psychometrika*, —) and the method presented here.

3. Study the material in Guilford, *Psychometric Methods*, pages 434 and 435, on Cook's index B and Clark's index. Compare these two indices.

4. The following item analysis information is available on a 35-item test. Which items should be eliminated in shortening the test to 30 items?

ITEM ANALYSIS INFORMATION FOR USE WITH PROBLEM 4

(These data were furnished through the courtesy of Dr. W. G. Mollenkopf
of the Educational Testing Service.)

Item Number	Proportion Answering Item Correctly	Standard Deviation of Item	Point Biserial Correlation of Item with		Relia-bility Index	Validity Index
			Total Test Score	Criterion Score		
	p_g	$s_g = \sqrt{p_g - p_g{}^2}$	r_{xg}	r_{yg}	$r_{xg}s_g$	$r_{yg}s_g$
1	.800	.400	.280	.203	.112	.081
2	.814	.389	.393	.152	.153	.059
3	.731	.443	.142	.126	.063	.056
4	.807	.395	.256	.327	.101	:129
5	.241	.428	.409	.168	.175	:072
6	.379	.485	.266	.188	.129	:091
7	.717	.451	.233	.186	.105	.084
8	.772	.420	.200	.200	.084	.084
9	.634	.482	.203	.212	.098	.102
10	.559	.497	.237	.213	.118	.106
11	.641	.480	.375	.273	.180	.131
12	.621	.485	.400	.291	.194	.141
13	.241	.428	.285	.313	.122	.134
14	.441	.497	.270	.245	.134	.122
15	.324	.468	.385	.239	.180	.112
16	.628	.483	.290	.157	.140	.076
17	.138	.345	.287	.165	.099	.057
18	.483	.500	.414	.232	.207	.116
19	.097	.296	.253	.267	.075	.079
20	.455	.498	.301	.309	.150	:154
21	.340	.474	.441	.255	.209	.121
22	.280	.449	.434	.165	.195	.074
23	.667	.471	.193	.208	.091	.098
24	.457	.498	.327	.207	.163	.103
25	.435	.496	.278	.222	.138	.110
26	.378	.485	.227	.196	.110	.095
27	.149	.356	.213	.247	.076	.088
28	.305	.460	.143	.191	.066	.088
29	.320	.467	.435	.330	.203	.154
30	.545	.498	.143	.118	.071	.059
31	.560	.496	.381	− .008	.189	− .004
32	.356	.479	.476	.194	.228	.093
33	.713	.452	.257	.150	.116	.068
34	.558	.497	.366	.215	.182	.107
35	.308	.462	.266	.182	.123	.084

Item Analysis Information for Use with Formula 1

(These data were furnished through the courtesy of Dr. W. G. Mollenkopf
of the Educational Testing Service.)

Bibliography

Abelson, H. H. (1927) *The Improvement of Intelligence Testing.* Contributions to Education, No. 273. New York: Bureau of Publications, Teachers College, Columbia University.

Ackerson, L. (1933) In disagreement with E. A. Lincoln's article, "The unreliability of reliability coefficients." *J. Educ. Psychol.,* **24,** 233–235.

Adams, H. F. (1936) Validity, reliability and objectivity. *Psychol. Monogr.,* **47,** 329–350.

Adkins, D. C. (1937) *A Comparative Study of Methods of Selecting Items.* Dissertation on file in library of Ohio State University. Pp. 338.

Adkins, D. C. (1938) A rational comparison of item-selection techniques. *Psychol. Bull.,* **35,** 655.

Adkins, D. C., *et al.* (1947) *Construction and Analysis of Achievement Tests.* U. S. Government Printing Office. Pp. xvii + 292.

Adkins, D. C., and Toops, H. A. (1937) Simplified formulas for item selection and construction. *Psychometrika,* **2,** 165–171.

Aitken, A. C. (1934) Note on selection from a multivariate normal population. *Proc. Edinburgh Math. Soc.,* **4,** 106–110.

Aitken, A. C. (1937) The evaluation of a certain triple-product matrix. *Proc. Roy. Soc. Edinburgh,* **57,** 172–181.

Alexander, H. W. (1947) The estimation of reliability when several trials are available. *Psychometrika,* **12,** 79–99.

Allcock, H. J., and Jones, J. R. (1932) *The Nomogram: The Theory and Practical Construction of Computation Charts.* New York: Pitman Publishing Corporation. Pp. viii + 209.

Anastasi, A. (1934) Influence of practice upon test reliability. *J. Educ. Psychol.,* **25,** 321–335.

Anderson, J. E. (1935) The effect of item analysis upon the discriminative power of an examination. *J. Appl. Psychol.,* **19,** 237–244.

Arnold, J. N. (1935) Nomogram for determining validity of test items. *J. Educ. Psychol.,* **26,** 151–153.

Arnold, J. N., and Dunlap, J. W. (1936) Nomographs concerning the Spearman-Brown formula and related functions. *J. Educ. Psychol.,* **27,** 371–374.

Asker, William (1924) Reliability of tests requiring alternate responses. *J. Educ. Research,* **9,** 234–240.

Ayres, L. P. (1911) *A Scale for Measuring the Quality of Handwriting of School Children.* Publication on Measurement in Education, Division of Education, Russell Sage Fund Bulletin 113.

Ayres, L. P. (1915) *A Measuring Scale for Ability in Spelling.* New York: Russell Sage Foundation.

Babitz, Milton, and Keys, Noel. (1940) A method for approximating the average intercorrelation coefficient by correlating the parts with the sum of the parts. *Psychometrika,* **5,** 283–288.

Barry, R. F. (1939) An analysis of some new statistical methods for selecting test items. *J. Exp. Educ.*, **7**, 221–228.

Barthelmess, H. M. (1931) *The Validity of Intelligence Test Elements.* Contributions to Education, No. 505. New York: Bureau of Publications, Teachers College, Columbia University.

Baxter, B. (1941) An experimental analysis of the contributions of speed and level in an intelligence test. *J. Educ. Psychol.*, **32**, 285–296.

Bedell, Ralph. (1940) Scoring weighted multiple keyed tests on the IBM counting sorter. *Psychometrika*, **5**, 195–201.

Bennett, G. K. (1947) The evaluation of pairs of tests for guidance use. *Amer. Psychol.*, **2**, 287.

Bennett, G. K., and Doppelt, J. E. (1948) The evaluation of pairs of tests for guidance use. *Educ. and Psychol. Meas.*, **8**, No. 3, 319–325.

Bernstein, E. (1924) Quickness and intelligence. *Brit. J. Psychol. Monogr.*, **3**, 1–55.

Bijou, S. W. (1947) *The Psychological Program in AAF Convalescent Hospitals.* Report 15, AAF Aviation Psychology Program Research Reports, U. S. Government Printing Office. Pp. viii + 256.

Binet, A. (1899) Attention et adaptation. *Année Psychol.*, **6**, 248–404.

Binet, A., and Henri, V. (1895) La psychologie individuelle. *Année Psychol.*, **2**, 411–465.

Bingham, W. V. (1932) Reliability, validity and dependability. *J. Appl. Psychol.*, **16**, 116–122.

Bingham, W. V. (1937) *Aptitudes and Aptitude Testing.* New York: Harper and Brothers. Pp. xii + 390.

Bliss, E. F. (1929) The difficulty of an item. *J. Educ. Psychol.*, **20**, 63–66.

Bôcher, Maxime. (1907) *Introduction to Higher Algebra.* New York: The Macmillan Company. Pp. xi + 321.

Bolles, M. M., and Zubin, J. (1939) A graphic method for evaluating differences between frequencies. *J. Appl. Psychol.*, **23**, 440–449.

Bolton, T. L. (1892) Growth of memory in school children. *Amer. J. Psychol.*, **4**, 362–380.

Boring, E. G. (1919) Mathematical versus scientific significance. *Psychol. Bull.*, **16**, 335–338.

Boring, E. G. (1920) The logic of the normal law of error in mental measurement. *Amer. J. Psychol.*, **31**, 1–33.

Bradford, L. P. (1940) The effect of practice upon standard errors of estimate. *Psychol. Monogr.*, **52**, No. 3, 56–71.

Bray, C. W. (1948) *Psychology and Military Proficiency.* Princeton, N. J.: Princeton University Press. Pp. 242.

Brigham, C. C. (1932) *A Study of Error.* New York: College Entrance Examination Board. Pp. xiii + 384.

Brogden, H. E. (1946a) An approach to the problem of differential prediction. *Psychometrika*, **11**, 139–154.

Brogden, H. E. (1946b) Variation in test validity with variation in the distribution of item difficulties, number of items, and degree of their intercorrelation. *Psychometrika*, **11**, 197–214.

Brown, William. (1910) Some experimental results in the correlation of mental abilities. *Brit. J. Psychol.*, **3**, 296–322.

Brown, William, and Thomson, Godfrey. (1925) *The Essentials of Mental Measurement.* 3rd Ed. London: Cambridge University Press. Pp. viii + 216.

Brownell, W. A. (1933) On the accuracy with which reliability may be measured by correlating test halves. *J. Exp. Educ.*, **1**, 204–215.

Buros, O. K. (1936) *Educational, Psychological, and Personality Tests of 1933, 1934, and 1935.* New Brunswick, N. J.: School of Education, Rutgers University. Pp. 83. Reviews 1–503.

Buros, O. K. (1937) *Educational, Psychological, and Personality Tests of 1936.* New Brunswick, N. J.: School of Education, Rutgers University. Pp. 141. Reviews 504–868.

Buros, O. K. (1938) *The 1938 Mental Measurements Yearbook.* New Brunswick, N. J.: School of Education, Rutgers University. Pp. xiv + 415. Reviews 869–1181.

Buros, O. K. (1941) *The 1940 Mental Measurements Yearbook.* New Brunswick, N. J.: School of Education, Rutgers University. Pp. xxi + 674. Reviews 1182–1684.

Buros, O. K. (1949) *The Third Mental Measurements Yearbook.* New Brunswick, N. J.: School of Education, Rutgers University. Pp. xiv + 1047.

Burt, Cyril. (1936) Supplement. In *The Marks of Examiners*, by Hartog, P. J., and Rhodes, E. C. London: Macmillan and Company. Pp. xix + 344.

Burt, Cyril (1943) Validating tests for personnel selection. *Brit. J. Psychol.*, **34**, 1–19.

Burt, Cyril. (1944) Statistical problems in the evaluation of Army tests. *Psychometrika*, **9**, 219–235.

Calandra, Alexander. (1941) Scoring formulas and probability considerations. *Psychometrika*, **6**, 1–9.

Carr, H. A. (1938) Reliability vs. the validity of test scores. *Psychol. Rev.*, **45**, 435–440.

Carroll, J. B. (1945) The effect of difficulty and chance success on correlations between items or between tests. *Psychometrika*, **10**, 1–19.

Carter, H. D. (1942) How reliable are the common measures of difficulty and validity of objective test items? *J. Psychol.*, **13**, 31–39.

Carter, L. F. (1947) *Psychological Research on Navigator Training.* Report 10, AAF Aviation Psychology Program Research Reports, U. S. Government Printing Office. Pp. ix + 186.

Casanova, T. (1939*a*) A test of the assumptions of linearity and homoscedasticity made in estimating the correlation in one range from that obtained in a different range. *J. Exp. Educ.*, **7**, 245–249.

Casanova, T. (1939*b*) A simple graphical method for determining the significance of a difference. *J. Educ. Psychol.*, **30**, 289–294.

Casanova, T. (1941) Analysis of the effect upon the reliability coefficient of changes in variables involved in the estimation of test reliability. *J. Exp. Educ.*, **9**, 219–228.

Cattell, J. McK. (1890) Mental tests and measurements. *Mind*, **15**, 373–381.

Cattell, J. McK., and Farrand, L. (1896) Physical and mental measurements of the students of Columbia University. *Psychol. Rev*, **3**, 618–648.

Chapanis, Alphonse. (1937) A note on the validity and difficulty of items in form A of the Otis self-administering tests of mental ability. *J. Exp. Educ.*, **5**, 246–248.

Chapanis, Alphonse. (1941) Notes on the rapid calculation of item validities. *J. Educ. Psychol.*, **32**, 297–304.

Chapman, J. C., and Cook, S. (1923) The principle of the single variable in a speed of reading cross-out test. *J. Educ. Res.*, **8**, 389–396.

Chesire, L., Saffir, M., and Thurstone, L. L. (1933) *Computing Diagrams for the Tetrachoric Correlation Coefficient.* University of Chicago Bookstore.

Churchman, C. W., Ackoff, R. L. and Wax, Murray. (1947) *Measurement of Consumer Interest.* Philadelphia: University of Pennsylvania Press. Pp. 213.

Clark, E. L. (1928) A method of evaluating the units of a test. *J. Educ. Psychol.*, **19**, 263–285.

Cleeton, G. V. (1926) The optimum difficulty of group test items. *J. Appl. Psychol.*, **10**, 327–340.

Conrad, H. S. (1941) Comparable Measures. *Encycl. Educ. Res.*, 340–344. Ed., W. S. Monroe. New York: The Macmillan Company.

Conrad, H. S. (1943) *Item Analysis of Navy Aptitude Tests.* OSRD; Publications Board, No. 13302. Washington, D. C.: U. S. Department of Commerce, 1946. Pp. 117.

Conrad, H. S. (1944a) *Characteristics and Uses of Item-Analysis Data.* OSRD; Publications Board, No. 13296. Washington, D. C.: U. S. Department of Commerce, 1946. Pp. 82. Also published in *Psychol. Monogr: Gen. and Appl.*, 1948, **62**, No. 8. (Whole No. 295.) Pp. 49.

Conrad, H. S. (1944b) *Statistical Analysis of the Mechanical Knowledge Test.* OSRD; Publications Board, No. 13320. Washington, D. C.: U. S. Department of Commerce, 1946. Pp. 14.

Conrad, H. S. (1945) *A Statistical Evaluation of the Basic Classification Test Battery* (Form I). OSRD; Publications Board, No. 13294. Washington, D. C.: U. S. Department of Commerce, 1946. Pp. 105.

Conrad, H. S., and Satter, G. A. (1945) *The Use of Test Scores and Quality-Classification Ratings in Predicting Success in Electrician's Mates School.* OSRD; Publications Board, No. 13290. Washington, D. C.: U. S. Department of Commerce, 1946. Pp. 35.

Cook, S. W. (1947) *Psychological Research on Radar Observer Training.* Report 12, AAF Aviation Psychology Program Research Reports. U. S. Government Printing Office. Pp. x + 340.

Cook, W. W. (1932) *The Measurement of General Spelling Ability Involving Controlled Comparisons between Techniques.* Iowa City, Iowa: University of Iowa Studies in Education, Vol. VI, No. 6.

Cook, W. W. (1941) Tests, achievement. *Encycl. Educ. Res.*, 1283–1301. Ed., W. S. Monroe. New York: The Macmillan Company.

Copeland, H. A. (1934) Note on the effect of teaching on the reliability coefficient of an achievement test. *J. Appl. Psychol.*, **18**, 711–716.

Cosby, C. B., and Weatherly, J. H. (1943) A simple method for the construction of nomographs. *J. Lab. Clin. Med.*, **28**, 1468–1473.

Courtney, D., Bucknam, M. E., and Durrell, D. (1946) Multiple choice recall versus oral and written recall. *J. Educ. Res.* **39**, 458–461.

Cramér, Harald. (1945) *Mathematical Methods of Statistics.* Stockholm: Hugo Gebers. Princeton, N. J.: Princeton University Press (1946). Pp. xvix + 575.

Crawford, A. B., and Burnham, P. S. (1932) Entrance examinations and college achievement, II. *School and Society*, **36**, 378–384.

Crawford, A. B., and Burnham, P. S. (1946) *Forecasting College Achievement —Part I.* New Haven, Conn.: Yale University Press. Pp. 291.

Crawford, M. P., *et al.* (1947) *Psychological Research on Operational Training in the Continental Air Forces.* Report 16, AAF Aviation Psychology Program Research Reports, U. S. Government Printing Office. Pp. vii + 367.

Cronbach, L. J. (1947) Test "reliability": its meaning and determination. *Psychometrika,* **12,** 1–16.

Cronbach, L. J. (1949) *Essentials of Psychological Testing.* New York: Harper and Brothers. Pp. xiii + 475.

Crooks, W. R., and Ferguson, L. W. (1941) Item validities of the Otis self-administering tests of mental ability for a college population. *J. Exp. Educ.,* **9,** 229–232.

Crum, W. L. (1923) Note on the reliability of a test with special reference to the examination set by the College Entrance Board. *Amer. Math. Monthly,* **30,** 296–301.

Culler, E. A. (1926) Studies in psychometric theory. *J. Exp. Psychol.,* **9,** 271–298.

Cureton, E. E. (1931) Errors of measurement and correlation. *Arch. Psychol.,* **19,** No. 125. Pp. 63.

Cureton, E. E. (1933) Validation against a fallible criterion. *J. Exp. Educ.,* **1,** 258–263.

Cureton, E. E., and Dunlap, J. W. (1929) A nomograph for estimating the reliability of a test in one range of talent when its reliability is known in another range. *J. Educ. Psychol.,* **20,** 537–538.

Cureton, E. E., and Dunlap, J. W. (1930) A nomograph for estimating a reliability coefficient by the Spearman-Brown formula and for computing its probable error. *J. Educ. Psychol.,* **21,** 68–69.

Dailey, J. T. (1947) *Psychological Research on Flight Engineer Training.* Report 13, AAF Aviation Psychology Program Research Reports, U. S. Government Printing Office. Pp. vii + 227.

Davidson, W. M., and Carroll, J. B. (1945) Speed and level components in time-level scores: a factor analysis. *Educ. and Psychol. Meas.,* **5,** 411–427.

Davis, F. B. (1944) A note on correcting reliability coefficients for range. *J. Educ. Psychol.,* **35,** 500–502

Davis, F. B. (1946) *Item-Analysis Data: Their Computation, Interpretation, and Use in Test Construction.* Harvard Education Papers, No. 2. Cambridge, Mass.: Graduate School of Education, Harvard University. Pp. 42.

Davis, F. B. (1947) *The AAF Qualifying Examination.* Report 6, AAF Aviation Psychology Program Research Reports, U. S. Government Printing Office. Pp. xvii + 266.

Deemer, W. L. (1942) A method of estimating accuracy of test scoring. *Psychometrika,* **7,** 65–73.

Deemer, W. L. (1947) *Records, Analysis and Test Procedures.* Report 18, AAF Aviation Psychology Program Research Reports, U. S. Government Printing Office. Pp. vii + 621.

Denney, H. R., and Remmers, H. H. (1940) Reliability of multiple-choice measuring instruments as a function of the Spearman-Brown prophecy formula, II. *J. Educ. Psychol.,* **31,** 699–704.

Dickey, J. W. (1930) On the reliability of a standard score. *J. Educ. Psychol.,* **21,** 547–549.

Dickey, J. W. (1934) On estimating the reliability coefficient. *J. Appl. Psychol.,* **18,** 103–115.

Donahue, W. T., Coombs, C. H., and Travers, R. M. W. (1949) *The Measurement of Student Adjustment and Achievement.* Ann Arbor, Mich.: University of Michigan Press. Pp. 256.

Douglass, H. R. (1934) Some observations and data on certain methods of measuring the predictive significance of the Pearson product-moment coefficient of correlation. *J. Educ. Psychol.*, **25**, 225–232.

Douglass, H. R., and Cozens, F. W. (1929) On formula for estimating the reliabilities of test batteries. *J. Educ. Psychol.*, **20**, 369–377.

Dressel, P. L. (1940) Some remarks on the Kuder-Richardson reliability coefficient. *Psychometrika*, **5**, 305–310.

DuBois, P. H. (1932) A speed factor in mental tests. *Arch Psychol.*, **22**, No. 141. Pp. 38.

DuBois, P. H. (1942) A note on the computation of bi-serial R in item validation. *Psychometrika*, **7**, 143–146.

DuBois, P. H. (1947) *The Classification Program.* Report 2, AAF Aviation Psychology Program Research Reports, U. S Government Printing Office. Pp. xiv + 394.

Duncan, W. J., Frazer, R. A., and Collar, A. R. (1938) *Elementary Matrices.* London: University of Cambridge Press.

Dunlap, J. W. (1933) Comparable tests and reliability. *J. Educ. Psychol.*, **24**, 442–453.

Dunlap, J. W. (1936a) Note on the computation of bi-serial correlation in item evaluation. *Psychometrika*, **1**, 51–58.

Dunlap, J. W. (1936b) Nomograph for computing bi-serial correlations. *Psychometrika*, **1**, 59–60.

Dunlap, J. W. (1940) Note on the computation of tetrachoric correlation. *Psychometrika*, **5**, 137–140.

Dunlap, J. W., DeMello, Adrian, and Cureton, E. E. (1929) The effects of different directions and scoring methods on the reliability of a true-false test. *School and Society*, **30**, 378–382.

Dunlap, J. W. and DiMichael, S. (1938) An abac for determining the mean deviation of a class from the general mean. *Psychometrika*, **3**, 41–43.

Dunlap, J. W., and Kurtz, A. K. (1932) *Handbook of Statistical Nomographs, Tables, and Formulas.* New York: World Book Company. Pp. vii + 163.

Edgerton, H. A. (1932) A graphic method of finding standard errors and probable errors of differences. *J. Educ. Psychol.*, **23**, 56–57.

Edgerton, H. A., and Kolbe, L. E. (1936) The method of minimum variation for the combination of criteria. *Psychometrika*, **1**, 183–187.

Edgerton, H. A., and Thomson, K. F. (1942) Test scores examined with the Lexis ratio. *Psychometrika*, **7**, 281–288.

Edgerton, H. A., and Toops, H. A. (1928a) A formula for finding the average intercorrelation coefficient for unranked raw scores without solving any of the individual intercorrelations. *J. Educ. Psychol.*, **19**, 131–138.

Edgerton, H. A., and Toops, H. A. (1928b) A table for predicting the validity and reliability coefficients of a test when lengthened. *J. Educ. Res.*, **18**, 225–234.

Ekman, Gösta. (1947) *Reliabilitet och Konstans.* Stockholm: Hugo Gebers. Pp. 291.

Engelhart, M. D. (1942) Unique types of achievement test exercises. *Psychometrika*, **7**, 103–115.

Engelhart, M. D. (1946) Suggestions with respect to experimentation under school conditions. *J. Exp. Educ.*, **14**, 225–244.

Engelhart, M. D. (1947) Suggestions for writing achievement exercises to be used in tests scored on the electric scoring machine. *Educ. and Psychol. Meas.*, **7**, 357–374.

Ferguson, G. A. (1941a) The factorial interpretation of test difficulty. *Psychometrika*, **6**, 323–329.

Ferguson, G. A. (1941b) A bi-factor analysis of reliability coefficients. *Brit. J. Psychol.*, **31**, 172–182.

Ferguson, G. A. (1942) Item selection by the constant process. *Psychometrika*, **7**, 19–29.

Finney, D. J. (1944) The application of probit analysis to the results of mental tests. *Psychometrika*, **9**, 31–39.

Finney, D. J. (1947) *Probit Analysis*. London: Cambridge University Press. Pp. 256.

Fisher, R. A. (1921) Studies in crop variation. I. An examination of the yield of dressed grain from Broadbalk. *J. Agric. Sci.*, **11**, 107–135.

Fisher, R. A. (1946) *Statistical Methods for Research Workers*. 10th Ed. London: Oliver and Boyd. Pp. xvi + 356.

Fisher, R. A. (1947) *The Design of Experiments*. 4th Ed. London: Oliver and Boyd. Pp. ix + 240.

Fisher, R. A., and MacKenzie, W. A. (1923) Studies in crop variation. II. The manurial response of different potato varieties. *J. Agric. Sci.*, **13**, 311–320.

Fitts, P. M., Jr. (1947) *Psychological Research on Equipment Design*. Report 19, AAF Aviation Psychology Program Research Reports, U. S. Government Printing Office. Pp. xii + 276.

Flanagan, J. C. (1935) *Factor Analysis in the Study of Personality*. Palo Alto, Calif.: Stanford University Press. Pp. x + 103.

Flanagan, J. C. (1936) A short method for selecting the best combination of test items for a particular purpose. *Psychol. Bull.*, **33**, 603–604.

Flanagan, J. C. (1937a) A proposed procedure for increasing the efficiency of objective tests. *J. Educ. Psychol.*, **28**, 17–21.

Flanagan, J. C. (1937b) A note on calculating the standard error of measurement and reliability coefficients with the test-scoring machine. *J. Appl. Psychol.*, **23**, 529.

Flanagan, J. C. (1939a) General considerations in the selection of test items and a short method of estimating the product moment coefficient from data at the tails of the distribution. *J. Educ. Psychol.*, **30**, 674–680.

Flanagan, J. C. (1939b) *A Bulletin Reporting the Basic Principles and Procedures Used in the Development of Their System of Scales Scores*. New York: Cooperative Test Service, American Council on Education. Pp. v + 41.

Flanagan, J. C. (1940) Item analysis by test scoring machine graphic item counter, *Proc. Educ. Res. Forum*, August 26–31, pp. 89–94. Endicott, N. Y.: International Business Machines Corporation. Pp. 127.

Flanagan, J. C. (1948) *The Aviation Psychology Program in the Army Air Forces*. Report 1, AAF Aviation Psychology Program Research Reports, U. S. Government Printing Office. Pp. xii + 316.

Foran, T. G. (1931) A note on methods of measuring reliability. *J. Educ. Psychol.*, **22**, 383–387.

Forlano, G., and Pintner, R. (1941) Selection of upper and lower groups for item validation. *J. Educ. Psychol.*, **32**, 544–549.

Franzen, Raymond. (1943) *A Method for Selecting Combinations of Tests and Determining Their Best "Cut-Off Points" to Yield a Dichotomy Most Like a Categor-*

ical Criterion. National Research Council. Civil Aeronautics Administration, Division of Research, Report 12, Washington, D. C.

Franzen, Raymond, and Derryberry, Mayhew. (1932a) Note on reliability coefficients. *J. Educ. Psychol.*, **23**, 559–560.

Franzen, Raymond, and Derryberry, Mayhew. (1932b) Reliability of group distinctions. *J. Educ. Psychol.*, **23**, 586–593.

Frederiksen, Norman (1945) *A Further Study of the Validity of the Arithmetical Computation Test.* OSRD; Publications Board, No. 13306. Washington, D. C.: U. S. Department of Commerce, 1946, pp. 12.

Freeman, F. N. (1917) A critique of the Yerkes-Bridges-Hardwick comparison of the Binet-Simon and point scales. *Psychol. Rev.*, **24**, 484.

Freeman, F. N. (1939) *Mental Tests: Their History, Principles, and Applications.* Rev. Ed. Cambridge, Mass.: The Riverside Press (Houghton Mifflin). Pp. ix + 503.

Freeman, F. S. (1928) Power and speed: their influence upon intelligence test scores. *J. Appl. Psychol.*, **12**, 631–635.

Freeman, F. S. (1931) The factors of speed and power in tests of intelligence. *J. Exp. Psychol.*, **14**, 83–90.

Freeman, F. S. (1932) The factor of speed. *J. Gen. Psychol.*, **6**, 462–468.

Frisch, Ragnar. (1934) *Statistical Confluence Analysis by Means of Complete Regression Systems.* Publication 5. Oslo University Economics Institute. Pp. 192.

Fulcher, J. S., and Zubin, Joseph. (1942) The item analyzer: a mechanical device for treating the four-fold table in large samples. *J. Appl. Psychol.*, **26**, 511–522.

Furfey, P. H. (1926) An improved rating scale technique. *J. Educ. Psychol.*, **17**, 45–48.

Galton, Francis. (1886a) Family likeness in stature. *Proc. Roy. Soc. London*, **40**, 42–73.

Galton, Francis. (1886b) Regression toward mediocrity in hereditary stature. *Roy. Anthrop. Inst. Jour.*, **15**, 246–263.

Gardner, E. F. (1947) *The Determination of Units of Measurement Which Are Consistent with Inter and Intra Grade Differences in Ability.* Thesis presented to faculty of Graduate School of Education, Harvard University.

Garrett, H. E. (1943) The discriminant function and its use in psychology. *Psychometrika*, **8**, 65–79.

Garrett, H. E. (1947) *Statistics in Psychology and Education.* 3rd Ed. New York: Longmans, Green and Company. Pp. xii + 465.

Gibbons, C. C. (1940) The predictive value of the most valid items of an examination. *J. Educ. Psychol.*, **31**, 616–621.

Gibson, J. J. (1947) *Motion Picture Testing and Research.* Report 7, AAF Aviation Psychology Program Research Reports, U. S. Government Printing Office. Pp. xi + 267.

Gilbert, J. A. (1894) Researches on the mental and physical development of school children. *Studies Yale Lab.*, **2**, 40–100.

Goodenough, F. L. (1936) Critical note on the use of the term reliability in mental measurement. *J. Educ. Psychol.*, **27**, 173–178.

Goodenough, F. L. (1949) *Mental Testing, Its History, Principles, and Applications.* New York: Rinehart and Company. Pp. xix + 609.

Gordon, Kate. (1924) Group judgments in the field of lifted weights. *J. Exp. Psychol.*, **7**, 398–400.

Green, B. F., Jr. (1950a) A note on the calculation of weights for maximum battery reliability. *Psychometrika*, **15**, 57–61.

Green, B. F., Jr.   (1950b)   A test of the equality of standard errors of measurement. *Psychometrika*, **15,** 251–257.

Greene, E. B.   (1943)   An analysis of random and systematic changes with practice. *Psychometrika*, **8,** 37–52.

Griffin, H. D.   (1930)   Nomogram for checking the reliability of test scores. *J. Appl. Psychol.*, **14,** 609–611.

Griffin, H. D.   (1932a)   Constructing a prediction chart. *J. Appl. Psychol.*, **16,** 406–412.

Griffin, H. D.   (1932b)   How to construct a nomogram. *J. Educ. Psychol.*, **23,** 561–577.

Griffin, H. D.   (1937)   Simple graphic aids for harassed psychometricians. *Psychometrika*, **2,** 69.

Grossnickle, L. T.   (1942)   The scaling of test scores by the method of paired comparisons. *Psychometrika*, **7,** 43–64.

Guiler, W. S.   (1929)   Validation of methods of testing spelling. *J. Educ. Res.*, **20,** 181–189.

Guilford, J. P.   (1936a)   The determination of item difficulty when chance success is a factor. *Psychometrika*, **1,** 259–264.

Guilford, J. P.   (1936b)   *Psychometric Methods.*   New York: McGraw-Hill Book Company.   Pp. xvi + 566.

Guilford, J. P.   (1937)   The psychophysics of mental test difficulty. *Psychometrika*, **2,** 121–133.

Guilford, J. P.   (1941a)   The phi coefficient and chi square as indices of item validity. *Psychometrika*, **6,** 11–19.

Guilford, J. P.   (1941b)   The difficulty of a test and its factor composition. *Psychometrika*, **6,** 67–77.

Guilford, J. P.   (1941c)   A simple scoring weight for test items and its reliability. *Psychometrika*, **6,** 367–374.

Guilford, J. P.   (1942)   *Fundamental Statistics in Psychology and Education.*   New York: McGraw-Hill Book Company.   Pp. xii + 333.

Guilford, J. P., and Lacey, J. I.   (1947)   *Printed Classification Tests, Parts I and II.*   Report 5, AAF Aviation Psychology Program Research Reports, U. S. Government Printing Office.   Pp. xi + 919.

Gulliksen, Harold.   (1936)   The content reliability of a test. *Psychometrika*, **1,** 189–194.

Gulliksen, Harold.   (1944)   *Selection of Test Items by Correlation with an External Criterion, as Applied to the Mechanical Comprehension Test—OQT 0–2.*   OSRD; Publications Board, No. 13319.   Washington, D. C.: U. S. Department of Commerce, 1946.   Pp. 11.

Gulliksen, Harold.   (1945)   The relation of item difficulty and interitem correlation to test variance and reliability. *Psychometrika*, **10,** 79–91.

Gulliksen, Harold.   (1949a)   Item selection to maximize test validity. *Proceedings of the 1948 Invitational Conference on Testing Problems—"Validity, Norms and the Verbal Factor,"* pp. 13–17.   Princeton, N. J.: The Educational Testing Service.   Pp. 117.

Gulliksen, Harold.   (1949b)   History of and present trends in testing. *The Sixth Yearbook of the National Council on Measurements Used in Education 1948–1949,* pp. 1–22.   Fairmont, W. Va.: National Council on Measurements Used in Education.   Pp. 72 + 43.

Gulliksen, Harold.   (1950)   The reliability of speeded tests. *Psychometrika*, **15,** 259–269.

Gulliksen, Harold, and Wilks, S. S. (1950) Regression tests for several samples. *Psychometrika*, **15**, 91–114.

Guttman, Louis. (1945) A basis for analyzing test-retest reliability. *Psychometrika*, **10**, 255–282.

Guttman, Louis. (1946) The test-retest reliability of qualitative data. *Psychometrika*, **11**, 81–95.

Hamilton, C. H. (1950) Bias and error in multiple choice tests. *Psychometrika*, **15**, 151—168.

Handy, Uvan, and Lentz, T. F. (1934) Item value and test reliability. *J. Educ. Psychol.*, **25**, 703–708.

Hawkes, H. E., Lindquist, E. F., and Mann, C. R. (1936) *The Construction and Use of Achievement Examinations*. Boston: Houghton Mifflin Company. Pp. vii + 497.

Hayes, S. P., Jr. (1946) Diagrams for computing tetrachoric correlation coefficients from percentage differences. *Psychometrika*, **11**, 163–172.

Henry, L. J. (1934) A comparison of the difficulty and validity of achievement test items. *J. Educ. Psychol.*, **25**, 537–541.

Hertzman, Max. (1936) The effects of the relative difficulty of mental tests on patterns of mental organization. *Arch. Psychol.*, **28**, No. 197. Pp. 69.

Hildreth, G. H. (1939) *A Bibliography of Mental Tests and Rating Scales*. New York: The Psychological Corporation. Pp. xxiv + 295. 2nd Ed.

Hobbs, Nicholas. (1947) *Psychological Research on Flexible Gunnery Training*. Report 11, AAF Aviation Psychology Program Research Reports, U. S. Government Printing Office. Pp. viii + 508.

Hoel, P. G. (1947) *Introduction to Mathematical Statistics*. New York: John Wiley and Sons. Pp. x + 258.

Holmes, H. W. (1917) *A Descriptive Bibliography of Measurement in Elementary Subjects*. Cambridge, Mass.: Harvard University Press. Harvard Educational Bulletin 5. Pp. vii + 46.

Holzinger, K. J. (1921) On the assumption that errors of estimate are equal in narrow and wide ranges. *J. Educ. Res.*, **4**, 237–239.

Holzinger, K. J. (1923a) An analysis of the errors in mental measurement. *J. Educ. Psychol.*, **14**, 278–288.

Holzinger, K. J. (1923b) Note on the use of Spearman's prophecy formula for reliability. *J. Educ. Psychol.*, **14**, 302–305.

Holzinger, K. J. (1924) On scoring multiple response tests. *J. Educ. Psychol.*, **15**, 445–447.

Holzinger, K. J. (1928) *Statistical Methods for Students in Education*. Boston: Ginn and Company. Pp. viii + 372.

Holzinger, K. J. (1932) Reliability of a single test item. *J. Educ. Psychol.*, **23**, 411–417.

Holzinger, K. J., and Clayton, Blythe. (1925) Further experiments in the application of Spearman's prophecy formula. *J. Educ. Psychol.*, **16**, 289–299.

Holzinger, K. J., and Swineford, F. (1934) Selected references on statistics and the theory of test construction. *School Rev.*, **42**, 459–465.

Horst, A. P. (1932a) The chance element in the multiple choice test item. *J. Gen. Psychol.*, **6**, 209–211.

Horst, A. P. (1932b) The difficulty of multiple choice test item alternatives. *J. Exp. Psychol.*, **15**, 469–472.

Horst, A. P. (1933) The difficulty of a multiple choice test item. *J. Educ. Psychol.*, **24**, 229–232.

Horst, A. P. (1934a) The economical collection of data for test validation. *J. Exp. Educ.*, **2**, 250–253.

Horst, A. P. (1934b) Item analysis by the method of successive residuals. *J. Exp. Educ.*, **2**, 254–263.

Horst, A. P. (1934c) Increasing the efficiency of selection tests. *The Personnel J.*, **12**, 254–259.

Horst, A. P. (1936a) Obtaining a composite measure from different measures of the same attributes. *Psychometrika*, **1**, 53–60.

Horst, A. P. (1936b) Item selection by means of maximizing function. *Psychometrika*, **1**, 229–244.

Horst, A. P. (1941) *The Prediction of Personal Adjustment.* SSRC Bulletin 48. Pp. 455.

Horst, A. P. (1948) Regression weights as a function of test length. *Psychometrika*, **13**, 125–134.

Horst, A. P. (1949) Determination of optimal test length to maximize the multiple correlation. *Psychometrika*, **14**, 79–88.

Hotelling, Harold. (1933) Analysis of a complex of statistical variables into principal components. *J. Educ. Psychol.*, **24**, 417–441, 498–520.

Hotelling, Harold. (1935) The most predictable criterion. *J. Educ. Psychol.*, **26**, 139–142.

Hotelling, Harold. (1936) Relations between two sets of variates. *Biometrika*, **28**, 321–377.

Hovland, C. I., and Eberhart, J. C. (1935) New method of increasing the reliability of the true-false examination. *J. Educ. Psychol.*, **26**, 388–394.

Hoyt, Cyril. (1941) Test reliability obtained by analysis of variance. *Psychometrika*, **6**, 153–160.

Hull, C. L. (1928) *Aptitude Testing.* New York: World Book Company. Pp. xiv + 535.

Jackson, Dunham. (1924) The trigonometry of correlation. *Amer. Math. Monthly*, **31**, 275–280.

Jackson, R. W. B. (1939) Reliability of mental tests. *Brit. J. Psychol.*, **29**, 267–287.

Jackson, R. W. B. (1940a) Some pitfalls in the statistical analysis of data expressed in the form of I. Q. scores. *J. Educ. Psychol.*, **31**, 677–685.

Jackson, R. W. B. (1940b) *Application of the Analysis of Variance and Covariance Method to Educational Problems.* Bulletin 11, Department of Educational Research, University of Toronto, Toronto, Canada. Pp. 103.

Jackson, R. W. B. (1942) Note on the relationship between internal consistency and test-retest estimates of the reliability of a test. *Psychometrika*, **7**, 157–164.

Jackson, R. W. B., and Ferguson, G. A. (1941) *Studies on the Reliability of Tests.* Bulletin 12. Department of Educational Research, University of Toronto, Toronto, Canada. Pp. 132.

Jastrow, J., and Morehouse, G. W. (1892) Some anthropometric and psychologic tests on college students. *Am. J. Psychol.*, **4**, 420–428.

Jenkins, W. L. (1946) A quick method for multiple *r* and partial *r*'s. *Educ. and Psychol. Meas.*, **6**, 273–286.

Johnson, P. O., and Neyman, J. (1936) Tests of certain linear hypotheses and their applications to some educational problems. *Statistical Research Memoirs*, **1**, 57–93.

Jones, E. S. (1938) Reliability in marking examinations. *J. Higher Educ.*, **8**, 436–439.

Jordan, R. C.   (1935)   An empirical study of the reliability coefficient.   *J. Educ. Psychol.*, **26**, 416–426.

Kaitz, H. B.   (1945*a*)   A note on reliability.   *Psychometrika*, **10**, 127–131.

Kaitz, H. B.   (1945*b*)   A comment on the correction of reliability coefficients for restriction of range.   *J. Educ. Psychol.*, **36**, 510–512.

Karlin, J. E.   (1942)   A factorial study of auditory function.   *Psychometrika*, **7**, 251–279.

Kelley, T. L.   (1914)   *Educational Guidance.*   Contributions to Education, No. 71. New York: Bureau of Publications, Teachers College, Columbia University.

Kelley, T. L.   (1916)   A simplified method of using scaled data for purposes of testing.   *School and Society*, **4**, 34, 71.

Kelley, T. L.   (1919)   The measurement of overlapping.   *J. Educ. Psychol.*, **10**, 458–461.

Kelley, T. L.   (1921)   The reliability of test scores.   *J. Educ. Res.*, **3**, 370–379.

Kelley, T. L.   (1923*a*)   A new method for determining the significance of differences in intelligence and achievement scores.   *J. Educ. Psychol.*, **14**, 321–333.

Kelley, T. L   (1923*b*)   The principles and techniques of mental measurement. *Amer. J. Psychol.*, **34**, 408–432.

Kelley, T. L.   (1923*c*)   *Statistical Methods.*   New York: The Macmillan Company. Pp. xi + 390.

Kelley, T. L.   (1924)   Note on the reliability of a test.   *J. Educ. Psychol.*, **15**, 193–204.

Kelley, T. L.   (1925)   The applicability of the Spearman-Brown formula for the measurement of reliability.   *J. Educ. Psychol.*, **16**, 300–303.

Kelley, T. L.   (1927)   *Interpretation of Educational Measurements.*   New York: World Book Company.   Pp. xiii + 363.

Kelley, T. L.   (1934)   The scoring of alternative responses with reference to some criterion.   *J. Educ. Psychol.*, **25**, 504–510.

Kelley, T. L.   (1939)   The selection of upper and lower groups for the validation of test items.   *J. Educ. Psychol.*, **30**, 17–24.

Kelley, T. L.   (1942)   The reliability coefficient.   *Psychometrika*, **7**, 75–83.

Kelley, T. L.   (1947)   *Fundamentals of Statistics.*   Cambridge, Mass.: Harvard University Press.   Pp. 755.

Kelly, R. L.   (1903)   Psychophysical tests of normal and abnormal children—a comparative study.   *Psychol. Rev.*, **10**, 345–372.

Kemp, E. H., and Johnson, A. P.   (1947)   *Psychological Research on Bombardier Training.*   Report 9, AAF Aviation Psychology Program Research Reports, U. S. Government Printing Office.   Pp. x + 294.

Kolbe, L. E., and Edgerton, H. A.   (1936)   A table for computing biserial *r*.   *J. Exp. Educ.*, **4**, 245–251.

Kreezer, G. L., and Bradway, K. P.   (1939)   The direct determination of the probable error of measurement of Binet mental age.   *J. Educ. Res.*, **33**, 197–214.

Kroll, A.   (1940)   Item validity as a factor in test validity.   *J. Educ. Psychol.*, **31**, 425–436.

Kuder, G. F.   (1937)   Nomograph for point bi-serial *r*, and bi-serial *r*, and four-fold correlations.   *Psychometrika*, **2**, 135–138.

Kuder, G. F., and Richardson, M. W.   (1937)   The theory of the estimation of test reliability.   *Psychometrika*, **2**, 151–160.

Kurtz, A. K.   (1937)   The simultaneous prediction of any number of criteria by the use of a unique set of weights.   *Psychometrika*, **2**, 95–101.

Lanier, L. H. (1927) Prediction of the reliability of mental tests and tests of special abilities. *J. Exp. Psychol.*, **10**, 69–113.

Larson, S. C. (1931) The shrinkage of the coefficients of multiple correlation. *J. Educ. Psychol.*, **22**, 45–55.

Lawshe, C. H. (1942) A nomograph for estimating the validity of test items. *J. Appl. Psychol.*, **26**, 846–849.

Lee, A. (1927) Supplementary table for determining correlation from tetrachoric groupings. *Biometrika*, **19**, 354–404.

Lee, J. M., and Symonds, P. M. (1934) New type or objective tests: a summary of investigations (October, 1931–October, 1933). *J. Educ. Psychol.*, **25**, 161–184.

Lentz, T. F., Hirshstein, Bertha, and Finch, J. H. (1932) Evaluation of methods of evaluating test items. *J. Educ. Psychol.*, **23**, 344–350.

Lentz, T. F., and Whitmer, E. F. (1941) Item synonymization: a method for determining the total meaning of pencil-paper reactions. *Psychometrika*, **6**, 131–139.

Lepley, W. M. (1947) *Psychological Research in the Theaters of War*. Report 17, AAF Aviation Psychology Program Research Reports, U. S. Government Printing Office. Pp. vi + 202.

Lev, Joseph. (1938) Evaluation of test items by the method of analysis of variance. *J. Educ. Psychol.*, **29**, 623–630.

Lincoln, E. A. (1932) The unreliability of reliability coefficients. *J. Educ. Psychol.*, **23**, 11–14.

Lincoln, E. A. (1933) Reliability coefficients are still unreliable. *J. Educ. Psychol.*, **24**, 235–236.

Lindquist, E. F. (1940) *Statistical Analysis in Educational Research*. Boston: Houghton Mifflin Company. Pp. xi + 266.

Lindquist, E. F., and Cook, W. W. (1933) Experimental procedures in test evaluation. *J. Exp. Educ.*, **1**, 163–185.

Loevinger, Jane. (1947) A systematic approach to the construction and evaluation of tests of ability. *Psychol. Monogr.*, **61**, 1–49.

Long, J. A. (1934) Improved overlapping methods for determining validities of test items. *J. Exp. Educ.*, **2**, 264–268.

Long, J. A., Sandiford, Peter, *et al.* (1935) *The Validation of Test Items*. Bulletin of the Department of Educational Research, Ontario College of Education, No. 3. Pp. 126.

Lord, F. M. (1944*a*) Alignment chart for calculating the four fold point correlation coefficient. *Psychometrika*, **9**, 41–42.

Lord, F. M. (1944*b*) Reliability of multiple-choice tests as a function of number of choices per item. *J. Educ. Psychol.*, **35**, 175–180.

Lorr, Maurice. (1944) Interrelationships of number-correct and limen scores for an amount-limit test. *Psychometrika*, **9**, 17–30.

Lovell, C. (1944) The effect of special construction of test items on their factor composition. *Psychol. Monogr.*, **56**, No. 6, 1–26.

McCall, W. A. (1922) *How to Measure in Education*. New York: The Macmillan Company. Pp. xii × 416.

McLeod, L. S. (1929) The interrelations of speed, accuracy, and difficulty. *J. Exp. Psychol.*, **12**, 431–443.

McNamara, W. J., and Dunlap, J. W. (1934) A graphical method for computing the standard error of bi-serial *r*. *J. Exp. Educ.*, **2**, 274–277.

McNamara, W. J., and Weitzman, E. (1946) The economy of item analysis with the IBM graphic item-counter. *J. Appl. Psychol.*, **30**, 84–90.

Mangold, Sister Mary Cecilia. (1927) *Methods for Measuring the Reliability of Tests.* Catholic University of America, Education Research Bulletins, Vol. 2, Catholic Education Press. Pp. 32.

Maurer, K. M. (1946) *Intellectual Status at Maturity as a Criterion for Selecting Items in Preschool Tests.* Institute of Child Welfare, Monograph 21. Minneapolis, Minn.: The University of Minnesota Press. Pp. 166.

Melton, A. W. (1947) *Apparatus Tests.* Report 4, AAF Aviation Psychology Program Research Reports, U. S. Government Printing Office. Pp. xxi + 1056.

Merrill, W. W., Jr. (1937) Sampling theory in item analysis. *Psychometrika*, **2**, 215–224.

Miller, N. E. (1947) *Psychological Research on Pilot Training.* Report 8, AAF Aviation Psychology Program Research Reports, U. S. Government Printing Office. Pp. xix + 488.

Mollenkopf, W. G. (1948) *Variation of the Standard Error of Measurement.* Thesis, Department of Psychology, Princeton University. Pp. 86. Also published in *Psychometrika* (1949), **14**, 189–229.

Mollenkopf, W. G. (1950) Predicted differences and differences between predictions. *Psychometrika*, **15**, 409–417.

Monroe, P. (Editor) (1939) *Conference on Examinations at Dinard, France, September 16–19, 1938.* New York: Bureau of Publications, Teachers College, Columbia University. Pp. xiii + 330.

Monroe, W. S. (1923a) *An Introduction to the Theory of Educational Measurements.* Boston: Houghton Mifflin Company. Pp. xxiii + 364.

Monroe, W. S. (1923b) *The Theory of Educational Measurements.* Boston: Houghton Mifflin Company. Pp. 364.

Monroe, W. S., *et al.* (1928) *Ten Years of Educational Research, 1918–1927.* Bureau of Educational Research Bulletin, College of Education, University of Illinois, No. 42.

Monroe, W. S. (1934) A note on efficiency of prediction. *J. Educ. Psychol.*, **25**, 547–548.

Monroe, W. S., DeVoss, J. C., and Kelly, F. J. (1924) *Educational Tests and Measurements.* Boston: Houghton Mifflin Company. Pp. xxvii + 521.

Monroe, W. S., and Engelhart, M. D. (1936) *Scientific Study of Educational Problems.* New York: The Macmillan Company. Pp. xv + 504.

Moore, C. C. (1940) The rights-minus-wrongs method of correcting chance factors in the T-F examination. *J. Genet. Psychol.*, **57**, 317–326.

Mosier, C. I. (1936) A note on item analysis and the criterion of internal consistency. *Psychometrika*, **1**, 275–282.

Mosier, C. I. (1940) Psychophysics and mental test theory. I. Fundamental postulates and elementary theorems. *Psychol. Rev.*, **47**, 355–366.

Mosier, C. I. (1941) Psychophysics and mental test theory. II. The constant process. *Psychol. Rev.*, **48**, 235–249.

Mosier, C. I. (1943) On the reliability of a weighted composite. *Psychometrika*, **8**, 161–168.

Mosier, C. I., and McQuitty, J. V. (1940) Methods of item validation and abacs for item-test and critical ratio of upper-lower difference. *Psychometrika*, **5**, 57–65.

Mosteller, Frederick. (1946) On some useful "inefficient" statistics. *Annals Math. Stat.*, **17**, 377–408.

Muenzinger, K. F. (1927) Critical note on the reliability of a test. *J. Educ. Psychol.*, **18**, 424–428.

Mursell, J. L. (1947) *Psychological Testing.* New York: Longmans, Green and Company. Pp. 449.

National Society for the Study of Education. (1916) *Standards and Tests for the Measurement of the Efficiency of Schools and School Systems.* 15th Yearbook, Part I. Bloomington, Ill.: Public School Publishing Company. Pp. 172.

National Society for the Study of Education. (1918) *The Measurement of Educational Products.* 17th Yearbook, Part II. Bloomington, Ill.: Public School Publishing Company.

National Society for the Study of Education. (1922) *Intelligence Tests and Their Use.* 21st Yearbook, Parts I and II. Bloomington, Ill.: Public School Publishing Company.

Neyman, J. (1937) Outline of a theory of statistical estimation based on the classical theory of probability. *Phil. Trans.* **236**-A, 333–380. London: Royal Society.

Neyman, J., and Pearson, E. S. (1933) On the problem of the most efficient test of statistical hypotheses. *Phil. Trans.* **231**-A, 289–337. London: Royal Society.

Neyman, J., and Pearson, E. S. (1936a) Contributions to the theory of testing statistical hypotheses. I. Unbiassed critical regions of type A and type A_1. *Statistical Research Memoirs,* **1,** 1–37.

Neyman, J., and Pearson, E. S. (1936b) Sufficient statistics and uniformly most powerful tests of statistical hypotheses. *Statistical Research Memoirs,* **1,** 113–137.

Norsworthy, Naomi. (1906) The psychology of mentally deficient children. *Arch. Psychol.,* **1,** 1–111.

Nygaard, P. H. (1923) The advantages of the probable error of measurement as a criterion of the reliability of a test or scale. *J. Educ. Psychol.,* **14,** 407–413.

Orleans, J. S. (1937) *Measurement in Education.* New York: Thomas Nelson and Sons. Pp. xvi + 461.

Osburn, W. J. (1933) The selection of test items. *Rev. Educ. Res.,* **3,** 21–32, 62–65.

Otis, A. S. (1916) Reliability of spelling scales involving a deviation formula for correlation. *School and Society,* **4,** Part I, 676–683; Part II, 716–722; Part III, 750–756; Part IV, 793–796.

Otis, A. S. (1922a) The method for finding the correspondence between scores in two tests. *J. Educ. Psychol.,* **13,** 529–545.

Otis, A. S. (1922b) A method of inferring the change in a coefficient of correlation resulting from a change in the heterogeneity of the group. *J. Educ. Psychol.,* **13,** 293–294.

Otis, A. S. (1925) *Statistical Method in Educational Measurement.* New York: World Book Company. Pp. xi + 339.

Otis, A. S., and Davidson, P. E. (1912) Reliability of standard scores in adding ability. *Elem. School Teacher,* **13,** 91–105.

Otis, A. S., and Knollin, H. E. (1921) The reliability of the Binet scale and of pedagogical scales. *J. Educ. Res.,* **4,** 121–142.

Paterson, D. G., and Tinker, M. A. (1930) Time-limit versus work-limit methods. *Amer. J. Psychol.,* **42,** 101–104.

Paulsen, G. (1931) A coefficient of trait variability. *Psychol. Bull.,* **28,** 218–219.

Peak, H., and Boring, E. G. (1926) The factor of speed in intelligence. *J. Exp. Psychol.,* **9,** 71–94.

Pearson, E. S., and Wilks, S. S. (1933) Methods of statistical analysis appropriate for k samples of two variables. *Biometrika,* **25,** Nos. 3 and 4, 353–378.

Pearson, Karl. (1896) Mathematical contributions to the theory of evolution. III. Regression, heredity, and panmixia. *Phil. Trans.* **187**-A, 253–318. London: Royal Society.

Pearson, Karl. (1900) Mathematical contributions to the theory of evolution. VII. On the correlation of characters not quantitatively measurable. *Phil. Trans.* **195**-A, 1–47. London: Royal Society.

Pearson, Karl. (1903*a*) Mathematical contributions to the theory of evolution. XI. On the influence of natural selection on the variability and correlation of organs. *Phil. Trans.* **200**-A, 1–66. London: Royal Society.

Pearson, Karl. (1903*b*) On a general theory of the method of false position. *Phil. Mag.*, **4**, 658–668, 6th series.

Pearson, Karl. (1904) On the laws of inheritance in man. II. On the inheritance of the mental and moral characters in man and its comparison with the inheritance of the physical characters. *Biometrika*, **3**, 131–160.

Pearson, Karl. (1907) Mathematical contributions to the theory of evolution. XVI. On further methods of determining correlation. Drapers' Company, *Research Memoirs*, Biometric Series IV. Pp. 39. London: Cambridge University Press.

Pearson, Karl. (1910*a*) On a new method of determining correlation between a measured character A and a character B of which only the percentage of cases wherever B exceeds (or falls short of) a given intensity is recorded for each grade of A. *Biometrika*, **7**, 96–105.

Pearson, Karl. (1910*b*) On a new method of determining correlation when one variable is given by alternatives and the other by multiple categories. *Biometrika*, **7**, 248–257.

Pearson, Karl. (1912) On the general theory of the influence of selection on correlation and variation. *Biometrika*, **8**, 437–443.

Peel, E. A. (1947) A short method for calculating maximum battery reliability. *Nature*, **159**, 816.

Peel, E. A. (1948) Prediction of a complex criterion and battery reliability. *Brit. J. Psychol.*, **1**, 84–94.

Peters, C. C., and VanVoorhis, W. R. (1940) *Statistical Procedures and Their Mathematical Bases*. New York: McGraw-Hill Book Company. Pp. xiii + 516.

Peterson, D. A. (1944) The Preparation of Norms for the Fleet Edition of the General Classification Test. OSRD; Publications Board, No. 13295. Washington, D. C.: U. S. Department of Commerce, 1946. Pp. 17.

Pintner, R., and Forlano, G. (1937) A comparison of methods of item selection for a personality test. *J. Appl. Psychol.*, **21**, 643–652.

Preston, M. G. (1940) Concerning the determination of trait variability. *Psychometrika*, **5**, 275–281.

Read, C. B. (1939) A note on reliability by the chance halves method. *J. Educ. Psychol.*, **30**, 703–704.

Remmers, H. H. (1931) The equivalence of judgments to test items in the sense of the Spearman-Brown formula. *J. Educ. Psychol.*, **22**, 66–71.

Remmers, H. H., and Adkins, R. M. (1942) Reliability of multiple-choice measuring instruments as a function of the Spearman-Brown prophecy formula, VI. *J. Educ. Psychol.*, **33**, 385–390.

Remmers, H. H., and Ewart, Edwin. (1941) Reliability of multiple-choice measuring instruments as a function of the Spearman-Brown prophecy formula, III. *J. Educ. Psychol.*, **32**, 61–66.

Remmers, H. H., and House, J. M.   (1941)   Reliability of multiple-choice measuring instruments as a function of the Spearman-Brown prophecy formula, IV. *J. Educ. Psychol.*, **32**, 372–376.

Remmers, H. H., Karslake, Ruth, and Gage, N. L.   (1940)   Reliability of multiple-choice measuring instruments as a function of the Spearman-Brown prophecy formula, I. *J. Educ. Psychol.*, **31**, 583–590.

Remmers, H. H., and Sageser, H. W.   (1941)   Reliability of multiple-choice measuring instruments as a function of the Spearman-Brown prophecy formula, V. *J. Educ. Psychol.*, **32**, 445–451.

Remmers, H. H., Shock, N. W., and Kelley, E. L.   (1927)   An empirical study of the validity of the Spearman-Brown formula as applied to the Purdue rating scale. *J. Educ. Psychol.*, **18**, 187–195.

Remmers, H. H., and Whisler, L.   (1938)   Test reliability as a function of method of computation.   *J. Educ. Psychol.*, **29**, 81–92.

Richardson, M. W.   (1935)   Abac for Computing Tetrachoric Coefficients in Item Analysis. Chicago: University of Chicago Board of Examinations.

Richardson, M. W.   (1936a)   The relation of difficulty to the differential validity of a test. *Psychometrika*, **1**, 33–49.

Richardson, M. W.   (1936b)   Notes on the rationale of item analysis. *Psychometrika*, **1**, 69–76.

Richardson, M. W., and Adkins, D. C.   (1938)   A rapid method of selecting test items.   *J. Educ. Psychol.*, **29**, 547–552.

Richardson, M. W., and Kuder, G. F.   (1939)   The calculation of test reliability coefficients based on the method of rational equivalence.   *J. Educ. Psychol.*, **30**, 681–687.

Richardson, M. W., and Stalnaker, J. M.   (1933)   A note on the use of bi-serial *r* in test research. *J. Gen. Psychol.*, **8**, 463–465.

Rogers, D. C.   (1933)   An argument for centile ranks.   *J. Educ. Psychol.*, **24**, 107–117.

Ross, C. C.   (1947)   *Measurement in Today's Schools.*   New York: Prentice-Hall, Inc. Pp. 551.

Royer, E. B.   (1941)   A machine method for computing the biserial correlation coefficient in item validation. *Psychometrika*, **6**, 55–59.

Ruch, G. M.   (1929)   *The Objective or New Type Examination.*   Chicago: Scott, Foresman and Company. Pp. 478.

Ruch, G. M., Ackerson, Luton, and Jackson, J. P.   (1926)   An empirical study of the Spearman-Brown formula as applied to educational test material.   *J. Educ. Psychol.*, **17**, 309–313.

Ruch, G. M., and Degraff, M. H.   (1926)   Corrections for chance and "guess" versus "do not guess" instructions in multiple response tests.   *J. Educ. Psychol.*, **17**, 368–375.

Ruch, G. M., and Stoddard, G. D.   (1925)   Comparative reliabilities of five types of objective examinations. *J. Educ. Psychol.*, **16**, 89–103.

Ruch, G. M., and Stoddard, G. D.   (1927)   *Tests and Measurements in High-School Instruction.*   New York: World Book Company. Pp. xix + 381.

Ruger, G. J.   (1918)   *Bibliography of Psychological Tests.*   New York: Bureau of Educational Measurements. Pp. 116.

Rulon, P. J.   (1930)   A graph for estimating reliability in one range, knowing it in another. *J. Educ. Psychol.*, **21**, 140–142.

Rulon, P. J.   (1939)   A simplified procedure for determining the reliability of a test by split-halves. *Harvard Educ. Rev.*, **9**, 99–103.

Rulon, P. J. (1946) On the validity of educational tests. *Harvard Educ. Rev.*, **16**, 290–296.

Rulon, P. J. (1947) Validity of educational tests. (An article in *National Projects in Educational Measurement*. A Report of the 1946 Invitational Conference on Testing Problems, sponsored by the Committee on Measurement and Guidance.) American Council on Education Studies.

Sargent, S. S. (1940) Thinking processes at various levels of difficulty. *Arch. Psychol.*, **35**, No. 249. Pp. 58.

Satter, G. A. (1944) *Selection of Items for the U. S. Navy General Classification Test (Form 2) and the U. S. Navy Tests of Reading and Arithmetical Reasoning (Form 2)*. OSRD: Publications Board, No. 13298. Washington, D. C.: U. S. Department of Commerce, 1946. Pp. 43.

Satter, G. A., and Conrad, H. S. (1945) *Predicting Success in Service School from the Order of Assignment*. OSRD: Publications Board, No. 13292. Washington, D. C.: U. S. Department of Commerce, 1946. Pp. 35.

Satter, G. A., and Frederiksen, Norman. (1945) The Construction and Validation of an Arithmetical Computation Test. OSRD Report No. 4556, Jan. 8, 1945. Pp. 44. (See Stuit, 1947, pp. 468.)

Scates, D. E. (1947) Fifty years of objective measurement and research in education. *J. Educ. Res.*, **41**, 241–264.

Schrader, W. B., and Conrad, H. S. (1948) Tests and measurements. *Rev. Educ. Res.*, **18**, 448–468.

Segel, David. (1933) A note on an error made in investigations of homogeneous grouping. *J. Educ. Psychol.*, **24**, 64–66.

Sharp, S. E. (1899) Individual psychology: a study in psychological methods. *Amer. J. Psychol.*, **10**, 329–391.

Sims, V. M. (1929) The reliability and validity of four types of vocabulary tests. *J. Educ. Res.*, **20**, 91–96.

Sims, V. M., and Knox, L. B. (1932) The reliability and validity of multiple response tests when presented orally. *J. Educ. Psychol.*, **23**, 656–662.

Skaggs, E. B. (1927) Some critical comments on certain prevailing concepts and methods used in mental testing. *J. Appl. Psychol.*, **11**, 503–508.

Slocombe, C. S. (1927a) The Spearman prophecy formula. *J. Educ. Psychol.*, **18**, 125–126.

Slocombe, C. S. (1927b) A further note on the Spearman prophecy formula; a correction. *J. Educ. Psychol.*, **18**, 347–348.

Smith, B. O. (1938) *Logical Aspects of Educational Measurement*. New York: Columbia University Press. Pp. x + 182.

Smith, Max. (1934) *The Relationship between Item Validity and Test Validity*. Contributions to Education, No. 621. New York: Bureau of Publications, Teachers College, Columbia University.

Snedecor, G. W. (1946) *Statistical Methods*. 4th Ed. Ames, Iowa: Iowa State College Press. Pp. xvi + 485.

Social Science Research Council. (1949) *Studies in Social Psychology in the Army*. Vol. I, *The American Soldier: Adjustment during Army Life*. Vol. II, *The American Soldier: Combat and Its Aftermath*. Vol. III, *Experiments on Mass Communication*. Vol. IV, *Measurement and Prediction* (1950). Princeton, N. J.: Princeton University Press.

Spearman, Charles. (1904a) The proof and measurement of association between two things. *Amer. J. Psychol.*, **15**, 72–101.

Spearman, Charles. (1904b) "General intelligence" objectively determined and measured. *Amer. J. Psychol.*, **15**, 201–292.

Spearman, Charles. (1907) Demonstration of formulae for true measurement of correlation. *Amer. J. Psychol.*, **18**, 161–169.

Spearman, Charles. (1910) Correlation calculated with faulty data. *Brit. J. Psychol.*, **3**, 271–295.

Spearman, Charles. (1913) Correlations of sums and differences. *Brit. J. Psychol.*, **5**, 417–426.

Spearman, Charles. (1927) *The Abilities of Man.* New York: The Macmillan Company. Pp. vi + 415 + xxxiii.

Stalnaker, J. M. (1938) Weighting questions in the essay-type examination. *J. Educ. Psychol.*, **29**, 481–490.

Stalnaker, J. M. (1940) Computing difficulty index and validity index in item analysis by electric accounting machines, *Proc. Educ. Res. Forum*, August 26–31, pp. 80–88. Endicott, N. Y.: International Business Machines Corporation. Pp. 127.

Stalnaker, J. M., and Richardson, M. W. (1933) A note concerning the combination of test scores. *J. Gen. Psychol.*, **8**, 460–463.

Starch, D., and Elliot, E. C. (1912) Reliability of grading high-school work in English. *School Rev.*, September, 442–457.

Starch, D., and Elliot, E. C. (1913a) Reliability of grading high-school work in mathematics. *School Rev.*, April, 254–259.

Starch, D., and Elliot, E. C. (1913b) Reliability of grading high-school work in history. *School Rev.*, December, 676–681.

Stead, W. H., Shartle, C. L., *et al.* (1940) *Occupational Counseling Techniques.* New York: American Book Company. Pp. ix + 273.

Stephenson, William. (1934) Factorizing the reliability coefficient. *Brit. J. Psychol.*, **25**, 211–216.

Stern, William. (1914) *The Psychological Methods of Testing Intelligence.* Translated from the German by Guy Montrose Whipple. Cornell University; Educational Psychol. Monograph, No. 13. Baltimore: Warwick and York. Pp. x + 160.

Stouffer, S. A. (1936) Reliability coefficients in a correlation matrix. *Psychometrika*, **1**, 17–20.

Stuit, D. B. (Ed.) (1947) *Personnel Research and Test Development in the Bureau of Naval Personnel.* Princeton, N. J.: Princeton University Press. Pp. xxiv + 513.

Swineford, Frances. (1936a) Validity of test items. *J. Educ. Psychol.*, **27**, 68–78.

Swineford, Frances. (1936b) Biserial r versus Pearson r as measures of test-item validity. *J. Educ. Psychol.*, **27**, 471–472.

Swineford, Frances. (1946) Graphical and tabular aids for determining sample size when planning experiments which involve comparisons of percentages. *Psychometrika*, **11**, 43–49.

Swineford, Frances, and Holzinger, K. J. (1933 to 1948) Selected references on statistics, the theory of test construction, and factor analysis. *School Rev.*, **41–56**. (This is an annotated bibliography which has appeared annually in the June issue of the *School Review;* according to present plans it will continue to be issued annually.)

Symonds, P. M. (1927) *Measurement in Secondary Education.* New York: The Macmillan Company. Pp. 605.

Symonds, P. M. (1928) Factors influencing test reliability. *J. Educ. Psychol.*, **19**, 73–87.

Symonds, P. M.   (1929)   Choice of items for a test on the basis of difficulty.   *J. Educ. Psychol.*, **20**, 481–493.

Taylor, C. W.   (1950)   Maximizing predictive efficiency for a fixed total testing time.   *Psychometrika*, **15**, 391–406.

Thompson, G. G., and Witryol, S. L.   (1946)   The relationship between intelligence and motor learning ability, as measured by a high relief finger maze.   *J. Psychol.*, **22**, 237–246.

Thomson, G. H.   (1940)   Weighting for battery reliability and prediction.   *Brit. J. Psychol.*, **30**, 357–366.

Thomson, G. H.   (1946)   *The Factorial Analysis of Human Ability.*   Boston: Houghton Mifflin Company.   London: University of London Press.   Pp. xvi + 386.

Thomson, G. H.   (1947)   The maximum correlation of two weighted batteries.   *Brit. J. Psychol.*, Statistical Section, **1**, 27–34.

Thomson, G. H.   (1948)   Note on the relations of two weighted batteries.   *Brit. J. Psychol.*, Statistical Section, **1**, 82–83.

Thorndike, E. L.   (1907)   Empirical studies in the theory of measurement.   *Arch. Psychol.*, **1**, No. 3, 1–45.

Thorndike, E. L.   (1919)   *An Introduction to the Theory of Mental and Social Measurements.*   2nd Ed., Revised and Enlarged.   New York: Bureau of Publications, Teachers College, Columbia University.   Pp. xi + 277.

Thorndike, E. L.   (1922)   On finding equivalent scores in tests of intelligence.   *J. Appl. Psychol.*, **6**, 29–33.

Thorndike, E. L., et al.   (1927)   *The Measurement of Intelligence.*   New York: Bureau of Publications, Teachers College, Columbia University.   Pp. xxvi + 616.

Thorndike, R. L.   (1947)   *Research Problems and Techniques.*   Report No. 3, AAF Aviation Psychology Program Research Reports, U. S. Government Printing Office.   Pp. viii + 163.

Thorndike, R. L.   (1949)   *Personnel Selection (Test and Measurement Techniques).*   New York: John Wiley and Sons.   Pp. viii + 358.

Thouless, R. H.   (1936)   Test unreliability and function fluctuation.   *Brit. J. Psychol.*, **26**, 325–343.

Thouless, R. H.   (1939)   The effect of errors of measurement on correlation coefficients.   *Brit. J. Psychol.*, **29**, 383–403.

Thurstone, L. L.   (1919)   A method for scoring tests.   *Psychol. Bull.*, **16**, 235–240.

Thurstone, L. L.   (1925)   A method of scaling psychological and educational tests.   *J. Educ. Psychol.*, **16**, 433–451.

Thurstone, L. L.   (1926)   The mental age concept.   *Psychol. Rev.*, **33**, 268–278.

Thurstone, L. L.   (1927a)   Equally often noticed differences.   *J. Educ. Psychol.*, **18**, 289–293.

Thurstone, L. L.   (1927b)   The unit of measurement in educational scales.   *J. Educ. Psychol.*, **18**, 505–524.

Thurstone, L. L.   (1928a)   A note on the Spearman-Brown formula.   *J. Exp. Psychol.*, **11**, 62–63.

Thurstone, L. L.   (1928b)   The absolute zero in intelligence measurement.   *Psychol. Rev.*, **35**, 175–197.

Thurstone, L. L.   (1931a)   *The Reliability and Validity of Tests.*   Ann Arbor, Mich.: Edwards Brothers.   Pp. 113.

Thurstone, L. L.   (1931b)   The indifference function.   *J. Soc. Psychol.*, **2**, No. 2, 139–167.

Thurstone, L. L.   (1932)   *The Theory of Multiple Factors.*   Ann Arbor, Mich.: Edwards Brothers.   Pp. vii + 65.

Thurstone, L. L. (1935a) *The Vectors of Mind.* Chicago: The University of Chicago Press. Pp. 266.

Thurstone, L. L. (1935b) *Fundamentals of Statistics.* New York: The Macmillan Company. Pp. xvi + 237.

Thurstone, L. L. (1937) Ability, motivation, and speed. *Psychometrika,* **2,** 249–254.

Thurstone, L. L. (1938) Primary mental abilities. *Psychometric Monogr.,* **1** Chicago: The University of Chicago Press. Pp. ix + 121.

Thurstone, L. L. (1944) *A Factorial Study of Perception.* Chicago: The University of Chicago Press. Pp. 148.

Thurstone, L. L. (1947a) The calibration of test items. *The American Psychologist,* **2,** No. 3, 103–104.

Thurstone, L. L. (1947b) *Multiple Factor Analysis.* Chicago: The University of Chicago Press. Pp. 535.

Thurstone, L. L., and Thurstone, T. G. (1941) Factorial Studies of Intelligence. *Psychometric Monogr.,* **2.** Chicago: The University of Chicago Press. Pp. 94.

Thurstone, T. G. (1932) The difficulty of a test and its diagnostic value. *J. Educ. Psychol.,* **23,** 335–343.

Toops, H. A. (1923) *Tests for Vocational Guidance of Children Thirteen to Sixteen.* Contributions to Education, No. 136. New York: Bureau of Publications, Teachers College, Columbia University.

Toops, H. A. (1941) The L-method. *Psychometrika,* **6,** 249–266.

Toops, H. A. (1944) The criterion. *Educ. and Psychol. Meas.,* **4,** 271–297.

Toops, H. A., and Edgerton, H. A. (1927) An abac for determining the probable correlation over a larger range knowing it over a shorter one. *J. Educ. Res.,* **16,** 382–385.

Toops, H. A., and Symonds, P. M. (1922) What shall we expect of the A. Q.? *J. Educ. Psychol.,* **13,** 513–528.

Trabue, M. R. (1916) *Completion-Test Language Scales.* Contributions to Education, No. 77. New York: Bureau of Publications, Teachers College, Columbia University. Pp. 118.

Travers, R. M. W. (1939) The use of a discriminant function in the treatment of psychological group differences. *Psychometrika,* **4,** 25–32.

Travers, R. M. W. (1942) A note on the value of customary measures of item validity. *J. Appl. Psychol.,* **26,** 625–632.

Trimble, O. C. (1934) The oral examination: its validity and reliability. *School and Society,* **39,** 550–552.

Tucker, L. R. (1946) Maximum validity of a test with equivalent items. *Psychometrika,* **11,** 1–13.

Tucker, L. R. (1948) The problem of differential criteria (an article in *Exploring Individual Differences, A Report of the 1947 Invitational Conference on Testing Problems*), pp. 63–70. Washington, D. C.: American Council on Education. Pp. vii + 110.

Turnbull, W. W. (1946) A normalized graphic method of item analysis. *J. Educ. Psychol.,* **37,** 129–141.

Turney, A. H. (1932) The cumulative reliability of frequent short objective tests. *J. Educ. Res.,* **25,** 290–295.

Uhrbrock, R. S. (1936) Analysis of 4378 test items. *Psychol. Bull.,* **33,** 737 (abstract).

Uhrbrock, R. S., and Richardson, M. W. (1933) Item analysis: the basis for constructing a test for forecasting supervisory ability. *The Personnel J.*, **12**, No. 3, 141–154.

United States Army Air Forces Aviation Psychology Program Research Reports. U. S. Government Printing Office.

Report No.
1. Flanagan, J. C. (1948) *The Aviation Psychology Program in the AAF.*
2. DuBois, P. H. (1947) *The Classification Program.*
3. Thorndike, R. L. (1947) *Research Problems and Techniques.*
4. Melton, A. W. (1947) *Apparatus Tests.*
5. Guilford, J. P., and Lacey, J. I. (1947) *Printed Classification Tests.*
6. Davis, F. B. (1947) *The AAF Qualifying Examination.*
7. Gibson, J. J. (1947) *Motion Picture Testing and Research.*
8. Miller, N. E. (1947) *Psychological Research on Pilot Training.*
9. Kemp, E. H., and Johnson, A. P. (1947) *Psychological Research on Bombardier Training.*
10. Carter, L. F. (1947) *Psychological Research on Navigator Training.*
11. Hobbs, Nicholas. (1947) *Psychological Research on Flexible Gunnery Training.*
12. Cook, S. W (1947) *Psychological Research on Radar Observer Training.*
13. Dailey, J. T. (1947) *Psychological Research on Flight Engineer Training.*
14. Wickert, F. (1947) *Psychological Research on Problems of Redistribution.*
15. Bijou, S. W. (1947) *The Psychological Program in AAF Convalescent Hospitals.*
16. Crawford, M. P., et al. (1947) *Psychological Research on Operational Training in the Continental Air Forces.*
17. Lepley, W. M. (1947) *Psychological Research in the Theaters of War.*
18. Deemer, W. L., Jr. (1947) *Records, Analysis, and Test Procedures.*
19. Fitts, P. M. (1947) *Psychological Research on Equipment Design.*

United States War Department. (1943) *Army Instruction.* Technical Manual. 21–250. U. S. Government Printing Office. Pp. 227.

United States War Department. (1946) *Personnel Classification Tests.* Technical Manual 12–260. U. S. Government Printing Office. Pp. 90.

University of Chicago. (1937) *Manual of Examination Methods.* 2nd Ed. By Technical Staff, The Board of Examinations, University of Chicago. University of Chicago Bookstore. Pp. 177.

Vincent, L. E. (1924) *A Study of Intelligence Test Elements.* Contributions to Education, No. 152. New York: Bureau of Publications, Teachers College, Columbia University. Pp. 37.

Votaw, D. F. (1933) Graphical determination of probable error in validation of test items. *J. Educ. Psychol.*, **24**, 682–686.

Votaw, D. F. (1934) Notes on the validation of test items by comparison of widely spaced groups. *J. Educ. Psychol.*, **25**, 185–191.

Votaw, D. F., Jr. (1947) Testing Compound Symmetry in a Normal Multivariate Distribution. Ph.D. Thesis. Princeton, N. J.: Princeton University. Pp. 63. Also published in *Annals Math. Stat.*, 1948, **19**, pp. 447–473.

Walker, D. A. (1931) Answer pattern and score scatter in tests and examinations. *Brit. J. Psychol.*, **22**, 73–86.

Walker, D. A. (1936) Answer pattern and score scatter in tests and examinations. *Brit. J. Psychol.*, **26**, 301–308.

Walker, D. A. (1940) Answer pattern and score scatter in tests and examinations. *Brit. J. Psychol.*, **30**, 248–260.

Walker, H. M. (1929) *Studies in the History of Statistical Method with Special Reference to Certain Educational Problems.* Baltimore: The Williams and Wilkins Company. Pp. viii + 229.

Weichelt, J. A. (1946) A first-order method for estimating correlation coefficients. *Psychometrika*, **11**, 215–221.

Weidmann, C. C. (1930) Reliability or consistency coefficient. *School and Society*, **31**, 674.

Weidmann, C. C., and Newens, L. F. (1933) The effect of directions preceding true-false and indeterminate statement examinations upon distributions of test scores. *J. Educ. Psychol.*, **24**, 97–106.

Wesman, A. G. (1949) The effect of speed on item-test correlation coefficients. *Educ. and Psychol., Meas.*, **9**, 51–57.

Whelden, C. H., and Davis, F. J. J. (1931) A method for judging the discrimination of individual questions on true-false examinations. *J. Educ. Psychol.*, **22**, 290–306.

Wherry, R. J. (1940) An approximation method for obtaining a maximized multiple criterion. *Psychometrika*, **5**, 109–115.

Wherry, R. J. (1944) Maximal weighting of qualitative data. *Psychometrika*, **9**, 263–266.

Wherry, R. J. (1946) Test selection and suppressor variables. *Psychometrika*, **11**, 239–247.

Wherry, R. J., and Gaylord, R. H. (1943) The concept of test and item reliability in relation to factor pattern. *Psychometrika*, **8**, 247–264.

Wherry, R. J., and Gaylord, R. H. (1944) Factor pattern of test items and tests as a function of the correlation coefficient, content, difficulty and constant error factors. *Psychometrika*, **9**, 237–244.

Wherry, R. J., and Gaylord, R. H. (1946) Test selection with integral gross score weights. *Psychometrika*, **11**, 173–183.

Whipple, G. M. (1914) *Manual of Mental and Physical Tests.* Baltimore: Warwick and York. Vol. I. Pp. 354.

Whipple, G. M. (1915) *Manual of Mental and Physical Tests.* Baltimore: Warwick and York. Vol. II. Pp. 336.

Wickert, F. (1947) *Psychological Research on Problems of Redistribution.* Report No. 14, AAF Aviation Psychology Program Research Reports. U. S. Government Printing Office. Pp. vii + 298.

Wilks, S. S. (1938) Weighting systems for linear functions of correlated variables when there is no dependent variable. *Psychometrika*, **3**, 23–40.

Wilks, S. S. (1943) *Mathematical Statistics.* Princeton, N. J.: Princeton University Press. Pp. 284.

Wilks, S. S. (1946) Sample criteria for testing equality of means, equality of variances, and equality of covariances in a normal multivariate distribution. *The Annals Math. Stat.* **17**, 257–281.

Wilks, S. S. (1948) *Elementary Statistical Analysis.* Princeton, N. J.: Princeton University Press. Pp. xi + 283.

Wissler, Clark. (1901) The correlation of mental and physical tests. *Psychol. Monogr.*, **3**, No. 16, 1–62.

Wolfle, Dael. (1940) Factor Analysis to 1940. *Psychometric Monogr.* No. 3. Pp. 69. University of Chicago Press.

Wood, B. D. (1926a) Studies of achievement tests. I. *J. Educ. Psychol.*, **17**, 1–22.

Wood, B. D. (1926b) Studies of achievement tests. II. *J. Educ. Psychol.*, **17**, 125–139.

Wood, B. D. (1926c) Studies of achievement tests. III. Spearman-Brown reliability predictions. *J. Educ. Psychol.*, **17**, 263–269.

Woodrow, Herbert. (1932) Quotidian variability. *Psychol. Rev.*, **39**, 245–256.

Woodrow, Herbert. (1937) The scaling of practice data. *Psychometrika*, **2**, 237–247.

Working, H., and Hotelling, H. (1929) The application of the theory of error to the interpretation of trends. *J. Amer. Stat. Assn.*, **24**, 73–85.

Yerkes, R. M., Bridges, J. W., and Hardwick, R. S. (1915) *A Point Scale for Measuring Mental Ability.* Baltimore: Warwick and York. Pp. 218

Yule, G. U. (1897) On the theory of correlation. *J. Roy. Stat. Soc.*, **60**, 812–854.

Yule, G. U. (1912) On the methods of measuring the association between two attributes. *J. Roy. Stat. Soc.*, **75**, 579–642.

Yule, G. U. (1924) *An Introduction to the Theory of Statistics.* 7th Ed. London: Charles Griffin and Company. Pp. xv + 415.

Yule, G. U., and Kendall, M. G. (1940) *An Introduction to the Theory of Statistics.* 12th Ed. Rev. London: Charles Griffin and Company. Pp. xiii + 570.

Zubin, Joseph. (1934) The method of internal consistency for selecting test items. *J. Educ. Psychol.*, **25**, 345–356.

Zubin, Joseph. (1939) Nomographs for determining the significance of the differences between the frequencies of events in two contrasted series or groups. *J. Amer. Stat. Assn.*, **34**, 539–544

APPENDIX A

Equations from Algebra, Analytical Geometry, and Statistics, Used in Test Theory

Elementary algebra assumed for test theory

Expansion of binomials:

$$(x + y)^2 = x^2 + 2xy + y^2$$

$$(x - y)^2 = x^2 - 2xy + y^2$$

$$(x + y)^n = x^n + nx^{n-1}y + \frac{n(n-1)}{2} x^{n-2}y^2 + \cdots + \frac{n!}{r!(n-r)!} x^{n-r}y^r$$

$$+ \cdots + nxy^{n-1} + y^n$$

Factorial notation:

$$n! = n(n-1)(n-2) \cdots (3)(2)(1)$$

Expansion of polynomials:

$$(a + b + \cdots + y + z)^2 = a^2 + b^2 + \cdots + y^2 + z^2$$

$$+ 2ab + \cdots + 2ay + 2az + \cdots$$

$$+ 2by + 2bz + \cdots + 2yz$$

$$(a + b + \cdots + y + z)(A + B + \cdots + Y + Z)$$

$$= aA + aB + \cdots + aY + aZ + bA + bB + \cdots + bY + bZ + \cdots$$

$$+ yA + yB + \cdots + yY + yZ + zA + zB + \cdots + zY + zZ$$

Solution of simultaneous linear equations:

$$ax + by = c$$

$$dx + ey = f$$

$$x = \frac{\begin{vmatrix} c & b \\ f & e \end{vmatrix}}{\begin{vmatrix} a & b \\ d & e \end{vmatrix}} = \frac{ce - bf}{ae - bd}$$

$$y = \frac{\begin{vmatrix} a & c \\ d & f \end{vmatrix}}{\begin{vmatrix} a & b \\ d & e \end{vmatrix}} = \frac{af - cd}{ae - bd}$$

The solution of a quadratic equation:

$$ax^2 + bx + c = 0$$

$$x = \frac{-b \pm \sqrt{b^2 - 4ac}}{2a}$$

Analytical geometry assumed for test theory

Equation of the straight line:

$$y = ax + b$$

where a is the slope of the line, and
  b is the intercept on the y-axis.

Equation of a circle with its center at the origin and radius r:

$$x^2 + y^2 = r^2$$

General equation of a circle:

$$(x - a)^2 + (y - b)^2 = r^2$$

where r is the radius,
  a is the abscissa value for the center, and
  b is the ordinate for the center.

Equation of a hyperbola with asymptotes $x = 0$ and $y = 0$:

$$xy = c$$

Equation of hyperbola with asymptotes $x = a$ and $y = b$:

$$(x - a)(y - b) = 0$$

Equation of hyperbola with asymptotes $x\sqrt{a} \pm y\sqrt{b} = 0$:

$$ax^2 - by^2 = c$$

Equation of an ellipse:

$$ax^2 + by^2 = c$$

Equation of a parabola:

$$y = ax^2 + bx + c$$

The treatment of conics may be generalized as follows:

$A'x'^2 + B'x'y' + C'y'^2 + D'x' + E'y' + F' = 0$ (General equation of the second degree represents any conic section.)

$x' = x \cos \phi - y \sin \phi$ (Transformation used to change the general equation of the second degree to a standard form.)

$y' = x \sin \phi + y \cos \phi$

where $\tan 2\phi = \dfrac{B'}{A' - C'}$

$$\sin \phi = \sqrt{\frac{1 - \cos 2\phi}{2}}$$

$$\cos \phi = \sqrt{\frac{1 + \cos 2\phi}{2}}$$

By use of the foregoing transformation any equation of the second degree can be rotated to the following standard form, such that the coefficient of the xy term is zero.

$Ax^2 + Cy^2 + Dx + Ey + F = 0$ (Standard form for the general second-degree equation. Represents any conic section [with axes parallel to the coordinate axes].)

If A and C have *unlike* signs, this equation represents a *hyperbola* with axes parallel to the coordinate axes.

If A and C have the *same* sign, this equation represents **an** *ellipse* with axes parallel to the coordinate axes.

If A equals C, this equation represents a circle.

If A or C equals *zero*, this equation represents a parabola with its axis parallel to a coordinate axis.

If A equals C equals *zero*, this equation represents a straight line.

Elementary statistics assumed in test theory

$$X_i = \text{gross score of individual } i$$

$$N = \text{number of persons in sample}$$

$$\bar{X} \ \text{ or } \ M_X = \frac{\sum\limits_{i=1}^{N} X_i}{N} \qquad \text{(mean)}$$

$$x_i = X_i - M_X \qquad \text{(deviation score)}$$

$$\sum_{i=1}^{N} x_i = 0 \qquad \text{(mean deviation score)}$$

$$s_x^2 = \frac{\sum\limits_{i=1}^{N} x_i^2}{N} = \frac{\sum\limits_{i=1}^{N} X_i^2}{N} - M_X^2 \qquad \begin{array}{l}\text{(variance of a specified} \\ \text{sample)}\end{array}$$

$$_\mu s_x^2 = \frac{\sum\limits_{i=1}^{N} x_i^2}{N-1} \qquad \begin{array}{l}\text{(estimate of variance in} \\ \text{universe from which} \\ \text{sample is drawn)}\end{array}$$

See Yule and Kendall (1940), pages 434–436, for a discussion of the use of N and $N-1$ in the denominator of the formula for variance.

$$\sum_{i=1}^{N} x_i^2 = \sum_{i=1}^{N} X_i^2 - NM_X^2 \qquad \begin{array}{l}\text{(gross score formula for sum of} \\ \text{squares of deviations from the} \\ \text{mean)}\end{array}$$

$$r_{xy} = \frac{\Sigma xy}{N s_x s_y} = \frac{\Sigma xy}{\sqrt{\Sigma x^2 \Sigma y^2}} \qquad \begin{array}{l}\text{(deviation score formula for} \\ \text{correlation)}\end{array}$$

$$r_{xy} = \frac{\Sigma XY - NM_X M_Y}{\sqrt{\Sigma X^2 - NM_X^2} \ \sqrt{\Sigma Y^2 - NM_Y^2}}, \qquad \begin{array}{l}\text{(gross score formula for} \\ \text{correlation)}\end{array}$$

$$r_{xy} s_x s_y = \frac{\Sigma xy}{N} = \frac{\Sigma XY - NM_X M_Y}{N} \qquad \text{(covariance)}$$

$$\dot{y} = r_{xy} \frac{s_y}{s_x} x \qquad \text{(deviation score formula for regression of } y \text{ on } x \text{ used to estimate } y \text{ from } x)$$

$$\dot{Y} = r_{xy} \frac{s_y}{s_x} X + M_Y - r_{xy} \frac{s_y}{s_x} M_X \qquad \text{(gross score formula for regression of } Y \text{ on } X)$$

$$\dot{x} = r_{xy} \frac{s_x}{s_y} y \qquad \text{(deviation score formula for regression of } x \text{ on } y \text{ used to estimate } x \text{ from } y)$$

$$\dot{X} = r_{xy} \frac{s_x}{s_y} Y + M_X - r_{xy} \frac{s_x}{s_y} M_Y \qquad \text{(gross score formula for regression of } X \text{ on } Y)$$

$$s_{y.x} = s_y \sqrt{1 - r_{xy}{}^2} \qquad \text{(error of estimate, error made in estimating } y \text{ from } x)$$

$$s_{x.y} = s_x \sqrt{1 - r_{xy}{}^2} \qquad \text{(error of estimate, error made in estimating } x \text{ from } y)$$

$$r_{xy.z} = \frac{r_{xy} - r_{xz} r_{yz}}{\sqrt{1 - r_{xz}{}^2}\,\sqrt{1 - r_{yz}{}^2}} \qquad \text{(partial correlation, the correlation between } x \text{ and } y \text{ for a constant value of } z)$$

$$s_{x-y} = \sqrt{s_x{}^2 + s_y{}^2 - 2 r_{xy} s_x s_y} \qquad \text{(standard deviation of a difference)}$$

$$s_{x+y} = \sqrt{s_x{}^2 + s_y{}^2 + 2 r_{xy} s_x s_y} \qquad \text{(standard deviation of a sum)}$$

$$s_{x-y} = \sqrt{s_x{}^2 + s_y{}^2} = s_{x+y} \qquad \text{(standard deviation of a sum or difference for the special case of } zero \text{ correlation)}$$

$$A_{ig} = 1 \quad \text{or} \quad 0 \qquad \text{(score of individual } i \text{ on item } g)$$

$$p_g = \frac{\displaystyle\sum_{i=1}^{N} A_{ig}}{N} \qquad \text{(proportion of individuals answering item } g \text{ correctly)}$$

$$q_g = 1 - p_g \qquad \text{(proportion of individuals answering item } g \text{ incorrectly)}$$

$$s_g{}^2 = p_g q_g = p_g - p_g{}^2 \qquad \text{(variance of item } g)$$

$$\overline{X}_{g+} = \frac{\sum\limits_{i=1}^{N} X_i A_{ig}}{N p_g} \qquad \text{(average test score for persons answering item } g \text{ correctly)}$$

$$\overline{X}_{g-} = \frac{\sum\limits_{i=1}^{N} X_i (1 - A_{ig})}{N q_g} \qquad \text{(average test score for persons answering item } g \text{ incorrectly)}$$

z_g = normal curve ordinate corresponding to the area indicated by p_g or q_g

$$N z_g = \frac{N}{\sigma_x \sqrt{2\pi}} e^{(-x^2/2\sigma_x{}^2)} \qquad \text{(ordinate of normal curve)}$$

where N = number of cases,

σ_x = standard deviation of distribution,

π = 3.1416, and

$$e = 2.7183 = \lim_{n \to \infty} \left(1 + \frac{1}{n}\right)^n$$

$$bis^r xg = \left(\frac{\overline{X}_{g+} - \overline{X}_{g-}}{s_x}\right)\left(\frac{p_g q_g}{z_g}\right)$$

$$bis^r xg = \left(\frac{\overline{X}_{g+} - \overline{X}}{s_x}\right)\left(\frac{p_g}{z_g}\right)$$

(equivalent formulas for biserial correlation of item g with score x)

$$pt\text{-}bis^r xg = \left(\frac{\overline{X}_{g+} - \overline{X}_{g-}}{s_x}\right)\sqrt{p_g q_g}$$

$$pt\text{-}bis^r xg = \left(\frac{\overline{X}_{g+} - \overline{X}}{s_x}\right)\frac{\sqrt{p_g}}{\sqrt{q_g}}$$

(equivalent formulas for point-biserial correlation of item g with score x)

Use of the summation sign

If k represents a constant, and x, y, z, and w represent variables, the major principles in the use of the summation sign may be indicated in the following equations. Since all summations are assumed to be over persons, the subscripts and limits are not given.

$\Sigma(x + y) = \Sigma x + \Sigma y$ (The sum of $x + y$ is equal to summation x plus summation y.)

$\Sigma(x - y) = \Sigma x - \Sigma y$ (The sum of a set of differences is equal to the difference of the two sums.)

$\Sigma kx = k\Sigma x$ (The sum of a constant k times a variable x is equal to the constant multiplied by summation x.)

$\Sigma k = Nk$ (The sum of a constant term is equal to N times the constant term.)

Combinations of these principles with elementary algebra is illustrated in the following equations.

$$\Sigma k(x + y) = k\Sigma x + k\Sigma y$$

$$\Sigma(kx + y)(z + w) = k\Sigma xz + \Sigma yz + \Sigma yw + k\Sigma xw$$

The score matrix

$$
\begin{array}{ccccc}
X_{11} & X_{12} & X_{13} & \cdots & X_{1K} \\
X_{21} & X_{22} & X_{23} & \cdots & X_{2K} \\
X_{31} & X_{32} & X_{33} & \cdots & X_{3K} \\
\cdot & \cdot & \cdot & & \cdot \\
\cdot & \cdot & \cdot & & \cdot \\
\cdot & \cdot & \cdot & & \cdot \\
X_{N1} & X_{N2} & X_{N3} & \cdots & X_{NK}
\end{array}
$$

The foregoing matrix represents the scores of N persons on each of K tests. The first subscript designates the persons (from 1 to N); and the second subscript designates the tests (from 1 to K). The scores in any given column are the scores of all the persons on one test, and the scores in any row are the scores of one person on all the tests.

The general term in this matrix may be written

$$X_{ig} \qquad\qquad (i = 1 \cdots N; g = 1 \cdots K)$$

X_{ig} indicates the score of the ith person on the gth test. The notation in parentheses shows that i varies from 1 to N and g from 1 to K.

The mean of any particular test (g) is written as follows in the double subscript notation:

$$M_{\cdot g} = \frac{\displaystyle\sum_{i=1}^{N} X_{ig}}{N}$$

The period is used to indicate the position of the subscript over which we have summed. This is read: The mean of the gth test is equal to the summation of X sub i g for test g from i equals 1 to i equals N, divided by the number of persons.

Using this same double subscript notation, it is possible to express the average score on all the tests for any one person. This is written

$$M_{i\cdot} = \frac{\sum\limits_{g=1}^{K} X_{ig}}{K}$$

which is read: The average score of the ith person equals the sum of the scores (X_{ig}) for that person, from g equals 1 to g equals K, divided by K (the number of tests). The period is used in place of subscript g since summation was over this subscript.

The average score of all persons on all the tests would be expressed with a double summation notation,

$$M_{\cdot\cdot} = \frac{\sum\limits_{i=1}^{N} \sum\limits_{g=1}^{K} X_{ig}}{NK}$$

This is read: M is defined as the summation of X_{ig} with respect to g from g equals 1 to g equals K, summed with respect to i from i equals 1 to i equals N, divided by N times K.

Wherever we are dealing with several persons and tests, the double subscript notation is desirable to avoid ambiguity. If no ambiguity arises, it is permissible to omit the subscripts after X, and also to omit the limits above and below the summation sign.

It should be noted that the matrix of scores is not symmetric. The score of the second person on the third test is different from the score of the third person on the second test.

$$(X_{23} \neq X_{32})$$

On the other hand, the variance-covariance matrix or the intercorrelation matrix is symmetric. The correlation (or covariance) of test 2 with test 3 is identical with that of test 3 with test 2.

The correlation matrix

$s_1{}^2$	$r_{12}s_1s_2$	$r_{13}s_1s_3$	$\cdots$	$r_{1K}s_1s_K$
$r_{12}s_1s_2$	$s_2{}^2$	$r_{23}s_2s_3$	$\cdots$	$r_{2K}s_2s_K$
$r_{13}s_1s_3$	$r_{23}s_2s_3$	$s_3{}^2$	$\cdots$	$r_{3K}s_3s_K$
$\cdot$	$\cdot$	$\cdot$		$\cdot$
$\cdot$	$\cdot$	$\cdot$		$\cdot$
$\cdot$	$\cdot$	$\cdot$		$\cdot$
$r_{1K}s_1s_K$	$r_{2K}s_2s_K$	$r_{3K}s_3s_K$	$\cdots$	$s_K{}^2$

The foregoing matrix shows the variances and covariances for a set of K tests or items. The variance of the sum of the tests (or items) is the sum of the terms in this variance-covariance matrix. This sum may be written in several different ways,

$$\sum_{g=1}^{K} \sum_{h=1}^{K} r_{gh} s_g s_h \qquad\qquad (r_{gg} = r_{hh} = 1)$$

In order to show explicitly the difference between the variances and covariances, we may write

$$\sum_{g=1}^{K} s_g^2 + \sum_{\substack{g=1 \\ (g \neq h)}}^{K} \sum_{h=1}^{K} r_{gh} s_g s_h$$

Sometimes the second term is written without the two summation signs and the upper limit used to designate the *number* of terms as follows:

$$\sum_{g=1}^{K} s_g^2 + \sum_{g \neq h=1}^{K^2-K} r_{gh} s_g s_h$$

With this notation it is understood that, since the terms where $g = h$ are omitted, there are $K^2 - K$ terms in the second summation. Since the terms above the principal diagonal are identical with those below it, this sum for a symmetric matrix is sometimes written

$$\sum_{g=1}^{K} s_g^2 + 2\sum_{g > h=1}^{K-1} r_{gh} s_g s_h$$

APPENDIX B

Table of Ordinates and Areas
of the Normal Curve

TABLE OF THE NORMAL CURVE

ORDINATES (z) AND CUMULATIVE AREA (A) OF THE RIGHT HALF OF THE NORMAL
CURVE OF DISTRIBUTION OF UNIT AREA

For cumulative of whole curve, read $.5 \pm A$ for $\pm x/\sigma$. Ordinates are represented
in terms of the total area as unity.

x/σ	z	A	x/σ	z	A
0.00	0.39894	0.00000	0.50	0.35207	0.19146
0.01	0.39892	0.00399	0.51	0.35029	0.19497
0.02	0.39886	0.00798	0.52	0.34849	0.19847
0.03	0.39876	0.01197	0.53	0.34667	0.20194
0.04	0.39862	0.01595	0.54	0.34482	0.20540
0.05	0.39844	0.01994	0.55	0.34294	0.20884
0.06	0.39822	0.02392	0.56	0.34105	0.21226
0.07	0.39797	0.02790	0.57	0.33912	0.21566
0.08	0.39767	0.03188	0.58	0.33718	0.21904
0.09	0.39733	0.03586	0.59	0.33521	0.22240
0.10	0.39695	0.03983	0.60	0.33322	0.22575
0.11	0.39654	0.04380	0.61	0.33121	0.22907
0.12	0.39608	0.04776	0.62	0.32918	0.23237
0.13	0.39559	0.05172	0.63	0.32713	0.23565
0.14	0.39505	0.05567	0.64	0.32506	0.23891
0.15	0.39448	0.05962	0.65	0.32297	0.24215
0.16	0.39387	0.06356	0.66	0.32086	0.24537
0.17	0.39322	0.06749	0.67	0.31874	0.24857
0.18	0.39253	0.07142	0.68	0.31659	0.25175
0.19	0.39181	0.07535	0.69	0.31443	0.25490
0.20	0.39104	0.07926	0.70	0.31225	0.25804
0.21	0.39024	0.08317	0.71	0.31006	0.26115
0.22	0.38940	0.08706	0.72	0.30785	0.26424
0.23	0.38853	0.09095	0.73	0.30563	0.26730
0.24	0.38762	0.09483	0.74	0.30339	0.27035
0.25	0.38667	0.09871	0.75	0.30114	0.27337
0.26	0.38568	0.10257	0.76	0.29887	0.27637
0.27	0.38466	0.10642	0.77	0.29659	0.27935
0.28	0.38361	0.11026	0.78	0.29431	0.28230
0.29	0.38251	0.11409	0.79	0.29200	0.28524
0.30	0.38139	0.11791	0.80	0.28969	0.28814
0.31	0.38023	0.12172	0.81	0.28737	0.29103
0.32	0.37903	0.12552	0.82	0.28504	0.29389
0.33	0.37780	0.12930	0.83	0.28269	0.29673
0.34	0.37654	0.13307	0.84	0.28034	0.29955
0.35	0.37524	0.13683	0.85	0.27798	0.30234
0.36	0.37391	0.14058	0.86	0.27562	0.30511
0.37	0.37255	0.14431	0.87	0.27324	0.30785
0.38	0.37115	0.14803	0.88	0.27086	0.31057
0.39	0.36973	0.15173	0.89	0.26848	0.31327
0.40	0.36827	0.15542	0.90	0.26609	0.31594
0.41	0.36678	0.15910	0.91	0.26369	0.31859
0.42	0.36526	0.16276	0.92	0.26129	0.32121
0.43	0.36371	0.16640	0.93	0.25888	0.32381
0.44	0.36213	0.17003	0.94	0.25647	0.32639
0.45	0.36053	0.17364	0.95	0.25406	0.32894
0.46	0.35889	0.17724	0.96	0.25164	0.33147
0.47	0.35723	0.18082	0.97	0.24923	0.33398
0.48	0.35553	0.18439	0.98	0.24681	0.33646
0.49	0.35381	0.18793	0.99	0.24439	0.33891

Reprinted by permission from *Business Statistics*, by George R. Davies and Dale
Yoder, Second Edition, pages 582–585. New York: John Wiley and Sons, Inc.

TABLE OF THE NORMAL CURVE—*Continued*

x/σ	z	A	x/σ	z	A
1.00	0.24197	0.34134	1.50	0.12952	0.43319
1.01	0.23955	0.34375	1.51	0.12758	0.43448
1.02	0.23713	0.34614	1.52	0.12566	0.43574
1.03	0.23471	0.34850	1.53	0.12376	0.43699
1.04	0.23230	0.35083	1.54	0.12188	0.43822
1.05	0.22988	0.35314	1.55	0.12001	0.43943
1.06	0.22747	0.35543	1.56	0.11816	0.44062
1.07	0.22506	0.35769	1.57	0.11632	0.44179
1.08	0.22265	0.35993	1.58	0.11450	0.44295
1.09	0.22025	0.36214	1.59	0.11270	0.44408
1.10	0.21785	0.36433	1.60	0.11092	0.44520
1.11	0.21546	0.36650	1.61	0.10915	0.44630
1.12	0.21307	0.36864	1.62	0.10741	0.44738
1.13	0.21069	0.37076	1.63	0.10567	0.44845
1.14	0.20831	0.37286	1.64	0.10396	0.44950
1.15	0.20594	0.37493	1.65	0.10226	0.45053
1.16	0.20357	0.37698	1.66	0.10059	0.45154
1.17	0.20121	0.37900	1.67	0.09893	0.45254
1.18	0.19886	0.38100	1.68	0.09728	0.45352
1.19	0.19652	0.38298	1.69	0.09566	0.45449
1.20	0.19419	0.38493	1.70	0.09405	0.45543
1.21	0.19186	0.38686	1.71	0.09246	0.45637
1.22	0.18954	0.38877	1.72	0.09089	0.45728
1.23	0.18724	0.39065	1.73	0.08933	0.45818
1.24	0.18494	0.39251	1.74	0.08780	0.45907
1.25	0.18265	0.39435	1.75	0.08628	0.45994
1.26	0.18037	0.39617	1.76	0.08478	0.46080
1.27	0.17810	0.39796	1.77	0.08329	0.46164
1.28	0.17585	0.39973	1.78	0.08183	0.46246
1.29	0.17360	0.40147	1.79	0.08038	0.46327
1.30	0.17137	0.40320	1.80	0.07895	0.46407
1.31	0.16915	0.40490	1.81	0.07754	0.46485
1.32	0.16694	0.40658	1.82	0.07614	0.46562
1.33	0.16474	0.40824	1.83	0.07477	0.46638
1.34	0.16256	0.40988	1.84	0.07341	0.46712
1.35	0.16038	0.41149	1.85	0.07206	0.46784
1.36	0.15822	0.41309	1.86	0.07074	0.46856
1.37	0.15608	0.41466	1.87	0.06943	0.46926
1.38	0.15395	0.41621	1.88	0.06814	0.46995
1.39	0.15183	0.41774	1.89	0.06687	0.47062
1.40	0.14973	0.41924	1.90	0.06562	0.47128
1.41	0.14764	0.42073	1.91	0.06438	0.47193
1.42	0.14556	0.42220	1.92	0.06316	0.47257
1.43	0.14350	0.42364	1.93	0.06195	0.47320
1.44	0.14146	0.42507	1.94	0.06077	0.47381
1.45	0.13943	0.42647	1.95	0.05959	0.47441
1.46	0.13742	0.42786	1.96	0.05844	0.47500
1.47	0.13542	0.42922	1.97	0.05730	0.47558
1.48	0.13344	0.43056	1.98	0.05618	0.47615
1.49	0.13147	0.43189	1.99	0.05508	0.47670

TABLE OF THE NORMAL CURVE—*Continued*

x/σ	z	A	x/σ	z	A
2.00	0.05399	0.47725	2.50	0.01753	0.49379
2.01	0.05292	0.47778	2.51	0.01709	0.49396
2.02	0.05186	0.47831	2.52	0.01667	0.49413
2.03	0.05082	0.47882	2.53	0.01625	0.49430
2.04	0.04980	0.47932	2.54	0.01585	0.49446
2.05	0.04879	0.47982	2.55	0.01545	0.49461
2.06	0.04780	0.48030	2.56	0.01506	0.49477
2.07	0.04682	0.48077	2.57	0.01468	0.49492
2.08	0.04586	0.48124	2.58	0.01431	0.49506
2.09	0.04491	0.48169	2.59	0.01394	0.49520
2.10	0.04398	0.48214	2.60	0.01358	0.49534
2.11	0.04307	0.48257	2.61	0.01323	0.49547
2.12	0.04217	0.48300	2.62	0.01289	0.49560
2.13	0.04128	0.48341	2.63	0.01256	0.49573
2.14	0.04041	0.48382	2.64	0.01223	0.49585
2.15	0.03955	0.48422	2.65	0.01191	0.49598
2.16	0.03871	0.48461	2.66	0.01160	0.49609
2.17	0.03788	0.48500	2.67	0.01130	0.49621
2.18	0.03706	0.48537	2.68	0.01100	0.49632
2.19	0.03626	0.48574	2.69	0.01071	0.49643
2.20	0.03547	0.48610	2.70	0.01042	0.49653
2.21	0.03470	0.48645	2.71	0.01014	0.49664
2.22	0.03394	0.48679	2.72	0.00987	0.49674
2.23	0.03319	0.48713	2.73	0.00961	0.49683
2.24	0.03246	0.48745	2.74	0.00935	0.49693
2.25	0.03174	0.48778	2.75	0.00909	0.49702
2.26	0.03103	0.48809	2.76	0.00885	0.49711
2.27	0.03034	0.48840	2.77	0.00861	0.49720
2.28	0.02965	0.48870	2.78	0.00837	0.49728
2.29	0.02898	0.48899	2.79	0.00814	0.49736
2.30	0.02833	0.48928	2.80	0.00792	0.49744
2.31	0.02768	0.48956	2.81	0.00770	0.49752
2.32	0.02705	0.48983	2.82	0.00748	0.49760
2.33	0.02643	0.49010	2.83	0.00727	0.49767
2.34	0.02582	0.49036	2.84	0.00707	0.49774
2.35	0.02522	0.49061	2.85	0.00687	0.49781
2.36	0.02463	0.49086	2.86	0.00668	0.49788
2.37	0.02406	0.49111	2.87	0.00649	0.49795
2.38	0.02349	0.49134	2.88	0.00631	0.49801
2.39	0.02294	0.49158	2.89	0.00613	0.49807
2.40	0.02239	0.49180	2.90	0.00595	0.49813
2.41	0.02186	0.49202	2.91	0.00578	0.49819
2.42	0.02134	0.49224	2.92	0.00562	0.49825
2.43	0.02083	0.49245	2.93	0.00545	0.49831
2.44	0.02033	0.49266	2.94	0.00530	0.49836
2.45	0.01984	0.49286	2.95	0.00514	0.49841
2.46	0.01936	0.49305	2.96	0.00499	0.49846
2.47	0.01889	0.49324	2.97	0.00485	0.49851
2.48	0.01842	0.49343	2.98	0.00471	0.49856
2.49	0.01797	0.49361	2.99	0.00457	0.49861

TABLE OF THE NORMAL CURVE—*Continued*

x/σ	z	A	x/σ	z	A
3.00	0.00443	0.49865	3.50	0.00087	0.49977
3.01	0.00430	0.49869	3.51	0.00084	0.49978
3.02	0.00417	0.49874	3.52	0.00081	0.49978
3.03	0.00405	0.49878	3.53	0.00079	0.49979
3.04	0.00393	0.49882	3.54	0.00076	0.49980
3.05	0.00381	0.49886	3.55	0.00073	0.49981
3.06	0.00370	0.49889	3.56	0.00071	0.49981
3.07	0.00358	0.49893	3.57	0.00068	0.49982
3.08	0.00348	0.49897	3.58	0.00066	0.49983
3.09	0.00337	0.49900	3.59	0.00063	0.49983
3.10	0.00327	0.49903	3.60	0.00061	0.49984
3.11	0.00317	0.49906	3.61	0.00059	0.49985
3.12	0.00307	0.49910	3.62	0.00057	0.49985
3.13	0.00298	0.49913	3.63	0.00055	0.49986
3.14	0.00288	0.49916	3.64	0.00053	0.49986
3.15	0.00279	0.49918	3.65	0.00051	0.49987
3.16	0.00271	0.49921	3.66	0.00049	0.49987
3.17	0.00262	0.49924	3.67	0.00047	0.49988
3.18	0.00254	0.49926	3.68	0.00046	0.49988
3.19	0.00246	0.49929	3.69	0.00044	0.49989
3.20	0.00238	0.49931	3.70	0.00042	0.49989
3.21	0.00231	0.49934	3.71	0.00041	0.49990
3.22	0.00224	0.49936	3.72	0.00039	0.49990
3.23	0.00216	0.49938	3.73	0.00038	0.49990
3.24	0.00210	0.49940	3.74	0.00037	0.49991
3.25	0.00203	0.49942	3.75	0.00035	0.49991
3.26	0.00196	0.49944	3.76	0.00034	0.49992
3.27	0.00190	0.49946	3.77	0.00033	0.49992
3.28	0.00184	0.49948	3.78	0.00031	0.49992
3.29	0.00178	0.49950	3.79	0.00030	0.49992
3.30	0.00172	0.49952	3.80	0.00029	0.49993
3.31	0.00167	0.49953	3.81	0.00028	0.49993
3.32	0.00161	0.49955	3.82	0.00027	0.49993
3.33	0.00156	0.49957	3.83	0.00026	0.49994
3.34	0.00151	0.49958	3.84	0.00025	0.49994
3.35	0.00146	0.49960	3.85	0.00024	0.49994
3.36	0.00141	0.49961	3.86	0.00023	0.49994
3.37	0.00136	0.49962	3.87	0.00022	0.49995
3.38	0.00132	0.49964	3.88*	0.00021	0.49995
3.39	0.00127	0.49965	3.90	0.00020	0.49995
3.40	0.00123	0.49966	3.91	0.00019	0.49995
3.41	0.00119	0.49968	3.92	0.00018	0.49996
3.42	0.00115	0.49969	3.94	0.00017	0.49996
3.43	0.00111	0.49970	3.95	0.00016	0.49996
3.44	0.00107	0.49971	3.97	0.00015	0.49996
3.45	0.00104	0.49972	3.98	0.00014	0.49997
3.46	0.00100	0.49973	4.00	0.00013	0.49997
3.47	0.00097	0.49974	4.02	0.00012	0.49997
3.48	0.00094	0.49975	4.04	0.00011	0.49997
3.49	0.00090	0.49976	4.06	0.00011	0.49998

* For skipped x/σ items below, read values next preceding.

APPENDIX C

Sample Examination Questions in Statistics
for Use as a Review Examination at the Beginning
of the Course in Test Theory [1]

The following two experiments were performed:

Experiment 1. The average of the men on a physical sciences test is 243.0. The average of the women is 226.5. The standard error of the difference is 5.0.

Experiment 2. The average of the men on an English test is 158.4. The average of the women is 182.4. The standard error of this difference is 16.0.

Mark the following statements according to this code:

    1. Applicable to experiment 1
    2. Applicable to experiment 2
    0. Applicable to neither experiment 1 nor to experiment 2

_____ It would be worth while repeating this experiment with twice as many cases in each group.

_____ It would be worth while repeating this experiment with four times as many cases in each group.

_____ Since chance variation will not explain the results of this experiment, it is plausible to assume that there is a sex difference in the ability involved in this test.

_____ Since chance variation will explain the results of this experiment, I do not feel that it is worth while to investigate this problem any further.

_____ Differences larger than those obtained in this experiment would occur only one time out of a thousand if the two groups differed only by chance.

_____ There is only one chance out of a thousand that the difference between the two groups was due to the influence of chance.

_____ The difference of means is significant.

_____ The difference of means is not significant.

[1] If students are not required to memorize formulas, items such as these are suitable for "open-book" examinations.

An intelligence test and an arithmetic test are given to a group of 1000 students. The correlation coefficient, means, standard deviations, and parameters of both regression lines are computed. In rechecking the results it is found that the intelligence test has been scored accurately, but there were a number of errors in the scoring of the arithmetic test. Assume that these errors are *completely random* errors.

For each of the measures listed below write:

    1. If the correct value is *larger* than the value already computed.
    2. If the correct value is *smaller* than the value already computed.
    3. If the two values are the *same*.

_____ The standard error of the mean of the arithmetic scores.

_____ The standard deviation of the distribution of intelligence scores.

_____ The mean arithmetic test score.

_____ The standard deviation of the errors made in predicting arithmetic test score from intelligence test score.

_____ The coefficient of alienation.

_____ The coefficient of correlation between intelligence and arithmetic.

_____ The variance of the predicted arithmetic test scores (that is, predicted from the regression of arithmetic test score on intelligence test score).

_____ The variance of the observed arithmetic test scores minus the variance of the predicted arithmetic test scores.

_____ The ratio of the standard deviation of the predicted intelligence test scores (that is, predicted from the arithmetic score) to the standard deviation of the observed intelligence test scores.

_____ The square of the alienation coefficient plus the square of the correlation coefficient.

_____ The product of the alienation coefficient and the standard deviation of the distribution of observed scores.

_____ The slope of the regression of arithmetic on intelligence.

_____ The standard deviation of the arithmetic test.

_____ The slope of the regression of intelligence on arithmetic.

Before each of the following items write the number of the *one* formula from the following list of six that is most directly connected with the problem to be solved. Be sure *not* to make *any* calculations, just indicate the *one best* formula in each case.

1. $M + 3s_m$ $\left(s_m = \dfrac{s}{\sqrt{N}} \right)$

2. $\dfrac{M_1 - M_2}{s_d}$ $\left(s_d = \sqrt{s_1^2/N_1 + s_2^2/N_2} \right)$

3. $\dfrac{M_1 - M_2}{s'_d}$ $\left(s'_d = \sqrt{(1/N)(s_1^2 + s_2^2 - 2r_{12}s_1s_2)} \right)$

4. ks_y

5. $\dfrac{\Sigma xy}{Ns_xs_y}$

6. $r\left(\dfrac{s_y}{s_x}\right) X + M_y - r\left(\dfrac{s_y}{s_x}\right) M_x$

_____ How can I estimate the geometry score of a student from his performance in algebra?

_____ How far wrong is one likely to be when using arm-length to estimate height.

_____ A sample of 100 Wistar adult white rats has an average weight of 342.5 grams; the standard deviation of the distribution of weight is 9.3 grams. What are reasonable upper and lower limits for the average weight of all Wistar adult white rats?

_____ Which of two aptitude tests would it be better to use for estimating grades in this college?

_____ An experiment is performed using two persons (one brother and one sister) from each of a hundred families. An intelligence test is given to these two hundred persons. Do brothers score higher than their sisters?

_____ An instructor has two classes. In one there are 150 students, and in the other there are 136 students. The same intelligence test is given to the entire group of 286 students. Is the average intelligence of one class clearly higher than that of the other?

_____ I want to predict the speed with which a rat will learn maze B from its performance in maze A.

_____ Are rats more active on days when they have thyroid extract than on control days when they do not get the extract?

Before each statement given below, put a circle around the number(s) indicating the assumption(s) which must be made if the statement is to be regarded as correct. Use the following code:

1. A zero point which is not arbitrary.
2. A constant unit of measurement.
3. The assumed mean is approximately equal to the true mean.
4. The cases are evenly distributed within the class interval.
5. The number of cases in a class interval varies inversely with the distance from the mean.
6. The two distributions have the same number of cases.
7. The two distributions have the same mean.
8. The statement is correct as it stands, no assumption being involved.

1 2 3 4 5 6 7 8   The differences between brothers can be measured by taking the differences of their test scores.

1 2 3 4 5 6 7 8   The differences between brothers can be measured by taking the ratios of their test scores.

1 2 3 4 5 6 7 8   The mean may be computed by grouping the data in class intervals.

1 2 3 4 5 6 7 8   The simplest method of calculating the mean is by using grouped data and an equivalent scale with an assumed mean and an arbitrary origin.

1 2 3 4 5 6 7 8   The standard deviation of a distribution may be calculated by using grouped data and an equivalent scale with an assumed mean and an arbitrary origin.

1 2 3 4 5 6 7 8   The mean may be calculated from the formula $M = \Sigma X/N$.

1 2 3 4 5 6 7 8   The median may be calculated from a frequency distribution plotted in class intervals of ten.

1 2 3 4 5 6 7 8   A class of students is divided into two sections for the purpose of administering a given test. The standard deviation of the total class can be calculated from the means, standard deviations, and number of cases for each section.

1 2 3 4 5 6 7 8   In the case just mentioned, the mean of the total class can be calculated if one knows the mean and number of cases for each section.

1 2 3 4 5 6 7 8   John is twice as intelligent as James.

1 2 3 4 5 6 7 8   If a class in geometry has been given three tests during the semester, the final ranking of the students can be determined by summing these three scores for each student.

All applicants for admission to the university are given an English examination and a scholastic aptitude test. In 1933 the standards for admission based entirely on scholastic aptitude scores were raised. As a result the size of the entering class decreased markedly.

Mark the following items:

    1. If it will probably be larger in the freshman class of 1932.
    2. If it will probably be larger in the freshman class of 1933.
    3. If it will probably be about the same in both classes.
    4. If not enough data are given, or if code numbers given above do not apply.

_____ Mean score on the scholastic aptitude test.

_____ Standard deviation of the English examination.

_____ Pearson correlation coefficient between English and aptitude scores.

_____ Variance of the English scores as estimated from the aptitude test scores.

_____ The standard deviation of the errors of prediction of English from aptitude test scores.

_____ Coefficient of alienation.

_____ Slope of the line of regression of English on aptitude scores.

_____ Slope of the line of regression of aptitude on English scores.

_____ The ratio of the standard error of estimate (that is, error made in estimating aptitude scores from English scores) to the standard deviation of the aptitude scores.

_____ Standard deviation of aptitude scores.

For each of the statements below write:

    1. If it applies to the mode.
    2. If it applies to the median.
    3. If it applies to the mean.
    4. If it applies to none of these terms.

_____ The abscissa of the highest point on the frequency distribution.

_____ The ordinate of the highest point on the cumulative frequency curve.

_____ The x-value of the steepest part of the cumulative frequency curve.

_____ The point halfway between the two extreme values of the distribution.

_____ The score value so chosen that exactly 50 per cent of the scores are higher than it.

_____ The measure which lends itself most readily to algebraic treatment.

Calculate the mean and standard deviation of the following distribution:

Score	Frequency
160–174	10
145–159	22
130–144	45
115–129	18
100–114	5

Present *all* your calculations in an orderly data sheet.

Suppose that after you have computed a mean, mode, median, range, and standard deviation on the data shown in the above tabulation, you find that two scores that are tabulated as 146 in the distribution are erroneous and should be tabulated as 129. *Do not calculate means or standard deviations;* answer simply from the *general trend* of the data.

The value of the mean already computed is (the same as, larger than, smaller than) the correct value.

The value of the mode already computed is (the same as, larger than, smaller than) the correct value.

The value of the median already computed is (the same as, larger than, smaller than) the correct value.

The value of the standard deviation already computed is (the same as, larger than, smaller than) the correct value.

The value of the range already computed is (the same as, larger than, smaller than) the correct value.

Given originally a symmetrical distribution of 500 cases with a mean of 100 and a σ of 25.

Add to this a second symmetrical distribution of 100 cases with individual scores ranging from 110 to 126.

Before each of the measures listed below write:

1. If the measure is increased by adding the second distribution.
2. If the measure is decreased by adding the second distribution.
3. If the measure is not affected by adding the second distribution.
4. If it is impossible to tell what will happen from the information given.

_____ Mean

_____ Median

_____ Range

_____ Mode

_____ Standard deviation

_____ Average deviation

Below are shown curves for six distributions, some of which are cumulative frequency curves and others are column diagrams.

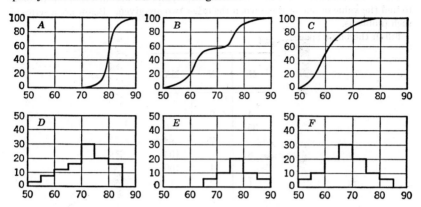

Encircle the correct alternative, or alternatives, in each of the parentheses. Be sure to distinguish carefully between *distribution*, which is the *general* term, and column diagram and cumulative frequency curve, which refer to *specific* types of plots.

The *column diagram* with the smallest standard deviation (*A, B, C, D, E, F*, None)

The *column diagram* with the smallest mode............ (*A, B, C, D, E, F*, None)

The *column diagram* with the largest mean............. (*A, B, C, D, E, F*, None)

The *column diagram* with the smallest range........... (*A, B, C, D, E, F*, None)

The *column diagram* with the smallest *N*.............. (*A, B, C, D, E, F*, None)

The *cumulative frequency curve* with the smallest standard
deviation.. (*A, B, C, D, E, F*, None)

The *cumulative frequency curve* with the largest mean.... (*A, B, C, D, E, F*, None)

The *cumulative frequency curve* with the largest mode.... (*A, B, C, D, E, F*, None)

The *distribution* with the largest range................ (*A, B, C, D, E, F*, None)

The *distribution* with the smallest range............... (*A, B, C, D, E, F*, None)

The *distribution* with the largest median.............. (*A, B, C, D, E, F*, None)

The *distribution*(s) which is (are) negatively skewed and
unimodal.. (*A, B, C, D, E, F*, None)

The *distribution*(s) which is (are) positively skewed and
unimodal... (*A, B, C, D, E, F*, None)

The *distribution*(s) which is (are) bimodal.............. (*A, B, C, D, E, F*, None)

Fill in the spaces in the following table:

The relationships between the three terms M, N, and ΣX are such that it is possible to find the value of one of them when the other two are given. Below are a series of such problems.

Fill in the blank spaces.

M	N	ΣX
4	6	
35		140
	7	84
8		104
	4	100
7	9	

If the mean of a given set of scores (X) is 12 and the number of cases is 15, find $\Sigma(X - k)$, where k is 5.

$Ans.$ $\Sigma(X - k) =$ _____

If ΣX is 133 and ΣY is 95, the mean of the X-scores is 7 and the mean of the Y-scores is 5. What is the value of $\Sigma(X - Y)$?

$Ans.$ $\Sigma(X - Y) =$ _____

If 25 students took both a vocabulary test and an intelligence test, and the following averages were found:

Vocabulary test average $= 56$; intelligence test average $= 51$; then

The sum of all the scores in the vocabulary test is _____

The sum of all the scores in the intelligence test is _____

The sum of all the scores in both tests is _____

If each student is given a composite score, which is found by taking his vocabulary test score and adding to it the intelligence test score multiplied by 2, the average of this set of 25 composite scores will be

_____

If each student is given a composite score, which is found by subtracting his intelligence test score from his vocabulary test score, the average of these composite scores will be

_____

If a new vocabulary score is found by deducting 10 from each student's original vocabulary test score, the sum of these new scores will be

_____

And the average of these new scores will be

In the following problems c and k represent constants; also M (the mean) and N (the number of cases) are constants. X and Y are variables, S indicates "the sum of." Simplify each of the following expressions.

$$\overset{N}{\underset{1}{S}} MX =$$

$$\overset{N}{\underset{1}{S}} (NY + c - XM + X^2) =$$

$$\overset{N}{\underset{1}{S}} (kX + cY) =$$

$$\overset{N}{\underset{1}{S}} (Y - c) =$$

$$\overset{N}{\underset{1}{S}} (YN) =$$

$$\overset{N}{\underset{1}{S}} (k + Y) =$$

$$\overset{N}{\underset{1}{S}} (2XM) =$$

$$\overset{N}{\underset{1}{S}} [(X + Y)(X - Y)] =$$

$$\overset{N}{\underset{1}{S}} (2M^2) =$$

$$\overset{N}{\underset{1}{S}} [(X + Y)Y] =$$

$$\overset{N}{\underset{1}{S}} (NM^2) =$$

$$\overset{N}{\underset{1}{S}} [(X + Y)^2] =$$

$$\overset{N}{\underset{1}{S}} (M^2 - kX) =$$

$$\overset{N}{\underset{1}{S}} [(X - Y)(Y + kX)] =$$

$$\overset{N}{\underset{1}{S}} (MX + Y^2 + cY) =$$

If U, V, W, and Z are variables and a, b, c, and d are constants, simplify the following expressions:

$$\Sigma abd =$$

$$\Sigma VaWc =$$

$$\Sigma(U + c)(Z - d) =$$

In a positively skewed distribution:

The mode is generally (larger than, smaller than, the same as) the median.
The mode is generally (larger than, smaller than, the same as) the mean.
The mean is generally (larger than, smaller than, the same as) the median.

Each of the following cases shows a discrepancy between the mean as calculated from the formula $M = \Sigma X/N$ and the mean calculated by grouped data and an arbitrary origin.

Before each of the following cases place the number of the *one* comment that best applies.

Comments:

1. There must be an error in computation or tabulation.
2. If the arbitrary origin were placed nearer to the mean of the distribution, the discrepancy between the two means would be partially corrected.
3. Such a discrepancy between the two means is reasonable.
4. There is either some error in computation or tabulation, or else poor judgment has been shown in choosing the limits for the class intervals.
5. Such a discrepancy between the two means is reasonable when one has such a large standard deviation.

	$\Sigma X/N$	Mean Calculated with Class Interval and Arbitrary Origin	Class Interval	Arbitrary Origin	Standard Deviation of Distribution
____ Case A	38.38	43.28	10	75.0	15
____ Case B	38.38	37.90	5	37.5	10
____ Case C	38.38	36.71	3	38.0	12
____ Case D	156.93	151.72	10	150.0	50
____ Case E	592.41	598.38	50	525.0	175
____ Case F	417.36	405.92	25	200.0	50

APPENDIX D

Sample Examination Items in Test Theory [1]

After each of the following statements, encircle the letter or letters of *all* the statements which apply. Use the following code.

O = a statement that could not reasonably be true.
T = a statement that is unconditionally true.
A = true if the mean error is assumed to be zero.
B = true if the correlation between errors and true score is zero.
C = true if the correlation between two sets of errors is zero.
D = true if the standard deviation of two sets of errors are the same.

The observed score is equal to the true score plus the error... O T A B C D

Equivalent forms of a test will have the same standard deviation... O T A B C D

The average true score is equal to the average observed score. O T A B C D

The true variance is equal to the error variance plus the observed variance... O T A B C D

The error variance is equal to the observed variance multiplied by the difference between unity and the reliability coefficient.. O T A B C D

The average error is equal to the sum of the errors divided by the number of errors.................................... O T A B C D

The true variance is equal to the reliability coefficient multiplied by the observed variance.......................... O T A B C D

The correlation between true scores and observed scores is equal to the square of the reliability coefficient........... O T A B C D

The square root of the difference between unity and the reliability coefficient is equal to the correlation between observed scores and error scores............................. O T A B C D

The observed variance less the true variance is equal to the error variance... O T A B C D

[1] If students are not required to memorize formulas, items such as these are suitable for "open-book" examinations.

447

Miscellaneous formulas applicable to a single test:

r = reliability of the test.
r_r = reader reliability of the test.
e = the standard error of measurement.
σ = the true standard deviation.
s = the standard deviation of the test scores.
d = the standard deviation of the difference between scores on comparable halves of the test.

1. σ^2/s^2

2. e/s

3. σ/s

4. $\sqrt{r}$

5. $\sqrt{1-r}$

6. $\sigma^2 + e^2$

7. r/r_r

8. $\dfrac{s^2 - d^2}{s^2 + d^2}$

For each of the following items write the number of the *one* or *more* formulas that are clearly indicated. Be sure to give *all* the answers that are *correct*.

_____ The reliability coefficient.

_____ The correlation between true scores and observed scores.

_____ The correlation between errors and observed scores.

_____ The correlation between comparable halves of a test.

_____ The total test variance.

_____ The content reliability of the test.

_____ The true variance divided by the reliability coefficient.

_____ The Spearman-Brown formula would need to be used on this quantity in order to get the reliability of the test.

_____ This will decrease with an increase in the length of the test.

_____ The index of reliability.

Given the following information from the manual on each of two standardized spelling tests:

	Mean	Standard Deviation	Reliability
Test A	100	20	.81
Test B	200	40	.95

Estimate the standard error of measurement of test A.   _____

Estimate the standard error of measurement of test B.   _____

Estimate the correlation between true scores and observed scores for test A.

Student X scores 100 in test A. What is the standard error of this score?

What is a reasonable upper limit for the true score of student X?

What is a reasonable lower limit for the true score of student X?

Student Y scores 300 in test B. What is the standard error of this score?

What is a reasonable upper limit for the true score of student Y?

What is a reasonable lower limit for the true score of student Y?

What is the standard deviation of the true scores in test A?

What is the standard deviation of the true scores in test B?

What is the mean of the true scores in test A?

What is the mean of the error scores in test B?

Give the index of reliability for test B.

What is the correlation between true scores and error scores for test A? _____

What is the correlation between observed scores and errors for test B? _____

Student Z receives a standard score of 1.5 in test A. What is his gross score?

What is the standard error of the standard score of 1.5?

What is the probable upper limit for the true standard score of student Z?

What is the probable lower limit for the true standard score of student Z?

Test A is selected by you and given to your class with the following results, $M = 100; \sigma = 40$. Comment on these results.

_____

_____

_____

_____

Test B is selected by you and given to your class with the following results, $M = 250; \sigma = 30$. Comment on these results.

_____

_____

_____

_____

An arithmetic test is reported to have a standard error of measurement of 10.

Estimate the reliability of this test when it is given to a class with mean 100 and standard deviation 20.   _____

Estimate the reliability of this test when it is given to a class with mean 200 and standard deviation 10.   _____

Estimate the reliability of this test when it is given to a class with mean 150 and standard deviation 40.   _____

Various standard error formulas, together with erroneous formulas:

r_{11} = reliability coefficient of test 1.

r_{12} = the correlation between tests 1 and 2 which are not necessarily different forms of the same test.

σ_1 = the standard deviation of the test scores for test 1.

1. $\sigma_1\sqrt{1 - r_{11}}$ 6. $\sigma_1\sqrt{2}\sqrt{1 - r_{11}^2}$

2. $\sigma_1\sqrt{1 - r_{11}^2}$ 7. $\sigma_1\sqrt{2}\sqrt{1 - r_{12}}$

3. $\sigma_1\sqrt{1 - r_{12}}$ 8. $\sigma_1\sqrt{2}\sqrt{1 - r_{12}^2}$

4. $\sigma_1\sqrt{1 - r_{12}^2}$ 9. $\sigma_1\sqrt{r_{11}}\sqrt{1 - r_{11}}$

5. $\sigma_1\sqrt{2}\sqrt{1 - r_{11}}$

For each of the following items write the number of the *one* formula which is *most* clearly suggested.

_____ By how much does this student's test score deviate from his true score?

_____ What is the extent of the error I am likely to make in estimating college grades by a scholastic aptitude test?

_____ Mr. A is using one form of the Otis test, Mr. B is using a parallel form of the same test. By how much are their scores for the same people likely to differ?

_____ I have given ten different forms of this test to Mr. X. Can I estimate the standard deviation of this distribution of ten scores?

_____ The formula for the standard error of measurement.

_____ The formula for the standard error of substitution.

_____ The formula for the standard error of estimate.

_____ The standard deviation of the distribution of differences between scores on parallel forms of a test.

_____ The smallest standard error in the group.

_____ The standard deviation of the errors made in regarding the obtained score as the true score.

_____ The error made in predicting true score from the fallible scores.

Indicate the type of scores to which each of the following statements refers by using the following code. Give the *one best* answer for each item.

1. Raw score.	5. Absolute scores.
2. Standard score.	6. Mental age scores.
3. Percentile scores.	7. I.Q. scores.
4. Normalized scores.	8. None of the foregoing scores.

_____ Gives a linear plot with chronological age for ages 2 to 10 years, if the average score for large groups is used.

_____ This distribution must be Gaussian.

_____ The frequency distribution of these scores is rectangular.

_____ These scores are linearly related to raw scores.

_____ The origin of these scores is at zero ability.

_____ The unit of measure is in some testable sense constant at different points on the scale.

_____ In groups that are homogeneous with respect to attainment level, this score is likely to be correlated negatively with chronological age.

_____ There is a procedure for checking to see whether or not these scores may be applied to a given set of data.

_____ If the raw score distribution is Gaussian, the plot of these scores against standard scores will be linear.

_____ The result of the plot of these scores against normalized scores is the integral of the normal probability curve.

_____ These scores are comparable from distribution to distribution, in the sense that different groups have the same mean and standard deviation.

_____ These scores assume that all differences in the frequency distributions for different groups are due solely to the peculiarities of the test.

_____ These scores assume that after all rank order is the important thing to consider.

Derive the equation for the correlation between the observed test score and the true test score.

As indicated below, be sure to distinguish between definitions, assumptions, and the derivation.

Definitions used	(15 lines)
Assumptions used	(5 lines)
Derivation	(15 lines)
Final equation	(1 line)

Test x and test y are two different power tests of the *same ability*.

Test x is a 400-item test, test y is a 1600-item test.

Both these tests are given to group A ($N = 2000$), and to group B ($N = 1000$), with the following results.

	Mean	σ	Group	Test
Case 1	200	25	A	x
Case 2	170	16	B	x
Case 3	700	90	A	y
Case 4	600	60	B	y

A number of different statistics, such as reliability, validity, error of measurement, were computed for each of the four cases indicated above.

In column I compare the statistics for the *same* test and *different* groups.

Write   A if it will probably be larger in group A.

         B if it will probably be larger in group B.

         S if it will probably be about the same (except for sampling errors) in both groups.

         O if the data given do not suggest which will be larger.

         N if the statement is nonsense.

         = if they must be identical for both groups.

In column II compare the statistics for the *same* group and *different* tests.

Write   x if it will probably be larger for test x.

         y if it will probably be larger for test y.

         S if it will probably be about the same (except for sampling errors) in both tests.

         O if the data given do not suggest the relative magnitudes of the two quantities.

         N if the statement is nonsense.

         = if they must be identical for both tests.

I Same Tests, Different Groups	II Same Groups, Different Tests	
———	———	The reliability coefficient.
———	———	The standard error of measurement.
———	———	The true standard deviation.
———	———	The validity coefficient, for example, correlation with college grades.
———	———	Reliability for infinite length.
———	———	The observed variance minus the error variance.
———	———	The correlation between observed scores and error scores.
———	———	The standard error of substitution.
———	———	The correlation between true scores and error scores.
———	———	The validity coefficient when corrected for attenuation.

Five *comparable forms* of a test are administered to the same class. It is necessary to predict the correlation between the average of the first two and the average of the last three forms.

Start with the definition of $r_{\left(\frac{x_1+x_2}{2}\right)\left(\frac{x_3+x_4+x_5}{3}\right)}$ and show that with certain conventional test theory assumptions, the required formula is $\dfrac{r\sqrt{6}}{\sqrt{1+3r+2r^2}}$, where r is the reliability of a single form of the test.

For each step indicate at the right the assumption made, the definition used, or the operation performed.

Derivation	Assumption, Definition, or Operation
(one page)	

A test of arithmetic ability is given to each of three classes. In class A the testing conditions are excellent. In class B the testing conditions are about the same as in class A, except that an oversight of the tester allows the class two minutes more than given to class A to work the test. In class C the testing conditions are not uniform; after the test was over it was found that about one-third of the class had misunderstood the nature of the test and had answered the questions with a bias that influenced the correctness of the responses. The following were the results obtained:

	Mean	S.D.	Average Number of Items Attempted	Average Number of Errors	N
Class A	50	5	100	2.1	100
Class B	55	6	120	1.9	124
Class C	45	7	90	2.4	81

No person in any of the three classes finished the test. There were practically no items skipped.

For each of the questions below write the number of the item that best applies. Use the following code:

1. Class A.　　　　　5. False.
2. Class B.　　　　　6. Can't tell from data given.
3. Class C.　　　　　7. Nonsense.
4. True.

_____ Would the reliability of the test be greater as calculated on class B or on class A?

_____ In which class would the test reliability be greatest?

_____ Would the test reliability be greater when calculated on class A or on class C?

_____ Which class was best on the ability tested?

_____ The reliability of the test calculated on the combined scores of classes A and C would be greater than that calculated on the combined scores of classes A and B.

_____ The Kuder-Richardson formula for reliability can legitimately be applied to the results of class A.

_____ The Kuder-Richardson formula could legitimately be applied to class B.

_____ The Kuder-Richardson formula could legitimately be applied to class C.

_____ If an intelligence test were given to the three classes, which class would most likely have the lowest mean score?

_____ The correlation between the scores in class A and class B would probably be higher than that for classes A and C.

Miscellaneous formulas:

r_{11} = a reliability coefficient.
r_{12} = a validity coefficient.
σ = the true standard deviation of the test.
s = the standard deviation of the test scores.
e = the standard error of measurement.
n = the number of times a test is increased in length.
1 = subscript designating the test.
0 = subscript designating the criterion.

1. $\dfrac{r_{10}}{\sqrt{r_{11}}}$

2. $\dfrac{r_{10}}{\sqrt{r_{00}}}$

3. $\dfrac{r_{10}}{\sqrt{r_{11}r_{00}}}$

4. σn

5. $e\sqrt{n}$

6. $ns^2(nr + 1 - r)$

7. $s\sqrt{n}\,\sqrt{nr + 1 - r}$

8. $\sigma^2 n^2$

9. $e^2 n$

For each of the following items write the number of the *one* formula that is *most* clearly suggested.

____ The true correlation between test and criterion.

____ The error variance of a test when it is increased in length.

____ The standard deviation of the raw scores of the augmented test.

____ If I quadruple the length of this test and give it again to the same group of students, what will happen to the true variance?

____ I should like to know how much this test would correlate with my criterion, if it were possible to measure the criterion with a reliability of unity.

____ Can I estimate the correlation that would exist between college grades and intelligence, if it were not for the errors of measurement in both variables?

____ This test has a standard deviation of 20 and a reliability of .80. What will the standard deviation probably be if I quadruple the length of the test?

Give the numerical answer to the foregoing question here _____.

____ This aptitude test has a reliability coefficient of .81, a validity coefficient of .64, a standard deviation of 30, and an error of measurement of 13+. I should like to estimate the validity coefficient the test would have if it were made perfect, and correlated with the same criterion scores as before.

Give the numerical answer to the foregoing question here _____.

____ Does the error of measurement of a test increase, diminish, or remain constant as the test is increased in length?

____ If I quadruple the length of this test would I expect any change in the standard deviation of the true scores?

Formulas showing the relationship between test length, heterogeneity, reliability, and validity:

r_{11} = reliability coefficient for test of unit length.

r_{01} = validity coefficient for test of unit length.

R_{11} = reliability coefficient when altered by increasing either the length of the test or the heterogeneity of the group.

R_{01} = validity coefficient altered by increasing the *length of the test*.

m, n as either coefficients or subscripts indicate the length of the augmented test.

σ = standard deviation of scores of the test of unit length.

Σ = standard deviation of scores of the test when it is altered either by increasing the length of the test or the heterogeneity of the group.

1. $\dfrac{nr_{11}}{1 + (n-1)r_{11}}$

5. $\dfrac{r_{01}}{\sqrt{\dfrac{1 - r_{11}}{n} + r_{11}}}$

2. $\dfrac{R_{11}(r_{11} - 1)}{r_{11}(R_{11} - 1)}$

6. $\dfrac{1 - r_{11}}{\dfrac{r_{01}^{2}}{R_{01}^{2}} - r_{11}}$

3. $\sigma_1 \sqrt{\dfrac{1 - r_{11}}{1 - R_{11}}}$

7. $\sqrt{R_{mm}R_{nn}}$

4. $1 - \dfrac{\sigma_1^{2}}{\Sigma_1^{2}}(1 - r_{11})$

For each item write the number of the *one* formula that is *most* clearly suggested. Give only one answer except where multiple answers are indicated.

_____ This test has a reliability of .81. I should like to raise the reliability to .95.

_____ In working with test X, Mr. B reports a reliability of .84 with mean 112, standard deviation 35. Mr. C uses the same test and reports that he gets a reliability of .95.

_____ I have a vocabulary test of 300 items with mean 210, standard deviation 15, and reliability .76. Can I estimate its correlation with another similar vocabulary test of 500 items, with a reliability of .81, mean 351, and standard deviation 21?

_____ These formulas depend upon the assumption that the standard error of measurement of a test is invariant with respect to variations in the heterogeneity of the group taking the test. (Multiple answer possible.)

_____ This intelligence test has a reliability of .80, but its correlation with grades is only .50. I wonder if I could make the test so long that its validity would increase to .70.

_____ A given college entrance examination has a reliability of .80, mean 190, and standard deviation 15. The same examination is given next year, and it is discovered that the average score is 180 and the standard deviation is 25.

_____ On this vocabulary test, I find that the odd-even correlation is .81.

_____ This 30-minute test has such a low validity that I wonder if its validity would be appreciably changed by making it into a 2-hour test. There would be space in the testing program for a test as long as that.

_____ The 2-hour final examination that I have been giving for the last two years has a distressingly low reliability. Would it be worth while to consider giving a 6-hour final of the same type?

_____ This formula can be readily derived from the correction for attenuation.

A test is given to two different groups with these results:

	Mean	σ	N
Group A	100	20	200
Group B	150	10	400

Mark each of the following items:

A if it will be larger in group A.
B if it will be larger in group B.
S if it will be about the same in both groups.
O if one cannot tell from the data given.
N if the statement is nonsense.

_____ The reliability coefficient of the test.

_____ The standard error of measurement of the test.

_____ The average achievement level of the group.

_____ The reliability coefficient of the test if it is made four times as long.

_____ The correlation between the scores of group A and the scores of group B.

_____ The ratio of the standard deviation of odd-item scores to the standard deviation of even-item scores.

_____ The standard deviation of the difference between odd-item scores and even-item scores.

_____ The slope of the line of regression of even-item scores on odd-item scores.

_____ The true variance.

_____ The correlation between true scores and error scores.

Given a test with a reliability coefficient (r_{11}) .84, length (k) 100, and standard deviation (σ) 20.

Estimate each of the following, giving:

  (*a*) The general formula expressed in symbolic form.
  (*b*) The numerical answer for the particular case.

1. Reliability coefficient if the test is altered to length N ($N = 250$).

  (*a*) Formula

  (*b*) Numerical answer

2. Length necessary if one is content to use a test with a reliability of .72.

  (*a*) Formula

  (*b*) Numerical answer

3. The error variance for length N ($N = 250$).

  (*a*) Formula

  (*b*) Numerical answer

4. The true score variance for length N ($N = 250$).

  (*a*) Formula

  (*b*) Numerical answer

5. The obtained standard deviation for length N ($N = 250$).

  (*a*) Formula

  (*b*) Numerical answer

6. The correlation between the test of length k (100) and length N (250).

(a) Formula

(b) Numerical answer

A class of 200 students is given the L and M forms of the Stanford Binet test.

Below are given a number of different ways of estimating the reliability coefficient of the Stanford Binet.

In column A mark each of these methods:

    1 if it is the best method of estimating reliability.
    + if it is a reasonably good method of estimating reliability.
    0 if it is a method that could not give an estimate of reliability.

In column B mark each of these methods:

    + if it is necessary to use the Spearman-Brown correction.
    0 if it is not necessary to use this correction.

A B

____   ____ Correlation of score on odd items with score on even items on form L.

____   ____ Correlation of score on the first half of the test, with score on the second half on form M.

____   ____ Correlation of score on form M with score on form L.

____   ____ Use of the Kuder-Richardson formula (simplest form using only mean standard deviation and number of items) on the items of form L.

____   ____ Give form M again and correlate scores on the first giving with those on the second for form M.

A and B are comparable halves of a test. $r_{AB} = .60$. The standard deviation of A is 14, and its mean is 103; corresponding figures for B are 26 and 106, respectively. Comment on the foregoing data with special reference to the reliability of the total test.

---

1 and 2 are comparable halves of a test. $r_{12} = .90$. The mean and standard deviation of part 1 are respectively 147 and 34; the corresponding figures for part 2 are 148 and 33. Comment on the foregoing data with special reference to the reliability of the total test.

A test of some simple mechanical ability in which practice has no effect is given twice to a class of 100 students. The standard deviation of each of the distributions is 10.0, the correlation between the two scores is .64. Assume that the distribution is normal, homoscedastic, etc.

1. What is the probability that the score of any given student on the first test will deviate by more than 6 score points from his score on the second test?

(a) Appropriate
     formula

(b) Numerical value
     of appropriate
     standard error

(c) Probability

---

2. What is the probability that the score of any given student on the first test will deviate by more than 6 score points from the prediction made from scores on the second test?

(a) Appropriate
     formula

(b) Numerical value
     of appropriate
     standard error

(c) Probability

---

3. What is the probability that the score of any given student on the first test will deviate by more than 6 score points from his true score?

(a) Appropriate
     formula

(b) Numerical value
     of appropriate
     standard error

(c) Probability

Answers to Problems

Note: Where discussions or derivations are called for, the answers are not given.

Chapter 2

1.

Test	Index of Reliability	Standard Deviation of True Scores	Correlation between Observed and Error Scores	Error of Measurement
A	.95	14.25	.30	4.50
B	.92	23.64	.40	10.28
C	.88	9.94	.47	5.31
D	.93	71.14	.36	27.54
E	.87	19.05	.49	10.73

2.

	True Score Limits (Approximately 0.3 per cent level)
(a) 115 on test A	101.50–128.50
(b) 211 on test B	180.16–241.84
(c) 31 on test C	15.07– 46.93
(d) 500 on test D	417.38–582.62
(e) 100 on test E	67.81–132.19

3.

Test	Minimum Difference	
	$C = 2$	$C = 3$
A	(12.726) 13	(19.089) 20
B	(29.072) 30	(43.608) 44
C	(15.017) 16	(22.525) 23
D	(77.883) 78	(116.825) 117
E	(30.344) 31	(45.517) 46

Chapter 3

1.   A. $T = X - E$ D. $r_{E_1 E_2} = 0$

B. $M_E = 0$ E. $\bar{X}_1 = \bar{X}_2 = \cdots = \bar{X}_k$

C. $r_{TE} = 0$ F. $s_1 = s_2 = \cdots = s_k$

Chapter 4

1.

	s_d	s_d	s_e	s_e
A.	5.66	5.43	4.00	3.67
B.	3.74	3.47	2.65	2.24
C.	20.84	20.47	14.74	14.21
D.	12.10	11.76	8.56	8.07
E.	10.08	9.51	7.13	6.30

12.   (a) $s_e = 6.30$ (c) $135.9 > T_A > 98.1$
(b) $s_e = 6.30$ (d) $113.9 > T_B > 76.1$

Chapter 6

3.

Test	Estimated Reliability
A	.98
B	.84
C	.93
D	.95
E	.91

Chapter 7

3.   (a) 619.35; (b) 198.69; (c) 3.18; (d) 5.50; (e) 31 items; (f) 300 items; (g) 27 items.

Chapter 8

3. $$\overline{s^2} = s_1{}^2$$

$$\overline{r_{ij} s_i s_j} = r_{11} s_1{}^2$$

where $s_1{}^2$ is the variance of one unit test,

$\overline{s^2}$ is the average variance of all unit tests,
r_{11} is the reliability of one unit test, and

$\overline{r_{ij} s_i s_j}$ is the average covariance of all unit tests.

4.   (a) .97; (b) .96; (c) 3.89 times as long or 78 items; (d) 50 items; (e) 32 items; (f) .88; (g) 240 items.

Chapter 9

1. (a) $r_{I\,I} \gtreqless r_{11}$ and (b) $r_{\infty\infty} = \sqrt{\dfrac{r_{11}}{r_{I\,I}}}.$

2. Assumed that $(r_{\infty\infty}\sqrt{r_{I\,I}})$ is not greater than $\sqrt{r_{11}}.$

4. .90.

5. .64.

6. (a) Mean 55, standard deviation 13.15, reliability .90, validity .76.

    (b) 34 new items, .54 new validity.

    (c) Test E.

    (d) Test A.

    (e) Test A.

    (f)   A   B   C   D   E

       .96   .68   .87   .89   .92

    (g) .77.

    (h) $k = 3.86$ or 4.

    (i) True variance of test C = 100.75   (true variance of test C increased to 300 items = 906.75).

        Error variance of test C = 13.74   (error variance of test C increased to 300 items = 41.22).

    (j) Reliability of lengthened test = .97.

        Reliability of lengthened criterion = .82.

        Validity of lengthened measures = .79.

    (k) .77.

7. Test X items.

Chapter 10

2. (a) Reliability about .93. (b) Standard deviation about 6.2. (c) Yes. (d) No. (e) Time limit decreased. (f) Test E is unsuitable for sectioning a group with standard deviation of 3.9.

Chapter 11

5. (a) .84; (b) 26.9.   **6.** (a) .90; (b) 42.7.   **7.** (a) .60; (b) 320.95.   **9.** 13.3

10. (a) .57; (b) 13.3.

Chapter 12

3. $R_{YZ} = .80.$ $R_{XZ} = .77.$

Chapter 14

Note. To facilitate computational checks, quantities such as D, B, s^2 (or u), s^2r (or w), and v as well as L, and $-N \log_{10} L$ are given.

In answering the question "Are the tests parallel?" the following convention was used:

    Yes   indicates p-value greater than .05.

    No   indicates p-value less than .01.

    ?   indicates p-value between .05 and .01.

    —   indicates that the test for equality of means cannot be made because the data are not in agreement with H_{vc} (or $\hat{H}_{vc}$).

1. $D = 279,215.81$; $s^2 = 194.2733$; $s^2r = 170.7367$; $v = 1.7034$.

	$-N \log_{10} L$	df	Are the tests parallel?
$L_{mvc} = .8181$	17.44	6	No
$L_{vc} = .9408$	5.30	4	?

	$[-N(k-1) \log_{10} L]$		
$L_m = .9325$	12.14	2	No

2(a). $D = 491.39363$; $s^2 = 10.4931$; $s^2r = 5.620087$; $v = 14.5956$.

	$-N \log_{10} L$	df	Are the tests parallel?
$L_{mvc} = .002435$	1568.1	11	No
$L_{vc} = .1552$	485.47	8	No

	$[-N(k-1) \log_{10} L]$		
$L_m = .2503$	1082.77	3	—

2(b). No.

2(c). $D = 140.09132$; $s^2 = 17.574598$; $s^2r = 12.829812$; $v = 0.1168$.

	$-N \log_{10} L$	df	Are the tests parallel?
$L_{mvc} = .9477$	13.998	2	No
$L_{vc} = .9711$	7.644	1	No
$L_m = .9760$	6.330	1	—

2(d). $D = 8.0254985$; $s^2 = 3.411593$; $s^2r = 1.872942$; $v = 0.1761$.

	$-N \log_{10} L$	df	Are the tests parallel?
$L_{mvc} = .8857$	31.626	2	No
$L_{vc} = .9870$	3.408	1	No
$L_m = .8973$	28.236	1	—

3(a). $D = 39,750.431$; $s^2 = 24.47055$; $s^2r = 13.0306$; $v = 0.2604$.

	$-N \log_{10} L$	df	Are the tests parallel?
$L_{mvc} = .3905$	51.45	11	No
$L_{vc} = .4177$	47.77	8	No

	$[-N(k-1) \log_{10} L]$		
$L_m = .9778$	3.69	3	—

3(b). $D = 9239.3439$; $s^2 = 25.337167$; $s^2r = 11.130033$; $v = 0.2714$.

	$-N \log_{10} L$	df	Are the tests parallel?
$L_{mvc} = .9260$	4.21	6	Yes
$L_{vc} = .9618$	2.13	4	Yes

$$[-N(k-1)\log_{10} L]$$

$L_m = .9813$	2.07	2	Yes

3(c). $D = 552.37637$; $s^2 = 26.63625$; $s^2r = 12.4363$; $v = 0.1678$.

	$-N \log_{10} L$	df	Are the tests parallel?
$L_{mvc} = .98395$	0.8845	2	Yes
$L_{vc} = .99558$	0.2429	1	Yes
$L_m = .98832$	0.6426	1	Yes

3(d). $D = 351.65226$; $s^2 = 22.30485$; $s^2r = 12.0692$; $v = 0.00201$.

	$-N \log_{10} L$	df	Are the tests parallel?
$L_{mvc} = .99927$	0.0397	2	Yes
$L_{vc} = .99946$	0.02974	1	Yes
$L_m = .99980$	0.01134	1	Yes

3(f). $\hat{D} = 377{,}668.24$; $\hat{B} = 2364.63$; $u_x = 24.2706$; $w_x = 11.0902$; $v_x = 0.3836$.

	$-N \log_{10} L$	df	Are the tests parallel?
$\hat{L}_{mvc} = .8681$	7.740	8	?
$\hat{L}_{vc} = .9194$	4.599	6	Yes
$\hat{L}_m = .9442$	3.142	2	?

3(g). $\hat{D} = 465{,}126.99$; $\hat{B} = 2408.2694$; $u_x = 25.3372$; $w_x = 11.1300$; $v_x = 0.2714$.

	$-N \log_{10} L$	df	Are the tests parallel?
$\hat{L}_{mvc} = .9213$	4.486	8	Yes
$\hat{L}_{vc} = .9568$	2.417	6	Yes
$\hat{L}_m = .9629$	2.069	2	Yes

4. $\hat{D} = 1{,}866{,}681.57$; $\hat{B} = 72{,}588.09$; $u_x = 64.6667$; $w_x = 58.2833$; $v_x = 1.0$.

	$-N \log_{10} L$	df	Are the tests parallel?
$\hat{L}_{mvc} = .4717$	16.31650	8	No
$\hat{L}_{vc} = .6311$	9.995	6	No
$\hat{L}_m = .7475$	6.31950	2	—

Chapter 15

1. .82. **2.** .91. **3.** .85. **4.** (a) .92; (b) .89. **5.** .93. **6.** (a) .91; (b) .84; (c) .84.
8. (a) .89; (b) .96. **9.** (a) .87; (b) .84; (c) .84; (d) 5.04; (e) (35.9–66.1), (57.9–88.1);
(f) .93, .96, .98, .99; (g) about 484 items; (i) .48; (j) .97.

Chapter 16

1. (.89), (.85). **2.** (.81), (.74). **3.** (a) (.91); (b) (.88).

Chapter 17

1. $s_u = \sqrt{\dfrac{2}{500}(3200) + 1.544 - (1.544)^2} = 3.46$

2. Frequencies 372 21 13 11 15 9 9 10 5 5 10   5   2   3   3   2   2   0   1   2
Score   0   1   2   3   4 5 6   7 8 9 10 11 12 13 14 15 16 17 18 19

$$M_u = 1.54$$

$$s_u = 3.46$$

3. $.97 > R > .82$
$.97 > R' > .80$

4.

	Lower Bound for Reliability Coefficient	
A	.96	.96
B	.00	.71
C	.62	.76
D	.83	.85
E	−3.5 or zero	.59

5.

	Error of Measurement	Upper Bound
A	4.75	5.19
B	4.31	8.74
C	3.24	7.09
D	3.25	3.29
E	4.75	7.19

Chapter 19

2.

	$\bar{c}$	$\bar{c}^2$	Lowest Gross Score Exceeding $\bar{c} + 2\bar{c}$
(a)	10	5	15
(b)	50	25	61
(c)	4	3.2	8
(d)	20	16	29
(e)	1	0.9	3

9.

	a	b	c
Set A	5.34	4.11	6.56
B	6.65	2.24	11.07

10.
      (a) $w_i = 7.353A_i + 138.97$
      (b) $w'_i = 7.132B_i + 88.21$

11.
    (a) Mean $= 111.5039$; standard deviation $= 22.1712$
    (b) $w_i = 1.2658A_i - 74.174$
    (c) $w'_i = 1.036B_i - 67.419$

Chapter 20

1. .917. **2.** .00. **3.** $\dot{X}_h = .386X_a - .342X_s + .905X_e + 315.550$. **4.** .73.
5. (a) and (s). **6.** $\dot{X}_p = .2X_a + .9X_s + 97$. **7.** .721. **17.** (a) .57; (b) .63; (c) .69.

Chapter 21

4. Delete items 2, 5, 22, 31, 32.

Author Index

(Wherever more than ten references to a single name occur, the references for that name are further subdivided by topics. (p) indicates that the reference is in the problems at the end of the chapter. (n) after a page number indicates that the reference occurs in a footnote.)

Abelson, H. H., 397
Ackerson, Luton, 66, 86, 194, 397, 413
Ackoff, R. L., 400
Adams, H. F., 193, 397
Adkins, D. C., 266, 330, 364, 380, 381, 391, 397, 413
Adkins, R. M., 412
Aitken, A. C., 165, 166, 397
Alexander, H. W., 221, 397
Allcock, H. J., 397
Anastasi, Anne, 193, 397
Anderson, J. E., 397
Andrus, Lawrence, 218(p), 229(p)
Arnold, J. N., 67, 397
Asker, William, 397
Ayres, L. P., 368, 397

Babitz, Milton, 397
Barry, R. F., 398
Barthelmess, H. M., 398
Baxter, Brent, 398
Bedell, Ralph, 398
Bennett, G. K., 354, 398
Bernstein, Enoch, 398
Bijou, S. W., 398, 418
Binet, Alfred, 1, 398
Bingham, W. V., 398
Bliss, E. F., 368, 369, 398
Bôcher, Maxime, 159, 398
Bolles, M. M., 398
Bolton, T. L., 398
Boring, E. G., 398, 411
Bradford, L. P., 47(p), 398
Bradway, K. P., 408
Bray, C. W., 398
Bridges, J. W., 420
Brigham, C. C., 368, 398
Brogden, H. E., 355, 381, 398

Brolyer, Cecil R., 368
Brown, William, 65, 78, 398
Brownell, W. A., 399
Bucknam, M. E., 400
Burnham, P. S., 111, 133, 138, 400
Buros, O. K., 2, 399
Burt, Cyril, 165, 166, 399

Calandra, Alexander, 399
Carr, H. A., 399
Carroll, J. B., 67, 220, 374, 393, 399, 401
Carter, H. D., 399
Carter, L. F., 399, 418
Casanova, Teobaldo, 399
Cattell, J. McK., 1, 399
Chapanis, Alphonse, 399
Chapman, J. C., 399
Chesire, Leona, 400
Churchman, C. W., 400
Clark, E. L., 394(p), 400
Clayton, Blythe, 66, 86(p), 406
Cleeton, G. V., 400
Collar, A. R., 402
Conrad, H. S., 353, 400, 414
Cook, Sidney, 399
Cook, S. W., 400, 418
Cook, W. W., 363, 373, 374, 381, 394(p), 400, 409
Coombs, C. H., 402
Copeland, H. A., 112, 400
Cosby, C. B., 400
Courtney, Douglas, 400
Cozens, F. W., 402
Cramér, Harald, 400
Crawford, A. B., 111, 133, 138, 400
Crawford, M. P., 401, 418
Cronbach, L. J., 2, 193, 401
Crooks, W. R., 401

469

Topic Index

((p) after a page number indicates that the reference is in the problems at the end of the chapter. (n) indicates that the reference is in a footnote.)

475